DELICT

A Comprehensive Guide to the Law in Scotland

(2nd edition)

Francis McManus dedicates this book to Ann and Lucy

Eleanor Russell dedicates this book to John and Eilidh

DELICT

A Comprehensive Guide to the Law in Scotland

(2nd edition)

Francis McManus

Emeritus Professor of Law, Edinburgh Napier University

and

Eleanor Russell

Solicitor; Lecturer in Law, Glasgow Caledonian University

with

Josephine Bisacre

Solicitor; Senior Teaching Fellow, Heriot-Watt University

DUNDEE UNIVERSITY PRESS
2011

First published in Great Britain in 1998 by John Wiley & Sons Ltd

Second edition published in 2011 by
Dundee University Press
University of Dundee
Dundee DD1 4HN

www.dundee.ac.uk/dup

Reprinted 2014

ISBN 978–1–84586–042–4

No natural forests were destroyed to make this product;
only farmed timber was used and replanted.

British Library Cataloguing-in-Publication data
A catalogue record for this book is available on request from the British Library.

Typeset by Fakenham Prepress Solutions, Fakenham, Norfolk NR21 8NN
Printed by Bell & Bain Ltd, Glasgow

CONTENTS

CONTENTS

PREFACE

It is a trite saying, indeed, that the law does not stand still for the convenience of authors. However, this apothegm has added meaning for the authors when one recalls that it is now some 13 years since the first edition of this work was published. There have been many significant changes in the law since then. One of the most important developments in the law of delict has been the advent of human rights jurisprudence which has presented judges, as well as academics, with a considerable challenge.

This book is intended mainly for the use of undergraduates. However, we hope that the book will also be of some use to the practitioner. We have attempted to discuss the main areas of delictual liability in Scots law. However, lack of space precludes mention, far less discussion, of some areas.

Francis McManus wrote Chapters 1–8, 11–14 and 17–20. Eleanor Russell wrote Chapters 9, 10, 15, and 21–24. Josephine Bisacre wrote Chapters 16 and 25. The book therefore represents a joint effort.

We would like to thank Duncan Spiers, Zhongdong Niu and James MacDougall for commenting on draft chapters of the book. Francis McManus would like to thank Bonnie Holligan and Ann McManus for their help with literature searches. He would also like to thank the Carnegie Trust for the Universities of Scotland for its support in the preparation of this work; and the library staff of Edinburgh Napier University, the University of Edinburgh and that of the Institute of Advanced Legal Studies, London for their help. Eleanor Russell would like to thank Aidan O'Donnell, former Head of the Law Department at Glasgow Caledonian University, for his support and encouragement. She is also grateful to the members of the School Management Team (Law and Social Sciences) for granting the sabbatical leave which proved to be invaluable in bringing this work to fruition. Tom McDonnell, in particular, is owed a special debt of gratitude in this regard.

Finally, we would like to thank our respective families for their cheerful forbearance over the past 3 years.

We have attempted to state the law as at 31 March 2011 but have been able, at proof stage, to take account of some developments since that date.

Francis McManus
Eleanor Russell

TABLE OF CASES

TABLE OF LEGISLATION

STATUTES

STATUTORY INSTRUMENTS

EUROPEAN LEGISLATION

1 INTRODUCTION

In this work we attempt to provide an account of the law of delict. Our approach is to **1.1**
concentrate on what we consider to be the more important delicts. The law of delict
has developed neither uniformly nor coherently. Delict, unlike, for example, the law
of evidence or the law of contract, is, generally speaking, an un-integrated subject.
Indeed, what Tony Weir has observed in relation to the law of tort is perfectly apposite,
in our view, to the law of delict: that is to say, generally there is nothing connecting the
various delicts which we discuss, other than the binding of this book![1] That is not to
say, however, that there is *never* an overlap between certain delicts. For example, there
is some overlap between the law of negligence and the law of nuisance.

The law of negligence, itself, since the "big bang" of 1932 has experienced some **1.2**
exciting phases of development, where judges came close to giving themselves *carte
blanche* to widen the scope of negligence almost to the limits of human imagination,
as well as phases of slow, incremental growth, a process which began towards the end
of the 1980s. This restrictive, conservative approach to expanding the arc of the duty
of care remains to date. However, rules (including self-denying ordinances) mean all
things to all men – even judges! And, at times, we see the courts being quite willing to
break out of the judicial straightjacket which judges foisted on themselves in the 1980s.
One way for the court to get round any rule, of course, is simply to pay lip-service
to the sanctity of the rule and then proceed to decide the case on broader grounds of
"justice" which, of course, is always "trumps". The way in which the House of Lords
has treated the claims of disappointed beneficiaries of wills provides a good example
of such an approach. Again, recently, we have seen the Supreme Court "bending"
traditional, seemingly well-entrenched rules (which govern the law relating to factual
causation) in the law of negligence, in order to do justice to victims of mesothelioma.
Furthermore, that much-flogged unruly horse, public policy, is still very much alive
and kicking in the law. We see the courts denying, on policy grounds (which, here, are
based on the courts discouraging a surfeit of claims), claims for pure economic loss
and also claims by those witnessing accidents, by reason of which they suffer psychiatric injury, unless the pursuers are very closely related to the victims of the accident.
Reflecting on the current rules which govern liability for nervous shock, one gets the
distinct impression that the courts have, on grounds of public policy, placed artificial
barriers in the path of pursuers. Logic appears to be sacrificed to public policy. Indeed,
one is reminded here of the words of Burrough J in *Richardson* v *Mellish*[2] that public
policy is an unruly horse and, once one gets astride the saddle, the horse can take
one anywhere. Perhaps the unruly horse has taken the law of nervous shock to such

---

[1] T Weir, *Tort Law* (Preface) (Clarendon Press, 2002).
[2] (1824) 2 Bing 229 at 252.

a point that the law waxes asinine! One of the most complicated and grey areas of the law of negligence, in the authors' opinion, is the liability of public authorities. Actions in negligence against public bodies grow apace. We see here the courts displaying a great deal of discomfort in applying the common law rules of negligence to the plethora of powers and duties which statute has foisted on public bodies.

1.3   The law of delict has been forged by judicial decision making over the years. However, Parliament has intervened, from time to time, to reform the law. Sometimes the law has, to all intents and purposes, been completely reformed, as is the case with occupiers' liability. At other times, Parliament has reformed only parts of the common law, as is the case with the law of defamation and the law relating to liability for animals.

1.4   Finally, in recent years, the law of delict has had to come face to face with human rights jurisprudence. This, as we will see in the course of this work, has provided the courts with a formidable challenge. Human rights law has had a profound effect on the law relating to breach of confidence and also, to a lesser extent, the law of defamation. As far as other delicts are concerned – for example, the law of nuisance – judges have been more reserved in embracing human rights law.

1.5   By way of conclusion, while the law of delict, looked at in its entirety, may not represent a particularly tidy area of the law of Scotland, and, furthermore, may be castigated as primitive at times, the importance of delict is beyond dispute. The subject deserves careful study. Most of all, however, delict should be enjoyed.

2 NEGLIGENCE – DUTY OF CARE

In this chapter we look at the liability which lies in respect of harm caused by the defender's negligent conduct. Actions based on negligence represent the most important branch of the law of delict in terms of the number of cases brought before the courts. This chapter is devoted to what is often called "mainstream" negligence, in contradistinction to liability for nervous shock, negligent statements and pure economic loss which are dealt with separately. Therefore, attention will largely be focused on that part of the law of negligence in which the pursuer has sustained some form of harm either to his person or to his property by virtue of the negligent conduct of the defender. However, it should be stressed at the very outset that while liability in respect of nervous shock, economic loss and negligent statements are treated separately for the purposes of this work, judges, in deciding cases in these areas of law, have been influenced by the development of the law in mainstream negligence to a varying degree. It would, therefore, be imprudent to treat liability in terms of the law of negligence for nervous shock etc as existing in watertight compartments, and uninfluenced by the developments in mainstream negligence. **2.1**

In order to succeed in an action based on negligence it is necessary for the pursuer to prove that: **2.2**

(1) the defender owed him a duty of care;
(2) the duty of care has been breached;
(3) the defender's conduct caused the pursuer injury; and
(4) the injury was not too remote.

WHAT IS THE DUTY OF CARE?

In any negligence action, failing admission, the court must establish whether the defender owes a duty of care not to injure the pursuer. In essence, the court is required to decide whether the factual circumstances before it fall within the compass of the law of negligence. **2.3**

It is usual to commence a discussion on the duty of care with the celebrated case of *Donoghue* v *Stevenson*,[1] which was decided in 1932 and is the most important case in the modern law of negligence. However, this was certainly not the first negligence case to be decided by the courts. For example, it had been established by the courts, before the end of the 19th century, that an occupier of land owed a duty of care to those who entered **2.4**

---

[1] 1932 SC (HL) 31.

that land, that a doctor owed a duty of care to his patient, and that a road-user owed a duty of care to other road-users and also pedestrians, in terms of the law of negligence.

2.5   The facts in *Donoghue* were homely. Mrs Donoghue went to a café in Paisley with a friend. The latter bought Mrs Donoghue some ice cream and ginger beer. The ginger beer was manufactured by Stevenson. The café proprietor poured some ginger beer into the glass which contained the ice cream. Mrs Donoghue drank some of the mixture. As Mrs Donoghue's friend poured more ginger beer into Mrs Donoghue's glass, Mrs Donoghue noticed the remains of a decomposing snail in her glass. Mrs Donoghue became ill. It will be observed, of course, that there was no contract between Mrs Donoghue and Stevenson. She, therefore, was required to base her action in delict. She had to establish that Stevenson owed her a duty of care in terms of the law of negligence. By a majority, the House of Lords decided in her favour. The leading judgment was given by Lord Atkin. His Lordship stated:[2]

> "The rule that you are to love your neighbour becomes in law you must not injure your neighbour. You must take reasonable care to avoid acts or omissions which you can reasonably foresee would be likely to injure your neighbour. Who is my neighbour? Persons who are so closely and directly affected by my act that I ought reasonably to have them in contemplation as being so affected when I am directing my mind to the acts or omissions which are called in question."

2.6   Lord Atkin, therefore, based the "duty of care" test on the principle of foreseeability. In other words, if one can foresee that one's conduct would be likely to injure one's neighbour, the law imposes a duty on one not to injure him. Lord Atkin was not attempting to enunciate a formula, of general application, which could be applied to any negligence scenario. There is no doubt that his Lordship was fully aware that there were certain areas where the law had resolutely set its face against imposing a duty of care on the ground of policy. For example, it was well settled by 1932 that, with certain exceptions, the courts would not recognise claims in respect of pure economic loss or liability for pure omissions. Lord Atkin, therefore, did not intend his "foreseeability" test to apply to these situations. Rather, the "foreseeability" test was to be enlisted to determine liability in novel situations which came before the courts. Indeed, the Atkinian "foreseeability" test provided the judiciary with ample scope for creativity. Never again was the law of negligence to be so rigidly hide-bound within the limits of the then existing categories of duty of care. Before proceeding further, one should note that *Donoghue* establishes the principle that the scope of the duty of care owed by the defender to the pursuer is confined to the particular type of harm which the pursuer sustains. In *Donoghue*, of course, the duty of care imposed on Messrs Stevenson by the court was not to physically injure Mrs Donoghue, the consumer of the offensive ginger beer, by the nature and the composition of that beer. For example, if Mrs Donoghue had fainted on discovering her ginger beer was contaminated, whereupon her friend, in witnessing this, had suffered a heart attack, no duty would have been owed by Stevenson to the friend. This point is neatly illustrated in the recent Court of Appeal case of *Jain* v *Trent Strategic Health Authority*.[3] In that case the claimants, who were proprietors of a nursing home, alleged that they had sustained economic loss as a

---

[2] 1932 SC (HL) 31 at 44.
[3] [2008] QB 246. See R Bagshaw, "Negligence making business activities illegal: *Jain* v *Trent Strategic Health Authority*" (2009) 17 Torts Law Journal 295.

result of the negligent cancellation of the registration in respect of the home. The court held that since the object of the statute which governed the regulation of the home was to protect the vulnerable residents of the home from harm, the defendants did not owe the claimants a duty of care to protect them from economic loss.[4]

Several examples can be given of the Atkinian "foreseeability" test being applied in pristine form. In *Beaumont* v *Surrey County Council*,[5] a teacher discarded a long piece of elastic in an open bin in a classroom. The elastic was used in horseplay between pupils. The plaintiff lost an eye. The education authority was held liable on the basis that the injury in question was foreseeable.[6] Another case, the facts of which were completely different from those in *Beaumont*, is the Court of Appeal case of *Ministry of Housing* v *Sharp*.[7] In that case the clerk of a local land registry issued an erroneous certificate to the purchaser of land over which the plaintiffs had a charge (ie they had real rights over the land in question). The upshot of this was that the plaintiffs automatically lost their interest over the land concerned. The plaintiffs successfully sued the registrar for the clerk's negligence. Lord Denning MR stated:[8] "I have no doubt that the clerk is liable. He was under a duty at common law to use due care. That was a duty which he owes to any person – incumbrancer or purchaser – whom he knew or ought to have known might be injured if he made a mistake." It was during the same year that *Sharp* was decided, that the "neighbour" principle attained its high-water mark in the House of Lords case of *Home Office* v *Dorset Yacht Co*.[9] There, a party of borstal trainees were working on Brownsea Island in Poole Harbour, under the supervision and control of three borstal officers. During the night, seven of them escaped and went aboard a yacht which was anchored nearby. They could not navigate the yacht properly and it collided with a yacht belonging to the Dorset Yacht Company, which successfully sued the Home Office in negligence. Lord Reid stated:[10] "The time has come when we can and should say that [Lord Atkin's "neighbour" principle] ought to apply unless there is some justification or valid explanation for its exclusion."

2.7

THE TWO-STAGED APPROACH

However, such a sanguine approach to the "neighbour" principle did not survive the decade. The change was brought about by the House of Lords case of *Anns* v *Merton Borough Council*.[11] In that case the plaintiffs were lessees of flats which had been built under plans passed by a local authority in respect of whose legal duties and obligations Merton Borough Council had succeeded. The block in which the flats were situated had been built on foundations which were of an inadequate depth in terms of the relevant building byelaws. The defendant local authority building inspectors had failed to notice this during the course of their visits to the site. The plaintiffs sued the local authority. The basic question which the House was required to decide was

2.8

---

[4] See also *Calvert* v *William Hill Credit Ltd* [2008] All ER (D) 155. See P Mitchell, "Problem gambling and the law of negligence" (2010) 18 Torts Law Journal 1.
[5] (1968) 66 LGR 580.
[6] For a discussion of a teacher's duty of care, see L Barnes, "Trips, slips and bangs: pupil injury claims and the teacher's duty of care" 2009 JR 190.
[7] [1970] 2 QB 223.
[8] *Ibid* at 268.
[9] [1970] AC 1004.
[10] *Ibid* at 1027.
[11] [1977] 2 All ER 492.

whether the local authority owed the plaintiffs a duty of care in the law of negligence. The House held that such a duty was owed to the plaintiffs. Lord Wilberforce stated:[12]

> "[The] position has now been reached that in order to establish that a duty of care arises in a particular situation, it is not necessary to bring the facts of that situation within those of previous situations in which a duty of care has been held to exist. Rather, the question has to be approached in two stages. First, one has to ask whether, as between the alleged wrongdoer and the person who has suffered damage there is a sufficient relationship of proximity or neighbourhood such that, in the reasonable contemplation of the former, carelessness on his part may be likely to cause damage to the latter – in which case a *prima facie* duty of care arises. Secondly, if the first question is answered affirmatively, it is necessary to consider whether there are any considerations which ought to negative, or to reduce or limit the scope of duty or the class of person to whom it is owed or the damages to which a breach of it may give rise ..."

2.9 Thus, the so-called "two-staged" approach to the duty of care was enunciated. By this approach, in order to ascertain whether a duty of care was owed by the defender to the pursuer, one was required to ascertain whether there was a sufficient relationship of proximity between the defender and the pursuer. This first stage embraced Lord Atkin's "neighbour" principle. If the defender should have foreseen that his conduct would injure the pursuer then, *prima facie*, a duty of care would arise. The second stage consisted of ascertaining whether there were any policy considerations which would militate against the imposition of a duty of care. One can readily see here that Lord Wilberforce's test offered the judiciary considerable scope for expanding the existing categories of the duty of care, since the only apparent check on expanding the existing categories of negligence in terms of Atkinian foreseeability was public policy.

2.10 A case which neatly illustrates the two-staged approach to the duty of care is the House of Lords case of *McLoughlin v O'Brian*,[13] which concerned liability for nervous shock. The gist of the case was whether the defendant, a lorry driver who had negligently collided with a car being driven by the husband of the plaintiff, owed a duty of care to the plaintiff in respect of the nervous shock she sustained when witnessing her seriously injured family in hospital. The House of Lords held that a duty of care did exist between the defendant and the plaintiff. Lord Wilberforce,[14] himself, after establishing that there was a sufficient relationship of proximity between the defendant and the plaintiff in terms of the scene of the accident, and also in terms of time and place, went on to consider the application of the second limb of *Anns* to the facts of the case. In his view, first, there were no grounds for accepting an argument based on the premise that, by admitting a claim for nervous shock in such circumstances, this would lead to a proliferation of such claims. Second, Lord Wilberforce rejected the suggestion that an extension of liability would be unfair to defendants, in that it would impose damages out of all proportion to the negligent conduct in question and would also result in an additional burden being placed on insurers and ultimately, road-users. Third, to admit such "aftermath" claims would not lead to evidentiary difficulties. In other words, in his Lordship's view, there were no policy reasons for rejecting such a claim. The plaintiff, therefore, succeeded.

---

[12] [1977] 2 All ER 492 at 498.
[13] [1982] 1 AC 410.
[14] *Ibid* at 421.

THE RETREAT FROM *ANNS*

However, the expansive approach to the duty of care which was enunciated in *Anns* **2.11** (described as "extreme" by Rougier J in *John Monroe Ltd v London Fire Authority*[15]) was relatively short-lived. The judiciary were beginning to have some doubts about the two-staged approach. The first sign of such a change in judicial attitudes to the two-staged approach to the duty of care came in the House of Lords case of *Governors of the Peabody Fund v Sir Lindsay Parkinson*.[16] In that case the plaintiffs submitted plans for the construction of a housing development. The plans, which were approved by the local authority, made provision for the installation of drains of a flexible construction. However, drains of a rigid construction were installed. The local authority building inspectors failed to notice this. The upshot of this was that the drains had to be replaced. This considerably delayed construction, thereby causing loss to the plaintiffs. Lord Keith,[17] in effect, refused to treat the two-staged test as an inflexible rule in respect of all situations where a duty of care had to be established. In his Lordship's view, it was necessary to ascertain whether a relationship of proximity, in Lord Atkin's sense, existed. However, the scope of the duty must depend on all the circumstances of the case. Lord Keith then went on to state that, in determining whether or not the law imposed a duty of care of a particular scope upon the defendant, it was material to take into consideration whether it was just and reasonable to do so. While *Peabody* did not overrule the two-staged test which was enunciated in *Anns*, the principle was significantly weakened.

The momentum against *Anns* continued with the decision of the Privy Council **2.12** in *Yuen Kun-Yeu v Attorney General of Hong Kong*.[18] In that case the appellants had deposited money with a deposit-taking registered company which went into liquidation. The appellants lost their money. The Hong Kong Commissioner of Deposit-taking Companies had a statutory power to grant, refuse or revoke the registrations of such companies. The appellants maintained that the company had been run fraudulently and also that the Commissioner had been negligent in discharging his functions, in that, despite cogent reasons for suspecting that the company was being run fraudulently, he had done nothing. In other words, the main question which had to be determined by the Board was whether the Commissioner owed a duty of care to the appellants. The Privy Council, in rejecting the proposition that a duty of care was owed, concurred with the reasoning of Brennan J in the Australian case of *Sutherland Shire Counties v Heyman*,[19] where he advocated that the law should develop novel categories of negligence incrementally and by analogy with established categories rather than by a massive extension of a *prima facie* duty of care, restrained only by indefinable considerations which ought to negative or to reduce or limit the scope of the duty of class of person to whom it is owed. Lord Keith[20] in *Yuen Kun-Yeu* expressed the view that the two-staged test which was formulated by Lord Wilberforce in *Anns* had been elevated to a degree of importance greater than it merited.

---

[15] [1996] 4 All ER 318.
[16] [1985] AC 210.
[17] *Ibid* at 240.
[18] [1987] 2 All ER 705.
[19] (1985) 60 ALR 1 at 43–44.
[20] [1987] 2 All ER 705 at 710.

2.13   The retreat from *Anns* was completed with the decision of the House of Lords in *Caparo* v *Dickman*.[21] In that case the plaintiffs were shareholders in a company. Relying on an audit made by the defendants, the plaintiffs purchased further shares in the company and made an unsuccessful takeover bid. The plaintiffs lost money. They sued the auditors in negligence. The House of Lords held that no duty of care was owed by the defendants to the plaintiffs. A relation of proximity or neighbourhood was required to exist between the parties. The judgment of Lord Bridge is instructive. His Lordship stated:[22]

> "What emerges (from case law) is that, in addition to the foreseeability of damage, necessary ingredients in any situation giving rise to a duty of care are that there should exist between the party owing the duty and the party to whom it is owed a relationship characterised by the law as one of 'proximity' or 'neighbourhood' and that the situation should be one in which the court considers it fair, just and reasonable that the law should impose a duty of a given scope upon the one party for the benefit of the other. But it is implicit in the passages referred to that the concepts of proximity and fairness embodied in these additional ingredients are not sustainable of any such precise definition as would be necessary to give them utility as practical tests, but amount in effect to little more than convenient labels to attach to the features of different specific situations which, on a detailed examination of all the circumstances, the law recognises pragmatically as giving rise to a duty of a given scope. Whilst recognising, of course, the importance of the underlying general principles common to the whole field of negligence, I think the law has now moved in the direction of attaching greater significance to the more traditional categorisation of distinct and recognisable situations as guides to the existence, the scope and the limits of the varied duties of care which the law imposes."

2.14 Another important factor which influenced the House's decision was that the provisions of the Companies Act 1985 imposed a duty on the defendant auditors to shareholders as a class and that the duty did not extend to an individual shareholder except in respect of some class activity.

2.15   Therefore, as far as the modern law of negligence is concerned, in order to establish whether the defender owes the pursuer a duty of care it must be shown that:

    (1) the loss in question is reasonably foreseeable;
    (2) there is a relationship of proximity between the parties;
    (3) it is fair, just and reasonable that a duty of care be imposed; and
    (4) that such an imposition of a duty of care is not contrary to public policy.

2.16 Superimposed on these rules (the first three of such rules have come to be known as the "tripartite test") and, indeed, acting as a powerful break, is the general requirement that any extension to the duty of care should be incremental, with the court expanding the ambit of the duty of care only if the facts of the case before it are either "foursquare" with previous decided cases or analogous to them.

---

[21] [1990] 2 AC 605.
[22] *Ibid* at 617.

THE INCREMENTAL APPROACH ILLUSTRATED

A good illustration of the application of the incremental approach to the duty of care **2.17** is seen in the Privy Council case of *Davies v Ratcliffe*.[23] In that case a statutory body, the Finance Board, issued a licence to the Isle of Man Bank to allow it to carry out banking activities. The licence was revoked by the Board but, before this, the appellants had invested money in the Bank and had suffered financial loss. The appellants claimed that their financial loss was attributable to the fact that the respondents had carried out their licensing functions negligently. It was held that no duty of care existed between the Board and the appellants. It was held[24] that it was not sufficient that the loss in question was foreseeable. It was also necessary to establish proximity between the parties. "Proximity" in this context meant a relationship between the parties which rendered it just and reasonable that liability for negligence might be imposed on the defendant for the loss or the damage which was suffered. It was not desirable to attempt to state, in broad and general propositions, the circumstances in which such proximity might or might not exist. Rather, it was preferable that the law should develop novel categories of negligence incrementally and by analogy with established categories. That process was of particular importance in cases where the plaintiff claimed damages in respect of pure financial loss.

In the cases discussed thus far where the tripartite test has been applied, the courts **2.18** have had to consider whether a duty of care has been owed in terms of economic loss which has been sustained by the pursuer. What is the position, however, where the pursuer has sustained harm either to his person or to his property? Can one argue, here, that the learning in *Caparo* is redundant? This very issue came before the House of Lords in *Marc Rich and Co AG v Bishop Rock Marine Co Ltd (The Nicholas H)*.[25] The case mainly concerned an action by cargo owners, Marc Rich, against the owners of a vessel (the *Nicholas H*), namely Bishop Rock Marine, and also a marine classification society, NKK. The facts of the case were that during a voyage the *Nicholas H* developed a crack in her hull. It was feared that the crack presented a danger. The owners of the vessel, therefore, requested NKK to examine the ship. A surveyor did so on behalf of the defendants. The vessel was allowed to proceed to port in order to allow temporary repairs to be carried out. Temporary repairs were carried out on the vessel. The surveyor then recommended that the vessel could sail. Shortly after her departure from port, cracks began to reappear. The ship sank a few days later. The main question which the House was required to answer was whether NKK owed a duty of care to the plaintiffs. As stated above, NKK was a classification society. It was a non-profit-making, non-governmental organisation which was registered in Japan as a foundation related to public interests. Its founding instrument described its function as being "to promote the improvement and development of various matters relating to ships ... so as to safeguard the safety of life and property at sea". The plaintiffs submitted that, given that they had sustained physical damage to property in which they had a proprietary interest, the only requirement in order to establish the requisite duty of care between the defendants and the plaintiffs was proof of foreseeability. The House rejected this contention. Rather, the question of whether a duty of care existed

---

[23] [1990] 1 WLR 821.
[24] *Ibid*, per Lord Goff at 826.
[25] [1996] AC 211.

depended also on fairness, justice and reasonableness, in addition to foreseeability and proximity, regardless of the nature of the relevant harm (ie whether physical harm or economic loss). In the instant case, the shipowners were primarily responsible for the vessel sailing in a seaworthy condition. The role of NKK was a subsidiary one. The carelessness of the NKK surveyor did not involve the direct infliction of physical damage. Furthermore, there was no contract between the cargo owners and the NKK surveyor. Indeed, the cargo owners were possibly not aware that NKK had surveyed the vessel. The cargo owners simply relied on the shipowners to keep the vessel seaworthy and to look after the cargo. The dealings between shipowners and cargo owners were based on a contractual structure, the Hague Rules and tonnage limitation on which the insurance of international trade depended. If one were to recognise a duty of care by classification societies, this would have a substantial impact on international trade. In all the circumstances, the recognition of a duty would be unfair, unjust and unreasonable as against the shipowners who would ultimately have to bear the cost of holding classification societies liable. Such an obligation was also at variance with the relationship between shipowners and cargo owners which was based on an internationally agreed contractual structure. The imposition of a duty of care would also be unfair, unjust and unreasonable towards classification societies because they acted for the collective welfare, namely the safety of lives and ships at sea. Furthermore, unlike shipowners, a classification society would not have the benefit of any limitation provisions.

2.19   We see the incremental approach to the duty of care being applied in terms of personal injury by the Court of Appeal in *Barrett* v *Ministry of Defence*.[26] There, an off-duty naval airman engaged in a bout of heavy drinking at a naval establishment. He became inebriated and then unconscious. He was later found dead, having choked on his own vomit. The widow of the deceased claimed damages against the Ministry of Defence on the basis that it had failed to enforce its own standards of discipline in order to protect the deceased airman from drinking himself to death. The court held that up to the time it assumed responsibility for his well-being, the defendant did not owe the deceased a duty of care in law. The fact that it was foreseeable that the deceased would sustain injury if he drank too much was insufficient to ground liability. Rather, it was fair, just and reasonable for the law to leave a responsible adult to assume responsibility for his own actions in consuming alcoholic drink. Beldam LJ stated:[27] "To dilute self-responsibility and to blame one adult for another's lack of self-control is neither just nor reasonable and, in the development of the law of negligence, an increment too far."[28]

BREAKING OUT OF THE STRAIGHTJACKET

2.20   Whereas the incremental approach to the duty of care certainly acted as a powerful brake on the courts introducing novel categories of duty of care, the capacity of judges for creativity in the field of the law of negligence was not completely eroded. The House of Lords case of *Page* v *Smith*[29] illustrates this point quite neatly. The facts

---

[26] [1995] 1 WLR 1217.
[27] *Ibid* at 1224.
[28] See also *Mulcahy* v *Ministry of Defence* [1996] QB 732.
[29] [1995] 2 WLR 644.

of the case were that the plaintiff was involved in a minor collision between his car and another, driven by the defendant. The plaintiff was uninjured. However, he had been suffering from a condition known as myalgic encephalomyelitis (chronic fatigue syndrome), which he claimed had become permanent as a result of the accident. It will be seen later[30] that the courts draw a distinction between primary and secondary victims of nervous shock. Whereas primary victims have actually participated in the very traumatic events as a result of which they have sustained nervous shock, secondary victims have sustained harm simply by witnessing such an event. Traditionally, as far as primary victims of nervous shock are concerned, the courts have insisted, in general conformity with the law of negligence, that the type of harm which the pursuer sustains must be reasonably foreseeable.[31] This was not the case in *Page* since it was not reasonably foreseeable that the plaintiff would suffer nervous shock given the nature of the accident. However, the House (by a majority) held that the plaintiff could recover, on the basis that the law already recognised that the defendant owed a duty of care not negligently to inflict physical harm on the plaintiff. One should not draw a distinction between psychiatric injury and bodily injury. It was sufficient, therefore, that in the circumstances one should have foreseen some form of physical injury to the plaintiff. In the last analysis, the House, by refusing to distinguish between bodily injury and psychiatric harm, expanded the scope of the duty of care to allow the plaintiff to recover damages in a situation where the law had previously denied redress.

Another case which illustrates that the capacity for judicial inventiveness is perhaps not **2.21** as moribund as appeared after *Caparo* is the House of Lords case of *White* v *Jones*.[32] There, solicitors who were acting for a testator negligently failed to carry out instructions to prepare a new will. The upshot of this was that the intended beneficiaries failed to receive the money which the testator desired they should. The former sued the solicitors. The House held that the defendants owed the plaintiffs a duty of care. Indeed, the conceptual difficulties which the plaintiffs faced seemed formidable, if not insurmountable, in that:

(1) it is well established that a solicitor who acts on behalf of a client owes a duty of care only to his client;
(2) a plaintiff cannot normally recover in delict or tort for pure financial loss;
(3) if the plaintiffs were allowed to recover in the instant case, the decision could open the floodgates to claims against solicitors by indeterminate classes of people, including those affected by an *inter vivos* transaction.

Lord Goff, however, sidestepped these difficulties.[33] Uppermost in the mind of his **2.22** Lordship was the injustice that would be done if solicitors were not liable to beneficiaries for negligently preparing wills. The law of negligence required to be extended to fill such a gap. The decision in *White* represents the law of Scotland.[34] However, in

---

[30] See Chapter 5.
[31] *The Wagon Mound* [1961] AC 388. See Chapter 8.
[32] [1995] 2 AC 207.
[33] *Ibid* at 268.
[34] See, eg, *Holmes* v *Bank of Scotland* 2002 SLT 544 and *Robertson* v *Watt*, unreported, IH – 4 July 1995. For a useful discussion of the delictual liability of solicitors in relation to the preparation of wills, see J Kerrigan, "Negligence in will-making – a line in the sand" 2010 SLT 77. *White* was distinguished in the Outer House case of *McLeod* v *Crawford* 2010 SLT 1035, where it was held that *White* applied only to intended beneficiaries.

the Outer House case of *McLeod* v *Crawford*[35] it was held that a solicitor does not owe a duty of care to the family of a client in respect of the accuracy of the advice which is given to the client. *White* was distinguished here.

2.23   A good example of judicial inventiveness post *Caparo* is *Spring* v *Guardian Assurance*.[36] In that case, the House of Lords held that the author of an employee reference which is given to a potential employer owes a duty of care to the employee in respect of the accuracy of the reference. In short, the *Hedley Byrne* v *Heller* principle was extended to cover the facts of the case.

2.24   Another interesting example of the incremental approach to the duty of care can be seen in the Court of Appeal case of *Watson* v *British Boxing Board of Control*.[37] This case concerned liability for head injuries sustained by Michael Watson, who was a professional boxer, in his title fight with Chris Eubank. The fight was regulated by the British Boxing Board of Control (BBBC). Watson claimed that the BBBC had failed to take adequate measures to ensure that he received immediate and effective medical attention should he sustain injury during the fight. The Court of Appeal held that there was sufficient proximity between the parties to ground a duty of care in law. The basis for the decision was that since the BBBC had complete control over the contest it was fair, just and reasonable to conclude that a duty of care existed. Lord Phillips MR[38] set store by the following factors:

(1) Watson was one of a defined number of boxing members of the BBBC.
(2) A primary stated object of the BBBC was to look after its boxing members' physical safety.
(3) The BBBC encouraged and supported its boxing members in the pursuit of an activity which involved inevitable physical injury.
(4) The BBBC controlled the medical assistance which could be provided.
(5) The BBBC had access to specialist expertise in relation to medical care.
(6) If Watson had no remedy against the BBBC, he had no remedy at all.
(7) Boxing members of the BBBC, including Watson, could reasonably rely on the former to look after their safety.

2.25   The application of the threefold test which was enunciated in *Caparo* is neatly illustrated in the House of Lords case of *Mitchell* v *Glasgow City Council*.[39] The facts of the case were both simple and straightforward. The widow and daughter of a local authority tenant raised an action against a local authority in respect of the tenant's death. The deceased had died as a result of head wounds he received in an assault on him by another tenant who had previously threatened to kill him. The local authority had been aware of a long history of previous incidents of threatening behaviour by the other tenant towards the deceased. Written warnings had been issued to the tenant by the local authority in respect of his tenancy and a meeting was eventually held by the local authority and the tenant to discuss this. It was following that meeting that the tenant attacked and murdered the deceased. The pursuers

---

[35] 2010 SLT 1035.
[36] [1995] 2 AC 296.
[37] [2001] 2 WLR 1256.
[38] *Ibid* at 1281.
[39] 2009 SC (HL) 21. For an interesting discussion of this case, see J O'Sullivan, "Liability for the criminal acts of third parties" [2009] CLJ 270.

sought damages against the local authority, *inter alia*, on the ground that the local authority had a duty to evict the tenant and to have warned the deceased about the meeting. The House held that the local authority was under no such duty to warn the deceased. The local authority had not assumed any responsibility for the safety of the tenant. Foreseeability of injury was not enough of itself to impose a duty of care. Interestingly, Lord Hope swept aside the suggestion that the tripartite test, which was enunciated in *Caparo*, was not part of the law of Scotland.[40] For his Lordship, the test was really no more than an expression of the idea that lies at the heart of every judgment about legal policy.

2.26 The application of the tripartite test was discussed recently by the Inner House in *Hines* v *King Sturge*.[41] In that case, the pursuers sought damages from the defenders who were managing agents of premises from which they operated their businesses. The said premises were damaged in a fire. The pursuers averred that the defenders, as managing agents, had control of the building and that the maintenance of the fire alarm system and monitoring system was the defenders' responsibility. In short, the pursuers argued that the defenders owed them a duty of care. The Inner House, by a majority, in allowing proof before answer, held, *inter alia*, that the "foreseeability" test, as expounded in *Caparo*, could be satisfied where the defenders either knew or ought to have known that if the fire alarm system was not operating effectively, the premises would be at risk. The Inner House also decided that it could possibly be argued successfully that there was proximity between the parties and also that it could possibly be established that it was fair, just and reasonable to impose a duty of care.

2.27 It has already been observed[42] that the *Caparo* tripartite test falls to be applied not simply in relation to circumstances where the pursuer has sustained financial loss, but also where the pursuer has sustained physical harm to his property. However, does the test also apply to a situation where the pursuer sustains injury to his person? This point was decided by the Court of Appeal in *Everett* v *Comojo (UK) Ltd t/a The Metropolitan*.[43] The facts of the case were simple. The claimants visited a nightclub. They were attacked and seriously injured by another guest. They claimed that the club had failed to adopt appropriate measures to prevent the assault from taking place. The court held that the club owed the claimants a duty of care in terms of the law of negligence. After stating[44] that the three elements were not completely separate considerations and overlapped to some extent, Smith LJ expressed the view that the relationship between the management of the club and its guests was of sufficient proximity to justify the existence of a duty of care. The management was in control of the premises. It could regulate who entered, who was refused entry and who was to be removed after entry. There was also an economic relationship between the two. Given the relationship between the consumption of alcohol and violence, it was foreseeable that one guest might attack another. After stating[45] that the common law duty of care is an extremely flexible concept and is adaptable to the very wide range of circumstances to which it has to be applied, his Lordship considered that it was fair, just and

---

[40] 2009 SC (HL) 21 at 31.
[41] 2011 SLT 2.
[42] At p 9, above.
[43] [2011] PIQR 211. See also *Gibson* v *Orr* 1999 SC 420, which is discussed below.
[44] [2011] PIQR 211 at 219.
[45] *Ibid* at 221.

reasonable that it should govern the relationship between the managers of a hotel or nightclub and their guests in relation to the actions of third parties on the premises.

LIABILITY FOR OMISSIONS

2.28 The next issue for discussion is to what extent, if any, the law imposes a duty on the defender to save his neighbour from injury. Omissions, like economic loss, are notoriously a category of conduct for which Lord Atkin's generalisation in *Donoghue* v *Stevenson*[46] offers limited help.[47] The general rule is that there is no duty of affirmative action in the law of negligence.[48] In other words, subject to certain exceptions, I am under no duty to save my neighbour who is in a dangerous situation. I can smugly watch him walk towards a dangerous cliff without shouting a warning. I can idly stand by and watch a baby drown in a shallow pool of water, provided that I do not stand in a special relationship to the child.[49]

However, there are certain circumstances in which the law does impose an affirmative duty on the defender to take affirmative action. These situations will now be considered.

OCCUPIER OF LAND

2.29 The law imposes a duty of care on the defender not to allow his property to become a known source of danger to neighbouring proprietors. This was established in the trilogy of cases, namely *Sedleigh Denfield* v *O'Callaghan*,[50] *Goldman* v *Hargrave*[51] and *Leakey* v *National Trust*,[52] which we will discuss in the chapter on the law of nuisance.[53] In these cases the respective courts were prepared to assimilate the law of nuisance with the law of negligence in respect of both the nature and scope of the duty owed by the occupier of land to a neighbouring proprietor. In the aforementioned cases, the land of the defendants had become physically unsafe either by human conduct, as in *Sedleigh-Denfield*, or by an act of nature, as in *Goldman*. To what extent, if any, is the above learning applicable to a situation where the land becomes a source of danger by virtue of the illegal conduct of trespassers? This question fell to be answered in the House of Lords case of *Smith* v *Littlewoods*.[54] In that case, trespassers entered the defenders' premises which were unoccupied at the time. The trespassers set the premises on fire. The fire spread to and damaged neighbouring property which belonged to the pursuer. The defenders were held not liable in terms of the law of negligence since, on the facts of the case, the intervention by the trespassers was not foreseeable. The House held that unless the occupier had actually created the source of danger whence the damage arose, the occupier of the land would not be liable

---

[46] [1932] AC 562.
[47] Per Lord Hoffmann in *Stovin* v *Wise* [1996] AC 923 at 943.
[48] *Smith* v *Littlewoods* [1987] AC 241, per Lord Goff at 270.
[49] L Eldridge, *Modern Tort Problems* (1941) at p 12.
[50] [1940] AC 880.
[51] [1967] 1 AC 645.
[52] [1980] 1 All ER 17.
[53] See Chapter 11.
[54] [1987] AC 241.

for damage which was caused by the acts of third parties trespassing on the land of the defender unless the perpetration of such damage was highly probable. In other words, the law does not normally impose an affirmative duty on an occupier of land to prevent third parties, on that land, damaging adjoining property.

"CONTROL" SITUATION

The law requires a person who stands in a particular relationship with, and therefore exercises some form of control over, that person, to protect that person from harm in certain circumstances. The relationships of parent–child, employer–employee, occupier of land–visitor, school governors–pupil have all attracted a duty of care on the person exercising the relevant control. However, the list of situations where the law imposes an affirmative duty on the defender is not closed. Indeed, the courts have been willing to impose a duty of care by way of analogous reasoning on a relationship where a duty of care has previously been held to exist. For example, in the Canadian case of *Moddejonge v Huron County Board of Education*,[55] a person who acted as the co-ordinator of outdoor educational programmes was found liable in negligence when a student drowned on a field trip. Again, in *Smith v Horizon Aero Sports Ltd*,[56] a parachute instructor was held to owe a duty of care to his student. In the aforementioned cases the school–pupil relationship was extended to cover the facts of the case. An example of the occupier of land–visitor relationship being extended by way of analogy is neatly illustrated in *Jordan House Ltd v Menow*.[57] In that case, the employees of the defendant hotel had served the plaintiff with drink until he became patently drunk. He was subsequently ejected from the hotel in a state in which it was quite clear that he could not look after himself. He was hit by a car while he was crossing the road and was injured. It was held that the proprietors of the hotel owed an affirmative duty of care to a drunken customer to the effect that he should not be turned out of the former's premises if it would be unsafe to do so.[58] A further example of the extension of the category of relationships where the law has placed an affirmative duty on the defender is seen in the Canadian Supreme Court case of *Horsley v MacLaren*,[59] where it was held that the owner of a private boat was under a common law duty, in terms of the law of negligence, to attempt to rescue a passenger who had fallen overboard.

2.30

Where the defender exercises control over both the pursuer and the third party who injures the pursuer, the case for the imposition of a duty is particularly strong. The *Everett* case, which was discussed above, serves as a good example of this.

2.31

In some cases the relevant control which the defender exercises is in relation to either (a) a dangerous situation, *or* (b) a potentially dangerous situation. The Outer House case of *Gibson v Orr*[60] illustrates (a). In that case, a bridge which carried a public road collapsed. The attention of the police was drawn to the danger which was posed to traffic. The police coned off the north side of the bridge and left a police vehicle with its lights flashing on that side so that it would be visible to vehicles approaching from

2.32

---

[55] [1972] 2 OR 437.
[56] (1981) 19 CCLT 89 (BCSC).
[57] (1973) 38 DLR (3d) 105.
[58] For a useful discussion of the duties of the duty of occupiers of licensed premises to their customers, see C Hare, "Am I my (drunken) neighbour's keeper?" [2010] CLJ 16.
[59] [1971] 2 Lloyd's Rep 410.
[60] 1999 SC 420.

the south side of the road. The police then left the scene of the accident without having received confirmation that any warning or barrier had been placed on the south side of the bridge. Shortly after this, a car, which approached the bridge from the south side, fell into the river. The pursuer survived but the other occupants of the car were killed. It was held that, by virtue of the police having taken control of the hazard in question, they came under a duty of care to the pursuer.[61]

2.33 The Outer House case of *Wilson v Chief Constable of Lothian and Borders Police*[62] illustrates category (b). In that case the police were called to a domestic incident. The husband (W) of the pursuer was removed in the police car but he was not arrested. W was in an inebriated condition. After causing a disturbance in the car, W was released in the early hours of the morning on the outskirts of Edinburgh, in adverse weather conditions. W subsequently died of hypothermia. It was held that, by virtue of the control which the police exercised over W, they owed him a duty of care in terms of the law of negligence.

ASSUMPTION OF RESPONSIBILITY/DETRIMENTAL RELIANCE

2.34 If, through my conduct, I encourage the pursuer (to whom I stand in no special relationship) to rely on me (in other words, I assume responsibility towards him), and I then proceed to conduct a rescue, do I automatically owe the pursuer a duty of care in law? In the US case of *H R Moch Co v Rensselar Water Co*,[63] Judge Cardozo, in discussing the duty of affirmative action, stated in somewhat quaint language: "if conduct has gone forward to such a stage that inaction would commonly result, not negatively merely in withholding a benefit, but positively or actively in working an injury, there exists a relation out of which arises a duty to go forward". Therefore, if I see my neighbour's garden shed burn and I proceed to train my garden hose on the fire for a short time, the upshot of which is that my neighbour reasonably forgoes the opportunity to summon firefighters by deciding to rely on my help instead, the law will impose an affirmative duty on me to continue putting out the fire and, furthermore, to do so without negligence. This general principle was neatly illustrated in the US case of *Zelenko v Gimbel Bros.*[64] In that case, the plaintiff was taken ill at the defendant's premises. The latter kept him in isolation for 6 hours to the detriment of his health. It was held that the defendant owed him a duty of care in law.

2.35 Another case which illustrates that the assumption of responsibility towards the pursuer grounds liability for pure omissions is the House of Lords case of *White v Jones*, which has already been considered above.[65] It will be recalled that, in *White*, the defendant solicitors failed to follow instructions to prepare a new will for the testator, as a consequence of which the plaintiffs lost money. It was held that since the defendant solicitors had assumed responsibility for their conduct, they were liable for their acts of omission as well as commission. Again, in another case discussed above, namely *Watson v British Boxing Board of Control*, one of the factors which prompted the

---

[61] See, however, *Ancell v McDermott* [1993] 4 All ER 355.
[62] 1989 SLT 97.
[63] 159 NE 896 (1928) at 898.
[64] (1935) 158 Misc 904, 287 NYS 134.
[65] See p 11.

Court of Appeal to hold that the Board owed a common law duty of care to the boxer, Watson, was that he had relied on the Board to look after his safety in the ring.

DEFENDER CREATES DANGEROUS SITUATION

The defender may come under a duty to take the necessary prophylactic action **2.36** to either rescue the pursuer, abate the relevant danger, or warn the pursuer of the relevant danger, if the defender creates a dangerous situation. This is neatly illustrated in the Court of Appeal case of *Kimber v Gaslight and Coke Co.*[66] In that case, workmen, who were carrying out work to a private house, removed floorboards from part of a landing in the house. A visitor put her foot in the hole and was injured. It was held that the workmen who had created the dangerous condition were under a duty to warn the plaintiff of the existence of the hole. Such a duty arose quite independently of the occupation of the premises. Similarly, in the Court of Appeal case of *Fisher v Ruislip-Northwood UDC,*[67] the plaintiff was injured when his car collided with a surface air-raid shelter during the hours of darkness. It was held that the defendant local authority was under a duty to give the plaintiff adequate warning of the danger. Again, in the Inner House case of *Mooney v Lanark County Council,*[68] the tenant of a new council house entered into occupation of the house before the entrance path to the premises had been completed. A metal toby protruded from the surface of the path. The pursuer, who was visiting the wife of the tenant, tripped over the toby and was injured. It was held that, since the defender local authority had created the danger, it was under a duty to warn visitors to the premises about the danger.

Finally, in the Court of Appeal case of *Kane v New Forrest District Council,*[69] a **2.37** planning authority required a developer to construct a footpath before allowing a development to commence. The footpath ended on the inside of a bend of a road which had impaired visibility to road-users. The claimant was struck by a car when emerging from the footpath. In a striking-out action, the court accepted the proposition that the claimant had a powerful case, in terms of the law of negligence, that the planning authority owed him a duty of care in law since it had created the danger in question.

DEFENDER DERIVES ECONOMIC BENEFIT FROM HIS RELATIONSHIP WITH PURSUER

There is some Commonwealth authority to the effect that, if the pursuer derives some **2.38** economic advantage from his relationship with the defender, the courts are inclined to hold that a duty of care is owed by the defender to the pursuer. In *Crocker v Sundance Northwest Resorts Ltd,*[70] the defendant company operated a ski complex. A competitor was allowed to enter a race despite the fact that he was visibly drunk. He was injured. It was held, on appeal, that since the defendants derived economic advantage from the

---

[66] [1918] 1 KB 584. See also *A C Billings & Sons v Riden* [1958] AC 240.
[67] [1945] KB 584.
[68] 1954 SC 245.
[69] [2002] 1 WLR 312. See also *Yetkin v Mahmood* [2011] 2 WLR 1073.
[70] (1988) 44 CCLT 192.

competitor, the latter was owed a duty of care by the former. Finally, in *Everett*,[71] one of the reasons the Court of Appeal felt justified in holding that the defendant club owed a duty of care to the claimant, who had been seriously injured by another patron, was that the club derived an economic advantage from the presence of the claimant on the premises.

DUTY OF CARE AND PUBLIC AUTHORITIES

2.39   We now examine the concept of duty of care in terms of the liability of public authorities in the law of negligence. Public authorities, unlike private individuals, normally derive their powers and duties from statute. Sometimes such powers are either misused or not used at all, the upshot of which is that the pursuer sustains some type of harm to either his person or property. The subject represents a grey and, indeed, untidy area of the law of delict. The subject is also vast.[72] For the purposes of this section of the chapter we have discussed delictual liability under separate functions or authorities: for example, "The police". However, this is done simply for the sake of convenience. The separate categories of functions or authorities should not be regarded as self-contained or watertight categories in terms of the law of negligence.

THE POLICE

2.40   The most important function of the police is, of course, the prevention of crime. We have already observed that, subject to certain exceptions, the courts are unwilling to impose liability on the defender for acts of third parties.[73] However, is this learning applicable to the police? Are the police liable in delict for failing to prevent a criminal from harming members of the public?[74]

2.41   The general rule is that the courts are unwilling to impose an affirmative duty on the police to prevent third parties from inflicting harm on the public. This is well illustrated in the House of Lords case of *Hill v Chief Constable of West Yorkshire*.[75] There, the mother of one of the Yorkshire Ripper's victims sued the Chief Constable for failure to apprehend the Ripper. It was held that whereas it was reasonably foreseeable that, if the "Ripper" (Peter Sutcliffe) was not apprehended, he would inflict serious bodily harm on members of the public, no duty of care was owed by the police to his victim. There was no proximity between the police and the victim. Furthermore, it was against public policy to hold the police civilly liable for failure to apprehend a criminal. Lord Keith stated:[76] "A great deal of time, trouble and expense might be expected to have to be put to the preparation of the defence to the action and attendance of witnesses at

---

[71] See p 13 above.

[72] For a more detailed discussion of the subject, see C Booth and D Squires, *The Negligence Liability of Public Authorities* (2006). See also D Nolan, "The liability of public authorities for failing to confer benefits" (2011) 127 LQR 260.

[73] See p 14.

[74] For a useful discussion of the potential liability of the police to prevent crime, see D Walsh, "Police liability for negligent failure to prevent crime: enhancing accountability by clearing the public policy fog" (2011) KLJ 27. See also M Burton, "Failing to protect victim's rights and police liability" (2009) 72 MLR 283.

[75] [1989] AC 53.

[76] *Ibid* at 63.

the trial. The result would be a significant diversion of police manpower and attention from their most important function, that of suppression of crime."

In the Court of Appeal case of *Calveley* v *Chief Constable of Merseyside Police*,[77] a **2.42** police constable sued his police authority in respect of the anxiety, vexation and injury to his reputation he had allegedly sustained by virtue of the manner in which disciplinary proceedings against him had been conducted by a police investigating officer. It was held that the latter did not owe a common law duty of care to the officer. If the law imposed such a duty it would prejudice the fearless and efficient discharge by police officers of their vitally important public duty of investigating crime.[78]

The decision in *Hill* fell to be considered again by the House of Lords most recently[79] **2.43** in *Van Colle* v *Chief Constable of the Hertfordshire Police*.[80] The basic question before the House was as follows: if the police are alerted to a threat that D may kill or inflict violence on V, and the police take no action to prevent that occurrence, and D does kill or inflict violence on V, may V or his relatives obtain civil redress against the police, and, if so, how and in what circumstances?[81] Since *Hill*, of course, the Human Rights Act 1998 has incorporated the ECHR into domestic law. The Convention provides that "everyone's life shall be protected by law. No one shall be deprived of his life intentionally".[82] Furthermore, in the ECHR case of *Osman* v *UK*[83] the court held that the liability of the state would only lie in such circumstances if it was established that the authorities either knew, or ought to have known, at the time, of the existence of a real and immediate risk to the life of an individual by a third party and that the necessary measures were not taken. The fundamental question which the House had to consider was the extent, if any, to which the policy of the common law was required to be reconsidered in the light of such jurisprudence. The House was firmly of the view that *Hill* was not undermined by *Osman*. Indeed, the House was of the view that the right to life which was enshrined in the Convention had no influence on the development of the law of negligence in this area. In short, Convention rights could sit quite comfortably beside the rights which were conferred by the common law.[84]

FIRE AUTHORITIES, AMBULANCE SERVICE AND COASTGUARD

Whereas public policy decreed that the plaintiff should fail in *Hill* in an action which **2.44** was based on the defendants' failing to apprehend a third party timeously, do similar considerations apply in relation to firefighters in terms of the performance of their statutory duties? In the Outer House case of *Duff* v *Highlands and Islands Fire Board*,[85] the defenders had been called out to the house adjoining that of the pursuer twice in one evening. On their first visit, the fire brigade left while the house was still on fire. The fire brigade was recalled but it was unable to put out the fire. The fire spread to the pursuer's premises, which were destroyed. It was claimed on behalf of the defenders

---

[77] [1989] QB 136.
[78] *Ibid* at 150.
[79] See also *Brooks* v *Commissioner of Police of the Metropolis* [2005] 1 WLR 1495.
[80] [2008] UKHL 50. See also *Thomson* v *Scottish Ministers* [2011] CSOH 90.
[81] *Ibid*, per Lord Bingham at [1].
[82] Art 2.
[83] (1998) 29 EHRR 245.
[84] For a useful discussion of *Van Colle*, see C McIvor, "Getting defensive about police negligence: the Hill principle, the Human Rights Act 1998 and the House of Lords" [2010] CLJ 133.
[85] *The Times*, 3 November 1995.

that it was contrary to public policy for the law to hold that a duty of care was owed by the defenders to the pursuer, on the basis that the imposition of a duty of care might tend to encourage a defensive approach to their operations. However, this argument was rejected by Lord Macfadyen, who expressed the view that the manner in which operational duties of the defenders were performed was not immune from challenge at common law. It was open to the court to ascertain whether such a duty of care had been breached in any given factual situation. However, a different approach was taken by the court in *Church of Jesus Christ of Latter-Day Saints (Great Britain)* v *Yorkshire Fire and Civil Defence Authority*.[86] In that case a fire brigade failed to extinguish a fire at the plaintiffs' premises because the defendant fire authority had failed to ensure that certain fire hydrants at the premises were in working order. It was held that to permit common law claims in negligence to be made against a fire service would impose a new burden which would be detrimental to the service and a distraction from its proper task of fighting fires. The imposition of a duty of care would create the possibility of massive financial claims which would be an unreasonable burden on the taxpayer. It was for the individual to insure his property against fire – it was not for the community to do so for him. Again, in *John Munroe (Acrylics) Ltd* v *London Fire and Civil Defence Authority*,[87] certain individuals caused an explosion on wasteland not far from the plaintiff's premises. This caused a scattering of flaming debris over a fairly wide area. Debris fell on to the plaintiff's premises. Fire engines arrived in response to emergency calls, by which time the burning debris and the fires on the wasteland had been extinguished, and there was no visible evidence of any continuing fire. Believing that the fires were out and that the danger had passed, the fire crews left. The fire crews, however, had not inspected the plaintiff's premises which abutted on one side of the wasteland where there was combustible material. Fire damaged the premises. Rougier J held that the fire authority did not owe the plaintiff a duty of care at common law. There was insufficient proximity between the fire brigades and the owner of any property which was on fire to impose a duty of care at common law on the fire authority. Furthermore, it was contrary to public policy to impose a common law duty of care on a fire authority for failing to extinguish a fire. A number of factors combined to make it contrary to public policy to impose such a duty:

(1) no extra standard of care would be achieved;
(2) a common law duty of care would lead to defensive firefighting;
(3) the efficiency of the emergency services should be tested but not in private litigation;
(4) the fire brigade acted for the collective welfare of the community;
(5) successful claims against any fire authority would have to be subscribed by the general public – it was preferable that the floodgates should remain closed to such claims.

2.45   As is the case with the police (as seen in *Gibson* v *Orr*, above), the courts are more willing to impose liability regarding claims which are made in relation to the performance of operational duties of the fire services. For one thing, of course, it is easier for the courts to ascertain whether the requisite standard of care has been breached.

---

[86] *The Times*, 9 May 1996.
[87] [1996] 4 All ER 318.

This is illustrated in *Duff* v *Highlands and Islands Fire Board*,[88] where it was held that it was not contrary to public policy to impose a duty of care on the defenders. *Duff* can be contrasted with *Capital and Counties plc* v *Hampshire County Council*.[89] There, the plaintiffs were tenants of a commercial building. A fire in one block was attended by the fire brigade. The plaintiff tenants' building was attended by the fire brigade; it was equipped with a sprinkler system in its roof space. In the course of fighting the fire, the station officer in charge of the operation ordered that the sprinkler system be shut down. The fire went out of control as a result of this action. The building was destroyed. The court held that the defendants owed the plaintiffs a duty of care in law. The very act of shutting down the sprinkler system generated a relationship of proximity between the defendants and the plaintiffs. Furthermore, there were no policy grounds for excluding liability on the part of the defendants.[90]

2.46 The question of whether the ambulance service owes a duty of care to the public in the way in which it responds to "999" calls was considered by the Court of Appeal in *Kent* v *Griffiths*.[91] The facts of the case were simple. The claimant suffered an asthma attack. Her doctor summoned an ambulance. The ambulance service promised to send an ambulance immediately, to convey her to hospital. The ambulance arrived at the claimant's home unreasonably late, by which time she had suffered brain damage. The court held that the ambulance service should be regarded as part of the health service in relation to which the law already imposed a duty of care in relation to its treatment of patients. A distinction was drawn between the ambulance service responding to an emergency call and the police or the fire service responding to requests for assistance. In the last analysis, the defendants did owe a duty of care to the claimant.

2.47 *Kent* was followed recently in the Outer House case of *Aitken* v *Scottish Ambulance Service*.[92] In that case the pursuer was the mother of a young woman who had suffered an epileptic fit. An ambulance was called by the pursuer's son. However, the ambulance arrived late despite the son being reassured that an ambulance was on its way after making the original call. The woman died as a result of her fit. The issue to be determined was whether the defenders owed the pursuer a duty of care to attend to the deceased timeously. In allowing proof before answer, Lord Mackay was of the opinion that it would be possible for the pursuer to establish at proof that, by the defenders' eliciting information about the deceased's medical history from her brother, advising him that an ambulance was on its way, giving him advice as to how his sister was to be treated until the ambulance arrived, and also despatching a rapid response unit, the defenders had established a relationship of proximity with the deceased.[93] In reaching such a conclusion, the Lord Ordinary set store by the fact that the routine which had been followed by the defenders fell to be categorised as operational in nature as opposed to the exercise of a discretionary policy decision.[94]

---

[88] 1995 SLT 1362.
[89] [1996] 4 All ER 336.
[90] The *Capital and Counties*, *John Munroe* and *Church of Jesus Christ* decisions were upheld on consolidated appeals to the Court of Appeal: [1997] QB 1004.
[91] [2001] QB 36.
[92] [2011] CSOH 49.
[93] *Ibid* at [61].
[94] *Ibid* at [62].

2.48   Finally, in the first-instance case of *OLL Ltd* v *Secretary of State for the Home Department*[95] (which was a striking-out action), it was held that the coastguard did not owe a duty of care to those in danger by negligently misguiding either its own personnel or other people outside its own service in response to an emergency call.

HIGHWAY AUTHORITIES

2.49   Roads can be very dangerous. The design and layout of a public road as well as the lack of appropriate warning signs may pose a potential danger to road-users. Again, it is patently obvious that un-gritted roads in winter can be particularly hazardous. To what extent, if any, then, is a highway authority liable to members of the public who suffer harm by virtue of the manner in which such an authority exercises its functions in relation to public roads?

2.50   The leading case is the House of Lords case of *Stovin* v *Wise (Norfolk County Council third party)*.[96] In that case, the plaintiff was injured when his motorcycle collided with a car which was driven by the defendant, who was turning out of a side road. The defendant's visibility had been limited because a bank on adjacent railway land obstructed her view of the corner in question. The defendant joined the highway authority as third party to the proceedings. The Court of Appeal held that a duty of care was owed at common law by the highway authority to the plaintiff. In reaching this decision, the court was influenced by the fact that many of the duties and powers which were imposed on the highway authority under the Highways Act 1980 had, as their principal object, the promotion of the safety of road-users. However, the House of Lords, by a majority of three to two, reversed the decision of the court.[97] The House rejected the proposition that, simply because the Highways Act conferred a variety of powers on the highway authority to make roads in its area convenient and safe, this automatically resulted in the law imposing a common law duty of care to the plaintiff to remove the obstruction which caused the accident. However, in determining whether such a duty was owed at common law it was not simply a question of statutory construction. Rather, one had to have regard to the policy of the statute. Furthermore, if a public authority was to be held liable at common law for failing to exercise a statutory power, it would require to be shown: (a) that it was irrational not to have exercised that power, so that there was, in effect, a public law duty to act; and (b) that there were exceptional grounds for holding that the policy of the statute required compensation to be paid to persons who suffered loss because the power was not exercised.[98] In the instant case, the question of whether anything should be done about the junction was firmly within the highway authority's discretion. As the authority was not under a public law duty to effect the work in question, the first condition, (a), was not satisfied. As far as (b) was concerned, the majority of the House[99] also expressed doubt (*obiter*) that, even if the authority ought, as a matter of public law, to have done the work, there were any grounds upon which it could be said that the

---

[95] *The Times*, 22 July 1997.
[96] [1994] 3 All ER 467.
[97] [1996] AC 923.
[98] *Ibid* at 953 (per Lord Hoffmann).
[99] *Ibid* at 957.

public law duty should give rise to compensate persons who had suffered loss because the relevant function was not performed.

The House of Lords was again required to consider the liability of a highway **2.51** authority in negligence in *Gorringe* v *Calderdale Metropolitan Borough Council*.[100] In that case the claimant was injured in a road traffic accident. Her vehicle was in collision with a bus which had been hidden behind a sharp crest in the road until just before the claimant's vehicle reached the top. The layout of the road probably caused the appellant to believe, mistakenly, that the bus was on her side of the road. She brought an action against the highway authority, claiming, *inter alia*, that the highway authority owed her a duty of care at common law to institute proper highway safety measures, including the provision of adequate road signs. In short, the fundamental question which the House had to answer was whether the highway authority was liable at common law for its omission. The House held that the Road Traffic Act 1988,[101] which imposed a broad duty on highway authorities to prepare and carry out a programme designed to promote and improve road safety, did not create a common law duty of care and thus a private right of action.

It is instructive to compare the judgments of their Lordships. According to Lord **2.52** Steyn,[102] in order to ascertain whether a statute confers private rights on the claimant in terms of the law of negligence, one is required to consider whether the statute excludes a private law remedy. His Lordship went on to doubt the utility of the public law concept of unreasonableness as a condition precedent to the court imposing liability on a public authority in terms of the law of negligence. In turn, Lord Hoffmann also rejected public law concepts in determining whether a duty of care was owed by the highway authority to the defendant.[103] His Lordship found it difficult to imagine a case in which a common law duty of care could be founded simply on the failure, however irrational, to provide some benefit which a public authority had power to provide. Lord Scott was of the view that if, on construction, the relevant statute precluded an action for breach of statutory duty,[104] that would automatically preclude an action at common law in terms of the law of negligence.[105] Both Lord Rodger[106] and Lord Brown[107] considered that it was against public policy that drivers should sue highway authorities in negligence. Rather, liability should fall on those who cause the accident in question.

The above cases were reviewed by the Court of Appeal in *Sandhar* v *Department of* **2.53** *Transport*.[108] The facts of this case were simple. The claimant's husband lost control of his vehicle on an icy road which had not been gritted. He was killed. It was claimed that the highway authority owed the deceased a common law duty of care in the law of negligence because the highway authority had assumed responsibility to perform salting operations. The court held that in order for an assumption of responsibility to be sufficient to create a duty of care, a particular relationship with either an individual or individuals was normally required. An assumption of responsibility could not be

---

[100] [2004] PIQR 521.
[101] Road Traffic Act 1988, s 39.
[102] [2004] PIQR 521 at 524.
[103] *Ibid* at 531.
[104] See Chapter 10.
[105] [2004] PIQR 521 at 542.
[106] *Ibid* at 549.
[107] *Ibid* at 551.
[108] [2005] 1 WLR 1632.

based on a general expectation. Reliance on an assumption of responsibility was also necessary for liability to lie. There was no evidence, in the instant case, to the effect that the deceased had relied on the highway authority. The highway authority did not, therefore, owe a duty of care to the deceased at common law.

SOCIAL WORK AND EDUCATION AUTHORITIES

2.54 In *X* v *Bedfordshire County Council*,[109] the House of Lords essentially had to determine whether a social work authority owed children a common law duty of care to prevent them from being sexually abused by third parties. The House refused to do so. One of the reasons for this decision was that to impose a duty of care in terms of the law of negligence would encourage social work departments to adopt a defensive attitude to their duties.[110] In the same appeal, the House was required to decide whether an education authority owed to pupils with special needs a duty of care to assess such needs. It was held that where a school accepted a pupil, it assumed responsibility not only for his physical well-being but also for his educational needs. A duty of care was, therefore, owed by the authority to the pupil.[111]

2.55 The House of Lords case of *Barrett* v *Enfield London Borough Council*[112] (which was a striking-out action) is instructive in the present context. B had been placed in the care of a local authority. He claimed damages for personal injury arising out of negligence by the local authority. The alleged breaches of duty included failure to arrange for his adoption, or to provide him with appropriate and properly monitored placements, or to obtain appropriate psychiatric treatment for him. The House held that public policy considerations, which meant that it would not be fair, just and reasonable to impose a common law duty of care on a local authority when deciding whether or not to take a child into care in respect of suspected child abuse, did not have the same force once B had been taken into care. Another reason for the House allowing the case to go to trial was the fact that, once B had been taken into care, one could ascertain whether the standard of care which the law demanded of the defendant had been attained. In other words, the ability of the court to ascertain the requisite standard of care the law demanded of the defendant had a reflexive effect on whether the court should impose a duty of care in the law of negligence.

FACTUAL DUTY OF CARE

2.56 What we have been looking at so far is the law relating to the courts' imposing a duty of care in relation to novel situations. However, once a court does decide that the defender owes a duty of care to the pursuer, the court must then consider whether, on the facts of the case, the defender owes the pursuer a factual duty of care by reason of

---

[109] [1995] 2 AC 633.
[110] *Ibid* at 750 (per Lord Browne-Wilkinson). See also *Lawrence* v *Pembrokeshire CC* [2007] EWCA Civ 446.
[111] See also *Phelps* v *Hillingdon LBC* [2000] 3 WLR 776 and *Carty* v *Croydon LBC* [2005] 1 WLR 2312 where the House of Lords held that when an education officer entered into a relationship with a child or assumed responsibility towards a child with special educational needs, he might owe a duty of care to the child in terms of the law of negligence. See also *Connor* v *Surrey CC* [2011] QB 429 and S Tofaris, "Negligence Liability of Public Bodies: Locating the Interface between Public and Private Law" [2011] CLJ 294.
[112] [2001] 2 AC 550.

posing a danger to the pursuer. This important point can be illustrated by two famous cases. The first is American.

In *Palsgraf* v *Long Island Rail Co*,[113] Mrs Palsgraf was standing on a railway platform **2.57** when two men ran to catch a train. The second man, X, was carrying a small, ostensibly innocuous, package. The defendants' servants, in attempting to assist X in boarding the train, carelessly dislodged the package from his arms. The package fell. An explosion ensued, since the package contained fireworks. A heavy weighing machine, which was situated at the other end of the platform, was dislodged by the explosion. The plaintiff was injured by the machine. The court held that the defendants were not liable for their careless act. The defendants could not have foreseen that their careless act would have harmed the plaintiff. Judge Cardozo, speaking for the majority of the court, held that there was no liability because there was no negligence between the parties. Negligence required to be founded upon the foreseeability of harm to the person who was actually injured, not to someone else.

The Scottish equivalent of *Palsgraf* is the House of Lords case of *Bourhill* v *Young*.[114] **2.58** There, a pregnant fishwife had just alighted from a tram when she heard the sound of a road accident. The accident had been caused by the negligence of a motorcyclist, John Young, who was overtaking the tram in which Mrs Bourhill had been travelling. Young collided with a car which was turning right and into his direction of travel. Mrs Bourhill sustained nervous shock. She sued the estate of the deceased. The House held that whereas motorcyclists and cyclists who use the roads owe a duty of care to fellow road-users and pedestrians, on the facts of the case, the defender did not owe the pursuer a duty of care. The former could not reasonably foresee that someone where Mrs Bourhill was situated when the accident took place would have suffered nervous shock. She was not within the relevant risk area vis-à-vis the defender.

---

[113] 248 NY 339 (1928).
[114] 1942 SC (HL) 78.

3 THE DUTY OF CARE – NEGLIGENT MISSTATEMENTS

In this chapter we shall consider the potential liability in negligence for loss caused by   **3.1**
the defender making a statement on which the pursuer relies. For example, suppose
that Cyril advises Tony to invest his life savings in a certain foreign bank. Tony relies
on that advice. However, the bank collapses soon after Tony opens his account and
Tony loses his money. Could Tony sue Cyril in delict? Again, it is mid-winter. One
night I am driving my car along a road. Driving conditions are poor. My "Sat Nav"
instructs me to take the first exit from the approaching roundabout. I do so, only to
collide with metal barriers which have been used to block off that exit. Could I sue the
manufacturers of the "Sat Nav" in delict?

Before we examine the relevant case law on liability for negligent misstatements,   **3.2**
it is worth addressing our minds to the words of Lord Pearce in *Hedley Byrne* v *Heller*[1]
where he stated: "Words are more volatile than deeds. They travel fast and far afield.
They are used without being expended." Liability for unlimited sums of money to an
unlimited class of individuals is something that the courts are unwilling to encourage.
The law therefore requires to be circumspect in allowing claims for loss which is caused
by negligent statements, lest the courts be inundated with claims. In sharp contrast to
negligent conduct which results in physical harm to the pursuer, negligent misstatements can potentially reach the whole world through the medium of newspapers and
the internet, encouraging those to whom the words are published to rely on them and
possibly sustain harm. Until the *Hedley Byrne* case, which we will now discuss, the
courts were disinclined to impose liability in respect of negligent statements on the
ground of policy.

In *Hedley Byrne* v *Heller* the plaintiff asked its bank, National Provincial, to obtain   **3.3**
information regarding the financial state of a firm called Easypower for which the
plaintiff was carrying out advertising work. Heller, Easypower's bankers, passed on
information about Easypower to the plaintiffs. The information was erroneous, in
that it indicated that Easypower was financially sound. In actual fact, Easypower was
not. The plaintiff lost money. The plaintiff then sued Heller. The House of Lords held
that in the absence of the disclaimer (that is, a statement disclaiming liability in negligence) which had been made by the defendants to the plaintiffs, they would have been
liable for the loss which had been caused by the plaintiffs relying on the statement.
According to Lord Morris,[2] if someone possessed of a special skill undertakes, quite
irrespective of contract, to apply that skill for the assistance of another person, a duty
of care will arise. According to Lord Devlin, the relationship between the defendant
and plaintiff required to be similar to that existing under contract before the law would

---

[1] [1964] AC 465 at 534.
[2] *Ibid* at 502.

hold the defendant liable for a negligent statement.[3] Therefore, for his Lordship, the relationship between the parties required to be close for the court to conclude that the defender owed the pursuer a duty of care.

3.4 It is of fundamental importance to the operation of the rule in *Hedley Byrne* that the defender intends the pursuer to rely on the former's statement and that, in turn, the pursuer relies on the representation. Such intention on the part of the defender to assume responsibility for the accuracy of the statement requires to be assessed objectively by the court.[4]

3.5 *Hedley Byrne*, therefore, establishes that there requires to be close proximity between the parties before liability will lie for a negligent statement. In *Caparo* v *Dickman*,[5] Lord Oliver was of the opinion that the relationship between the defendant and the plaintiff required to possess four features before liability would fall on the former:

(1) the advice is required for a purpose either specific or generally described, which is made known to the adviser at the time the advice is given;
(2) the defendant knows that the advice will be communicated to the advisee, either individually or as a member of an ascertained class in order that it should be used by the advisee for that purpose;
(3) the defendant knows that the advice is likely to be acted upon without independent enquiry;
(4) the plaintiff acts on the advice.

3.6 Foreseeability, in as much as the defender knows that his words will be relied on by the pursuer, is, therefore, not enough to ground liability. This point was emphasised in the Court of Appeal case of *Galoo Ltd* v *Bright Graham Murray*.[6] In that case, the third plaintiff, a public limited company, by a written agreement, purchased 51 per cent of the shares in the second plaintiff, a limited company owning all the shares in the first plaintiff. The defendants, who were the auditors of the first and second defendants, were required under the agreement to calculate the net profits and to deliver copies of the accounts to the third plaintiff. The third plaintiff made loans to the first and second plaintiffs on the strength of the information contained in the accounts, which, it was claimed, had been negligently prepared. The court held, *inter alia*, that mere foreseeability that a potential bidder for shares might rely on the company's audited accounts did not impose on the auditor a duty of care either to the bidder or to the lender. Such a duty would arise only if the auditor was expressly made aware that a particular bidder or lender might rely on the accounts without independent enquiry. Therefore, since it was not alleged that the third plaintiff would rely on the accounts for the purpose of calculating the purchase price under the share purchase agreement, the facts of the case disclosed no cause of action. Glidewell LJ stated:[7]

---

[3] [1964] AC 465 at 529.
[4] *Possfund Custodian Trustee Ltd* v *Diamond* [1996] 1 WLR 1351 at 1364. See also *Customs and Excise Commissioners* v *Barclays Bank* [2006] 3 WLR 1 and *Precis (521)* v *William M Mercer Ltd* [2005] EWCA Civ 114.
[5] [1990] 2 AC 605 at 638. See Chapter 2.
[6] [1994] 1 WLR 1360.
[7] *Ibid* at 1382.

"Mere foreseeability that a potential bidder may rely on the audited accounts does not impose on the auditor a duty of care to the bidder, but if the auditor is expressly made aware that a particular identified bidder will rely on the audited accounts or other statements approved by the auditor, and intends that the bidder should so rely, the auditor will be under a duty of care to the bidder for the breach of which he may be liable."[8]

The need for the pursuer to establish that the defender intended that the former **3.7** rely on him was discussed in *Goodwill v British Pregnancy Advisory Service*.[9] There, the defendants arranged for a vasectomy to be performed on X. Afterwards, the defendants informed X that the vasectomy had been successful and that X no longer needed to use any other method of contraception. Several years later, X commenced a sexual relationship with the plaintiff, who had been advised by X that the vasectomy had been successful. She became pregnant. She sued the defendants, alleging that they owed her a duty of care in law. However, the Court of Appeal held that the defendants were not liable since the plaintiff could not have known that their advice would be communicated to the plaintiff and also relied on by her without independent enquiry.

As we have just observed, it is not sufficient that it is foreseeable that the pursuer will **3.8** act on the statement made by the defender. Some form of special relationship between the parties is required. What, then, is the nature of such a relationship? In the Privy Council case of *Mutual Life v Evatt*,[10] the plaintiff was a policyholder in Mutual Life. The plaintiff claimed that Mutual Life gratuitously gave him negligent information on the financial state of an associated company, on the strength of which he invested in that company and lost money. It was held that Mutual Life were not liable since giving advice on financial matters was not part of the company's business. However, in the Court of Appeal case of *Esso v Mardon*[11] a large oil company, Esso, gave misleading information to the potential tenant of a garage as to the throughput of the garage. The court held that Esso owed the plaintiff a duty of care in negligence. According to Lord Denning MR, it was sufficient that Esso professed to have, and did in fact have, special knowledge or skill in estimating the throughput of the filling station.[12]

The authors suggest that *Esso* represents the correct approach as to the status **3.9** of the maker of the statement. That is to say, for liability to lie, the maker of the statement must be possessed of knowledge (which may be either general or specific) or information which is of such a character that the maker of the statement assumes responsibility to exercise reasonable care in giving the pursuer information on which the latter relies. Whether the defender has assumed responsibility for the accuracy of his statement is judged objectively.[13]

There is a strong presumption that if the maker of the statement is in the business **3.10** of dispensing advice (ie the defender has "general" knowledge which he applies to

---

[8] See also *Royal Bank of Scotland v Bannerman Johnstone Maclay* 2005 SLT 579 (where a bank had relied on the negligently prepared accounts of a company and had thereby incurred loss): the Lord Justice-Clerk (Lord Gill) stated (at 585) that mere knowledge that the company would supply the audited accounts to a third party was not enough to impose a duty of care. However, subject to limited exceptions, it was not necessary that the defender should intend the pursuer to rely on the relevant statement.

[9] [1996] 1 WLR 1397.

[10] [1971] AC 793.

[11] [1976] 1 QB 801.

[12] *Ibid* at 820.

[13] *Customs and Excise Commissioners v Barclays Bank* [2006] 3 WLR 1, per Lord Bingham at 6 and Lord Hoffmann at 14.

the subject-matter of a given enquiry) such responsibility is assumed and the maker of the statement would be liable. The defender would also be liable if he was (as in *Esso*) privy to information which is not widely available (ie specific information) and which he gives to the pursuer in such circumstances that reliance must be placed on its accuracy. Again, if the defender has some financial interest in the matter on which the advice is given, the courts seem readily inclined to hold the defender liable.[14]

3.11   In the House of Lords case of *Smith* v *Eric Bush*,[15] a valuer who was commissioned by a building society to value a house prepared his survey report negligently; a copy was given to the mortgagor. Relying on the report, the latter purchased the house without obtaining independent advice. She sustained financial loss. She sued the valuer. The House held that the valuer owed her a duty of care in the law of negligence on the basis that the report would probably be relied on by the mortgagor in considering whether she would purchase the house. For Lord Templeman[16] the relationship between the plaintiff mortgagor and the valuer was akin to contract. For Lord Jauncey[17] the valuer had, by virtue of his proximate relationship to both the mortgagees and the mortgagor, assumed responsibility for the accuracy of his report. For his Lordship, it was of critical importance that the plaintiff would rely on the report without taking independent advice.

3.12   Another interesting example of the application of the *Hedley Byrne* principle is found in the House of Lords case of *Henderson* v *Merrett Syndicates Ltd*.[18] In that case the plaintiffs were Lloyds "names" who were members of syndicates that were managed by the defendant underwriting agents. The relationship between the "names" and members' agents was regulated by either agency or sub-agency agreements which gave the agent absolute discretion in respect of underwriting business conducted on behalf of the "name". There was an implied term in the agreement that the agent would exercise due care and skill in the exercise of their functions as managing agents. The plaintiffs brought proceedings against the defendants, alleging that the defendants had been negligent in the conduct and management of the plaintiffs' syndicates. The House held, in applying the *Hedley Byrne* principle, that a duty of care was owned in tort to the plaintiffs. In reaching its decision, the House, in effect, broadened the decision in *Hedley Byrne* to embrace liability for providing professional services. Furthermore, the concept of special skill could be broadened to embrace special knowledge. *Henderson* also emphasises the point that there can be concurrent liability in both contract and delict.

3.13   According to Lord Browne-Wilkinson in *White* v *Jones*,[19] the categories of cases in which a special relationship (on which liability for the making of a negligent misstatement can be prefaced) can be held to exist are not closed. However, in his Lordship's view, only two categories had been identified thus far, namely:

(1) where there is a fiduciary relationship; and
(2) where the defendant has voluntarily answered a question or tenders skilled advice or services in circumstances where he knows or ought to know that an identified plaintiff will rely on his answers or advice.

---

[14] See, eg, *Anderson (W B)* v *Rhodes* [1967] 2 All ER 850.
[15] [1990] 1 AC 831.
[16] *Ibid* at 846.
[17] *Ibid* at 871.
[18] [1994] 3 All ER 506.
[19] [1995] 1 All ER 691 at 716. See above.

If such a special relationship exists between the defender and the pursuer, the former **3.14** is liable for both acts of commission and also acts of omission: that is to say, as far as the latter is concerned, for failure to provide the pursuer with appropriate information which would have allowed him to avoid the relevant loss.[20]

ADVICE GIVEN ON INFORMAL OCCASIONS

Negligent information which is given on purely informal occasions generally does **3.15** not attract liability since the law tends to the view that there is no assumption of responsibility on that occasion. Therefore, I would not be able successfully to sue a tax accountant whom I ask for advice in the course of a train journey. In other words, the solemnity, or lack of solemnity, of the occasion in which the advice is given, has a bearing on the degree of assumption of responsibility on the part of the defender to the pursuer.

However, there may be certain ostensibly "social" occasions on which a duty of care **3.16** will be held to arise for negligent misstatements. For example, in the Court of Appeal case of *Chaudhry* v *Prabhakar*[21] the plaintiff wished to buy a second-hand car. The first defendant was a close friend of the plaintiff but was not a mechanic. The plaintiff asked the defendant if he could try to find her a second-hand car which had not been involved in an accident. He agreed to do so without remuneration. The defendant did find a car and took it to the plaintiff. He told her that it was in very good condition and that he highly recommended it. The plaintiff asked him if the car had been involved in an accident, to which the latter replied that it had not. Furthermore, the defendant assured her that the car did not require to be examined by a mechanic. However, it soon transpired that the car had, indeed, been involved in a serious road accident and was, as a consequence, unroadworthy. It had been bought as salvage. It was claimed on behalf of the defendant that he was simply under a duty to be honest. However, the court, by a majority, held that the defendant was liable in negligence. Stuart-Smith LJ found the defendant liable on the basis that the defendant, in purchasing the car, had acted as the agent of the plaintiff. The former, therefore, owed the latter a duty of care based on that relationship. Stoker LJ stated *obiter*[22] that, even if the defendant had not conceded that he owed the plaintiff a duty of care, he would have found the defendant liable in negligence. In his Lordship's view, the defendant had gone beyond what was required of him as a friend. This very assumption of responsibility by the defendant was enough by itself to bring the *Hedley Byrne* principle into play.

However, the concept of assumption of responsibility in the context of liability for **3.17** negligent misstatements is an elusive concept, to be sure, and is in the process of being developed by the courts. There is no comprehensive list of guiding principles to help the courts determine when an assumption of responsibility can be said to arise.[23] The courts, therefore, develop this area of the law on a case-by-case basis.

---

[20] See, eg, *Commissioner of Police of the Metropolis* v *Lennon* [2004] EWCA Civ 130. See also *Henderson* v *Merrett* [1995] 2 AC 605.
[21] [1989] 1 WLR 29.
[22] *Ibid* at 37.
[23] Per Arden LJ in *Precis (521)* v *William M Mercer* [2005] EWCA Civ 114 at [24].

MANNER IN WHICH THE INFORMATION IS IMPARTED

3.18   In ascertaining whether the defender has assumed responsibility towards the pursuer, the court takes into account the manner in which the negligent information has been imparted. A good example of this is seen in the Court of Appeal case of *Howard Marine* v *Ogden*.[24] There, the plaintiffs, who were civil engineering contractors, asked a barge owner the capacity of a barge which they intended to use to convey clay. The defendant gave wrong advice. However, the advice was given orally. As far as the claim at common law was concerned, the court held that the defendant was simply under a duty to be honest. In the last analysis, there was no assumption of responsibility on the part of the defendant for the accuracy of his statement.

RELEVANT TIME ASSUMPTION OF RESPONSIBILITY ASCERTAINED

3.19   The relevant time at which one ascertains whether the defender has assumed responsibility for the accuracy of his statement falls at the time the statement is made, in contrast to the time when the statement is relied on.[25]

DEFENDER EXERCISING STATUTORY DUTIES

3.20   To what extent, if any, is the maker of a statement, or the relevant public body, liable for making a statement if the statement is made in the course of the defender discharging a public duty? For example, if a local authority building control officer, who, in the course of inspecting my house which is in the course of construction, negligently informs me that it must be provided with thermal insulation and fire-resistant materials of a much higher specification than the current building standard regulations require, could I successfully sue the inspector for the additional costs which I incur by virtue of my acting on such advice? The leading case on this issue is the Court of Appeal case of *Welton* v *North Cornwall DC*.[26] In that case an environmental health officer negligently required the owner of food premises to carry out works which, in point of fact, were unnecessary to secure compliance with the relevant food hygiene legislation. Acting on this advice, the owners of the premises incurred substantial expenditure. After discovering that the bulk of the work they had been advised to have carried out was unnecessary, the owners sued the local authority, claiming damages for the unnecessary expenditure. The court held that the owner could recover from the local authority at common law under the rule in *Hedley Byrne* v *Heller*. According to Rose LJ,[27] in determining whether a local authority was liable for loss which was

---

[24] [1978] QB 574.
[25] *McCullagh* v *Lane Fox* [1996] PNLR 205.
[26] [1997] 1 WLR 570.
[27] *Ibid* at 581.

caused by one relying on the negligent advice of officials, one had to determine into which of three categories the relevant facts fell:

(1) If the negligent advice was given in the course of statutory enforcement, such as the institution of legal proceedings, the service of improvement notices and closing orders, such negligent advice would attract liability unless the imposition of liability was inconsistent with or had a tendency to discourage the due performance of the statutory duty.

(2) If the advice was part and parcel of the local authority's advisory service, insofar as the advice in question was part and parcel of the local authority's system for discharging its statutory duties, liability would be excluded so as not to impede the due performance of these duties. However, if the advice went beyond that, the advice was capable of attracting liability, and the fact that the service was offered by way of statutory duty was irrelevant.

(3) If the conduct in question was outwith the scope of the relevant legislation – that is to say that the officer imposed detailed requirements which were coupled with threats of closure and close supervision – liability would lie at common law.

As far as the second category is concerned, it may, however, be difficult in practice **3.21** to determine whether the advice tendered by a public official is part and parcel of a local authority's system for discharging its statutory duties. The dividing line between what is actually required by law of the public and, on the other hand, what is simply desirable from a public health viewpoint, and falling within a local authority's advisory service, is often fine.

STATEMENT MADE TO SOMEONE OTHER THAN THE PURSUER BY REASON OF WHICH PURSUER SUSTAINS LOSS

Thus far we have been discussing a situation where the defender makes a negligent **3.22** misstatement either directly or indirectly to the pursuer who relies on the statement to his detriment. What is the position, however, where the statement is made to a third person who acts on it in such a way that the pursuer suffers loss? For example, X, who wishes to invest money in Y (a company), is misinformed by Z that Y is financially unsound, as a consequence of which X does not invest in Y. Y, therefore, loses money it would otherwise have obtained. Could Y sue Z in delict? We can see here, of course, that the maker of the statement, Z, has made the representation to a third person, X, and not the person who sustained loss, namely Y. Could the principle in *Hedley Byrne* be extended to allow Y to recover in such a situation? This is the fundamental question which fell to be answered in *Ministry of Housing and Local Government* v *Sharp*.[28] Here, the Ministry had registered a planning charge in the local land register after the payment of compensation to N who had been refused planning permission to develop his land. Any later developer of the land would have had to pay money to the Ministry before development could take place. Two years later, planning permission was

---

[28] [1970] 1 All ER 1009.

granted. A prospective purchaser of the land requested an official search in the register of local land charges. However, the certificate omitted to mention the Ministry's charge because of the carelessness of a clerk who was employed by the relevant local authority. The plaintiffs accepted the fact that the purchaser was not liable to repay the sum because the certificate (which showed no charge) was, by virtue of English land law, conclusive in his favour. The Court of Appeal held, *inter alia*, the clerk liable for his negligence at common law. Lord Denning MR swept aside any suggestion that the rule in *Hedley Byrne* was founded upon a voluntary assumption of responsibility by the defendant to the plaintiff. Rather, in his Lordship's view,[29] "[T]he duty of care arose not from any voluntary assumption of responsibility but from the fact that the person making [the statement] knows or ought to know that others, being his neighbours in this regard, would act on the faith of the statement being accurate. That is enough to bring the duty into existence". In other words, if it is foreseeable that the statement will be relied on, a duty of care will lie.

3.23   The law was taken further forward in the House of Lords case of *Spring* v *Guardian Assurance*.[30] In that case, a former employer gave a reference to a potential employer of the plaintiff. The reference was negligently prepared. As a consequence of the unfavourable nature of the reference, the plaintiff failed to secure employment. He suffered economic loss. He sued his former employer, contending that the latter owed him a duty of care in the law of negligence. The majority of the House accepted that such a duty was owed by invoking the concepts of mainstream negligence. Of interest, in the present discussion, is that Lord Goff[31] was willing to extend the rule in *Hedley Byrne* to cover a situation where the plaintiff suffered economic loss by virtue of a third party relying on a statement to the detriment of the plaintiff.

DEGREE OF RELIANCE REQUIRED

3.24   What degree of reliance on the negligent misstatement does the pursuer require to prove in order to succeed in an action in delict? Is it necessary that the negligent advice given to me by someone plays the sole role in inducing me to act to my detriment, or, does it simply suffice that such advice played some part, albeit a minor part, in inducing me so to act? For example, suppose I commission a surveyor to survey a house in the Pentland Hills which I am considering purchasing. The report as to the physical condition of the house is satisfactory. However, the survey has been carried out negligently and fails to reveal that the foundations of the house are defective, the building has no damp-proof course and also that the private water supply to the house is contaminated. Prior to commissioning the survey, my financial adviser urged me to purchase the house in order that I could convert it into a cafeteria and make a handsome profit. I purchase the house, only to discover that it is worthless. While I am encouraged by the surveyor's favourable report, it is, in fact, the advice given by my financial adviser that weighs more heavily on my mind when I make a decision to purchase the house. In such circumstances, could I succeed in an action in delict against the surveyor?

---

[29] [1970] 1 All ER 1009 at 1018–1019.
[30] [1996] 2 AC 296.
[31] *Ibid* at 316.

The leading case on this point is the Court of Appeal case of *JEB Fasteners Ltd* **3.25**
v *Marks Bloom*.[32] In that case the plaintiffs entered into negotiations to take over a
manufacturing company which had started to trade in the same products as the plaintiffs. During the negotiations, the defendants, who were the company's accountants
and who also knew that the plaintiffs were negotiating to take over the company,
produced audited accounts for the company's first year. The accounts were certified
as correct. In turn, they were made available to the plaintiffs. However, the accounts
were partially inaccurate. In short, the accounts presented a somewhat sanguine view
of the company. The plaintiffs decided to take over the company, their prime motive
being to acquire the services of the company's two directors who had considerable
experience in the trade. The takeover was unsuccessful. The plaintiffs lost money. They
brought an action against the defendants, claiming damages for breach of the defendant's duty of care to the plaintiffs. However, the court held that since the plaintiffs had
not relied on the negligent advice to any material degree in making their unsuccessful
bid, they could not succeed in a claim in negligence against the defendants. According
to Donaldson LJ,[33] if the negligent advice plays a subsidiary role in the mind of the
decision-taker it is not relied on in terms of the rule in *Hedley Byrne*. Stephenson LJ was
of the view[34] that if the misrepresentation plays a real and substantial part, though not
by itself a decisive part, in inducing the pursuer to act to his detriment, that is sufficient to ground liability.

---

[32] [1983] 1 All ER 583.
[33] *Ibid* at 588.
[34] *Ibid* at 589.

4

THE DUTY OF CARE – PURE ECONOMIC LOSS

The question we shall be addressing in this chapter is the extent, if any, to which **4.1** the defender is liable for causing loss which ranks in the eyes of the law as pure economic loss. However, before we proceed to discuss the subject it is important to establish precisely what is meant by the expression "pure economic loss". Put simply, such loss is not founded on any physical injury to the pursuer. Rather, the injury the pursuer sustains sounds in pure monetary terms. For example, if I am knocked down and injured by the defender's negligent driving, as a result of which I am injured and have to take time off work, I would have sustained economic loss. However, such loss would not rank as pure economic loss since it derives from physical damage. In contrast, however, if the local authority archives, at which a historian is working, are destroyed by a fire which is negligently started by a workman, as a result of which the historian cannot complete a book he is in the course of writing, the loss to the historian would rank as pure economic loss, since, whereas he undoubtedly has suffered pecuniary loss, none of his own property has been damaged.

The general rule is that the common law duty to take care to avoid causing injury **4.2** to others is restricted to physical injury, either of the person or of the property of the pursuer. In other words, there is no liability for pure economic loss. The reason for this approach is founded on policy. The courts fear that if claims for pure economic loss were allowed it would encourage a multiplicity of claims or, in the words of Chief Justice Cardozo: "Recovery of economic loss in the absence of physical damage or personal injury would expose defendants to liability in an indeterminate time to an indeterminate class."[1] This somewhat apocalyptic vision of the consequences of allowing claims for pure economic loss was graphically illustrated by Gibbs J in the High Court of Australia case of *Caltex Oil Ltd* v *The Willenstaad*.[2] His Lordship stated:

> "If a person committing an act of negligence were liable for all economic loss foreseeably resulting therefrom, an act of careless inadvertence might expose the person guilty of it to claims unlimited in number and crippling in amount. For example, if, through the momentary inattention of an officer, a ship collided with a bridge, and as a result, a large suburban area, which included ships and factories, was deprived of its main means of access to a city, great loss might be suffered by tens of thousands of persons, but to require the wrongdoer to compensate all those who suffered pecuniary loss would be to impose upon him a burden out of all proportion to his wrong."

---

[1] *Ultramares Corp* v *Touch* 255 NY 170 (1931) at 179.
[2] (1976) 136 CLR 529 at 551.

4.3   The traditional approach of the courts is neatly illustrated by the Court of Appeal case of *Spartan Steel & Alloys Ltd* v *Martin & Co (Contractors) Ltd*.[3] The plaintiffs had a factory where they manufactured steel. The factory obtained electricity by direct cable from a power station. Martins were building contractors and they used power-driven tools. While carrying out excavating work, a shovel fractured a cable. The electricity power supply to the factory was shut off. This caused a "melt", which was being prepared, to be damaged. During the time the electricity was shut off (ie 14½ hours), it was established that the plaintiffs could have put more "melts" through the furnace. They brought an action against Martins to recover all damages which they had incurred. The court held that the plaintiffs were entitled to recover the loss which was consequent on the physical damage they had sustained by virtue of the lost profits in relation to the melt that had been destroyed. However, the plaintiffs could not recover damages for the lost profits of the "melts" that could have been put through the furnace had the power supply not been affected. According to Lord Denning MR:[4]

> "If claims for pure economic loss were permitted for this particular hazard there would be no end of claims. Some might be genuine, but many others might be inflated or even false. A machine might not have been in use anyway, but it would be easy to put it down to the cut in supply. It would be well-nigh impossible to check the claims."

4.4   Another case which illustrates the same judicial stance to pure economic loss is *Weller* v *The Foot and Mouth Disease Research Institute*.[5] In that case there was an escape of the foot and mouth disease virus from the defendant's premises. Cattle were infected on the neighbouring land. The cattle could not be sent to market for auction. Auctioneers lost money as a consequence since they were unable to earn any commission on the sale of the cattle. They sued the defendants. It was held that since the auctioneers had simply suffered pure economic loss, they could not recover damages. Again, in the Inner House case of *Dynamco* v *Holland*,[6] contractors negligently carried out building operations. An underground electricity cable carrying power to a factory was damaged. Whereas no property of the occupiers was damaged, production in the factory was interrupted. It was held that the occupiers could not recover in delict since the loss sustained ranked as pure economic loss. Another interesting case which illustrates the same point is *London Waste Ltd* v *Amec Civil Engineering Ltd*.[7] In that case the plaintiffs generated electricity from the burning of waste. Electricity, in turn, was fed into the grid. The defendant was a building contractor. One day when carrying out road improvements, with part of the work involving sheet-piling, a subcontractor of the defendant severed the cable carrying the electricity to the grid. As a result, the plaintiffs suffered financial loss by not being able to supply the grid. It was held that the plaintiffs could not recover for this loss since it ranked as pure economic loss.

4.5   Until the early 1980s it seemed that the approach displayed by the courts to claims for pure economic loss was too well entrenched in law to warrant serious challenge. However, the law seemed to have been turned on its head (or, at least, taken a new

---

[3] [1972] 3 All ER 557.
[4] *Ibid* at 564.
[5] [1966] 1 QB 569.
[6] 1971 SC 257.
[7] (1996) 53 Const LR 66.

twist) by the decision of the House of Lords in *Junior Books Ltd* v *Veitchi Co Ltd*.[8] In that case a specialist subcontractor, Veitchi, laid a floor in a factory which was being constructed for Junior Books Ltd. There was no contractual relationship between Junior Books and Veitchi. It was alleged that the floor had been negligently laid and required replacement. Junior Books successfully sued Veitchi for this pure economic loss. The House of Lords held that Junior had relied on the skill and experience of Veitchi. The relationship between the parties was as close as it could be short of actual privity of contract. *Junior Books* was thought to have been a landmark in negligence law. It allowed (or seemed to allow) recovery for pure economic loss. Later cases, however, show the courts reasserting their former approach to disallowing pure economic loss claims.

One case which neatly illustrates this is *Muirhead* v *Industrial Tank Specialities*.[9] The **4.6** plaintiff was a fish merchant who ran a lobster factory. The lobsters were fattened up in tanks which were fed oxygen by pumps manufactured by the defendants. One day, the equipment failed. Denied oxygen, the lobsters died. The plaintiffs sued the defendants for the price of the lobsters and the cost of repairing the pumps, as well as the loss which resulted from the pumps not being used. The Court of Appeal held that the plaintiffs could only recover in respect of the dead lobsters. The claim for damages in relation to lost profits which accrued from the pumps not being able to be used ranked as pure economic loss. There had been no reliance by the plaintiff on the manufacturer. Furthermore, there was also insufficient proximity between the parties. The plaintiff, therefore, failed to recover.

Similarly, in the House of Lords case of *Leigh and Sillivan Ltd* v *Aliakmon Shipping* **4.7** *Co Ltd*,[10] the plaintiffs contracted to buy a quantity of steel coils which were to be shipped from Korea. The plaintiffs had expected to resell the coils. Contrary to the expectation of the parties, the property in the coils did not pass to the plaintiff buyers under the contract. The coils were damaged during the voyage. The plaintiffs sued the shipowner defendants whose negligence had caused the damage. It was held that since the plaintiffs did not have either legal ownership or a possessory title to the coils at the time the damage took place, they failed in their action, since the loss in question ranked as pure economic loss.[11] Again, in *Nacap Ltd* v *Moffat Plant Ltd*[12] the pursuers laid a pipeline on behalf of the British Gas Corporation. While the pipeline was being laid by the pursuers, it was damaged by the defender. The pursuers were contractually liable for any damage caused to the pipeline. The pursuers brought an action for damages in respect of the financial loss they had sustained. The Inner House followed the *ratio* in *The Aliakmon* and held that since the pursuers neither owned nor had a possessory right or title to the property which was damaged, the loss ranked simply in terms of pure economic loss in respect of which the pursuers could not recover.

The House of Lords case of *D & F Estates Ltd* v *Church Commissioners*[13] is also inter- **4.8** esting. In that case the first defendants (D1) commissioned the third defendants (D3) to build a block of flats. D3 engaged subcontractors to carry out plastering work, which was carried out negligently. The plaster had to be replaced. The plaintiffs, who had

[8] [1983] 1 AC 520.
[9] [1986] QB 507.
[10] [1986] AC 785.
[11] See K Low, "Equitable title and economic loss" (2010) 126 LQR 507.
[12] 1987 SLT 221.
[13] [1989] AC 177.

bought a lease from D1, the owners of the flats, brought an action against the builders, claiming the cost of repairing the plaster. It was held, however, that the loss in question simply ranked as pure economic loss since no property, other than the flats themselves, had been damaged.

4.9   Another case which illustrates the resoluteness on the part of the courts to deny claims for pure economic loss is the Court of Appeal case of *Simaan General Contracting Co v Pilkington Glass Ltd*.[14] In that case a new building was being constructed in Abu Dhabi. Furthermore, Simaan were the main contractors. Feal were subcontractors and were responsible for fitting glass in the building. Pilkington Glass supplied the wrong type of glass to the subcontractors, which was then fitted by them into the building. Simaan suffered financial loss in replacing the units. Simaan sued Pilkington in tort. The Court of Appeal held, however, that there was no liability in tort because the loss which Simaan had suffered was pure economic loss. Furthermore, Simaan had not relied on Pilkington. The court did concede that where a specialist subcontractor was vetted, selected and also nominated by a building owner, it might be possible to conclude that the nominated subcontractor had assumed a direct responsibility to the building owner. However, according to the court, it could not be said in the instant case that the defendant had assumed such responsibility.

4.10   Another important case which illustrates the same point is the Court of Appeal case of *Greater Nottingham Co-op Society v Cementation Piling & Foundations Ltd*.[15] The main contract between the Society and the main contractors provided for an extension and alteration works to the Society's premises. Cementation was a nominated subcontractor. The Society also entered into a collateral contract with Cementation. That contract did not make any provision as to the manner in which the subcontracted work was to be carried out. Cementation carried out the piling work negligently. The Society sued Cementation for the financial loss which the former had incurred in having to revise their building schedule. However, the Society failed in their action. The court held that the loss which the Society had sustained ranked as pure economic loss. In reaching its decision the court took into account the fact that the Society had the opportunity to provide for such loss by way of appropriate terms in the collateral contract, but had failed to do so. In short, there was no assumption of responsibility on the part of Cementation to avoid causing the Society such loss.

4.11   The pendulum has, therefore, decidedly swung away from *Junior Books*. A leading case which illustrates this approach is *Murphy v Brentwood DC*.[16] In that case a local authority building inspector failed to notice that the foundations of a house, which was under construction, were of adequate depth to support the weight of the building. The upshot of this was that the walls of the building began to crack. The plaintiff owner sustained financial loss since his house could only be sold at a reduced price. He sued the local authority in negligence. However, the House of Lords rejected his claim on the basis that, since the relevant damage was confined to the house itself, the claim ranked as pure economic loss and was, therefore, irrecoverable. In coming to this decision, the House rejected, *inter alia*, the so-called complex structure theory which had gained some academic support, to the effect that if one considered a building as consisting of different components (ie the foundations, walls, roof), and (say) the

---

14 [1988] QB 758.
15 [1988] 2 All ER 971.
16 [1990] 3 WLR 414. See also *Robinson v P E Jones (Contractors) Ltd* [2011] EWCA Civ 9.

foundations were negligently constructed, by reason of which the walls began to crack (as in the instant case), one could now construe such damage as physical damage in that the damaged component was a separate entity from that from which the danger derived.

Murphy, then, is authority for the proposition that if a building is negligently **4.12** constructed, for the purposes of the law of delict, one has to regard the building as an integrated entity. Therefore, injury which is inflicted by the builder to any part of that building automatically ranks as pure economic loss and is, therefore, irrecoverable in the law of delict. Such a form of loss would be analogous to Mrs Donoghue, on discovering that her ginger beer was in an imperfect condition, simply pouring her drink down the sink. However, if a subcontractor were negligently to carry out work on an *existing* building, the upshot of which is that parts of that building are damaged, he would be responsible for injury inflicted upon other property, and would, therefore, be liable in delict. For example, in the Outer House case of *Parkhead Housing Association Ltd* v *Phoenix Preservation Ltd*,[17] the owners of a tenement building entered into a contract with main contractors for the renovation of the premises. The main contractors appointed specialist subcontractors to install a damp-proof course in the building. It was alleged that the damp-proof course had been negligently installed, thereby resulting in an outbreak of damp and also dry rot in the ground floor of the premises. In the Outer House, Lord Prosser expressed the view that where either a contractor or a subcontractor does work on an existing building, such damage to one part which is caused by a hidden defect in another part may qualify as damage to other property and therefore ranks as physical damage.[18]

Murphy was considered in the Outer House case of *Stevenson* v *A & J Stephen* **4.13** *(Builders) Ltd*.[19] In that case the owners of a house damaged in a fire sought damages from the builders of the house, who were also feudal superiors of the owners, on the ground that the builders had failed to construct a fire stop between the garage which adjoined the house and the house itself. The pursuers maintained that the builders had shown a fire stop in the plans which had been lodged for building control purposes, and that the fire stop had complied with the relevant regulations. The pursuers also claimed that the defenders had obtained a completion certificate, after work had been completed, on the strength that the work had been satisfactorily carried out. Lord Osborne, in allowing proof before answer, was prepared to accept that, even if one assumed that the loss in question ranked as pure economic loss (his Lordship was unsure whether the damage which had been caused by the fire was economic loss), it was arguable that the pursuers could recover in a delictual claim. His Lordship laid considerable store by the fact that the representation the defenders had made in applying for the completion certificate was of fundamental importance in establishing a special relationship between the pursuers and the defenders which, in turn, could render the latter liable for economic loss.

However, in the authors' view, it would seem that the loss in question was pure **4.14** economic loss, since, first, the house and the garage were an entity and, second, the damage in question arose from within the building itself. The *type* of harm which emanates from the relevant defect, it is suggested, is quite irrelevant for the purposes of

[17] 1990 SLT 812.
[18] *Ibid* at 816.
[19] 1996 SLT 140.

determining whether harm should rank as pure economic loss. For example, suppose Mrs Donoghue's bottle of ginger beer, instead of containing a decomposing snail, had contained an excess of gas which was caused by the negligence of Messrs Stevenson and had, as a consequence, exploded, but at the same time not injuring any of the customers in the café. Such loss would still rank as pure economic loss. Furthermore, it seems difficult to accept the proposition that the defenders' representation to the local authority as regards the state of the premises established a special relationship between the defenders and the pursuers. Indeed, in relation to such a representation, the pursuers were mere passive bystanders.

4.15   Other evidence of the courts' displaying of a willingness to allow a claim for pure economic loss where the relationship between the plaintiff and defendant is sufficiently proximate is seen in the Court of Appeal case of *Barclays Bank Ltd* v *Fairclough Building Ltd*.[20] In that case, Barclays Bank engaged Fairclough Building Ltd to carry out maintenance work at two large warehouse units. Part of the work involved cleaning the unit's corrugated asbestos cement roofs. The cleaning of the roof was subcontracted to Carne (Structural Repair) Co Ltd, which, in turn, subcontracted the work to Trendleway Ltd. However, the latter carried out the work negligently. The result of this was that asbestos penetrated the building. A prohibition notice was served on Barclays, forbidding further work being carried out in the building until the situation was remedied. Barclays recovered the cost of carrying out the remedial work against Fairclough Ltd. Carne then sued Trendleway Ltd, contending that the latter were in breach of an implied warranty to the effect that the work be carried out with reasonable skill. The court held that Trendleway owed Carne a duty of care in tort as well as contract, to avoid causing economic loss by failing to exercise the care and skill of a competent contractor. The imposition of such liability did not expose Trendleway to the risk of an unrestricted number of claims.

4.16   A more recent example of the courts displaying unwillingness to allow recovery for pure economic loss is seen in the House of Lords case of *McFarlane* v *Tayside Health Board*.[21] In that case a couple were negligently advised that a vasectomy had been performed satisfactorily. The couple relied on that advice and refrained from using contraceptives. Mrs McFarlane became pregnant. The couple sued the defender health board, *inter alia*, for the cost of bringing up the child. However, it was held that such loss ranked as pure economic loss and was, therefore, irrecoverable. In short, whereas the doctor who performed the ineffective vasectomy thereby assumed a duty of care to his patient to prevent a pregnancy, that duty did not extend to avoiding the costs that were associated with bringing up a child if one happened to be born.[22]

4.17   The issue of liability for pure economic loss was considered by the Court of Appeal in *London Borough of Islington* v *University College London Hospital NHS Trust*.[23] As a result of a hospital's negligence, Mrs J suffered a stroke. As a consequence she was unable to look after herself. She was provided with residential care by the claimant authority which acted, in this respect, under its statutory duty to her. She was unable to pay for her care. The claimant, therefore, sought to recover the cost from the hospital. At first instance, the claim was rejected. The Court of Appeal dismissed the

---

[20] [1995] PIQR P152.
[21] [2000] 2 AC 59.
[22] *Ibid*, per Lord Slynn at 76.
[23] [2006] PIQR 3.

appeal. Whereas the loss sustained by the claimant was reasonably foreseeable, in the last analysis, the defendant Trust did not owe the claimant a duty of care to prevent it from sustaining pure economic loss deriving from its having to provide care assistance for a patient. According to Buxton LJ, there was no identifiable public policy which required the court to extend the law of negligence by providing a novel duty of care to local authorities in the circumstances of the case.[24]

THE COMMONWEALTH – A MORE FLEXIBLE APPROACH TO PURE ECONOMIC LOSS?

While the strong arm of public policy firmly dictates the denial of recovery for claims **4.18** for pure economic loss, it could, however, be argued that the judiciary have been too deferential to public policy and have, as a consequence, denied claims which are founded on pure economic loss in circumstances where considerations of fairness, justice and also public policy dictated otherwise. Indeed, some Commonwealth decisions illustrate a departure from the traditional United Kingdom judicial stance of denying recovery for claims of pure economic loss. For example, in the Privy Council case of *Invercargill City Council* v *Hamlin*,[25] which related to an appeal from the Court of Appeal of New Zealand, the plaintiff owners of a house sued a local authority for negligently carrying out its inspectorial duties in relation to the house when it was being built, by virtue of the local authority failing to observe that its foundations were inadequate. As a consequence, the walls of the house began to crack with the passage of time. It was held that community standards and expectations demanded the imposition of a duty of care between the local authority and the builder. The decision in this case, of course, sharply contrasts with *Murphy* v *Brentwood District Council*,[26] which we have already discussed.[27]

Some non-building cases also point to a more flexible approach to recovery for pure **4.19** economic loss. A good example of this is seen in *Caltex Oil* v *The Willemstad*.[28] In that case, a dredge owned by the defendant negligently collided with and also fractured an underwater pipe which was owned by AOR and carried the plaintiff's petroleum from its refinery across Botany Bay. The plaintiff, therefore, had to transfer the oil products by alternative means. The High Court of Australia held that the plaintiff was entitled to recover the cost of alternatively transporting its products until the pipe was repaired from the defendant. This form of loss, of course, was pure economic loss. However, it was held that to allow the plaintiff to recover such costs would not open the floodgates since the defendant knew of the risk to Caltex as a specific individual, in contradistinction to simply that of a member of a general class. Furthermore, the loss that was claimed was in respect of expenditure which was necessarily incurred by someone who, to the knowledge of the defendant, relied on the use of the pipe. There was,

---

[24] [2006] PIQR 3 at 42. For a discussion of this case, see J Spencer, "Liability for purely economic loss again: small earthquake in Chile, not many dead" [2006] CLJ 13.
[25] [1996] 1 All ER 756.
[26] [1990] 2 All ER 908.
[27] See p 40.
[28] (1976) 136 CLR 529.

therefore, sufficient proximity between the defendant and the plaintiff to establish a duty of care in law between the former and the latter.

4.20   A similar bold approach to a claim for pure economic loss was displayed again in the Canadian case of *Canadian National Railway Co* v *Norsk Pacific Steamship* (*The Jervis Crown*).[29] In that case, the defendant's vessel collided with a bridge which crossed the Fraser River. The bridge was put out of commission. The railway company whose trains used the bridge sued the owners of the ship for the loss sustained by the former in not being able to use the bridge. By a majority, the Supreme Court of Canada held that the plaintiff could recover for the pure economic loss which it had sustained. In the view of the majority of the court, there was sufficient proximity between the negligent act and the loss to ground liability. While the court recognised that the law should be chary of awarding damages for pure economic loss, there was no doctrinal bar to admitting such claims if one adopted an incremental approach, that is to say, if one judged each case on its own particular facts. In the instant case, a decision in favour of the defendant would not manifest the odious spectre of indeterminate liability to an unlimited class of claimants.[30]

---

[29] (1992) 91 DLR (4th) 289.
[30] For a discussion of Canadian case law on the subject of pure economic loss, see P Giliker, "Revisiting pure economic loss: lessons to be learnt from the Supreme Court of Canada" (2005) 25 LS 49.

5

THE DUTY OF CARE –
NERVOUS SHOCK

In this chapter we will be looking at nervous shock which has been caused by **5.1**
the negligent conduct of the defender. For example, while I am walking along
the pavement I see a car being driven along the road by Derek. He is driving too
fast. The car goes into a skid. I think it is about to hit me. It narrowly misses me.
However, I sustain nervous shock as a consequence. Could I sue Derek for the
nervous shock or psychiatric injury I have sustained as a result of his negligent
conduct? One of the major problems associated with this form of injury is the
acute awareness on the part of the courts that the crude application of the Atkinian
"foreseeability" test would often allow too many people to recover for psychiatric
injury. For example, if one were to vary the above facts slightly and suppose that,
instead of Derek's car posing a risk to me, the car collides with a cyclist who is
seriously injured, the upshot of which being that 40 people who are standing
at a nearby bus-stop sustain nervous shock, could all of the bystanders recover
damages from Derek? We see here, of course, that if, indeed, all 40 people could
recover, Derek's potential liability would be substantial. Furthermore, the problem
could be compounded by some of the bystanders falsely claiming to have sustained
psychiatric injury. Nervous shock, therefore, requires to be treated differently from
physical injury lest the floodgates be opened too readily to potential pursuers. We
will see how the courts have attempted to shape the law which, to a large extent,
has travelled in a compartment of its own. However, before we proceed to discuss
the case law on the subject, it should be borne in mind that "nervous shock" or
psychiatric injury is a legal term of art. In the House of Lords case of *Page* v *Smith*,[1]
Lord Keith described nervous shock as "a reaction to an immediate and horrifying
impact, resulting in some recognisable psychiatric illness. There must be some
serious mental disturbance outside the range of normal human experience".

THE DEVELOPMENT OF THE LAW

During the 19th century the courts displayed a robust approach to claims for nervous **5.2**
shock and denied pursuers the right to recover damages. Indeed, in the House of
Lords case of *Lynch* v *Knight*,[2] Lord Wensleydale expressed the view that mental
pain or anxiety was "something which the law cannot value and does not pretend
to redress". Such an approach was based, first, on the esoteric nature of the subject,

---

[1] [1996] AC 155 at 167.
[2] (1861) 9 HLC 577 at 590.

and, second, on the jejune state of medical knowledge during this period.[3] However, encouraging signs that the courts were willing to countenance claims for psychiatric injury were seen in *Wilkinson* v *Downton*.[4] In that case the plaintiff's husband had gone to the races for the day. The defendant visited the plaintiff in her house and told her, by way of a practical joke, that her husband was lying, seriously injured, in a pub some miles away. As a consequence, the plaintiff suffered nervous shock. At first instance, she successfully recovered in tort from the defendant on the basis that the latter had wilfully done an act which was calculated (ie the natural consequences of which were) to cause physical harm to the plaintiff. It will be noted, of course, that the injury sustained by the plaintiff in *Wilkinson* was intentionally inflicted. However, as far as liability for psychiatric injury caused by negligence on the part of the defender was concerned, the courts made a tentative start by allowing the plaintiff to recover if he suffered nervous shock by virtue of fear of physical injury to himself. For example, in *Dulieu* v *White and Sons*[5] the plaintiff, who was pregnant, was working behind the bar of a public house. An employee of the defendant negligently drove a horse and van into the bar. The plaintiff feared that she would be injured. She sustained nervous shock. It was held that since the defendant owed her a duty of care, she was entitled to recover damages.

5.3   A more generous approach to injury by way of nervous shock was seen in the Court of Appeal case of *Hambrook* v *Stokes*.[6] In that case, the employee of the defendants left a lorry at the top of a hill, with the brake off. The lorry took off of its own accord, ran down the hill, hurtled past the plaintiff, and ultimately crashed into a building, where the lorry came to rest. The plaintiff had just left her children at the foot of the hill but they were out of her sight when the collision took place. The plaintiff immediately feared for the safety of her children. She was then told by a passer-by that a child whose description matched that of her child had been injured. The plaintiff sustained nervous shock. The court held that the plaintiff was entitled to recover, notwithstanding the fact that she did not fear for her own safety. In other words, it was sufficient that the plaintiff feared injury to her children. Whereas *Hambrook* did extend the law relating to nervous shock, one important limitation the court imposed was that, in order to recover, it was necessary that the plaintiff witnessed the traumatic event with her own unaided senses.

5.4   The next important landmark case in the progression of the law relating to nervous shock was the House of Lords case of *Bourhill* v *Young*,[7] which we have already discussed.[8] It will be recalled that a pregnant fishwife sustained nervous shock by witnessing the immediate aftermath of an accident in which the defender, who was riding a motorcycle at the time, was killed. The House of Lords held that the pursuer could not succeed since it was not foreseeable that someone situated where the pursuer was at the time the accident occurred would have sustained injury by way of nervous shock. However, in terms of the subject-matter currently being discussed, the House of Lords in *Bourhill* did approve of the learning in *Dulieu* and *Hambrook* and

---

[3] See also the Privy Council case of *Victorian Railway Commissioners* v *Coultas* (1888) LR 13 App Cas 222 where the Privy Council held that compensation for psychiatric injury was not recoverable.
[4] [1897] 2 QB 57.
[5] [1901] 2 KB 669.
[6] [1925] 1 KB 141.
[7] 1942 SC (HL) 78.
[8] At p 25, above.

reaffirmed the courts' acceptance of the fact that nervous shock does rank as a form of physical injury in respect of which the law will allow one to be compensated.

CONCEPTUAL PROBLEMS

One of the main conceptual problems the courts have grappled with is whether to address the facts of a particular nervous shock case from either a "duty of care" or a "remoteness of damage" perspective. For example, in the Court of Appeal case of *King* v *Phillips*[9] a taxicab driver omitted to look where he was driving. He reversed his taxi over a child who was riding a tricycle at the time. The child sustained only slight injury as a consequence. However, the child's mother, who was looking out of her window at the time the accident took place, heard the child scream. She also saw his tricycle under the taxi. She sustained nervous shock as a consequence. The scene of the accident was situated some 64–73 metres from the point where it was witnessed by the plaintiff. The court held that the plaintiff failed in her action. For Singleton LJ this was a "no duty" situation in the Atkinian sense, in that the plaintiff was not within the requisite area of risk. Interestingly, in describing the nature of the risk to which the law demanded the plaintiff should be exposed before a duty of care existed in terms of the law of negligence, his Lordship found it difficult to draw a distinction between a risk consisting of physical injury and one consisting of nervous shock.[10] For Denning LJ (as he then was), the defendant owed the plaintiff a duty of care in law but the type of damage which the latter had sustained was too remote.[11] However, it should be mentioned that this case was decided before case of *The Wagon Mound*[12] (which we will discuss later).

5.5

THE CURRENT LAW

We now take a look at the modern law relating to nervous shock. Discussion will be divided into two main categories, namely:

5.6

(1) primary victims; and,
(2) secondary victims.[13]

Category (1) governs a situation where the pursuer is actively participating in the very events which give rise to his injury, whereas category (2) deals with a situation where the pursuer has simply witnessed a traumatic event whereby he sustains nervous shock. As far as category (2) is concerned, it must be emphasised that, normally, the pursuer must prove that he has suffered psychiatric injury by witnessing a traumatic event, in contradistinction to suffering such injury by dint of being exposed to an adverse state of affairs over a prolonged period of time.[14] For example, suppose that

5.7

---

[9] [1953] 1 QB 429.
[10] *Ibid* at 437.
[11] *Ibid* at 442.
[12] [1961] AC 388.
[13] The Scottish Law Commission has recommended the abolition of these two categories: Report on *Damages for Psychiatric Injury* (Scot Law Com No 196, 2004) at p 4.
[14] See, eg, *McLoughlin* v *O'Brien* [1982] 2 WLR 982.

my wife is seriously injured in a road accident by the negligence of the defender. I do not witness the accident itself. However, I suffer a mental breakdown from observing her disability over a period of months. As far as the law currently stands, I could not recover, since my injury does not derive from my witnessing the event.

5.8   In certain circumstances the pursuer may be able to found an action in terms of being both a primary and a secondary victim of nervous shock. This point is illustrated in the House of Lords case of *W v Essex County Council* (which was a striking-out action).[15] The claimants sued a local authority in negligence. The basis of their claim was that the local authority had negligently placed a known child sex-abuser in their care, the result of which being that G had abused their children. The parents claimed that they had sustained psychiatric injury as a result. The House felt itself unable to reject the proposition that, if the facts which were alleged could be proved, the parents could be regarded as being both primary *and* secondary victims of psychiatric injury.

5.9   However, the law allows the recovery of damages in relation to injury caused by nervous shock if such injury is partly attributable to witnessing a traumatic event and partly attributable to the pathological consequences of grief and bereavement. This was decided in *Vernon v Bosley (No 1)*.[16] In that case the defendant was carrying the plaintiff's children in her car. She drove the car negligently. She lost control of the car, which careered down a bank, into a fast-flowing river running alongside the road. The defendant managed to escape but the children were trapped in the car. The plaintiff and his wife were called to the scene of the accident and proceeded to watch the rescue services making an abortive attempt to rescue the children. They perished. The plaintiff claimed that as a result of the accident he suffered both nervous shock and also severe post-traumatic stress disorder which was complicated by a severe grief reaction. The Court of Appeal, by a majority, held that damages were recoverable in respect of the nervous shock, which had been either caused or contributed to by negligence on the part of the defendant, notwithstanding the fact that the illness could also have been attributable to the consequences of bereavement which the plaintiff also suffered. There were no policy grounds for excluding injury brought about by such means.

PRIMARY VICTIMS OF NERVOUS SHOCK

5.10   The courts have traditionally been more willing to allow claims for nervous shock occasioned to those who have been participating in some way in the traumatic event in question, as opposed to having simply witnessed that event. Such an approach is hardly surprising since there are fewer compelling policy reasons to exclude liability for this form of injury than for injury caused to someone who simply witnesses a traumatic event. Certainly, to admit claims of primary victims of nervous shock would not open up a frightful vista of potential limitless liability on the part of the defender to a vast number of claimants. Participation in the particular events giving rise to psychiatric injury is the very touchstone of liability. This point is neatly illustrated in *Dooley v Cammell Laird and Co Ltd*.[17] In that case a crane driver recovered damages when the rope of the crane he was operating snapped because it was faulty, causing

---

[15] [2001] 2 AC 592.
[16] [1997] 1 All ER 577.
[17] [1951] 1 Lloyd's Rep 271.

the load he was lifting to fall into the hold of the ship from which the load was being lifted. The plaintiff believed that he had killed some men who had been working in the hold. He thereupon sustained nervous shock. He successfully recovered damages from his employers.

The requirement that the pursuer participates in the events occasioning his injury **5.11** was forcefully emphasised in *Robertson v Forth Road Bridge Joint Board (No 2)*.[18] In that case the pursuers, Robertson and Rough, were working on the Forth Road Bridge. Rough noticed a large piece of metal sheeting lying on the carriageway. He therefore enlisted the assistance of the pursuer and another colleague, Smith, to remove the sheet. The metal sheet was loaded on to the back of a pick-up van. However, because of its size, the sheet protruded over one side. Smith, therefore, sat on top of the sheet. Robertson drove the van. Rough followed behind in another vehicle. As the vehicles were travelling towards the end of the bridge, a gust of wind blew Smith and the metal sheet off the back of the van and over the side of the bridge. Smith was killed. In an action against their employers both Robertson and Rough claimed that they had suffered nervous shock as a result of witnessing the accident. However, the Inner House of the Court of Session rejected their claim. It did not suffice that the pursuers could prove that they had sustained nervous shock in the workplace. Indeed, there was no separate category of liability governing liability for nervous shock in the workplace. Rather, the ordinary rules which governed liability for nervous shock applied. Since the pursuers had not been participating in the traumatic event in question, they ranked simply as mere bystanders in the eye of the law, and could therefore recover only if they had a close emotional relationship with the victim (see below).

The leading case on nervous shock and primary victims is now *Page v Smith*.[19] The **5.12** facts of that case were that the plaintiff was involved in a collision between his car and the car driven by the defendant. The plaintiff was uninjured. However, he had been suffering from a condition known as myalgic encephalomyelitis or chronic fatigue syndrome. The plaintiff claimed that, as a result of the accident, his medical condition had become permanent. By a majority, the House of Lords held the defendant liable, notwithstanding the fact that it was not reasonably foreseeable, on the facts of the case, that the plaintiff would sustain nervous shock. According to Lord Lloyd,[20] once it was established that the defendant was under a duty of care to avoid causing personal injury to the plaintiff, it mattered not whether the injury in fact sustained was physical, psychiatric or both. It was enough to ask whether the defendant should reasonably have foreseen that the plaintiff might suffer physical injury as a result of the defendant's negligence, so as to bring him within the range of the defendant's duty of care. It was unnecessary to ask, as a separate question, whether the defendant should reasonably have foreseen injury by shock; and it was irrelevant that the plaintiff did not, in fact, suffer any external physical injury.[21]

The application of the *ratio* in *Page v Smith* is neatly illustrated in the Outer House **5.13** case of *Salter v UB Frozen and Chilled Foods Ltd*.[22] In that case the pursuer was employed

---

[18] 1994 SLT 56. For a discussion of *Robertson*, see F McManus, "Nervous Shock in the Workplace" 1995 JR 240.
[19] [1996] AC 155.
[20] *Ibid* at 190.
[21] For a useful discussion of *Page*, see S Bailey and D Nolan, "The *Page v Smith* Saga: a tale of inauspicious origins and unintended consequences" [2010] CLJ 495.
[22] 2003 SLT 1011.

in a factory as a forklift truck operator. One day, two fellow employees were stock-taking in a cold store of the factory. They were lifted in a cage by the truck. When the cage reached the highest level the men had to duck in order to avoid contact with the roof beams. However, one of the stocktakers who was being lifted by the pursuer's truck failed to do so. His head collided with a beam and he was fatally injured. The pursuer sustained psychiatric injury by witnessing the horrific injuries his colleague had sustained. It was held that the pursuer was entitled to recover since he had actively participated in the traumatic events which had given rise to his injury.[23]

Practical difficulties with the "participation" test

5.14   We have now seen that in order to rank as a primary victim of nervous shock it is necessary for the pursuer to prove that he participated in the traumatic events which caused his injury. However, in practice it may not always be easy to determine whether the pursuer has participated in such events. For example, one could consider the case of a building contractor's foreman standing on the ground, observing a roofer replace broken tiles on the roof of a building which is under construction. Unfortunately, the employer has failed to take adequate safety precautions. The roofer slips from the roof and falls to his death. The foreman, who is unrelated to the roofer, sustains psychiatric injury as a result. In the light of the above case law, the foreman would fail in an action based on nervous shock, since he merely witnessed the traumatic event. Suppose, however, the foreman was shouting instructions to the roofer when the latter fell. Could one then argue that, instead of ranking as a mere bystander, the foreman would now be deemed to be participating in the traumatic event and, therefore, could recover damages from his employer? The authors suggest that no decisive answer can be given to this important question.[24]

Work-related psychiatric injury

5.15   Since the mid-1990s, in a number of cases employees have sued their employers for creating a work environment, the nature of which has caused the employees to succumb to psychiatric illness. The first reported case featuring this form of injury was the first-instance case of *Walker* v *Northumberland County Council*.[25] In that case the plaintiff was employed by a local authority as an officer with managerial duties for social services in certain areas of Northumberland. The population in that area grew with the passage of time. However, there was no commensurate increase in staffing levels. The stress levels among staff increased. From 1985 onwards, the plaintiff produced reports that were intended to draw his superiors' attention to the work pressures to which both he and his staff were subjected. In 1986, the plaintiff suffered a nervous breakdown. He remained off work until early 1987. During his absence his workload had increased.

---

[23] See also the interesting Court of Appeal case of *Young* v *Charles Church (Southern) Ltd* (1997) 39 BMLR 146. In that case the victim, Cook, was erecting a structure consisting of scaffolding poles. He was assisted by two labourers, one of whom was the plaintiff, Young. As Young turned away in order to fetch another pole, Cook raised a long pole. It came in contact with an overhead power cable. Cook was electrocuted. Young was within about 6 feet from Cook when the accident took place. It was held that Young had participated in the traumatic events which gave rise to his injury. Therefore, he ranked as a primary victim in the eye of the law.
[24] For an example of the difficulty confronting the courts, see *Campbell* v *North Lanarkshire Council* 2000 SCLR 373.
[25] [1995] ICR 702. For a discussion of *Walker*, see T Burns and F McManus, "Mental health in the workplace" [1995] 2 PILMR 73.

There was also a backlog of paperwork for him to deal with. He subsequently had a second mental breakdown and was then dismissed by the local authority on the ground of permanent ill health. The plaintiff then sued the local authority for breach of its duty in failing to take reasonable steps to avoid exposing him to a health-endangering workload. Colman J held that an employer owes an employee a duty of care not to cause him psychiatric damage by the volume or character of the work he is required to perform. The local authority had breached that duty to the plaintiff. The former had failed to take the preventative measures which were commensurate with the foreseeable risk that the plaintiff would sustain psychiatric harm.

In the Outer House case of *Fraser* v *State Hospitals Board for Scotland*,[26] a former **5.16** charge nurse at the defenders' hospital sued the hospital board, alleging that he had developed a depressive disorder as a result of a punitive work regime. In deciding that the defenders owed a common law duty of care to their employees, to avoid exposing them to the unnecessary risk of injury, Lord Carloway refused to draw a distinction between physical and psychiatric injury. The law imposed a duty of care on an employer in relation to each form of injury.[27] However, the pursuer failed in his action since he could not prove that the defenders had failed to take adequate precautions to protect him from psychiatric injury. In other words, the likelihood of the pursuer sustaining such injury warranted no greater precautions than the defenders had actually taken.[28]

SECONDARY VICTIMS OF NERVOUS SHOCK

As we noted above, a secondary victim of nervous shock is one who has sustained **5.17** psychiatric injury by reason of having witnessed some form of traumatic event. Basically, the pursuer suffers nervous shock by witnessing someone being injured or, less frequently, an inanimate object being damaged, the upshot of which is that the pursuer sustains a sudden assault on his senses.[29] The leading case on the subject of psychiatric injury sustained by secondary victims is the House of Lords case *Alcock* v *Chief Constable of South Yorkshire*.[30] In that case the defendant was responsible for the policing of a football match which took place in the Hillsborough Stadium in Sheffield. There was overcrowding in part of the stadium, caused by the negligence of the police. Ninety-six spectators died as a result of being crushed. Many more were seriously injured. Pictures of the harrowing event were broadcast live on television. The plaintiffs were all either related to, or friends of, the spectators who were involved in the disaster. Some witnessed the traumatic events from parts of the stadium itself, while others saw the events on television. However, all plaintiffs alleged that they had suffered nervous shock. The House of Lords held that, in order for a plaintiff to succeed, it was necessary for them to prove that the injury sustained by the plaintiff was reasonably foreseeable and that the relationship between the plaintiff and the defendant was sufficiently proximate. As far as the latter was

---

[26] 2001 SLT 1051.
[27] *Ibid* at 1055.
[28] See also *Cross* v *Highlands and Islands Enterprise* 2001 SLT 1060; *Barber* v *Somerset* Council [2004] 1 WLR 1089; and *Dickins* v *O*$_2$ [2008] EWCA Civ 1144.
[29] The Scottish Law Commission has recommended the abolition of this requirement: Report on *Damages for Psychiatric Injury* (Scot Law Com No 196, 2004) at p 4.
[30] [1991] 3 WLR 1057.

concerned, the relationship between the plaintiff and the victim required to be one of love and affection. Such affection would be presumed to exist in certain situations, such as when a parent, child, husband or wife was injured. In other cases, however, the requisite bond of affection would require to be proved. This would be the case in respect of remoter relationships: for example, between cousins. The plaintiff had also to establish propinquity in respect of his sustaining the shock, in terms of both time and space to the accident or its immediate aftermath. Finally, the plaintiff had to sustain nervous shock by witnessing the event in question with his own unaided senses. It is instructive to look at the judgments.

5.18   According to Lord Keith,[31] the question of whether the plaintiffs could recover had to be resolved by invoking the concept of reasonable foreseeability. It was reasonably foreseeable that the plaintiff would suffer nervous shock when someone with whom the former had close ties of love and affection was injured. Such close ties could be present in family relationships or those of close friendship. The closeness of the tie would, however, require to be proved by the plaintiff, though was no doubt capable of being presumed in appropriate cases. As far as the case of a bystander who was unconnected with the victims of the accident was concerned, the problem was more difficult. Psychiatric injury to him would not ordinarily be within the range of reasonable foreseeability. However, such individuals could not, perhaps, be entirely excluded from it if the circumstances of the catastrophe occurring very close to the bystander were particularly horrific. His Lordship then went on to state[32] that it was necessary that the plaintiff should suffer nervous shock by virtue of seeing or hearing either the traumatic event itself or its immediate aftermath. The viewing of such an event on television could not be equiparated with actually witnessing such an event with one's unaided senses.

5.19   For Lord Ackner,[33] as far as claims for nervous shock were concerned, the "reasonable foreseeability" test as expounded by Lord Atkin in *Donoghue v Stevenson* was appropriate for determining liability in nervous shock, provided that one remembered that the concept of proximity was integrated in the test. Who, then, was one's neighbour as far as liability for nervous shock was concerned? In ascertaining this, there was a need to modify the "foreseeability" test in order to limit the extent of admissible claims. This limiting exercise had to be effected by considering:

(1) the class of persons whose claim should be recognised;
(2) the proximity of the plaintiff to the scene of the accident; and
(3) the means by which the shock is caused.

5.20 As far as (1) was concerned, only those who had a close emotional tie with the victim should be able to recover. However, if the accident was particularly horrific, a mere bystander who was unrelated to the victim could possibly recover since it was foreseeable that a strong-willed person in those circumstances would suffer nervous shock. For example, his Lordship stated that he would not be prepared to rule out a potential claim by a passer-by who sustained nervous shock by witnessing a petrol

---

[31] [1991] 3 WLR 1057 at 1100.
[32] *Ibid* at 1101, 1102.
[33] *Ibid* at 1105.

tanker career out of control into a school in session.[34] For (2), the plaintiff's proximity to the accident required to be close, in both time and space.[35] However, it was not necessary that the plaintiff witnessed the accident with his own unaided senses. It sufficed that he witnessed the immediate aftermath of the accident. In the instant case, one plaintiff had identified his brother in the mortuary some 8 hours after the accident. This did not, in Lord Ackner's opinion, constitute the immediate aftermath of the accident. Finally, as far as (3) was concerned, the shock was required to come about by directly witnessing the relevant traumatic event as opposed to the plaintiff simply watching it on television.[36] However, it was possible that in certain circumstances the witnessing of events on television could be regarded as equivalent to the direct perception of such events. Lord Ackner gave the example (which Nolan LJ had given in the same case in the Court of Appeal) of a situation where it was reasonable to anticipate that television cameras, while filming and transmitting pictures of a special event of children travelling in a balloon, showed the balloon bursting into flames.

For Lord Oliver, the touchstone of liability as far as secondary victims of nervous **5.21** shock were concerned, was the proximity or directness of the relationship between the plaintiff and the defendant.[37] The notion of proximity in such a context depended largely on the court's perception of what is the reasonable area for the imposition of liability, rather than upon any logical process of analogical deduction. Proximity, here, was an amalgam of the directness of the perception of the events, coupled with the relationship between the plaintiff and the victim.[38] His Lordship went on to warn against confining liability only to close relatives of the victims of accidents. Furthermore, in certain circumstances where the traumatic event was of horrific proportions, a bystander who was unrelated to the victim could possibly recover.

In the Court of Appeal case of *McFarlane* v *EE Caledonia Ltd*,[39] the plaintiff was **5.22** employed on an oil rig which was owned and operated by the defendants. One night, when the plaintiff was off duty and on a support vessel, a series of massive explosions took place on the rig. The closest the plaintiff came to the fire was 100 metres when the support vessel moved in towards the rig in an attempt to fight the fire and also render assistance. The plaintiff brought an action against the defendants on the ground that he had suffered nervous shock as a result of witnessing the horrific events. The court held that he could not recover since he ranked as a mere bystander.

The Hillsborough disaster formed the basis of more litigation. In the House of **5.23** Lords case of *White* v *Chief Constable of South Yorkshire*,[40] a large number of police officers brought claims for psychiatric injury which they had suffered as a result of tending the victims of the tragedy. At first instance it was held that, given the fact that the plaintiffs simply ranked as secondary victims of nervous shock and, furthermore, since they were not rescuers, they could not recover in damages against the defendant, notwithstanding that the relationship which they enjoyed in relation to the defendant was analogous to that of employer and employee. The Court of Appeal reversed that decision on the ground that the defendant's duty to the plaintiffs derived from

[34] [1991] 3 WLR 1057 at 1106.
[35] *Ibid* at 1107.
[36] *Ibid* at 1108.
[37] *Ibid* at 1113.
[38] *Ibid* at 1118.
[39] [1994] 2 All ER 1.
[40] [1998] 3 WLR 1509.

the employer–employee relationship. The defendant was, therefore, under a duty to protect the plaintiffs from psychiatric injury, irrespective of whether the latter ranked either as primary or as secondary victims. The defendant successfully appealed to the House of Lords. Essentially, the majority of the House took the view that the police who were at the stadium at the time the accident took place and had witnessed the traumatic events were to be regarded as secondary victims of nervous shock and also were to be treated no differently than other bystanders. The fact that the police were employed at the time the accident took place was irrelevant.[41]

5.24   The Outer House case of *Keen* v *Tayside Contracts*[42] serves as a good example of the application of the law in the wake of *Alcock* and *White*. In *Keen*, a roadworker claimed damages from his employers for post-traumatic stress disorder. The pursuer had been instructed by his supervisor to attend the scene of a road accident in order to assist the rescue services. He witnessed crushed and burned bodies in a car. For Lady Paton, the facts of the case represented a classic case of nervous shock in that the pursuer was exposed to one single horrific incident during which he was forced to witness the physical suffering and death of other human beings, as a result of which he developed symptoms of psychiatric injury.[43] The pursuer, therefore, ranked as a secondary victim of nervous shock. It was immaterial that he witnessed the traumatic events in the course of his employment. He therefore failed in his action.

The pursuer's relationship with the traumatic event

5.25   It is not necessary that the secondary victim of nervous shock should actually witness the relevant traumatic event. It suffices that he should witness the immediate aftermath of the event. The leading case is now *McLoughlin* v *O'Brian*.[44] The plaintiff's husband and children were seriously injured when their car came in collision with a vehicle being negligently driven by the defendant. The plaintiff suffered psychiatric illness after seeing her family lying seriously injured in hospital some 2 hours after the accident had taken place. The House of Lords held that the plaintiff could recover damages from the defendant. It sufficed that the plaintiff had sustained nervous shock by experiencing the immediate aftermath of the accident. Furthermore, to allow such a claim did not flout public policy.[45]

Rescuers

5.26   We have seen that the law adopts a bold stance in relation to claims advanced by those who have simply witnessed a traumatic event, by denying them a remedy unless they have a bond of love and affection with the victim of the accident. However, what is the position as far as a rescuer is concerned? In the first-instance case of *Chadwick* v *British*

---

[41] For an interesting discussion of the law relating to primary and secondary victims of nervous shock, see P Handford, "Psychiatric injury in breach of a relationship" (2007) 27 LS 26. See also P Handford, "Psychiatric injury in the workplace" [1999] Tort Law Rev 126.
[42] 2003 SLT 500.
[43] *Ibid* at 509.
[44] [1983] 1 AC 410.
[45] See also *Galli-Atkinson* v *Seghal* [2003] Lloyd's Rep Med 285: mother able to recover after seeing body of daughter in mortuary 2 hours after the relevant accident had taken place. See also *Ravenscroft* v *Rederiaktiebologet Transatlantic, The Times*, 6 April, 1992: mother sees son dead in hospital some time after accident. Held: no liability – too remote in time for plaintiff to recover. Cf *Taylor* v *Somerset Health Authority* [1993] 4 Med LR 34.

Railways Board,[46] there was a serious railway accident in London in which 90 people lost their lives. The plaintiff, who lived near the scene of the accident, assisted with the rescue activities. As a result of his experiences he suffered psychiatric injury. He sued the defendants. It was held that, since it was reasonably foreseeable that the plaintiff would suffer nervous shock, he could recover. It was irrelevant that the plaintiff did not fear for his own safety. Whereas *Chadwick* was approved in *McLoughlin* v *O'Brian*,[47] in *White* Lord Goff expressed the view that the circumstances in *Chadwick* were wholly exceptional and that it would be very rare that a person bringing aid and comfort to victims would be held to have suffered foreseeable psychiatric injury as a result.[48]

In the first-instance case of *Wigg* v *British Railways Board*,[49] a train driver came upon the body of a person soon after he had been struck by a door of the train the plaintiff had been driving and which had pulled away from a railway station. A guard had negligently allowed the train to commence its journey. The plaintiff sustained nervous shock. Tucker J was prepared to treat the plaintiff as a rescuer since he had attempted to comfort the victim whom he mistakenly believed was alive. It was foreseeable that the plaintiff would suffer nervous shock. He recovered damages from the Board. In the authors' view, Homer, indeed, nodded on this occasion!   **5.27**

Whether or not a person is to be regarded as a rescuer is a question of fact which falls to be decided on the particular facts of the case. Trivial or peripheral assistance on the part of the pursuer is not sufficient to allow him to rank as a rescuer.[50]   **5.28**

Injury to inanimate objects

Thus far we have been considering liability for psychiatric injury in respect of pursuers who have sustained such injury by witnessing injury to third parties. We now consider to what extent, if any, the courts are willing to entertain claims in respect of the pursuer witnessing harm being inflicted on inanimate objects. For example, suppose I employ an electrician to rewire my house. The wires in my study are negligently installed, as a result of which my study goes on fire. I manage to flee from my house in time and so avoid being injured. However, I suffer psychiatric injury on seeing my precious law books slowly perish in the flames. Could I successfully sue the electrician?   **5.29**

In *Owens* v *Liverpool Corporation*,[51] the plaintiffs, who were relatives of the deceased, suffered nervous shock when they witnessed his coffin, which was being carried in a hearse they were following, colliding with and being overturned by a runaway tram operated by the defendant local authority. It was held that the plaintiffs could recover. However, the authority of *Owens* was doubted by Lord Oliver in *Alcock*[52] and may not represent good law.   **5.30**

Another case which concerned nervous shock being sustained by the witnessing of damage being caused to an inanimate object was *Attia* v *British Gas*.[53] In that case, the plaintiff suffered nervous shock from witnessing the destruction of her home by fire. The fire had been caused by the defendant's negligently installing central   **5.31**

---

[46] [1967] 1 WLR 912.
[47] [1983] 1 AC 410, per Lord Bridge at 438.
[48] *White* v *Chief Constable of South Yorkshire* [1998] 3 WLR 1509 at 1532.
[49] *The Times*, 4 February 1986.
[50] Per Lord Griffiths in *White* v *Chief Constable of South Yorkshire* [1998] 3 WLR 1509 at 1514.
[51] [1938] 4 All ER 727.
[52] [1991] 3 WLR 1057 at 1114.
[53] [1988] QB 304.

heating in the premises. The Court of Appeal, in deciding a preliminary issue, held that she could recover for such harm if she could prove at the trial that it was reasonably foreseeable. To what extent *Attia* represents good law is, in the authors' view, doubtful. However, if *Attia* does represent good law, one would have the ironic situation where the Atkinian "foreseeability" test applies without any embellishment in relation to nervous shock suffered by a pursuer witnessing damage being inflicted upon an inanimate object, whereas, in contrast, a pursuer would require to establish a bond of love and affection in relation to the victim of an accident which the former witnesses. In short, it would potentially be easier to recover damages in relation to harm being inflicted upon inanimate objects than upon humans! The law would wax asinine, indeed, if this were so.

Sensitive pursuers

5.32   It is trite law that the courts will not protect the oversensitive.[54] This general principle finds expression in the law relating to psychiatric injury by the rule that the courts will not countenance claims for nervous shock in respect of traumatic events which would not have affected those of reasonable fortitude.[55]

CONCLUSIONS

5.33   The authors would endorse Lord Steyn's assessment of the law relating to psychiatric injury as being a patchwork quilt of distinctions which are difficult to justify.[56] Indeed, the authors feel little need to depart from the observation made in the first edition of this work, to the effect that, as far as secondary victims of nervous shock are concerned, the courts have been over-mindful of the menacing spectre of encouraging false claims. The panoply of artificial rules which the courts have incorporated in the law relating to nervous shock sustained by secondary victims flouts the norms of fairness. The *Alcock, White* and *Robertson* decisions poignantly epitomise the law's somewhat harsh approach to secondary victims, such policy drawing sustenance largely from public policy. Indeed, looking at the development of the law, one is forcefully reminded of the *dictum* of Burrough J to the effect that public policy is an unruly horse and once you get astride it you never know where it will carry you.[57] Perhaps the law relating to nervous shock has been taken to a point where both fairness and justice are almost completely sacrificed?

---

[54] See, eg, *Heath v Brighton Corporation* (1908) 24 TLR 414.
[55] See, eg, *Wigg v British Railways Board, The Times,* 4 February 1986; *Brice v Brown* [1984] 1 All ER 997.
[56] *White v Chief Constable of South Yorkshire* [1998] 3 WLR 1509 at 1547.
[57] *Richardson v Mellish* (1824) 2 Bing 229 at 252.

6 BREACH OF DUTY OF CARE – STANDARD OF CARE

What we have discussed thus far is whether the defender owes the pursuer a duty of care in law. If it is, indeed, ascertained that the defender does owe the pursuer a duty of care, the latter needs to prove that the former has breached the duty of care. This is done by proving that the defender has failed to attain the standard of care that the law requires of him. The law sets the requisite standard of care in any given situation. Whether the defender meets that standard is a question of fact to be determined in the light of the circumstances of the case.[1]

6.1

THE CRITERION OF THE REASONABLE MAN

Whether the defender is negligent or not is judged objectively. No account is taken of individual disabilities or idiosyncrasies, except in relation to children, who are judged in terms of the standard of children of the age of the defender.[2] Therefore, it matters not, in the eyes of the law, that I am clumsy and have a very poor sense of direction and speed: I fall to be judged by the standard of care which is set by the normal adult. In *Blyth* v *Birmingham Waterworks Co*,[3] Alderson B stated: "Negligence is the omission to do something which a reasonable man guided upon those considerations which ordinarily regulate the conduct of human affairs would do or doing something which a prudent and reasonable man would not do."

6.2

The application of the objective test was graphically illustrated in the leading case of *Nettleship* v *Weston*.[4] In that case the defendant asked the plaintiff, a friend and not a professional driving instructor, if he would give her driving lessons in her husband's car. After being assured that there was fully comprehensive insurance cover, he agreed to do so. During the lesson, the defendant stopped at a junction and then proceeded to turn left slowly. However, she failed to allow the steering wheel to return to its original position, the upshot of which was that the car travelled in a perfect curve, mounted the nearside pavement and struck a lamp-post. The plaintiff sustained a fractured knee. He sued the defendant, claiming that she had breached the duty of care which she owed to him in law. The trial judge dismissed the action on the basis that the defendant was simply under a duty to do her best and that she had discharged that duty in the circumstances. The Court of Appeal, however, allowed the plaintiff's appeal. In essence, the court was of the view that no account should be

6.3

---

[1] *McCann* v *J R McKellar* 1969 SC (HL) 1.
[2] See, eg, *Yachuk* v *Oliver Blais Co Ltd* [1949] AC 386.
[3] (1856) 11 Ex 781 at 784.
[4] [1971] 2 QB 691.

taken of the fact that the defendant was a learner driver in determining whether she had attained the standard of care the law demanded of her. Megaw LJ (who dissented on a different point) stated[5] that a general standard was preferable to the vagaries of a fluctuating standard.

6.4   It is instructive to contrast *Nettleship* with the Australian case of *Cook* v *Cook*.[6] In that case, the defendant, who did not hold a driver's licence, was invited to gain experience by driving a car in which the plaintiff was a passenger. The defendant collided with a concrete post. The plaintiff was injured. The High Court of Australia held that the requisite standard of care which was applicable fell to be determined objectively, but that standard was required to be adjusted to meet the special relationship under which it arose. The special relationship between the plaintiff and the defendant transformed the relationship between driver and passenger in such a way that it was unreal to regard the relevant relationship as being simply one of driver and passenger. The apposite standard of care to be applied, in effect, was circumscribed by that relationship and was, therefore, that which could reasonably be expected of an unqualified and inexperienced driver.

6.5   In some circumstances the law places an obligation on the defender to enlist the aid of experts or specialists to perform a particular task, in which case the standard of care the defender requires to attain is judged by that of the relevant professional. The law imposes such a duty to delegate the performance of a task when the work involves highly specialised skill and knowledge and creates serious dangers if not properly carried out. The leading case is the Court of Appeal case of *Wells* v *Cooper*.[7] In that case, a householder fixed screws in a door handle himself. However, the handle came away when the plaintiff pulled it. He was injured. The court held that the task the defendant had performed was of a trifling nature and did not require the services of a tradesman. The defendant had not, therefore, breached the duty of care he owed to the plaintiff.

Application of the objective test

6.6   The application of the objective test as far as the standard of care is concerned is seen in *The Lady Gwendolene*.[8] In that case, a brewing company, Guinness, owned a ship which was regularly used for the carriage of their stout from Dublin to Liverpool and Manchester. This ship was involved in a collision. The plaintiff's ship was damaged. The defendant shipowners claimed that since they, the owners, were a brewing company, not a shipping line, a lower standard of care would be applicable. However, the Court of Appeal held that one required to gauge the defendant's conduct by reference to the standard of a reasonably prudent shipowner.

6.7   The application of the objective test is well illustrated in the House of Lords case of *Glasgow Corporation* v *Muir*.[9] There, the manageress of the defender's tearoom gave a church party permission to use the tearoom to eat pre-packed lunches. A child was

---

5 [1971] 2 QB 691 at 707.
6 (1986) 162 CLR 376.
7 [1958] 2 QB 265.
8 [1965] P 294.
9 1943 SC (HL) 3.

scalded when a tea urn, which was being carried through the tearoom by members of the party, overturned. Lord Macmillan stated:[10]

> "The standard of foresight of the reasonable man is in one sense an impersonal test. It eliminates the personal equation and is independent of the idiosyncrasies of the particular person whose conduct is in question. Some persons are by nature unduly timorous and imagine every path beset with lions, others of more robust temperament fail to foresee or nonchalantly disregard even the most obvious dangers. The reasonable man is presumed to be free both from over-apprehension and from over-confidence ..."

The rule that one adopts an objective approach in ascertaining whether the standard of care has been attained by the defender is inflexibly applied. A good example of such an approach is seen in *Roberts v Ramsbottom*.[11] In that case the defendant suffered a stroke while driving his car. His ability to drive was impaired. Twenty minutes later his car collided with a car being driven by the plaintiff, who was injured. It was held that the standard of care the law demanded of the defendant was to be determined objectively. Therefore, the standard of the reasonably competent driver was applicable to the situation. The defendant was, therefore, liable.[12]   **6.8**

HOW IS THE STANDARD OF CARE DETERMINED?

What we consider here are the various factors the courts take into account in order to determine whether the duty of care the defender owes to the pursuer has been breached.   **6.9**

STATE OF CURRENT KNOWLEDGE

The court takes into account, where relevant, the state of current knowledge. The leading case here is *Roe v Minister of Health*.[13] In 1947, the plaintiff went into hospital for a minor operation. He was given a spinal injection. The fluid used for the injection was kept in an ampoule, that is, a very small glass container, which in turn was kept in a phenol solution. The phenol seeped into the ampoule through invisible cracks in its wall. At that time it was not known that this was possible. The plaintiff was paralysed from the waist downwards. He sued the Minister of Health responsible for the hospital concerned. The plaintiff did not succeed, however, since the hospital had acted in a way in which any other reasonable hospital would have acted in the situation. The state of current knowledge was not such that the law imposed a duty on the defendant to act in any other way than it had done.   **6.10**

MAGNITUDE OF RISK

The greater the risk of injury, the greater the amount of precautions the defender is required to take. In *Blyth v Birmingham Waterworks Co*,[14] the defendant Water Board   **6.11**

---

[10] [1943] AC 448 at 457.
[11] [1981] 1 All ER 7.
[12] See also *Mansfield v Weetabix Ltd* [1998] 1 WLR 1263.
[13] [1954] 2 QB 66.
[14] (1856) 11 Ex 781.

laid a water mains 18 inches in depth. One year there was an extremely severe frost which penetrated the ground as far as the water mains. The water mains burst and the flood damaged the plaintiff's premises. It was held that the Water Board was not negligent because it had taken reasonable precautions in the circumstances.

6.12   The leading modern case on standard of care is *Bolton* v *Stone*.[15] The plaintiff, while standing in a quiet suburban highway outside her house, was struck by a cricket ball. The plaintiff was 100 yards from the batsman and the ball had cleared a 17-foot fence, 78 yards from the batsman. Similar hits had occurred only about six times in the previous 30 years. It was held by the House of Lords that since the likelihood of injury was small, the plaintiff had not established that the defendant had broken his duty of care.[16]

RISK OF SERIOUS INJURY

6.13   The risk of serious injury (ie gravity of consequences) is taken into account in determining whether the duty of care has been breached. What is being said here is that the court considers not only the magnitude of the risk involved in the activity which is being undertaken by the defender, but also the gravity of the consequences of an accident if it did take place. The leading case on this issue is *Paris* v *Stepney Borough Council*.[17] In that case the plaintiff had only one good eye. He was struck in his good eye by a chip from a bolt. He claimed that his employers should have provided and also required him to wear goggles while he was carrying out work. It was held by the House of Lords that, notwithstanding the fact that the plaintiff was just as capable of carrying out his work as a person with normal vision (and, therefore, the risk of an accident occurring to him was no greater than that in respect of a fully sighted person), it was necessary for the employer, when considering which preventative measures should be taken, to take into account the consequences of any accident occurring to the plaintiff.

UTILITY OF THE DEFENDER'S ACTIVITY

6.14   The social utility or usefulness of the relevant activity in which the defender is engaging is taken into account. The greater the utility, the more likely it is that the court will hold that the relevant standard of care has been attained. The leading case is *Watt* v *Hertfordshire County Council*.[18] The plaintiff was a fireman. The fire station at which the plaintiff was working received an emergency call that a woman was trapped under a lorry. Two of the plaintiff's colleagues threw a heavy jack on to the lorry in which they were to travel to the scene of the accident. However, the lorry was not equipped to carry such a jack. Jacks were normally carried to accidents in a purpose-made lorry. No such lorry was available. During the rescue journey, the jack rolled away from its original position on the lorry and injured the plaintiff. The Court of Appeal held that the duty of care the defendant owed to the plaintiff had not been breached. In reaching

---

[15] [1951] AC 850. See also *Hilder* v *Associated Portland Cement* [1961] 1 WLR 1434.
[16] See also *Brisco* v *Secretary of State for Scotland* 1996 Rep LR 169 and *Gillon* v *Chief Constable of Strathclyde Police* 1996 Rep LR 165.
[17] [1951] AC 367.
[18] [1954] 1 WLR 835.

its decision, the court took into account the social utility of the journey, namely the rescuing of an injured person. However, it should be emphasised that simply because the defender is involved in an activity which has some social worth or utility does not exonerate him from the need to take care. This point was decided in *Ward* v *London County Council.*[19] In that case the driver of a fire engine, responding to an emergency call, drove through a red traffic light and injured the plaintiff. It was held that the defendant could not use the reason that he was involved in a journey of social worth as an excuse for his breach of duty of care.

PRACTICALITY OF PRECAUTIONS

The easier it is to take measures to counteract the risk in the particular circumstances **6.15** concerned, the more likely the courts will hold that the appropriate duty of care has been breached. In the House of Lords case of *Latimer* v *AEC Ltd,*[20] the floor of the defendant's factory was flooded by an exceptionally heavy rainstorm. Oil which was kept in troughs was washed out on to the factory floor. The defendant put sawdust on the floor, but there was not enough sawdust to cover the entire factory floor. The plaintiff, a factory worker, slipped on the floor and injured himself. He sued the factory occupier. It was held that the defendant was not liable since he had taken all appropriate precautions short of closing the factory. The decision has been criticised on the ground that commercial profitability was given too much prominence by the court over personal security of the workers.

AVAILABILITY OF RESOURCES

To what extent, if any, is it relevant for the court to take into account the level of **6.16** resources the defender has at his disposal when ascertaining whether he has breached his duty of care? For example, suppose an employer decided to reduce the number of workmen who were normally employed to convey heavy sacks from one part of the factory to another, as a consequence of which an employee is forced to lift a sack which would formerly have been carried by two men, and injures his back. Could the employer claim, by way of defence, that he had not breached his duty of care to the employee? On the authority of *Walker* v *Northumberland County Council*[21] the answer would be in the negative. In that case the plaintiff suffered a nervous breakdown which had been caused by the strain of carrying out his professional duties. He sued his employer, a local authority. The authority was held liable. The court stated, *obiter*, that the defendant could not shelter behind a policy not to increase staff.

However, in certain situations the courts seem willing to take into account the **6.17** defender's lack of resources. In *Goldman* v *Hargrave,*[22] which concerned the law of nuisance as well as the law of negligence, the defendant failed to extinguish a fire in a tree which had been started by lightning. The fire spread and the plaintiff's premises were damaged. The Privy Council, in ascertaining whether the duty of care had been broken, considered it legitimate to judge the defendant in the light of his

---

[19] [1938] 2 All ER 341.
[20] [1953] AC 643.
[21] [1995] ICR 702.
[22] [1967] 1 AC 645.

individual circumstances as opposed to those of a hypothetical landowner. *Goldman* was approved by the Court of Appeal in *Leakey* v *National Trust*.[23]

EMERGENCY SITUATIONS (AGONY OF THE MOMENT)

6.18 If the defender is placed in a sudden emergency situation, which is not of his own creation, his actions must be judged in the light of those circumstances. For example, in the Court of Appeal case of *Marshall* v *Osmond*,[24] a suspect was struck by a police car as he left his vehicle to make an escape. It was held that the police had not been negligent. Again, in the Privy Council case of *Ng Chun Pui* v *Lee Chuen Tat*,[25] the driver of a coach who had braked, swerved and skidded when another vehicle had cut across his path had acted reasonably in an emergency.

CHILDREN

6.19 Children are delictually responsible for their conduct. In *Campbell* v *Ord and Maddison*,[26] it was stated *obiter* that a child of 4 years of age could be negligent in law. As far as the determination of the requisite standard of care demanded of a child is concerned, the law sets the relevant standard by reference to the age of the child in question. The authority on this point derives from cases concerned with contributory negligence. In the Privy Council case of *Yachuk* v *Oliver Blais Co Ltd*,[27] the defendant sold petrol to a child who burned himself with it. It was held that the degree of care which the law could demand the child to take of himself depended on his particular age. Again, in the Court of Appeal case of *Gough* v *Thorne*,[28] it was held not to be contributorily negligent for a girl aged 13, who was crossing the road, not to look forward and see whether anything else was travelling along the road. Lord Denning MR stated[29] that a judge should find a child guilty of contributory negligence only if he or she is of such an age as one could reasonably expect to take precautions for his or her own safety.[30]

---

[23] [1980] 1 All ER 17.
[24] [1983] QB 1034.
[25] (1988) 132 SJ 1244.
[26] (1873) 1 R 149.
[27] [1949] AC 386.
[28] [1966] 1 WLR 1387.
[29] *Ibid* at 1390.
[30] See also *Orchard* v *Lee*, *The Times*, 14 April 2009; and *Mullin* v *Richards* [1998] 1 WLR 1304.

7 FACTUAL CAUSATION

Notwithstanding the fact that the defender owes a duty of care to the pursuer and **7.1** also that that duty has been breached, the pursuer will fail in his action unless he can prove that the negligent conduct in question has actually caused the injury in question. For example, suppose that Ian, a surveyor, negligently surveys a house which I am contemplating purchasing. Ian fails to notice that the walls of the house are badly cracked. The survey is carried out on behalf of a building society from which I wish to obtain a mortgage. The report is sent to me by post. However, I fail to open the letter which contains the report. I purchase the house, only to discover that it is of little value. I could not successfully sue Ian in delict simply because his negligent conduct did not cause the relevant loss.

There are two main tests which the courts use to ascertain whether D's conduct **7.2** caused the loss in question, namely:

- the "but for" test; and
- the "material contribution" test.

THE "BUT FOR" TEST

In order to ascertain whether the defender's conduct has caused the pursuer's injury, **7.3** the court enquires: "But for the defender's conduct, would the pursuer have sustained the injury in question?" The leading case is *Barnett v Chelsea and Kensington Hospital Management Committee*.[1] In that case, three nightwatchmen drank tea which made them vomit. They went to the casualty department of the local hospital. The casualty officer was informed by a nurse about the men. However, he decided not to see them. Instead, he told them to go home and consult their own doctors. A few hours later, one of them died from arsenic poisoning. It was held that, while the hospital did owe the man a duty of care in law, since the plaintiff would have died anyway, the defendants were not liable. In other words, there was no causal link between the negligent conduct of the defendant hospital board and the injury which was sustained by the plaintiff. Again, in the House of Lords case of *The Empire Jamaica*,[2] a collision was caused by the negligence of the officer who was on watch on the defendant's ship. While there was no doubt that the owners of the ship were vicariously liable for the officer's negligence, under the relevant merchant shipping legislation, they were entitled to limit their liability if the collision was without their actual fault.

---

[1] [1969] 1 QB 428.
[2] [1957] AC 386.

As far as the owners of the ship were concerned, the only fault attributable to them was that the officer in charge did not hold the necessary mate's certificate. However, it was established during the trial that if the owners had, indeed, applied for such a certificate it would have been granted. In other words, the lack of the certificate had not caused the damage in question. They were, therefore, able to limit their liability. Furthermore, in the House of Lords case of *McWilliams* v *Sir William Arrol and Co Ltd*,[3] a workman was employed by the defenders. He was killed when he fell off a roof. It was claimed by his widow that the defenders were negligent in failing to provide him with a safety harness. It was accepted by the House that the harness would have prevented the fall. However, the pursuer failed in her action because the defenders proved that her husband would not have worn the harness in any event. In other words, the defenders' omission was not the cause of his fall. Again, in the House of Lords case of *Kay* v *Ayrshire and Arran Health Board*,[4] the pursuer claimed that his son's deafness had been caused by a penicillin overdose while he had been a patient in a hospital run by the defenders. The latter claimed, however, that the child's deafness had been caused by meningitis. The House held that the pursuer had not established that the overdose had a causal link with the deafness and, therefore, the pursuer failed in his action.

7.4   In order to succeed, the pursuer is required to prove a causal link between the defender's conduct and the pursuer's injury, on a balance of probabilities.[5] The burden of proof remains on the pursuer throughout the trial.[6]

THE "MATERIAL CONTRIBUTION" TEST

7.5   The courts are willing to accept that the defender has caused harm to the pursuer if the defendant's negligent act has materially contributed to the pursuer's injury as opposed to being the sole cause of it. For example, if A negligently starts a fire on his premises and the fire spreads to his neighbour C's premises, and damages it, A, of course, would be liable to C in the law of delict, since A caused the relevant harm. However, if B also negligently started a fire on his own premises, and that fire combines with the fire A started, and the fires merge and burn C's premises, the latter fire could also be said to have "caused" the fire in question.

7.6   Again, if X and Y play loud music in their respective premises, and the noise from each premises combines to annoy Z, a neighbouring proprietor, both X and Y would be liable in nuisance, provided that the noise generated by either X or Y had materially contributed to the nuisance. In the above scenarios both A and B, in the first, and C and D in the second, would be said to be jointly and severally liable for the harm which has been caused. It should be added, however, that it would be irrelevant in either example if the conduct of either A (in the first example) or X (in the second example) would have been insufficient in itself to cause the injury in question.

---

[3] 1962 SC (HL) 70.
[4] 1987 SC (HL) 145.
[5] *Wardlaw* v *Bonnington Castings Ltd* 1956 SC (HL) 26; *Kay's Tutor* v *Ayrshire and Arran Health Board* 1987 SC (HL) 145. See also *Gregg* v *Scott* [2005] 2 AC 176.
[6] *Wilsher* v *Essex Area Health Authority* [1988] 1 All ER 871.

The role of the principle of material contribution in terms of factual causation is **7.7** seen in the House of Lords case of *Wardlaw* v *Bonnington Castings*.[7] There, the pursuer's disease was caused by an accumulation of dust in his lungs. The dust in question came from two sources. The defenders (who were the pursuer's employers) were not responsible for one source, but they could have prevented the other. The dust from the latter source (ie the "illegal" dust) was not, in itself, sufficient to cause the disease. However, the pursuer succeeded because the illegal dust had made a material contribution to his injury. Again, in the House of Lords case of *McGhee* v *National Coal Board*,[8] the pursuer contracted dermatitis from the presence of brick dust on his skin. It was proved that some exposure to brick dust was the inevitable consequence of working with brick. However, the employers had failed to provide washing facilities, in contravention of the relevant legislation. The pursuer was, therefore, forced to cycle home each day with dust on his skin. The House held that the pursuer could succeed, if he could prove that the state of affairs brought about by the failure to provide washing facilities materially contributed to his illness. The interesting Court of Appeal case of *Vernon* v *Bosley*[9] illustrates the same principle. In *Vernon*, the defendant was carrying the plaintiff's daughters as passengers in a car she was driving. The defendant drove the car negligently. The car crashed and fell into a fast-flowing river. The defendant managed to escape but the children were trapped. The plaintiff and his wife were called to the scene of the accident where they watched the rescue services make an abortive attempt to rescue the children. The children perished. The plaintiff claimed that he suffered nervous shock and psychological trauma by witnessing the immediate aftermath of the accident. He further claimed that he had developed a severe post-traumatic stress disorder which was complicated by a severe grief reaction caused by the defendant's negligence. However, the defendant contended, *inter alia*, that the damage sustained by the plaintiff had come about either wholly or partly as a result of his reaction to grief. The Court of Appeal held, following *Bonnington* above, that where the plaintiff's injury was attributable to two possible causes it was sufficient that the "illegal" cause (here, the nervous shock that stemmed from the plaintiff witnessing the immediate aftermath of the accident) materially contributed to the injury in question.

However, the need for the pursuer to prove that the defender's conduct either **7.8** caused or materially contributed to his injury may be unfair to the pursuer. Indeed, in *Fairchild* v *Glenhaven Funeral Services Ltd*,[10] the House of Lords held that in certain circumstances one could depart from the well-established rules governing factual causation. In *Fairchild*, F had been employed at different times, and for different periods, by more than one employer. F's employers, E1 and E2, had been subject to a legal duty to prevent F from inhaling asbestos dust. However, both E1 and E2 had failed to take the relevant preventative measures. F contracted mesothelioma, from which he died. The question the House had to answer was whether F could recover against either E1 or E2, or against both E1 and E2. On the current limits of scientific knowledge he was unable to prove, on the balance of probabilities, that his mesothelioma was actually caused by his inhaling asbestos dust during his employment by one or other or both of his employers (ie E1 and E2). The House held that F could

---

[7] 1956 SC (HL) 26.
[8] [1972] 3 All ER 1008.
[9] [1997] 1 All ER 577.
[10] [2002] 3 All ER 305. See R Merkin and J Steele, "Compensating Mesothelioma Victims" (2011) 127 LQR 329.

recover against both E1 and E2 on the ground that, in certain special circumstances, the court could depart from the usual "but for" test of causation and treat a lesser degree of causation as sufficient: namely, that the defendant's breach of duty had materially contributed to causing the disease by materially increasing the risk that the disease would be contracted. *McGhee* was, therefore, followed. Any injustice that might be involved in imposing liability in these circumstances was heavily outweighed by the injustice of denying redress to the victim. According to Lord Bingham:[11]

> "It can probably be said to be unjust to impose liability on a party who has not been shown, even on a balance of probability, to have caused the damage complained of. On the other hand, there is a strong policy argument in favour of compensating those who have suffered grave harm at the expense of their employers who owed them a duty to protect them against that very harm and failed to do so when the harm can only have been caused by breach of that duty and when science does not permit the victim accurately to attribute, as between several employers, the precise responsibility for the harm he has suffered."

7.9 The law was taken further by the House of Lords in *Barker* v *Corus (UK) Ltd*[12] where, on facts which were similar to those in *Fairchild*, it was held appropriate to apportion liability between the defendants in accordance with the degree of risk to which they had exposed the claimant by virtue of their negligence.

7.10 As far as liability in respect of mesothelioma is concerned, the Compensation Act 2006[13] reverses *Barker* and makes the person who is at fault jointly and severally liable (ie *in solidum*) with any other person.

7.11 In both *Fairchild* and *Barker*, the employee was exposed to contamination from an "illegal" source, or sources, in the workplace. Indeed, the key requirement in *Fairchild* was that all the exposures were related to employment, and were due to breaches of duty, and also, that it was impossible to prove which exposure had caused the disease.[14] However, in *Sienkiewicz* v *Greif (UK) Ltd*,[15] the question which fell to be answered by the House of Lords was whether the learning in *Fairchild* and *Barker* was applicable to a situation where simply *one* source to which the claimant had been exposed was work related and the other source was not. In *Sienkiewicz*, the claimant's mother had been exposed to asbestos dust between 1966 and 1984 during the period of her employment with the defendant. However, due to the location of her home, she had also been exposed to low levels of asbestos in the general environment. The House held that the learning in *Fairchild* and *Barker* applied to the facts of the case and, therefore, the defendant was liable. According to Lord Phillips,[16] the underlying premise in both *Fairchild* and *Barker* was that it was not possible to determine causation unless medical science enabled one to do so with certainty. However, the law of causation dealt not with certainties but with probabilities. His Lordship went on to state[17] that both *Fairchild* and *Barker* developed the common law by equating "materially increasing the risk" with "contributing to the cause" in specified and limited circumstances which

---

[11] [2002] 3 All ER 305 at 334.
[12] [2006] 2 WLR 1027.
[13] Section 3.
[14] See K Amirthalingam, "Causation, risk and damage" (2010) 126 LQR 162 at 164.
[15] [2011] 2 WLR 523. See P Easton, "Game of Chance" 2011 SJ (April) 15.
[16] [2011] 2 WLR 523 at 544.
[17] *Ibid* at 548.

include ignorance of how causation in fact occurs. The law was capable of further development.

SUPERVENING EVENTS

It may sometimes happen that an event occurs after the occurrence of the defender's **7.12** negligent act (but before the relevant proof or trial) which, in practical terms, eclipses the effects of the original delictual act. To what extent, if any, can the defender in such circumstances successfully argue that he is only liable to compensate the pursuer for the consequences of his negligent act up to the time the supervening act takes place? The House of Lords was required to answer this question in *Baker* v *Willoughby*.[18] In that case the plaintiff sustained an injury to his leg by virtue of the defendant's negligence. The plaintiff's leg was partially disabled. Later, but before the trial, the plaintiff was shot in the leg during an armed robbery. His leg had to be amputated. The House held that the plaintiff could still recover damages in respect of the original negligent act of the defendant. However, in the Court of Appeal case of *Cutler* v *Vauxhall Motors*,[19] the plaintiff grazed his ankle in an accident at work for which his employers were liable in negligence. The graze caused ulceration of the leg for which the plaintiff required an immediate operation to remove varicose veins. The court held that, since the plaintiff would have needed the operation within 5 years anyway, this fact could be taken into account when it was awarding damages to the plaintiff. Again, in the House of Lords case of *Jobling* v *Associated Dairies*,[20] the plaintiff was injured by virtue of the defendant's negligence. He suffered back pain that was somewhat disabling. However, before the trial, he suffered serious illness completely unconnected with the accident. That illness completely incapacitated him. The House held that the effect of the illness should be taken into account when one was deciding the amount of damages which should be awarded to the plaintiff.

The important question which falls to be answered, of course, is whether the **7.13** learning in *Jobling* is simply confined to personal injury cases, or is of more general application. For example, suppose my next-door neighbour, in carrying out building operations on his land, damages part of the foundations of my house, which becomes structurally unstable as a result. I decide to sue him to recover damages to cover the costs of necessary remedial works. However, before the trial, the entire foundations of my house are severely damaged by subsidence because my house is situated in a former shale mining area. Could my neighbour successfully claim that his negligent act has now been entirely eclipsed by the supervening event? In the absence of authority, it is suggested that the supervening act should, indeed, be taken into account in the award of damages.

LOSS OF CHANCE

Does the law take into account damage caused by the loss of chance, in determining **7.14** the defender's liability? For example, if the defender, a medical practitioner, wrongly

---

[18] [1970] AC 467.
[19] [1971] 1 QB 418.
[20] [1982] AC 794.

diagnoses that the pursuer has a benign tumour, as a result of which the latter does nothing to have it removed, but it subsequently transpires that the tumour is, indeed, malignant, by which time nothing can be done to remedy the situation, the defender can be said to have denied the pursuer the chance, or opportunity, to take appropriate remedial action. We say that the pursuer has denied the pursuer a *chance* of recovery simply because one does not really know whether it would have made any difference to the pursuer if the correct advice had been timeously given to him. For example, such diagnosis might have revealed that nothing could have been done to cure him anyway or, if something could have been done, there is a possibility that the pursuer would have rejected any treatment. We now consider how the courts have dealt with a loss of chance in terms of the law of negligence.

7.15   In *Kenyon v Bell*,[21] a young child's eye was injured in a domestic accident. The injury was treated in a hospital casualty ward. The pursuer was sent home. However, the condition of the eye worsened considerably. The eye had to be surgically removed. It was claimed that the doctor who had treated the girl had been negligent, as a result of which the pursuer had lost her eye, or, such negligence had denied the pursuer a material chance of saving the eye. However, Lord Guthrie, in the Outer House refused to accept that the loss of chance of saving the eye was a legally recognised harm.

7.16   The right to recover in relation to a lost chance was again considered in *Yeoman v Ferries*.[22] There, an employee consulted a solicitor in order to ascertain whether he could sue his employer in respect of an industrial injury. The solicitor had some discussion with the employer but they failed to achieve any settlement. The solicitor did not instruct an action to be raised against the employer. The claim against the employer became time barred. The employee then raised against the solicitor an action which was based on professional negligence. In the Outer House it was held that the pursuer could sue the solicitor for depriving him of the loss of the chance to sue his employer.

7.17   The right to recover for a lost chance was considered by the House of Lords in *Hotson v East Berkshire Area Health Authority*.[23] In that case a boy fell out of a tree and injured his hip. He was taken to a hospital where he was misdiagnosed. His condition was, in fact, serious. He developed avascular necrosis. However, he was not given the proper treatment. By the time the mistake was discovered, it was too late for anything to be done. It was proved that the plaintiff had only a 25 per cent chance of avoiding permanent disability if a correct diagnosis had been made. Therefore, the plaintiff claimed that since he had a 25 per cent chance of recovery, the defendant should pay him 25 per cent of the full compensation recoverable by reason of the negligent act. However, the House of Lords held that, since in 75 per cent of such cases avascular necrosis develops, the plaintiff had failed to prove on a balance of probabilities that the negligence of the defendant had materially contributed to his condition. The plaintiff, therefore, failed in his action. However, the House did not reject the proposition that one could not sue in respect of a lost chance in the law of tort.

7.18   The right to recover for a lost chance was again explicitly recognised in *Kyle v P & J Stormonth Darling WS*.[24] The pursuer had been the defender in a sheriff court action where decree had been pronounced against him. That decision had

---

[21] 1953 SC 125.
[22] 1967 SC 255.
[23] [1987] 2 All ER 909.
[24] 1992 SLT 264.

been unsuccessfully appealed to the sheriff principal and, thereafter, an appeal was marked (ie scheduled) to the Court of Session. The appeal had to be abandoned because the defender failed to lodge and deliver relevant papers before the court. The pursuer then raised an action of damages, alleging professional negligence and breach of contract against his solicitors. Lord Prosser, allowing proof before answer, held that since the pursuer had a reasonable prospect of success in the litigation in which he was involved, the loss of the right to appeal to the court had deprived him of a legal right in respect of which he could seek redress in the law of delict. The Inner House, on appeal, held that the loss of the right to pursue a claim in the courts could form the basis of an action in delict.

The issue of lost chance was discussed again in *Allied Maples Group Ltd* v *Simmons* **7.19** *and Simmons*.[25] There, a retailing company instructed the defendant solicitors to act for them in the takeover of assets of a company, among which were four department stores leased by a subsidiary. The defendants negligently advised the plaintiffs about the agreement. Certain contingent claims were made against the plaintiffs by the lessors of the property. The plaintiffs only became aware of claims a year later. The plaintiffs then brought an action against the defendants, contending that, on the balance of probabilities, there was a real chance the plaintiffs would successfully have re-negotiated the contract with the vendor. The plaintiffs succeeded at first instance. The defendants appealed. The Court of Appeal, in dismissing the appeal, held:

(1) that the establishment of a causal link between the defendants' negligence and the plaintiffs' loss, where the negligence consisted of some positive act, was a question of historical fact to be determined on the balance of probabilities, in which case, once established, the fact was taken as true and the plaintiff was entitled to recover his damages in full;

(2) that where the quantification of the plaintiffs' loss depended upon future uncertain events it was to be decided on the court's assessment of the risk materialising;

(3) that where the defendants' negligence consisted of an omission, causation depended on the answer to the hypothetical question of what the plaintiff would have done if the defendant had not been guilty of the omission, which was a matter of inference to be determined from all the circumstances; and

(4) that where the plaintiffs' loss depended on the hypothetical action of a third party, the plaintiff was entitled to succeed if he could show that there was a real or substantial, rather than a speculative, chance that the third party would have acted so as to confer the benefit or avoid the risk to the plaintiff.

Stuart-Smith LJ[26] referred to the House of Lords case of *Spring* v *Guardian Assurance*,[27] **7.20** where it was held that an employer who negligently gave a bad reference for the plaintiff, their ex-employee, might be liable to him in damages. The case was remitted to the Court of Appeal for the assessment of damages, the plaintiff's case being that he had failed to obtain employment with a third party because of the adverse reference. The defendant's case was based on the fact that the third party would not

[25] [1995] 1 WLR 1602.
[26] *Ibid* at 1613.
[27] [1994] 3 All ER 129.

have employed him anyway. Lord Lowry[28] expressed the opinion, *obiter*, that once the duty of care is held to exist and the defendant's negligence is proved, the plaintiff only requires to show that by reason of that negligence he has lost a reasonable chance of employment and has thereby sustained loss. He does not have to prove that "but for" the negligent reference the third party would have employed him.

7.21   Hobhouse LJ stated[29] that the plaintiffs were not obliged to prove more than that they had lost something of substance. They had done so by showing that they had a measurable chance of negotiating better terms in the agreement. When such a chance was established, it was up to the trial judge to assess the value of what the plaintiff had lost.

7.22   In the House of Lords case of *Gregg* v *Scott*[30] the issue was whether the claimant could sue a doctor in negligence in respect of his failing properly to diagnose the claimant's cancerous condition, with the result that the claimant's chance of survival for 10 years (which was considered to be a cure) had been reduced from 42 per cent to 25 per cent. By a bare majority, the House of Lords held that, in accordance with the general rules of causation, a claimant must prove, on the balance of probabilities, that the defendant's negligence caused the harm in question. There could be no remedy in tort simply for a reduction in the chance of recovery from illness.[31]

---

[28] [1994] 3 All ER 129 at 154.
[29] *Allied Maples Group Ltd* v *Simmons and Simmons* [1995] 1 WLR 1602 at 1621.
[30] [2005] 2 WLR 268.
[31] See K Lockhart, "*Loss of chance in medical negligence*: *Gregg* v *Scott*" 2005 SLT 93.

8 REMOTENESS OF DAMAGE (LEGAL CAUSATION)

The law will not allow the pursuer to recover for harm which has been inflicted **8.1** by the negligent conduct of the defender if the injury is too remote. Before we commence a detailed discussion of the subject it is instructive to consider the following scenarios.

(a) Lex, a delict lecturer, goes out jogging. He falls into a hole in the pavement which has been excavated by local authority workmen but has not been properly guarded. Lex breaks his leg and has to take considerable time off work. Jock replaces Lex, but is not an expert in delict. The quality of his lectures is poor. As a result of such poor teaching, X (a part-time law student) fails his delict exam. As a consequence of this, X does not get a pay rise he would have received had he passed the delict exam. X is distraught. He commits suicide. Could X's estate sue the local authority for X's death?

(b) Alan, a builder, lays the foundations of Tom's house at an inadequate depth. Cracks develop in the walls. The house becomes dangerous. Tom and his wife therefore have to leave the house and move to rented accommodation, in a poorer part of the town. While they live there, Tom is mugged by a gang of skinheads and injured. Can Tom sue Alan, in delict, for the personal injuries he sustains?

There is a causal link, in the first scenario, between Lex falling into the hole and X **8.2** committing suicide, and, in the second, between Alan negligently building Tom's house and Tom being mugged. Indeed, a logician, a philosopher and also a historian would encounter little difficulty in linking the harm which the pursuer sustains with the negligent conduct of the respective defenders in both (a) and (b). However, in each of the above scenarios the relevant injury would be too remote to attract legal redress.

In ascertaining whether any given damage is too remote the law adopts a practical **8.3** approach. Such an approach is well illustrated in the Inner House case of *Blaikie* v *British Transport Commission*.[1] In that case the widow of a train driver brought an action against the defenders, claiming that, as a result of their negligence, the boiler of the train which the deceased drove was in serious risk of exploding, in consequence of which the deceased had been put to great physical effort to extinguish the fire. He collapsed and died of a heart attack. However, it was held by the Inner House that the injury was too remote. The Lord Justice-Clerk stated:[2]

---

[1] 1961 SC 44.
[2] *Ibid* at 48.

"The law has always had to come to some sort of compromise with the doctrine of causation. The problem is a practical rather than an intellectual one. It is easy and usual to bedevil it with subtleties, but the attitude of the law is that expediency and good sense dictate that for practical purposes a line has to be drawn somewhere, and that in drawing it the Court is to be guided by the practical experience of the reasonable man rather than by the theoretical speculations of the philosopher."

REMOTENESS

8.4 How, then, do the courts ascertain whether the damage the pursuer sustains is too remote in order to render the defender liable in negligence?

There are two competing rules which were used by the courts to determine liability in negligence in such situations, namely:

(1) the "directness" test; and
(2) the "foreseeability" test.

THE "DIRECTNESS" TEST

8.5 Under the "directness test" the defender was held responsible for all loss, which directly flowed from his original act of negligence. The genesis of the rule is found in *Re Polemis*.[3] In that case, a chartered vessel was unloading in Casablanca. The servants of the charterers negligently let a plank of wood drop into the hold of the ship. Part of the cargo was a quantity of petrol. The petrol had leaked out of its containers during the voyage. The fall of the plank caused a spark which caused the petrol to explode. The ship was completely destroyed. The Court of Appeal held that the charterers were responsible for the loss of the ship since such loss was the direct consequence of the act of negligence in question. Scrutton LJ stated:[4]

"[T]he fact that the damage the negligent act causes is not the exact kind of damage one would expect is immaterial, so long as the damage is in fact caused sufficiently directly by the negligent act ... Once the act is negligent, the fact that its exact operation was not foreseen is immaterial. In the present case it was negligent in discharging cargo to knock down the planks of the temporary staging, for they might easily cause some damage either to workmen or cargo or the ship. The fact that they did directly produce an unexpected result, a spark in the atmosphere of vapour which caused a fire, does not relieve the person who was negligent from the damage which his negligent act directly caused."

8.6 Therefore, according to this view, it matters not whether the *kind* of damage sustained by the pursuer is foreseeable, as long as the origins of such damage can be linked to the original negligent act of the defender. In such circumstances, liability will lie.

---

[3] [1921] 3 KB 560.
[4] *Ibid* at 577.

THE "FORESEEABILITY" TEST

The competing test to the "directness" test is found in the Privy Council case of *The*   **8.7**
Wagon Mound.[5] In that case, OT Ltd were charterers of a ship which was known as the
Wagon Mound. It was moored in a wharf in Sydney, Australia. OT's servants allowed a
large quantity of oil to be spilled. The oil spread to another wharf where another ship
was under repair. Sparks from the welding operations in that part of the harbour fell
onto the water. Either rags or cotton waste which was floating on the water caught fire.
The wharf was damaged. The Privy Council held that while the damage in question
was the direct cause of the spillage, it was, at the same time, unforeseeable. Therefore,
the defendants were not liable. The foresight of the hypothetical reasonable man in the
position of the defender determines liability.

It is the rule in *The Wagon Mound*, in contrast to that in *Re Polemis*, which currently   **8.8**
finds favour with the courts in determining whether the harm which has been caused
by a negligent act is too remote to allow the pursuer to recover.[6]

What need one foresee?

The defender need not actually foresee the occurrence of the accident in which the   **8.9**
pursuer sustains harm. Rather, it suffices that he can foresee that the relevant *kind* of
harm would occur if the accident actually occurred. This was decided in *Galashiels Gas
Co Ltd v O'Donnell*.[7] In that case the defenders had a lift at their gasworks. The lift was
ostensibly in a safe working order. However, on one occasion something went wrong.
The lift fell to the bottom of the shaft. The pursuer and others were killed. The House
of Lords held that the defenders were liable, since a reasonable man, if advised of the
way in which the lift went wrong, would have foreseen that the deceased would have
been killed.

The precise series (or concatenation) of events, which occurred as a result of the   **8.10**
negligent conduct of the defender, need not have been foreseen by him for liability to
lie. This particular point was established in the House of Lords case of *Hughes v Lord
Advocate*.[8] In that case the pursuer, aged 8, and his uncle, aged 10, were playing in a
public road. Their attention was attracted to an unattended canvas shelter situated
over an uncovered manhole. The boys entered the manhole and decided to explore
it. They enlisted the aid of a ladder and a paraffin lamp which had been left outside
the tent. The pursuer tripped against the lamp, which fell into the manhole. The
paraffin, which leaked from the lamp on its coming into contact with the bottom of the
manhole, vaporised with the heat of the lamp. There was an explosion. The pursuer
lost his balance and fell into the manhole. He sustained serious injury. The House of
Lords held that the defenders were liable for the harm the pursuer had sustained since,
notwithstanding the fact that the precise concatenation of events which had taken
place was not reasonably foreseeable, the type of harm (ie harm by burning) which he
had sustained was foreseeable. Lord Morris stated:[9]

---

[5] [1961] AC 388.
[6] See also *Simmons v British Steel* 2004 SC (HL) 94.
[7] [1949] AC 275. The action in this case was for breach of statutory duty (see Chapter 10).
[8] [1963] SC (HL) 31.
[9] *Ibid* at 43.

"The circumstances that an explosion as such would not have been contemplated does not alter the fact that it could reasonably have been foreseen that a boy who played in and about the canvas shelter, and played with the things that were thereabouts, might get hurt and might in some way burn himself. That is just what happened. The pursuer did burn himself, though his burns were more grave than would have been expected. The fact that the features or developments of an accident may not reasonably have been foreseen does not mean that the accident itself was not foreseeable."[10]

Degree of foreseeability required

8.11 We have established thus far that the type of injury the pursuer sustains needs to be foreseeable. However, what degree of foreseeability is required before the defender would be liable for the harm he causes? In the first-instance case of *Tremain* v *Pike*,[11] the plaintiff was employed by the defendant as a herdsman. He contracted Weil's disease (Leptospirosis) from rats' urine, because the defendant had allowed the rat population in his farm to become too large. It was held that the injury suffered by the plaintiff was too remote since, while some form of injury from rat bites was foreseeable, it was not reasonably foreseeable that the plaintiff would develop Weil's disease. If *Tremain* represents good law then a high degree of foreseeability is required. The authors suggest that *Tremain* sets too high a ceiling as far as the level of foreseeability is concerned. It is, indeed, difficult to predict the outcome of a particular case as far as this area of the law is concerned. However, one gets the impression that judges approach the issue intuitively. A good example of such an approach is seen in the Court of Appeal case of *Lamb* v *Camden London Borough Council*.[12] In that case contractors, who were replacing a sewer on behalf of a local council, broke a water main, causing the house nearby, which was owned by the plaintiff but let to others, to be vacated because it was unsafe. The house became a sitting target for squatters. Indeed, they soon moved into the house. They were ultimately ejected but, by then, the squatters had inflicted substantial damage on the premises. The plaintiff sued the local authority to recover the costs of repairing the premises. However, the Court of Appeal held that the damage which had been done by the squatters was too remote. The judgment of Watkins LJ is instructive. His Lordship stated:[13]

8.12 " 'This doctrine of remoteness of damage is one of very considerable obscurity and difficulty.' " So wrote the editor of *Salmond on Torts*, 17th ed (1977) p 538. If I did not consciously share that opinion previously from a fairly long acquaintance with the subject I have to confess to feelings of apprehension of never emerging out of the maze of authorities on the subject of remoteness into the light of a clear understanding of it. On my way to providing an answer to the question raised in this appeal I have sometimes felt like Sir Winston Churchill must have when he wrote (in *My Early Life*):
'I had a feeling once about mathematics, that I saw it all – depth beyond depth was revealed to me – the byss and the abyss. I saw, as one might see the transit of Venus – or even the Lord Mayor's show, a quantity passing through infinity and changing its sign from plus to minus. I saw exactly how it happened and why the tergiversation was inevitable: and how one step involved all the others. It was like politics ... but it was after dinner and I let it go!'

---

[10] See also *Jolley* v *Sutton LBC* [2000] 1 WLR 1082.
[11] [1969] 1 WLR 1556.
[12] [1981] QB 625.
[13] *Ibid* at 644.

This appeal involves but a single issue. Was the damage done to Mrs Lamb's house by squatters too remote to be a consequence of the defendant's initial negligent and damaging act which partly destroyed support for the house for which they have to compensate her?"

His Lordship continued:[14]   8.13

"A robust and sensible approach to this very important area of the study of remoteness will more often than not produce, I think, an instinctive feeling that the event or act being weighed in the balance is too remote to sound in damages for the plaintiff. I do not pretend that in all cases the answer will come easily to the inquirer. But that the question must be asked and answered in all these cases I have no doubt ... To return to the present case, I have the instinctive feeling that the squatters' damage is too remote."

Serious manifestations of thing foreseen

If the relevant harm which the pursuer sustains is foreseeable, the defender will   8.14
be liable even though the *extent* of the harm is much greater than that which could reasonably have been foreseen. A good example of the application of this principle can be seen in *Vacwell Engineering Co Ltd* v *BDH Chemicals Ltd.*[15] In that case the defendants, who were manufacturers and distributors of chemicals, sold chemicals to the plaintiffs. The former were unaware that the chemicals sold to the plaintiffs were of an explosive character. The plaintiffs were similarly unaware of the qualities of the chemical. In the course of the plaintiffs' process it was necessary to remove the labels from the ampoules which contained the chemical. The plaintiffs' scientists did this with water in a sink. Several ampoules were accidentally dropped into the sink. A violent explosion ensued. One scientist was killed and another was seriously injured. Property was also damaged. It was held that, notwithstanding the fact that the magnitude of the explosion was not reasonably foreseeable, it was not too remote to preclude recovery.

Vacwell should be contrasted with the Court of Appeal case of *Doughty* v *Turner.*[16]   8.15
There, the plaintiff, who was employed at the defendant's factory, was injured when another workman inadvertently knocked an asbestos cover into a cauldron of very hot molten liquid. The extreme heat caused the cover to undergo a chemical change. Water was released which turned into steam. The liquid erupted from the cauldron. The plaintiff was injured. The court held that the plaintiff could not recover since the eruption of the liquid could not be described as a variant of the dangers which could arise from splashing. In the authors' view, however, this case certainly does not rest comfortably with *Hughes* v *Lord Advocate,*[17] which was distinguished. It could plausibly be argued that the injury in *Doughty* caused by the liquid coming into contact with the plaintiff was a foreseeable consequence of the lid being dropped into the cauldron. In other words, the injury the plaintiff sustained emanated from a known source of danger, namely a cauldron which contained molten liquid. The precise concatenation of events by means of which the injury occurred (that is, the way in which the liquid came to be splashed on the plaintiff) would, in the light of the reasoning in *Hughes*, be irrelevant.

---

[14] [1981] QB 625 at 647.
[15] [1971] 1 QB 88.
[16] [1964] 1 All ER 98.
[17] 1963 SC (HL) 31 (see above).

"THIN SKULL" RULE

8.16 We have now established that in order to recover for the harm which has been caused by the defender, the harm requires to be foreseeable. However, this rule may, at times, redound to the detriment of the pursuer. Consider the following scenario.

8.17 I am walking along the pavement one day when I am knocked over by a skate-boarder who is navigating negligently. I fall to the ground. I sustain a fractured skull simply because my skull is thinner, and therefore more fragile, than the normal human skull. Could the skateboarder argue, by way of defence, that he is not liable for my injury, simply because such injury is not reasonably foreseeable? The *type* of injury here, namely a wound to my head, is certainly foreseeable. The *extent* of the injury is not. However, the law would allow me to recover in respect of my injury on the basis of the so-called "thin skull" rule, which is applicable to negligently inflicted harm in general and is not simply confined to personal injuries.[18] In other words, the rule would allow me to recover from the defender in respect of the full extent of my injuries which directly derive from a state of affairs (or type of harm) that was reasonably foreseeable.

8.18 A good illustration of the application of the "thin skull" rule is seen in *Smith* v *Leech Brain and Co.*[19] In that case the plaintiff suffered a burn on his lip as a result of the defendant's negligence. The burn caused the plaintiff to contract cancer, since the tissues of his lips were in a pre-malignant state. He died within 3 years of the accident. The defendants argued that they were not responsible for his death since it could not have been foreseen. It was held, however, that the "thin skull" rule applied to the facts of the case. The defendants were required to "take" the victim as they "found" him. The defendants were, therefore, liable.[20] Again, in the Court of Appeal case of *Robinson* v *Post Office*,[21] the plaintiff was employed by the defendant. He fell down a ladder as a result of the defendant's negligence and cut his leg. The plaintiff's doctor gave him an anti-tetanus injection. The plaintiff developed encephalitis. The court held the defendant liable on the basis that some form of adverse reaction to the injection on the part of the plaintiff should have been foreseen by the defendant. The "thin skull" rule seems to have been stretched to the limit in this case. Similarly, in the Australian case of *Sayers* v *Perrin*,[22] as a result of the defendant's negligence, the plaintiff suffered an electric shock when a poliomyelitis virus was already present in his body. He developed poliomyelitis. It was held that the defendant was liable for this illness since it was the direct result of a state of affairs which was foreseeable.

"THIN SKULL" RULE AND IMPECUNIOSITY

8.19 What is the effect of the thin skull on a pursuer who is poor? Does the law require a defender who has inflicted harm on a poor person to take his victim as he finds him? For example, if my car is seriously damaged by the defender and I am too poor to buy

---

[18] Professor Thomson argues that the rule is, indeed, confined to personal injuries: J Thomson, *Delictual Liability* (4th edn, 2009), para 16.4.
[19] [1962] 2 QB 105.
[20] See also *McKillen* v *Barclay Curle and Co Ltd* 1967 SLT 41.
[21] [1974] 1 WLR 1176.
[22] [1966] Qd R 89.

a replacement, as a result of which I have to hire a car at an inflated cost, would I be able to recover the cost of hire?

Traditionally, the law adopted a bold stance towards impecuniosity in that the **8.20** courts would not allow the pursuer to recover for loss which derived from his own poverty. The leading case on this point is *Liesbosch (Dredger)* v *SS Edison*.[23] In that case, the plaintiffs were under a contract to complete a piece of work within a given time. Their dredger was sunk by the negligence of the defenders. The plaintiffs were too poor to buy a substitute dredger. The plaintiffs were put to much greater expense in fulfilling the contract because they were required to hire a substitute dredger at an exorbitant rate. The substitute was also much more expensive to work than the *Liesbosch*. The House of Lords held that the plaintiffs were entitled to recover:

(1) the market price of a substitute dredger;
(2) the cost of adaptation, transport and insurance of the substitute vessel;
(3) compensation for the loss on the contract for the period between the sinking of the *Liesbosch* and the time when a substitute dredger could have been available.

The claim for the extra expenses due to the poverty of the plaintiffs was rejected on **8.21** the ground that this was an extraneous matter and, therefore, too remote to warrant recovery.

However, courts have not felt particularly comfortable with the decision in *Liesbosch* **8.22** and are inclined to distinguish it. For example, in *Martindale* v *Duncan*[24] the plaintiff's taxi was damaged by the negligence of the defendant. The plaintiff was unable to bear the cost of repairs himself. His car was off the road for a period of 14 weeks, which included the period in which he had waited for the defendant's insurers to agree to pay for the relevant repairs. The defendants contended that the plaintiff should have had the repairs done immediately, and, therefore, on the authority of *Liesbosch*, claimed that they were liable to pay only the cost of a substitute vehicle during the period when the car could have been taken to a garage for repairs and for the likely time it would take until the completion of such repairs. However, the Court of Appeal held that the defendant was liable for the cost of hire during the 14-week period. Again, in *Mattocks* v *Mann*,[25] the Court of Appeal held that the plaintiff was entitled to recover the cost of hiring a replacement vehicle during a period of delay in the repair of her own vehicle, notwithstanding the fact that the delay was brought about by the plaintiff's lack of money.

The decision in *Liesbosch* again came under scrutiny in the House of Lords case **8.23** of *Lagden* v *O'Connor*.[26] In that case the claimant's car was damaged as a result of the defendant's negligence. The car was required to be repaired at a garage. However, the claimant was unemployed. He could not afford to pay for the hire of a replacement car while his own car was off the road. He therefore signed an agreement with a credit hire company whereby it provided a hire car at no cost to him by way of a 26-week credit facility in order to allow for the company to recover its charges from the negligent driver's insurers. The agreement also included an insurance policy to provide

---

[23] [1933] AC 449.
[24] [1973] 1 WLR 574.
[25] [1993] RTR 13.
[26] [2004] 1 AC 1067.

payment in the event of non-recovery. These fees were higher than the equivalent rate charged by traditional car hire firms. The defendant admitted liability. However, he disputed the claim for damages, which included a sum of money that was included in the credit hire company's charges. The House held that in determining the question of damages payable to an injured party whose expenditure had been augmented by his impecuniosity, the court was not precluded from considering the injured party's lack of means as a factor which was too remote. In short, the defendant was required to take the victim as he found him. By a majority, the House held that the claimant was entitled to recover the whole of the cost of hiring the car. The decision of the House in *Liesbosch* was departed from.

8.24   The question which, of course, falls to be answered is whether the decision of the House in *Langden* is confined to motor insurance claims or has a more general application. It is the authors' view that the decision in *Liesbosch* does not represent modern law and, therefore, should not be followed.

BREAKING THE CHAIN OF CAUSATION

8.25   It sometimes happens that an event occurs between the negligent act of the defender and the pursuer sustaining harm. The effect of this intervening act is, in the eye of the law, to break the link between the negligent act of the defender and the subsequent harm. In other words, the intervening act has the effect of eclipsing the original negligent act of the defender and, therefore, negates liability. The intervening act would be said to be a *novus actus interveniens*.

WHAT IS A *NOVUS ACTUS INTERVENIENS*?

8.26   We will now go on to discuss how the courts ascertain whether an intervening act ranks as a *novus actus interveniens* or, alternatively, as a *causa causans*, that is to say, an act which is not independent from the original act of negligence and, therefore, falls to be regarded as a link between the defender's act of negligence and the subsequent damage. The courts have never really felt comfortable with this particular aspect of the law of negligence. It remains a grey area of the law. Indeed, judges have scrupulously refrained from enunciating a formula by means of which one can categorise any given act either as a *novus actus interveniens* or, alternatively, as a *causa causans*. The courts seem content to approach the concept of *novus actus interveniens* on a case-by-case basis. One therefore requires to study case law in order to obtain an understanding of how the courts distinguish a *causa causans* from a *novus actus interveniens*. However, it should be noted that in some of the case law cited below, judges concentrate simply on whether the relevant independent act ranks as a *causa causans*, with scant reference being made to the concept of *novus actus interveniens*.

"NATURAL AND REASONABLE" INTERVENING ACTS

In *The Oropesa*,[27] two vessels (the *Manchester Regiment* and the *Oropesa*) collided, owing   **8.27**
partly to the negligence of the defendant. After about 80 minutes, the captain of the
Manchester Regiment decided to discuss salvage arrangements with the captain of
the *Oropesa*. He embarked in a lifeboat with some of his crew, including the son of
the plaintiffs. However, the boat capsized in the heavy seas after half an hour. The son
was drowned. It was held that the action of the captain did not constitute a *novus actus
interveniens*. According to Lord Wright:[28]

> "[T]he hand of casualty lay heavily on [the *Manchester Regiment*] and that the conduct both
> of the master and of the deceased was directly caused by and flowed from it. There was an
> unbroken sequence of cause and effect between the negligence which caused the *Oropesa* to
> collide with the *Manchester Regiment* and their action which was dictated by the exigencies of
> the position. To break the chain of causation it must be shown that there is something which
> I will call ultroneous, something unwarrantable, a new cause which disturbs the sequence of
> events, something which can be described as either unreasonable or extraneous or extrinsic
> ... When a collision takes place by the fault of the defending ship in an action for damages,
> the damage is recoverable if it is the natural and reasonable result of the negligent act, and
> it will assume this character if it can be shown to be such a consequence as in the ordinary
> course of things would flow from the situation which the offending ship had created."

In other words, according to his Lordship, if the intervening act was the natural and   **8.28**
reasonable result of the original act of negligence, it fell to be categorised as *causa
causans*. Otherwise, such an act ranked as a *novus actus interveniens*.

INTERVENING ACT "REASONABLY LIKELY"

In *Rouse* v *Squires*,[29] the first defendant negligently collided with the plaintiff who was   **8.29**
driving his car on a road. The second defendant then negligently collided with the
plaintiff when the plaintiff was stranded in his car in the middle of the road. The Court
of Appeal held that the first defendant was liable for the subsequent damage, since the
intervening act of the second defendant did not break the chain of causation between
the first and the second negligent acts. The intervening act (ie the second negligent act)
was, as a consequence of the original act of negligence, reasonably likely to occur.[30]

"UNREASONABLE" INTERVENING ACTS

Sometimes conduct which is castigated by the courts as "unreasonable" is deemed   **8.30**
capable of breaking the chain of causation. For example, in *McKew v Holland, Hannen
and Cubitts (Scotland) Ltd*,[31] the pursuer was injured in an accident which had been
caused by the defender's negligence. The pursuer's leg became numb and also tended
to give way without warning. One day, when he was descending stairs, he felt his leg
give way. The pursuer jumped to the bottom of the stair and sustained further injury.

---

27 [1943] P 32.
28 *Ibid* at 37.
29 [1973] QB 889.
30 *Ibid* at 901 (per Buckley LJ).
31 1970 SC (HL) 20.

The House of Lords held that the pursuer could not recover for this further loss since he had acted unreasonably in placing himself in such a position that he could do little to save himself if his leg did give way. Furthermore, such unreasonable conduct constituted a *novus actus interveniens* and so broke the chain of causation between the defender's negligent act and the injury sustained by jumping down the stairs.

8.31   However, what ranks as unreasonable conduct in terms of a given intervening act is sometimes difficult to predict. For example, in the Court of Appeal case of *Philco Radio and Television Corporation of Great Britain* v *J Spurling Ltd*,[32] the defendant negligently delivered parcels of flammable film scrap to the plaintiff's premises. A typist, by way of diversion, touched one of the parcels with a lighted cigarette. There was a violent explosion which seriously damaged the plaintiff's premises. It was held that the typist's conduct was not so unreasonable as to break the chain of causation between the defendant's original act of negligence and the subsequent damage. Again, in *Knightly* v *Johns*,[33] the first defendant was involved in a serious road accident in a tunnel. The second defendant, who was a police inspector, ordered the plaintiff, who was a police constable, to close the tunnel entrance to incoming traffic. In order to do this, the plaintiff had to drive against the flow of traffic. In the course of his journey along the tunnel he collided with a vehicle and was injured. The Court of Appeal held that the inspector's unreasonable instructions, to drive against the flow of traffic, broke the chain of causation between the first defendant's negligence and the subsequent injury.

8.32   An interesting example of the application of the concept of unreasonableness and causation is seen in *Crown River Cruises Ltd* v *Kimbolton Fireworks Ltd and London Fire and Civil Defence Authority*.[34] There, the plaintiffs operated pleasure barges on the River Thames. The first defendants provided a firework display to commemorate the Battle of Britain. One of the plaintiffs' vessels was set alight by a firework. The second defendants were called. They attended the blaze and then left. However, the fire recurred. It spread to a second barge (the *Suerita*), which was damaged. It was held, in effect, that since the conduct of the fire authority could not be castigated as unreasonable, it did not break the chain of causation between the original act of negligence by the first defendants and the subsequent damage to the *Suerita*. The first defendants were, therefore, liable for the damage to the vessel.

8.33   The application of the concept of unreasonableness in relation to what ranks as a *novus actus interveniens* was seen in the recent Court of Appeal case of *Spencer* v *Wincanton Holdings Ltd*.[35] In that case the claimant was employed by the defendant. The former was injured as a result of his employer's negligence. He lost part of his leg as a result of the injury. He required to wear a prosthesis in order to walk. However, he could not wear it while driving. One day, he attempted to fill his car with petrol without his prosthesis. He tripped and fell. He sustained further injury. The court held that the defendant was liable for this injury. In the last analysis, the fall in the petrol station was reasonably foreseeable at the time of the claimant's original accident. Furthermore, the claimant's conduct was not so unreasonable as to constitute a *novus actus interveniens*.

---

[32] [1949] 2 All ER 882.
[33] [1982] 1 All ER 851.
[34] [1996] 2 Lloyd's Rep 533.
[35] [2009] EWCA Civ 1404. For a discussion of this case, see K Hughes, "Causation: is it fair?" [2010] CLJ 230.

FORESEEABLE INTERVENING ACTS

In some cases, foreseeability is the touchstone employed by the courts to ascertain   **8.34**
whether the chain of causation has been broken. For example, in *Donaghy v NCB*,[36] a
young miner sued his employers under common law and also for breach of statutory
duty in respect of injuries he received when a detonator, which had been left in the
pursuer's workplace in breach of the relevant legislation, exploded when he hit it with
a hammer. The Inner House held that the act of the pursuer constituted a *novus actus
interveniens* since his act was not reasonably foreseeable. Again, in *Wieland v Cyril Lord
Carpets*,[37] the plaintiff suffered a neck injury due to the defendant's negligence. This
injury made it difficult for her to see properly through her bifocals. As a result, she
fell while she was descending stairs, as a consequence of which she sustained further
injuries. It was held that the defender was responsible for these subsequent injuries
since the accident was a foreseeable consequence of the defendant's original negligent
act.

The concept of foreseeability in relation to remoteness of damage is seen again in   **8.35**
Ward v Cannock Chase District Council.[38] There, the defendant local authority owned a
number of cottages situated in an area which was zoned for industrial development.
As the cottages became vacant, the local authority had boarded them up. With the
passage of time, the cottages were falling into disrepair and were being damaged by
vandals. The plaintiff had purchased two cottages at the end of a terrace. The local
authority ceased to maintain the other cottages in the terrace as they became vacant.
Vandals removed tiles, bricks and timbers from the buildings, the upshot of which
was that one night part of the terrace, which adjoined the plaintiff's house, collapsed,
bringing down part of the gable wall and the roof of the plaintiff's cottage. The plaintiff
obtained a court order requiring the local authority to repair his premises. While
his premises were vacant, vandals removed a water tank and did further damage.
Subsequently, vandals again broke into his property and stole, *inter alia*, machinery,
and livestock. The plaintiff sued the local authority. At first instance, it was held that
the local authority was liable for the damage caused to the plaintiff's premises by the
collapse of the adjoining premises. The local authority was also liable for the damage
to the plaintiff's premises caused by the acts of the vandals since such acts were
foreseeable. However, the loss caused by damage to and theft of the plaintiff's chattels
was not recoverable in that such loss was not a reasonably foreseeable consequence of
the local authority's breach of duty.

AGONY OF THE MOMENT

The law will not normally regard the automatic reaction to a dangerous situation   **8.36**
created by the negligence of the defender as a *novus actus interveniens*. Therefore,
the chain of causation between the original negligent act of the defender and the
subsequent harm to the pursuer will not be broken. The leading case here is *Scott v
Shepherd*.[39] In that case the defendant tossed a lighted squib among a group of people.

---

[36] 1957 SLT (N) 35.
[37] [1969] 3 All ER 1006.
[38] [1986] Ch 546.
[39] (1773) 2 WBL 892.

One of the group threw the squib away. It hit the plaintiff and injured him. It was held that the throwing away of the squib did not amount to a *novus actus interveniens*. Again, in *Brandon* v *Osborne, Garrett and Co Ltd*,[40] a skylight crashed from the roof of a shop where the plaintiff was standing with her husband. She injured her leg in trying to pull him out of danger. It was held at first instance that she could recover for the injury she sustained.

RESCUERS' ACTIONS AND CAUSATION

8.37   For policy reasons, the courts are not willing to regard any reasonable attempts made by a third party to effect a rescue as a *novus actus interveniens*. For example, in *Baker* v *T E Hopkins*,[41] the defendant company was employed to clean out a contaminated well in a farm. It was decided to use a pump powered by a petrol engine inside the well. This caused a build-up of carbon monoxide in the well. Two employees went down the well and were overcome by fumes. A medical practitioner descended the well in order to give them medical aid. He, himself, was overcome by the fumes and died. The Court of Appeal held that since the act of rescue was reasonable it did not amount to a *novus actus interveniens*. The defendant company was, therefore, liable for the practitioner's death.

SUICIDE AS *NOVUS ACTUS INTERVENIENS*

8.38   Victims of physical injury often suffer long-term effects. They can become severely depressed. Occasionally, such depression may lead to suicide. The question, of course, which requires to be answered in the context of the present discussion is whether the suicide of the victim of an accident ranks as a *novus actus interveniens*. The leading case is now the House of Lords case of *Corr* v *IBC Vehicles Ltd*.[42] In that case, the claimant's husband was employed by the defendant as a maintenance engineer. He sustained serious head injuries because of the malfunctioning of machinery in the defendant's factory. He became depressed and committed suicide. The claimant sued the defendant for his death. The House of Lords held that the suicide was both a direct and a foreseeable consequence of the negligence of the defendant. The latter was, therefore, liable for the victim's death. According to Lord Bingham,[43] the principle of *novus actus interveniens* rested on the principle of fairness. It was not fair to hold a tortfeasor liable, however gross his breach of duty was, for damage caused by some independent supervening act for which the tortfeasor was not responsible. His Lordship went on to approve decisions which had been taken by the courts to the effect that the informed conscious decision by a person who was not suffering from a depressive illness ranked as a *novus actus interveniens* in the eye of the law.[44] However, the more unsound the mind of the victim was, the less likely the suicide would rank as a *novus actus interveniens*. In the instant case, the victim's death was not as a result of a voluntary informed decision on his part. Rather, it was the response of a man suffering

---

[40] [1924] 1 KB 548.
[41] [1959] 1 WLR 966.
[42] [2008] 2 WLR 499.
[43] *Ibid* at 507.
[44] See, eg, *Dalling* v *R J Heale and Co Ltd* [2011] EWCA Civ 365.

from a severely depressive illness which impaired his capacity to make a reasoned and informed judgement about his future. His employer was therefore liable for his death.

Interestingly, Lord Scott was prepared to employ the "thin skull" rule to find **8.39** the employer liable for the victim's death.[45] According to his Lordship, the victim's depressive disorder was a result of the negligent act of the defendant. By virtue of *Page* v *Smith*, no distinction fell to be drawn between physical and psychiatric injury. Applying the "thin skull" rule, the death of the claimant by suicide was the direct result of the illness caused by the defendant's negligence.[46]

---

[45] [2008] 2 WLR 499 at 511–512.
[46] See also *Simmons* v *British Steel* 2004 SC (HL) 94.

9 PROFESSIONAL NEGLIGENCE

In recent decades there has been a growing commitment to civil rights generally and **9.1** most countries, including our own, have witnessed a rise in challenge to all professional groups. Various pressure groups and agencies have been developed to offer advice and to assist people in vindicating their rights. The increasing prevalence of "rights" language has led to the general public becoming more aware of the possibility of challenging professional advisers.

This chapter addresses the matter of professional negligence. The discussion will **9.2** focus on two main professional groups, namely medical practitioners and legal practitioners. In medical cases, the harm will normally be tangible, whereas in negligence cases against lawyers (and indeed other professionals such as surveyors, auditors and architects) the harm is more usually of an economic nature. The nature of the loss will, of course, dictate the test to be applied in determining whether the professional person owed the pursuer a duty of care. Particular attention will be paid to the medical profession, not only because the courts have been heavily influenced by policy considerations in medical negligence cases but also because the test which is applied to determine the standard of care in all professional negligence cases arose in a medical context.[1]

SUING IN CONTRACT OR DELICT

Clearly, in cases where the person suffering loss is a client of the professional person, **9.3** he may have a contractual remedy. In Scots law, the existence of a contractual remedy does not exclude a remedy based on the law of delict. In *Edgar* v *Lamont*,[2] the pursuer had sent for a doctor, but had done so as agent for her husband and on the basis that he was to pay for the doctor's services. The pursuer required to have her finger amputated after the doctor administered what was alleged to be improper treatment. The doctor argued that the contract was between himself and the pursuer's husband and that, accordingly, the pursuer had no title to sue. The court, however, concluded that while the doctor's duty to his patient might arise out of contract, it also arose from the law of delict where there was a direct relationship between the patient and the doctor. In cases where there is no contractual nexus between the professional person and the person suffering loss (as was the case in *Edgar* v *Lamont*), the latter's success will therefore clearly depend on his establishing delictual liability. Where a purchaser of a property wishes to sue a surveyor in respect of an allegedly negligent survey, the case will usually proceed under the law of delict as there is rarely a contract between the

---

[1] See *Hunter* v *Hanley* 1955 SC 200.
[2] 1914 SC 277.

prospective purchaser of property and the surveyor. The latter is normally instructed by the lender and so any contract is usually between the lender and the surveyor.

9.4   Where there is a contractual relationship, the pursuer, of course, may base his action on both the law of delict and breach of contract. This, in fact, was done in the solicitor's negligence case of *J G Martin Plant Hire Ltd* v *Macdonald*[3] where the pursuers raised an action on the basis of both contract and delict against their former solicitors, who had loosed an arrestment without authority.

9.5   The standard of care is usually the same in contract and delict. Contract, however, is a consensual obligation in which both parties are free to agree on specific contract terms. It is therefore possible, as a matter of contract, to bind oneself to a higher standard of duty than that of reasonable care. Indeed, as a matter of contract, one might even warrant a particular result. It was argued that a doctor had done precisely that in *Thake* v *Maurice*.[4] There, a patient underwent a sterilisation operation on a private basis. He and his wife subsequently raised an action against the surgeon following the birth of a child. The child had been conceived as a result of the recanalisation of the patient's vas. The patient alleged that the surgeon had stated that the vasectomy operation would be irreversible. The Court of Appeal held that this did not constitute a contractual warranty of permanent sterility. Neill LJ observed:[5]

> "Medicine, though a highly skilled profession, is not, and is not generally regarded as being, an exact science. The reasonable man would have expected the defendant to exercise all the proper skill and care of a surgeon in that speciality; he would not in my view have expected the defendant to give a guarantee of 100% success."

9.6   Of course, although parties to a contract are free to agree their specific contract terms, professional people will be subject to the constraints of the Unfair Contract Terms Act 1977, so they will be unable to exclude liability for personal injuries or death arising from a breach of duty and any other attempt to exclude liability will be ineffective unless it was fair and reasonable.[6]

THE STANDARD OF CARE

9.7   Some early guidance as to what is legally expected from a professional person was provided by Tindall CJ in *Lanphier* v *Phipos*:[7]

> "Every person who enters into a learned profession undertakes to bring to the exercise of it a reasonable degree of care and skill. He does not undertake, if he is an attorney, that at all events you shall gain your case, nor does a surgeon undertake that he will perform a cure; nor does he undertake to use the highest possible degree of skill."

---

[3] 1996 SLT 1192.
[4] [1984] 2 All ER 513; reversed [1986] 1 All ER 479.
[5] [1986] 1 All ER 479 at 510.
[6] Unfair Contract Terms Act 1977, s 16.
[7] (1838) 8 C & P 475 at 478.

More recently, the position was articulated by McNair J in *Bolam* v *Friern Hospital* **9.8**
Management Committee[8] in the following terms:

"[W]here you get a situation which involves the use of some special skill or competence, then the test as to whether there has been negligence or not is not the test of the man on top of the Clapham omnibus, because he has not got this special skill. The test is the standard of the ordinary skilled man exercising the profession and professing to have that special skill."

It is clear from this *dictum* that, in determining whether a breach of duty has occurred, **9.9**
the court judges the defender's behaviour according to the standard of care expected in the defender's profession. To establish negligence, therefore, the pursuer must establish that the defender's behaviour fell short of what is expected from the reasonable doctor, lawyer, surveyor, etc.

MEDICAL NEGLIGENCE

At one time it was extremely uncommon for patients to sue their doctors. This is **9.10**
evident from the *dicta* of Lord Young in *Farquhar* v *Murray*,[9] which arose out of the allegedly negligent treatment of the pursuer's finger. His Lordship remarked at the outset of his dissenting judgment:[10] "This action is certainly one of a particularly unusual character. It is an action of damages by a patient against a medical man. In my somewhat long experience I cannot remember having seen a similar case before."

In recent years, however, claims against doctors have increased dramatically.[11]
Indeed, medical negligence is now a "substantial and significant category"[12] of the law of negligence. The Pearson Commission,[13] which reported in 1978, observed that claims against medical practitioners had been uncommon 50–60 years previously. It noted, however, that the introduction of the NHS had led to an increase in claims. The late 1970s witnessed a further rise in the number of claims and the number of actions and level of awards again rose dramatically towards the end of the 1980s. In February 2011, the No-fault Compensation Review Group, chaired by Professor Sheila McLean, reported that total awards and costs have risen more or less steadily over the period from 1998 to 2009, and that the average sum awarded has risen significantly over that period.[14]

There is a number of reasons for the public's increased propensity to sue in respect **9.11**
of medical negligence. In the early part of the 20th century, a hospital was simply seen as the location at which a doctor administered treatment. The doctor was seen as a professional exercising independent judgement. With the introduction of the NHS in 1948, the nature of hospitals shifted from charitable status to state financing. Doctors

---

[8] [1957] 1 WLR 582 at 586.
[9] (1901) 3 F 859.
[10] *Ibid* at 862.
[11] Mason and Laurie observe that "[t]here is concern in both medical and governmental circles over the growing incidence of personal injury actions against doctors and over the cost to the health system of compensating the victims" (J K Mason and G T Laurie, *Mason and McCall Smith's Law and Medical Ethics* (8th edn, 2011) at p 122).
[12] *M* v *Newham LBC; X (Minors)* v *Bedfordshire CC* [1994] 2 WLR 554, per Staughton LJ at 584.
[13] Royal Commission on Civil Liability and Compensation for Personal Injury (Cmnd 7054, 1978).
[14] See *No-fault Compensation Review Group – Report and Recommendations*, para 2.21.

began to be viewed as employees of the relevant health authority and vicarious liability in a medical context began to develop.[15] Not surprisingly, patients were more willing to seek damages from an impersonal state institution, a relatively anonymous defender, rather than the individual doctor who had been treating them. The introduction of legal aid in the 1950s contributed to the rising tide of litigation by making it financially feasible for a large sector of the population to sue.

9.12   Another reason for the increase in medical negligence litigation is that there has been an increase in litigation consciousness generally. In the context of medicine, this has been fuelled by media reporting of substantial medical negligence awards and the pursuit of massive drug injury claims. The legal campaigns waged on behalf of the victims of Thalidomide and the anti-arthritis drug Opren (in the 1970s and late 1980s respectively), and the litigation waged on behalf of the brain damaged victims of the pertussis (whooping cough) vaccine received considerable media attention. Such protracted litigation undoubtedly alerts the public mind to the possibility of using legal mechanisms as a means of obtaining redress.

9.13   Scientific progress, somewhat ironically, may also have led to an increase in litigation for a number of reasons. Major advances in medicine and reports of medical successes increase the public's expectations of medicine. Resort to the law may follow when such expectations are not met. Furthermore, medical advances have an obvious effect on the volume of treatment being administered, thus increasing the opportunity for negligence to occur. Innovative techniques are often of an intricate and high-risk nature and can themselves give rise to injury. Moreover, the advance of technology arguably depersonalises medicine and increases the information gap between doctor and patient, making the patient more inclined to challenge in the event of medical failure.

9.14   The emergence of certain pressure groups, which campaign on behalf of victims, has also had an impact on the number of claims being pursued. The most well-known association in the medical context is AvMA (Action against Medical Accidents), which was founded in 1982. This group has greatly assisted pursuers in gaining access to legal and medical expertise.

9.15   Finally, notions of consumerism are increasingly pervading the practice of medicine. It has been pointed out that the relationship of patients and the NHS is gradually being redefined in terms of "value for money".[16] Such an atmosphere encourages the use of market remedies, of which recourse to the law is an obvious example.[17]

THE NEGLIGENCE ACTION IN A MEDICAL CONTEXT

9.16   Most cases arising from alleged medical malpractice are brought under the law of negligence. Although resort is frequently had to the negligence action, the Pearson

---

[15] See Roe v Ministry of Health [1954] 2 QB 66 (Court of Appeal held that an anaesthetist was the servant or agent of the hospital and the hospital was liable for his acts on the principle of respondeat superior); Cassidy v Ministry of Health [1951] 2 KB 243; Hayward v Royal Infirmary of Edinburgh; MacDonald v Glasgow Western Hospitals 1954 SC 453. Of course, while many cases proceed today on the basis of the vicarious liability of a health authority/NHS Trust in respect of the negligence of its employees, liability can also be incurred by an authority/trust on the basis of a direct duty of the hospital to care for patients. See the observations of Mustill LJ in Wilsher v Essex Area Health Authority [1987] QB 730 at 747.

[16] H Teff, Reasonable Care – Legal Perspectives on the Doctor–Patient Relationship (1994) at p 24.

[17] That the position is now far removed from the days of Farquhar v Murray is evident from cases such as McFarlane v Tayside Health Board 2000 SC (HL) 1 where damages were sought in respect of the birth of a healthy child following a negligent misstatement as to the effectiveness of a vasectomy operation!

Commission, when it reported in 1978, was not happy about its success rate in a medical context. The purpose of the negligence action is to redress grievances. If the action is successful, the aggrieved individual is awarded compensation, the purpose of which, in theory, at least, is to restore him to the position he would have been in, had he not been injured. A further feature of the negligence action is the need to attribute fault and this may represent one of the most problematic aspects of the medical negligence action.[18] Moreover, the desire to redress grievances and the need to attribute fault can be mutually exclusive as was graphically illustrated by the Thalidomide tragedy. The drug Thalidomide, an anti-emetic, was manufactured by a German company, Chemie Grunenthal. The Distillers company bought the formula and marketed the drug in the UK. The drug was given to pregnant women to prevent morning sickness. Some of these women subsequently gave birth to babies with deformed or "flipper" limbs. Ultimately, the Distillers company made *ex gratia* payments to those children who appeared to have been harmed by the drug. This resulted, in large measure, from public pressure exerted through the media. However, had the cases proceeded to proof or trial, the Thalidomide victims would almost certainly have encountered difficulties on the question of attribution of fault. From a legal point of view, a defender is responsible only for the *foreseeable* consequences of his acts or omissions. At the time of the Thalidomide tragedy, it was not necessary to test pregnant animals for toxicity levels and Distillers could have argued that it had, in fact, carried out all the testing which it was obliged by its own professional practice to do. The company could therefore have argued that, legally, it was not at fault.

BASIC ELEMENTS OF THE MEDICAL NEGLIGENCE ACTION

As with other negligence actions, the pursuer in a medical negligence action requires to show that he was owed a duty of care, that the duty was breached and that the breach caused the harm complained of. The second and third components of the action, namely breach of duty and causation, are notoriously more difficult to establish in a medical context than in other contexts. The findings of the Pearson Commission would tend to support this view. The Commission observed that, while some 86 per cent of general negligence cases were successful, only 30–40 per cent of medical negligence cases resulted in an award of damages. **9.17**

DUTY OF CARE

Of the three elements of the medical negligence action, the easiest to establish is the first, namely the existence of a duty of care. Because most medical negligence cases involve personal injury, Lord Atkin's "neighbourhood" test in *Donoghue* v *Stevenson*[19] will apply. We need not rehearse the details of *Donoghue* v *Stevenson* here. Suffice to say that the existence of a duty of care in relation to personal injury cases depends on the concepts of proximity and foreseeability. In a medical context, the doctor's acceptance of the patient for treatment is therefore sufficient to establish the existence of the duty.[20] **9.18**

---

[18] A Review Group led by Professor Sheila McLean has recently recommended the adoption of a no-fault system of liability in relation to medical injury (see discussion below).
[19] 1932 SC (HL) 31.
[20] See *Jones* v *Manchester Corporation* [1952] 2 QB 852, per Denning LJ at 867.

The concept of holding out or undertaking is fundamental to the duty issue. Thus, it was said in *R v Bateman*[21] that "[i]f a person holds himself out as possessing special skill and knowledge, and he is consulted as possessing such skill and knowledge, by or on behalf of a patient, he owes a duty to the patient to use due caution in undertaking the treatment".[22] A general practitioner will therefore owe a duty of care to any patient whom he accepts on to his list.

9.19   However, consistent with the general law of negligence, a doctor is not required to be a Good Samaritan. Therefore, a doctor attracts no liability if he ignores the call "Is there a doctor on the train?" and the heart attack victim on board subsequently dies for want of speedy treatment. The doctor does not adopt a duty of care in such a situation. If, however, he chooses to intervene, then he does adopt a duty[23] and will be liable in the event of his negligence.

9.20   As far as hospital authorities are concerned, some guidance on the question of duty of care was provided in *Cassidy v Minister of Health*:[24]

> "[A]uthorities who run a hospital ... are in law under the self-same duty as the humblest doctor; whenever they accept a patient for treatment, they must use reasonable care and skill to cure him of his ailment. The hospital authorities cannot, of course, do it by themselves: they have no ears to listen through the stethoscope, and no hands to hold the surgeon's knife. They must do it by the staff which they employ; and if their staff are negligent in giving the treatment, they are just as liable for that negligence as is anyone else who employs others to do his duties for him. What possible difference in law I ask, can there be between hospital authorities who accept a patient for treatment, and railway or shipping authorities who accept a passenger for carriage? None whatever. Once they undertake the task, they come under a duty to use care in the doing of it, and that is so whether they do it for reward or not."

9.21   An open Accident and Emergency unit has a duty to treat or at least assess a patient who presents himself there.[25] What is the position, however, where an accident victim arrives at a hospital and is turned away because the hospital does not accept accident and emergency victims? The notices positioned on the main road directing potential patients to the hospital state quite clearly that the hospital does not accept accident and emergency victims. Should the victim's condition deteriorate in the time taken to find a hospital which will accept him, does he have a right of action against the original hospital in respect of the deterioration in his condition? The answer is "no" because the first hospital did not undertake to treat him: in other words, it did not owe him a duty of care.[26]

---

[21] (1925) 94 LJ KB 791.
[22] *Ibid*, per Lord Hewart CJ at 794. (This *dictum* was subsequently quoted with approval by Lord Blades in *Crawford v Campbell* 1948 SLT (Notes) 91 at 91.) See, also, K Norrie, *Delict* (J M Thomson (ed)) (SULI, 2007) at para 19–23): "[H]olding oneself out as possessing a special skill in order to attract ... a patient ... subjects one to the standard of the ordinarily competent possessor of that skill."
[23] See *Everett v Griffiths* [1920] 3 KB 163.
[24] [1951] 2 KB 343, per Denning LJ at 360.
[25] *Barnett v Chelsea & Kensington HMC* [1969] 1 QB 428.
[26] See the observations of Nield J in *Barnett* (above), where a distinction is drawn between a casualty department which closes its doors and says no patients can be received (in which case no duty of care arises) and the the circumstances in *Barnett* where three nightwatchmen entered the defendant's hospital "without hindrance" and were given erroneous advice (in which case a duty of care did arise).

Griffiths points out[27] that the duty extends beyond the diagnosis and treatment **9.22** of patients to other matters such as the examination of patients for employment purposes[28] and for quantification of personal injury claims. He notes that claims have arisen against doctors where, subsequent to allegedly negligent medical examinations, pursuers have accepted inadequate sums of damages.

As far as the patient is concerned, the duty issue is not generally problematic. **9.23** However, greater difficulty arises where it is contended that a duty is owed by the doctor to a third party.[29] In *Goodwill v BPAS*[30] it was held that no duty of care was owed to the future sexual partner of a man who had undergone a vasectomy operation. The man had been advised that he no longer required to use contraception. However, the vasectomy naturally reversed some 3 years later. This resulted in pregnancy and the birth of a child to the plaintiff, who sought damages for financial loss. When the advice was given to the patient, the plaintiff was not his partner but merely a member of an immeasurably large class of women who might in future have sexual relations with him. Accordingly, she was not owed a duty of care.[31]

In *JD v East Berkshire Community Health NHS Trust*[32] three cases were brought **9.24** against health care authorities by the parents of young children in respect of psychiatric harm allegedly resulting from unfounded allegations of child abuse. The House of Lords held that the child was the doctor's patient in whose best interests the doctor was obliged to act. Although the interests of parent and child normally coincided, this was not the case where the possibility of abuse arose. Where the doctor's suspicions were aroused, he required to act single-mindedly in the interests of the child without regard to the possibility of a claim by the parent. Given the seriousness of child abuse as a social problem, health care professionals should not be subject to conflicting duties. Accordingly, it was not fair, just and reasonable that a duty of care be imposed in relation to the parents.[33]

BREACH OF DUTY – THE TEST IN *HUNTER* v *HANLEY*[34]

The second element of the medical negligence action, namely *breach* of duty, presents **9.25** a more formidable hurdle for the pursuer, not least because in determining whether a doctor has breached his duty the court relies on expert professional opinion. In an ordinary negligence action, a defender is liable if he fails to exercise reasonable care. In,

---

[27] J R Griffiths, "Medical Negligence – An Update of the Law" 1995 SLPQ 25. See, also, *Baker v Kaye* [1997] IRLR 219. Compare, however, *Kapfunde v Abbey National* (1999) 46 BMLR 176 where a job applicant failed to secure a job in the face of an unfavourable medical report and the English Court of Appeal held that no duty was owed to protect the job applicant from economic loss.

[28] See, eg, *Johnstone v Traffic Commissioner* 1990 SLT 409.

[29] In *Sidaway v Bethlem Royal Hospital Board of Governors* [1985] AC 871 Lord Diplock stated (at 890) that "a doctor's duty of care, whether he be general practitioner or consulting surgeon or physician is owed to that patient and none other, idiosyncracies and all."

[30] [1996] 1 WLR 1397.

[31] See, also, *Palmer v Tees Health Authority* [1999] Lloyd's Rep Med 351.

[32] [2005] 2 AC 373.

[33] See, also, *Fairlie v Perth and Kinross Healthcare NHS Trust* 2004 SLT 1200. There, the pursuer sought damages from the Trust in respect of the alleged negligence of a psychiatrist in the treatment of his daughter. His daughter had undergone recovered memory therapy and had then alleged that her father had abused her. Lord Kingarth held that there was nothing to indicate that the doctor came at any stage into a special relationship with the pursuer such that he owed him a duty of care.

[34] Note that the discussion here focuses on orthodox medicine. As far as alternative medicine is concerned, see *Shakoor v Situ* [2001] 1 WLR 410.

say, a negligent driving case, the judge or sheriff will usually be in a position to make a determination as to whether the driving in question is of a reasonable standard. Most judges and sheriffs drive. However, few judges have a detailed knowledge of medicine. What is "reasonable" in a medical context will usually be outwith judicial knowledge. Indeed, in *Hotson* v *East Berkshire Area Health Authority*,[35] Lord Harwich freely admitted[36] to the "deficiencies in [his] own medical understanding". The judge must therefore rely on other medical practitioners to guide him. Therefore, medical practitioners routinely testify as to whether the conduct of their fellow doctor was negligent. The main criticism of this approach is that the medical evidence rather than being persuasive has tended to be treated as more or less determinative of the issue. The courts have historically displayed a reluctance to argue with the expert evidence in medical cases. As Brazier and Cave[37] have observed: "In claims against other professionals, the courts rigorously scrutinised expert evidence to ensure that evidence of professional opinion could be demonstrated to be responsible and reasonable. In claims against doctors, it appeared that as long as suitably qualified expert witnesses endorsed the defendant's conduct, English judges simply deferred to the doctors." Given that doctors generally are reluctant to criticise one another, perhaps mindful that they too may be defending a civil suit at some time in the future, the pursuer in a medical case is faced with a difficult task.[38]

9.26   What test is employed by the Scottish courts in determining whether there has been a breach of duty by a medical practitioner? The leading case is *Hunter* v *Hanley*,[39] a jury trial resulting from an injury caused to a patient when a needle broke and became embedded in her hip. The patient alleged that the needle used by the doctor was unsuitable in that it was too fine for the particular type of injection in question. The trial judge (Lord Patrick) directed the jury in the following terms: "There must be such a departure from the normal and usual practice ... as can reasonably be described as gross negligence." On appeal, however, the trial judge's direction was said to be wrong and the Lord President (Clyde) formulated the test as follows:[40] "The true test for establishing negligence in diagnosis or treatment on the part of a doctor is whether he has been proved to be guilty of such failure as no doctor of ordinary skill would be guilty of if acting with ordinary care."[41] His Lordship went on to say:[42]

> "To establish liability by a doctor where deviation from normal practice is alleged, three facts require to be established. First of all it must be proved that there is a usual and normal practice. Secondly it must be proved that the defender has not adopted that practice, and thirdly (and this is of crucial importance) it must be established that the course the doctor

---

[35] [1987] 2 All ER 909.
[36] *Ibid* at 913.
[37] M Brazier and E Cave, *Medicine, Patients and the Law* (4th rev edn, 2007), p 162.
[38] The judiciary appears to be aware of the tendency of the medical profession to stick together. See, eg, *Whitehouse* v *Jordan* [1981] 1 WLR 246 at 253 where Lord Wilberforce makes "allowance for professional loyalty" in weighing the evidence of the medical witness. See, also, Lord Fraser at 264–265: "It would be natural for Dr Skinner to feel professional and personal loyalty towards Mr Jordan, who was his superior and also his friend."
[39] 1955 SC 200.
[40] *Ibid* at 217.
[41] Lord President Clyde's "true test" in *Hunter* v *Hanley* was later approved by Lord Scarman in *Maynard* v *West Midlands Regional Health Authority* [1984] 1 WLR 634 and by Lord Scarman and Lord Bridge in *Sidaway* v *Bethlem Royal Hospital Board of Governors* [1985] AC 871.
[42] 1955 SC 200 at 217.

adopted is one which no professional man of ordinary skill would have taken if he had been acting with ordinary care."[43]

The position of the specialist practitioner should be noted. "[S]pecialists within a **9.27** structured profession are subject to the standard of the ordinary specialist."[44] It should also be noted that the circumstances in which a doctor treats a patient will also be relevant. It has been judicially stated that "[a]n emergency may overburden the available resources, and, if an individual is forced by circumstances to do too many things at once, the fact that he does one of them incorrectly should not lightly be taken as negligence".[45]

A few years after *Hunter*, the case of *Bolam v Friern Hospital Management Committee*[46] **9.28** came before an English court. The facts were that the plaintiff had sustained fractures following the administration of electro-convulsive therapy. No relaxant drugs or manual restraints had been used. While one school of thought supported the use of such measures, another school of thought was of the view that such measures simply increased the risk of fracture. McNair J formulated the appropriate test to be applied in the following manner:[47] "A doctor is not guilty of negligence if he has acted in accordance with a practice accepted as proper by a responsible body of medical men skilled in that particular art."[48] Negligence was not to be inferred simply because a body of opinion took a different view. In *Defreitas v O'Brien*,[49] it was held that a small number of medical practitioners could constitute a "responsible body of medical opinion". The matter is not to be resolved, therefore, on the basis of a head count.

In *Maynard v West Midlands Regional Health Authority*,[50] a conflict between two schools **9.29** of thought arose once again but on this occasion the matter ultimately proceeded to the House of Lords. The plaintiff's medical advisers took the view that while the most likely diagnosis of her illness was tuberculosis there was also a possibility that she had Hodgkin's disease. Because of the potentially fatal effects of the latter condition, the doctors decided to carry out a procedure, known as a mediastinoscopy, to obtain a biopsy, rather than wait a period of weeks for the results of a sputum test. As a result of a risk inherent in this procedure, the plaintiff's vocal cords were damaged and her speech became impaired. The biopsy was negative and it transpired that the plaintiff was, in fact, suffering from tuberculosis. She sued the health authority and, at first

---

[43] For application of the *Hunter v Hanley* test, see *Kennedy v Steinberg* 1998 SC 379; *Gerrard v Edinburgh NHS Trust Royal Infirmary* 2005 1 SC 192. (In neither case was the doctor found to have been negligent.) Compare *Learmont v Vernon* [2007] CSOH 204 (defender was held to have been professionally negligent as the three facts stated in the *dictum* of LP Clyde in *Hunter* were established).

[44] Norrie, *Delict*, para 19–24. See, also, the observations of Lord Bridge in *Sidaway v Bethlem Royal Hospital Board of Governors* [1985] AC 871 at 897: "In the field of neuro-surgery it would be necessary to substitute for Lord President Clyde's phrase 'no doctor of ordinary skill', the phrase 'no neuro-surgeon of ordinary skill'.

[45] *Wilsher v Essex Area Health Authority* [1987] QB 730, per Mustill LJ at 749.

[46] [1957] 1 WLR 582.

[47] Although there has been considerable academic debate as to whether the *Hunter* and *Bolam* tests represent one and the same test, it is significant that McNair J in *Bolam*, after propounding his test, observed (at 122): "I do not think there is much difference in sense. It is just a different way of expressing the same thought."

[48] [1957] 1 WLR 582 at 587. *Bolam* was approved by the House of Lords in *Whitehouse v Jordan* [1981] 1 WLR 246 (in respect of treatment), *Maynard v West Midlands Regional Health Authority* [1984] 1 WLR 634 (in respect of diagnosis) and *Sidaway v Board of Governors of Bethlem Royal Hospital* [1985] AC 871 (in respect of advice and information giving).

[49] [1995] 6 Med LR 128.

[50] [1984] 1 WLR 634.

instance, was successful. Although some experts approved of the doctors' actions, Comyn J preferred the evidence of the plaintiff's expert, who stated, that, in his view, the case had almost certainly been one of tuberculosis and it was wrong to undertake the procedure. The judge's decision was overturned by the Court of Appeal. The case proceeded to the House of Lords and, in affirming the Court of Appeal's decision, their Lordships made it clear that it is not for the court to choose between conflicting medical views. Lord Scarman, delivering the leading judgment, stated:[51]

> "[A] doctor who professes to exercise a special skill must exercise the ordinary skill of his speciality. Differences of opinion and practice exist, and will always exist, in the medical as in other professions. There is seldom any one answer exclusive of all others to problems of professional judgment. A court may prefer one body of opinion to the other but that is no basis for a conclusion of negligence."

9.30 His Lordship went on to say:[52]

> "[A] judge's preference for one body of distinguished professional opinion to another … is not sufficient to establish negligence in a practitioner whose actions have received the seal of approval of those whose opinions, truthfully expressed, honestly held, were not preferred. For in the realm of diagnosis and treatment, negligence is not established by preferring one respectable body of opinion to the other."

Lord Scarman therefore refused to make a choice between the two schools of thought.

9.31 In *Gordon* v *Wilson and Ors*,[53] the pursuer argued that the defender was negligent in not referring her to a specialist at an earlier stage. She averred that a benign brain tumour thus became larger and more invasive than it would have been at an earlier stage. Following surgery, she lost nerve function and suffered loss of hearing and other sensations. A responsible body of medical opinion took the view that a reasonable doctor would have referred her to a specialist at an earlier stage. However, another responsible body of opinion took the view that a reasonable doctor would not have referred until the stage at which the defender doctor had done so. The pursuer's action therefore failed.[54]

9.32 When *Bolam*, *Maynard* and *Gordon* v *Wilson* are viewed in light of the *Defreitas* case (which provides that a small number of doctors is sufficient to constitute a responsible body of opinion), the difficulty facing the pursuer becomes evident. If a doctor is supported by a responsible body of medical opinion, he is entitled to be absolved of liability even if a greater number of experts thinks that the course of action adopted was wrong.

9.33 In *Phillips* v *Grampian Health Board*,[55] the pursuer averred a negligent failure to diagnose testicular cancer. Lord Clyde endorsed the *Hunter* v *Hanley* test and pointed out: "As was indicated in *Maynard* preference between one body of competent medical

---

[51] [1984] 1 WLR 634 at 638.
[52] *Ibid* at 639.
[53] 1992 SLT 849.
[54] The case has been described as one which illustrates "the formidable difficulties facing a pursuer in an action of medical negligence" (J Thomson, *Delictual Liability* (4th edn, 2009), p 167). Norrie, however, points out that "[t]his was *not* the court preferring one professional opinion over the other, but the failure of the pursuer to satisfy the test in *Hunter* v *Hanley*" (Norrie, *Delict*, para 19–34).
[55] [1991] 3 Med LR 16.

opinion and another is not enough to enable the pursuer to succeed. The existence of the opposing body of evidence, unless it is entirely rejected, is fatal to the case."

As the above passage indicates, the defender's experts may have their evidence 9.34 rejected or discredited. In *Sidaway v Board of Governors of Bethlem Royal Hospital*,[56] Lord Donaldson MR, in the Court of Appeal, said that the practice followed by the defender must be *rightly* accepted as proper by a responsible body of medical opinion. Thus, Lord Donaldson appears to assert a judicial right to pronounce that a particular practice is unacceptable.

The power of the courts to review and evaluate the medical evidence was again 9.35 underlined in *Bolitho v City and Hackney Health Authority*.[57] The House of Lords stressed that the body of evidence relied upon must rest upon a *logical* basis. There, a child suffered respiratory failure, cardiac arrest and brain damage after a hospital doctor failed to attend him while he was in a state of respiratory distress. The doctor argued that, had she attended, she would not have intubated the child and that accordingly her failure to attend would have made no difference to the outcome. The course of not intubating in such circumstances was one which was supported by a body of opinion. The House of Lords held that, in applying the *Bolam* test, the court must be satisfied that the exponents of the body of opinion relied upon had demonstrated that such opinion had a logical basis and had directed their minds to the question of comparative risks and benefits and had reached a defensible conclusion. If, in a rare case, it had been demonstrated that the professional opinion was incapable of withstanding logical analysis, the judge was entitled to hold that it could not provide the benchmark by reference to which the doctor's conduct fell to be assessed. However, in most cases the fact that distinguished experts in the field were of a particular opinion would demonstrate the reasonableness of that opinion. In the instant case, since the judge had directed himself correctly and there had been good reason for acceptance of the defendants' expert opinion, it had not been proved that the doctor's failure to attend had caused the injuries complained of.[58]

Mason and Laurie state that "*Bolitho* undoubtedly devalues the trump card which *Bolam* presented to the medical profession, but only in limited circumstances".[59] Brazier and Cave observe that "*Bolitho* returns *Bolam* to its proper limits. Doctors, like solicitors and all other professionals, are subject to legal scrutiny".[60]

It should be noted that there is a marked reluctance on the part of the courts to 9.36 allow the operation of *res ipsa loquitur* in medical negligence cases,[61] although the maxim has operated successfully on rare occasions.[62]

---

[56] [1984] 1 All ER 1018, CA; [1985] AC 871, HL.
[57] [1998] AC 232.
[58] For further discussion of *Bolitho*, see *Marriott v West Midlands RHA* [1999] Lloyd's Rep Med 23; *Penny v East Kent AHA* [2000] Lloyd's Rep Med 41; *Wisniewski v Central Manchester Health Authority* [1998] Lloyd's Rep Med 223; *Gerrard v Edinburgh NHS Trust Royal Infirmary* 2005 1 SC 192; *Lowe v Yorkhill NHS Trust* [2007] CSOH 111; *Birch v University College London Hospital NHS Foundation Trust* (2008) 104 BMLR 168 (in *Birch*, *Bolitho* was applied in the context of information disclosure).
[59] Mason and Laurie, *Mason and McCall Smith's Law and Medical Ethics* at p 139.
[60] Brazier and Cave, *Medicine, Patients and the Law* at p 164.
[61] In *Fletcher v Bench* (1973) 4 BMJ 117, CA, Megaw LJ pointed out that if it was accepted that negligence was automatically established if something went wrong and it was unexplained then "few dentists, doctors and surgeons, however competent, conscientious and careful they might be, would avoid the totally unjustified and unfair stigma of professional negligence probably several times in the course of their careers".
[62] See *Mahon v Osborne* [1939] 2 KB 14; *Cassidy v Ministry of Health* [1951] 2 KB 343. For further discussion of the maxim, see Chapter 23.

9.37   Let us now examine a number of cases to ascertain what the courts have considered to constitute negligence on the part of a medical practitioner.

KEEPING UP TO DATE

9.38   In *Crawford* v *Board of Governors of Charing Cross Hospital*,[63] the question of keeping up to date arose. In that case, a patient underwent a bladder operation during which a blood transfusion was administered. He had lost the use of one arm as a result of polio some time previously. As a result of his arm being held in a certain position during the transfusion, he developed brachial palsy and thus lost the use of his good arm. Six months previously, *The Lancet* had carried an article discrediting that particular technique of blood transfusion. The anaesthetist in question had failed to read the article. The Court of Appeal held that failure to read one recent article in a medical journal was not negligent.[64] Denning LJ observed: "It would, I think, be putting too high a burden on a medical man to say that he has to read every article appearing in the current medical press." Ignoring a series of warnings, however, may amount to negligence. Denning LJ in *Crawford* pointed out that "the time may come in a particular case when a new recommendation may be so well proved and so well known, and so well accepted that it should be adopted".[65]

FAILURE TO MAKE AN ACCURATE DIAGNOSIS

9.39   The question of a failure to make an accurate diagnosis was raised in *Newton* v *Newton's New Model Laundry*.[66] There, a doctor was held to have been negligent where he had failed to diagnose a broken kneecap in a man who had fallen some 12 feet on to a concrete floor.[67]

NEGLIGENT TREATMENT

9.40   The leading case on negligent treatment is *Whitehouse* v *Jordan*.[68] There, a woman of 4 feet 10 inches had refused to allow an X-ray of her pelvis to be taken during her pregnancy and had also refused to submit to an internal examination. She encountered great difficulty in labour with her first child, who was subsequently born brain damaged. She alleged negligence against the senior registrar who had attempted to deliver the child by forceps. After six attempts, he had proceeded to a caesarean section delivery. The mother claimed that the defendant had pulled too long and too hard on the forceps and that this had caused her child's injury. At the original hearing of the case, the trial judge concluded that the doctor had been negligent. In the Court

---

[63] (1953) *The Times*, 8 December, CA.
[64] See, also, *Dwan* v *Farquhar* [1988] Qd R 234; *H* v *Royal Alexandra Hospital for Children* [1990] 1 Med LR 297.
[65] That the standard of care which patients can expect will change in light of new knowledge is illustrated by the Creutzfeldt-Jakob disease litigation – see the discussion in Mason and Laurie, *Mason and McCall Smith's Law and Medical Ethics* at pp 150–152.
[66] (1959) *The Times*, 3 November.
[67] See, also, *Langley* v *Campbell, The Times*, 6 November 1975 (a doctor was held negligent where he had failed to diagnose malaria in a patient who had recently returned from East Africa); *Tuffil* v *East Surrey Area Health Authority, The Times*, 15 March 1978 (a doctor was held negligent in failing to diagnose amoebic dysentery in a patient who had spent many years in the tropics).
[68] [1981] 1 WLR 246.

of Appeal, however, that decision was reversed and Lord Denning MR pronounced that, at most, the doctor had been guilty of an error of judgement and a doctor, in his view, could not be liable for such an error of judgement. Although the House of Lords agreed with the finding of the Court of Appeal to the effect that the doctor had not been negligent, their Lordships expressed disapproval of Lord Denning's statements in relation to errors of judgement. Quoting from the words of McNair J in *Bolam*, Lord Edmund-Davies observed:[69] "'The test is the standard of the ordinary skilled man exercising or professing to have that special skill.' If a surgeon fails to measure up to that standard in any respect ('clinical judgement' or otherwise), he has been negligent ..."

Lord Fraser stated:[70]   **9.41**

"Merely to describe something as an error of judgement tells us nothing about whether it is negligent or not. The true position is that an error of judgement may, or may not, be negligent; it depends on the nature of the error. If it is one that would not have been made by a reasonably competent professional man professing to have the standard and type of skill that the defendant held himself out as having, and acting with ordinary care, then it is negligent. If, on the other hand, it is an error that such a man, acting with ordinary care, might have made, then it is not negligent."[71]

Doctors must take a proper case history from the patient prior to commencing   **9.42** treatment. In *Chin Keow* v *Government of Malaysia*[72] liability was established against a clinic where a patient had been injected with penicillin and died an hour later. She was allergic to penicillin but there had been a failure to examine her records or make enquiries of the patient herself.

Another issue which requires to be considered under the heading of "treatment"   **9.43** is the question of a departure from accepted practice. Lord President Clyde in *Hunter* v *Hanley* warned against construing such departures as negligence when he stated:[73] "[I]n regard to allegations of deviation from ordinary professional practice ... such a deviation is not necessarily evidence of negligence. Indeed it would be disastrous if this were so, for all inducement to progress in medical science would then be destroyed." The departure or deviation from accepted practice will only constitute negligence if, in terms of *Hunter* v *Hanley*, it is one which "no doctor of ordinary skill would be guilty of if acting with ordinary care".

BREAKING BAD NEWS

In *AB* v *Tameside and Glossop Health Authority*,[74] the defendants discovered that one   **9.44** of their health workers was HIV positive. Patients who had had obstetric treatment were advised by letter that they were at a very remote risk of having been infected by HIV. The patients claimed that the authority had breached its duty of care to them by

---

[69] [1981] 1 WLR 246 at 258.
[70] *Ibid* at 263.
[71] For an error of judgement which did amount to negligence, see *Boustead* v *North West Strategic Health Authority* [2008] EWHC 2375 (QB). (The case concerned a delay in performing a caesarean section in the face of foetal distress.)
[72] [1967] 1 WLR 813.
[73] 1955 SC 200 at 217.
[74] *The Times*, 27 November 1996.

advising of the risk by letter. They claimed that it was reasonably foreseeable that a recipient of the standard letter might suffer shock and psychiatric illness as a result. The best method of avoiding such a risk was for a suitably qualified person to give the information face to face. At first instance, the judge concluded that the defendants had not exercised due care. On appeal, however, it was held that the judge had applied the wrong standard of care. The standard which the judge had applied required the authority to employ the best method of imparting the information irrespective of the circumstances. The correct test of negligence, however, was whether the defendant had exercised *reasonable* care in the circumstances, and, applying that test, the Court of Appeal concluded that the health authority had not breached its duty in breaking the news in the way in which it had.

PROTECTING PATIENTS FROM SELF-HARM

9.45 In *Rolland* v *Lothian Health Board*[75] a patient who was suffering from a mental condition jumped from a hospital window. Although a tendency to violence was a well-known feature of the condition in question, there was no evidence of a patient ever having attempted to jump from a hospital window previously. In holding that such irrational action on the patient's part was not reasonably foreseeable, the judge stated:

> "[W]hat occurred could not in my opinion have been reasonably foreseeable. It was different in kind to what could have been foreseen such as a patient leaving by the door or setting herself alight with a cigarette lighter. What in fact occurred, namely the pursuer's jumping or falling from a window, was a type of occurrence which could not in my opinion have been reasonably foreseeable. It is quite different in kind from what could have been foreseen and the consequence must therefore be that the defenders are not liable."

9.46 In *Hay* v *Grampian Health Board*,[76] on the other hand, negligence was established in circumstances where a voluntary psychiatric patient hanged herself in a bathroom while two nurses were attending other patients. The patient was resuscitated but suffered severe brain damage. She had a history of depressive illness and was known to be a high suicide risk. Staff were required to keep her under close observation, which involved knowing where she was at all times.

CONSENT CASES

9.47 To legitimise any medical intervention it is essential that the patient consents to it. Sometimes, the basis of a patient's claim against a doctor is not that his treatment was carried out negligently but that the doctor failed to make an adequate disclosure of the risk inherent in the treatment and that the patient has suffered as a result of that risk materialising. The patient might thus argue that he did not provide a real consent. Because consent to medical treatment involves the issue of the autonomy of the patient, one could advance a compelling argument that it should be isolated from the generality of the doctor's duty – in other words, it should not be treated under mainstream negligence theory because that approaches the issue from the doctor's

---

[75] Outer House, 1981, unreported.
[76] 1995 SLT 652.

perspective (his duty) rather than from the patient's perspective (his rights to receive information). Scots law, however, declines to treat the issue of consent as a distinct one. Indeed, judges in both Scotland and England appear content to analyse the question as simply another aspect of the doctor's duty.

The leading case is *Sidaway* v *Governors of Bethlem Royal Hospital*,[77] a House of Lords   **9.48** decision in an English appeal. The plaintiff underwent surgery to relieve pressure on a nerve root. She had been advised of the risk of damage to a nerve root during surgery but not of the risk of damage to the spinal cord. The second risk, which was a risk of less than 1 per cent, materialised and the plaintiff suffered paralysis as a result. Some neurosurgeons would have advised the patient of the risk of damage to the spinal cord but because others would not have so advised her, the plaintiff's case failed. The House of Lords held that a doctor is not negligent if a responsible body of medical opinion supports his decision not to advise the patient of the risk. Lord Bridge, however, did assert a judicial right to reject the medical evidence in consent cases when he stated:[78] "I am of opinion that the judge might in certain circumstances come to the conclusion that disclosure of a particular risk was so obviously necessary to an informed choice on the part of the patient that no reasonably prudent medical man would fail to make it."

The *Sidaway* decision was strongly endorsed in the Scottish decision of *Moyes* v   **9.49** *Lothian Health Board*.[79] There, the pursuer underwent a CT scan in 1981. This failed to disclose the cause of her trouble. She was subsequently advised to undergo an angiography. During that procedure, the pursuer suffered a stroke. There had been a 0.2–0.3 per cent risk of this occurring. Lord Caplan observed:[80]

> "As I see it the law in both Scotland and England has come down firmly against the view that the doctor's duty to the patient involves at all costs obtaining the informed consent of the patient to specific medical treatments ... I can read nothing in the majority view in *Sidaway* which suggests that the extent and quality of warning to be given by a doctor to his patient should not in the last resort be governed by medical criteria. The risks inherent in a particular operation or procedure, the manner in which the operation may affect or damage a particular patient, the medical need for the operation and the ability of the patient to absorb information about his situation without adding damage to his health, are all matters where the doctor, with his own clinical experience and the benefit of the experience of other practitioners, is best able to form a judgment as to what the patient can safely be told in the exercise of medical care."[81]

Although the law of assault will generally provide a remedy to a patient where   **9.50** treatment has been administered without any consent being given at all, it is clear from the authorities that, where the issue is one of non-disclosure of a risk, the patient's remedy lies in the law of negligence, not assault. In *Sidaway*, Lord Scarman indicated

---

[77] [1985] AC 871.
[78] *Ibid* at 900.
[79] 1990 SLT 444.
[80] *Ibid* at 449.
[81] Norrie argues persuasively that, notwithstanding the decision in *Chester* v *Afshar* [2005] 1 AC 134 (see discussion below under causation), levels of disclosure are to be determined by the normal *Hunter* v *Hanley* test (Norrie, *Delict*, para 19–24).

that "it would be deplorable to base the law in medical cases of this kind on the torts of assault and battery".[82]

CAUSATION

9.51 The third part of the pursuer's task in a medical negligence action, namely proving causation, can also present considerable difficulty. The most well-known case on this subject is *Barnett v Chelsea & Kensington Hospital Management Committee*.[83] Barnett, while on duty with two fellow nightwatchmen, drank some tea with them and vomited for 3 hours. He presented himself at casualty where the nurse on duty contacted the doctor on duty. The doctor declined to come down to examine Barnett, advising instead that he be told to contact his own doctor in the morning. However, Barnett died during the night and his widow raised an action against the hospital management committee. The action was unsuccessful. Although a breach of duty was clearly made out, the plaintiff failed to establish causation. The deceased had in fact been suffering from arsenic poisoning (the arsenic having been present in the tea) and it was that which was the cause of death, not the doctor's breach of duty.

9.52 In medical negligence cases the causation issue can be particularly problematic. Doctors are generally consulted because the patient's body is diseased in some way. If the patient ends up in a worse condition following medical intervention, it is often difficult to establish whether that deterioration was due to the original disease process or whether it was due to negligent medical intervention. This point is highlighted in a number of important cases.

9.53 In *Kay's Tutor v Ayrshire and Arran Health Board*,[84] a 2-year-old child was admitted to hospital with suspected meningitis. A massive overdose of penicillin was administered and the child went into convulsions and developed temporary paralysis down one side of his body. Fortunately, the child made a recovery from the meningitis, the convulsions and paralysis but it transpired that he had become deaf. Although the health board admitted liability in respect of the paralysis and convulsions, it refuted liability in respect of the child's deafness. The House of Lords was required to determine whether the overdose or the meningitis had caused the deafness. The evidence indicated that meningitis had often caused deafness in the past but there was no case of an overdose of penicillin ever having caused deafness. In the light of that evidence, their Lordships concluded that it was the meningitis which had caused the child's deafness.

9.54 *Wilsher v Essex Area Health Authority*[85] again illustrates the difficulty in proving causation in a medical context. A baby was born prematurely and was admitted to a neonatal intensive care unit. Extra oxygen was administered to him but he had been incorrectly catheterised (the catheter had been inserted into his vein rather than his artery) with the result that he received too much oxygen. The child subsequently

---

[82] See, however, *Bartley v Studd*, Medical Law Monitor, vol II, 8 Oct 1995. There, the plaintiff claimed that her ovaries had been removed without her consent during a hysterectomy operation. The High Court ruled that she was entitled to judgment for battery and negligence for unlawful removal of her ovaries. It was held that the "hostility" required for a finding of battery did not require any finding of malevolence on the part of the defender – it was sufficient that the touching was against the will of the plaintiff.

[83] [1969] 1 QB 428.

[84] 1987 SLT 577.

[85] [1988] AC 1074.

developed retrolental fibroplasia (RLF), which condition causes gradual blindness. There were five possible causes for the condition, the excess oxygen being one of them. It was clearly established that there had been a breach of duty. What was in issue was the question of causation. The judge at first instance held that, as a breach of duty was established, the burden of proving that that breach of duty did not cause the injury moved to the defendants. In other words, in the trial judge's view, it was for the defendants to prove that the plaintiff's injuries (RLF) resulted from one of the other possible causes. When the case reached the House of Lords, their Lordships disagreed with the approach of the trial judge and stressed that the burden of proof remains on the plaintiff even where a breach of duty is proved or admitted. Their Lordships ordered a retrial on the basis that a breach of duty and an injury did not raise a presumption that the injury was caused by the breach. A causal link between the two required to be established.

In *Chester* v *Afshar*[86] the claimant suffered repeated episodes of low back pain and   **9.55** was referred for surgery to a consultant neurosurgeon. Following surgery, the claimant suffered a rare complication known as cauda equina syndrome, a risk in respect of which the neurosurgeon had failed to warn her. The judge had not found that the neurosurgeon had been negligent in the *actual performance* of the surgery. However, he had found that the neurosurgeon had failed to warn the claimant of the small risk that the operation could adversely affect her, and that, had she been warned of the risk, she would not have undergone the surgery at the time she did. On appeal, the House of Lords held, by majority, that the surgeon was liable to the patient when that risk materialised, even though the risk was not increased by the failure to warn and the patient had not shown that she would never have had an operation carrying the same risk.

The duty of a surgeon to warn of the dangers inherent in an operation was intended   **9.56** to help minimise the risk to the patient. It was also intended to enable the patient to make an informed choice whether to undergo the treatment recommended and, if so, at whose hands and when. The neurosurgeon had violated the claimant's right to choose for herself, even if he had not increased the risk to her. The function of the law was to enable rights to be vindicated and to provide remedies when duties had been breached. Unless that was done, the duty to warn would be a hollow one. On policy grounds, a majority of their Lordships held that the claimant should recover. Thus, the House of Lords departed from the strict rules of causation in order to assist the claimant, this concession being made on the basis that it was necessary in order to protect the patient's right to self-determination.

LOSS OF CHANCE

Another problem with causation occurs where the alleged negligence does not neces-   **9.57** sarily cause the resultant injury but rather deprives the pursuer of a chance of recovery from his original affliction. It is interesting to note the manner in which the courts have examined the causation issue in loss of chance cases. It has been argued[87] that the approach of the courts is more favourable to the medical profession than it is to, say, the legal profession.

---

[86] [2005] 1 AC 134.
[87] See A F Phillips, "Lost Chances in Delict – All or Nothing?" 1995 JR 401.

9.58   In *Hotson* v *East Berkshire Area Health Authority*,[88] the plaintiff sustained a hip injury when he was 13 after falling from a rope on which he was swinging. The hospital which he attended failed to diagnose the problem and it was only some 5 days later, after he had suffered considerable pain, that the problem was detected and treated. The plaintiff developed avascular necrosis. Evidence indicated that, had the plaintiff been promptly treated, he would still have had a 75 per cent chance of developing this disease. The negligent delay in his diagnosis and treatment led to the inevitable onset of the disease – in other words, it became a certainty that he would develop the disease. The trial judge and the Court of Appeal, classifying the issue as one of quantum, awarded damages in respect of the 25 per cent loss of chance of a full recovery. The House of Lords, on further appeal, disagreed with this approach and held that, on a balance of probabilities, it was the fall which had caused the avascular necrosis, not the negligent treatment. The plaintiff thus failed at the causation hurdle and no damages were awarded in respect of the onset of avascular necrosis.

9.59   The question of loss of chance arose once again in *Gregg* v *Scott*[89] and resulted in a divided House of Lords. There, the claimant visited the defendant because he had a lump under his arm. The defendant negligently misdiagnosed the claimant's condition as benign. A year later, another general practitioner referred the claimant to hospital for an examination and it was discovered that he had cancer of a lymph gland. Sadly, by that time, the tumour had spread to the claimant's chest. The claimant suffered pain and required a course of chemotherapy. He was left with poor prospects of survival. He sued the defendant, alleging that the defendant should have referred him to hospital and that, if he had done so, his condition would have been diagnosed earlier and there would have been a high likelihood of cure. The judge held that, on the expert evidence, the delay in diagnosis had reduced the claimant's chances of surviving for more than 10 years from 42 per cent to 25 per cent. The judge therefore dismissed the action because the delay had not deprived the claimant of the prospect of a cure, meaning surviving more than 10 years, because, at the time of the misdiagnosis, the claimant had less than a 50 per cent chance of surviving more than 10 years anyway. The Court of Appeal dismissed the claimant's appeal. On further appeal to the House of Lords, the claimant submitted that the reduction in his chances of survival was a compensatable head of damage. The House of Lords dismissed the appeal. On the judge's findings, it had not been shown that, *on the balance of probabilities*, the delay in commencing the claimant's treatment had affected the course of his illness or his prospects of survival, which had never been as good as even. Their Lordships further held that liability for the loss of a chance of a more favourable outcome should not be introduced into personal injury claims. Lord Phillips stated[90] that "there is a danger, if special tests of causation are developed piecemeal to deal with perceived injustices in particular factual situations, that the coherence of our common law will be destroyed".

9.60   Lord Nicholls and Lord Hope dissented, taking the view that the significant reduction in the prospects of a successful outcome which the defendant's negligence caused was a loss for which the claimant ought to be compensated. In the view of the minority, what had to be valued was what the claimant had lost, and the principle on which that loss had to be calculated was the same, irrespective of whether the

---

[88] [1987] 2 All ER 909.
[89] [2005] AC 176.
[90] *Ibid* at para 172.

prospects were better or less than 50 per cent. Lord Nicholls pointed out[91] that the majority approach "means that a patient with a 60 per cent chance of recovery reduced to a 40 per cent prospect by medical negligence can obtain compensation. But he can obtain nothing if his prospects were reduced from 40 per cent to nil".

It is interesting to contrast the approach taken in medical loss of chance cases with **9.61** that taken in legal loss of chance cases. The legal loss of chance cases are discussed in detail below in relation to negligence of members of the legal profession. There appears to be some inconsistency in approach as between the medical and legal cases. Despite the striking similarities between the two types of case, the medical claimants appear to be treated less generously than those claiming loss of chance as a result of solicitors' negligence. Phillips[92] observes that there is no justification in principle for the difference in analysis of loss of medical chance and loss of legal chance cases. Phillips believes that the distinction might be the result of an unarticulated public policy and he questions whether there would in fact be a flood of claims if the distinction had not been drawn.

POLICY ISSUES

For policy reasons, the judiciary has tended to adopt a very conservative attitude **9.62** towards medical negligence claims and this approach pervades the various judgments in this field. Mason and Laurie observe that "there has been a degree of policy-based judicial reluctance to award damages against doctors".[93] It has been argued that frequent findings of liability will lead to defensive medicine – a form of medical practice which is more concerned with protecting the doctor's legal position than it is with the patient's well-being. The medical profession argues that overzealous attribution of liability in relation to diagnostic errors will simply result in expensive, time-wasting and potentially damaging procedures being adopted. Unnecessary X-rays and caesarean sections are often cited as examples of such defensive practices, the doctor being fearful of a subsequent civil suit if he fails to spot a fracture or continues with a difficult natural delivery. It is also believed in some quarters that doctors are deliberately avoiding what are perceived to be high-risk areas of practice such as obstetrics and that this may result in a shortfall of required expertise in a given area and thus be damaging to the interests of the community as a whole. Some members of the judiciary have displayed a deep-seated fear of the practice of defensive medicine, a practice which is considered to be widespread in the United States. Fear of the American experience does pervade a number of judgments.[94] For example, in *Roe* v *Ministry of Health*,[95] Denning LJ's speech discloses a fear that overzealous attribution of liability to the medical profession may have deleterious consequences for the general public. His Lordship stated:[96] "[W]e should be doing a disservice to the community at large if we were to impose liability on hospitals and doctors for everything that happens to

---

[91] [2005] AC 176 at para 121.
[92] Phillips, "Lost Chances in Delict – All or Nothing?" 1995 JR 401.
[93] Mason and Laurie, *Mason and McCall Smith's Law and Medical Ethics*, p 133.
[94] See, for example, the *dicta* of Purchas LJ in *Greater Nottingham Co-op* v *Cementation Ltd* [1988] 3 WLR 396 (at 409) and the observations of Lord Scarman in *Sidaway* v *Governors of Bethlem Royal Hospital* [1985] 1 AC 871 at 887.
[95] [1954] 2 QB 66.
[96] *Ibid* at 87.

go wrong. Doctors would be led to think more of their own safety than of the good of their patients." Earlier in his judgment, Denning LJ warned:[97] "It is so easy to be wise after the event and to condemn as negligence that which is only a misadventure. We ought always to be on our guard against it especially in cases against hospitals and doctors." It is significant that Denning LJ uses the word *especially*. It would suggest that, in his view, the medical profession deserves special treatment. In *Bolam*, McNair J quoted extensively from Denning LJ's judgment in *Roe* and endorsed his *dicta* as "wise words".[98] Fears of defensive medicine were again expressed in *Whitehouse v Jordan*[99] and in *Sidaway v Governors of Bethlem Royal Hospital*.[100]

9.63   It is suggested, however, that it is unwise to regard the American experience as an example of what might happen in this country given the fundamental differences which exist in the realms of both healthcare provision and litigation practice. A private health system on the American model, where healthcare is charged on a "fee for service" basis, could be said to encourage excessive testing. Most people in the UK, however, still rely on the NHS.

9.64   As far as litigation is concerned, in the USA, a contingency fee system operates which undoubtedly makes it easier for a patient to litigate. (Under a contingency fee system, if the case fails the client pays nothing, whereas if he succeeds the lawyer takes a percentage of the award of damages.) Moreover, damages in Scotland are designed to compensate, whereas in the US, the jury is empowered to award punitive damages in appropriate circumstances. American juries are undoubtedly aware that the lawyers are "taking a cut" and, mindful of that fact, may well inflate the award.

POSSIBLE REFORM

9.65   The current system of medical negligence litigation is enormously expensive and some would claim that it is patently unjust. In *Whitehouse v Jordan*,[101] it will be remembered that the plaintiff failed to recover compensation despite divisions both in the medical evidence and on the Bench. However, the opposite outcome might be said to have been unfair to the defendant as he did receive support from a number of eminent experts in his field. One of the most problematic aspects of the negligence action is the need to attribute fault. This is a point which has attracted comment not only from academics but also from the Bench. In *Ashcroft v Mersey Area Health Authority*[102] a patient sought compensation in respect of facial paralysis following an ear operation. The expert evidence as to whether such damage might result in the absence of negligence was split and the plaintiff therefore failed to recover. It was clearly with some reluctance that Kilner Brown J dismissed the action and his Lordship observed:[103] "Where an injury is caused which never should have been caused, common sense and natural justice indicate that some degree of compensation ought to be paid by someone." There appears to be some support for the introduction of a no-fault system under which a patient who is harmed by medical treatment would receive compensation

---

[97] [1954] 2 QB 66 at 83.
[98] *Bolam v Friern Hospital Management Committee* [1957] 1 WLR 582 at 593.
[99] [1980] 1 All ER 650, per Lawton LJ at 659.
[100] [1985] AC 871, per Lord Scarman at 887 and per Lord Diplock at 893.
[101] [1981] 1 WLR 246.
[102] [1983] 2 All ER 245.
[103] *Ibid* at 246.

without the need to prove fault. Such systems exist in both New Zealand and Sweden. The possibility of establishing a no-fault system in Scotland was considered in 2003 but the Report of the Expert Group on Financial and Other Support, 2003 (under the chairmanship of Lord Ross) declined to recommend the introduction of a general no-fault compensation scheme at that time. More recently, the Cabinet Secretary for Health and Wellbeing (Nicola Sturgeon) announced in June 2009 that she was establishing the No-fault Compensation Review Group to be chaired by Professor Sheila McLean of the University of Glasgow. The Group's remit was to look at the issue of no fault liability. The Group issued its Report (*No-fault Compensation Review Group – Report and Recommendations*) in February 2011. The Group examined well-established no-fault schemes such as those in New Zealand and Sweden. The Working Group's Research Team[104] noted that previous research indicated that when an error has occurred, patients expect doctors to make a meaningful apology, provide an explanation and take steps to prevent recurrence. The Report identifies a number of problems with the current system of litigation of medical negligence claims in Scotland (including inadequacy of funding provided by Legal Aid, difficulties experienced by pursuers in finding a solicitor to take on their cases, length of time until resolution, adversarial culture and its attendant problems (eg delay in disclosure of expert opinions or information) and the disproportionality of legal expenses when compared with the value of a claim). The Report noted that the concept of no fault is not entirely alien to UK law.[105] "The group was of the view that a no-fault system in itself would contribute directly to a more open and less defensive culture."[106] The Report recommends (*inter alia*) that:

(1) consideration be given to the establishment of a no-fault scheme for medical injury, along the lines of the Swedish model (the Swedish scheme is confined to medical injury and includes recourse to the courts, ie patients remain entitled to bring a claim in delict);

(2) the scheme should cover all medical treatment injuries that occur in Scotland;

(3) any compensation awarded should be based on need, rather than on a tariff-based system;

(4) it should extend to all registered healthcare professionals in Scotland, and not simply to those employed by NHS Scotland;

(5) claimants who fail under the no-fault scheme should retain the right to litigate and a claimant who fails in litigation should have a residual right to claim under the no-fault scheme (although any financial award made under the no-fault scheme should be deducted from any award subsequently made as a result of litigation);

(6) appeal from the adjudication of the no-fault scheme should be available to a court of law (this is required in terms of human rights law).

It remains to be seen whether these proposed reforms will be implemented.

---

[104] Farrell *et al* (2010).

[105] For example, the Criminal Injuries Compensation Authority and the Vaccine Damage Payments Act 1979 currently operate on a no-fault basis.

[106] *No-fault Compensation Review Group – Report and Recommendations*, para 6.5.

THE DAMAGES AWARD

9.66 There are no special rules governing the award of damages to the victims of medical negligence. The pursuer will be able to claim both *solatium* and patrimonial loss. It should, however, be noted that the rules on provisional damages have greatly assisted medical negligence pursuers in particular. Such pursuers have often suffered severe physical disability with the likelihood of deterioration at some point in the future. Owing to the rules on limitation of actions,[107] the pursuer must generally commence proceedings within 3 years and, if it were not for the rules on provisional damages, the pursuer may go undercompensated. If he is awarded provisional damages, he will be entitled to return to court should the feared deterioration materialise.

PROFESSIONAL LIABILITY OF THE LEGAL PROFESSION

9.67 In recent years, lawyers, like other professional groups, have been increasingly exposed to civil litigation.

THE SOLICITOR IN HIS DEALINGS WITH HIS CLIENT

9.68 Professional liability may attach to a solicitor as a result of a breach of contract.[108] Where a solicitor breaches the duty of care which he owes to his client, he may also be sued in delict. The client may proceed against the solicitor both in contract and delict.[109] As far as his delictual liability is concerned, the solicitor will be judged according to the general test of professional negligence expounded in *Hunter* v *Hanley*.[110] A reasonable solicitor should know that his client's rights will be extinguished through the process of prescription or rendered unenforceable through the process of limitation, if not pursued timeously. Thus, in *Duncan* v *Ross, Harper & Murphy*,[111] a solicitor who had failed to raise his client's personal injury action within the 3-year limitation period was in breach of duty to his client (although the pursuer failed to recover damages there as the illegality defence would have prevailed against him even if the action had been raised timeously). A solicitor instructed in relation to the purchase of property owes a duty to his client to enquire as to his mortgage arrangements and to warn the client of the danger of concluding missives prior to the loan arrangements being finalised.[112] A solicitor engaged to prepare a deed is expected to ensure that it is properly executed.[113] A solicitor who acts for a lender should ensure that the deed is drawn up in a proper manner so as to render it effective as a security[114] but is not generally considered to be

---

[107] See Chapter 24.
[108] Contract may, of course, provide for a standard of duty higher than that of reasonable care. For example, the express terms of a contract may require that a particular result is achieved: see *Mortgage Corporation Ltd* v *Mitchells Roberton* 1997 SLT 1305.
[109] See *J G Martin Plant Hire Ltd* v *Macdonald* 1996 SLT 1192.
[110] 1955 SC 200.
[111] 1993 SLT 105.
[112] *Buckland* v *Mackesy* (1968) 208 EG 969, CA.
[113] *Currie* v *Colquhoun* (1883) 2 S 407.
[114] *Sim* v *Clark* (1831) 10 S 85.

responsible if it transpires that the security is insufficient to cover the loan. In *Midland Bank plc v Cameron, Thom, Peterkins & Duncans*,[115] Lord Jauncey posited the question: "Is it ... to be taken that the solicitor charged with the preparation of the security document is, at his own hand, to undertake independent verification of the security subjects? I do not consider that a simple instruction to prepare security documents can import so far reaching a duty." In the English case of *National Home Loans Corporation plc v Giffen, Couch & Archer*[116] it was held that a solicitor who acts for both lender and borrower in a transaction is under a duty to inform the lender about the prospective borrower's arrears on another loan and the threat of legal proceedings against him. These were matters which a reasonably competent solicitor would realise would have a material impact on the lender's decision to approve the loan.

Occasionally, the basis of the client's complaint is that the solicitor's negligence **9.69** has resulted in a lost chance for the client. We have already considered the matter of loss of chance in a medical context. As far as legal advisers are concerned, the leading case is *Kyle v P & J Stormonth Darling*.[117] There, the defender was a firm of solicitors. A client's appeal to the Court of Session was held to be abandoned owing to the defender's failure to comply with a court rule. Counsel's opinion had been obtained to the effect that the client would have had a reasonable prospect of success in an appeal to the Court of Session. Furthermore, the client had been successful in his application for legal aid for the appeal, whereas his opponent had not. The client sued the firm of solicitors, alleging both negligence and breach of contract, both of which were admitted. However, the defender argued that the loss of chance to pursue the appeal was not in fact a legal wrong and, furthermore, it argued that there should have been an averment in the pleadings that the appeal would probably have been successful. The Inner House took the view that the loss of the right of appeal was sufficient to constitute a legal wrong and it was not necessary for the pursuer to aver that he would probably have succeeded in the appeal.[118]

THE SOLICITOR'S LIABILITY IN RELATION TO THOSE WHO ARE NOT CLIENTS

Lawyers will sometimes offer advice to those who are not clients and in such cases **9.70** they may nevertheless be liable in delict where the *Henderson v Merrett*[119] or *Caparo*[120] criteria for liability are satisfied. In other words, there must be a voluntary assumption of responsibility by the defender coupled with reliance by the pursuer or it must be fair, just and reasonable to impose a duty. In *Midland Bank plc v Cameron, Thom, Peterkin & Duncans*,[121] the pursuer, a bank, lent a sum of money to a client of a firm of solicitors. The bank's decision to lend was partly based on information pertaining to the client's financial circumstances, which had been supplied by the solicitors. The information was inaccurate and the money was lost. The bank sued the solicitors. The Lord Ordinary (Jauncey) observed that, in certain circumstances, a solicitor can incur

---

[115] 1988 SLT 611.
[116] *The Times*, 31 December 1996.
[117] 1993 SC 57.
[118] Contrast the approach taken in the medical loss of chance cases, discussed above.
[119] *Henderson v Merrett Syndicates Ltd* [1995] 2 AC 145.
[120] *Caparo Industries v Dickman* [1990] 2 AC 605.
[121] 1988 SLT 611.

liability to a third party. His Lordship stated:[122] "I have no hesitation in concluding ... that situations can arise in which a solicitor owes a duty not only to his client but to a third party who relies upon what the solicitor tells him." His Lordship then went on to set out four criteria which determine whether a solicitor will owe a duty of care to a third party:

"(1) the solicitor must assume responsibility for the advice or information furnished to the third party; (2) the solicitor must let it be known to the third party expressly or impliedly that he claims, by reason of his calling, to have the requisite skill or knowledge to give the advice or furnish the information; (3) the third party must have relied upon that advice or information as a matter for which the solicitor has assumed personal responsibility; and (4) the solicitor must have been aware that the third party was likely so to rely."

SOLICITOR ACTING ON BEHALF OF CLIENT BUT CAUSING LOSS TO THIRD PARTY

9.71   What is the position where a solicitor, rather than giving advice to a person who is not a client, occasions loss to a third party by reason of failing to implement his client's instructions? Such a scenario may arise where a solicitor is instructed to prepare a will, but, owing to his delay, the client dies before the will is prepared. Alternatively, through negligence on the part of the solicitor, the client's will is ineffective. In situations such as these, intended beneficiaries, who are not themselves clients of the negligent solicitor, will suffer loss. This loss will be purely economic in nature. Does the solicitor owe the intended beneficiary a duty of care in a situation such as this? Traditionally, the Scottish courts have resisted the imposition of a duty of care in these circumstances.

9.72   In *Robertson v Fleming*,[123] a decision of the House of Lords in a Scottish appeal, a solicitor was held not to owe a duty of care to a creditor of his client. The solicitor had failed to make effective certain security documents in favour of the creditor. When the client subsequently became insolvent, the creditor suffered a loss. Lord Campbell LC stated:[124]

"I never had any doubt of the unsoundness of the doctrine ... that A employing B, a professional lawyer, to do any act for the benefit of C ... if through the gross negligence ... of B in transacting the business, C loses the benefit intended for him by A, C may maintain an action against B ... If this were law a disappointed legatee might sue the solicitor employed by a testator to make a will in favour of a stranger, whom the solicitor never saw or before heard of if the will were void for not being properly signed or attested ... I am clearly of opinion that this is not the law of Scotland."

9.73   However, the English courts took a somewhat different view in *Ross v Caunters*.[125] There, a solicitor failed to draw a testator's attention to the fact that the will should not be witnessed by the spouse of a beneficiary. The will was witnessed by the plaintiff's husband and was thus invalid under statute. The intended beneficiary did not receive

---

[122] 1988 SLT 611 at 616.
[123] (1861) 23 D (HL) 8, 4 Macq 167.
[124] 4 Macq 167 at 177.
[125] [1980] Ch 297.

her legacy and it was held that the solicitor did owe her a duty of care. The solicitor was aware of the identity of the intended beneficiary and that she would suffer loss in the event of the will being ineffective.

9.74 In *Weir* v *J M Hodge*,[126] it was with some reluctance that that the Lord Ordinary (Weir) followed the decision in *Robertson* v *Fleming*, a case which he considered to be "out of sympathy with the modern law of negligence". In *MacDougall* v *Clydesdale Bank Trs*,[127] Lord Cameron of Lochbroom also followed the decision in *Robertson* v *Fleming* although the pursuer in that case was not the direct beneficiary but the legatee of the beneficiary who would have inherited but for the invalid will.

9.75 The continued viability of *Robertson* v *Fleming* must now be in some doubt, however, following the decision of the House of Lords in *White* v *Jones*.[128] The facts of the case were as follows. Following a family feud, the testator made a will excluding his two daughters from his estate. There was a subsequent reconciliation and the testator instructed his solicitors to prepare a fresh will leaving legacies of £9,000 to each of his daughters. The solicitor negligently delayed in drawing up the will and the testator died without the new will having been executed. As a result, the deceased's daughters, the plaintiffs, were deprived of their legacies. They sued their father's solicitor. The House of Lords, by majority, held that the plaintiffs should be allowed to recover. Lord Goff provided a detailed analysis of the decision in *Ross* v *Caunters* as well as a number of decisions from other jurisdictions. Having made reference to the passage quoted above from *Robertson* v *Fleming*, Lord Goff stated:[129]

> "Statements such as these no doubt represented the law as understood in this country over a century ago. Moreover, as I have already observed, the general rule today is that, subject to his duties to the court and the professional duties imposed upon his profession, a solicitor when acting for his client owes no duties to third parties. But the problem which arises in the present case relates to the particular position of an intended beneficiary under a will or proposed will to which the solicitor has negligently failed to give effect in accordance with the instructions of his client, the testator; and the question is whether exceptionally a duty of care should be held to be owed by the solicitor to the disappointed beneficiary in those circumstances. I myself do not consider that the existence of such a duty of care can simply be dismissed by reference to the sweeping statements made in *Robertson* v *Fleming*. For the law has moved on from those days."

His Lordship continued:[130]   **9.76**

> "In my opinion ... your Lordships' House should in cases such as these extend to the intended beneficiary a remedy under the *Hedley Byrne* principle by holding that the assumption of responsibility by the solicitor towards his client should be held in law to extend to the intended beneficiary who (as the solicitor can reasonably foresee) may, as a result of the solicitor's negligence, be deprived of his intended legacy in circumstances in which neither the testator nor his estate will have a remedy against the solicitor."

9.77 Lord Goff clearly discerned a potential injustice if a duty was not recognised in this situation. His Lordship was at pains to ensure that the plaintiffs' loss did not

---

[126] 1990 SLT 266.
[127] 1994 SLT 1178.
[128] [1995] 2 AC 207.
[129] *Ibid* at 259.
[130] *Ibid* at 268.

go unremedied and accorded precedence to the need to "do practical justice". If no duty was recognised in this situation, the plaintiffs' case would fall into a legal *lacuna* which ought to be filled. Lord Goff was clearly unimpressed with the floodgates argument which was advanced on behalf of the appellants. His Lordship stated:[131] "... the ordinary case is one in which the intended beneficiaries are a small number of identified people. If by any chance a more complicated case should arise to test the precise boundaries of the principle in cases of this kind, that problem can await solution when such a case comes forward for decision."

9.78   It follows that *White* v *Jones* is limited to the case of the disappointed legatee. Thus, in *McLeod* v *Crawford & Ors*[132] a solicitor was held to owe no duty of care to the family of a client to whom advice had been provided in respect of a personal injury. Distinguishing *White* v *Jones*, Lord Woolman stated:[133] "The chief feature of Lord Goff's *dictum* [in *White* v *Jones*] may be said to be its circumscription. He framed the extension to the existing law in a very limited way. It applied only to intended beneficiaries. There is no suggestion that he had in mind any broader extension of the liability owed by solicitors to third parties."[134]

9.79   Although *White* (limited as it is in its application) was a decision of the House of Lords in an English appeal, it appears to have been accepted by the Scottish courts.[135]

THE LEGAL LIABILITY OF ADVOCATES

9.80   Special mention ought to be made of the position of advocates in relation to the conduct of litigation. Advocates in Scotland (and barristers in England) have traditionally enjoyed immunity from civil suit in relation to the conduct and management of a case in court.[136] In *Rondel* v *Worsley*,[137] the House of Lords was called upon to determine whether the immunity of counsel was still capable of justification. There, a barrister was sued by the plaintiff, who had been convicted and sentenced in respect of a crime. Following his release from prison, the plaintiff sued the barrister for professional negligence, claiming that the barrister had conducted his criminal defence improperly and that this had resulted in his conviction. The House of Lords, however, held unanimously that barristers enjoyed immunity from civil suit in respect of the conduct and management of a case in court. This immunity was required on the grounds of public policy in order to prevent the retrying of cases. A barrister should also be in a position, it was thought, to carry out his duties fearlessly and independently.

9.81   However, more recently, in *Arthur J S Hall* v *Simons*[138] the House of Lords, in an English appeal, held that barristers should no longer have immunity from suit

---

[131] [1995] 2 AC 207 at 269.
[132] 2010 SLT 1035.
[133] *Ibid* at para 23.
[134] See, also, *Fraser* v *McArthur Stewart* 2009 SLT 31 and *Matthews* v *Hunter & Robertson* [2008] CSOH 88 for further discussion of the limits of the *White* v *Jones* principle.
[135] See *Robertson* v *Watt & Co* (2nd Div) 4 July 1995, unreported; *Holmes* v *Bank of Scotland* 2002 SLT 544.
[136] See, eg, *Batchelor* v *Pattison and Mackersy* (1876) 3 R 914 where the view was expressed in the Inner House that the public interest required counsel to be immune from suit. The Lord President pointed out that not only does an advocate owe duties to his client but he also owes duties to his profession, to the court and to the public.
[137] [1969] 1 AC 191.
[138] [2002] 1 AC 615.

in respect of professional negligence in relation to the conduct of either a civil or a criminal case. However, in the Scottish case of *Wright* v *Paton Farrell*,[139] the Inner House took the view that solicitors and advocates conducting *a criminal defence* should continue to enjoy immunity from suit at the instance of a dissatisfied client. The position in Scotland as regards the conduct of a civil case remains uncertain.

It is clear from *Saif Ali* v *Sydney Mitchell & Co*[140] that a barrister or advocate might **9.82** incur liability in relation to advice: for example, an opinion on a point of law. In *Pritchard Joyce & Hinds (a firm)* v *Batcup & Anor*[141] the English Court of Appeal considered the standard of competency required of barristers. A standard of reasonable competence is required but it is not necessary for the legal adviser to discern any claim a client may theoretically have. Just because a piece of advice is incorrect, it does not follow that the barrister is automatically negligent. In *Fraser* v *Bolt Burdon*[142] it was held that, given the environment in which it is given, legal advice "at the door of the court" need not be right but should be careful. In the circumstances, and applying the *Bolam* test (discussed above), a firm of solicitors and the barristers whom they instructed had not been negligent in advising their client to settle her claim for negligence immediately before the trial was due to commence.

OTHER PROFESSIONAL GROUPS

As noted at the outset, the test in *Hunter* v *Hanley* has been extended to other profes- **9.83** sional groups such as surveyors,[143] engineers,[144] architects[145] and teachers[146] among others.[147]

GENERAL POINTS

THE INEXPERIENCED PROFESSIONAL

As a matter of *fact* the inexperienced professional is unlikely to possess as much **9.84** knowledge and expertise as a more experienced professional. However, *the law* will not make allowances for inexperience.[148] At the Court of Appeal stage of *Wilsher* v *Essex Area Health Authority*,[149] the legal position of the inexperienced doctor was considered. An argument was put forward to the effect that the standard of care

---

[139] 2006 SLT 269.
[140] [1978] 3 All ER 1033.
[141] [2009] EWCA Civ 369.
[142] [2009] EWHC 2906.
[143] See *Gillies Ramsay Diamond* v *PJW Enterprises Ltd* 2003 SLT 162; *Sneesby* v *Goldings* [1995] EGLR 102.
[144] *Strathclyde RC* v *W A Fairhurst & Partners* 1997 SLT 658.
[145] *Kelly* v *City of Edinburgh District Council* 1983 SC 97; *Wagner Associates* v *Joseph Dunn (Bottlers) Ltd* 1986 SLT 267; *Atwal Enterprise Ltd* v *Toner t/a Donal Toner Associates* 2006 SLT 537.
[146] *Scott* v *Lothian RC* 1999 Rep LR 15. See, also, A Bowen, "Teachers as professionals: *Hunter* v *Hanley* rides again" 1999 SLT (News) 11.
[147] For a fuller discussion of the law of professional negligence as it applies to other professional groups, see Norrie, *Delict*, paras 19–45 to 19–49.
[148] See *Jones* v *Manchester Corporation* [1952] 2 QB 852 (patient died after maladministration of anaesthetic by doctor qualified for only 5 months).
[149] [1987] QB 730; [1988] 1 All ER 871.

to be expected from a junior doctor was not the same as what was expected from a more experienced doctor. This argument was rejected. The standard expected of a professional person is determined by the nature of the post which he occupies. The standard required from a professional does not vary according to his length of experience.[150] The same standard is required of a GP who qualified last week as is required from the GP who has been in practice for 20 years. Likewise, the consultant obstetrician elevated to that post last week is expected, as a matter of law, to display the same expertise as a consultant with many years of experience in the same discipline. A newly qualified solicitor is expected to meet the same standard as his more experienced colleagues. However, as a matter of practice, it would be imprudent for an employer to rely too heavily on inexperienced employees owing to the concept of vicarious liability.

THE TIRED, STRESSED OR ILL PROFESSIONAL

9.85 Similarly, no concession is made to a professional person on the grounds that he or she is tired, stressed or ill at the time at which any alleged negligence occurred.[151] As Norrie has observed, "these facts do not change what the client is entitled to expect in the way of care".[152]

TIME AT WHICH NEGLIGENCE IS JUDGED

9.86 The question of negligence is judged not according to knowledge possessed at the date of proof but rather according to knowledge possessed as at the date of the alleged negligence. This is well illustrated in the case of *Roe* v *Ministry of Health*.[153] There, two patients underwent minor surgery. It was not necessary to administer a general anaesthetic. Instead, the patients were to receive a local anaesthetic given by way of lumbar puncture using the anaesthetic Nupercaine. The Nupercaine had been stored in glass ampoules which were in turn stored in a solution of phenol. This means of storing the anaesthetic had been employed to ensure that the anaesthetic remained sterile as, in the past, on occasion, the needle of the hypodermic syringe had contacted the outside of the ampoule and thus the anaesthetic was rendered non-sterile. It was hoped to prevent such contamination by storing the ampoules in the sterilising solution. Unknown to the anaesthetist, however, the ampoules contained hairline cracks which were incapable of detection by the human eye. As a result the phenol solution percolated through the molecular flaws in the glass. The patients were therefore injected with a mixture of anaesthetic and phenol. They were paralysed as a result. The negligence action, which came to trial in 1954, was unsuccessful. At the time of the accident, in 1947, the occurrence could not have been foreseen. Such an accident had never happened before. Obviously, following the catastrophic injuries to the plaintiffs, the risk became well documented. However, the medical staff, whose actions were subject to scrutiny in the civil action, were to be judged, not with the benefit of hindsight, but according to the state of knowledge possessed at the date of the operation. Denning LJ

---

[150] See *Djemal* v *Bexley Health Authority* [1995] 6 Med LR 269.
[151] See *Barnett* v *Chelsea & Kensington Hospital Management Committee* [1969] 1 QB 428, per Nield J at 437.
[152] Norrie, *Delict* at para 19–24.
[153] [1954] 2 KB 66.

articulated the position in the following terms: "We must not look at the 1947 accident with 1954 spectacles." Morris LJ stated:[154] "[C]are has to be exercised to ensure that conduct in 1947 is only judged in the light of knowledge which then was or ought reasonably to have been possessed."

---

[154] [1954] 2 KB 66 at 92.

10 BREACH OF STATUTORY DUTY

INTRODUCTION

As we have seen, delictual liability may attach to a defender as a result of a breach **10.1** of a common law duty of care. Liability may also attach to a defender as a result of a breach of statutory duty. It is important to note at the outset that not all breaches of statutory duty give rise to delictual liability. In this chapter we will examine the circumstances in which breach of a statutory duty *does* give rise to delictual liability. Breach of statutory duty is an increasingly important area of the law, owing to the vast volume of legislation emanating from both the Westminster and Scottish Parliaments.[1] Acts of Parliament and statutory regulations[2] set out detailed rules of conduct in the fields of road traffic, housing, education, childcare, employment, etc. Many of these statutory provisions, such as, for example, those imposing requirements with respect to falling objects in the workplace,[3] are aimed at accident prevention. Statutory duties are usually additional to common law duties[4] unless the statute expressly provides that they are to supersede the common law duties.[5] The pursuer can accordingly base his action on either the statutory or common law ground or indeed on both grounds.[6]

In Scotland, the traditional approach[7] has been to regard breach of statutory duty as **10.2** a separate and distinct cause of action from breach of common law duty (negligence).[8] This is also the case in England. In *London Passenger Transport Board* v *Upson*[9] Lord Wright stated:[10]

---

[1] It should be noted that breach of EU Treaty provisions may also give rise to an action for breach of statutory duty: see *Garden Cottage Foods* v *Milk Marketing Board* [1984] AC 130, per Lord Diplock at 141. A detailed consideration of the European dimension is, however, beyond the scope of this work. For a fuller discussion, see K Stanton *et al*, *Statutory Torts* (2003), Chapter 6.

[2] The action for breach of statutory duty applies not only to statutes but also to subordinate legislation.

[3] See Workplace (Health, Safety and Welfare) Regulations 1992 (SI 1992/3004).

[4] See *Matuszczyk* v *NCB* 1953 SC 8, where Lord Keith stated at 16: "[I]f some duty is imposed by statute on a workman which would also be his duty at common law, I see no reason to hold that the common law duty has been superseded and ceases to exist."

[5] The Nuclear Installations Act 1965, s 12(1), for example, excludes a concurrent cause of action under the common law.

[6] See *Millar* v *Galashiels Gas Co Ltd* 1949 SC (HL) 31; *McLellan* v *Dundee City Council* 2009 Rep LR 61; *Ruddy* v *Monte Marco and M & H Enterprises Ltd* [2008] CSOH 40; *Welsh* v *Brady* 2009 SLT 747.

[7] See *Millar* v *Galashiels Gas Co Ltd* 1949 SC (HL) 31.

[8] Lord Wright's *dicta* in *McMullan* v *Lochgelly Iron & Coal Co* 1933 SC (HL) 64 would appear to derogate from this general approach. His Lordship's approach in *McMullan* is akin to the US approach. His Lordship appears to have had a change of heart in *London Passenger Transport Board* v *Upson* [1949] AC 155.

[9] [1949] AC 155.

[10] *Ibid* at 168–169.

"[A] claim for damages for breach of a statutory duty ... is a specific common law right which is not to be confused in essence with a claim for negligence. The statutory right has its origins in the statute, but the particular remedy of an action for damages is given by the common law in order to make effective, for the benefit of the injured plaintiff, his right to the performance by the defendant of the defendant's statutory duty ... It is not a claim in negligence in the strict or ordinary sense ... whatever the resemblances, it is essential to keep in mind the fundamental differences of the two classes of claim."

10.3 The distinction between the two causes of action (that is, breach of statutory duty on the one hand and common law negligence on the other hand) is further illustrated by the fact that one cause of action may succeed while the other fails. In his judgment in *London Passenger Transport Board* v *Upson*, Lord Wright, referring to regulations in respect of pedestrian crossings, stated:[11] "I have desired before I deal specifically with the regulations to make it clear ... that a claim for their breach may stand or fall independently of negligence."

10.4   Thus, it is possible for a claim based on breach of statute to succeed while a claim on the same facts based on negligence fails. For example, in *Millar* v *Galashiels Gas Co Ltd*[12] a workman was killed after falling down a lift shaft in his employer's factory owing to the failure of a brake mechanism of a lift. His widow's subsequent action based on breach of common law duty failed because there was no proof of lack of reasonable care. Insofar as it related to breach of the Factories Act 1937, the action was successful because the duty imposed by the Act was an absolute one. In other words, the mere fact that the brake mechanism had failed was sufficient to establish breach of statutory duty on the employer's part.

10.5   Conversely, there are cases where a claim in negligence has succeeded and a statutory claim has failed, as in *Bux* v *Slough Metals Ltd*.[13] In *Bux*, an employer had fulfilled his statutory duty under the Non-Ferrous Metals (Melting and Founding) Regulations 1962,[14] which required him to supply safety goggles to an employee. The employer was nevertheless liable in negligence when the employee, a diecaster, was injured by molten metal being thrown into his eye. It was established in evidence that the injured employee would have worn the goggles had he been instructed to do so in a firm manner followed up by supervision. The employer's failure to so instruct and supervise the employee constituted a breach of his common law duty to provide a safe system of work.

10.6   Where an action is brought based on both negligence and breach of statutory duty, it is more common for the latter claim to succeed as statutes generally impose a standard higher than that of reasonable care.[15]

---

[11] [1949] AC 155 at 169.
[12] 1949 SC (HL) 31.
[13] [1974] 1 All ER 262.
[14] SI 1962/1667.
[15] The pursuer may, however, succeed on several grounds of action: see *Beggs* v *Motherwell Bridge Fabricators Ltd* 1998 SLT 1215 where the pursuers were successful in establishing breaches of the Factories Act 1961, the Occupiers' Liability (Scotland) Act 1960 and the duty of care owed at common law.

DIFFERENCES BETWEEN BREACH OF STATUTORY DUTY AND NEGLIGENCE

In Scots law, there are clear differences between breach of statutory duty and **10.7** negligence.

First, the respective duties derive from different conceptual bases. In statutory **10.8** cases, the relevant statute imposes the duty. In negligence, on the other hand, the court determines whether a duty of care at common law is owed. It has been said that a common law duty cannot grow "parasitically" out of a statutory duty which was not intended to be owed to individuals.[16]

Second, the standard of duty may differ in the two causes of action. In the negli- **10.9** gence action the standard is that of reasonable care, whereas, in the action for breach of statutory duty, the standard is fixed by Parliament and is usually higher, for example strict or absolute liability.

A third difference relates to the application of the defence of *volenti non fit injuria*. **10.10** The defence of *volenti* is available to a defender in negligence cases where the pursuer, knowing of a risk of injury, voluntarily accepted that risk. The defence of *volenti* is rarely available in breach of statutory duty cases, however.[17]

Fourth, the two causes of action are treated separately from a pleading point **10.11** of view. So, while the two grounds of action may be combined in the one action, separate and distinct averments should be made in respect of each ground detailing the different bases of the claim and the different standards of duty which apply. The statutory case will benefit the pursuer when the duty is framed in absolute or strict terms. This is illustrated by the case of *Millar v Galashiels Gas Co Ltd*,[18] discussed above, in which the claim based on the absolute statutory duty succeeded, while the claim in negligence failed.

Finally, and this is now of historical interest only, the action for breach of statutory **10.12** duty was not subject to the defence of common employment, which defence often served to defeat claims brought *in negligence* by employees against their employer.[19] This feature of the action for breach of statutory duty therefore invested the statutory ground of action with a considerable advantage over the negligence action from the perspective of the injured employee.

WHEN DOES AN ACTION FOR BREACH OF STATUTORY DUTY LIE?

Essentially, the availability of the action for breach of statutory duty depends on **10.13** the intention of Parliament. Some statutes expressly state that breach of their provi-

---

[16] See *Gorringe v Calderdale MBC* [2004] 1 WLR 1057, per Lord Scott at para 71.
[17] See *Baddeley v Earl Granville* (1887) 19 QBD 423; *Wheeler v New Merton Board Mills* [1933] 2 KB 669. The Occupiers' Liability (Scotland) Act 1960, however, specifically allows the defence of *volenti*: see s 2(3).
[18] 1949 SC (HL) 31.
[19] The doctrine of common employment was abolished in 1948, the Law Reform (Personal Injuries) Act 1948, s 1(1) providing that "[I]t shall not be a defence to an employer who is sued in respect of personal injuries caused by the negligence of a person employed by him, that that person was at the time the injuries were caused in common employment with the person injured."

sions will give rise to a civil remedy in delict. For example, the Copyright, Designs and Patents Act 1988 provides that "an infringement is actionable ... as a breach of statutory duty" (see ss 103 and 194).

10.14 There are other statutes which specifically exclude a civil action for breach of their provisions.[20] The most well-known example of this is found in s 47(1) of the Health and Safety at Work etc Act 1974, which provides that breach of any of the general duties in ss 2–8 of the Act does not give rise to civil liability for breach of statute. The appropriate method of enforcement for breach of these duties is criminal prosecution.

10.15 It should be noted, however, that the *regulations* made under the Health and Safety at Work etc Act 1974 *do* create civil liability unless otherwise provided.[21] An important series of health and safety regulations was introduced by the UK in 1992. These regulations, which are often referred to as the "six-pack regulations", are based on the principle of risk assessment and were brought into effect under the Health and Safety at Work etc Act 1974 in order to implement a series of European Directives. Some of the original regulations have been superseded by later regulations. The regulations are as follows:

Workplace (Health, Safety and Welfare) Regulations 1992 (SI 1992/3004);
Provision and Use of Work Equipment Regulations 1998 (SI 1998/2306);
Personal Protective Equipment at Work Regulations 1992 (SI 1992/2966);
Health and Safety (Display Screen Equipment) Regulations 1992 (SI 1992/2792);
Manual Handling Operations Regulations 1992 (SI 1992/2793);
Management of Health and Safety at Work Regulations 1999 (SI 1999/3242).

Breaches of the above regulations *do* give rise to an action for breach of statutory duty.[22]

10.16 These two categories of statute clearly present little difficulty. In one category, it is quite clear that civil liability may ensue as a result of statutory breach. In the other category, it is clear that civil liability will not result from statutory breach (although liability may arise nevertheless as a result of breach of a common law duty). In both cases, Parliament's intention has been made clear explicitly in the statute itself.

10.17 Greater difficulty is encountered where Parliament has not addressed the question of civil liability and it is to such cases which we now turn. At one time, the view taken was that where a statute prohibited certain conduct and someone was injured as a result of breach, that person could sue the person in breach of statute.[23] As statutory activity increased, however, this early view began to involve the danger of very wide-ranging liability and gradually it came to be discarded. In *Atkinson* v *Newcastle & Gateshead Waterworks*,[24] Lord Cairns LC expressed doubts as to the early approach and pointed out that actionability depends on the *particular* statute. Thus, a more restrictive approach to the action for breach of statute began to develop.

---

[20] See, eg, the Guard Dogs Act 1975, s 5(2) and the Safety of Sports Grounds Act 1975, s 13.
[21] Health and Safety at Work etc Act 1974, s 47(2).
[22] The Management of Health and Safety at Work Regulations 1999 (SI 1999/3242) originally excluded liability for their breach but have been civilly actionable since 2003: see the Management of Health and Safety at Work and Fire Precautions (Workplace) (Amendment) Regulations 2003 (SI 2003/2457). See *McLellan* v *Dundee City Council* 2009 Rep LR 61; *Wallace* v *Glasgow City Council* [2011] CSIH 57.
[23] *Couch* v *Steel* (1854) 3 El & Bl 402.
[24] (1877) 2 Ex D 441.

In the modern law of delict, the basic proposition is that a breach of statutory duty **10.18** does not by itself give rise to any private law cause of action.[25] The pursuer must establish that Parliament intended a civil right of action for breach of statute. The fundamental question is: "Did Parliament intend an action for breach of statutory duty to lie at the instance of a person injured by the breach, when it enacted the duty in question?"

In their search for Parliament's intention, the courts have tended to rely on **10.19** certain presumptions which have developed over the years. These presumptions are discussed in more detail below. It is also important not to underestimate the role which policy plays in decision making in this area.[26] Numerous cases have been brought successfully for breach of the Factories Acts and the Mines and Quarries Act. The courts consider that, as a matter of policy, the action should be available to the injured employee.

In other cases, policy considerations have led the courts to disallow the action. **10.20** Thus policy considerations no doubt played a role in *R* v *Deputy Governor of Parkhurst Prison, ex parte Hague*,[27] where the court denied the action to a prisoner complaining of unlawful segregation in breach of r 43 of the Prison Rules 1964.

PREREQUISITES FOR AN ACTION FOR BREACH OF STATUTORY DUTY

Let us now turn to look at what the pursuer has to establish in an action for breach of **10.21** statutory duty.

The pursuer must show:

(1) that there was a statutory *duty* in force which was imposed on the *defender* and which applied to the situation in question;
(2) that the duty was intended to protect, *inter alios*, the pursuer;
(3) that the statute intended to confer a civil action;
(4) that the harm suffered was of a kind which the statute was intended to prevent;
(5) that there has been a breach of the statutory obligation;
(6) that the breach caused the harm complained of.

Let us now look at these points in more detail.

THERE MUST HAVE BEEN A STATUTORY DUTY IN FORCE WHICH WAS IMPOSED ON THE DEFENDER AND WHICH APPLIED TO THE CIRCUMSTANCES IN QUESTION

The first point to note is that the statute must impose a duty rather than a power on **10.22** the defender. In other words, the statute must be mandatory as opposed to permissive.

---

[25] See Lord Browne-Wilkinson in *X (Minors)* v *Bedfordshire CC* [1995] 2 AC 633 at 731.
[26] The role occupied by policy was expressly acknowledged by Lord Macnaghten in *Pasmore* v *Oswaldtwistle Urban Council* [1898] AC 387 where his Lordship stated at 397–398 that the outcome "must depend on the scope and language of the Act which creates the obligation and on considerations of policy and convenience".
[27] [1992] 1 AC 58.

It must direct the defender to adopt or avoid a certain course of conduct. It is not enough that the statute simply permits the defender to adopt or avoid a certain course of conduct.

10.23   The second point to note is that the duty must have been imposed on the defender.[28] In *ICI* v *Shatwell*,[29] an employee raised an action against his employer for personal injury. The plaintiff's action failed as the statutory duty under consideration was incumbent on himself and his brother rather than on the defendant employer. James and George Shatwell were employees of ICI and were both experienced shotfirers. Statutory regulations governing the industry stated that "No shotfirer shall fire any round of shots ... unless he has tested the circuit for continuity ... A shotfirer shall not make any such test unless all persons in the vicinity have withdrawn to a place of safety and he himself has taken proper shelter". The brothers acted in breach of these regulations and suffered injury. The court concluded that the duty was incumbent on the brothers themselves and not on ICI, which was accordingly not in breach of statutory duty. Finally, the duty must apply to the circumstances in question.[30] Many statutes, for example, apply only to certain types of premises. Thus, many actions averring breach of statutory duty under the Factories Acts have been defeated on the basis that the premises in question were not a "factory." Thus, in *Wood* v *London County Council*,[31] an action averring breach of the Factories Act failed when the court concluded that a hospital kitchen was not a factory. Thus, the legislation did not apply to the premises in question.[32] The limited sphere of operation of the statute again proved crucial in *Chipchase* v *British Titan Products Co Ltd*.[33] There, a workman was injured when he fell from a platform which was 6 feet above the ground. Statutory regulations provided that any working platform from which a person was liable to fall more than 6 feet 6 inches had to be at least 34 inches wide. The platform on which the plaintiff was working was only 9 inches wide. The plaintiff's action failed as the regulations had no application in the circumstances of the case.[34]

10.24   In *Given* v *James Watt College*[35] the pursuer, who was employed as a kitchen assistant by the defender, suffered injury at work. At the relevant time, she was standing in the vicinity of a drinks dispensing machine when it malfunctioned, hissed loudly and emitted quantities of steam. It then emitted a flash, which caused the pursuer to jump back and fall heavily on the floor. She raised an action against her employer alleging,

---

[28] See *Harrison* v *National Coal Board* [1951] AC 639; *Coutts* v *J M Piggins* 1983 SLT 320; *King* v *RCO Support Services Ltd and Yorkshire Traction Co Ltd* [2001] ICR 608; *Nisbet* v *Orr and North Lanarkshire Council* 2002 GWD 13–444. Cf *Smith* v *Cammell Laird & Co Ltd* [1940] AC 242; *Donaghey* v *Boulton & Paul Ltd* [1968] AC 1.

[29] [1965] AC 656.

[30] See *Gill* v *Humberstone & Co Ltd* [1963] 1 WLR 929; *Gorringe* v *Calderdale MBC* [2004] 1 WLR 1057; *Shine* v *London Borough of Tower Hamlets* [2006] EWCA Civ 852; *King* v *Carron Phoenix Ltd* 1999 Rep LR 51; *Hughes* v *Grampian Country Food Group* 2007 SLT 635; *Smith* v *Northamptonshire CC* [2009] 4 All ER 557; *Bruce* v *Ben Odeco Ltd* 1996 SC 389; *Munro* v *Aberdeen City Council* 2009 SLT 964. Cf *Matthews* v *Glasgow City Council* 2006 SC 34; *Spencer-Franks* v *Kellogg Brown and Root Ltd* 2008 SC (HL) 159; *Littlejohn* v *Wood & Davidson Ltd* 1997 SLT 1353.

[31] [1941] 2 KB 232.

[32] See, also, *Longhurst* v *Guildford, Godalming and District Water Board* [1963] AC 265. Note that the Workplace (Health, Safety and Welfare) Regulations 1992 (SI 1992/3004), which were introduced to replace the Factories Act, apply to workplaces in general and are not restricted to factories.

[33] [1956] 1 QB 545. See, also, *Ruine* v *Roger* 1997 SLT (Notes) 46.

[34] See, also, *Ashbridge* v *Christian Salvesen plc* 2006 SLT 697 where the Control of Substances Hazardous to Health Regulations 1999 (SI 1999/437) were held not to apply to a caustic soda solution of less than 0.5%, such a concentration being below the limits referred to in the list of hazardous substances.

[35] 2007 SLT 39.

inter alia, breach of reg 5(1) of the Provision and Use of Work Equipment Regulations 1998.[36] The college argued that that provision did not apply to the circumstances in question. In its view, the regulation could be prayed in aid only by an employee who was actually using work equipment in the course of his work at the time when the accident occurred. It did not protect someone in Mrs Given's position who was merely passing by or standing near the machine in question. That argument was rejected by the Lord Ordinary (Emslie) who declared:[37]

> "I am not attracted by a suggested interpretation which would permit recovery to (say) a lathe operator injured by the catastrophic failure of his machine while he was actually using it, but none at all to (a) an apprentice or trainee observing the work; (b) a supervising foreman or manager; (c) a neighbouring lathe operator working on his own machine; or (d) the original lathe operator while in the vicinity of the machine either before or after actual operation. Similarly, I am not attracted by a suggested interpretation on which the sudden collapse of a hoist or scaffolding would afford no right of action to an employee hurt while working underneath. In my view such limitations would ... lead to a strange situation in which work equipment would somehow float in and out of the scope of the regulations during the course of a working day and in which extremely difficult questions would arise as to the point at which the statutory protections might be held to apply or to fly off."

His Lordship concluded that, on an application of the definitional provisions in regs 2(1) and 3(2), the machine was provided by the college for use by canteen employees, it was fully operational and available for such use at the material time. It was thus "work equipment" as defined for the purposes of the Regulations and held that qualifying character at the time the accident occurred. The pursuer's statutory case against the defender was accordingly made out.

10.25

THE DUTY MUST BE INTENDED TO PROTECT, *INTER ALIOS,* THE PURSUER

To succeed in an action for breach of statutory duty the pursuer must establish that he was one of those for whose benefit the statutory duty was imposed.[38] The leading case is *Cutler* v *Wandsworth Stadium*.[39] There, the plaintiff, a bookmaker, raised an action against a licensed dog track, Wandsworth Stadium, in respect of its refusal to allow him space on the track premises to carry on bookmaking. The plaintiff argued that the occupier of the stadium operated his own bookmaking business (the totalisator) and had denied him access in order to safeguard his own monopoly. The plaintiff, who lost revenue owing to the defendant's refusal to admit him, founded on the Betting and Lotteries Act 1934 which provided in s 11(2) that the track occupier "shall take such steps as are necessary to secure that ... there is available for the bookmakers space on the track where they can conveniently carry on bookmaking in connection with dog races run on the track". The House of Lords concluded, however, that the provision was intended to protect the public by providing competition rather than to protect bookmakers such as the plaintiff, whose action accordingly failed. Lord Reid posed

10.26

---

[36] SI 1998/2306.
[37] 2007 SLT 39 at para 31.
[38] See *Knapp* v *Railway Executive* [1949] 2 All ER 508.
[39] [1949] AC 398.

the question:[40] "For whose benefit was this subsection intended? The appellant's case is that it was primarily if not solely for the benefit of bookmakers. I do not think so. I think that it was primarily intended for the protection of those members of the public who might wish to bet on these tracks."

10.27   Again, in *Brown v Carlin*[41] the pursuer went on to the defender's premises and was splashed with petrol and burned. He raised an action averring breach of the Highly Flammable Liquids and Liquefied Petroleum Gases Regulations 1972,[42] which were made under the Factories Act 1961. However, the Act was only intended for the protection of persons employed, in whatever capacity and by whomsoever, in premises covered by the Act. As the pursuer was merely a casual visitor to the premises, he was not someone for whose protection the Act was intended to provide. He therefore failed in his action based on statutory breach.

10.28   Similarly, in *Donaldson v Hayes Distribution Services Ltd*[43] the relevant statutory provisions were held to afford no protection to the injured party, who was simply a visitor to the workplace. There, the pursuer suffered injury when she was crushed between a reversing lorry and a loading bay at a shopping centre. She based her action, *inter alia*, on alleged breach of reg 17 of the Workplace (Health, Safety and Welfare) Regulations 1992.[44] The Inner House held, however, that the Workplace Regulations were designed to implement the Workplace Directive which applied exclusively for the protection of *workers*. When she sustained injury, the pursuer had been present in a workplace not as a worker but as a visitor, and, as such, she did not fall within the scope of protection of the Regulations.

10.29   In *Pullar v Window Clean Ltd and Scottish Special Housing Association*,[45] Pullar, a window cleaner, was sent to clean the second-floor window of a building which was owned and occupied by the second-named defenders. He could not clean the outside of the window from inside. He therefore went outside on to the sill where he lost his balance, fell and was injured. He raised an action averring, *inter alia*, breach of statutory duty by the SSHA. He averred that in terms of s 52 of the Edinburgh Corporation (Streets, Buildings and Sewers) Order Confirmation Act 1926, the SSHA had a duty to ensure that the window was constructed to allow the outside of it to be cleaned from inside. On appeal to the Inner House, Lord President Clyde concluded[46] that s 52 did not "constitute a charter for window cleaners" but formed part of the building code for the city and as such did not ground an action for breach of statutory duty. The main purpose of the provision was the maintenance and improvement of the safety of buildings, not the safety of window cleaners.[47]

---

[40] [1949] AC 398 at 416.
[41] 1996 SCLR 739.
[42] SI 1972/917.
[43] 2005 1 SC 523.
[44] SI 1992/3004.
[45] 1956 SC 13.
[46] *Ibid* at 22.
[47] The Lord President, in delivering his judgment, also appears to have been influenced by the fact that compliance with the provision was secured by the penalty provisions of s 34 "which appear to ... be adequate for the purpose" (1956 SC 13 at 22).

THE STATUTE INTENDED TO CONFER A CIVIL ACTION

We have noted that before an action for breach of statutory duty will lie there must be **10.30** evident a legislative intention to allow such an action.[48]

The modern approach is illustrated by the House of Lords' decision in *X (Minors)* **10.31** v *Bedfordshire County Council*,[49] where five separate appeals were brought before their Lordships.

In *Bedfordshire*, five siblings claimed that they had suffered a catalogue of parental **10.32** abuse over a period of 5 years. They claimed that the local authority had breached duties imposed on it by the childcare legislation by failing to investigate the matter properly or to protect the children from further harm, despite receiving reports from the NSPCC, neighbours, the family GP and relatives.

In one of the appeals, *M* v *Newham London Borough Council*, a minor plaintiff, M, **10.33** and her mother sought damages from the local authority, the Area Health Authority and a consultant psychiatrist for both breach of statutory duty and negligence. The facts of the case were that a psychiatrist had interviewed M in the presence of a local authority social worker to determine whether M had been sexually abused and, if so, by whom. Having concluded that the child had been sexually abused, the psychiatrist and the social worker wrongly identified the mother's cohabitee as the abuser, with the result that court orders were obtained to remove M from her mother. The error was eventually detected. Both M and her mother subsequently claimed damages for psychiatric injury as a result of their separation of almost a year.

Their Lordships, in considering the two cases, concluded that the childcare legis- **10.34** lation did not give rise to a claim for breach of statutory duty. Lord Browne-Wilkinson, delivering the leading judgment, pointed out[50] that the purpose of the legislation was "to establish an administrative system designed to promote the social welfare of the community". Difficult and sensitive decisions often had to be made (on the basis of disputed facts) about whether to split the family in order to protect the child. His Lordship concluded:[51]

> "in such a context it would require exceptionally clear statutory language to show a parlia-
> mentary intention that those responsible for carrying out these difficult functions should
> be liable in damages, if, on subsequent investigation with the benefit of hindsight, it was
> shown that they had reached an erroneous conclusion and therefore failed to discharge their
> statutory duties ... When one turns to the actual words used in the primary legislation ...
> they are inconsistent with any intention to create a private law cause of action."

The decision demonstrates that the court must have regard to the statutory wording in **10.35** order to ascertain whether there exists a parliamentary intention to confer a civil right of action on those who suffer loss or injury as a result of the statutory breach.

In another of the five appeals, *Keating* v *Bromley London County Council*, their **10.36** Lordships required to consider the breach of statutory duty claim in the context of

---

[48] Reference may now be made to *Hansard* in an effort to determine Parliament's intention: see *Pepper* v *Hart* [1993] 1 All ER 42. Scrutiny of the parliamentary proceedings has not always proved particularly productive, however: see the comments of Russell LJ in *Richardson* v *Pitt-Stanley* [1995] QB 123 at 128 and those of the sheriff principal (Bowen) in *Quinn* v *McGinty* 1999 SLT (Sh Ct) 27 at 29.
[49] [1995] 2 AC 633.
[50] *Ibid* at 747.
[51] *Ibid*.

education legislation. The plaintiff claimed, *inter alia*, that the local authority had failed to provide him with adequate primary and/or secondary education. Again, the House could not discern a parliamentary intention to allow an action for breach of statutory duty. Lord Browne-Wilkinson discussed a number of reasons why the action should not be allowed. First, the wide-ranging duties imposed on local authorities under the education legislation were of an unspecific and discretionary nature and such duties are not generally considered to give rise to a right of action. Also, the legislation involved the parents in every stage of the decision-making process and gave them rights of appeal. His Lordship concluded:[52]

> "Although for present purposes, I am prepared to assume that the plaintiff, as a child having special educational needs, was a member of a class for whose protection the statutory provisions were enacted, I can find nothing in either set of statutory provisions which demonstrates a parliamentary intention to give that class a statutory right of action for damages."

10.37   The matter, therefore, is one of statutory construction. It is difficult to generalise as to when an action will lie for breach of statutory duty. Much will depend on the policy considerations involved and the context of the statute. In *Cutler* v *Wandsworth Stadium*,[53] the facts of which case are recounted above, Lord Simonds did "not propose to try to formulate any rules by reference to which such a question can infallibly be answered".[54] His Lordship went on to say that: "[t]he only rule which in all circumstances is valid is that the answer must depend on a consideration of the whole Act and the circumstances including the pre-existing law in which it was enacted".[55]

10.38   In *Morrison Sports Ltd* v *Scottish Power plc*[56] the pursuers in three related actions sought damages in respect of fire damage to properties which they owned or occupied. The damage was said to result from alleged breaches of the Electricity Supply Regulations 1988[57] by the defenders. An action for breach of statutory duty was denied by the Supreme Court. There were provisions in both the parent legislation and the 1988 Regulations which pointed to the conclusion that the Regulations were to be enforced by the Secretary of State and those appointed to act on his behalf, rather than by individuals raising private actions. That conclusion was buttressed by the fact that it was difficult to identify any limited class of the public for whose protection the 1988 Regulations were enacted, and on whom Parliament had intended to confer a private right of action for breach thereof.

10.39   The "construction" approach is further illustrated in the case of *Issa and Another* v *Hackney London Borough Council*.[58] The plaintiffs' parents were granted a tenancy of council accommodation in London in 1985. The plaintiffs, at that time, were aged 9 and 7 and both suffered from asthma. The premises were badly affected by condensation and mould growth and were prejudicial to health. In 1989, the council pled guilty to offences under Pt III of the Public Health Act 1936 and was fined. In 1992, the

---

[52] [1995] 2 AC 633 at 769.
[53] [1949] AC 398.
[54] *Ibid* at 407.
[55] *Ibid.*
[56] 2011 SC (UKSC) 1.
[57] SI 1988/1057.
[58] [1997] 1 WLR 956.

plaintiffs brought an action against the council seeking damages in respect of ill health allegedly suffered as a result of the state of the premises, which, they claimed, had aggravated their asthmatic conditions. It was common ground that the availability of the civil action for breach of statutory duty depended on the construction of Pt III of the 1936 Act as a whole. The Court of Appeal, in delivering its judgment, stressed that the effect of Pt III of the 1936 Act had to be judged at the date of its enactment. Their Lordships concluded, in a unanimous judgment, that there were no grounds for construing the Act so as to incorporate the creation of a civil cause of action. As a matter of practice, the courts, in seeking to determine Parliament's intention, frequently have resort to a number of presumptions. These presumptions will now be considered along with other considerations which appear to influence judicial determination in this area.

The first presumption

In *Doe dem Murray, Lord Bishop of Rochester* v *Bridges*[59] Lord Tenterden stated:[60]   **10.40**
"[W]here an Act creates an obligation and enforces the performance in a specified manner, we take it to be a general rule that performance cannot be enforced in any other manner." The first presumption is therefore that if the statute provides a specific means of enforcement of the statutory duty, then the presumption is that Parliament did not intend the additional remedy of an action for statutory breach. Thus, if there is a criminal sanction set out in the statute, such as a fine, the presumption is against the action for breach of statutory duty.[61] It is important to note that the specific means of enforcement need not be a financial remedy. Therefore, a remedy by way of complaint to a Minister can preclude a remedy by way of action for breach of statutory duty.[62]

The case of *Atkinson* v *Newcastle & Gateshead Waterworks*[63] illustrates the application   **10.41**
of the first presumption. The defendant company was under a duty imposed by the Waterworks Clauses Act 1847, to fix fireplugs at intervals along the street and to keep them charged up with water to the prescribed pressure. A fire broke out at the plaintiff's premises. There was insufficient water in the pipes to allow the fire to be fought satisfactorily. The plaintiff's premises were destroyed. He raised an action for breach of statutory duty against the water company. The action was unsuccessful because the statute provided for the imposition of a £10 fine for breach of the duty.[64]

Similarly, in *Cutler* v *Wandsworth Stadium*,[65] discussed above, the Betting and   **10.42**
Lotteries Act 1934 provided a criminal sanction for breach of its provisions. Therefore,

---

[59] (1831) 1 B & Ad 847.
[60] *Ibid* at 859.
[61] See *Pullar* v *Window Clean Ltd and Scottish Special Housing Association* 1956 SC 13; *Square* v *Model Farm Dairies (Bournemouth) Ltd* [1939] 2 KB 365; *Balmer* v *Hayes* 1950 SC 477; *Coutts* v *J M Piggins Ltd* 1983 SLT 320; *Phillips* v *Brittania Hygienic Laundry Co Ltd* [1923] 2 KB 832; *Tan Chye Choo* v *Chong Kew Moi* [1970] 1 WLR 147; *Issa and Anor* v *Hackney LBC* [1997] 1 WLR 956; *W L Tinney & Co Ltd* v *John C Dougall Ltd* 1997 SLT (Notes) 58.
[62] See *Pasmore* v *Oswaldtwistle UDC* [1898] AC 387 (a remedy by way of complaint to the Local Government Board was held to preclude a right of action upon the Public Health Act 1875); *Phelps* v *Hillingdon LBC* [2001] 2 AC 619 (a right of action under the education legislation was denied in respect of a failure to identify the plaintiff's dyslexia, there being an appeals procedure in place in respect of the relevant process as well as the possibility of judicial review).
[63] (1877) LR 2 Ex D 441.
[64] Note, also, the comments of Lord Cairns LC at 446 to the effect that if liability were to be imposed "[the company] would virtually become gratuitous insurers of the safety from fire".
[65] [1949] AC 398.

the general presumption applied and denied a civil right of action to the disappointed bookmaker who had been excluded from the grounds. Lord Reid stated:[66] "The sanction of prosecution appears to me to be appropriate and sufficient for the general obligation imposed."

10.43   *Lonrho Ltd* v *Shell Petroleum Co*[67] provides a further illustration of the application of the first presumption. The case concerned an alleged breach by Shell of the sanctions orders which had been imposed in relation to trade with the breakaway regime of Ian Smith in Southern Rhodesia. A criminal sanction was provided for breach and in those circumstances the presumption was against the availability of an action for breach of statutory duty.

10.44   The first presumption (against the action for breach of statutory duty where there is a specific mode of enforcement contained in the statute) has two exceptions. These exceptions were set out by Lord Diplock in his judgment in *Lonrho*:[68] "The first is where on the true construction of the Act it is apparent that the obligation or prohibition was imposed for the benefit or protection of a particular class of individuals, as in the case of the Factories Acts and similar legislation." The first exception makes clear that, even if the statutory provision does provide its own enforcement machinery, an action for breach of statutory duty may nevertheless lie, provided that the statute was designed to protect a particular class of individuals as opposed to the public in general.

10.45   This exception explains why the courts have allowed actions for breach of the Factories Acts 1937 and 1961 at the instance of injured employees, notwithstanding the imposition of criminal penalties for breach of the legislation. Workers have traditionally been regarded as a particular class and much litigation has occurred over the years in relation to injuries alleged to have resulted from breaches of the factories legislation. The *locus classicus* is *Groves* v *Lord Wimborne*.[69] There, the occupier of a factory was required to fence dangerous machinery under the Factory and Workshop Act 1878. Breach of this provision carried a fine of £100. A boy who was employed in the factory caught his arm in part of the machine which was unfenced. His arm required to be amputated. Notwithstanding the imposition of a fine, his action for breach of statutory duty was allowed. The statute provided that the whole or part of the fine might, if the Secretary of State so determined, be payable to the injured employee. However, the Court of Appeal emphasised that there was no guarantee that the victim would receive any part of the fine and, in any event, the upper limit of £100 seemed insufficient compensation for death or very severe injury.

10.46   The application of the class protection exception is not limited to personal injury cases. In *Rickless* v *United Artists Corporation*[70] the class protection exception was mobilised in relation to breaches of the Dramatic and Musical Performers' Protection Act 1958. There, a film was produced without the consent of the performer (Peter Sellars) or his representatives having been obtained. Despite the existence of a criminal

---

[66] [1949] AC 398 at 418.
[67] [1982] AC 173.
[68] *Ibid* at 185.
[69] [1898] 2 QB 402. See, also, *Kelly* v *Glebe Sugar Refining Co* (1893) 20R 833. For further examples of the class protection exception in the context of personal injury (or fatal) cases, see *Black* v *Fife Coal Co Ltd* 1912 SC (HL) 33 (see, in particular, the observations of Lord Kinnear at 45); *Littlejohn* v *Wood & Davidson Ltd* 1997 SLT 1353; *Solomons* v *Gertzenstein Ltd* [1954] 2 QB 243; *Ziemniak* v *ETPM Deep Sea Ltd* [2003] 2 Lloyd's Rep 214.
[70] [1988] QB 40.

penalty, an action upon the statute was permitted, the protection of a limited class, namely performers, being the clear intention of the legislation.

The court requires to consider whether the legislation was passed primarily for the benefit of society at large or whether it was passed primarily to protect a particular class of individuals. If a class of individuals receives only an incidental benefit from the legislation this will be insufficient to found an action. Rather, the legislation must be intended *primarily* for their benefit. Thus, in *Cutler*, discussed above, the House of Lords concluded that there was no action for breach of statutory duty available to the disappointed bookmaker because the legislation in question was passed primarily for the benefit of the general public.[71]   **10.47**

The "class protection" approach has not escaped criticism. In *Phillips* v *Brittania Hygienic Laundry*,[72] Atkin, LJ commented:[73] "It would be strange if a less important duty, which is owed to a section of the public, may be enforced by an action, while a more important duty which is owed to the public at large cannot." One of the obvious difficulties with the class protection approach is that it is difficult to determine in advance the amount of common identity necessary to constitute a defined class.[74] This imbues the law with an unacceptable level of uncertainty. For example, while employees have traditionally been regarded as a distinct class,[75] road users have often not been so regarded.[76] It is difficult to understand why this should be so.   **10.48**

The second exception to the presumption of non-actionability where there is an alternative mode of enforcement is set out by Lord Diplock in *Lonrho*:[77] "The second exception is where the statute creates a public right ... and a particular member of the public suffers ... 'particular, direct, and substantial' damage 'other and different from that which was common to all the rest of the public'."   **10.49**

In *Lonrho*, the sanctions orders prohibiting the supply of oil to Southern Rhodesia were breached. This resulted in the prolongation of the illegal regime. The plaintiffs suffered loss as their pipeline was out of commission for longer than would have been the case had the illegal regime been brought to an end more swiftly. There was   **10.50**

---

[71] The courts have tended to view welfare legislation as being intended to protect the public at large rather than any particular class of it: see *X (Minors)* v *Bedfordshire CC* [1995] 2 AC 633, per Lord Browne-Wilkinson at 731–732; *O'Rourke* v *Camden LBC* [1998] AC 188, per Lord Hoffmann at 193. For other cases in which plaintiffs were unable to bring themselves within the "class protection" exception, see *Bollinger* v *Costa Brava Wine Co Ltd* [1960] Ch 262 (where it was held that the Merchandise Marks Act 1887 was designed to protect the purchasers of goods which might be misleadingly described rather than rival traders such as the plaintiffs); *Richardson* v *Pitt-Stanley* [1995] QB 123 (where a majority of the Court of Appeal held the Employers' Liability (Compulsory Insurance) Act 1969 did not have as its sole purpose the safeguarding of an injured employee against a barren judgment – its purpose might just as readily be said to be the protection of the employer against a disastrously large claim (cf *Quinn* v *McGinty* 1999 SLT (Sh Ct) 27)).

[72] [1923] 2 KB 832.

[73] *Ibid* at 841.

[74] See, eg, *Johanneson* v *Lothian RC* 1996 SLT (Sh Ct) 74, where the pursuer submitted that "persons occupying or frequenting the premises" (of a local authority school) was a reasonably definable class whereas the defender took the view that the class was too wide and insufficiently defined. In the event, the sheriff principal did not require to decide the point.

[75] *Groves* v *Lord Wimborne* [1898] 2 QB 402; *Black* v *Fife Coal Co Ltd* 1912 SC (HL) 33.

[76] See the comments of Bankes LJ in *Phillips* v *Brittania Hygienic Laundry Co Ltd* [1923] 2 KB 832 at 840 and those of Somervell LJ in *Solomons* v *Gertzenstein Ltd* [1954] 2 QB 243 at 255. See, however, *McArthur* v *Strathclyde RC* 1995 SLT 1129 where Lord Abernethy was prepared to regard road users as a distinct class and the observations of Pill LJ in *Roe* v *Sheffield City Council* [2004] QB 653 at para 49. The judicial approach taken to road users is by no means uniform.

[77] [1982] AC 173 at 185.

a criminal penalty for the breach of the sanctions orders. This, therefore, gave rise to the presumption that no additional remedy was available. The House of Lords then considered whether either of the two exceptions, discussed above, applied. Their Lordships dismissed the first exception as inapplicable as the sanctions orders were not imposed for the benefit of a particular class. The second exception was similarly inapplicable. The statutory provisions did not create any public right to be enjoyed by all Her Majesty's subjects who wished to avail themselves of it. Lord Diplock quoted with approval from Fox, LJ in the court below: "I cannot think that they were concerned with conferring rights either on individuals or the public at large. Their purpose was the destruction, by economic pressure, of the UDI regime in Southern Rhodesia; they were instruments of state policy in an international matter."[78] Lord Diplock pointed out that a mere prohibition on members of the public generally from doing what it would otherwise be lawful for them to do is not enough to give rise to a public right on which a claim for breach of statutory duty can be based. The writers are unaware of any case in which Lord Diplock's second exception to the first presumption has been successfully invoked.

The second presumption

10.51   The second presumption, like the first, finds expression in the *dictum* of Lord Tenterden in *Doe dem Murray, Lord Bishop of Rochester v Bridges*.[79] His Lordship stated:[80] "If an obligation is created [by an Act], but no mode of enforcing its performance is ordained, the common law may, in general, find a mode suited to the particular nature of the case." Thus, if a statute does not provide any criminal or other sanction, it is presumed that the action for breach of statutory duty *is* available. If it were not so, the provision in question would have no effective force or, as Lord Simonds stated in *Cutler*,[81] "the statute would be but a pious aspiration". The courts, in short, are reluctant to hold that a statutory provision is, in effect, toothless.[82]

10.52   In *Dawson v Bingley Urban District Council*[83] the defendant provided a notice indicating the wrong position of a fireplug. This contravened s 66 of the Public Health Act 1875. When a fire broke out at the plaintiff's premises, there was a delay in extinguishing it owing to the fire brigade's inability to find the exact position of the fireplug. The plaintiff was held entitled to a private law remedy for breach of statutory duty because the statute did not provide a penalty.

10.53   More recently, in *Kirvek Management and Consulting Services Ltd v Attorney General of Trinidad and Tobago*[84] the Privy Council allowed a right of action based on breach of the Court Funds Investment Act 1980. Sums lodged with the court as security for costs were not held in an interest-bearing account as directed by the statute. Following settlement of the action, the funds were returned to the plaintiff without interest. No

---

[78] [1982] AC 173 at 186.
[79] (1831) 1 B & Ad 847.
[80] *Ibid* at 859.
[81] [1949] AC 398 at 407.
[82] In *X (Minors) v Bedfordshire CC* [1995] 2 AC 633 Lord Browne-Wilkinson articulated the position as follows (at 731): "If the statute provides no other remedy for its breach and the Parliamentary intention to protect a limited class is shown, that indicates that there may be a private right of action since otherwise there is no method of securing the protection the statute was intended to confer."
[83] [1911] 2 KB 149.
[84] [2002] 1 WLR 2792.

enforcement procedure was stipulated in the Act itself and, in those circumstances, the Privy Council held that a private law right of action was available in respect of the breach of statutory duty.

The third presumption

Aside from the two presumptions extracted from *Doe dem Murray*, there is another **10.54** presumption which assists in ascertaining Parliament's intention.

If the statute does not provide a specific mode of enforcement but adequate common **10.55** law remedies are available, then the presumption is that Parliament did not intend an action for breach of statutory duty to lie. For example, in *J Bollinger v Costa Brava Wine Co Ltd*,[85] the defendants, a Spanish company, marketed a Spanish wine, using the name "champagne". The plaintiffs were manufacturers of champagne from the Champagne region in France and brought an action against the defendants, alleging infringement of the Merchandise Marks Act 1887. The court held that the statute did not give a rival trader a right to sue for breach of statutory duty. In reaching its decision the court was influenced by the fact that the Act preserved the right to proceed with a common law action for passing off.[86]

The existing common law remedy (which leads to the presumption against the **10.56** action for breach of statutory duty) need not be a delictual remedy. If the pursuer has an adequate remedy for breach of contract, the presumption against the action for breach of statutory duty still operates.[87] What is the position, however, if the pursuer could seek judicial review? Professor Thomson[88] points out that judicial review is a procedure rather than a remedy and submits that, although the position is unclear, the right to seek judicial review should not be presumed to exclude the possibility of civil action upon the statute. Stanton *et al*, on the other hand, suggest that "the existence of standard … administrative law remedies should be regarded as raising a presumption of non-actionability".[89] Certainly, in many cases where judicial review has been available, an action upon the statute has been denied.[90]

It is important to note that the presumptions are not in all cases determinative of **10.57** the issue. Should the statutory intention point towards a different conclusion, then the presumptions must yield to that statutory intent.[91]

---

[85] [1960] Ch 262.
[86] Note, however, that in the context of industrial safety, the existence of the negligence action does not bar the action for breach of statutory duty.
[87] See *McCall v Abelesz* [1976] QB 585; *W L Tinney & Co Ltd v John C Dougall Ltd* 1977 SLT (Notes) 58; *Square v Model Farm Dairies (Bournemouth), Ltd* [1939] 2 KB 365.
[88] J Thomson, *Delictual Liability* (4th edn, 2009), p 215.
[89] K Stanton *et al*, *Statutory Torts* (2003), para 2.040.
[90] See *Olutu v Home Office* [1997] 1 WLR 328; *R v Deputy Governor of Parkhurst Prison, ex parte Hague* [1992] 1 AC 58; *Clunis v Camden & Islington Health Authority* [1998] QB 978; *O'Rourke v Camden LBC* [1998] AC 188; *Phelps v Hillingdon LBC* [2001] 2 AC 619; *Cullen v Chief Constable of the Royal Ulster Constabulary* [2003] 1 WLR 1763. For a fuller discussion of this matter, see E Russell, *Delict* (J M Thomson (ed)) (SULI, 2009), paras 6.63–6.69.
[91] See Lord Diplock's judgment in *Lonrho Ltd v Shell Petroleum Co* [1982] AC 173 and Lord Bridge's judgment in *R v Deputy Governor of Parkhurst Prison, ex parte Hague* [1992] 1 AC 58. See, also, Lord Browne-Wilkinson in *X (Minors) v Bedfordshire CC* [1995] 2 AC 633 at 731.

Lord Browne-Wilkinson's "two-stage" approach

10.58 In *X (Minors)* v *Bedfordshire County Council*,[92] Lord Browne-Wilkinson advanced a two-stage approach to the question of whether a particular statutory provision is civilly actionable. His Lordship stated:[93] "... a private law cause of action will arise if it can be shown, as a matter of construction of the statute, that the statutory duty was imposed for the protection of a limited class of the public and that Parliament intended to confer on members of that class a private right of action for breach of the duty." While the class protection criterion clearly features in this approach, it is being used here in a different manner from its traditional use. It will be remembered that under the presumptions approach, membership of a class justifies an exception to the presumption of non-actionability where a penal sanction exists. Under Lord Browne-Wilkinson's approach, it acts as a precondition for the action for breach of statutory duty. If class membership can be demonstrated, it remains for the pursuer to show that Parliament intended members of that class to have a right of action.[94]

Other guidelines

10.59 Apart from the approaches discussed above, there are other factors which influence decision making in this area: for example, the type of loss which has been occasioned.[95] Where the pursuer has been physically injured or where his property has been damaged the courts are more willing to infer a parliamentary intention to allow the action than, say, in a case of pure economic loss.[96] Thus, the courts traditionally allow the action for breach of statutory duty where employees have been physically injured[97] but do not generally allow the action where the loss is purely economic in nature, as was the case in *Cutler*, where it will be remembered that the disappointed bookmaker failed to recover.[98]

---

[92] [1995] 2 AC 633.

[93] *Ibid* at 731.

[94] For an application of this approach, see *Todd* v *Adams* [2002] 2 Lloyd's Rep 293 where the first but not the second hurdle was held to be satisfied. The two-stage test was again applied in *St John Poulton's Trustee in Bankruptcy* v *Ministry of Justice* [2010] 3 WLR 1237. Again, the first but not the second hurdle was satisfied.

[95] See the observations of Lord Bridge in *Pickering* v *Liverpool Daily Post and Echo Newspapers plc* [1991] 2 AC 370 at 420. The case concerned publication of unauthorised information about a patient's application for discharge to a mental health review tribunal. This was said not to be capable of causing loss of a kind for which the law awards compensation.

[96] See J F Clerk and W H B Lindsell, *Torts*, (A Dugdale and M Jones (eds), 20th rev edn, 2010), para 9–12. See, also, *Richardson* v *Pitt-Stanley* [1995] QB 123 where Stuart-Smith LJ observed at 132: "In my opinion, the court will more readily construe a statutory provision so as to provide a civil cause of action where the provision relates to the safety and health of a class of persons rather than where they have merely suffered economic loss." It would be to go too far, however, to state that claims under the relevant statute are necessarily destined to failure where the losses are economic in nature. Indeed, in *Monk* v *Warbey* [1935] 1 KB 75, *Rickless* v *United Artists Corporation* [1988] QB 40 and *Kirvek Management and Consulting Services Ltd* v *Attorney General of Trinidad and Tobago* [2002] 1 WLR 2792 an action on the statute was permitted in circumstances where the losses were economic in nature. See, also, the comments of Sh Pr Bowen in *Quinn* v *McGinty* 1999 SLT (Sh Ct) 27 at 29: "I am unimpressed, unlike the majority in *Richardson*, by the fact that other statutes in which civil liability has been found tend to deal with physical injury. That ... certainly did not arise in the *Lonrho* v *Shell* case which related purely to economic losses and in which there was no suggestion that this alone excluded the possibility of a civil claim."

[97] See, eg, *Groves* v *Lord Wimborne* [1898] 2 QB 402; *Black* v *Fife Coal Co Ltd* 1912 SC (HL) 33; *National Coal Board* v *England* [1954] AC 403, HL.

[98] For a further case of pure economic loss where an action on the relevant statute was denied, see *Wentworth* v *Wiltshire CC* [1993] QB 654.

The more specific the duty, the more likely an action is to lie.[99] General admin- **10.60** istrative duties involving wide discretion on the part of the defender are less likely to generate an action upon the statute. This point was articulated by Lord Browne-Wilkinson in *X (Minors) v Bedfordshire County Council*,[100] where his Lordship stated:[101] "The cases where a private right of action for breach of statutory duty have been held to arise are all cases in which the statutory duty has been very limited and specific as opposed to general administrative functions imposed on public bodies and involving the exercise of administrative discretions."[102]

Legislation which is regulatory in nature is not generally found to generate an **10.61** action for breach of statutory duty. In *R v Deputy Governor of Parkhurst Prison, ex parte Hague*,[103] a prisoner claimed that he had been unlawfully segregated from other prisoners. A statutory case based upon alleged breach of the Prison Rules 1964 was rejected. Lord Jauncey observed:[104] "The rules are regulatory in character, they provide a framework within which the prison regime operates but they are not intended to protect prisoners against loss, injury and damage nor to give them a right of action in respect thereof."

Finally, the prevailing judicial policy is against allowing the action for breach of **10.62** statutory duty in relation to breaches of duties imposed on public authorities. In *T (A minor) v Surrey County Council*[105] a child was injured by a childminder who had been implicated in a previous case involving non-accidental injuries to a child in her care. The local authority, however, had failed to remove her name from the register. In other words, the authority failed to maintain its register of childminders adequately. Such failure was contrary to certain statutory provisions contained in the Nurseries and Childminders Regulation Act 1948. Failure by the authority to meet its implied obligations under the Act to suspend the childminder was held not to confer a private law right of action for breach of statutory duty. Scott Baker J stated[106] that there seemed to be "considerable reluctance on the part of the courts to impose upon local authorities any liability for breach of a statutory duty other than that expressly imposed in the statute".[107]

THE HARM SUFFERED IS OF A KIND WHICH THE STATUTE WAS INTENDED TO PREVENT

An action for breach of statutory duty will be available only if the harm suffered by **10.63** the pursuer is of a kind which the statutory provision was intended to prevent. Thus, the defender will only be liable if the harm suffered falls within the scope of the risk contemplated by the statute. In the leading case of *Gorris v Scott*,[108] the Contagious

---

[99] See the observations of Pill LJ in *Roe v Sheffield City Council* [2004] QB 653 at para 49.
[100] [1995] 2 AC 633.
[101] *Ibid* at 732.
[102] See, also, the observations of Stuart-Smith LJ, delivering the judgment of the Court of Appeal, in *Capital and Counties plc v Hampshire CC* [1997] QB 1004 at 1050.
[103] [1992] 1 AC 58.
[104] *Ibid* at 172.
[105] [1994] 4 All ER 577.
[106] *Ibid* at 597.
[107] Such reluctance is illustrated in the House of Lords' decisions in *X (Minors) v Bedfordshire CC* [1995] 2 AC 633, *Phelps v Hillingdon LBC* [2001] 2 AC 619 and *O'Rourke v Camden LBC* [1998] AC 188.
[108] (1874) LR 9 Exch 125.

Diseases (Animals) Act 1869 provided that sheep and cattle be carried in pens of certain specifications when being transported by sea. The defendant disregarded these provisions and the plaintiff's sheep were washed overboard in rough weather and drowned. This would not have occurred had pens been provided. The plaintiff's action for breach of statutory duty was unsuccessful because the purpose of the statute was to prevent the spread of disease (murrain). The harm which materialised (drowning) was outwith the scope of risks envisaged by the Act.[109] Similarly, in *Nicholls v F Austin (Leyton) Ltd*,[110] a girl was injured when a piece of wood flew off a circular saw. The House of Lords concluded that she had no action for breach of statutory duty because the purpose of fencing, as required by the Factories Act 1937, was to "keep the worker out, not to keep the machine or its product in".[111]

10.64   The House of Lords adopted a similar approach in *Carroll v Andrew Barclay & Sons Ltd*[112] and *Close v Steel Co of Wales Ltd*.[113] In *Carroll*, a driving belt, which was unfenced, broke off transmission machinery and hit a worker on the head. The worker's action averring breach of the Factories Act 1937 failed. The statute was designed to prevent persons coming into contact with the machinery, not to guard against ejection of broken parts. In *Close*, fragments of a shattered drill flew off and struck the plaintiff. The subsequent action for breach of statutory duty failed. The court held that, although fencing would have avoided the injury, the purpose of the statute was to prevent contact with the machine as opposed to preventing the ejection of fragments.

10.65   The above cases illustrate a very narrow interpretation by the judiciary of the relevant statutory purpose. In other cases, however, the courts have taken a more liberal approach. Thus, if the pursuer's injury is of a kind which the statute aimed to prevent, it is immaterial that the harm occurred in a way not contemplated by the statute.[114] In *Donaghey v Boulton & Paul Ltd*,[115] statutory regulations required that crawling boards be provided where work was being done on roofs covered with fragile materials through which a person was liable to fall more than 10 feet. The defendants did not comply with this requirement and the plaintiff fell through a hole in the roof on which he was working. This would not have occurred had the boards been provided. His action based on breach of statutory duty was allowed notwithstanding that the main purpose of the legislation was to prevent falls through fragile material in the roof. The general object was to prevent men working on the roof falling to the ground. Lord Reid pointed out[116] that, as long as the injury was not totally different in kind from that which the statute aimed to prevent, it was irrelevant that it happened in a way not precisely contemplated.

10.66   A more liberal judicial approach was again taken in *Grant v National Coal Board*.[117] It was held that s 49 of the Coal Mines Act 1911, which required roofs of a travelling

---

[109] See, also, *Fytche v Wincanton Logistics plc* [2004] 4 All ER 221; *Wentworth v Wiltshire CC* [1993] 2 All ER 256; *Vibixa Ltd v Komori UK Ltd; Polestar Jowetts Ltd v Komori UK Ltd* [2006] 1 WLR 2472.

[110] [1946] AC 493.

[111] *Ibid*, per Lord Simonds at 505.

[112] 1948 SC (HL) 100.

[113] [1962] AC 367.

[114] Note the analogy here with negligence cases such as *Hughes v Lord Advocate* 1963 SC (HL) 31.

[115] [1968] AC 1.

[116] *Ibid* at 26.

[117] 1956 SC (HL) 48. *Gerrard v Staffordshire Potteries* [1995] ICR 502 and *Cullen v North Lanarkshire Council* 1998 SC 451 offer further illustrations of a more generous judicial approach to statutory provisions.

road in a mine to be secure, covered not only the risk of being hit from above by falling material, but also the risk of derailment of a bogie caused by fallen debris lying on the road. The rationale for the decision was that the object of the Act was to improve safety conditions and its provisions were not therefore to be construed narrowly.

THERE HAS BEEN A BREACH OF THE STATUTORY OBLIGATION

The pursuer must also establish that the statutory duty has been breached. This will involve questions of statutory interpretation. There is no uniform standard imposed by statutes.[118] Some statutes impose an unqualified or absolute obligation[119] while other statutes qualify the obligation in some way.[120] **10.67**

In order to succeed in negligence, the pursuer is required to establish that the defender failed to take reasonable care. That standard is sometimes imposed by statutes, the most notable example being the Occupiers' Liability (Scotland) Act 1960. It is, however, more usual for statutes to impose a higher standard such as strict liability[121] or an absolute duty. If strict liability applies, the pursuer does not require to establish fault. Strict liability is not, however, as high a standard as absolute liability because in strict liability cases there are certain limited defences available to the defender. In other words, liability is not *absolute*. In neither strict nor absolute liability cases will it avail the defender to show that he exercised reasonable care – in other words, liability may attach to the defender under the statute even when he has not been at fault.[122] Thus, in *Millar* v *Galashiels Gas Co Ltd*,[123] statutory liability attached to the defender in respect of the failure of the brake mechanism in a lift even although negligence could not be proved. The statutory duty in question was absolute in nature.[124] **10.68**

Many cases have been brought averring breaches of the Factories Act 1961. Lord Upjohn pointed out in *Nimmo* v *Alexander Cowan & Sons Ltd*[125] that a "great variety of **10.69**

---

[118] It has been said that "strict liability is not an invariable characteristic of the tort, even if it is the most common one": see K M Stanton, "New forms of the tort of breach of statutory duty" (2004) 120 LQR 324 at 332.
[119] See *Hamilton* v *National Coal Board* 1960 SC (HL) 1 (where s 81(1) of the Mines and Quarries Act 1954 was held to impose an absolute and continuing obligation on mineowners to keep a winch in a proper and efficient state); *Bruce* v *Ben Odeco Ltd* 1996 SC 389 (where reg 5(1) of the Offshore Installations (Operational Safety, Health and Welfare) Regulations 1976 was considered – see the discussion below); *Robb* v *Salamis* 2007 SC (HL) 71, where Lord Hope observed (at para 24) that regs 4 and 20 of the Provision and Use of Work Equipment Regulations 1998 (SI 1998/2306) were designed "to ensure that work equipment which is made available to workers may be used by them without impairment to their safety or health". His Lordship then asserted that "[t]his is an absolute and continuing duty".
[120] Williams has observed that "[t]he language used in legislation seems to be largely haphazard, yet it is upon the accident of language that the issue is made to turn". See G Williams, "The effect of penal legislation in the law of tort" (1960) 23 MLR 233 at 243.
[121] See, eg, Pt 1 of the Consumer Protection Act 1987.
[122] See the observations of Rigby LJ in *Groves* v *Lord Wimborne* [1898] 2 QB 402 at 412–413 and those of Lord Wright in *Smith* v *Cammell, Laird & Co Ltd* [1940] AC 242 at 264. See, also, *Riddell* v *Reid* 1942 SC (HL) 51.
[123] 1949 SC (HL) 31.
[124] The relevant section of the Factories Act 1937 provided that "[e]very hoist or lift shall be of good mechanical construction, sound material and adequate strength, and be properly maintained". The Act defined "maintained" as "maintained in an efficient state, in efficient working order and in good repair". The decision in *Millar* remains relevant in pointing to the absolute nature of the obligation in modern legislation which is similarly worded: see, eg, *Stark* v *The Post Office* [2000] ICR 1013; *Given* v *James Watt College* 2007 SLT 39. In *Given*, Lord Emslie, in the context of reg 5(1) of the Provision and Use of Work Equipment Regulations 1998 (SI 1998/2306), stated (at para 26): "the obligation to 'maintain in an efficient state' is absolute in nature, so that the emergence of any defect or malfunction automatically constitutes a breach irrespective of whether that defect or malfunction could have been foreseen or avoided".
[125] 1967 SC (HL) 79 at 104.

phraseology … has been employed in the drafting of the sections of the Factories Act and similar legislation".

10.70   In recent years there has been an overhaul of safety legislation. The modern legislation (see the "six-pack regulations" to which reference is made above) contains variations in the standards imposed – some duties are qualified, some are not.

10.71   A modern example of an absolute duty is found in reg 19 of the Workplace (Health, Safety and Welfare) Regulations 1992.[126] The regulation requires that "escalators and moving walkways shall function safely". In absolute liability cases, the mere non-observance of a state of affairs will result in liability.[127] It is irrelevant that it is impractical to comply or that compliance renders the work in question impossible.[128] This is illustrated in *John Summers & Sons Ltd* v *Frost*.[129] The Factories Act 1937 imposed a duty on factory owners to fence dangerous machinery. Frost's thumb was injured as a result of the incomplete fencing of a grinding wheel in a factory. The machine was guarded at the top only. The defendant argued that the machine was fenced so far as was reasonably practicable and that complete compliance with the statute would render the machine unusable. The House of Lords rejected that argument. It held that the obligation in question was absolute. Non-compliance therefore established breach.

10.72   In *Bruce* v *Ben Odeco Ltd*,[130] the Inner House had occasion to consider reg 5(1) of the Offshore Installations (Operational Safety, Health and Welfare) Regulations 1976.[131] The regulation provides that: "All parts of every offshore installation and its equipment shall be so maintained as to ensure the safety of the installation and the safety and health of the persons thereon." In that case, a mechanic was employed on a drilling rig in the North Sea. He was injured when his foot slipped on the metal surface of a floor on which there was a slippery substance. The court held that the regulation imposed an absolute obligation but that the obligation was directed at the *structural integrity* of the installation which had to be kept in a proper state of repair. The presence on the floor of a slippery substance was a transient condition which was not due in any way to a lack of maintenance of the structure of the floor.

10.73   We have seen that some statutes impose absolute liability whereas others such as the Occupiers' Liability (Scotland) Act 1960 impose a duty of reasonable care. Another group of statutes requires certain precautions to be taken "so far as is reasonably practicable".[132] A modern example of such a provision is found in reg 12(3) of the Workplace (Health, Safety and Welfare) Regulations 1992. The obligation to keep floors free from obstructions, articles or substances which may cause a person to slip, trip or fall is to be complied with "so far as is reasonably practicable". In *Edwards* v *National Coal Board*,[133] the court considered what is meant by the term "reasonably practicable":

> "Reasonably practicable is a narrower term than physically possible and seems to me to imply that a computation must be made … in which the quantum of risk is placed in one

---

[126] SI 1992/3004.
[127] See the observations of Lord Radcliffe in *Brown* v *National Coal Board* [1962] AC 574 at 592 and those of Lord Jenkins in *Hamilton* v *National Coal Board* 1960 SC (HL) 1 at 18.
[128] See *Gill* v *Donald Humberstone & Co Ltd* [1963] 1 WLR 929, and, in particular, the comments of Lord Devlin at 942.
[129] [1955] AC 740.
[130] 1996 SC 389.
[131] SI 1976/1019.
[132] See, eg, *Black* v *Fife Coal Co* 1912 SC (HL) 33; *Cavanagh* v *Godfreys of Dundee Ltd* 1997 SLT (Sh Ct) 2.
[133] [1949] 1 KB 704.

scale and the sacrifice involved in the measures necessary for averting the risk (whether in money, time or trouble) is placed in the other, and that, if it be shown that there is a gross disproportion – the risk being insignificant in relation to the sacrifice – the defendants discharge the onus on them … The questions he has to answer are: (a) what measures are necessary and sufficient to prevent any breach … (b) are these measures reasonably practicable?"[134]

In *Neil v Greater Glasgow Health Board*,[135] Lord Abernethy considered the concept of **10.74** reasonable practicability in relation to s 29(1) of the Factories Act 1961. That section provided: "There shall, so far as is reasonably practicable, be provided and maintained safe means of access to every place at which any person has at any time to work, and every such place shall, so far as is reasonably practicable, be made and kept safe for any person working there." The pursuer was injured when part of a machine he was working on tipped. His action, insofar as it was based on common law negligence, failed because the accident was unforeseeable. However, the ground of action based on breach of s 29(1) of the Factories Act 1961 was successful because the clamping of the machine to the floor had been a reasonably practicable step for the defenders to take and could have been taken before the accident to prevent its occurrence, the clamping being a quick, simple and inexpensive operation.

Other statutory provisions may provide that "all practicable measures" be taken **10.75** to achieve a certain result.[136] Where a particular duty is framed in terms of what is (reasonably) practicable, the burden of proving that a particular step was not (reasonably) practicable falls on the defender.[137]

Finally, it should be noted that, in determining whether a particular statutory **10.76** provision has been breached, the interpretation placed on certain statutory words may be crucial. The courts, for example, may have to determine whether a particular piece of machinery was "dangerous", or whether a piece of equipment was "properly maintained". There is a considerable body of case law which provides guidance on how the courts are likely to interpret words encountered in statutory provisions.

THE BREACH CAUSED THE HARM COMPLAINED OF

In cases involving breach of statutory duty it is necessary for the pursuer to establish **10.77** that the defender's breach of statutory duty caused or materially contributed[138] to his injury. Thus, the need to prove causation is a fundamental requirement of a statutory breach case in exactly the same way as it is in negligence cases. The standard of proof is the same as in common law negligence: that is, the pursuer must prove causation on a balance of probabilities.[139]

In *McWilliams v Sir Wm Arrol & Co Ltd and Another*,[140] a steel erector, who had not **10.78** been wearing a safety belt, was killed when he fell from a lattice tower at a shipyard.

---

[134] [1949] 1 KB 704, per Asquith LJ at 712. See, also, *Braham v J Lyons & Co Ltd* [1962] 1 WLR 1048.
[135] 1996 SC 185.
[136] For a consideration of such a statutory formulation, see *Adsett v K & L Steelfounders & Engineers Ltd* [1953] 1 WLR 773.
[137] *Nimmo v Alexander Cowan & Sons Ltd* 1967 SC (HL) 79; *Gibson v British Insulated Callenders Construction Co Ltd* 1973 SC (HL) 15.
[138] See *Holtby v Brigham & Cowan (Hull) Ltd* [2000] ICR 1086.
[139] See *Wardlaw v Bonnington Castings Ltd* 1956 SC (HL) 26.
[140] 1962 SC (HL) 70.

The belts had been removed to another site. His widow raised an action on the basis that safety belts had not been provided. She averred negligence against his employers and, as against the occupiers of the site, she alleged both negligence and breach of the Factories Act 1937. Her action was unsuccessful as she failed to establish a causal link between the breach of statutory duty and her husband's death. It was proved that the deceased did not normally wear a safety belt and that in the past he had worked at greater heights and, on these occasions, he had neither worn nor asked for a safety belt. Safety belts were commonly regarded by the workforce as being unduly cumbersome. Therefore, the pursuer failed to establish, on the balance of probabilities, that the occupiers' breach of the Factories Act caused her husband's death.[141]

10.79   In situations where the defender's breach of statutory duty is a *factual* or "but for" cause of the pursuer's loss, the defender may nonetheless be relieved of liability for the ultimate loss where there is a *novus actus interveniens* which breaks the chain of causation. The *novus actus* thus becomes the real, effective or *legal* cause of the pursuer's loss.[142]

10.80   *Ginty* v *Belmont Building Supplies Ltd*[143] raises an interesting point in relation to causation and liability for breach of statutory duty. The plaintiff was employed by roofing contractors. Statutory provisions which placed a duty on both plaintiff and defendant required the use of crawling boards on fragile roofs. The defendants provided the boards. The plaintiff did not use them and fell through the roof. Both the plaintiff and the defendant were in breach of the statutory duty to use the boards. However, the plaintiff was unsuccessful in his action for breach of statutory duty. Pearson J pointed out[144] the "special feature" of the case that both plaintiff and defendant were in breach of statutory duty and he posited[145] what he termed was "the important and fundamental question in a case like this ... Whose fault was it? ... If the answer to that question is that in substance and reality the accident was solely due to the fault of the plaintiff, so that he was the sole author of his own wrong, he is disentitled to recover". The court will ascertain whether the employer's fault is simply co-extensive with the employee's fault as in *Ginty*, or, alternatively, whether it transcends or is independent of the employee's fault. Furthermore, *Ginty* makes clear that if the defender is also at fault to some degree (for example by failing to exercise proper supervision or by giving inadequate instructions), then the pursuer will be entitled to recover some damages, subject, of course, to reduction in respect of contributory negligence.

DEFENCES

CONTRIBUTORY NEGLIGENCE

10.81   In an action for breach of statutory duty, the defender may seek to rely on the defence of contributory negligence.[146] The onus of proving that the pursuer was contributorily

---

[141] See, also, *Lineker* v *Raleigh Industries Ltd* [1980] ICR 83.
[142] That the concept of *novus actus interveniens* applies in breach of statutory duty cases was accepted in *Horton* v *Taplin Contracts Ltd* [2003] ICR 179.
[143] [1959] 1 All ER 414.
[144] *Ibid* at 423.
[145] *Ibid* at 424.
[146] See *Cakebread* v *Hopping Bros (Whetstone) Ltd* [1947] KB 641; *Boyle* v *Kodak Ltd* [1969] 1 WLR 661; *Mullard* v *Ben Line Steamers Ltd* [1970] 1 WLR 1414; *King* v *RCO Support Services Ltd and Yorkshire Traction Co Ltd* [2001]

negligent rests on the defender.[147] Prior to the Law Reform (Contributory Negligence) Act 1945 contributory negligence was a complete defence to an action.[148] Now, under the 1945 Act, an apportionment of damages is made depending on the relative blame-worthiness of the parties and the award of damages made to the pursuer is reduced accordingly. In *Smith v Chesterfield & District Co-operative Society*,[149] a girl who was operating a pastry-making machine collected stray pieces of dough and deliberately pushed them towards the moving rollers. The court concluded that dangerous parts of the machine had not been securely fenced as required by s 14 of the Factories Act 1937. The girl, however, was partly to blame for the ensuing injury and the damages were reduced by 60 per cent on account of her contributory negligence. In *Robb v Salamis (M and I) Ltd*[150] the pursuer sustained injury when descending from his bunk on an offshore installation. He descended by way of a removeable ladder but failed to ascertain that it was properly secured before doing so. Although successful in estab-lishing a breach of the Provision and Use of Work Equipment Regulations 1998 by his employers, the pursuer was held to have been 50 per cent contributorily negligent. It would have been "only sensible"[151] for the pursuer to have checked the stability of the ladder before putting his weight on it.

There is some evidence that the courts are less likely to categorise a pursuer's **10.82** conduct as contributorily negligent where an absolute obligation has been imposed on the defender.[152] Thus, in *Flower v Ebbw Vale Steel, Iron and Coal Co Ltd*,[153] Lawrence J stated that "it is not for every risky thing which a workman in a factory may do in his familiarity with the machinery that a plaintiff ought to be held guilty of contributory negligence".[154] Of course, *Flower* pre-dated the 1945 Act. At that time, contributory negligence operated as a complete defence to an action. The courts were accordingly faced with an "all or nothing" decision. More recently it has been said that "the need for such extreme caution is less obvious now that the complete defence which was afforded by a finding of contributory negligence has been replaced by the provisions which the Act of 1945 made for reducing the amount of damages".[155] Indeed, in a recent case where a risk had been consciously accepted by a skilled employee, in circum-stances where precautions might easily have been taken, it was said that the injured

---

ICR 608; *Tasci v Pekalp of London Ltd* [2001] ICR 633; *Ellis v Bristol City Council* [2007] ICR 1614; *McLellan v Dundee City Council* 2009 Rep LR 61.

[147] See *John Summers & Son Ltd v Frost* [1955] AC 740 and in particular the observations of Lord Keith of Avonholm at 777.

[148] See the observations of Lord Atkin in *Caswell v Powell Duffryn Associated Collieries Ltd* [1940] AC 152 at 164–165 (although, there, the deceased workman was not found to have been contributorily negligent).

[149] [1953] 1 WLR 370.

[150] 2007 SC (HL) 71.

[151] *Ibid*, per Lord Rodger at para 54.

[152] See the observations of Lord Tucker in *Staveley Iron and Chemical Co Ltd v Jones* [1956] AC 627 at 648. See, also, the warning sounded by Sachs LJ in *Mullard v Ben Line Steamers Ltd* [1970] 1 WLR 1414 to the effect that "the courts must be careful not to emasculate [statutory] regulations by the side-wind of apportionment". More recently, Lord McCluskey has stated that "the court must be cautious about making a finding of contributory negligence against a workman based simply upon his departing marginally from the ordinary routine. The whole purpose of a provision such as s 14 [of the Factories Act 1961] is to avoid the risk of accident to the inadvertent workman or passer by" (*McNeill v Roche Products Ltd* 1989 SLT 498 at 504). See, also, *McGowan v W & J R Watson Ltd* 2007 SC 272.

[153] [1934] 2 KB 132.

[154] *Ibid* at 140. The *dictum* was endorsed by the House of Lords in *Caswell v Powell Duffryn Associated Collieries Ltd* [1940] AC 152 and again in *John Summers & Son Ltd v Frost* [1955] AC 740.

[155] Per Lord Hope in *Reeves v Commissioner of Metropolitan Police* [2000] 1 AC 360 at 384.

employee could "properly be required to bear the greater responsibility".[156] In another case,[157] in which the pursuer suffered burns to both feet in an accident at work, breaches of the Provision and Use of Work Equipment Regulations 1998[158] and the Personal Protective Equipment at Work Regulations 1992[159] were found to be established but the pursuer was held to be 50 per cent contributorily negligent. He knew that it was dangerous to open a sludge door if there was water in the tank which he was draining down, because the tank contained a hot caustic solution which would come out if the sludge door was opened. His attitude towards checking the level of water in the tank before opening the sludge door was described as "cavalier in the extreme".[160]

VOLENTI NON FIT INJURIA

10.83 Many breach of statutory duty cases arise in an industrial context. The defence of *volenti non fit injuria* (a wrongful act is not done to one who is willing) is generally excluded in an employment context as it is not generally thought that the employee has any real freedom of choice as he is working under economic pressure.[161] In such circumstances, it is not appropriate to consider the worker to be *volens* in relation to risks incurred in carrying out his duties. Thus, in the case of the employee suing his employer for breach of statutory duty, the defence of *volenti* will not normally apply.[162] In limited circumstances, however, the defence of *volenti* will be available. Thus in *ICI* v *Shatwell*,[163] the employer was able to rely on the defence. Two experienced shotfirers were subject to a specific statutory duty. They embarked on a course of conduct which was in breach of that duty and suffered injury. One shotfirer sought to hold the employer vicariously liable in respect of the other shotfirer's breach of statutory duty. He did not succeed. Public policy no doubt played a part in the decision making in that case. It is important to note that the employer in *ICI* v *Shatwell* was not himself in breach of any statutory duty.[164]

10.84   On a more general level, the defence is normally excluded in cases of statutory duty as it would be contrary to public policy to allow individuals to consent to risks against which statute has provided protection. This is illustrated in *Wheeler* v *New Merton Board Mills Ltd*.[165] A boy was employed to clean blades in a machine. He was in the habit of doing so without stopping the machine. After some months of this practice, he lost his hand. In the ensuing court action, it was held that the defendant employer could not rely on the defence of *volenti*.

10.85   In some instances, the statute under consideration specifically allows the defence of *volenti*. This is the case with the Occupiers' Liability (Scotland) Act 1960[166] and the Animals (Scotland) Act 1987.[167]

---

[156] *Sherlock* v *Chester City Council* [2004] EWCA Civ 201. However, such cases of conscious acceptance of a risk have to be clearly distinguished from those involving only momentary inattention or inadvertence on the part of the worker, as was acknowledged by Latham LJ at para 32 in *Sherlock*.

[157] *Ashbridge* v *Christian Salvesen plc* 2006 SLT 697.

[158] SI 1998/2306.

[159] SI 1992/2966.

[160] 2006 SLT 697, per Lord Glennie at para 26.

[161] See, eg, *Smith* v *Baker & Sons* [1891] AC 325.

[162] See, eg, *Baddeley* v *Earl Granville* (1887) 19 QBD 423; *Wheeler* v *New Merton Board Mills* [1933] 2 KB 669.

[163] [1965] AC 656.

[164] See, also, *Hugh* v *National Coal Board* 1972 SC 252.

[165] [1933] 2 KB 669.

[166] Section 2(3).

[167] Section 2(1)(b).

THE ILLEGALITY DEFENCE

The illegality defence – sometimes expressed as *ex turpi causa non oritur actio* – may also **10.86** operate as a defence in an action for breach of statutory duty. It operates as a complete defence in circumstances where the claim results from the pursuer's own illegal conduct. In *Clunis* v *Camden & Islington Health Authority*,[168] the plaintiff, who had a history of mental disorder, was discharged from hospital where he had been detained under the mental health legislation. The plaintiff alleged that, following his release, the district health authority had failed in its statutory duty under the Mental Health Act 1983 to arrange after-care for him. The plaintiff contended that this failure resulted in his killing a person in an unprovoked attack. This, in turn, led to his conviction for manslaughter on the grounds of diminished responsibility and his detention in a secure hospital. The plaintiff's claim against the authority was rejected by the Court of Appeal on the basis of *ex turpi causa non oritur actio*. Beldam LJ said[169] that "[t]he court ought not to allow itself to be made an instrument to enforce obligations alleged to arise out of the plaintiff's own criminal act". Although his culpability was reduced on account of his mental state, the plaintiff's condition was not such as to completely negate responsibility for his actions. Thus, it was to be assumed that the plaintiff knew what he was doing and that it was wrong. The plaintiff was therefore prevented from recovering compensation.[170]

DELEGATION

In general, delegation is no defence to an action for breach of statutory duty. The **10.87** defender cannot absolve himself of liability by saying that he delegated the duty to another.[171] One commentator has expressed the position as follows: "The performance may be delegated, but not the responsibility."[172] This principle is clearly stated by Lord Atkin in *McMullan* v *Lochgelly Iron Co*:[173] "[T]he duty is imposed upon the employer and it is irrelevant whether his servants had disregarded his instructions or whether he knew or not of the breach."[174] A person on whom a statutory duty is placed cannot discharge it by entrusting responsibility for it to another. The defence of delegation has, however, succeeded in exceptional circumstances such as where the statutory duty has been delegated to the injured employee himself who, in turn, is injured. A good example of such a situation is *Smith* v *A Baveystock & Co Ltd*.[175] The plaintiff was an experienced circular saw fitter. The adjustment of the guard on his own saw had been delegated to him. It was held that if the injury resulted from the fact that the saw

---

[168] [1998] QB 978.

[169] *Ibid* at 990.

[170] See, also, *Hewison* v *Meridian Shipping Services PTE Ltd* [2003] ICR 766.

[171] See *Groves* v *Lord Wimborne* [1898] 2 QB 402, per AL Smith LJ at 410, per Rigby LJ at 411 and per Vaughan Williams LJ at 418; *Bett* v *Dalmeny Oil Co* (1905) 7 F 787, per Lord M'Laren at 790; *Monk* v *Warbey* [1935] 1 KB 75, per Greer LJ at 80; *Braham* v *J Lyons & Co Ltd* [1962] 1 WLR 1048, per Lord Denning MR at 1051.

[172] Stanton, "New forms of the tort of breach of statutory duty" (2004) 120 LQR 324 at 338.

[173] 1933 SC (HL) 64 at 67.

[174] The same principle applies where an independent contractor's actions have put the employer in breach of statutory duty – as, for example, when the contractor has provided a faulty plank of wood which renders a gangway to be of unsound construction – see *Hosking* v *De Havilland Aircraft Co Ltd* [1949] 1 All ER 540.

[175] [1945] 1 All ER 531.

had been incorrectly adjusted then he had no right to damages because the task had been delegated to him.

PRESCRIPTION AND LIMITATION

10.88 The concepts of prescription and limitation apply to obligations and actions arising from breach of statutory duty. A detailed discussion of prescription and limitation can be found in Chapter 24.

VICARIOUS LIABILITY

10.89 The principle of vicarious liability applies to claims for breach of statutory duty as well as to claims grounded in negligence. There have been various judicial statements to this effect over the years[176] but the matter has now been put beyond doubt by the House of Lords' decision in *Majrowski* v *Guy's and St Thomas' NHS Trust*.[177] There, the House of Lords held that an employer could be vicariously liable in damages for harassment perpetrated by his employee in breach of the Protection from Harassment Act 1997. Lord Hope observed:[178]

> "There is no rule in Scots law which precludes a finding that the employer is liable vicariously for a breach of a statutory duty imposed on his employee. So far as conduct within the scope of the employee's employment is concerned, the doctrine respondeat superior applies irrespective of whether the duty the employee has breached was laid on him by the common law or by statute."

10.90 Lord Nicholls, similarly, could discern no reason to confine the doctrine of vicarious liability to common law wrongs and took the view that the policy considerations at the root of the doctrine applied to statutory obligations as much as to common law wrongs.[179] Accordingly, the principle of vicarious liability applies in respect of wrongs having a statutory source unless, of course, the statute expressly or impliedly displaces the doctrine. The possibility of the legislature disapplying the doctrine was addressed by Lord Hope in *Majrowski*. His Lordship stated[180] that "Parliament could have chosen, had it wished, to exclude the application of the doctrine [of vicarious liability] in the case of conduct by an employee amounting to harassment. But it chose not to do so. It provided expressly and deliberately in s 10(1) of the 1997 Act to the contrary."[181]

---

[176] See the *obiter* observations of Lord MacDermott in *Harrison* v *National Coal Board* [1951] AC 639 at 671 and the *dictum* of Lord Guthrie in *Nicol* v *National Coal Board* (1952) 102 LJ 357. See, also, the observations of Lord Keith in *Matuszczyk* v *National Coal Board* 1953 SC 8 at 15 and those of Lord Oaksey in *National Coal Board* v *England* [1954] AC 403 at 422.
[177] [2007] 1 AC 224.
[178] *Ibid* at para 58.
[179] *Ibid* at para 10.
[180] *Ibid* at para 58.
[181] Section 10(1) of the 1997 Act sets out the Scottish limitation provisions in respect of actions brought under the Act. That provision indicates that, in Scotland, employers may be vicariously liable for damages for harassment by their employees. Lord Hope concluded that that must be the case in England and Wales also because Parliament would not have intended "any difference in substance as between the two jurisdictions as to the scope of the civil remedy for harassment" (at para 63).

A COMPARATIVE PERSPECTIVE

In Scotland, breach of statutory duty is quite distinct from negligence and a pursuer **10.91** may succeed on one ground of action and fail on the other.[182] Different approaches are taken in other jurisdictions, however. In many jurisdictions within the United States, for example, statutory breach is integrated within the negligence framework. Thus, the statutory standard is adopted in place of the standard of reasonable care.[183] Failure to conform to the legislative standard is negligence *per se*.[184] The statute is said to "concretise" the common law duty. In other American states the approach is diluted somewhat so that breach of the statute amounts to *prima facie* evidence of negligence but is not determinative of the issue. It would be open to the defender to establish that breaching the statute was outwith his control and thus he could rebut the inference of negligence. This approach has been approved in Canada in *R v Saskatchewan Wheat Pool*.[185]

CONCLUSIONS

Regrettably, it is not possible to formulate a general rule which applies in all cases where **10.92** the issue of breach of statutory duty arises. It will be evident to the reader that this is an area of law where a degree of uncertainty exists. The action for breach of statutory duty has certainly played an important role in the realm of industrial safety. In other areas, the courts have been less amenable to its introduction and it has been suggested that, in recent times, there has been a "slight hardening of the courts' approach, against finding a remedy in damages for breach of statutory duty".[186] It would be fair to say that (with the exception of industrial safety cases) it is often difficult to predict in what circumstances the courts will allow the action for breach of statutory duty.

Essentially, the question as to whether an action for breach of statutory duty will **10.93** lie depends on the intention of Parliament. The courts therefore become involved in questions of construction. The construction approach has been subject to academic criticism. It has been doubted whether it is coherent to speak about the intention of "such a large and diverse group of politicians".[187] Fleming has described the search for Parliament's intention as a "barefaced fiction because ... the legislature's silence on the question ... rather points to the conclusion that it either did not have it in mind or deliberately omitted to provide for it".[188] In any event, it is far from easy in some cases to determine Parliament's intention. The difficulties encountered in determining

---

[182] See *Millar v Galashiels Gas Co Ltd* 1949 SC (HL) 31.
[183] The refusal of our courts to adopt the "statutory negligence" approach is a decision which Stanton says "should be applauded". He goes on to assert that "[t]he imperialistic nature of the tort of negligence has swamped and distorted too many areas of tort". See Stanton, "New forms of the tort of breach of statutory duty" (2004) LQR 324 at 333.
[184] See Thayer, "Public Wrong and Private Action" (1914) 27 Harv L Rev 317.
[185] (1983)143 DLR (3d) 9 (Sup Ct of Canada). Such an approach has also attracted the support of Glanville Williams: see G Williams, "The effect of penal legislation in the law of tort" (1960) 23 MLR 233.
[186] Per Staughton LJ in *X (Minors) v Bedfordshire CC* [1994] 2 WLR 554 (at 578) (CA).
[187] See D Howarth, *Textbook on Tort* (1995), p 333.
[188] John G Fleming, *The Law of Torts* (9th edn, 1998), p 138. Stanton, too, suggests that in applying the construction approach "the court is seeking to discover something which is not there": see Stanton *et al*, *Statutory Torts* at para 2.009.

Parliament's intention have prompted judicial requests for Parliament to state its intention specifically or at least to use language which is less delphic. Thus Lord du Parcq commented in *Cutler* v *Wandsworth Stadium Ltd*:[189]

> "To a person unversed in the science or art of legislation it may well seem strange that Parliament has not by now made it a rule to state explicitly what its intention is in a matter which is often of no little importance, instead of leaving it to the courts to discover, by a careful examination and analysis of what is expressly said, what that intention may be supposed probably to be. There are no doubt reasons which inhibit the legislature from revealing its intention in plain words. I do not know, and must not speculate, what those reasons may be. I trust, however, that it will not be thought impertinent, in any sense of that word, to suggest respectfully that those who are responsible for framing legislation might consider whether the traditional practice, which obscures, if it does not conceal, the intention which Parliament has, or must be presumed to have, might not safely be abandoned."

10.94   These sentiments appear to have fallen on deaf ears. In *X (Minors)* v *Bedfordshire County Council*[190] both Sir Thomas Bingham MR[191] and Peter Gibson LJ,[192] in the Court of Appeal, felt compelled to express regret that Lord du Parcq's plea in *Cutler* had been ignored.

10.95   Certainly, there are presumptions which may be of assistance to the pursuer. These presumptions are not, however, devoid of difficulty.[193] The fact that the presumptions are not binding but must yield to a contrary statutory intention means that the uncertainty for the pursuer is not removed. Even where a presumption points clearly in one direction, the pursuer cannot be sure that the court will not conclude that Parliament's intention points the other way. In any event, it has already been noted that policy plays an important role in this area. The interaction of policy and presumptions makes it difficult to predict whether an action will lie in any given situation where a statute has been breached. The uncertainty which exists in this area has been emphasised by members of the judiciary. In *Ex parte Island Records*,[194] Lord Denning MR remarked[195] that Parliament "has left the courts with a guess-work puzzle. The dividing line between the pro-cases and the contra cases is so blurred and so ill-defined that you might as well toss a coin to decide it".

10.96   The difficulties encountered in this area of law could be removed if Parliament was simply to address the question of actionability specifically in each new piece of legislation. While such an approach, admittedly, cannot address the question of actionability in relation to statutes already on the statute book,[196] it would be a welcome step forward in clarifying the position for the future.[197]

---

[189] [1949] AC 398 at 410.
[190] [1994] 2 WLR 555.
[191] *Ibid* at 568.
[192] *Ibid* at 585.
[193] See, for example, the discussion in W J Stewart, "Fundamentally reconsidering statutory duty in delict" 2009 SLT (News) 99 at 100.
[194] [1978] Ch 122, CA.
[195] *Ibid* at 134–135.
[196] A considerable number of provisions has already been subject to judicial determination in relation to the question of actionability in which case the difficulty has been removed.
[197] In 1969, the Scottish Law Commission proposed that where a statute imposes a duty, actionability should be presumed unless express provision to the contrary is made: see *The Interpretation of Statutes* (Law Com No 21/Scot Law Com No 11, 1969) at para 38. The proposal was never implemented.

11 NUISANCE

INTRODUCTION

In this chapter we turn our attention to that branch of the law of Scotland which **11.1** specifically concerns itself with the protection of the enjoyment of land from external interference.[1] The law of nuisance, is, therefore, concerned with the law of neighbourhood.[2] Whereas the *raison d'être* of the law of nuisance is quite clear, it is, nonetheless, difficult to define.[3] According to Smith, a nuisance comprises an operation on the part of the defender which, taking into account the natural rights of his neighbours, is unreasonable or extraordinary on account of being unnatural, dangerous or offensive; and such operation must have caused material injury.[4] Walker, in turn, taking a more general approach, regards "nuisance" as a general term which is employed, rather loosely, to cover any use of property that causes trouble or annoyance to neighbours.[5] In essence, the law recognises that a proprietor of land has a right to the free and absolute use of his own property, but only to the extent that such use does not discomfit or annoy his neighbour.[6] In other words, the law recognises one's right to enjoy the physical possession of one's land by the law imposing a reciprocal duty on one's neighbour not to interfere with such enjoyment. The law of nuisance is, therefore, concerned with striking a balance between the competing rights or interests of proprietors in relation to land, each of whom has a right to enjoy his own land.[7] This potential conflict is pragmatically resolved by the courts imposing a duty on each not to use his land in such an unreasonable way that the pursuer's enjoyment of his land

---

[1] F McManus (ed), *Environmental Law in Scotland* (SULI) at para 3.01. *Clerk and Lindsell on Torts* (19th edn, 2006) at para 20–01 state that the essence of nuisance is a condition or activity which unduly interferes with the use or enjoyment of land. See, also, *Hunter v Canary Wharf Ltd* [1997] Env LR 488 at 536 where Lord Hope stated that the tort of nuisance was an invasion of the plaintiff's interest in the possession and enjoyment of land. See also S Todd (ed), *The Law of Torts in New Zealand* (4th edn, 2005).

[2] See *Lord Advocate v Rio Stakis Organisation* 1981 SC 104 at 110.

[3] In *Victoria Park Racing and Recreation Grounds Co Ltd v Taylor* (1937) 58 CLR 479 at 500, Rich J stated that nuisance covers so wide a field that no general definition of nuisance has been attempted but only a classification of the various types of nuisance.

[4] T B Smith, *Short Commentary on the Law of Scotland* (1962) at p 1132.

[5] D Walker, *Delict* (2nd edn, 1981) at p 955.

[6] N Whitty argues that originally Scots law imposed no general restraint on the use of property except *aemulato vicini* and the protection against direct damage. There was never a time when Scots law sought to protect even rural property free from all interference and annoyance: *SME* (Reissue) No 14, para 17.

[7] See, eg, the judgment of Lord Wright in *Sedleigh-Denfield v O'Callaghan* [1940] AC 880 at 903 and that of Lawton LJ in *Kennaway v Thompson* [1980] 3 All ER 329 at 333. Professor J Fleming argues that "The paramount problem in the law of nuisance is … to strike a tolerable balance between conflicting claims of neighbours, each invoking the privilege to exploit the resources and enjoy the amenities of his property without undue subordination to the reciprocal interests of the other": *The Law of Torts* (9th edn, 1998) at p 467.

is adversely affected.[8] The law was succinctly summarised by Lord President Cooper in *Watt* v *Jamieson*,[9] where his Lordship stated:

> "The balance in all such cases has to be held between the freedom of a proprietor to use his property as he pleases and the duty on a proprietor not to inflict material loss or inconvenience on adjoining proprietors or adjoining property and in every case the answer depends on considerations of fact and degree ... The critical question is whether what he is exposed to was *plus quam tolerabile* when due weight has been given to all the circumstances of the offensive conduct and its effects. If that is satisfied, I do not consider that our law accepts as a defence that the nature of the user complained of was usual, familiar and normal. Any type of use which in the sense indicated above subjects adjoining proprietors to substantial annoyance, or causes material damage to their property, is *prima facie* not a reasonable use."

11.2   However, importantly, the Lord President went on to state[10] that, in deciding whether a nuisance existed, the proper angle of approach was from the standpoint of the victim as opposed to that of the alleged offender.[11] Some authors have, therefore, argued that there is some doubt that the issue as to whether an activity is *plus quam tolerabile* (and therefore a nuisance) indeed involves a balancing of respective interests.[12] Such an approach really conforms to one that regards the law of nuisance as being solely based on the protection of an interest in land.[13] However, in the authors' view, this represents a misunderstanding of *Watt*. The reason is this. Simply because the law requires one to view the relevant adverse state of affairs from the standpoint of the victim does not automatically rule out one taking account of the nature of the conduct of the defender. Indeed, the Lord President (Lord Cooper) stated in *Watt* that in determining whether the relevant adverse state of affairs ranks as a nuisance in law: "The critical question is whether what he was exposed to was *plus quam tolerabile when due weight has been given*

---

[8] N Whitty, "Reasonable neighbourhood: the province and analysis of private nuisance in Scots Law" (1982) 27 JLSS 497 at 500. See, also, G Cross, "Does only the careless polluter pay?" (1995) 111 LQR 445 at 449. In *Cunard* v *Antifyre* [1933] 1 KB 551 at 557, Talbot J succinctly defined private nuisances as interferences by owners or occupiers of property with the use or enjoyment of neighbouring property.

[9] 1954 SC 56 at 58.

[10] *Ibid* at 57.

[11] A similar approach was approved by the First Division in *Lord Advocate* v *Reo Stakis Organisation Ltd* 1981 SC 104 at 108 (Lord Emslie). See also *City of Campbellton* v *Grays Velvet Ice Cream Ltd* (1982) 127 DLR (3d) 436 at 441, where Stratton JA stated that the gist of a private nuisance is a substantial and unreasonable interference with an occupier's use and employment of the land which he occupies. It is the impact of the defendant's activity on the plaintiff's interest which is the focus of attention and not the nature of the defendant's conduct.

[12] See J Rowan-Robinson and D McKenzie-Skene, "Environmental Protection and the Role of the Common Law: A Scottish Perspective" in *Environmental Protection and the Common Law* (2000) at p 243. G Cameron argues that the primary advantage in describing nuisance in terms of the interests invaded is that it avoids the difficulty in defining nuisance, given the confusing variety of circumstances in which the term has come to be applied: (1998) SLPQ 1 at 9. Buxton, in turn, regards nuisance as the actual infliction of the relevant harm, in contradistinction to the state of affairs whence the nuisance arises: R Buxton, "The negligent nuisance" (1996) 8 *Malaysia Law Review* 1 at 13. See also *Fritz* v *Hobson* (1880) 14 ChD 542 at 556, where Fry J stated that one should not attempt to ascertain the existence of a nuisance in terms of its duration but rather by its effect on the plaintiff. See also A Linden and B Feldthusen, *Canadian Tort Law* (8th edn) at p 559 where the authors state that "Nuisance is a field of liability. It describes a type of harm that is suffered rather than a kind of conduct that is forbidden."

[13] W Gordon argues that what constitutes a nuisance is to be determined as a matter of fact, looking at the operations from the point of view of the alleged wrongdoer, whose use of his land need not be unusual: *Scottish Land Law* (2nd edn, 1999) at p 811.

to all the surrounding circumstances of the offensive conduct and its effects"[14] (emphasis supplied).

In the authors' view, *Watt* is authority for the proposition that, in determining **11.3** whether a nuisance exists, one should commence by considering the nature of the impact of the state of affairs on the pursuer and decide whether such an impact falls to be protected by the law of nuisance. For example, does the law of nuisance offer any protection against the defender's building interfering with the reception of television signals?[15] However, one must also take into account other factors in order to determine whether the adverse state of affairs complained of constitutes a nuisance. Indeed, if one ignores the nature of the conduct of the defender and simply concentrates on the impact or inconvenience occasioned to the pursuer, many activities (such as road traffic, which generates noise) would often automatically constitute a nuisance in law.[16] In other words, the concept of *plus quam tolerabile*, as far as the law of nuisance is concerned, derives its hue, in no small measure, from the nature of the conduct of the defender.

Watt, therefore, is authority for the proposition that before an adverse state of affairs **11.4** can be categorised as a nuisance it must rank as *plus quam tolerabile* (ie unreasonable) in the eyes of the law. However, the concept of reasonableness in terms of the law of nuisance is, at best, vague, and, at worst, a meaningless shibboleth which offers little guidance as to whether a given adverse state of affairs ranks as a nuisance.[17] Indeed, some authors have gone so far as to express the view that the notion of reasonableness has now become redundant and misleading in many cases of private nuisance[18]

Watt also emphasises the point that whether any given state of affairs constitutes **11.5** a nuisance is a question of fact and degree.[19] For example, the louder the noise from my neighbour's karaoke machine, or the more intense the smoke from the fire my neighbour has erected in his garden, the more likely the courts will be inclined to classify the adverse state of affairs as a nuisance in law.

· ELEMENTS OF THE LAW OF NUISANCE

UNREASONABLE CONDUCT

We now consider the various factors a court takes into account when it determines **11.6** whether any particular adverse state of affairs ranks as a nuisance in law. At the outset, however, it is important to emphasise that it is only unreasonable conduct which is capable of being categorised as a nuisance in law.[20] A good modern illustration of this

---

[14] 1954 SC 56.

[15] See para 11.7, below.

[16] See also J Murphy, *Street on Torts* (12th edn, 2007) at p 431.

[17] However, an example of uncritical adherence to the concept of reasonableness is provided by P Osbourne, *The Law of Torts* (2nd edn, 2003) at p 343, where it is stated that the limits of tolerance are reached when the defendant's activities cause an unreasonable interference with the plaintiff's use, enjoyment and comfort of land.

[18] M Lee, "What is a private nuisance?" (2003) 119 LQR 298 at 298.

[19] See also *Mutter v Fyffe* (1848) 11 D 303, *Haddon v Lynch* [1911] VLR 230 and *Howarth v Canadian Red Cross Society* [1943] 2 WWR 692.

[20] *Watt v Jamieson* 1954 SC 56. See also *Western Silver Fox Ranch Ltd v Ross and Cromarty CC* 1940 SLT 144. See also *Pugliese v National Capital* (1977) 3 CCLT 18 at 51, where Howland JA stated that in determining

point is seen in the House of Lords case of *Baxter* v *Camden London Borough Council*.[21] In that case the appellants were local authority tenants who occupied flats which had been constructed or adapted for multiple occupation. However, the flats were inadequately soundproofed, the result being that the tenants could literally hear everything their neighbours were doing. The tenants, therefore, brought proceedings in nuisance against their landlords. The House of Lords held, however, that the noise in question did not rank as a nuisance in law since the noise emanated from the everyday and normal use of the flats in question. We have already seen above[22] that, in *Watt* v *Jamieson*,[23] the Lord President was of the view that in determining whether a given state of affairs ranked as a nuisance in law, one should assess the situation from the standpoint of the pursuer, and therefore it was quite irrelevant that the defender was making a normal and familiar use of his property. It has already been argued above[24] that *Watt* is not authority for the proposition that in determining whether a given state of affairs ranks as a nuisance one should assess the situation simply from the standpoint of the pursuer, and, therefore, that it is quite irrelevant that the defender was making normal and usual use of his property. In the authors' view, therefore, there is no necessary conflict in the approach adopted in *Watt* with that of the House of Lords in *Baxter*. On facts similar to those which were found in *Baxter*, a Scottish court would take a similar approach.

WHAT FACTORS ARE TAKEN INTO ACCOUNT?

11.7 We now look at the various factors the courts take into account when considering whether an adverse state of affairs constitutes a nuisance in law. One should bear in mind that the various factors listed below are not mechanically applied in every nuisance case. Rather, the courts have tended to emphasise several factors, often to the exclusion of others. For example, in *Fleming* v *Hislop*[25] the court simply focused on the intensity of the smell which emanated from the offending accumulation of mineral refuse situated on the defender's premises. It is difficult, therefore, to predict in advance what factors will determine the outcome of a case. The judges have refrained from constructing a hierarchy of the various factors in terms of their relative importance. Indeed, there is little academic discussion on this important point. It should be further emphasised that the factors discussed below are probably not exhaustive. While the law of nuisance is rather slow moving in comparison (say) with the law of negligence, with judges not really showing a great deal of creativity, judges have at times attempted some creativity, and it would seem that judges have not closed their minds to taking new factors into account. For example, in *Hunter* v *Canary Wharf Ltd*,[26] which concerned liability in the law of nuisance for the interference by a large building with the reception of television signals, Lord Cooke stated *obiter*:

---

whether a nuisance exists it is not sufficient to ask whether an occupier has made a reasonable use of his own property. One must ask whether his conduct is reasonable considering the fact that he has a neighbour.

[21] [1999] 4 All ER 449.
[22] At para 11.2.
[23] n17.
[24] See para 11.2.
[25] (1882) 10 R 426; (1886) 13 R (HL) 43.
[26] [1997] AC 655 at 711.

"[the] lineaments of the law of nuisance were established before the age of television and radio, motor transport and aviation, town and country planning, a 'crowded island' and a heightened public consciousness of the need to protect the environment. All these are now among the factors falling to be taken into account in the evolving law."

SOCIAL UTILITY

The social benefit which accrues from the activity that generates the state of affairs in question is taken into account by the court in determining whether a nuisance exists. Essentially, the more socially useful the activity is, the less likely the court would be willing to castigate the state of affairs complained of as a nuisance in law.[27] The courts have been inclined to recognise the concept of social or public utility in relation to factories.[28] However, as far as other forms of activity are concerned, the courts have displayed more reticence about taking into account social utility when determining whether a nuisance exists, preferring simply to take this factor into account when considering whether or not to grant an interdict.[29] Such reluctance is shown in the English case of *Dennis* v *Ministry of Defence*.[30] In that case the claimants owned and lived on a large estate situated in close proximity to RAF Wittering, home to the Harrier jet, which is a noisy aircraft. Indeed, the witnesses who gave evidence to the court described the noise from the aircraft as sometimes "intolerable". The claimants brought an action in nuisance against the MoD. At first instance, Buckley J had no hesitation in holding that the noise from the Harriers constituted a nuisance in law.[31] However, it was also beyond dispute that the flying of military aircraft in the very way that gave rise to the action in question redounded to the benefit of the general public.[32] Put simply, Britain needs its airforce, including aircraft which inevitably cause a great deal of noise. However, to weigh this factor in the judicial scales when determining whether the noise in question amounted to a nuisance would, in the view of Buckley J, have deprived the claimants of a judicial remedy under the common law.[33] In his Lordship's view, the growing *corpus* of human rights law dictated that the appropriate remedy under the law of nuisance should be that of damages as opposed to, for example, an injunction or a declaration.[34] Unfortunately, however, Buckley J did not discuss at all this somewhat revolutionary view of the impact of human rights law on the law of nuisance. In the last analysis, what his Lordship seemed to be saying was that where an activity has a manifest and palpable public benefit, one should not include that factor among those normally falling to be taken into account when determining whether a nuisance exists at common law, since this would automatically deprive the claimant of a remedy in law. Rather, in such a case, the public utility factor should be employed in order to select the appropriate remedy. In the authors' view the approach taken by Buckley J in *Dennis*, which has not been followed subsequently in England, does not

11.8

---

[27] *Harrison* v *Southwark and Vauxhall Water Co* [1891] 2 Ch 409.
[28] See, eg, *Bellew* v *Cement Ltd.* [1948] IR 61.
[29] See, eg, *Webster* v *Lord Advocate* 1984 SLT 13. See also *Miller* v *Jackson* [1977] QB 966.
[30] [2003] EHLR 297.
[31] *Ibid* at 311.
[32] *Ibid* at 315.
[33] *Ibid* at 316.
[34] See, however, *McKenna* v *British Aluminium Ltd* [2002] EnvLR 721, where Neuburger J supported the contention advanced by counsel to the effect that it would be inappropriate to extend the common law by way of the law of nuisance in order to give effect to Art 8 of the ECHR.

represent the law of Scotland. It is the authors' view that the substantive law governing rights in the law of nuisance should be kept quite separate from the law surrounding remedies. In short, the concept of public or social utility requires to be addressed when considering whether an adverse state of affairs constitutes a nuisance.

MOTIVE OF THE DEFENDER

11.9   If the relevant adverse state of affairs is caused simply in order to punish or annoy the pursuer, that is to say that the defender has acted out of spite, the courts lean heavily towards the view that the state of affairs in question ranks as a nuisance in law. The leading case is *Christie* v *Davey*.[35] In that case the plaintiff's family were musically inclined and frequently practised their instruments at home. This annoyed the defendant, who retaliated by banging trays on the party wall which separated his house from that of the plaintiff. It was held that the noise generated by the defendant amounted to a nuisance in law. Another example of the relevance of malice in the law of nuisance is seen in *Hollywood Silver Fox Farm* v *Emmett*.[36] Here, the plaintiff bred foxes on his land. The defendant, who was about to develop land which adjoined that of the plaintiff, objected to the presence of foxes, on the ground that he feared that this would deter people from purchasing houses on the estate. The defendant, therefore, caused guns to be fired on the boundary separating his premises from that of the plaintiff. As a result of this, vixen on the fox farm devoured their young. It was held that the defendant's conduct amounted to a nuisance in law.[37]

11.10   Finally, an interesting question that falls to be asked at this juncture is whether the relevance of malice in terms of the law of nuisance can be reconciled with the decision of the House of Lords in *Bradford* v *Pickles*.[38] The issue the House of Lords had to consider in that case was whether the owner of land could lawfully interfere (by sinking a shaft into his own land) with the passage of percolating water, which passed through his land in undefined channels to the land of the plaintiff, such interference being to the detriment of the plaintiff. The interference with the water was motivated by malice on the part of the defendant. The House of Lords held that a lawful act cannot be transformed into an unlawful act, however ill the motive of the person who performs the act in question might be. The plaintiff, therefore, had no remedy in law. However, in the authors' view the learning in *Bradford* is confined to the facts of that case and has no relevance in relation to the law of nuisance.[39]

LOCALITY

11.11   In determining whether a given state of affairs ranks as a nuisance, the courts take into account the nature of the relevant locality.[40] Essentially, the more typical the adverse

---

[35] [1893] 1 Ch 316.
[36] [1936] 2 KB 468.
[37] See also the House of Lords case of *Hunter* v *Canary Wharf Ltd* [1997] Env LR 488 where it was held that the erection of a tall building which interfered with the reception of television signals did not constitute an actionable nuisance. However, Lord Cooke stated *obiter* (at 534) that the malicious erection of a structure for the purpose of interfering with television reception could rank as a nuisance in law.
[38] [1895] AC 587.
[39] For a discussion of the relevance of *Bradford* v *Pickles* to the law of nuisance, see R Buckley, *The Law of Nuisance* (2nd edn, 1996), pp 17–18.
[40] See, eg, *Trotter* v *Farnie* (1830) 9 S 144.

state of affairs complained of is of the relevant area, the less likely that the state of affairs will rank as a nuisance. The rationale of this is that if the state of affairs is typical of a given locality, a reasonable person who resides in the locality is presumed to be less inclined to be annoyed by having become habituated, at least to some extent, to the nuisance in question. The leading case on the application of the locality factor is *Bamford* v *Turnley*,[41] where Pollock CB stated: "That may be a nuisance in Grosvenor Square, which would be none in Smithfield Market." Again, in *Inglis* v *Shotts Iron Co*,[42] the Lord Justice-Clerk stated: "Things which are forbidden in a crowded urban community may be permitted in the country. What is prohibited in enclosed land may be tolerated in the open." Of further interest is the earlier case of *Swinton* v *Pedie*,[43] where it was claimed by the pursuer that the erection of a slaughterhouse in the vicinity of the Edinburgh Academy would constitute a nuisance in law. Lord Gillies stated: "... and although Pall Mall or Grosvenor Square be equally open for the driving of cattle, as the roads in the vicinity to Smithfield Market, it is very evident that the establishment of a great slaughterhouse, however it may be arranged internally, would be a nuisance in either of the former of these places, though not in the last."[44]

However, whereas the courts may be less inclined to castigate as a nuisance a state   **11.12**
of affairs which is indigenous in the area, the courts are not prepared to accord the defender *carte blanche* to create a nuisance. This point is well illustrated in *Rushmer* v *Polsue and Alfieri Ltd*.[45] In that case the plaintiff resided in an area specially devoted to printing and allied trades. The defendants set up machinery which caused serious disturbance to the plaintiff and his family during night-time hours. At first instance, the court granted an injunction restraining the defendants from causing a noise nuisance. The House of Lords, on appeal, upheld the injunction restraining the defendants from carrying on their business as to cause a nuisance. Lord Loreburn LC[46] stated:

> "A dweller in towns cannot expect to have as pure air, as free from smoke, smell, and noise as if he lived in the country, and distant from other dwellings, and yet an excess of smoke, smell and noise may give a cause of action, but in each of such cases it becomes a question of degree, and the question is in each case whether it amounts to a nuisance which will give a right of action. This is a question of fact."[47]

However, the nature of the relevant locality is only important if the state of affairs   **11.13**
complained of affects personal comfort. That is to say, if the pursuer's property is injured by the state of affairs in question, the nature of the locality is redundant. The leading case on this point is *St Helens Smelting Co* v *Tipping*.[48] In that case, vapours from the defendant's works damaged the plaintiff's property. The House of Lords held it immaterial that the plaintiff's property was situated in an industrial area.[49]

---

[41] (1862) 31 LJQB 286 at 286.
[42] (1881) 8 R 1006 at 1021.
[43] (1837) 15 S 775.
[44] Lord Corehouse stated *ibid* at 779 that if the slaughterhouse were erected no parent would suffer his children to attend a school, close by a great slaughterhouse, where there would always be an assemblage of the lowest of the population including butchers' boys and servants and their associates. See also *Scott* v *Leith Police Commissioners* (1830) 8 S 845.
[45] [1907] AC 121.
[46] Citing Lord Halsbury in *Colls* v *Home and Colonial Stores* [1904] AC 179 at 185.
[47] [1907] AC 121 at 123.
[48] (1865) 11 HL Cas 642.
[49] For an interesting discussion of this case, see A Simpson, *Leading Cases in the Common Law*, Ch 7.

LOCALITY AND THE EFFECT OF PLANNING LAW

11.14 To what extent, if any, does planning permission have an effect on the locality factor in terms of the law of nuisance? For example, if a planning authority designated a given area which was formerly green belt, to be put to industrial use in the future, in the relevant development plan in terms of the Town and Country Planning (Scotland) Act 1997,[50] and then the planning authority proceeded to give planning permission for the erection of a factory on the relevant land, to what extent, if any, would this be taken into account by a court which had to decide whether smoke or noise from the factory affecting neighbours ranked as a nuisance in law?

11.15   In *Gillingham Borough Council* v *Medway (Chatham) Dock Co Ltd*,[51] a dock company obtained planning permission to operate the former naval dock in Chatham as a commercial port. Once the port was in operation, the plaintiff received complaints of noise emanating from the port. At first instance, Buckley J held[52] that in determining whether the noise amounted to a nuisance one had to ascertain the character of the neighbourhood by reference to the present character of the land in terms of the planning permission for use of the dockyard as a commercial port. Whereas the grant of planning permission could not authorise a nuisance, a planning authority could, through its development plans and decisions, change the character of a neighbour-hood.[53] However, in *Wheeler* v *Saunders Ltd*,[54] planning permission had been granted to allow the intensification of pig farming on a site already used for that purpose by the defendants. The smell from the farm began to annoy neighbouring landowners who raised an action in nuisance. It was claimed by the defendants, by way of defence, that the planning permission which had been given had the effect of sanctioning the alleged nuisance. This proposition was rejected by the Court of Appeal. In short, the court held that the grant of planning permission could not, in the eyes of the law, sanction the creation of a nuisance. However, Staughton LJ stated *obiter*[55] that it was possible for a planning authority, by giving planning permission, to change the character of land in terms of the law of nuisance.

11.16   In the recent Court of Appeal case of *Watson* v *Croft Promo-Sport Ltd*,[56] the defendants operated a motor racing circuit on land which had once been an aerodrome. The claimants instituted proceedings against the defendants, alleging that the use of the circuit by the defendants caused excessive noise and, therefore, constituted a nuisance in law. The defendants claimed, however, that while the noise from the circuit might cause some discomfort and inconvenience to the claimants, there was no actionable nuisance because the defendants' use of the circuit was reasonable, having regard to the nature and character arising from the grant of planning permission. Whereas the court reaffirmed the law that planning permission cannot sanction a nuisance, it was prepared to accept the proposition that "the implementation of planning permission may alter the nature and character of the locality as to shift the standard of reasonable

---

[50] As amended by the Planning etc (Scotland) Act 2006.
[51] [1993] QB 343.
[52] *Ibid* at 360.
[53] *Ibid* at 359.
[54] [1996] Ch 19.
[55] *Ibid* at 30.
[56] [2009] EWCA Civ 15.

user which governs the question of nuisance or not".[57] The court doubted whether there was some middle category of planning permission which, without implementation, would be capable of affecting private rights unless such effect was specifically authorised by Parliament.[58]

DURATION AND INTENSITY

Essentially, the length of time that a state of affairs exists as well as its intensity are **11.17** taken into account by the court when considering whether a nuisance exists. In the leading case of *Bamford* v *Turnley*,[59] Pollock CB stated:

> "A clock striking the hour, or a bell ringing for some domestic purpose, may be a nuisance if unreasonably loud and discordant, of which the jury alone must judge; but although not unreasonably loud, if the owner from some whim or caprice made the clock strike the hour every 10 minutes, or the bell ring continually, I think that a jury would be justified in considering it to be a very great nuisance."

As far as noise nuisances are concerned, the nature of the noise is a relevant factor in **11.18** the court deciding whether the noise ranks as a nuisance. The more pleasant sounding the noise is, the less likely it will rank as a nuisance.[60]

TIME OF DAY

The time of day during which an adverse state of affairs exists is only relevant in **11.19** relation to noise nuisances and, perhaps, light nuisance. The courts are more inclined to regard night noise as a nuisance than that which takes place during the day.[61] The obvious rationale of the rule is that night noise is more likely to disturb than noise which takes place during the day.

SENSITIVITY OF THE PURSUER

It is a general rule in law that the courts are unwilling to assist the oversensitive. In **11.20** *Armistead* v *Bowerman*,[62] the defender was involved in moving timber. The timber was dragged across a stream as a consequence of which the bed of the stream became disturbed. The silt flowed downstream and destroyed ova in the salmon hatchery owned by the pursuer. It was held that no liability lay as far as the law of nuisance was concerned, since the pursuer's use of the stream was, in the eyes of the law, too sensitive to attract the protection of the law. The leading case on the subject is *Heath* v *Brighton Corporation*,[63] where a priest complained about the noise and vibrations emanating from the defendant's premises. The plaintiff was denied a remedy in

---

[57] Per Richards LJ at para 32, with whom his fellow judges agreed.
[58] *Ibid* at para 33. For a general discussion of the effect of planning permission on the law of nuisance, see F McManus, "Planning Permission, the Law of Nuisance and Human Rights" (2011) 19 Tort Law Rev 29. See also F Moor, "Planning for Nuisance?" (2011) 3 JLBE 65.
[59] (1862) 31 LJQB 286 at 292.
[60] *Webster* v *Lord Advocate* 1984 SLT 13 at 16.
[61] *Bamford* v *Turnley* (1862) 31 LJQB 286; *De Keyser's Royal Hotel Ltd* v *Spicer Bros Ltd* (1914) 30 TLR 257.
[62] (1888) 15 R 814.
[63] (1908) 24 TLR 414.

terms of the law of nuisance since the only reason he was discomfited was because he possessed hypersensitive hearing.

11.21 The rule that the law will not provide any help to the oversensitive also applies in relation to physical injury to property. For example, in *Robertson v Kilvert*[64] the plaintiff kept paper in his premises. However, the paper was of a delicate nature and was particularly vulnerable to heat. The paper was damaged by the heat generated from the defendant's premises. The plaintiff failed in his action. Again, in *Bridlington Relay Ltd v Yorkshire Electricity Board*,[65] the plaintiff company carried on a business of providing a relay system of sound and television broadcasts, and erected a mast on its own land for that purpose. The defendant electricity board commenced to erect an overhead power line, situating two of its pylons within 250 yards of the mast. On a *quia timet* action by the claimant for an injunction, Buckley J held, *inter alia*, that since the business of the claimant required an exceptional degree of immunity from interference, an action in nuisance failed.[66] Again, in *Hunter v Canary Wharf Ltd*,[67] the House of Lords held that the interference with the reception of television signals by the presence of a large building did not constitute a nuisance in law. However, the House did not rule out the possibility that the interference of television reception could never rank as a nuisance in law. *Hunter* serves as a good example of the difficulty the courts have experienced in clearly defining the forms of external influences against which an occupier of land can be protected by the law of nuisance.

11.22 The above cases were reviewed by the Court of Appeal in *Network Rail Infrastructure Ltd (formerly Railtrack) v C J Morris*.[68] In that case it was claimed that Railtrack's signalling system had caused electromagnetic interference to the electric guitars being played in the claimant's recording studios which were situated some 80 metres away. The court held[69] that amplified guitars fell into the category of extraordinarily sensitive equipment which did not attract the protection of the law of nuisance.

SOCIAL UTILITY OF THING INTERFERED WITH

11.23 There is scant authority in Scots law as to what extent, if any, a court takes into account the social utility of that which is interfered with by the conduct of the defender. The leading cases have concerned television reception. In *Bridlington Relay Ltd v Yorkshire*,[70] which concerned liability for interference with television signals, Buckley J took into account the fact that, in the main, television simply served a recreational function in society and, therefore, he accorded it a lowly status in deciding whether the interference ranked as a nuisance in law.[71] However, in the House of Lords case of *Hunter v Canary Wharf Ltd*,[72] which concerned the potential liability in nuisance comprising the presence of a tall building interfering with the

---

[64] (1889) 41 ChD 88.
[65] [1965] Ch 436.
[66] *Ibid* at 448. See, however, the Canadian case of *Nor-Video Services Ltd v Ontario Hydro* (1978) 84 DLR (3rd) 221 where damages were awarded for interference with the transmission of a cable television service.
[67] [1997] 2 WLR 684.
[68] [2004] EnvLR 861.
[69] *Ibid* at 867.
[70] [1965] Ch 436.
[71] Cf *Nor-Video Services Ltd v Ontario Hydro* (1978) 84 DLR (3d) 221.
[72] [1997] EnvLR 488.

reception of television signals, Lord Goff[73] expressed the view that, given that the function of television transcended the function of mere entertainment, interference with such an amenity might, indeed, in appropriate circumstances, be protected by the law of nuisance.

COULD THE ADVERSE STATE OF AFFAIRS HAVE BEEN AVOIDED BY THE PURSUER?

To what extent, if any, can the court take into account whether the pursuer could **11.24** have avoided being affected by the adverse state of affairs? Notwithstanding the fact that there is little authority on this point, the general rule is that the courts are unwilling to place the pursuer under a duty to take preventative or remedial action in the face of an adverse state of affairs affecting his property. This point is neatly illustrated in the Outer House case of *Webster* v *Lord Advocate*.[74] The pursuer, who lived in the vicinity of Edinburgh Castle esplanade, raised an action, alleging that both the noise from the performance of the Edinburgh Military Tattoo, and also the erection of scaffolding to accommodate seating on the Castle esplanade, amounted to a nuisance. The Lord Ordinary rejected the contention that the pursuer would be unable to succeed if it could be shown that the provision of double glazing to the windows of her flat would have reduced the ingress of noise to an acceptable level.[75]

IS THE STATE OF AFFAIRS TYPICAL OF MODERN LIFE?

What we consider here is whether the state of affairs which is complained of is typical, **11.25** not of a particular locality but, rather, in terms of society in general. The leading case is now *Hunter* v *Canary Wharf Ltd*.[76] In that case, the House of Lords held that the presence of a very tall building which interfered with the reception of television signals did not constitute an actionable nuisance. The Court of Appeal was influenced by the fact that buildings of that sort were not uncommon. Pill LJ seemed to suggest[77] that this factor may not be relevant if the given state of affairs consisted of an activity as opposed to a static state of affairs.

There is no Scottish authority on whether one should take into account whether **11.26** the state of affairs is typical of modern life. In the absence of authority, such a factor should be taken into account since the law of nuisance should be responsive to circumstances which have become accepted by society as being a feature of the modern world. Such an approach allows the law of nuisance to become dynamic and also responsive to the needs of society and, at the same time, to facilitate a fairer balance being struck between competing uses of land, a concept which underpins the law of nuisance.

---

[73] [1997] EnvLR 488 at 493.
[74] 1984 SLT 13.
[75] *Ibid* at 15.
[76] [1997] EnvLR 488.
[77] [1996] 1 All ER 482 at 489.

NEED FOR AN EMANATION FROM THE DEFENDER'S PREMISES

11.27 Generally, the adverse state which is the subject of a nuisance action comprises some form of pollution, whether it takes the form of noise, smoke, smell etc. However, the question to be considered at this juncture is whether, in order to bring an action in nuisance, it is essential that something emanates from the defender's property. In other words, can one successfully invoke a nuisance action in relation to a state of affairs confined to the premises of the defender? According to Bell, a nuisance could consist of a state of affairs which was "intolerably offensive to individuals in their dwelling houses, or inconsistent with the comfort of life, whether by stench (as the boiling of whale blubber), by noise (as a smithy in an upper floor) or by indecency (as a brothel next door)".[78]

11.28 In *Smith* v *Cox*,[79] it was held that the drying of cow hides within the site of a public road was a nuisance. There is some authority to the effect that proceedings which pose a threat to the safety of the pursuer can rank as a nuisance in law.[80] In *Thompson-Schwab* v *Costaki*,[81] it was held that since the plaintiff, who resided in nearby property, could see prostitutes and their clients leaving and entering the defendants' premises, this state of affairs ranked as a nuisance. Similarly, in *Laws* v *Florinplace*,[82] the defendants established a sex shop and cinema in the vicinity of the plaintiff's premises. It was claimed on the plaintiff's behalf that the defendant's activities would threaten the ordinary enjoyment of family life in the street where the plaintiff lived and would also be an embarrassment and a potential danger to young persons, especially young girls who might meet with indecent suggestions.[83] Vinelott J was of the view that, as far as the private law of nuisance was concerned, there was no need for a physical emanation from the defendant's premises. An interlocutory injunction was, therefore, granted. The issue as to whether it is necessary that there be some form of physical emanation from the defender's premises as a condition precedent to liability in nuisance was considered again in *Hunter* v *Canary Wharf Ltd*[84] where, as mentioned above,[85] the plaintiffs claimed damages for interference with television reception at their homes by a very tall tower. The House of Lords held that an action in nuisance failed. Their Lordships were of the opinion that the mere presence of a building which interfered with the reception of television signals could not rank as a nuisance in law. In other words, there was no emanation from the defendant's land. Unfortunately, there was little discussion as to whether an emanation from the defendant's premises was a condition precedent to liability in nuisance in general. However, Lord Goff expressed the view[86] that occasionally activities which take place on the defendant's land are so

---

[78] *Principles* (1829) (10th edn, 1899), para 974.
[79] 5 July 1810, FC.
[80] See, eg, *Ferguson* v *Pollok* (1901) 3 F 1140.
[81] [1956] 1 WLR 335.
[82] [1981] 1 All ER 659.
[83] *Ibid* at 663.
[84] [1999] 4 All ER 149.
[85] At para 11.23.
[86] at 432. [1999] 4 All ER 149.

offensive to neighbours as to constitute an actionable nuisance in law. The decision in *Thompson-Schwab* v *Costaki*[87] was specifically approved.

However, there is little authority on whether an emanation is required from the **11.29** defender's premises as far as Scots law is concerned. Probably, with the exception of brothels, sex shops, etc, there does require to be an emanation from the defender's premises in order that the adverse state of affairs can rank as a nuisance.

ISOLATED ESCAPES AND THE LAW OF NUISANCE

We now consider whether an isolated escape from the defender's property which **11.30** harms that of the pursuer can rank as a nuisance in law. For example, if a septic tank or oil tank situated in my garden were suddenly to rupture, with the result that my next-door neighbour's garden is flooded and his plants are destroyed, would one be liable in terms of the law of nuisance? The fundamental question arising here is whether a nuisance must arise from a state of affairs (that is to say, something which has a degree of permanence) or is it simply sufficient that the harm sustained by the pursuer emanates from an isolated escape? In *Attorney-General* v *PYA Quarries Ltd*,[88] Denning LJ (as he then was) expressed the view that a private nuisance always involves some degree of repetition or continuance. Textbook writers from various jurisdictions have also alluded to the need for a state of affairs to have a degree of permanence before it can rank as a nuisance.[89] In his seminal article on the law of nuisance, Newark expressed the view that although never laid down decisively in any case law, there were plenty of *dicta* scattered through the reports to support the view that the "true" nuisance must have some degree of permanence about it, since the plaintiff is required to show some act on the part of the defendant which disturbs the actual or prospective enjoyment of rights over land.[90] Newark went on to conclude that that which is temporary and evanescent cannot be a nuisance.[91]

In reality, it is suggested that escapes from land can conform to either one of two **11.31** models:

1   The first model comprises an escape of an inanimate thing or things from an adverse state of affairs which comprises either the land itself in its static condition or as a result of an activity which takes place on the land. An example of the former would be a rock outcrop, situated on the defender's land, becoming eroded, the upshot of which is that the rubble falls onto the pursuer's land and causes damage. An example of the latter state of affairs would be the escape of fumes from a cement works, to the pursuer's premises.

2   The second model consists of a situation where the relevant "escape" consists of people who have entered the defender's land, and either they use the land

---

[87] [1956] 1 WLR 335.
[88] [1957] 2 QB 169 at 192.
[89] See, eg, *Street on Torts* (5th edn, 1972) at p 219. The editor of the current edition (12th edn, 2007) at p 432 of the same work expresses a similar view. Writing from a New Zealand perspective, S Todd (ed), *The Law of Torts in New Zealand* (2nd edn, 1997) at p 543 puts forward the view that the concept of state of affairs is the basis of liability in nuisance. As far as the law of South Africa is concerned, R McKerron in *Delict* (7th edn, 1971) at p 228 was of the opinion that nuisance is a continuing wrong.
[90] F Newark, "The boundaries of nuisance" (1949) 65 LQR 480 at 489.
[91] *Ibid.* Newark excepted isolated escapes from accumulations which fell within the rule in *Rylands* v *Fletcher.* See also F McManus, "Liability for Isolated Escapes from Land in the Law of Nuisance" (2001) 3 Env L Rev 186.

in question as a "launching pad" or base from which to "attack" the pursuer's property or alternatively, they create a harmful situation on the land which, in turn, harms the pursuer's property. An example of the former would be where vandals congregate on the defender's land and then proceed to vandalise adjoining property. An example of the latter would be where vandals erect a bonfire on the defender's premises and the flames from the bonfire destroy adjoining property.

11.32 Each model will now be considered in the light of case law.

The escape of inanimate things from land

11.33 The courts have never really felt comfortable in dealing with escapes from land. Indeed, it seems very difficult to predict whether such escapes fall to be categorised in terms of the law of nuisance or the law of negligence. For example, in *British Celanese Ltd v A H Hunt (Capacitators) Ltd*,[92] metal foil strip was blown onto the plaintiff's land and came into contact with overhead cables which short-circuited, causing a power failure in the plaintiff's premises. The case was decided in terms of the law of negligence, in contrast to the law of nuisance. In *McLaughlan v Craig*[93] there was an accumulation of gas in the defender's premises which had been caused by a gas leak. An explosion ensued. The pursuer was injured. The case could have been decided in terms of the law of nuisance since the injury emanated from a state of affairs (that is the accumulation of gas) which culminated in an explosion. However, the case was argued and decided in terms of the law of negligence. This case should be contrasted with *Giblin v Middle Ward District Committee of Lanarkshire County Council*.[94] In that case, coal gas escaped from the defender's premises. The pursuer's mother, who occupied adjoining premises, was killed. It was held that the defender was liable in nuisance in respect of what in actual fact amounted to an isolated escape from land. Implicitly, the court held that there was no need for the pursuer to establish the existence of a state of affairs for which the defender was responsible in order to succeed.

11.34   The opportunity to discuss the relevance of isolated escapes from land to the law of Scotland arose in the House of Lords case of *RHM Bakeries (Scotland) Ltd v Strathclyde Regional Council*.[95] In that case the bakery premises of the pursuer were flooded as a result of the collapse of a sewer which was vested in the defenders. Therefore, the damage the pursuers sustained arose from an isolated escape. The pursuers raised an action against the defenders, *inter alia*, in terms of the law of nuisance. Whereas the case was decided on a different point, the House seemed to accept implicitly that an isolated escape could rank as a nuisance in Scots law. In other words, the existence of a state of affairs was not a condition precedent for liability in the law of nuisance.

"Escape" of people

11.35 Harm may be inflicted on land not only by natural or man-made hazards which exist on land. People themselves can inflict injury to the pursuer's land, in effect,

---

[92] [1969] 1 WLR 959.
[93] 1948 SC 599.
[94] 1927 SLT 563.
[95] 1985 SC (HL) 17.

by "escaping" from the defender's land to that of the pursuer. Therefore, one must consider the potential liability of an occupier of land in the law of nuisance for the conduct of persons who simply use that land as a means to inflict damage on the property of the pursuer. The fundamental problem confronting one who wishes to succeed in terms of the law of nuisance for the escape of people from land is that the courts have traditionally been reluctant to impose liability in the law of delict/tort in relation to the conduct of third parties.[96] As far as liability in the law of nuisance for harm inflicted by people who "escape" from land is concerned, the courts have had several opportunities to discuss such a form of liability.

In *Hussain* v *Lancaster City Council*,[97] the plaintiffs were the owners and occupiers **11.36** of both a shop and also residential property which were situated on a housing estate owned by the defendant council. The plaintiffs alleged that they had been the victims of a campaign of racial harassment, which consisted of attacks on their shop and also intimidation by people who gathered outside the shop. The plaintiffs sued the defendant in terms of both the law of nuisance and, also, negligence on the ground that the defendant had failed to prevent these undesirable activities. However, the Court of Appeal rejected the plaintiffs' claim under each head of action. As far as the claim in nuisance was concerned, the court held that the defendant was not liable, in that the adverse state of affairs did not derive from the manner in which the land (over which the defendant exercised control) affected the land of the plaintiffs. However, the court did not rule out the possibility that escapes by people onto the land of the plaintiff could rank as a nuisance in certain circumstances.

Shortly after *Hussain* was decided, the Court of Appeal had, once again, to **11.37** address the issue as to whether the escape of people from the defendant's land to that of the plaintiff could rank as a nuisance in *Lippiatt* v *South Gloucestershire Council*.[98] In that case the defendant council owned a strip of land which was occupied by a group of travelling people for a period of 3 years. The plaintiffs, who were tenant farmers and occupants of the adjacent land, brought proceedings against the council, alleging that the travellers had frequently trespassed on their land, also obstructed access to a field and carried out various unpleasant activities on it, including dumping rubbish, leaving excrement and tethering animals. Of interest, as far as the present discussion is concerned, is that the court held[99] that there was no rule in law which precluded a finding that activities taking place on the plaintiff's property (in contrast to that of the defendant) could rank as a nuisance.

While there is no authority on this point, it is the authors' view that as far as the **11.38** Scots law of nuisance is concerned, the adverse state of affairs which is the subject-matter of the action must take place on the land of the defender. In other words, it is the essence of the law of nuisance that the pursuer's enjoyment of land is indirectly invaded by either the acts or inactions of the defender.

---

[96] See, eg, *Murphy* v *Brentwood DC* [1990] 2 All ER 908; and *King* v *Liverpool City Council* [1986] 1 WLR 890.
[97] [1999] 4 All ER 125. The case was a striking-out action.
[98] [1999] 4 All ER 149.
[99] *Ibid* at 154.

REQUIREMENT OF *CULPA*

11.39 In English law nuisance liability is strict.[100] However, as far as the law of Scotland is concerned, the pursuer requires to prove *culpa* or fault on the part of the defender in order to succeed in a nuisance claim. The leading case is *RHM Bakeries Ltd* v *Strathclyde Regional Council*.[101] In that case bakery premises which belonged to the pursuer were flooded as a result of the collapse of a sewer which was under the control of the local authority. The pursuer sued the local authority on the ground of, *inter alia*, nuisance. It was held by the House of Lords that in order to succeed it was necessary for the pursuer to prove *culpa* on the part of the defender. Unfortunately, the House refrained from discussing the concept of *culpa* in relation to the law of nuisance. However, the Inner House had an opportunity to do so in *Kennedy* v *Glenbelle Ltd*.[102] The facts of the case were simple and straightforward. The pursuers were the heritable proprietors and tenants of tenement properties in Glasgow. The first defenders engaged the second defenders, a firm of consulting engineers, to advise on, design, direct and also supervise a scheme for the removal of a section or sections of wall within the premises. The pursuers raised an action against the defenders, claiming that, as a result of the work carried out in the basement, the pursuer's property had subsided. The basis of the action was that the carrying out of the renovation works in such a way that the pursuer's property was damaged amounted to a nuisance in law as well as in negligence. As far as the action in nuisance was concerned, the Inner House held that it was sufficient to prove in the instant case that a deliberate act had been done in the knowledge that damage would result from it. Lord Hope was of the view that *culpa* could be established by demonstrating negligence on the part of the defender, in which case the ordinary principles of the law of negligence would apply or *culpa* could be demonstrated by the fact that the defender was at fault in some other respect.[103] As far as this latter type of liability was concerned, *culpa* could either take the form of malice on the part of the defender or comprise a deliberate act on the part of the defender in that the defender knew that his action would result in harm to the pursuer or derive from the recklessness as to the consequences of his act. Here, Lord Hope identified a subspecies of recklessness, that is to say, a situation in which the defender has indulged in conduct that gives rise to a special risk of abnormal damage. In such a case, fault would be inferred. However, as far as liability in the instant case was concerned, the fact that the defenders knew that the deliberate removal of a section of the basement wall would result in damage to the pursuer's premises was sufficient to constitute the requisite *culpa* in order to ground liability in nuisance.[104]

11.40 However, Lord Kirkwood adopted a more "broad brush" approach to the concept of *culpa*. His Lordship endorsed the view of Lord Gifford in *Chalmers* v *Dixon*[105] to the effect that *culpa* is a flexible term and, therefore, much lighter fault may make a person liable in some circumstances than in others.[106] Lord Kirkwood concluded by stating

---

[100] *Cambridge Water Authority* v *Eastern Counties Leather Ltd* [1994] 2 AC 264.
[101] 1985 SC (HL) 17.
[102] 1996 SC 95. For a discussion of *culpa* and the law of nuisance, see F McManus, "*Culpa* and the Law of Nuisance" 1997 JR 259.
[103] *Ibid* at 100.
[104] *Ibid* at 101.
[105] (1876) 3 R 461 at 468.
[106] 1996 SC 95 at 102.

that before liability in damages for nuisance can be established there must be proof of a deliberate act or negligence or some other conduct from which *culpa* can be inferred.

The concept of *culpa* relating to the law of nuisance can now be summarised by stating that the requirement of *culpa* can be satisfied if it is proved that the defender has been negligent in some way. Here, negligence simply means negligence in the "duty of care" sense. Secondly, liability will lie if the defender has acted with malice towards the pursuer. Thirdly, liability will lie if the requisite state of affairs which harms the pursuer is brought about by either the deliberate or the reckless act of the defender. Fourthly, and most controversially, liability will lie if, through some fault of his, the defender brings into existence a state of affairs which ranks as hazardous. **11.41**

LIABILITY IN NUISANCE – WHO MAY BE SUED?

THE AUTHOR OF THE NUISANCE

The person who creates the nuisance, that is to say, the author of the nuisance, is liable in law.[107] He need have no interest in the land from which the nuisance arises.[108] For example, the organisers of a so-called "rave" held on a farmer's field could be held liable for any noise nuisance which is caused, notwithstanding the fact that the organisers have no proprietary interest in the land concerned. **11.42**

THE OCCUPIER OF LAND

The occupier of the land from which the nuisance emanates is normally liable in law.[109] The basis of liability is both the possession and also the control of the land from which the nuisance proceeds.[110] However, the occupier is not liable for an adverse state of affairs created by a third party – for example, by a trespasser, or by the act of nature – unless the occupier takes insufficient steps to abate the nuisance after he becomes aware of its presence, either actually or constructively, in which case the law will presume that he has adopted the nuisance. **11.43**

In *Sedleigh-Denfield* v *O'Callaghan*,[111] a local authority trespassed on the land of the defendant and then constructed a culvert on a ditch. One of the employees of the defendant knew of the existence of the culvert. Furthermore, the defendants also used the culvert in order to get rid of water from their own property. However, the culvert was not properly constructed, the upshot of which was that it became blocked by detritus. A heavy thunderstorm caused the ditch to flood, and the plaintiff's land became flooded. The House of Lords held the defendant liable in nuisance by virtue of both continuing and also adopting the nuisance in question. The defendant had continued the nuisance by virtue of failing to take the necessary remedial action after it became aware (through its servant) of the existence of the nuisance. The nuisance had been adopted by the defendant in using the culvert for its own purposes. **11.44**

---

[107] *Watt* v *Jamieson* 1954 SC 56.
[108] *Slater* v *McLellan* 1924 SC 854. See also *Marcic* v *Thames Water Utilities Ltd* [2004] 2 AC 42.
[109] *Sedleigh-Denfield* v *O'Callaghan* [1940] AC 880. See also *Smith* v *Scott* [1973] Ch 314.
[110] *Sedleigh-Denfield* v *O'Callaghan* [1940] AC 880 at 903 (per Lord Wright).
[111] *Ibid.*

11.45   However, it should be noted that in *Marcic v Thames Water Utilities Ltd*[112] the House of Lords held that the learning in *Sedleigh-Denfield* was inapplicable to determining the liability of a public utility in terms of whether it was liable to the claimant for damage caused by his property being inundated by effluent which had escaped from the defendant's sewer.[113]

11.46   The Privy Council had an opportunity to consider the law relating to nuisances created on the defender's land by third parties in *Goldman v Hargrave*.[114] In that case a tall gum tree, which was 100 feet high and situated on the defendant's land, was struck by lightning and then caught fire. The defendant cut the tree down the following day. However, he did not take any further steps to stop the fire from spreading, preferring simply to let the fire burn itself out. Several days later the weather changed. The wind became stronger and the air temperature increased. This caused the fire to revive and it spread over the plaintiff's land, which was damaged. The Privy Council held that the defendant was liable for the damage in that he had failed to remove the nuisance from his land. In so deciding, the court held that no distinction fell to be made between liability in terms of the law of negligence and the law of nuisance.[115] In deciding whether the defendant had failed to reach the standard of care which the law demanded, one was to take into account the defendant's knowledge of the hazard as well as his ability to foresee the consequences of not checking or removing it and also the ability to abate the nuisance.[116] However, in deciding whether the defendant had failed to attain the standard of care the law demanded of him, one was to adopt a subjective approach. One would, therefore, require to consider the resources of the defendant. One would also expect less of an occupier of small premises than that of larger property. In turn, less would be demanded of the infirm than of the able-bodied.

11.47   In *Leakey v National Trust for Places of Historic or Natural Beauty*,[117] the plaintiffs owned houses situated at the base of a steep conical hill which rejoiced in the name of "Burrow Mump". Part of the hill which adjoined the plaintiffs' land had become unstable. The condition of the hill was made known to the defendants by the plaintiffs. However, no remedial action was taken by the defendants. A few weeks later there was a substantial fall of earth and tree stumps from the hill on to the plaintiffs' land. The plaintiffs brought an action in nuisance. The Court of Appeal held the defendants liable. The court refused to draw a distinction between an adverse state of affairs which had been foisted on the defendant by man-made activities and that which arose by the operation of nature. The judgment of Megaw LJ is particularly interesting in that he discussed both the nature and the scope of the affirmative duty the law imposes on the occupier of land in relation to nuisances which, in effect, have been foisted upon him. In his Lordship's view, the extent of the harm to the plaintiff's premises should an accident occur, the practicability of preventative action, the cost of relevant works, and, also, the time which is available to take the necessary remedial action, were all relevant in determining liability.

---

[112] [2004] 2 AC 42.
[113] For a discussion of the *Marcic* decision and its relevance to Scotland, see F McManus, "*Marcic* rules OK? Liability in the law of nuisance in Scotland for escapes from overloaded sewers" (2008) *Water Law* 61.
[114] [1967] 1 AC 645.
[115] In *Delaware Mansions Ltd v Westminster City Council* [2001] 3 WLR 1007 at 1018, Lord Cooke expressed the view that in circumstances similar to those which featured in *Sedleigh-Denfield* and *Goldman*, the label "nuisance" or "negligence" was of no real significance.
[116] [1967] 1 AC 645 at 663 (per Lord Wilberforce). See also *Bybrook Barn Garden Centre Ltd v Kent County Council* [2001] EnvLR 30.
[117] [1980] QB 485.

The important question is whether *Sedleigh-Denfield*, *Goldman* and *Leakey* represent **11.48** the law of Scotland. Unfortunately, there is little authority on this point. However, the authors are of the view that these cases would be followed in Scotland. Yet the concept of *culpa* in the Scots law of nuisance is probably wider than the degree of fault necessary to ground liability in terms of the law which is set out in these three cases. It would, therefore, seem that in most cases a Scottish court would have no need to enlist the aid of these cases to determine liability for an occupier's failure to remove a nuisance from his land.

THE LANDLORD

A landlord is not liable for every nuisance emanating from his property which he has **11.49** leased.[118] Therefore, if I lease my flat to someone who proceeds to use the premises regularly for holding noisy parties, the upshot of which is that neighbours are annoyed, I would not be liable in terms of the law of nuisance. Rather, the landlord is only liable for a nuisance if he has either authorised the tenant to create a nuisance, or, if the creation of the nuisance is either certain or a highly probable result of the tenant's occupation of the premises concerned.[119]

THE LICENSOR OF THE NUISANCE

The person who authorises the creation of the nuisance is liable, especially if he makes **11.50** no attempt to either abate or remove the nuisance after he becomes aware of its existence. The leading case is *Webster* v *Lord Advocate*.[120] Here the pursuer claimed that the noise from both the performance of the Edinburgh Military Tattoo and also the erection of scaffolding to accommodate seating on the Edinburgh Castle esplanade amounted to a nuisance in law. The Lord Ordinary accepted that the Secretary of State for Scotland as occupier of the esplanade was liable in nuisance since he had licensed the creation of the nuisance. It was held irrelevant that the contract between the licensees, namely the Tattoo Policy Committee and the Secretary of State, contained a "no-nuisance" clause, since no attempt had been made by the latter either to monitor or to inspect the activities of the licensee or to enforce the clause. Therefore, if a licensor was capable and did, in fact, take steps to enforce such a clause, he could escape liability.

DEFENCES

We now consider several defences which have specific application to the law of **11.51** nuisance. Other defences which have a more general application in the law of delict are discussed in Chapter 21.

---

[118] *Smith* v *Scott* [1973] Ch 314.
[119] In *Smith* v *Scott*, *ibid* at 321, Pennycuik V-C was of the view that the proper test was that of "virtual certainty", which in his view was "another way of saying a high degree of probability". In *Tetley* v *Chitty* [1986] 1 All ER 663 at 671, McNeill J was of the view that the proper test for establishing liability in nuisance was whether the creation of the nuisance was the ordinary and necessary consequence of the lease or a natural and necessary consequence of the use of the land which was authorised by the landlord. See also *Dunn* v *Hamilton* (1837) 15 S 853 and *Caledonian Railway Co* v *Baird* (1876) 3 R 839.
[120] 1984 SLT 13.

STATUTORY AUTHORITY

11.52   The basis of this defence is that if Parliament has sanctioned the very state of affairs which constitutes the nuisance, this deprives the pursuer of a remedy. The defence has sole relevance to direct sanction by Parliament. For example, if the relevant adverse state of affairs has been approved by planning permission, such approval would not have a similar effect of denying the pursuer of a remedy.[121] The defence of statutory authority was invoked during the course of the 19th century against alleged nuisances from the operation of railways.[122] Indeed, much of the learning on the subject of the defence of statutory authority derives from the so-called "railway cases" which represent a particularly untidy area of law. Fortunately, the law embodied in the railway cases was reviewed and clarified by the House of Lords in the leading case of *Allen* v *Gulf Oil Refining Ltd*.[123] In that case a private Act of Parliament authorised a multinational company to acquire land, which was situated in a rural area, to construct an oil refinery. However, soon after the refinery commenced operations, residents who lived in the vicinity began to complain about the smell, noise and vibration which emanated from the plant. The House of Lords held that the Act had, by necessary implication, authorised both the construction and also the operation of the refinery, the inevitable consequence of which was the creation of the nuisance in question. Therefore, the plaintiffs failed in their action.

11.53   However, the defence of statutory authority does not apply if the relevant activities are being carried out negligently.[124]

11.54   Finally, if the relevant statute authorises the relevant activity to be carried out without causing a nuisance, the defence of statutory authority is inapplicable if the activity is carried on in such a manner as to cause a nuisance.[125]

PRESCRIPTION

11.55   The gist of this defence is that the law will not give a remedy to a pursuer who has failed to complain for 20 years or more in the face of a nuisance.[126] In order that the defence can succeed, the nuisance must have remained substantially constant over the prescriptive period,[127] and also constitute an actionable nuisance over that period.[128] Since, as explained above,[129] liability for nuisance in Scots law is prefaced on *culpa*, it automatically follows that the prescriptive period begins to run only when there is a convergence between fault on the part of the defender and the relevant adverse state of affairs. Furthermore, on the authority of both *Sturges* and *Webster*, the nuisance need not be in perpetual existence over the prescriptive period for the defence to succeed. It is sufficient that the nuisance manifests itself on a regular basis.

---

[121] *Wheeler* v *J J Saunders* [1996] Ch 19. See also *Watson* v *Croft Promo-Sport Ltd* [2009] EWCA Civ 15.
[122] See, eg, *Hammersmith and City Railway Co* v *Brand* (1869–70) LR 4 HL 171.
[123] [1981] AC 1001.
[124] See also *Tate and Lyle Industries Ltd* v *Greater London Council* [1983] 2 AC 509.
[125] *Hammersmith and City Railway Co* v *Brand* (1869–70) LR 4 HL 171.
[126] *Duncan* v *Earl of Moray* 9 June 1809, FC; *Collins* v *Hamilton* (1837) 15 S 902; and *Robertson* v *Stewarts and Livingston* (1872) 11 M 189; Prescription and Limitation (Scotland) Act 1973, s 7(1).
[127] *Webster* v *Lord Advocate* 1984 SLT 13.
[128] *Sturges* v *Bridgman* (1879) 11 Ch D 22.
[129] At para 11.39.

For the defence to succeed, the pursuer must have had either actual or constructive **11.56** knowledge of the nuisance.[130] The prescriptive period commences when the pursuer could have raised a successful action against the defender.[131]

Finally, if the defender does acquire a prescriptive right to continue a nuisance he **11.57** does not thereby acquire the right either to create another nuisance or increase the intensity of the nuisance in respect of which the prescriptive right has been acquired.[132]

It should be noted that the right to claim damages in terms of the law of nuisance **11.58** prescribes after 5 years.[133]

ACQUIESCENCE

The pursuer may also lose his right to raise an action in nuisance if he acquiesces in **11.59** the face of a nuisance. The defence of acquiescence is quite separate from the defence of prescription which has just been discussed.[134] The defence of acquiescence must be specifically pled.[135] For the defence to succeed there requires to be a clear, unequivocal and positive act on the part of the pursuer which indicates that he has consented to the nuisance in question. The person who is alleged to have acquiesced is required to have had both full knowledge of and also the power to stop that which is complained of.[136] Mere silence or passiveness in the face of the nuisance is insufficient to ground the defence.[137] Therefore, if I become aware that my land is being polluted by dust from a cement factory and I take no action, such awareness of the nuisance of itself would not disqualify me from raising an action. However, the occupation of the land which is affected by the nuisance, coupled with the knowledge of the existence of the nuisance, is capable of raising the presumption that the pursuer has acquiesced.[138] The longer the pursuer remains impassive in the face of the nuisance, the stronger is the presumption that he has acquiesced in its face. However, in *Colville* v *Middleton* it was held that 22 years' passive inaction was insufficient to ground the defence. Since the defence is based on implied consent, the defence is redundant if the pursuer objects timeously to the state of affairs in question.[139] Furthermore, the pursuer can only acquiesce in the face of the effects of a nuisance in contradistinction simply to the creation of the adverse state of affairs from which the nuisance arises.[140]

The act or acts of acquiescence can be implied from the facts and circumstances **11.60** of the case.[141] The defence does not apply if the nuisance in question differs either in nature or intensity from that which has been consented to.[142]

The courts are unwilling to infer acceptance or acquiescence of a given state of **11.61** affairs from the mere fact that the pursuer has "come to" the nuisance in question.

---

[130] *Liverpool Corporation* v *Coghill and Son* [1918] 1 Ch 307.
[131] *Ibid.*
[132] *Baxendale* v *MacMurray* (1867) LR 2 Ch 790; *McIntyre Bros* v *McGavin* [1893] AC 268; and *Webster* v *Lord Advocate* 1984 SLT 13.
[133] Prescription and Limitation (Scotland) Act 1973, s 6(1).
[134] *Collins* v *Hamilton* (1837) 15 S 902.
[135] *Buccleuch* v *Cowan* (1866) 5 M 214.
[136] *Earl of Kintore* v *Pirie* (1903) 5 F 818.
[137] *Cowan* v *Kinnaird* (1865) 4 M 236.
[138] *Colville* v *Middleton* 27 May 1817, FC.
[139] *Hill* v *Wood* (1863) 1 M 360.
[140] *Earl of Kintore* v *Pirie* (1903) 5 F 214.
[141] *Hill* v *Wood* (1863) 1 M 360 and *Houldsworth* v *Wishaw Magistrates* (1887) 14 R 920.
[142] *Colville* v *Middleton* 27 May 1817, FC.

The leading case is now *Webster* v *Lord Advocate*,[143] where the court swept aside the contention on the part of the defender that the pursuer, by choosing to reside in the vicinity of the Castle Esplanade in full knowledge that she would thereby expose herself to the noise generated by the Edinburgh Military Tattoo, had consented to the nuisance. Again, in *Miller* v *Jackson*[144] it was held to be no defence that the plaintiffs had decided to live in close proximity to a cricket pitch in the knowledge that by so doing they would expose themselves to the risk of being hit by cricket balls.[145]

REMEDIES

11.62   In order to raise an action in nuisance it is necessary that the pursuer has a proprietary interest in the land which is affected by the relevant nuisance. Therefore, someone who simply resides in the premises which are affected cannot successfully raise an action.[146] The remedies of damages, interdict and declarator which obtain generally in Scots law apply, of course, in the law of nuisance.[147] However, the authors would like to take the opportunity, at this juncture, to discuss the relevance of *culpa* to the law of interdict.

11.63   Some authors[148] hold the view that in sharp contrast to the case in which the pursuer sues the defender for damages, where *culpa* requires both to be averred and proved on the part of the defender, there is no need to do so when one simply raises an action for interdict.[149] However, it is the view of the authors that it is, indeed, necessary for the pursuer to aver and also prove *culpa* in an action for interdict given the fact that the grant of an interdict must be prefaced on the existence of either a wrong or a threatened wrong. Therefore, in order that any given state of affairs can rank as a nuisance (and therefore, a wrong) in law it must of necessity possess the stamp of *culpa* or fault from the very outset. It is illogical to talk, on the one hand, of the adverse state of affairs which ranks as a nuisance in law and, on the other, the culpable conduct of the defender which either created the nuisance or allowed it to remain in existence. They are indivisible. In conclusion, *culpa* is relevant to an action in nuisance where interdict is the only remedy the pursuer seeks.

---

[143] 1984 SLT 13.
[144] [1977] QB 966.
[145] See also *Watson* v *Croft Promo Sport Ltd* [2009] EWCA Civ 15.
[146] *Hunter* v *Canary Wharf Ltd*. [1997] EnvLR 488.
[147] See Chapter 22.
[148] See, eg, J Thomson, *Delictual Liability* (3rd edn, 2004) at p 192.
[149] See *Logan* v *Wang (UK) Ltd* 1991 SLT 580.

12 LIABILITY FOR ANIMALS

In this chapter we turn our attention to the law relating to liability for damage which **12.1** has been caused by animals.[1]

It is of course obvious that animals stand in quite a unique position as far as the **12.2** law of delict is concerned. Unlike other chattels, animals have a mind of their own. Animals can act unpredictably and, sometimes, quite violently towards each other and also to humans. The law, therefore, has had to treat animals in a special way. Indeed, in the House of Lords case of *Read* v *Lyons*[2] (the subject-matter of which did not relate to the liability of animals), Lord Simonds stated *obiter* that: "The law of torts has grown up historically in separate compartments and ... beasts have travelled in a compartment of their own." The law of delict has, perforce, had to deal with animals in a different way. In discussing the subject of liability for animals it is desirable, before focusing on the modern law, to look at how the law of Scotland has developed.

THE OLD LAW

At common law a person who was in charge of an animal was strictly liable for any **12.3** damage which was caused by the animal if:

(a) the animal was *ferae naturae* (that is, it belonged to a dangerous species); or
(b) the animal was *mansuetae naturae* (that is, it did not belong to a dangerous species) but, nonetheless, the animal had dangerous characteristics or tendencies.

Animals which fell into category (a) included lions, bears, wolves, gnus, apes and **12.4** monkeys.[3] As far as animals which fell into this category were concerned, the law imposed strict liability on the keeper of such animals for any injury they caused. In other words, liability lay quite irrespective of fault on the part of the defender.[4] Once a

---

[1] For a lengthier discussion of the law relating to liability for animals, see J Thomson (ed), *Delict* (2007), Ch 21.
[2] [1947] AC 156 at 182.
[3] Per Lord Moncrieff in *Burton* v *Moorhead* (1880–81) 8 R 892 at 895.
[4] See also *Hennigan* v *McVey* (1882) 9 R 411 where the Inner House held that a boar fell into the category of *ferae naturae* notwithstanding the fact that it was a domestic animal. Therefore, the defender was under a duty to take "absolute precautions". See also *Besozzi* v *Harris* (1858) 1 F and F 92 where it was held that a boar was presumed to be vicious. In the Court of Appeal case of *Filburn* v *The People's Palace and Aquarium Co* (1890) 25 QBD 258 it was held that an elephant was *ferae naturae* (see also *Behrens* v *Bertram Mills Circus Ltd* [1957] 2 QB 1). In *Marlor* v *Ball* (1900) 16 TLR 239 it was held that a zebra fell into the same category. In this interesting case the defendant was the proprietor of pleasure grounds in which he kept zebras. The zebras were kept in a stable. Each zebra was accommodated in a separate stall and was properly tied up by a halter. The plaintiff, having paid for admission to the grounds, found the door of the stable open. He entered the stable. He stroked one of the zebras whereupon the animal kicked out. The plaintiff fell into the next

member of a species of animal was deemed dangerous by the courts, the whole species automatically was to be regarded as *ferae naturae*.[5]

12.5   As far as animals which fell into category (b) were concerned, liability lay only if the animal concerned had evinced vicious tendencies in the past and such tendencies either were known, or should have been known, to the owner of the animal.[6] Furthermore, liability would lie if the animal was dangerous *sub modo*, that is to say, that the animal was dangerous only in a given situation. For example, in *McDonald v Smellie*,[7] a child was bitten on the leg by a dog which was not generally vicious but had nonetheless, in the past, behaved dangerously towards children. The defender owner knew of this trait. He was held liable for the injury caused by his dog.[8]

12.6   The rationale for the distinction the law made between animals which were *ferae naturae* and those which were *mansuetae naturae* was succinctly expressed by Devlin J[9] in *Behrens v Bertram Mills Circus*.[10] His Lordship stated:

> "The distinction between those animals which are *ferae naturae* by virtue of their genus and those which become so by the exhibition of a particular habit seems to me to be this: that in the case of the former it is assumed (and the assumption is true of a really dangerous animal such as a tiger) that whenever they get out of control they are practically bound to do injury, while in the case of the latter the assumption is that they will only do injury to the extent of the propensity they have peculiarly manifested."

THE MODERN LAW

LIABILITY UNDER THE ANIMALS (SCOTLAND) ACT 1987

12.7   We now consider the modern law relating to liability for damage caused by animals. However, it should be noted at the outset that the statute which we now discuss, that is to say the Animals (Scotland) Act 1987,[11] did not completely reform the law. Rather, the Act simply reformed the law relating to strict liability for animals.[12] The Act also replaces liability in terms of injury caused by straying animals and livestock in terms of the Winter Herding Act 1686 and damage inflicted by dogs to cattle and poultry in terms of the Dogs Act 1906.

---

stall where another zebra bit his hand. It was held that since the zebra fell into the category of a dangerous animal the defendant kept the animal at his peril. However, the court held that, notwithstanding this fact, the plaintiff must not have brought the injury on himself. In the instant case the plaintiff had done so by entering the stable and stroking the animal. The defendant was, therefore, not liable.

[5] *James v Wellington* [1972] NZLR 70.

[6] *Renwick v Rotberg* (1875) 2 R 855 and *Fraser v Bell* (1887) 14 R 811. See also *Smillie v Boyd* (1886) 14 R 150, *Clerk v Armstrong* (1862) 24 D 1315, *McIntyre v Carmichael* (1870) 8 M 570 and *Clerk v Armstrong* (1862) 24 D 1315.

[7] (1903) 5 F 955.

[8] See Erskine's *Principles of the Law of Scotland* (21st edn, 1911) (J Rankine (ed)) at pp 112–113.

[9] As he then was.

[10] [1957] 2 QB 1 at 18.

[11] The passing of the Act followed a period of gestation of almost a quarter of a century, including recommendations in 1963 of the Law Reform Committee for Scotland (Cmnd 2185); the passing of the Animals Act 1971 (applicable to England and Wales); a recommendation in 1978 by the Royal Commission on *Civil Liability and Compensation for Personal Injury* (Cmnd 7054) that the 1971 Act be applied to Scotland; a consultative memorandum (No 55) in 1982 by the Scottish Law Commission; and finally a report in 1985 by that Commission (Scot Law Com No 97); see also *Welsh v Brady* 2009 SLT 747 at 748 (opinion of the court).

[12] Animals (Scotland) Act 1987, s 1(8).

Under s 1(1) a person is liable for any injury[13] or damage caused by an animal if: **12.8**

(a) at the time of the injury or damage complained of he was the keeper of the animal;
(b) the animal belongs to a species whose members generally are by virtue of their physical attributes or habits likely (unless controlled or restrained) to injure severely or kill persons or animals or damage property to a material extent; and
(c) the injury or damage complained of is directly referable to such physical attributes or habits.

Species of animals includes sub-species.[14] **12.9**

For the purposes of s 1(1)(b), dogs and dangerous animals within the meaning **12.10** of s 7(4) of the Dangerous Wild Animals Act 1976 are deemed to be likely (unless controlled or restrained) to injure severely or kill persons or animals by biting or otherwise savaging, attacking or harrying.[15] It is a question of law for the court to decide whether the requirements of s 1(1)(b) are satisfied.[16]

In *Welsh* v *Brady*,[17] a dog walker raised an action against another dog walker for an **12.11** injury she received when the latter's black Labrador collided with her while running at great speed. The pursuer founded her action both on s 1(1)(b) of the Animals (Scotland) Act 1987 and also in terms of the common law of negligence. The Lord Ordinary in the Outer House found against the pursuer under both heads of action. She reclaimed. The Inner House was of the view that the form of injury the pursuer had sustained was not attributable to the characteristics which fell within the scope of s 1(1)(b) of the Act. In short, Labradors, by their very nature, are not likely to collide violently with individuals and injure them. The pursuer therefore failed in her action.[18]

Inter alia, cattle, horses, sheep and pigs are deemed to be likely (unless controlled **12.12** or restrained) to damage to a material extent land or the produce of land, whether harvested or not.[19] The Act goes on to provide that no liability lies under s 1 in respect of injury caused by an animal where the injury consists of disease transmitted by means which are unlikely to cause severe injury other than disease.[20] Therefore, no liability would lie if a visitor to my house became infected with a tropical disease from my tiger. However, if the visitor had been knocked against a rusty nail in a wall of my house by the tiger, the result being that he was infected by tetanus, I would be liable under the Act.

The Act also excludes liability in a situation where injury or damage is caused by **12.13** the mere fact that the animal is present on a road or other place.[21] Therefore, if I collide with a zebra while driving my car on a road, I would be unable to sue the keeper of the animal. However, if while driving on a road I find my way blocked by a zebra and I

---

[13] The expression "injury" includes death, any abortion or other impairment of physical or mental condition and any loss of or diminution in the produce of an animal and, subject to s 1(4) (discussed below), disease.
[14] Animals (Scotland) Act 1987, s 1(2).
[15] *Ibid*, s 1(3)(a). The expression "harry" is defined in s 7 as including chasing in such a way as may be likely to cause injury or suffering.
[16] *Foskett* v *McClymont* 1998 SC 96.
[17] 2009 SLT 747.
[18] See E Russell, "Liability for lively labradors" 2008 SLT 115.
[19] Animals (Scotland) Act 1987, s 2(3)(b).
[20] *Ibid*, s 1(4).
[21] *Ibid*, s 1(5).

proceed to attempt to push it off the road, whereupon I am bitten by the zebra, liability would lie under the Act.

Who is the animal's keeper?

12.14 The Act[22] defines the expression "keeper" as a person who owns the animal or has possession of it, or who has actual care and control of a child under the age of 16 who owns the animal or has possession of it.

Defences

12.15 The Act makes provision for exceptions to liability for injury inflicted by animals which are of a species falling within the scope of the Act.

General defences

12.16 Under s 2(1)(a), liability for injury or damage caused by animals does not lie if the injury or damage was due wholly to the fault of the person sustaining it or, in the case of injury sustained by an animal, the fault[23] of the keeper of the animal. The section also preserves the common law defence of *volenti non fit injuria*.[24] Furthermore, under s 1(6) any damages awarded to the pursuer in respect of any injury caused by an animal may be reduced in respect of the contributory negligence of the pursuer.[25]

Specific defences

12.17 The Act provides a defence if the injury or damage was sustained as a consequence of the person or animal sustaining the injury or damage coming on to land which was occupied by a person who was a keeper or by another person who authorised the presence on the land of the animal which caused the injury or damage, and, either:

    (i) the person sustaining the injury or damage was not authorised or entitled to be on the land (as the case may be); or

    (ii) no keeper of the animal sustaining the injury was authorised or entitled to be on the land.[26]

12.18 Furthermore, there is no exemption from liability if the animal causing the injury was kept on the land wholly or partly for the purpose of protecting persons or property unless the keeping of the animal was reasonable and, if the animal was a guard dog within the meaning of the Guard Dogs Act 1975, unless there was compliance with s 1 of that Act.[27]

---

[22] Animals (Scotland) Act 1987, s 5.

[23] The expression "fault" has the same meaning under the Act as it does in the Law Reform (Contributory Negligence) Act 1945, s 2(3)(a).

[24] For an example of the application of the defence of *volenti* in relation to the Animals Act 1971 (England and Wales), see *Cummings* v *Granger* [1977] 1 QB 397 and *Freeman* v *Higher Park Farm Ltd* [2009] PIQR P6. For a fuller discussion of the defence of *volenti*, see Chapter 21.

[25] Animals (Scotland) Act 1987, s 1(6).

[26] *Ibid*, s 2(1)(c).

[27] *Ibid*, s 2(2).

LIABILITY UNDER THE LAW OF NEGLIGENCE

As was stated above, the Animals (Scotland) Act 1987 only replaces strict liability **12.19** which the common law imposed in relation to injury caused by animals. In other words, the law of negligence which we have discussed[28] is also applicable to damage caused by animals.[29]

LIABILITY IN NUISANCE[30]

Finally, the conduct of animals, such as the creation of noise, can also render the **12.20** occupier of the relevant land liable in the law of nuisance.[31]

---

[28] See Chapter 2.

[29] See, eg, *Mitchil v Alstree* (1676) 1 Vent 295; *Hadwell v Righton* [1907] 2 KB 345; *Milne and Co v Nimmo* (1898) 25 R 1150; *McCairns v Wordie and Co* (1901) 8 SLT 354; *Aldham v United Dairies* [1940] 1 KB 507; *Cameron v Hamilton* 1955 SLT (ShCt) 74; *Henderson v John Stuart (Farms) Ltd* 1963 SC 245; *Draper v Hodder* [1972] 2 QB 556; *Hill v Lovett* 1992 SLT 994; *Swan v Andrew Minto* 1998 RepLR 42; *Wilson v Donaldson* [2004] EWCA 972; *Whippey v Jones* [2009] EWCA Civ 452.

[30] See Chapter 11 for a general discussion of the law of nuisance.

[31] See, eg, *Ball v Ray* (1873) 8 Ch App 467.

13 ASSAULT

Assault constitutes both a crime and a civil wrong or delict. As far as assault in terms **13.1** of the law of delict is concerned, the question to be answered is: to what extent, if any, does the law allow one to recover damages in respect of either intentional or threatened acts of violence? Bankton[1] divided such acts into:

- assault; and
- real injury.

As far as the delict of assault was concerned, this meant threatening to perpetrate an **13.2** act of physical violence on the person of the pursuer. The delict also included lying in wait for the pursuer and besetting his mansion in such a way whereby the pursuer's servants were unable to go in or out.

As far as real injury was concerned, the delict centred on both direct and wrongful **13.3** acts inflicted on the person of the pursuer by the defender. Bankton regarded such "real" injuries as analogous to the tort of trespass to the person in English law.[2] Examples of real injury included beating, striking, pushing and spitting upon the face of another.[3] The defender was liable to the pursuer in damages in respect of either assaults or real injuries.[4] However, the distinction between assault and real injury (or, as far as the law of England is concerned, assault and battery or trespass to the person) has not remained in Scots law. The expression "assault" is now used to embrace a situation where the pursuer is simply threatened with violence as well as circumstances where the act of violence actually takes place.

INGREDIENTS OF ASSAULT

The essence of the delict of assault is that the defender has either actually used, or **13.4** threatened to use, physical force against the person of the pursuer, with intention on the part of the defender and also without lawful excuse. The majority of assaults are constituted by the use of direct force against the person of the pursuer, for example by striking, kicking,[5] stabbing him, pulling his nose,[6] shooting him[7], hitting him with

---

[1] *Institutes of the Law of Scotland*, 1, 10, 37.
[2] For a general account of the tort of trespass to the person in English law, see W V H Rogers (ed), *Winfield & Jolowicz on Tort* (18th edn, 2010), ch 4.
[3] Bankton, *Institutes of the Law of Scotland*, 1, 10, 38.
[4] *Ibid*, 1, 10, 38.
[5] *McGregor* v *Murphy* (1895) 11 Sh Ct Rep 85.
[6] *Gordon* v *Stewart* (1842) 5 D 8.
[7] *McDonald* v *Robertson* (1910) 27 Sh Ct Rep 312.

an object,[8] or throwing him into water.[9] Professor Walker argues that it is an assault to make an immodest gesture to a woman which affronts her dignity.[10]

13.5 There need be no direct contact between the defender and the pursuer for an action in assault to lie. In the criminal case of *R* v *David Keay*,[11] the accused whipped a pony being ridden by the victim. The pony reared up and threw its rider. It was held that this constituted an assault. Again, in the celebrated English case of *Scott* v *Shepherd*,[12] A threw a lighted squib into a crowded marketplace. The squib fell upon the gingerbread stall of Y. A bystander, W, in order to prevent injury to himself and also damage to the wares of Y, picked up the squib and threw it away. The squib fell on the gingerbread stall of R, who, in order to save his own goods from injury, threw the squib further. It struck B in the face, exploded, and blinded him in one eye. It was held that A was liable to B for both trespass and also assault.

13.6 In the English criminal case of *R* v *Ireland*,[13] the defender admitted making a large number of telephone calls to three women and remaining silent when they answered. As a result, each woman had suffered psychological damage. The House of Lords held that, in the light of contemporary knowledge covering recognisable psychiatric injury, such injury fell to be construed as "bodily harm" within the meaning of the Offences against the Person Act 1861[14] and that, in the context of the Act, "inflict" included the infliction of psychiatric injury on another and was not confined to harm applied directly to the person of the victim. Furthermore, an assault might be committed by words or gestures alone, depending on the circumstances. The making of silent telephone calls, where such calls caused fear of immediate and unlawful violence, could make the caller guilty of an assault. *Ireland*, of course, illustrates the fact that there need be no direct physical contact between the defender and the pursuer.

13.7 It is not always necessary, in order to constitute an assault by means of applying some degree of force to the person of the pursuer, that the defender intends to injure the pursuer. For example, in *Harris* v *North British Railway*[15] it was held to be an assault to remove the pursuer forcibly from a train. To fondle, handle or kiss a woman against her will would constitute an assault.[16]

DEFENCES

SELF-DEFENCE

13.8 According to Bankton, it was lawful to strike someone in self-defence or in defence of one's wife, children, parents, master or servants or in defence of one's property.[17] One was also entitled to use force against the pursuer if one reasonably believed that one

---

[8] *Houston* v *McIndoe* 1934 SC 172.
[9] *Beaton* v *Drysdale* (1819) 2 Mur 151.
[10] D Walker, *Delict* (2nd edn, 1981) at p 490.
[11] (1837) 1 Swin 543.
[12] (1773) 2 WBl 892.
[13] [1998] AC 147.
[14] The Act applies only in England and Wales.
[15] (1891) 18 R 1009.
[16] *Hill* v *Fletcher* (1847) 10 D 7.
[17] Bankton, *Institutes*, 1, 10, 23.

was under imminent danger of attack.[18] The defence of self-defence still survives if the accused has acted in an honest, albeit mistaken, belief that he is under threat of imminent attack.[19] The force which the law allows the defender to use must be commensurate with the force offered to the defender.[20] However, the court will not measure with jewellers' scales the difference between the threat offered by the pursuer to the defender, and the force used by the defender towards the pursuer.[21] If the force offered by the defender by way of self-defence is excessive, such force will constitute an assault.[22]

NECESSITY

One can lawfully use force in order to restrain a person from doing harm either to oneself **13.9** or to a third party.[23] In *Leigh* v *Gladstone*[24] it was held to be lawful to force-feed a prisoner on the ground of necessity. One can also use force in order to prevent damage to property, or remove a trespasser from one's property, provided that one requests the trespasser to remove himself before any force is used.[25] Police officers may use reasonable force in order to make an arrest or to prevent the commission of crime.[26] Persons other than police officers are entitled to use reasonable force to detain without warrant those whom they see committing serious crimes. However, there require to be good grounds for a private citizen to make such an arrest. It is not sufficient that one simply suspects another person of committing an offence.[27] Prison warders, asylum attendants, railway servants and ship officers are entitled to use reasonable force in the performance of their duties.[28]

CONSENT

The pursuer cannot recover if he has freely consented to the assault in question.[29] It **13.10** is no defence, however, if the pursuer has been deceived by the defender as to the nature of the act which constitutes the assault. For example, in *R* v *Flattery*,[30] the defender professed to give medical and surgical advice for money. He advised X, a young woman, that a surgical operation required to be performed. Under the pretence of performing it, he had sexual intercourse with X. It was held that the defendant had committed an assault on the person of X. According to Mellor J:[31] "She consented to one thing, he did another materially different on which she had been prevented by his fraud from exercising her judgement and will."

While consent extorted by fear is no consent, consent unwillingly given ranks as **13.11** a valid consent in the eye of the law.[32] Consent may be given either expressly or by

---

[18] *Owens* v *HM Advocate* 1946 JC 119.
[19] *Ashley* v *Chief Constable of Sussex Police* [2008] 1 AC 962. See [2008] CLJ 461.
[20] *Lane* v *Holloway* [1968] 1 QB 379.
[21] *Cross* v *Kirkby, The Times,* 5 April 2000.
[22] *McDiarmid* v *Barrie* (1901) 18 Sh Ct Rep 47; *Hallowell* v *Niven* (1883–84) 11 R 217.
[23] *Knight* v *Inverness District Board of Control* 1920 2 SLT 157.
[24] (1909) 25 TLR 139.
[25] *Anderson* v *Barr and Cavens* (1847) 9 D 929.
[26] *Marchbank* v *Annan* 1987 SCCR 718.
[27] *Codona* v *Cardle* 1989 SCCR 287. See also *Ashley* v *Chief Constable of Sussex Police* [2008] 1 AC 962.
[28] *Brown* v *Hilson* 1924 JC 1.
[29] *Thomson* v *Devon* (1889) 15 Sh Ct Rep 209.
[30] (1876–77) 2 QBD 410.
[31] *Ibid* at 413.
[32] *Latter* v *Bradell* (1881) 50 LJQB 448.

implication.[33] That is to say, the law implies consent to the various forms of contact which one encounters in everyday life. For example, if two or more people meet in a narrow passage, and one touches the other gently, this form of contact does not constitute a battery.[34] Again, those who engage in sport implicitly consent to the physical contact associated with that sport. However, the law does not imply consent in respect of conduct which is carried out in a reckless and dangerous manner.[35]

CORPORAL PUNISHMENT

13.12 The law allows reasonable chastisement of child by a parent or another person in *loco parentis*.[36]

---

[33] *Thomson v Devon* (1899) 15 Sh Ct Rep 209.
[34] *Cole v Turner* (1704) 6 Mod Rep 149.
[35] *Condon v Basi* [1985] 1 WLR 866.
[36] *Skewis v Adams* (1914) 30 Sh Ct Rep 217. See now the Criminal Justice (Scotland) Act 2003, s 51(1). However, in *A v UK* [1998] FamLR 118 it was held that Art 3 of the European Convention on Human Rights (which provides that no one shall be subject to torture or inhuman or degrading treatment or punishment) had been breached when a stepfather caned with some considerable force a 9-year-old boy who was in his care.

14 DEFAMATION

Reflecting on the law of defamation, Faulks observed that the law of defamation has **14.1** two purposes, namely: to enable the individual to protect his reputation, and also to preserve the right to the freedom of speech. These two purposes necessarily conflict. The law of defamation was sound if it preserved a proper balance between them.[1]

THE ESSENTIALS OF DEFAMATION

In order to raise a successful action in defamation, the pursuer is required to prove the **14.2** following:

(1) the publication or communication of a defamatory statement;
(2) the statement is false;
(3) the publication concerns a living person; and
(4) the reputation of the pursuer is lowered.

PUBLICATION

There is no requirement in the law of Scotland that the defamatory statement **14.3** be made to a third party for liability to lie. For example, in *Stuart* v *Moss*[2] the defender, a theatre manager, engaged the pursuer, who was an actor, to perform in three towns. However, the actor failed to act up to the defender's expectation. The defender wrote a letter to the pursuer which stated: "You advertise what you are not capable of." The words were written to the pursuer alone. It was held that the defender was liable. Again, in *Mackay* v *McCankie*[3] it was held that a slanderous statement, which is in either oral or written form, and concerns the person to whom it is addressed, will found an action for damages even though no third parties read the statement.

The general rule is that the person who circulates a defamatory statement, for **14.4** example a publisher, printer or newsagent, is equally answerable with the author of the statement.[4] Similarly, a person who simply repeats a defamatory statement is liable, in addition to the maker of the original statement.[5]

---

[1] Faulks Report on *Defamation* (Cmnd 5909, 1975), para 19.
[2] (1885) 13 R 299.
[3] (1882–83) 10 R 537.
[4] Per Lord Kyllachy in *Wright and Greig* v *Outram* (1890) 17 R 596 at 599.
[5] *MacDonald* v *Martin* 1935 SC 621, *Fraser* v *Fraser* 2010 SLT (ShCt) 147 and *Lewis* v *Daily Telegraph Ltd* [1964] AC 234.

14.5   Whereas the law of England makes a distinction between defamation which takes a permanent form (in English law, "libel") and that which is of temporary form (in English law, "slander"), no such distinction falls to be made in the law of Scotland.[6]

Mode of communication

14.6 The defamatory statement or communication need not be in words. For example, the statement can take the form of a cartoon[7] or a waxwork model.[8]

FALSITY OF STATEMENT

14.7 The pursuer must aver, but need not prove, that the defamatory statement is false. If the statement is defamatory it is presumed to be untrue and the defender must prove that it is true.[9]

STATEMENT MUST BE ABOUT A LIVING PERSON

14.8 In order for the defamatory statement to be actionable it must be made of a living person.[10] In other words, one cannot defame the dead. One's reputation dies with one. A juristic person such as a bank or trading company can sue in defamation, provided its professional or commercial reputation is struck at.[11] However, a local authority cannot sue in respect of a defamatory statement which reflects on its governing reputation, since to allow it to do so would impose a substantial and unjustifiable restriction on freedom of expression.[12]

Words must refer to the pursuer

14.9 For liability to lie, the words complained of must refer to the pursuer.[13] However, it is irrelevant that the defender did not wish to refer to the pursuer.[14] Furthermore, the defamatory words need not contain a key or pointer to the pursuer for liability to lie.[15] In short, it simply suffices that the defamatory words would be understood by reasonable people to refer to the pursuer.[16] Where the pursuer is not named, the test is whether the words complained of would reasonably lead people who are acquainted with the pursuer to the conclusion that he was the person referred to.[17] Such strict

---

[6] For a discussion of the distinction between libel and slander in the law of England, see Winfield and Jolowicz, *Tort* (ed W Rogers) (17th edn, 2010) at p 570.
[7] *Tolley* v *Fry* [1931] AC 29.
[8] *Monson* v *Tussauds* [1894] 1 QB 671.
[9] *MacKellor* v *Duke of Sutherland* (1862) 24 D 1124.
[10] *Broon* v *Ritchie* (1904) 6 F 942. At the time of writing (2011) the Scottish Executive has published a consultation paper entitled "Death of a good name: defamation of the deceased", which invites views on whether the law of Scotland should, indeed, allow relatives to recover damages in respect of the defamation of a deceased relative.
[11] See *North of Scotland Banking Co* v *Duncan* (1857) 19 D 1156 and *South Hetton Coal Co* v *North Eastern News Association* [1894] 1 QB 133. See also *Jameel (Mohammed)* v *Wall Street Journal Europe SPRL* [2007] 1 AC 359.
[12] *Derbyshire CC* v *Times Newspapers* [1992] 3 WLR 28.
[13] *Knupffer* v *London Express* [1944] AC 116.
[14] *Hulton* v *Jones* [1910] AC 20.
[15] *Morgan* v *Odham's Press Ltd.* [1971] 1 WLR 1239. See also *Cassidy* v *Daily Mirror Newspapers* [1929] 2 KB 311 and *Hough* v *London Express Newspapers Ltd* [1940] 2 KB 507.
[16] *O'Shea* v *MGN Ltd* [2001] EMLR 40.
[17] *Knupffer* v *London Express* [1944] AC 116.

liability is mitigated, but at the same time not entirely removed, by the Defamation Act 1996,[18] which makes provision for an offer of amends in such circumstances. However, the strict liability the common law imposes here may now infringe Art 10 of Sch 1 to the Human Rights Act 1998 which makes provision for freedom of expression.[19]

Defamation of class

It is not defamatory to defame a class.[20] For example, if a newspaper were to publish **14.10** a letter to the effect that all solicitors were dishonest, an individual solicitor could not raise a successful action against either the author of the letter or the relevant newspaper. However, if the group which is defamed is small and, therefore, each individual member of the group can be identified, each individual member of the group could sue.[21] For example, if it were falsely alleged that the lecturers in a university law department (which comprised ten lecturers) were all poor academics and unworthy to be called "university law lecturers", each could sue.

REPUTATION OF PURSUER LOWERED

The question which falls to be answered now, of course, is: what ranks as defamatory **14.11** in the eye of the law? In *Sim v Stretch*,[22] Lord Atkin was of the view that in ascertaining if words were defamatory one would consider whether the words would tend to lower the pursuer in the estimation of right-thinking members of society generally? Faulks, in turn, was of the view that a statement was defamatory if it contained "matter which, in all the circumstances, would be likely to affect a person adversely in the estimation of reasonable people generally".[23] However, to date, neither judge nor academic writer has attempted to provide a comprehensive definition of what ranks as defamatory in law.[24] Indeed, such definitional problems resemble those concerning the law of nuisance.[25]

Generally, however, a defamatory statement involves some imputation against the **14.12** character or reputation of the pursuer, including his business or financial reputation. The notion of lowering the reputation of the pursuer in the mind of the general public is a common theme which runs through defamation cases.[26] It is a question of law as to whether the words in question are capable of being defamatory.[27] It is a matter of fact (possibly for the jury to decide) whether the actual words which were used by the defender of the pursuer were defamatory of the latter.

We now consider examples of what constitutes defamation. However, it must be **14.13** emphasised at the outset that what are considered below are simply *examples* of what

---

[18] Section 2.
[19] *O'Shea* v *MGN Ltd* [2001] EMLR 40.
[20] See, eg, *Sherlock* v *Beardsworth* (1816) 1 Mur 196.
[21] *Browne* v *Thomson and Co* 1912 SC 359.
[22] (1936) 52 TLR 669 at 671.
[23] Faulk's Report (n 1, above) at para 65.
[24] Per Sharp J in *Ecclestone* v *Telegraph Media Group Ltd* [2009] EWHC 2779 at para [15].
[25] See Chapter 11.
[26] See, eg, *Skuse* v *Granada Television Ltd* [1996] EMLR 278 and *Ecclestone* v *Telegraph Media Group Ltd* [2009] EWHC 2779.
[27] See, eg, *Adam* v *Ward* [1917] SC (HL) 14, *Russell* v *Stables Ltd* 1913 SC (HL) 14, *Gordon* v *John Leng* 1919 SC 415 and *Lewis* v *Daily Telegraph Ltd* [1964] AC 234.

the courts have considered defamatory. The list as to what ranks as defamatory is not closed.

Dishonesty

14.14   It is defamatory to allege that the pursuer is dishonest.[28]

Sexual immorality

14.15   It is defamatory to allege that the pursuer is sexually immoral. In *Morrison* v *Ritchie*,[29] false birth notices were inserted in a newspaper. The pursuer was married on 12 July 1901. The notice stated that a child was born to the pursuer and his wife one month later. This was held to be defamatory.

14.16   At one time, to allege that someone was a homosexual was clearly defamatory.[30] This may not be the case today.[31]

Improper, disgraceful or dishonourable conduct

14.17   It is defamatory to allege that the pursuer has conducted himself in an improper, disgraceful or dishonourable way. For example, in *McLaren* v *Robertson*[32] it was held to be defamatory to allege that the pursuer was the "Greatest Liar in the world". Again, in *McFarlane* v *Black*[33] the defender contended that the pursuer, who was a parliamentary candidate, spoke sarcastically about God's almighty Earth and sneered at Divine Government. It was held that the jury was entitled to hold that the words were defamatory. In *Gordon* v *John Leng and Co*[34] a newspaper article alleged that the pursuer, who was a colonel, had ordered men to surrender during the retreat from Mons in 1914 during the Great War. It was held that to impute such conduct to the pursuer was defamatory.

14.18   In *Cuthbert* v *Linklater*,[35] Wendy Wood, who was a famous Scottish Nationalist, raised an action against author Eric Linklater. In 1932, Wendy Wood had removed a Union Jack from Stirling Castle, rolled up the flag and then thrown it to a guard. However, in one of Linklater's novels, Beaty Bracken removes a Union Jack from Stirling Castle and places it in a public urinal. It was held that to impute such conduct to the pursuer was defamatory.

Imputations of criminal conduct

14.19   To allege that the pursuer has committed a serious crime such as murder[36] or theft[37] is defamatory. However, how serious the crime requires to be before the allegation ranks as defamatory is difficult to decide. There is little authority on this point.

---

[28] *Harkness* v *Daily Record* 1924 SLT 759.
[29] (1902) 4 F 645.
[30] *AB* v *XY* 1917 SC 15.
[31] *Quilty* v *Windsor* 1999 SLT 346.
[32] (1859) 21 D 183.
[33] (1886–87) 14 R 870.
[34] 1919 SC 415.
[35] 1935 SLT 94.
[36] *Monson* v *Tussauds* [1894] 1 QB 671.
[37] *Neville* v *C&A Modes* 1945 SC 175.

Unfitness for occupation or profession

14.20 To allege that the pursuer is unfit to perform the tasks demanded of him by his profession is defamatory. In *MacKellar* v *Duke of Sutherland*[38] it was held to be defamatory to state that a minister was incompetent in office. Again, in *McRostie* v *Ironside*[39] the defender stated that the pursuer carried on lawsuits for the purpose of creating money for himself in the wanton disregard of the interests of clients. This was held to be defamatory.

Insolvency and uncreditworthiness

14.21 To allege that the pursuer is either insolvent or lacks creditworthiness is defamatory.[40]

Unsoundness of mind

14.22 To allege that the pursuer is unsound in mind is defamatory.[41]

Loathsome disease

14.23 To allege that the pursuer is suffering from a loathsome disease is defamatory. This form of defamation is probably confined to allegations that the pursuer is suffering from a sexually transmitted disease.[42]

Victim of rape

14.24 Whereas the act of rape can elicit nothing but sympathy on the part of the general public for the victim, in *Youssoupoff* v *MGM*[43] it was held defamatory to allege that the pursuer had been raped by Rasputin. While this case has never been overruled, it may not represent the modern law of Scotland.

Objective approach adopted to ascertain meaning of words

14.25 In order to ascertain whether the words which are the subject-matter of the action are defamatory, one requires to ascertain what meaning such words would convey to the ordinary reader.[44] However, the judge decides how an ordinary man or woman would have analysed the article.[45] Furthermore, in order to ascertain how the ordinary reader would construe the alleged defamatory words, the article etc in which the offending words are contained requires to be read as a whole. This point was neatly illustrated in *Charleston* v *News Group Newspapers Ltd*.[46] In that case, two soap opera stars sued in respect of material published in the defendant's newspaper which depicted the claimants' faces superimposed upon two-near naked torsos engaged in sex. The article printed beneath the picture castigated the makers of a pornographic computer game

---

[38] (1859) 21 D 222.
[39] (1849) 12 D 74.
[40] *Russell* v *Stubbs* 1913 SC (HL) 14; *AB* v *CD* (1904) 7 F 22.
[41] *MacIntosh* v *Weir* (1875) 2 R 877.
[42] *A* v *B* 1907 SC 115; *Farrell* v *Boyd* 1907 SC 1154.
[43] (1934) 50 TLR 581.
[44] *Hunter* v *Ferguson* (1906) 8 F 574. See also *Freeguard* v *Marlet Ltd*, *The Times*, 15 January 2009.
[45] *Lewis* v *Daily Telegraph Ltd* [1964] AC 234. See also *Slim* v *Daily Telegraph Ltd* [1968] 2 QB 157, *Skuse* v *Granada Television Ltd* [1996] EMLR 278 and *Ecclestone* v *Telegraph Media Group Ltd* [2009] EWHC 2779.
[46] [1995] 2 AC 65.

which had generated the images in question. The House of Lords held that, taken as a whole, the picture and the article were not capable of being defamatory, in that the article, read as a whole, made the fact quite clear that the claimants had neither consented to being photographed in the manner depicted by the photograph, nor consented to their images being used for pornographic literature. In the last analysis, the picture which had been juxtaposed with the article did not bear a defamatory meaning.[47]

INNUENDO

14.26 Words which are innocent in themselves may, however, bear some secondary meaning which is capable of giving the words in question a defamatory meaning. In such circumstances, the pursuer must found his action on an innuendo. For example, making a waxwork model of a person who has been acquitted of a charge of murder might not be defamatory. However, placing the model of the person beside a room called "The Chamber of Horrors" which contains models of convicted murderers may be defamatory.[48] In *Morrison* v *Ritchie*,[49] considered above,[50] the publication of the relevant birth notice was patently innocuous. However, if it was known that the relevant couple had simply been married for a month, the words bear quite a different meaning.

14.27   In *Russell* v *Stubbs*,[51] Lord Shaw stated: "The innuendo must represent what is reasonable, natural or necessary inference from the words used, regard being had to the occasion and the circumstances of their publication." It is a matter of law for the court to determine whether the innuendo is one which the words used may reasonably bear. However, it is a matter of fact whether the words should be construed in that sense.[52] The relevant publication requires to be published to individuals who would construe the innuendo in the defamatory manner which is alleged.[53]

14.28   The application of the innuendo in the law of defamation is neatly illustrated in *Cassidy* v *Daily Mirror Newpapers Ltd*.[54] There the defendants published a newspaper photograph of a racehorse owner who was called Cassidy, and a Miss X. Alongside the photograph there was an announcement that the couple had just become engaged. However, the plaintiff was known among her acquaintances as the lawful wife of Cassidy. The defendants were unaware of this fact. The plaintiff successfully claimed that the publication bore an innuendo to the effect that reasonably minded people would have formed the impression that she was not the wife of Cassidy but, rather, was living with him in immoral cohabitation. Similarly, in *Tolley* v *Fry*,[55] the defendants, a firm of chocolate manufacturers, published a caricature of the plaintiff, who was a

---

[47] See also *Curran* v *Scottish Daily Record* 2010 SLT 377 and *Ecclestone* v *Telegraph Media Group Ltd* [2009] EWHC 2779.
[48] *Monson* v *Tussauds* [1894] 1 QB 671.
[49] (1902) 4 F 645.
[50] At n 50, above.
[51] 1913 SC (HL) 14 at 24.
[52] Per Lord Ross in *Fairbairn* v *SNP* 1979 SC 393 at 397. See also *Duncan* v *Associated Newspapers Ltd* 1929 SC 14.
[53] *Fullam* v *Newcastle Chronicle and Journal Ltd* [1977] 3 All ER 32.
[54] [1929] 2 KB 331.
[55] [1931] AC 333.

famous amateur golfer, depicting him playing golf in the company of a caddy who was holding up packets of the defendant's chocolate. A packet of Fry's chocolate protruded from Tolley's pocket. Below the caricature was a limerick in the following terms:

> "The caddie to Tolley said, Oh sir,
> Good shot Sir. That ball, see it go, Sir
> My word how it flies,
> Like a cartet of Frys,
> They're handy, they're good and priced low, Sir."

The caricature and limerick went on to describe the merits of Fry's chocolate. In the last **14.29** analysis, the whole publication was simply a vulgar advertisement for the defendant's goods. However, one can see that, on the face of it, there was nothing really defamatory about the advert. Indeed, the plaintiff did not allege this. Rather, he alleged that the advert bore an innuendo to the effect that he had either agreed or had permitted his portrait to be exhibited for the purpose of the advertisement of the defendant's chocolate, and that he had done so for gain and reward and had, thereby, prostituted his reputation as an amateur golfer for advertising purposes. The House of Lords held that the caricature was capable of bearing such an innuendo.

Words can only rank as defamatory at the time of publication. That is to say, facts **14.30** which come to light after the defamatory words are published cannot be founded upon in an action based on innuendo. This point is well illustrated in *Grappelli* v *Derek Block (Holdings) Ltd*.[56] In that case, the plaintiff was a musician of international repute. He employed managers or agents. In June 1976, the defendant arranged for the plaintiff to give concerts at various venues on specified dates. However, the bookings were made without the plaintiff's authority and had to be cancelled. When informing the managers of the various concert halls where the performances were scheduled to take place, the defendant stated that the plaintiff was ill and would never tour again. Later in the year, authentic notices appeared in a national newspaper giving dates of forthcoming concerts which included concerts on the same dates as those which had been cancelled but in different towns. The plaintiff brought action against the defendant, alleging that the false statement made by the defendant, to the effect that the plaintiff was seriously ill, gave rise to an innuendo that the plaintiff had given a reason which he knew to be false. However, it was held by the Court of Appeal that since the cause of action in defamation had to be known as soon as the words complained of were published, any extrinsic facts which were relied on to support an innuendo had to be known at the time of publication by those to whom they were published. Since no such extrinsic facts were known on the relevant date, the plaintiff failed. However, if the words in the relevant article are defamatory and simply the identification of the pursuer is omitted, a subsequent article which proceeds to identify the pursuer can be founded upon by him in a defamation action.[57]

It is sufficient to prove that there are people who might understand the words in a **14.31** defamatory sense. That is, there is no need for the pursuer to prove that some people actually did understand the words in a defamatory sense.[58]

---

[56] [1981] 2 All ER 272.
[57] *Hayward* v *Thomson* [1981] 3 All ER 450.
[58] *Hough* v *London Express Newspaper Ltd* [1940] 2 KB 507.

14.32   In some cases, however, the pursuer need not found on extrinsic facts. He may simply claim that the very words which are complained of have a slang or cant meaning in addition to the ordinary dictionary meaning of the word or words. For example, to say that someone is "bent" would not commonly nowadays be regarded as a comment on that person's physique but, rather, a comment on his sexual disposition.[59] The word "gay" would have a similar meaning.

DEFENCES

14.33 We now consider the defences which are specific to the law of defamation.

VERITAS (TRUTH)

14.34 The first defence is the defence of *veritas* (or truth),[60] which is commonly known as the defence of justification in the law of England. The rationale of this defence is that the law will not permit a man to recover damages in respect of an injury to his character which he does not possess.[61] The defence of *veritas* is a complete defence.[62] For example, if it were to be accurately reported in a newspaper that a distinguished politician was having an extramarital affair with a young woman and this was quite true, the newspaper publishers could avail themselves of the defence of *veritas* in any resultant defamation action. It is irrelevant that the defender is inspired by malice. Furthermore, the literal truth is not necessary for the defence to lie. It simply suffices that the statement is true in substance. In short, the defender must justify the sting of the charge made against the pursuer. This point is neatly illustrated in *Alexander* v *N E Railway*.[63] In that case, a statement that the plaintiff had been convicted of travelling in a train without a ticket, and had been fined £1, with 3 weeks' imprisonment in default of payment, was held to be capable of being justified by proof that the plaintiff had been convicted of the offence but had been sentenced to only 2 weeks' imprisonment in default of payment.

14.35   The Defamation Act 1952[64] now provides: "In an action for defamation in respect of words containing two or more distinct charges against the pursuer a defence of justification shall not fail by reason only that the truth of every charge is not proved if the words not proved to be true do not materially injure the pursuer's reputation having regard to the truth of the remaining charges."

14.36   Under the Rehabilitation of Offenders Act 1974[65] the defender cannot invoke the defence of *veritas* in relation to a spent conviction if the defamatory statement is proved to have been made with malice.

---

[59] *Allsop* v *Church of England Newspaper Ltd* [1972] 2 QB 161.
[60] For an interesting account of the defence of veritas or justification in English law, see E Descheemaeker, "'Veritas non est defamatio'? Truth as a defence in the law of defamation" (2011) 31 LS 1.
[61] *McPherson* v *Daniels* (1829) 10 B and C 263.
[62] Per Lord Nicholls in *Reynolds* v *Times Newspapers Ltd* [2001] 2 AC 127 at 192.
[63] (1865) 6 B and S 340.
[64] Section 5.
[65] Section 8(5).

INNOCENT DISSEMINATION

The Defamation Act 1996[66] provides a defence if the defender can show that he was   **14.37**
not the author, editor or publisher of matter complained of and that he took reasonable
care in relation to its publication and that he did not know or have reason to believe
that what he did caused or contributed to the publication of defamatory matter.

OFFER OF AMENDS

The Defamation Act 1996 makes provision for an offer of amends by the defender   **14.38**
in relation to a statement which is alleged to be defamatory, either generally or
specifically.[67] If the offer to make amends is accepted by the aggrieved party, the party
accepting the offer may not either bring or continue defamation proceedings in respect
of the publication.[68] The statutory offer to make amends is not a true defence in reality.[69]

ABSOLUTE PRIVILEGE

There are certain occasions on which it is for the benefit of the public that one should   **14.39**
be able to speak or write freely without fear of being sued for defamation. Such
occasions include the following.

Parliamentary proceedings

Statements made in either of the Houses of Parliament[70] and also reports and proceedings   **14.40**
published under the authority of either House in *Hansard* are protected.[71] Provisions
contained in an Act of the Scottish Parliament are also protected.[72] Statements made
in proceedings of the Scottish Parliament and also any publication of any statement
authorised by the Scottish Parliament are covered by absolute privilege.[73]

Judicial proceedings

Absolute privilege attaches to all statements made in judicial proceedings.[74] However,   **14.41**
protection does not extend to the entirely irrelevant answer of a witness to a question
which is put to him in court. For example, in answer to a question "Were you in
Edinburgh on 1st January 2011?" to which the witness replies "Yes and X [who has
nothing at all to do with the case] assaulted me on that day", the statement of the
witness would not be covered by qualified privilege.

In Scotland, the law does not confer absolute privilege to statements which are   **14.42**
made in civil proceedings. Parties to civil actions have only qualified privilege in
respect of such statements.[75]

---

[66] Section 1(1).
[67] Section 2(2).
[68] Section 3(2).
[69] A view to that effect was expressed by Morland J in *O'Shea* v *MGN Ltd* [2001] EMLR 943 at 953.
[70] Bill of Rights 1688, which was declared law by 1 Will & Mary, c 2 (1689).
[71] Parliamentary Papers Act 1840.
[72] Defamation Act 1996, s 17 (as amended by the Scotland Act 1998).
[73] Scotland Act 1998, s 41.
[74] *Hebditch* v *MacIlwaine* [1894] 2 QB 54.
[75] *Neill* v *Henderson* (1901) 3 F 387.

14.43 Fair and accurate reports of judicial proceedings are also covered by absolute privilege.[76]

Executive matters

14.44 Communications between certain officers of state are covered by the defence of absolute privilege as far as the law of defamation is concerned. In *Chatterton* v *Secretary of State for India*,[77] it was held that a letter from the Secretary of State for India to his Parliamentary Under-Secretary was covered by absolute privilege. However, it is unclear how high up the executive hierarchy the maker of the statement must be for the statement to be covered by absolute privilege.

14.45 If a statement is covered by absolute privilege, it is quite irrelevant that the maker of the statement is activated by malice.

QUALIFIED PRIVILEGE

14.46 There are certain circumstances where considerations of public policy and also the interests of society dictate that statements made on certain occasions should receive protection in terms of the law of defamation. Therefore, in certain circumstances the law allows the defender to avail himself of the defence of qualified privilege. However, in sharp contradistinction to the defence of absolute privilege, the defence of qualified privilege is vitiated by malice on the part of the defender. Privilege is not accorded by law either to communications or to the people who communicate them but, rather, to occasions.[78]

14.47 The categories of occasions covered by the defence of qualified privilege are not closed.[79] However, such occasions can roughly be included under the following headings:

Where A has a legal or moral or social duty to communicate a statement to B, and B, in turn, has a corresponding interest in receiving that statement; or where A has an interest to be protected and B is under a corresponding legal, moral or social duty to protect that interest.

14.48 In *Fraser* v *Mirza*,[80] a complaint by a member of the public to a Chief Constable about one of his police constables was held to be covered by qualified privilege. However, if the maker of the statement complains to the wrong person he loses the defence of qualified privilege.[81]

14.49 A person who gives a job reference is covered by qualified privilege.[82] However, if the statement is negligent, liability may lie.[83]

14.50 Whether the maker of the statement is under a moral or social duty to make the statement is a matter for the judge.[84] According to Lindley LJ, a moral or social duty

---

[76] Defamation Act 1996, s 14.
[77] [1895] 2 QB 189.
[78] Per Lord Hope in *Reynolds* v *Times Newspapers Ltd* [2001] 2 AC 127 at 229. See also *Horrocks* v *Lowe* [1975] AC 135. See also *Adam* v *Ward* [1917] AC 309 and *Fraser* v *Mirza* 1993 SC (HL) 27.
[79] *Per* Lord Cooke in *Reynolds* [2001] 2 AC 127 at 224.
[80] 1993 SLT 527.
[81] *Beach* v *Freeson* [1972] 1 QB 14.
[82] *Farquar* v *Neish* (1890) 17 R 716.
[83] *Spring* v *Guardian Assurance* [1995] 2 AC 296.
[84] *Stuart* v *Bell* [1891] 2 QB 341. See also *GKR Karate (UK) Ltd* v *Yorkshire Post Newspapers Ltd (No 2)* [2000] EMLR 410, per Sir Oliver Popplewell at 421.

meant a "duty recognised by English people of ordinary intelligence and moral principle, but at the same time not a duty enforceable by legal proceedings whether civil or criminal".[85] The duty to publish the relevant statement must exist at the time of its publication in order to attract the defence of qualified privilege.[86]

In the majority of reported cases, the interest to be protected comprises a property, **14.51** business or financial interest. However, other forms of interest have been recognised by the courts. For example, a complaint to a bishop that a clergyman had got into a fight with a schoolmaster was held to be covered by qualified privilege.[87] Again, in *Seray-Wurie* v *The Charity Commission of England and Wales*,[88] it was held that the publication of a report of inquiry held by the Charity Commission attracted qualified privilege. There the relevant interest revolved around the function of the Charity Commission both to investigate and to report on alleged misconduct or mismanagement in the administration of charities.

The defence of qualified privilege in relation to statements made to the public at large **14.52** was transformed by the House of Lords decision in *Reynolds* v *Times Newspapers Ltd*.[89] Indeed, this case has been described as the most significant development of the common law of defamation in recent times.[90] The facts of the case were quite straightforward. Essentially, *The Sunday Times* published an article which accused Reynolds, who was at the time Prime Minister of Ireland, of lying to the Irish Parliament. Reynolds sued the publishers of the newspaper in defamation. In turn, the defendants pleaded, *inter alia*, the defence of qualified privilege on the basis that the common law should recognise a generic form of qualified privilege which encompasses the publication by a newspaper of political matters affecting the people of the United Kingdom. However, the House refused to accept the proposition that the common law recognised such a defence.

Lord Nicholls, who gave the leading judgment, endorsed the decision of the Court **14.53** of Appeal to the effect that, in order to ascertain whether a situation attracted the defence of privilege in law, the court was required to consider, among other things, the nature, the status and also the source of the material which was published, as well as the circumstances of the publication.[91] For his Lordship, these were the very factors to be considered in ascertaining, first, whether the defender was under a duty to publish the relevant material, and, second, whether the public had an interest in receiving such material. The duty–interest test could not be carried out in isolation from these factors. His Lordship then went on to articulate the duty–interest test in terms of statements made by the media to the general public in the form of a "checklist" which is not exhaustive.[92] The relevant factors include the seriousness of the allegation, the nature of the information, the source of information, the steps taken to verify the information, and, whether comment was sought from the pursuer.

In the House of Lords case of *Jameel* v *Wall Street Journal*,[93] Lord Bingham expressed **14.54** the view that the decision in *Reynolds* built on the traditional foundations of qualified

[85] [1891] 2 QB 341 at 350.
[86] *Loutchansky* v *Times Newspapers Ltd* [2001] 3 WLR 404. See also *Clift* v *Slough BC* [2010] EWCA Civ 1171.
[87] *James* v *Boston* (1845) 2 C and K 4.
[88] [2009] EWCA Civ 153.
[89] [2001] 2 AC 127.
[90] *Joseph* v *Spiller* [2010] 3 WLR 1791 at 1812 (per Lord Phillips).
[91] *Ibid* at 197.
[92] *Ibid* at 205.
[93] [2007] 1 AC 359.

privilege but, at the same time, carried the law further in such a way that gave much greater weight than the earlier law had done to the value of informed public debate of significant public issues.[94] For Lord Scott, Lord Nicholls in *Reynolds* did not turn his back on the reciprocal duty–interest test for qualified privilege. Instead, Lord Nicholls had moulded the test so as to cater for the publication as a whole, as opposed to what a specific individual, or individuals, was or were entitled to know.[95]

14.55 The application of the so-called *"Reynolds* test" in relation to the defence of qualified privilege can be seen in *GKR Karate* v *Yorkshire Post Newspapers Ltd (No 2)*.[96] In that case, an article which appeared in a local newspaper circulated in the Leeds area made allegations about the claimant's conduct in selling karate lessons. It was alleged that the standard of lessons offered was of an inferior nature. Leeds families were, therefore, warned in the article not to buy lessons from the claimant's door-to-door salesmen. It was held at first instance that the defendant newspaper could avail itself of the defence of qualified privilege on the grounds that the public in Leeds had a legitimate interest in receiving the information, and the defendant newspaper was under a social and moral duty to communicate to the public in Leeds the particular information contained in the article. It was also in the public interest that the newspaper published the information which was the subject-matter of the action.

14.56 In *Flood* v *Times Newspaper Ltd*,[97] Lord Neuberger MR expressed the view that both the *Reynolds* decision and the advent of human rights jurisprudence have caused the courts to focus on the competing Convention rights, namely Arts 8 and 10 of Sch 1 to the Human Rights Act 1998 (the former guaranteeing the right to respect for family life, the latter guaranteeing freedom of expression), in a case where public interest privilege is raised to justify what would otherwise be a defamatory and inaccurate statement.

Reportage

14.57 We have already seen, in discussing the subject of publication, that the repetition of a defamatory statement renders the person who repeats the statement liable, in addition to the person who made the original statement.[98] However, in the wake of the *Reynolds* decision there has appeared a defence known as "reportage". The expression is now a term of art (ie a technical term) in the law of defamation. The first reported case where the defence of reportage featured was the Court of Appeal case of *Al-Fagih* v *HH Saudi Research and Marketing (UK) Ltd*,[99] where it was said[100] that reportage was a "convenient word to describe the neutral reporting of attributed allegations rather than their adoption by the newspaper". For example, if it was reported in the *Bruntsfield News* that X (a professor of law) had recently been seen lying drunk on Bruntsfield Links at lunchtime, and, subsequently, the *Craiglockhart Post* published an article about X, simply stating that it had been reported in the former newspaper that X had been seen

---

[94] [2007] 1 AC 359 at 376.
[95] *Ibid* at 402. However, Lord Hoffmann and Baroness Hale were of the opinion that, in effect, the *Reynolds* defence was *sui generis*.
[96] [2000] EMLR 410.
[97] [2010] EWCA Civ 804 at [41].
[98] See para 14.4.
[99] [2002] EMLR 13.
[100] Per Simon Brown LJ at [6]. For a general discussion of reportage, see J Besland, "Republication of Defamation under the Doctrine of Reportage – the Evaluation of Common Law Qualified Privilege in England and Wales" (2011) 310 JLS 89.

lying drunk on Bruntsfield Links, this would be reportage. One can see here, of course, that the *Craiglockhart Post* has simply reiterated the allegation made in the *Bruntsfield News*. That is to say, the *Craiglockhart Post* has not endorsed (that is, suggested that what was alleged of X was true) the statement made by the *Bruntsfield News* about X.

In *Roberts* v *Gable*,[101] the Court of Appeal held that there is no conflict between **14.58** the repetition rule and reportage, that is to say that, whereas the former is concerned with the defence of justification, the latter is concerned with the defence of privilege. To qualify as reportage, the report must have the effect of reporting, not the truth of the statement which was made, but rather the fact that it was made. The protection accorded by the defence of reportage would be lost if the journalist adopts the relevant report as his own, or if he fails to repeat the report in a fair, disinterested and neutral way. All the circumstances of the case and the factors listed in *Reynolds*, adjusted as may be necessary for the special nature of reportage, had to be considered in order to reach the conclusion that the article was the product of responsible journalism. Reportage was not confined to scandal-mongering. Reportage could, indeed, embrace serious allegations. The critical question was whether the public had the right to know that the relevant accusations were being made. Furthermore, for the defence of reportage to apply there was no need for the claimant to be a public figure.

Galloway v *Telegraph Group Ltd*[102] illustrates the defence of reportage, and also its **14.59** limits, quite neatly. In that case, serious allegations were made about an MP in the defendant's newspaper articles. The allegations were based on documents which had been found in Baghdad. The Court of Appeal held that, since *The Telegraph* had not simply neutrally reported the contents of these documents but had "embraced them with relish and even embellished them", the defence of reportage was inapplicable.

Another interesting case in which the defence of reportage was discussed was **14.60** the Court of Appeal case of *Charman* v *Orion Publishing Group Ltd.*[103] In that case the claimant, who was a former detective constable in the Metropolitan Police Force, raised an action in defamation in respect of certain passages which were contained in a book. The passages concerned a detailed account of his relationship with another officer and also a police informant. The defendants relied by way of defence on qualified privilege. One of the issues the court had to decide was the defence of reportage. According to Ward LJ,[104] the defence of reportage would be established if, judging the thrust of the report as a whole, the effect of the report was not to adopt the truth of what was being said but simply to record the fact that the defamatory statements had been made. The protection the law accorded by way of privilege in such circumstances would be lost if the relevant journalist adopted what had been said and made it his own or if he failed to report the story in a fair, disinterested and neutral way. However, in the instant case, the defining characteristic of reportage was missing in that the book which was the subject-matter of the action was not written to report the *fact* that allegations of corruption had been made against the claimant and the fact that he had denied them and, in turn, had accused the investigating officers of plotting against him. In the opinion of his Lordship the book was: "a piece of investigative journalism where [the journalist] was acting as the bloodhound sniffing out bits of the story from here and

---

[101] [2007] EMLR 16.
[102] [2006] EMLR 11.
[103] [2008] 1 All ER 750.
[104] *Ibid* at 765.

there, from published material and unpublished material, not as the watchdog barking to wake us up to the story already out there".

14.61   It can be concluded from the above authority that the defence of reportage is not a separate defence. Rather, reportage is simply a branch of the *Reynolds* defence which is applied to a particular form of journalistic reporting. In the authors' view there does, indeed, seem to be an uneasy tension between the defence of reportage and the well-established rule, discussed above,[105] to the effect that a person who repeats a defamatory statement is as liable as the person who uttered such a statement in the first place. The authors, therefore, eagerly await a Supreme Court ruling on this grey area of the law of defamation.

Protection of common interest

14.62   The defence of qualified privilege also applies if the defamatory statement is made by the defender in order to protect a common interest which he shares with the person to whom the statement is made. A good illustration of the application of such a principle is seen in *Watt* v *Longsdon*.[106] B was a foreign manager of the X Co. B wrote to Y, who was a director of the company, a letter containing gross charges of immorality, drunkenness and dishonesty on the part of the plaintiff, who was the managing director of the company abroad. B also wrote a letter to the plaintiff's wife along similar lines. The Court of Appeal held that B's letter to Y was covered by qualified privilege, since both B and Y had a common interest in the conduct of the affairs of the company. However, B's letter to the plaintiff's wife was not similarly privileged since no such common interest existed between them.

14.63   Another case which illustrates the same point is *Brady* v *Norman*.[107] In that case the claimant had been suspended from a trade union. He was subsequently dismissed as its general secretary. An article was printed in the union journal to the effect that the certification officer of the union had ruled that the claimant had been legitimately excluded from membership of the union for bringing the union into disrepute. The journal was also published on the union website. The defendant, who was the general secretary of the union, claimed the defence of qualified privilege. It was held, at first instance, that the defence failed on the basis that whereas some of the people on the distribution list of the journal had a legitimate interest in the affairs of the union, many of those to whom the journal was distributed did not. There was, therefore, no common interest to support the defence of qualified privilege.

Statutory privilege

14.64   The Defamation Act 1996[108] gives qualified privilege to any report or other statement mentioned in Sch 1 to the Act unless malice is shown. Other statutes – for example, the Freedom of Information Act 2000[109] – confer qualified privilege in certain circumstances.

Loss of qualified privilege

14.65   Privilege can be lost if:

---

[105] At para 14.4.
[106] [1930] 1 KB 130.
[107] [2008] EWHC 2481.
[108] Section 15(1).
[109] Section 79.

- the privilege is exceeded; or
- the defender is prompted by malice.

Excess of privilege

Privilege will be lost if a statement is made on an occasion which would otherwise **14.66** be privileged but the defender includes matter quite unconnected with that which would otherwise attract the defence of privilege.[110] For example, if one were to write to a client demanding payment for a legal opinion which one had prepared for him and one were to include a statement in one's letter "the fact that you are not paying me is quite disgraceful. You are a fraudster", the final sentence would deprive one of the defence of qualified privilege.

Privilege will also be lost if the statement is published to more persons than the occasion demands.[111]

Malice

The defence of qualified privilege will be lost if the defender uses the occasion on which **14.67** the statement is made for some improper purpose, or if he is motivated by spite.[112] The court will infer malice if the defender does not believe in the truth of his statement, or he was reckless as to whether the statement was true or false.[113] The honest belief in the veracity of one's statement will allow the defence to succeed. However, even if the defender thinks that the statement is true, privilege will be lost if the defender's main intention is to harm the pursuer. If the defender's motives are mixed, the improper motive must be the dominant one for the defence to be lost.[114]

FAIR COMMENT

In the Court of Final Appeal of Hong Kong case of *Tse wai Chun* v *Cheng*,[115] Lord **14.68** Nicholls stated that the purpose of the defence of fair comment was to facilitate the freedom of expression by commenting on matters of public interest. However, the law relating to this defence certainly constitutes a notoriously grey area of the law. Indeed, in the Supreme Court case of *Joseph* v *Spiller*,[116] which is now the leading case on the subject, Lord Phillips described the defence of fair comment as one of the most difficult areas of the law of defamation. His Lordship then went on to castigate the law of defamation *in toto* as "archaic" and also a "tangled web", and concluded that little had occurred in the last 20 years to unravel the tangle. This was particularly true of the defence of fair comment.[117] It is now necessary to look at *Joseph* in some detail.

The facts of the case were simple and straightforward. The claimants were members **14.69** of a group of musicians. In 2004, one of the claimants, who was the manager of the group, agreed that the group's live acts could be promoted by the defendants, who were an

---

[110] *Tuson* v *Evans* (1840) 12A & E 733.
[111] *De Buse* v *McCarthy* [1942] 1 KB 156 and *Brady* v *Norman* [2008] EWHC 2481.
[112] See *Adam* v *Ward* [1917] AC 309 and *Horrocks* v *Lowe* [1975] AC 135.
[113] *Fraser* v *Mirza* 1993 SC (HL) 27.
[114] *Horrocks* v *Lowe* [1975] AC 135.
[115] [2001] EMLR 777 at 778.
[116] [2010] 3 WLR 1791 at 1793.
[117] *Ibid* at 1794.

advertising agency. The terms and conditions of the agreement included a re-engagement clause which provided that any further bookings at any venue in the following 12 months should be arranged through the defendants. In 2007, the defendants complained to the claimants that the latter had arranged a performance directly with a venue, in breach of that condition. The claimants replied to the defendants by way of e-mail. The reply stated: "your contract … holds no water in legal terms". The defendants' response to the claimants' e-mail was swift. The defendants posted a notice on their website. That notice announced that the defendants were no longer accepting bookings for the claimants as, "following a breach of contract [the first claimant] had advised that the terms and conditions of … contracts hold no water in legal terms". The claimants brought libel proceedings against the defendants, averring that the statement which had been posted on their website meant that the claimants were grossly unprofessional and also that they were untrustworthy. The defendants claimed, *inter alia*, the defence of fair comment.

14.70   The Supreme Court,[118] in deciding in favour of the defendants, set out the following requirements for the defence of fair comment to succeed:

(a) the relevant statement must be comment, not fact;
(b) the matter in respect of which the comment is made is in the public interest;
(c) where that matter consists of facts which are alleged to have occurred, the facts are true;
(d) the comment is fair; and
(e) the statement is not made maliciously.

14.71   These requirements will now be discussed in turn.

(a) The relevant statement must be comment as opposed to fact

14.72   The defence of fair comment applies only if the words complained of are comment as opposed to fact. That is to say, the words must be an expression of opinion. For example, if I were to write of X, who is a football club manager of Y, in my newspaper, "X is a disgrace to his club", this would be a statement of fact. However, if I were to write, "Y has not won a game this season and, therefore, *X is a disgrace to his club*", the italicised phrase would rank as a comment.

The test which the courts employ to distinguish fact from comment is objective.[119] Here, the intention of the maker of the relevant statement is quite irrelevant. However, it is sometimes difficult to ascertain whether certain words are, indeed, opinion or fact. For example, in *Dakhyl* v *Labouchere*,[120] the plaintiff was described as "a quack of rankest species". The House of Lords held that this could be comment.

(b) The matter in respect of which the comment is made is in the public interest

14.73   In the Court of Appeal case of London *Artists Ltd* v *Littler*,[121] Lord Denning MR stated that there is no definition in the books as to what is a matter of public interest.

---

[118] [2010] 3 WLR 1791, per Lord Phillips at 1818.
[119] *London Artists Ltd* v *Littler Grade Organisation Ltd* [1969] 2 QB 375. See also *British Chiropractic Association* v *Singh* [2011] 1 WLR 133.
[120] [1908] 2 KB 325.
[121] [1969] 2 QB 375 at 391.

However, his Lordship was of the view that what ranked as that which fell within the public interest was not to be confined within narrow limits. His Lordship then went on to state that whenever a matter is such as to affect people at large, so that they may be legitimately interested in, or concerned at, what is going on, or what may happen to themselves or others, then it is a matter of public interest on which everyone is entitled to make fair comment. A few examples of what the courts would include as falling within the scope of public interest are: the closure of a theatrical play,[122] the conduct of those in public office,[123] and also the conduct of a publishing house,[124] all of which have been deemed to fall within the public interest.

(c) Where the matter consists of facts which are alleged to have occurred, the facts are true

In order to attract the defence of fair comment, the relevant comment requires to be **14.74** based on true facts, or statements which are privileged: for example, statements made in court by a witness.[125] Not all the facts need be stated in the comment. However, the comment requires to be based on a sufficient substratum of fact.[126] Furthermore, the comment should identify the subject-matter on which it is based in order to enable the reader of the comment to form his own view of the validity of the comment.[127] In *Joseph*, Lord Phillips emphasised that the rationale for the creation of the defence of fair comment was the desirability that a person should be entitled to express his views freely about a matter of public interest. If the subject-matter of the comment was not apparent from the comment, this justification for the defence would be lacking. The defamatory comment would be wholly unfocused.[128] However, where adverse comment is made generically or generally on matters which are in the public domain, there is no requirement that it is a prerequisite for fair comment that the readers should be in a position to evaluate the comment for themselves. However, it may be difficult to decide what falls within the public domain and, therefore, one can assume that the reader will automatically be familiar with the relevant facts in relation to which the comments are made. For example, in *Telnikoff* v *Matusevitch*,[129] the defendant wrote an article published in the *Daily Telegraph* which was highly critical of an article the plaintiff had written in a previous edition of the newspaper. The House of Lords held that the question as to whether the words complained of were capable of constituting statements of fact (that is, in order to determine whether the defence of fair comment could be sustained) was to be determined by consideration of the contents of the letter alone.

Sometimes the pursuer is not able to prove the truth of all the facts on which he **14.75** has made adverse comment. The Defamation Act 1952[130] provides that in an action for defamation the defence of fair comment shall not fail "by reason only that the truth

---

[122] *London Artists* v *Littler Grade Organisation Ltd* [1969] 2 QB 375.
[123] See *Campbell* v *Spottiswoode* (1863) 3 B & S 769 and *Langlands* v *Leng* 1916 SC (HL) 102.
[124] *Kemsley* v *Foot* [1951] 2 KB 34.
[125] *London Artists* v *Littler*. See also *Merivale* v *Carson* (1887) 20 QBD 275. See also *Brent Walker Group* v *Time Out Ltd* [1991] 2 QB 33.
[126] *Kemsley* v *Foot* [1952] AC 345.
[127] *Joseph* v *Spiller* [2010] 3 WLR 1791, per Lord Phillips at 1821.
[128] *Ibid* at 1821.
[129] [1992] 2 AC 343.
[130] Section 6.

of every allegation of fact is not proved if the expression of opinion is fair comment having regard to such of the facts alleged to in the words complained of as are proved".

(d) The comment is fair

14.76   An objective test is employed by the court in order to ascertain whether the comment is fair.[131] Wide latitude is given to the defender by the courts as to whether the comment is fair.

(e) The statement is not made maliciously

14.77   The defence of fair comment fails if the defender is motivated by malice. There is a considerable overlap between the requirements of (d) and (e). The law as to what constitutes malice in terms of the law of defamation was taken further by the Supreme Court in *Joseph*. There, Lord Phillips was of the view that the issue as to malice was no longer a subjective one, that is to say, whether the defendant honestly believed that the facts on which he commented justified his comment. Instead, the focus has been on the objective question, namely: could an obstinate and prejudiced person honestly have based the comment made by the defendant on the facts on which the defendant commented?[132] Lord Phillips went on to conclude that the defence of fair comment should be renamed "honest comment".[133] One can therefore see that, in the wake of *Joseph*, the defender may have been motivated to make the relevant comment out of malice towards the pursuer and, at the same time, avail himself of the defence of fair comment. It is, therefore, difficult to agree with Lord Phillips' suggestion to the effect that the defence of fair comment should be renamed the defence of "honest comment".

FAIR RETORT

14.78   The law allows a person, against whom an allegation has been made publicly, to deny the charge in strong language. Here, judicial indulgence is granted to the defender. In denying the allegation the pursuer has made against him, the defender may use strong words. However, the defence of fair retort does not confer *carte blanche* on the defender to defame the pursuer. The defender is required to confine his counter-attack to the subject-matter of the allegation the pursuer made against him. For example, in *Milne* v *Walker*,[134] the pursuer wrote a letter to a newspaper in which he claimed that the defender had supplied him with inferior goods. The latter replied in the same newspaper to the effect that the pursuer was a liar. It was held that the defence of fair retort was inapplicable since that the defender had simply accused the pursuer of being a liar. In other words, the defender had not confined his counter-attack on the pursuer to the supply of the goods in question.[135]

---

[131] *Merrivale* v *Carson* (1887) 20 QBD 275.
[132] *Joseph* v *Spiller* [2010] 3 WLR 1791 at 1823.
[133] *Ibid* at 1824.
[134] (1893) 21 R 155.
[135] See also *Gray* v *SSPCA* (1890) 17 R 1185.

RIXA

The defence of *rixa* is confined to words which are spoken in anger. According to **14.79** Cooper, the defence of *rixa* in Scots law has at its basis the same as that which distinguishes slander from libel in the law of England, that is to say that persons who sit down to write defamatory words certainly do so with some deliberation.[136]

For the defence of *rixa* to succeed, it requires to be proved that, viewed objectively, **14.80** the defender did not really utter words which were defamatory of the pursuer. In effect, if words are spoken in anger the courts attempt to give the least possible defamatory meaning to the words in question. For example, in *Christie v Robertson*,[137] the pursuer and defender bid for the same horse at an auction. Each was under the impression that the horse had been knocked down to him. As the defender was leading away the horse, the pursuer accused the defender of trying to steal the horse, whereupon the defender claimed that the pursuer should have been in the hands of the police at least 20 times during the past 5 years. The Inner House held that the words which were spoken of the pursuer were not to be understood in a defamatory sense.

The defence does not apply, however, if a definite charge or accusation is made **14.81** against the pursuer.

VERBAL INJURY

The expression "verbal injury" is a term which has been used since towards the end of **14.82** the 19th century. Verbal injury has become associated with words which harmed the pursuer but which were, at the same time, not defamatory. For example, in *Paterson v Welch*,[138] the defender stated that the pursuer had claimed that if children from the poorer classes were allowed to attend Madras College this would contaminate the genteel children who were currently attending the school. One can see, of course, that to allege that such a statement had been made was not defamatory. However, the Inner House decided that an action for verbal injury could succeed if it could be proved that:

(1) the statement is false;
(2) there was an intention on the part of the defender to injure the pursuer; and
(3) the pursuer sustained injury.

Verbal injury also includes slander of title, slander of property and also of **14.83** business.[139]

---

[136] *Cooper on Defamation and Verbal Injury* (1894) at p 89.
[137] (1889) 1 F 1155.
[138] (1893) 20 R 744.
[139] See also *Steele v Scottish Daily Record* 1970 SLT 53.

CONVICIUM

14.84 According to Professor Walker,[140] the law of Scotland recognises a quite separate action in the form of *convicium*. For this action to succeed, the learned author is of the view that the pursuer was required to prove that:

(1) the defender had maliciously communicated words concerning the pursuer;

(2) the words could have been either true or false;

(3) the words were calculated (that is if it was the natural tendency of the words) to bring the pursuer into public hatred, ridicule and contempt; and

(4) the words caused the pursuer loss, injury or damage.

14.85 However, there is little modern authority on *convicium*. In the authors' opinion, *convicium* is not a separate head of action in Scots law. Rather, words which expose the pursuer to hatred and ridicule are simply ways of injuring the pursuer and, thereafter, fall to be subsumed under the rubric of verbal injury.[141]

---

[140] D Walker, *Delict* (2nd edn, 1983) at pp 736 and 738.

[141] This approach is not inconsistent with the Inner House decision in *Steele* v *Scottish Daily Record* 1970 SLT 53 which concerned a claim founded (at least in the latter stages of the case) on verbal injury, not *convicium*.

15 ECONOMIC DELICTS[1]

In this chapter, we will examine a category of civil wrong known as the economic **15.1** delicts.[2] This category includes the following delicts:

(1) inducing breach of contract;
(2) causing loss by unlawful means;[3]
(3) conspiracy.

It has been said that "[t]he function of an action of damages is to provide a remedy **15.2** for interests that are recognised by the law as entitled to protection. Obvious examples are protection against injury to the person, to reputation and to privacy. Economic interests are entitled to protection too, such as a person's business or his property".[4] The economic delicts aim to protect against the infliction of economic harm. It will become evident to the reader from the cases discussed that these delicts occur most commonly (although not exclusively) in cases involving industrial strife.

GENERAL BACKGROUND

Competition is regarded as a socially desirable goal and something which is vital to **15.3** the functioning of a free market. The law, therefore, generally prefers to adopt a *laissez-faire* attitude, that is, it leaves citizens to operate in a free and competitive market. It should be noted at the outset that EU law plays a very important role in the realm of competition law and in particular the reader is referred to Arts 101 and 102 of the Treaty on the Functioning of the European Union in this regard. However, a study of EU competition law is not within the scope of this book.[5]

Competition is regarded as being in the public interest, and so the position which **15.4** was adopted by the common law was that an individual could harm another economically as long as he used lawful means to do so. Thus, the common law permitted trader A to put trader B out of business by, for example, offering a better service or

---

[1] For a more detailed analysis of this area of law, see G Gordon,"The Economic Delicts" in J M Thomson (ed), *Delict* (SULI, 2007; H Carty, *An Analysis of the Economic Torts* (2nd rev edn, 2010).
[2] Note, however, that this chapter is not concerned with the delict of passing off, which is considered in Chapter 16.
[3] The previously recognised delict of intimidation (see, eg, *Rookes v Barnard* [1964] AC 1129) now appears to have been subsumed under this head. See *OBG Ltd v Allan* [2008] 1 AC 1, per Lord Hoffmann at para 7 (wherein his Lordship describes intimidation as a "variant" of causing loss by unlawful means.) For a discussion of intimidation, see the first edition of this book.
[4] *Customs and Excise Commissioners v Total Network SL* [2008] 1 AC 1174, per Lord Hope at para 26.
[5] The reader is referred to the various specialist texts which exist. See, eg, M Furse, *Competition Law of the EC and UK* (6th edn, 2008).

by bettering trader B's price, neither of these courses of conduct being unlawful.[6] The common law position is neatly illustrated by the case of *Mogul Steamship Co Ltd v MacGregor, Gow & Co*.[7] The plaintiffs, who were shipowners, were excluded from an association of other shipowners. This association was designed (a) to secure a carrying trade exclusively for members of the association and (b) to increase profits for members of the association. A rebate was offered by the association to those shippers who shipped only with members and agents were prohibited, on pain of dismissal, from dealing with competing ship owners. When the plaintiffs sent ships (the *Pathan* and the *Afghan*) to port in an effort to obtain cargoes, the defendants (members of the association) sent more steamers to port and underbid the plaintiffs. The defendants also threatened to dismiss their agents in the event of their loading the plaintiffs' vessels and they sent a circular advising that the rebate would be withdrawn from anyone who shipped cargoes on the plaintiffs' ships. They also cut their own rates of freight to such an extent that the plaintiffs were obliged to lower their freight rates and so carry cargoes at unremunerative rates. The plaintiffs claimed damages for losses suffered as a result.

15.5   The House of Lords confirmed the decision of the Court of Appeal to the effect that the plaintiffs had no cause of action. The defendants had acted with a view to extending and safeguarding their trade and improving their profits (a lawful object) and they had not used any unlawful means in doing so. Lord Watson pointed out:[8] "If neither the end contemplated by the agreement, nor the means used for its attainment were contrary to law the loss suffered by the appellants was *damnum sine injuria*." His Lordship continued:

> "There is nothing in the evidence to suggest that the parties to the agreement had any other object in view than that of defending their carrying-trade during the tea season against the encroachments of the appellants and other competitors, and of attracting to themselves custom which might otherwise have been carried off by these competitors. That is an object which is strenuously pursued by merchants great and small in every branch of commerce; and it is, in the eye of the law, perfectly legitimate."

15.6   The motive of the defendants' conduct in *Mogul* was to secure an advantage for themselves. There was not, to quote Lord Hannen, any "malicious or sinister intent as against the plaintiffs".[9]

15.7   It became clear, a few years later, in *Allen* v *Flood*,[10] that even if an individual is actuated by spite, malice or ill will, he is entitled to harm another economically, provided he uses lawful means. In *Allen*, a trade union official advised his employers that if certain workers, who were employed as shipwrights, were not dismissed, then the union workers, who were boilermakers, would strike. Such a strike would have been entirely lawful as the boilermakers were employed on a day-to-day basis and

---

[6] "Competition between businesses regularly involves each business taking steps to promote itself at the expense of the other. One retail business may reduce its prices to customers with a view to diverting trade to itself and away from a competitor shop. Far from prohibiting such conduct, the common law seeks to encourage and protect it. The common law recognises the economic advantages of competition." Per Lord Nicholls in *OBG Ltd* v *Allan* [2008] 1 AC 1 at para 142.
[7] [1892] AC 25.
[8] *Ibid* at 42.
[9] *Ibid* at 59.
[10] [1898] AC 1.

were therefore under no duty to turn up for work on the next day. The employer acceded to this request and dismissed the shipwrights who subsequently raised an action against the TU official. However, the dismissal of the shipwrights had been executed lawfully. In summary, the TU official had used lawful means to persuade the employer to dismiss the plaintiffs lawfully. The House of Lords concluded that such conduct was not delictual/tortious even though the defendant had been motivated by malice.[11]

The common law position evidenced in *Allen v Flood*, that it is permissible to   **15.8** harm another economically by lawful means, is a natural corollary of a free market. However, the courts were not willing to sanction *all* types of economic harm. It soon became evident that they would be prepared to intervene when certain parameters were overstepped. Thus, in the late 19th and early 20th centuries, the courts began to recognise various economic delicts. These delicts constituted exceptions to the general approach illustrated in *Allen v Flood*. However, there were many areas of uncertainty[12] and the law in this area resembled something of a confusing mess.[13] In recent years the economic wrongs have been significantly recast by the House of Lords in *OBG Ltd v Allan*[14] and *Customs and Excise Commissioners v Total Network SL*.[15] *OBG* provided much-needed clarification of the law in this area, setting out the essential ingredients of the delicts of inducing breach of contract and causing loss by unlawful means respectively.[16] *Total*, on the other hand, addressed the issue of conspiracy. The modern law will now be considered.

INDUCING[17] BREACH OF CONTRACT

The first economic delict which we are going to consider is that of inducing breach   **15.9** of contract. If A induces or persuades B to breach his contract with C, then C can sue A in delict for inducing B to breach his contract with C. This is an additional remedy to the obvious contractual remedy which C has against B for breach of contract. The origin of liability for this delict would appear to be the English case of *Lumley v Gye*.[18] There, Johanna Wagner, a famous opera singer, contracted with the plaintiff, a theatre owner, to perform exclusively for him for a certain period. The plaintiff alleged that

---

[11] Contrast the American case of *Tuttle v Buck* (1909) 119 NW 946 where the court held a banker liable for *spitefully* driving a barber out of business by opening a rival barber's shop and undercutting him.

[12] This was acknowledged by Lord Nicholls in *OBG Ltd v Allan* [2008] 1 AC 1 (at para 139): "Judicial observations are not always consistent, and academic consensus is noticeably absent."

[13] See H Carty, "The economic torts in the 21st century" (2008) LQR 641 wherein the law is described as being in a "muddle" (at 641) and the author asserts that "[b]y the start of the 21st century a patchwork list of economic torts – with confusing intersections between them – had emerged".

[14] [2008] 1 AC 1. Gordon has expressed the view that *OBG* "simplifies [the law] by stripping away years of accumulated errors and misconceptions" (*Delict* at para 15.27).

[15] [2008] 1 AC 1174.

[16] The Lords further asserted that there was no in-between hybrid delict of "interfering with contractual relations", Lord Nicholls declaring (at para 189) that "[i]n so far as authorities suggest or decide otherwise they should not now be followed". The unified theory of liability – which had treated procuring breach of contract as one species of a more general delict of actionable interference with contractual rights – was resoundingly rejected in *OBG*.

[17] The term "procuring" a breach of contract is also sometimes encountered and *OBG* would appear to suggest that the terms are synonymous.

[18] (1853) 2 E & B 216.

the defendant, a rival theatre owner, had enticed and persuaded Wagner to refuse to perform. The court held that the plaintiff was entitled to sue the defendant as the defendant had deliberately violated the plaintiff's contractual right. Wightman J stated:[19] "It was undoubtedly prima facie an unlawful act on the part of Miss Wagner to break her contract, and therefore a tortious act of the defendant maliciously to procure her to do so." Although *Lumley* v *Gye* concerned a contract for personal service, subsequent English cases[20] demonstrated that the principle was not confined to such contracts.

15.10   Any doubts that this delict was also recognised in Scotland were dispelled in the case of *British Motor Trade Association* v *Gray*.[21] Lord Russell, in his judgment, endorsed the submission made by counsel, which he quoted:[22] "by the law of Scotland an actionable wrong is committed by one who intentionally and without lawful justification induces or procures some one to break a contract made by him with another, if damage has resulted to that other, provided the contract creates contractual relations recognised by law".

15.11   The facts of the case were as follows. After the Second World War, there was a shortage of new motor cars available for release to the public. The British Motor Trade Association (BMTA) was formed which was composed of manufacturers and their distributors. They devised a scheme, known as the "covenant scheme", by which every purchaser of a new car signed a tripartite agreement with the association and the car dealer binding himself not to resell the car within a certain period. Allan Gray, the respondent, was a motor car dealer in Glasgow. He was not a member of the association. Indeed, his name was on a "stop list" owing to his previous conduct breaching the rules relating to price protection. The BMTA alleged that he had purchased some 14 vehicles before expiry of the time limitation on resale. In other words, he was well aware that he was purchasing cars in respect of which there were valid agreements in force and that he had induced the original purchasers to breach their contracts with the BMTA. The Inner House, affirming the decision of the Lord Ordinary on this point, allowed the case to proceed to proof, holding that the averments disclosed a valid cause of action in Scots law.

15.12   The Lord President (Cooper) summed up the position as follows:[23]

"The full details regarding the acquisition of these fourteen cars will only be discovered at a proof, but the averments sufficiently disclose a deliberate course of conduct, pursued over an extended period, and involving the carrying on as a business venture of what I may describe as a 'black market' in cars, in wilful defiance of the Association's covenant scheme. The acceptance of the respondent's argument would mean that the respondent and others like-minded to himself are entitled so to proceed, and that the law is powerless to interfere. I do not think that it is."

15.13   The Lord President went on to say that, in England, inducing breach of contract was an actionable wrong, whereas, in Scotland, until recently, the only illustrations of the rule had been in relation to contracts of service.[24] However, the Lord President, under

---

[19] (1853) 2 E & B 216 at 238.
[20] See, eg, *Bowen* v *Hall* (1881) 6 QBD 333 and *Temperton* v *Russell* [1893] 1 QB 715.
[21] 1951 SC 586.
[22] *Ibid* at 603.
[23] *Ibid* at 598.
[24] See, eg, *Belmont Laundry Co Ltd* v *Aberdeen Steam Laundry Co Ltd* (1898) 1 F 45.

reference to *Findlay* v *Blaylock*[25] and *Crofter Hand Woven Scottish Tweed Co Ltd* v *Veitch*[26] (both discussed below), concluded that Scots law did not limit the rule to contracts of service alone. He declared himself "prepared to affirm expressly that it is only by accident that the Scottish illustrations have centred around the contract of service … that these are only instances of the wider rule, and that on principle the wider rule as more fully developed in England, must be considered as part of the law of Scotland".

A detailed analysis of the delict of inducing breach of contract was provided by **15.14** the House of Lords in *OBG Ltd* v *Allan*.[27] There, the claimants got into financial difficulty. An unsecured creditor purported to appoint administrative receivers and the receivers took control of the business. They terminated the contracts of the majority of the claimants' subcontractors and settled claims under contracts which the claimants had made. Shortly afterwards the claimants went into liquidation. They subsequently brought proceedings against the defendants, claiming that the receivers had been invalidly appointed and that they had suffered loss as a result of the receivers' wrongful interference with their contractual relations The House of Lords held that the requirements for liability for inducing breach of contract were not satisfied. There was no breach or non-performance of any contract by the contracting party and therefore no wrong to which accessory liability could attach.

The case makes clear that the purpose of the delict is the protection of contractual **15.15** rights against third parties (as opposed to the protection of economic interests).[28] Liability is incurred only if B breaks his contract with C as a result of A's actions. Liability arises because A is *accessory* to B's breach of contract.[29] Lord Nicholls put the matter in the following terms:[30]

> "[T]his tort provides a claimant with an additional cause of action. The third party who breached his contract is liable for breach of contract. The person who persuaded him to break his contract is also liable, in his case in tort. Hence this tort is an example of civil liability which is secondary in the sense that it is secondary, or supplemental, to that of the third party who committed a breach of his contract. It is a form of accessory liability."

Further elucidation was provided in *Global Resources Group* v *MacKay*,[31] where the Lord **15.16** Ordinary (Hodge) followed the approach adopted in *OBG* and set out five essential characteristics of the delict of inducing breach of contract:

(1) A breach of contract must occur. Without an *actual* breach of contract occurring, no liability for this delict can arise.[32] Interference with the contract which does not bring about a breach is not enough.

---

[25] 1937 SC 21.
[26] 1942 SC (HL) 1.
[27] [2008] 1 AC 1.
[28] See the observations of Lord Hoffmann at [2008] 1 AC 1, para 8.
[29] Thomson has remarked that "one does not have to be a purist to find the concept of a wrong of accessory liability as an unprincipled accretion to the Scots law of delict". (See J Thomson, "Redrawing the landscape of the economic wrongs" 2008 Edin LR 267 at 270.) Gordon argues, however, that "the difficulties presented by this particular transplantation are more apparent than real" (*Delict*, para 15–27). See, also, the observations of Lord Hodge in *Global Resources Group* v *MacKay* 2009 SLT 104 at para 11.
[30] [2008] 1 AC 1 at para 172.
[31] 2009 SLT 104.
[32] See, also, Lord Hoffmann in *OBG* at para 8 "[B]reach of contract is of the essence. If there is no primary liability, there can be no accessory liability." See also his Lordship's remarks at para 44.

(2) The inducing party must know that his actions will result in the contract being breached.[33]

(3) The inducing party must intend to induce the breach either as an end in itself or as the means by which he achieves some further end.[34] No intention *to harm* need be established.[35] Therefore. if A induces B to breach his contract with C, not owing to a desire to harm C but in an effort to secure B's services for himself (that being the "end" sought), the delict is committed.

(4) The inducement must take the form of persuasion, encouragement or assistance.[36]

(5) No lawful justification exists for the inducement of the breach of contract.

15.17 In relation to point (4) above, it should be noted that the inducement need not take the form of unlawful means. Indeed, the inducement may well be beneficial to the contract-breaker as it would be where it takes the form of a gift. Standing by and knowingly allowing parties to breach their contracts does not amount to inducement.[37] C must suffer loss as a result of the inducement but such loss will easily be inferred.[38]

15.18 The House of Lords had occasion to consider the mental element required for this delict in *Mainstream Properties Ltd* v *Young and Ors*.[39] There, Mainstream was a property development company. It employed Young and Broad as director and manager respectively. In breach of their contracts of employment, Young and Broad diverted the purchase of development land to a joint venture consisting of themselves and De Winter, the latter individual providing the necessary finance. Mainstream

---

[33] In *OBG* Lord Nicholls stated (at para 191): "A stranger to a contract may know nothing of the contract. Quite unknowingly and unintentionally he may procure a breach of the contract by offering an inconsistent deal to a contracting party which persuades the latter to default on his contractual obligations. The stranger is not liable in such a case." In *Rossleigh* v *Leader Cars Ltd* 1987 SLT 355 it was emphasised that to establish liability it was essential that the defenders had pursued a course of conduct, knowing of the contract and with the intention of procuring its breach. Lord Mayfield made clear that recklessness or turning a blind eye to whether a contract existed was not enough unless it was tantamount to intention. In *Global*, Lord Hodge expressed the view (at para 11) that "if A consciously decided not to inquire into the terms of the contract between B and C in the knowledge that there was a contract and that his actions were likely to induce a breach of that contract, that knowledge and the wilful turning of a blind eye as to the details of the contract would be sufficient knowledge".

[34] In *OBG* Lord Hoffmann had stated (at para 43): "[I]f the breach of contract is neither an end in itself nor a means to an end, but merely a foreseeable consequence, then … it cannot for this purpose be said to have been intended." It followed that *Millar* v *Bassey* [1994] EMLR 44 had been wrongly decided.

[35] See *South Wales Miners' Federation* v *Glamorgan Coal Co Ltd* [1905] AC 239. There, the miners' union said that its intention in calling a strike was to limit production of coal and thus increase its price. Rather than wishing to cause the mine owners loss, the union intended to make both owners and miners better off. This made no difference according to the House of Lords. It was sufficient that the union intended the employment contracts to be broken. The case therefore demonstrates that one may intend to procure a breach of contract without intending to cause loss.

[36] Note that *preventing* or *obstructing* a party from fulfilling his contractual obligations is not embraced by this delict but may fall under the heading of causing loss by unlawful means. The "crucial difference" between *inducement* and *prevention* was identified by Lord Nicholls in *OBG* at para 178.

[37] *Calor Gas Ltd* v *Express Fuels (Scotland) Ltd* 2008 SLT 123.

[38] "[D]amage … is of the essence of the wrong. But proof of specific damage is not required. Where breach of contract has been procured by a third party some damage will readily be inferred." (Per Lord Keith in *British Motor Trade Association* v *Gray* 1951 SC 586 at 604.) See, also, *Exchange Telegraph Co* v *Gregory* [1896] 1 QB 147 where Lord Esher MR stated (at 153): "Though I think there must be some damage to support an action for the infringement of the plaintiff's common law right, it is enough to shew that the act complained of was done in such a way as to be likely to damage the plaintiff, though proof of specific damage be not given."

[39] [2008] 1 AC 1. *Mainstream* was decided alongside *OBG*, at which time the House of Lords also considered a third appeal, viz *Douglas and Anor* v *Hello! Ltd and Ors*.

sought damages from De Winter for inducing breach of contract. The claim failed. De Winter had raised the question of conflict of interest with Young and Broad and had been assured that no such conflict existed because Mainstream had been offered and had refused the site. This was untrue but De Winter believed it. He therefore honestly believed that assisting Young and Broad with the joint venture would not involve them in any breach of contract. Accordingly, the House of Lords held that De Winter did not intend to cause a breach of contract.[40] The burden of proving that intention rested on Mainstream and they had failed to discharge that burden. Accordingly, the wrong of inducing breach of contract was not established.

THE DEFENCE OF JUSTIFICATION

A defence exists if the inducement of breach of contract is justified.[41] This is clear **15.19** from the *dicta* of Lord Russell in *British Motor Trade Association* v *Gray*:[42] "by the law of Scotland an actionable wrong is committed by one who intentionally and *without lawful justification* induces or procures some one to break a contract made by him with another, if damage has resulted to that other, provided the contract creates contractual relations recognised by law"(emphasis added). The words in italics emphasise the fact that, in some situations, a third party may lawfully induce a breach of contract between two other individuals. The question therefore arises as to what amounts to lawful justification in the eyes of the law. In *British Motor Trade Association* v *Gray*, Lord Russell[43] made clear that self-interest does not constitute justification. The same point was articulated forcefully by the Lord President:[44] "The suggestion that 'sufficient justification' for the respondent's conduct can be found in his own self-interest seems to me to be manifestly untenable, for such an exception would empty the rule of all intelligible content."

While it is clear that the pursuit of one's own economic interest does not constitute **15.20** sufficient justification, it is perhaps worth noting that Lord Nicholls in *OBG* indicated[45] that inducing a breach of contract was permissible "in order to protect an equal or superior right of [one's] own". No doubt the courts will provide further elaboration on this point in due course.

In *Brimelow* v *Casson*[46] the plaintiff was a theatrical manager. The defendants, **15.21** who were members of a committee called the Joint Protection Committee, induced theatre proprietors to break their contracts with the plaintiff in that they would no longer allow the plaintiff the use of their theatres. The defendants did this because the plaintiff was paying such low wages to his chorus girls that they were compelled to resort to prostitution to supplement their meagre earnings. The defendants' interest in maintaining standards in the theatrical profession was held to justify their inducement of the breach.

---

[40] Lord Nicholls stated at para 202: "An honest belief by the defendant that the outcome sought by him will not involve a breach of contract is inconsistent with him intending to induce a breach of contract."
[41] See *Glamorgan Coal Co* v *South Wales Miners' Federation* [1905] AC 239; *Edwin Hill & Partners* v *First National Finance Corp* [1989] 1 WLR 225.
[42] 1951 SC 586 at 603.
[43] *Ibid*.
[44] *Ibid* at 600.
[45] [2008] 1 AC 1 at para 193.
[46] [1924] 1 Ch 302.

15.22   The case of *Findlay* v *Blaylock*[47] also provides guidance as to what amounts to lawful justification. A woman raised an action against the father of her former fiancé, alleging that he had induced her former fiancé to break off the engagement. At that time, engagement was a binding contract in Scots law. The court concluded, in the circumstances of the case, that the father's inducement had been justified. His son was a minor and had entered into an unsuitable engagement with the pursuer and the defender was simply exercising parental guidance in good faith.

CAUSING LOSS BY UNLAWFUL MEANS

15.23   The delict of causing loss by unlawful means was recognised by the House of Lords in *OBG*. In the course of its judgment, the House of Lords made clear that this delict was quite separate and distinct from that of inducing breach of contract. Each delict had its own conditions for liability and while liability for inducing breach of contract was *accessory* in nature, liability in relation to causing loss by unlawful means was *primary*. In other words, the defender's liability in respect of the latter delict does not depend upon the commission of a wrong by a third party against the pursuer. On the contrary, causing loss by unlawful means is a "stand-alone" delict.[48]

15.24   The delict of causing loss by unlawful means should be distinguished from inducing breach of contract. One very significant difference is that before liability can arise in respect of the former delict, *unlawful means* must be employed.[49] The question arises as to what qualifies as "unlawful means". In *OBG* their Lordships did not speak with one voice on this issue. However, the majority view, which found expression in the judgment of Lord Hoffmann,[50] was that the term embraced acts against a third party which would be actionable by the third party[51] *and which affected the third party's freedom to deal with the pursuer*.[52] It follows that a wrong actionable in private law is a necessary ingredient of this delict.

15.25   Thus, this delict may arise where A steals essential equipment belonging to B so that B is no longer in a position to perform his contractual obligations vis-à-vis C. The act of theft is actionable at the instance of B and affects B's freedom to deal with C – it thus constitutes the unlawful means which is a prerequisite for liability. Likewise, if A vandalises B's machinery so that B cannot perform his contract with C, the act of vandalism is civilly actionable at B's behest and it also affects B's freedom to deal with C. Again, these actions would constitute the unlawful means required under this head. Were A physically to restrain B himself so that the contract could not be performed, such circumstances would also amount to unlawful means, as they are civilly actionable by B and also interfere with B's freedom to deal with C. A's own

---

[47] 1937 SC 21.
[48] Such was the terminology employed by Lord Nicholls in *OBG* at para 173.
[49] It will be remembered that, for liability to arise for inducement, the means used to induce the breach need not be unlawful.
[50] See paras 49–51. Lord Brown and Baroness Hale agreed with Lord Hoffmann on this point.
[51] This is subject to the qualification that acts against a third party will also amount to unlawful means if the only reason they are not actionable is because the third party has suffered no loss.
[52] Lord Nicholls (at paras 159 and 162) preferred a wider interpretation of "unlawful means" and took the view that the term covered *all* acts which a defender is not permitted to do (ie conduct which was prohibited by the civil *or criminal law*) provided the acts against B were instrumental in causing economic harm to C. Lord Walker expressed a preference for an "incremental approach" to unlawful means (at para 270).

breach of contract may also constitute unlawful means if that in turn prevents B from performing his contractual obligations to C. (There is no *inducement* here – rather it is a case of B being *prevented* from performing his contractual obligations owing to A's prior breach, the prior breach amounting to unlawful means.)

An attempt to rely on the wrong of causing loss by unlawful means was made in **15.26** *Douglas and Anor* v *Hello! Ltd and Otrs.*[53] The facts were as follows. The actors Michael Douglas and Catherine Zeta-Jones entered into an agreement with *OK!* magazine whereby the magazine was to have exclusive rights to publish their wedding photographs. The Douglases were to take reasonable steps to restrict access to the wedding so that no photographs were made available to third-party media. Despite tight security measures being put in place, the wedding was infiltrated by an individual who covertly took photographs. The photographer thereafter sold the photographs to *Hello!* magazine in which publication they were subsequently published. *OK!* sued *Hello!*, seeking damages for causing loss by unlawful means. The House of Lords held that no such wrong had been committed. The Douglases' freedom to deal with *OK!* had not been interfered with. All the freelance photographer and *Hello!* had done was to make *OK!*'s contractual rights less profitable than they would otherwise have been.[54]

For liability to arise in respect of this delict, A must *intend* to harm C. In *OBG*, Lord **15.27** Nicholls made the following observations:[55]

> "A defendant may intend to harm the claimant as an end in itself where, for instance, he has a grudge against the claimant. More usually a defendant intentionally inflicts harm on a claimant's business as a means to an end. He inflicts damage as the means whereby to protect or promote his own economic interests.
>
> Intentional harm inflicted against a claimant in either of these circumstances satisfies **15.28** the mental ingredient of this tort. This is so even if the defendant does not wish to harm the claimant, in the sense that he would prefer that the claimant were not standing in his way. Lesser states of mind do not suffice. A high degree of blameworthiness is called for, because intention serves as the factor which justifies imposing liability on the defendant for loss caused by a wrong otherwise not actionable by the claimant against the defendant. The defendant's conduct in relation to the loss must be deliberate. In particular, a defendant's foresight that his unlawful conduct may or will probably damage the claimant cannot be equated with intention for this purpose. The defendant must *intend* to injure *the claimant*."

In *Douglas* v *Hello!* (where *OK!*'s claim ultimately failed)[56] the House of Lords took **15.29** the view that *Hello!* did have the necessary intention to cause loss to *OK!*. Although the Court of Appeal had accepted evidence from *Hello!*'s editor-in-chief to the effect that *Hello!*'s intention had only been to maintain its own sales, the House of Lords took the view that causing loss to *OK!* was the means whereby *Hello!* had intended

---

[53] [2008] 1 AC 1. (This was one of three conjoined appeals, the others being *OBG Ltd v Allan* and *Mainstream Properties Ltd v Young*.)

[54] See, also, *McLeod v Rooney* 2009 SLT 449 where the pursuers' claim based on the intentional causing of loss by unlawful means was held to be irrelevant on the basis that the defender's alleged conduct did not restrict the freedom of the third party (in this case a company) to deal with the pursuers.

[55] [2008] 1 AC 1 at paras 164–166.

[56] The court held that the Douglases' freedom to deal with *OK!* had not been interfered with (see discussion above). Additionally, no unlawful means had been employed.

to secure its desired end. The loss was not merely a foreseeable consequence of attaining that end.

15.30   In *OBG*, the claimant was a civil engineering company which fell out with one of its main customers and got into financial difficulties as a result. Receivers were appointed and they took control of OBG's affairs, dismissing employees, terminating certain contracts, disposing of assets and settling claims which OBG had made. The company went into creditors' voluntary liquidation 10 days after the appointment of receivers. It transpired that the receivers' appointment had been invalid. In the subsequent legal proceedings it was held that there was no liability for causing loss by unlawful means. The receivers had neither employed unlawful means nor had they intended to cause OBG any loss.[57]

15.31   It seems likely that the defence of justification would be available in respect of this wrong, although the point has not yet been tested.[58]

15.32   Although inducing breach of contract and causing loss by unlawful means are independent delicts, each with its own conditions for liability, it does not follow that the two delicts are mutually exclusive. "[T]here is no reason why the same act should not create both accessory liability for procuring a breach of contract and primary liability for causing loss by unlawful means."[59]

CONSPIRACY

15.33 It will be remembered from *Allen* v *Flood*[60] (discussed above) that if A uses lawful means to harm B economically he is not delictually liable to B, even if the motive was to cause harm.

15.34   A few years after *Allen* v *Flood*, the House of Lords had to consider a slightly different issue in *Quinn* v *Leathem*.[61] This case, like so many of the others in this area of law, involved industrial conflict. Trade union officials had compelled an employer to dismiss a non-union employee. The House of Lords held that if A and B combine together with the intention of harming C, then A and B are liable in delict for harm caused to C as a result of their conspiracy against him. The reasoning behind this delict is that a person is expected to withstand harmful acts done by one other but is not expected to withstand harmful acts carried out by a combination of persons. Lord Bramwell pointed out in *Mogul Steamship Co Ltd* v *MacGregor, Gow & Co*[62] that "a man may encounter the acts of a single person, yet not be fairly matched against several".

15.35   The anomaly behind this reasoning has been noted by some writers.[63] It certainly seems strange that the law permits a massive company to harm another economically,

---

[57] Nor was the wrong of inducing breach of contract established because no contracts had been breached. Therefore, there was no wrong to which accessory liability could attach – see Lord Hoffmann at para 86.

[58] Gordon takes the view that "the circumstances in which such a defence may successfully be pled must be very limited indeed" (*Delict*, at para 15–45).

[59] Lord Hoffmann in *OBG* at para 37. See also his Lordship's observations at para 21. Lord Walker also acknowledged at para 264 that "in some factual situations" the two delicts might overlap.

[60] [1898] AC 1.

[61] [1901] AC 495.

[62] [1892] AC 25 at 45.

[63] See W J Stewart, *Delict* (4th edn, 2004), p 64. Winfield and Jolowicz point out: "The central issue has been why the 'magic of plurality' should make something unlawful if it is not unlawful when done by one person alone." (W V H Rogers, *Winfield & Jolowicz on Tort* (18th edn, 2010), pp 894–895).

yet strikes at a few smaller companies combining to do likewise. The large company may well wield greater economic power than the combination. The anomaly has also been judicially acknowledged, most notably by Viscount Simon LC in *Crofter Hand Woven Scottish Tweed Co Ltd* v *Veitch*:[64] "The action of a single tyrant may be more potent to inflict suffering on the continent of Europe than a combination of less powerful persons."[65]

Nevertheless, the rules on conspiracy remain firmly entrenched in Scots law. **15.36** Viscount Simon LC summed up the position in the *Crofter* case (the facts of which are stated below):[66] "there are cases in which a combination of individuals to act in a certain way, resulting in deliberate damage to others, is actionable, even though the same thing, if done by a single individual, without any element of combination would not expose him to liability". Lord Wright, in the same case, observed:[67]

> "The rule may seem anomalous, so far as it holds that conduct by two may be actionable if it causes damage, whereas the same conduct done by one, causing the same damage, would give no redress. In effect the plaintiff's right is that he should not be damnified by a conspiracy to injure him, and it is in the fact of the conspiracy that the unlawfulness resides."

THE ESSENTIALS OF CONSPIRACY

There are certain conditions which must be satisfied before liability for conspiracy **15.37** will arise. First, a number of persons must be involved. This means that there must be two or more participants in the conspiracy. These participants need not be of the same standing. Indeed, one party may be subordinate to the other. In these circumstances, however, the subordinate must still be able to exercise independent choice or, to use the words of Viscount Simon LC in *Crofter*,[68] the combination still exists if the subordinate "appreciated what he was about". Second, there must be a combination. This simply means that there must be concerted action by the conspirators. For example, in *Allen* v *Flood*[69] it was the TU official who said that there would be a strike. There was no concerted action or combination and hence no conspiracy. Third, those combining must have the intention of inflicting economic harm on the pursuer.[70] According to Viscount Simon LC, in *Crofter*, one has to establish: "what is in truth the object in the minds of the combiners when they acted as they did?" It has been pointed out elsewhere[71] that what must be established is that "the combiners should have acted in order that (not with the result that, even the foreseeably inevitable result) the claimant

---

[64] 1942 SC (HL) 1 at 8.
[65] See, also, *Lonrho Ltd* v *Shell Petroleum Co Ltd (No 2)* [1982] AC 173, per Lord Diplock at 189. His Lordship asserted that the wrong was "too well established to be discarded, however anomalous it may seem today". See, also, *Lonrho plc* v *Fayed* [1992] 1 AC 448, per Lord Bridge at 463 and 465, and *OBG*, per Lord Hoffmann at para 15.
[66] 1942 SC (HL) 1 at 9.
[67] *Ibid* at 23.
[68] *Ibid* at 6.
[69] [1898] AC 1.
[70] See *Berryland Books Ltd* v *BK Books Ltd* [2010] EWCA Civ 1440 where it was stated (at para 48) that the House of Lords' views in *OBG Ltd* on the mental requirements of the delict/tort of causing loss by unlawful means were equally applicable to the delict/tort of conspiracy. Nothing short of an actual intention to injure or reckless indifference would do. "Reckless indifference" in this context meant a conscious decision not to inquire into the existence of a fact.
[71] See Rogers, *Winfield & Jolowicz on Tort*, p 886.

should suffer damage". Finally, the pursuer must suffer an injury before liability is imposed.

LAWFUL MEANS CONSPIRACY AND UNLAWFUL MEANS CONSPIRACY

15.38   It is essential to distinguish two types of conspiracy. The first is where lawful means are used and the second is where unlawful means are used by the conspirators.

15.39   If lawful means are used, a conspiracy is delictual only if the *predominant* intention of the conspirators is to harm the pursuer. (We should remember at this stage that, on the authority of *Allen v Flood*, it is not delictual for one person to set out to harm another economically provided he uses lawful means to do so.)

15.40   If, on the other hand, the conspirators employ unlawful means, their conspiracy will be delictual as long as there is evident *an* intention to harm the pursuer,[72] even if that was not their primary or predominant motive.

15.41   Bearing this distinction in mind, let us now consider the facts of one of the leading cases on conspiracy, which is a decision of the House of Lords sitting in a Scottish appeal, that of *Crofter Hand Woven Scottish Tweed Co Ltd v Veitch*.[73] The pursuer, the Crofter Co, marketed cloth woven by the Isle of Lewis crofters using yarn imported from the Scottish mainland. Yarn was also spun on Lewis and the island spinners were members of the Transport and General Workers' Union (TGWU). The union wished to secure a higher rate of pay for its members who spun yarn on the island. The island employers intimated that they could not afford to increase wages. The TGWU therefore ordered its millowner members not to handle yarn from the mainland producers. The TGWU and millowners grouped together and instructed the union members employed at port not to handle the mainland yarn. The dockers, in obeying this instruction, were not in breach of contract as they had at no stage been asked by their employers to handle the imported yarn. Their Lordships held that since no unlawful means were involved, the conspiracy could be delictual only if the predominant motive was to harm the pursuer. However, their Lordships concluded that the predominant motive of the combination was to further the legitimate aim of the union, that being a better level of remuneration for its members. As harm to the pursuer was not the primary motive, the defenders were not liable.

15.42   It may be far from easy to isolate the predominant purpose of a particular course of action and to establish whether harm to the pursuer was the main object or was simply incidental to another legitimate object.[74] In *Crofter*, Viscount Simon stated:[75]

"The analysis of human impulses soon leads us into the quagmire of mixed motives, and even if we avoid the word 'motive', there may be more than a single 'purpose' or 'object'.

---

[72] See *Lonrho plc v Fayed* [1992] 1 AC 448; *Customs and Excise Commissioners v Total Network SL* [2008] 1 AC 1174.

[73] 1942 SC (HL) 1. It has been said that *Crofter* can "be seen as the final emergence of the tort of conspiracy in its modern form" (per Lord Walker in *Customs and Excise Commissioners v Total Network SL* [2008] 1 AC 1174 at para 66).

[74] Other legitimate objects might include improved working conditions and financial interests (such as increased wages as in *Crofter*). See, also, *Scala Ballroom v Ratcliffe* [1958] 3 All ER 220 where a trade union organised a boycott by its musician members of a dance hall which operated race discrimination in the form of a colour bar. The case demonstrates that the interests being furthered by the combination need not be the private interests of those combining.

[75] 1942 SC (HL) 1 at 10.

It is enough to say that, if there is more than one purpose actuating a combination, liability must depend on ascertaining the predominant purpose. If that predominant purpose is to damage another person and damage results, that is tortious conspiracy. If the predominant purpose is the lawful protection or promotion of any lawful interest of the combiners (no illegal means being employed), it is not a tortious conspiracy, even though it causes damage to another person."[76]

Crofter makes it clear that the determination of the predominant purpose is a broad question of fact. The onus of proving that the infliction of economic harm on the pursuer was the primary purpose of the combination rests with the pursuer.[77] Therefore, in a doubtful or borderline case, where the sides are equally balanced, the onus of proof will favour the defender. **15.43**

In *Customs and Excise Commissioners* v *Total Network SL*[78] the House of Lords once again had occasion to consider the delict of conspiracy. The defendant was a company which was incorporated in Spain and which had a bank account in the UK. The claimants alleged that the defendant had participated in 13 carousel frauds and was liable to them in damages for unlawful means conspiracy in sums equivalent to the amount of VAT lost as a result of the frauds. The unlawful means on which the commissioners relied was the commission of the common law offence of cheating the Revenue. Total argued that the commission of a crime alone was insufficient to constitute unlawful means for the purposes of grounding an action for conspiracy. Instead, Total argued that the conduct impugned would have to be independently actionable by the commissioners. The question for the House of Lords was therefore whether it was an essential requirement of the wrong of unlawful means conspiracy that the conduct which is said to amount to unlawful means should give rise to a separate action in tort/delict against at least one of the conspirators. The House of Lords held unanimously that criminal conduct at common law or by statute can constitute unlawful means for the purposes of conspiracy even though the acts relied upon are not in themselves actionable. It follows that, for the purposes of conspiracy, "unlawful means" has a meaning different from (and wider than) its meaning for the purposes of causing loss by unlawful means.[79] **15.44**

---

[76] Gordon has observed: "In practice, the predominant purpose requirement has the effect of excluding the possibility of liability in the great majority of cases which arise out of normal commercial trading or legitimate trade union type activity. This is because in such cases the court will ordinarily find it proved that, although the conspirators' motives may have been mixed (in that they may have wished, for instance, to profit by driving a competitor out of business), their main purpose was ultimately to advance their own self interest rather than to inflict harm. Successful lawful means conspiracy claims are rare indeed but not unknown" (*Delict*, at para 15–56).

[77] See *Crofter Hand Woven Scottish Tweed Co Ltd* v *Veitch* 1942 SC (HL) 1. It seems clear, however, from Viscount Maugham's judgment that the *provisional* burden may shift to the defender during the proof if the pursuer establishes that he suffered damage at the hands of a combination, where that damage was the natural and probable outcome of the acts in question. The defender would then require to establish what his purpose was and that it was legitimate.

[78] [2008] 1 AC 1174.

[79] The House of Lords in *Total* made a robust attempt to justify the different meanings attributed to the words "unlawful means" in the different contexts. Lord Mance, for example, stated (at para 123) that "there can be danger in what Lord Goff of Chieveley called "the temptation of elegance": *Henderson* v *Merrett Syndicates Ltd* [1995] 2 AC 145, 186 B–C. The two torts are different in their nature, and the interests of justice may require their development on somewhat different bases."

JUSTIFICATION

15.45 While the defence of justification is theoretically possible in unlawful means conspiracy, it has been observed that it is redundant in the context of lawful means conspiracy owing to the fact that a predominant intention to injure needs to be proved before liability is established under that head. If the conduct is justified at the outset, there is no liability and the defence is accordingly unnecessary.[80]

CONCLUDING REMARKS

15.46 There are some aspects of the law of economic delicts which remain uncertain even after the decisions of the House of Lords in *OBG* and *Total*.[81] Further refinement in this area of law appears likely. In particular, the failure of their Lordships in *OBG* to reach consensus on the meaning of "unlawful means" in the context of causing loss by unlawful means and the different construction given to that phrase in *Total* (in the context of unlawful means conspiracy) would appear to present a window for further debate.[82] In *Total*, Lord Walker observed[83] that "the development [of the economic delicts] has been a long and difficult process and may not yet be complete". Developments in this area are therefore awaited with interest.

---

[80] See Gordon, *Delict*, at para 15–58.

[81] These uncertainties are identified by Gordon (*Delict*, at para 15–68).

[82] Indeed, Lord Walker predicted as much in *OBG* where, having made reference to the competing views of Lord Hoffmann and Lord Nicholls as to the meaning of "unlawful means" in the context of causing loss by unlawful means, he stated (at 269): "I would respectfully suggest that neither is likely to be the last word on this difficult and important area of the law."

[83] [2008] 1 AC 1174 at para 89.

16 PASSING OFF

INTRODUCTION

If one person passes off his goods or services as being those of another, so as to cause **16.1** confusion to the public and loss of goodwill to another trader, that trader who has suffered loss may have a right of action. In Scotland the passing off action may have its origins in personality rights,[1] whereas the English law of passing off is considered as an economic tort.[2] Be that as it may, and the evidence is fairly thin, the law in the two countries has come together and has been judicially considered to be identical between England and Wales, and Scotland.[3]

When passing off takes place, existing customers of Business A may be misled into **16.2** thinking that the new product has something to do with Business A, and this may cause them to buy the new product, wrongly thinking it is produced by Business A. If the new product is inferior in quality to the product of Business A, Business A may suffer reputational damage and loss of goodwill as well as loss of revenue from lost sales. In any event, even if the new product is just as good as the existing one, Business A is likely to suffer loss of market. In some but not all cases, there may be a remedy at common law for passing off.

For example, a business advertises that its goods are "Marks & Spencer's Surplus" **16.3** when in fact the goods were not made for the well-known company Marks & Spencer plc at all and are of inferior quality to those sold in the well-known store. In such a case the goodwill of Marks & Spencer might be damaged, if Marks & Spencer's existing and potential customers are unhappy about the quality of the goods they buy from the rival business, and those who bought the goods have been misled about what they are in fact buying. Marks & Spencer will also be unhappy if some of their existing and potential customers defect to Marks & Spencer's Surplus, even if the goods supplied are just as good.

The purpose of the delict of passing off is to protect the *goodwill*[4] of traders from **16.4** being damaged by the activities of other traders. Often a trade mark may also be infringed by the same events,[5] and frequently both delicts are invoked in the same

---

[1] Per C Ng, "A common law of passing-off? English and Scottish perspectives" (2009) 13(1) *Edin LR* 134–139, referring to *dicta* in *Wilkie* v *McCulloch & Co* (1823) 2 S 413, (NS) 369.
[2] In *Perry* v *Truefitt* (1842) 6 Beav 66, Lord Langdale MR stated (at 73): "A man is not to sell his goods under the pretence that they are the goods of another man."
[3] Decision of Lord J-C Wheatley in *Lang Brothers Ltd* v *Goldwell Ltd* 1982 SLT 309 at 312. This case was brought by blenders of Scotch whisky against manufacturers of a drink called "Wee McGlen", which was a mixture of Scotch malt whisky and ginger wine made in England.
[4] This term is defined at para 16.10. See the remarks of Lord Diplock in *Warninck* v *J Townend & Sons* [1979] AC 731 (HL) at 742–743.
[5] Under ss 10 and 14 of the Trade Marks Act 1994, for infringement of a registered trade mark, and s 56 of the same Act, for infringement of a well-known mark, whether registered or not, which is entitled to protection under the Paris Convention. The differences between passing off and an action for infringement of trade

action. The trader whose goodwill has been harmed may seek a remedy, the principal remedy being interdict to prevent the wrong continuing. Damages may also be available.

16.5   Although many of the cases that come before the courts are concerned with misrepresentations relating to goods, passing off can relate also to services, and there can be passing off in relation to business names as well.[6]

16.6   In deciding passing off cases, judges must try to balance the benefits of free competition against the necessity of restraining those traders who have harmed the goodwill of others by passing off. In UK law there is no delict of unfair competition, unlike in many signatory countries of the Paris Convention.[7] This means that in UK law there are some seemingly hard cases where a trader suffers unfair trading at the hands of other traders where there may not be a remedy. Sometimes the dividing lines between successful and unsuccessful passing off cases are inconsistent. As Lord Scarman stated in *Cadbury Schweppes Pty Ltd* v *Pub Squash Co Pty Ltd*:[8]

> "Competition must remain free: and competition is safeguarded by the necessity for a plaintiff to prove that he has built up an 'intangible property right' in the advertised descriptions of his product: or in other words, that he has succeeded by such methods in giving his product a distinctive character accepted by the market. A defendant, however, does no wrong by entering a market and there competing with its creator. The line may be difficult to draw: but unless it is drawn, competition will be stifled."

WHAT ELEMENTS HAVE TO BE PROVED IN ORDER TO ESTABLISH THE DELICT OF PASSING OFF?

TWO DEFINITIONS

16.7   Various definitions of the delict have been attempted. In one case alone, two definitions were given by different judges. In *Warninck* v *J Townend & Sons Ltd* (the "Jif Lemon" case),[9] Lord Diplock and Lord Fraser of Tullybelton had different views of the essential elements that had to be proved. Lord Fraser considered that the following five matters had to be proved:

> "(1) that [the plaintiff's] business consists of, or includes, selling in England a class of goods to which the particular trade name applies; (2) that the class of goods is clearly defined, and that in the minds of the public, or a section of the public, in England, the trade name distinguishes that class from other similar goods; (3) that because of the reputation of the goods, there is goodwill attached to the name; (4) that he, the plaintiff, as a member of the class of

---

mark will be explored towards the end of this chapter. As well as an action for trade mark infringement, the acts that may amount to passing off may also give rise to actions for breach of other intellectual property rights including copyright, design rights, registered designs and patents.
[6] Eg *Ewing* v *Buttercup Margarine Co Ltd* [1917] 2 Ch 1 in which the claimant successfully contended that confusion would result between the name of his Scottish-based Buttercup Dairy Company and the defendant company's name; see also *Chill Foods (Scotland) Ltd* v *Cool Foods Ltd* 1977 SLT 38.
[7] See *L'Oréal SA* v *Bellure NV* [2008] RPC 9. In the UK, as well as passing off there are some provisions that protect traders from certain types of unfair competition by civil or criminal law or both, including the Business Protection from Misleading Marketing Regulations 2008 (SI 2008/1276).
[8] [1981] 1 WLR 193 at 200.
[9] [1979] AC 731.

those who sell the goods, is the owner of the goodwill in England which is of substantial value; (5) that he has suffered, or is really likely to suffer, substantial damage to his property in the goodwill by reason of the defendants selling goods which are falsely described by the trade name to which the goodwill is attached."[10]

Lord Diplock in turn defined the characteristics of a passing off action differently. He **16.8** stated that:

"(1) a misrepresentation (2) made by a trader in the course of trade, (3) to prospective customers of his or ultimate consumers of goods or services supplied by him, (4) which is calculated to injure the business or goodwill of another trader (in the sense that this is a reasonably foreseeable consequence) and (5) which causes actual damage to a business or goodwill of the trader by whom the action is brought or (in a *quia timet* action) will probably do so."[11]

However, judges in cases both before and after *Warninck* have preferred a definition **16.9** in terms of the "classic trinity" of goodwill, misrepresentation, and damage: these will be examined in turn.

THE ELEMENTS OF THE "CLASSIC TRINITY"

GOODWILL

Goodwill is a property right which only a trader can have. It cannot be held by a **16.10** private individual. The classic definitions of "goodwill" are those of Lord Macnaghten and Lord Linley in *Inland Revenue Commissioners* v *Muller & Co's Margarine*.[12] Lord Macnaghten defined "goodwill" as follows:

"It is the benefit and advantage of the good name, reputation and connection of a business. It is the attractive force which brings in custom. It is the one thing which distinguishes an old-established business from a new business at its first start. The goodwill of a business must emanate from a particular centre or source. However widely extended or diffused its influence may be, goodwill is worth nothing unless it has power of attraction sufficient to bring customers home to the source from which it emanates."[13]

Lord Linley defined "goodwill" in these terms: **16.11**

"Goodwill regarded as property has no meaning except in connection with some trade, business or calling. In that connection I understand the word to include whatever adds value to a business by reason of situation, name and reputation, connection, introduction to old customers, and agreed absence from competition ... In this wide sense, goodwill is insepa-rable from the business to which it adds value, and, in my opinion, exists where the business

---

[10] [1979] AC 731 at 755.
[11] *Ibid* at 742.
[12] [1901] AC 217.
[13] *Ibid* at 223.

is carried on. Such business may be carried on in one place or country or several, and if in several there may be several businesses, each having a goodwill of its own."[14]

16.12 The judges made it very clear that goodwill relates to the *business* as such, and not directly to brand names, business names, or the appearance of goods, or any such individual aspect of a business.[15] Both the pursuer and defender must be "traders". Although the concept of goodwill is normally associated with trade, from the cases it is evident that the judges have construed the concept of trade very widely, and have allowed passing off actions to be brought by trade and professional associations,[16] by writers and artists,[17] and by the British Broadcasting Corporation,[18] among others. Passing off actions are, however, inappropriate where either or both of the pursuer or defender are acting purely as private individuals.

16.13 Some judges have recognised that there can be goodwill deserving of protection by the courts, where a new product has not yet been brought to the market, but in relation to which there has been some advertising. In *Elida-Gibbs* v *Colgate-Palmolive*,[19] Colgate obtained an injunction against Elida-Gibbs, a trade rival, on the ground that Colgate had done some advertising of a new toothpaste (though through trade channels only, and not to the public), based on a tree concept. The day before the launch of the product to the public, Elida-Gibbs had advertised one of their own products using a tree theme.

16.14 Generally, the courts have held that goodwill is local in nature, and restricted to the territory in which the business is carried on. Lord Fraser of Tullybelton stated in *Warnink* v *J Townend Ltd*[20] that, for passing off to have occurred, the public within the jurisdiction of the court hearing the case must be aware of the reputation of the goods. And in some cases, the courts in the United Kingdom have not allowed a business which trades abroad, but which claims to have customers in the United Kingdom, to raise proceedings for passing off in a UK court.

16.15 This was the outcome in the "Crazy Horse" case, *Alain Bernardin et Compagnie* v *Pavilion Properties Ltd*.[21] In this case, the plaintiffs were the proprietors of the long-established place of entertainment known as "Crazy Horse". They sued the defendants in an action of passing off, on the ground that the defendants had opened an establishment in London under the name "Crazy Horse Saloon", which had adopted an op-art display incorporating a naked female body, similar to that used in the plaintiffs' premises in Paris. The London establishment had been advertised as "Crazy Horse comes to London", giving the impression that the London premises were associated with the Paris establishment. Pennycuick J refused to grant an injunction because, although the Paris establishment had been advertised in the United Kingdom, he considered that that fell short of the requirement for holding that there was goodwill in the United Kingdom. In his judgment, he made clear his reluctance in coming to that decision.[22]

---

[14] [1901] AC 217 at 235.
[15] *A G Spalding & Bros* v *A W Gamage Ltd* (1915) RPC 273; *Star Industrial Co Ltd* v *Yap Kwee Kor* [1976] FSR 256.
[16] *British Legion* v *British Legion Club (Street) Ltd* (1931) 48 RPC 555.
[17] *Marengo* v *Daily Sketch and Sunday Graphic Ltd* [1948] 1 All ER 406.
[18] *British Broadcasting Corporation* v *Talbot Motor Co Ltd* [1981] FSR 228.
[19] [1983] FSR 95.
[20] [1979] AC 731 at 755–756.
[21] [1967] RPC 581.
[22] The court in the "Budweiser" case *Anheuser-Busch Inc* v *Budjovicky Budvar NP* [1984] FSR 413 reached a similar decision.

In *William Grant & Sons Ltd* v *Glen Catrine Bonded Warehouse Ltd*,[23] the court in **16.16** Scotland held that a business could have a right of action in Scotland when whisky was sold for export, without reference to the law of the importing country where the customers were. Accordingly, if the facts were proved, goodwill could have been established in such a case. Conversely, sometimes an overseas business has been able to establish that goodwill exists in the United Kingdom, despite the lack of a presence in the country. For example, in *Maxim's* v *Dye*,[24] the court reached the opposite conclusion to that in the "Crazy Horse" decision, on similar facts, when the English proprietors of Maxim's restaurant in Paris successfully restrained the proprietors of a new Maxim's restaurant in Norwich from operating under that name, even though the proprietors of Maxim's restaurant in Paris had no business in England. However, it was established that the restaurant in Paris was patronised by English people, and on that basis it was held that it could have goodwill in England.

Sometimes goodwill can be even more local in its area of operation, depending on **16.17** the nature of the two parties' trading. It may be that the customers of each business are contained in separate geographical areas, in which case any restricting of the defender's business will be unnecessary, as there has been no misrepresentation and goodwill has not been harmed. In *Salon Services (Hairdressing Supplies) Ltd* v *Direct Salon Services Ltd*,[25] the pursuers and defenders both franchised the supply of hairdressing products to salons, but the court held that there was no passing off in this case, as the defenders' trade within Scotland was only in Fife and central Scotland, which were areas in which the pursuer did not trade, and where a descriptive name was used as opposed to an invented name, the balance of convenience favoured the recall of an interim interdict in this case.[26]

A trader who is giving up a certain line of trade would have no continuing **16.18** goodwill to protect if another trader supplied similar goods in similar containers. In *Alexander Ferguson & Co* v *Matthews McClay & Manson*,[27] a trader who was giving up selling a particular brand of paint was held to have no right of action when another trader started to sell paint under a different brand name but in the same tins.

MISREPRESENTATION

Hector MacQueen in *Stair Memorial Encyclopaedia: The Laws of Scotland*[28] states that "the **16.19** element of misrepresentation is the key that unlocks the door in a claim for passing off". In order to succeed in a passing off action, there must be a misrepresentation. In *Williamson* v *Meikle*,[29] there was evidence of some confusion in the minds of the public, but it was not proved that the defenders set out to deceive the public and no evidence that any customers actually were misled. Mere confusion in the minds of the public is not enough, as seen in *HFC Bank plc* v *HSBC Bank plc*.[30] In this case the claimant was

---

[23] 1995 SLT 936.
[24] [1977] FSR 364.
[25] 1988 SLT 414.
[26] For a more extensive discussion of passing off, see the article by H Carty, "Passing off and the concept of goodwill" (1994) *Journal of Business Law* Mar 139–154.
[27] 1989 SLT 795.
[28] 1993, vol 18 (with updates), para 1364.
[29] 1909 SC 1278.
[30] [2000] FSR 176.

not a High Street bank and was not well known in the UK, while the defendant was the well-known Midland Bank, which had rebranded itself in the UK as HSBC. The court did not find sufficient evidence of misrepresentation to ground a passing off action. For a definition of "misrepresentation", and a discussion of the requirements, see Chapter 3. It is important to note that the existence of the delict does not depend on whether the misrepresentation is innocent, fraudulent or negligent.[31] Often the misrepresentation is done deliberately, with the intention of profiting by it, but it is sufficient to establish the delict that the actions of the defender resulted in a loss of goodwill to the pursuer. Lord Hill Watson stated in *John Haig & Co Ltd v Forth Blending Co Ltd*[32] (the "Dimple Whisky" case):

> "The actings of a trader who copies a rival's established get-up need not be fraudulent and he need have no intention of obtaining any benefit from his rival's goodwill and reputation – indeed he may be ignorant of his existence – but if the result of his innocent actings are that the public are likely to be misled, he will be interdicted."

16.20 In *GNS Railway v Mann*,[33] Lord McLaren expressed a rather tentative view that fraud did not have to be proved or that at least the absence of evidence of fraud would defeat a claim of damages, although an interdict may still be granted. This will be discussed later in this chapter.

16.21 Nowadays, the judges tend to take the view that the misrepresentation should take place in a "common field of activity",[34] in other words, that the businesses are in the same line of business. From the case law, it is evident that this has not always been so. In 1898, the court was prepared to grant an injunction to protect the makers of Kodak cameras against the use of the word "Kodak" in the name of a bicycle specially designed for photographers, in *Eastman Photographic Materials Co Ltd v John Griffiths Cycle Corporation & Kodak Cycle Co Ltd*,[35] two somewhat different fields of activity. But more recently, in *Scottish Milk Marketing Board v Dryborough & Co Ltd*,[36] Lord Davidson in the Outer House of the Court of Session refused to grant an interim interdict because the two companies sold different products in entirely different markets (Scottish Pride milk products and Scottish Pride lager, respectively), and the likelihood of confusion in the minds of the public was considered to be fairly small. However, where one of the products is a "household name" the requirement for a common field of activity has been disregarded – *Lego Systems A/S v Lego M Lemelstrich*.[37] In this case, the manufacturer of Lego, the children's construction toy, with a worldwide reputation, successfully pursued a passing off action against a manufacturer of irrigation equipment.

16.22 When determining whether there has been a misrepresentation, the court will look at the particular market concerned. This may be a very local sector of the public: for example, the citizens of Kilmarnock in *Dunlop Pneumatic Tyre Co Ltd v Dunlop Motor Co Ltd*.[38] The court will look at the particular circumstances in which the misrepresen-

---

[31] Lord Kinnear in *Scottish Union and National Insurance Co Ltd* 1909 SC 318. See also *United Biscuits (UK) Ltd v ASDA Stores Ltd* [1997] RPC 513.
[32] 1954 SLT 2 at 6.
[33] (1899) 19R 1035.
[34] Phrase used by Wynn-Parry J in *McCulloch v May* (1948) 65 RPC 58.
[35] (1898) RPC 105.
[36] 1985 SLT 253.
[37] [1983] FSR 155.
[38] 1907 SC (HL) 15.

tation arises. For example, in the "Dimple Whisky" case,[39] in which the defenders were sued by Haig, the distillers of "Dimple Scots" whisky, which was sold in distinctive pinched glass bottles, for selling a rival whisky in a similarly shaped bottle, it was held relevant that people standing at the bar of a public house would not all be able to see the labels on the bottles, and the distinctive caps on the bottles would have been removed for the insertion of optic measure pouring devices. Thus the customers might well be assuming that what they were getting was "Dimple Scots" whisky from the shape of the bottle alone.

In *Johnston v Orr-Ewing*,[40] a picture of two elephants was used as a mark on yarn **16.23** in India, and the yarn came to be known as "two elephants". When another trader adopted a different picture of two elephants for his yarn, it was relevant evidence that the sector of the public that had been deceived was largely illiterate, and therefore would not have been able to differentiate the two labels by reading anything else written on the label.

Activities which have been held to amount to a misrepresentation

A misrepresentation may be made in relation to the origin of goods or the quality of **16.24** goods. For example, a retailer may attempt to sell a manufacturer's goods of inferior quality as being that manufacturer's best-quality goods. In *A G Spalding & Bros v A W Gamage Ltd*,[41] the plaintiffs produced a football known as the "Orb", and a later model known as the "improved Orb". The plaintiff sold some discarded Orb footballs to a rubber waste manufacturer, who sold them on to the defendant. The defendant sold these substandard footballs as being "improved Orb" but at a very cheap price. An injunction was granted. In another case, a public house was held to have passed off a lower grade of whisky as a better one in *Teacher v Levy*[42] by filling empty bottles of Teacher's best whisky with Teacher's cheapest grade of whisky. It may constitute passing off to sell second-hand goods as new, as in *General Electric Co v Pryce's Stores*,[43] where second-hand light bulbs were cleaned up and sold as new, for a very cheap price in a poor area.

One form of misrepresentation as to the origin of goods relates to "get-up" – in **16.25** other words, the distinctive appearance of the product, its distinctive labelling or the shape of the container.[44] One of the modern leading cases in this area is the "Jif Lemon" case, *Reckitt & Colman Products Ltd v Borden Inc*.[45] The facts of this case were that, during the 1950s, the respondents, Reckitt & Colman, had bought two companies in England that marketed fresh lemon juice in a natural-looking lemon-shaped squeeze container. The respondents managed to maintain a *de facto* monopoly in that product until the 1970s, when the appellants began to supply fresh lemon juice in bottles. The respondents began to compete with them, and also sold lemon juice in bottles. Thereupon, the appellants retaliated and also started producing lemon juice in lemon-shaped containers. Reckitt & Colman's container was yellow, and had a detachable

[39] *John Haig & Co v Forth Blending Co Ltd* 1954 SLT 2.
[40] (1882) 7 App Cas 219 (HL).
[41] (1915) 32 RPC 273.
[42] (1905) 23 RPC 117.
[43] (1933) 50 RPC 232.
[44] As in the "Dimple Whisky" case discussed above. See also *Alexander Ferguson & Co v Matthews MacClay & Manson* 1989 SLT 795.
[45] [1990] 1 All ER 873 (HL).

label attached to the neck of the container, and had the name "Jif" embossed on to the container, although the name was not very distinct. The label would generally be removed before use. Borden's lemon was called "ReaLemon", and was similar to the Jif lemon, except that it had a green cap instead of a yellow cap, a small flat area to enable the lemon to stand up, and a different label. The House of Lords dismissed the appeal by Borden against an injunction to restrain Borden from passing off their plastic lemon as being that of Reckitt & Colman. The reasoning for holding that there had been passing off was that it was not the lemon-shaped container that was protected by the injunction, but the get-up of the product, in that what was being misrepresented was the *contents*, that is, the lemon juice. The lemon-shaped container in the United Kingdom was so associated with the respondent company that shoppers would be confused by the sight of the appellants' products on the supermarket shelves, and would assume they were buying "Jif" lemons. The House of Lords quoted Walton J, the trial judge, who had stated:

> "The question is not whether the judge himself would be deceived by the defendant's get-up: the question is whether, in the light of all the admissible evidence, the judge is persuaded that an ordinary average shopper, shopping in the places in which the article is available for purchase, and under the usual conditions ... is likely to be deceived ... one is typically dealing with a shopper in a supermarket, in something of a hurry, accustomed to selecting between various brands when there is a choice, but increasingly having to choose in relation to a wide range of brands between the supermarket's 'own brand' and one other brand, and no more."[46]

16.26 Misrepresentation can relate to business names in exactly the same way as with brand names. In *Chill Foods (Scotland) Ltd* v *Cool Foods Ltd*,[47] interim interdicts were granted against Cool Foods Ltd trading in frozen foodstuffs without differentiating that business from that of Chill Foods (Scotland) Ltd in their marketing literature. Cool Foods Ltd had been set up by one of the directors and shareholders of Chill Foods (Scotland) Ltd, and traded in a similar, though not identical, line of business. Lord Maxwell said:

> "While it is well settled that intention to cause confusion is not an essential element of a 'passing off' case, the existence of such intention will make the proof of the likelihood of passing off easier. In the circumstances of this case the promoters of Cool Foods Ltd, having selected a name for their company so similar to the petitioners', can hardly complain if, at this stage, a deliberate intention to mislead is suspected."[48]

16.27 The law permits a person to trade under his/her own name, or to incorporate his/her own name into a business name, as long as it is not done with intent to deceive. Where the names are not identical, a minor difference may be sufficient to differentiate the two businesses. In *Dunlop Pneumatic Tyre Co Ltd* v *Dunlop Motor Co*,[49] the Dunlop Motor Co, a small garage in Kilmarnock, owned by two brothers called Dunlop, with a purely local trade, was sued by the mighty tyre manufacturer Dunlop Pneumatic Tyre

---

[46] [1987] FSR 505 at 512.
[47] 1977 SLT 38.
[48] *Ibid* at 41.
[49] 1907 SC (HL) 15.

Co Ltd with a worldwide trade. The House of Lords held that there was no passing off, as the names were not identical, and, in any event, Dunlop was a common name in Scotland. It was also significant that the nature of the two businesses was far from identical.

A particular problem arises in relation to names which were attached to goods by the original manufacturer, who may have enjoyed a *de facto* monopoly in relation to those goods for some time. When other people legitimately start to manufacture or supply those goods, they may attempt to use the name under which the items have always been known. In such a case, the original manufacturer often attempts to prevent the new manufacturer or supplier from doing so by interdict, claiming that there has been passing off. Legal challenges were made to the use of the words "vacuum cleaner",[50] "shredded wheat",[51] "linoleum",[52] and "cellular clothing".[53] In order to succeed, the pursuer will have to prove that the name has not become a generic name, but remains exclusively associated with the pursuer's product (a "fancy name"). Lord Shand stated in *Cellular Clothing Co Ltd* v *Maxton & Murray:*[54] **16.28**

> "I confess I have always thought and still think, that it should be made almost impossible for anyone to obtain the exclusive right to the use of a word or term which is in ordinary use in our language and which is descriptive only ... As to the proof itself, I have only to say this: it must not be forgotten that it is on the pursuers that the *onus* lies in seeking to appropriate as their own a descriptive term such as the word 'cellular'."

The courts attempt to distinguish generic names from so-called "fancy names", which can be protected by a passing off action because they bear no direct relation to the "character or quality of the goods which are to be sold under that name",[55] and have not developed secondary meanings as words that have entered the English language as the name for the class of goods and which can often find their way into English dictionaries. **16.29**

Extended form passing off

Some manufacturers and suppliers have sought to use the passing off action to protect their goodwill in relation to the use of words that denote not that the goods necessarily were made by them, but that the goods have a particular provenance: they may be made in a certain region, or comply with certain standards of manufacture. This is an extension of the traditional form of the passing off action, considering that many people rather than just one person are entitled to use the word. Champagne,[56] Scotch whisky,[57] advocaat,[58] Harris tweed [59]and vodka[60] have all given rise to such actions. **16.30**

---

[50] *British Vacuum Cleaner Co Ltd* v *New Vacuum Cleaner Co Ltd* [1907] 2 Ch 312.
[51] *Canadian Shredded Wheat Co Ltd* v *Kellogg Co of Canada Ltd* [1938] 1 All ER 618 (PC).
[52] *Linoleum Manufacturing Co* v *Nairn* [1878] 7 Ch 834.
[53] *Cellular Clothing Co Ltd* v *Maxton & Murray* (1899) 1 F (HL) 29.
[54] *Ibid* at 34.
[55] See the words of Lord Shand in *Cellular Clothing Co Ltd* v *Maxton & Murray* (1899) 1 F (HL) 29 at 33.
[56] *J Bollinger* v *Costa Brava Wine Co Ltd* [1961] 1 WLR 277.
[57] *John Walker & Sons Ltd* v *Henry Ost & Co Ltd* [1970] 1 WLR 917 (whisky mixed with sugar cane in Ecuador).
[58] *Erven Warninck* v *J Townend & Sons Ltd* [1979] AC 731 (confusion between Dutch advocaat and "Keeling's Old English Advocaat" even though they were different drinks).
[59] *Argyllshire Weavers Ltd* v *A Macaulay (Tweeds) Ltd* 1965 SLT 21.
[60] *Diageo North America Inc* v *Intercontinental Brands (ICB) Ltd* [2011] RPC 2.

16.31   In *J Bollinger* v *Costa Brava Wine Co Ltd*,[61] 12 champagne-producing companies, representing all the champagne-producing companies in the Champagne region of France, raised a passing off action against the defendants who produced a sparkling wine in Spain, from using the appellation "Champagne" or "Spanish Champagne" in relation to their product. The court awarded an injunction. Champagne is also protected by European Union Regulations on designation of origin. In *Taittinger* v *Allbev*,[62] the defendants had produced a non-alcoholic beverage called "Elderflower Champagne", which had a mushroom-shaped, wired cork similar to that of a champagne bottle. The appearance of the bottle was similar to a champagne bottle, although the label did state that the drink was non-alcoholic. An action was raised based on passing off and on breach of the EU Regulation regulating the use of the word "Champagne". On both grounds, injunctions were awarded because of the risk of confusion, and the risk of damage to the uniqueness of the word "champagne", with consequent damage to the goodwill of the champagne houses in France.

16.32   The term "Scotch whisky" is also heavily protected by regulation. Like champagne, it is protected by an EU Regulation[63] and also by various pieces of UK law, notably the Scotch Whisky Act 1988 and the Scotch Whisky Regulations 2009,[64] which provide detailed definitions of various terms in reg 3 including "Scotch Whisky" and "Single Malt Scotch Whisky". Various successful cases have been brought based on both breach of the EU Regulation and passing off, including *Scotch Whisky Association* v *Glen Kella Distillers Ltd*[65] in which the challenged product ("white whisky") was not made in the way laid down in the EU Regulation, by single distillation and maturation.

16.33   The pursuer in extended form passing off actions should have an interest to protect, and a trade association may fail to establish this, as was the case in *Chocosuisse Union des Fabricants Suisses de Chocolat* v *Cadbury Ltd*[66] ("Swiss" chocolate).

DAMAGE

16.34   The third requirement in the "classic trinity" (goodwill, misrepresentation and damage) is that damage must be caused to the pursuers or, if damage has not occurred yet, the court must be convinced that damage is likely to occur if a remedy is not granted. In *British Telecommunications plc* v *One in a Million Ltd*,[67] the court held that even the threat of passing off was sufficient, where One in a Million Ltd had registered the names of various household names as domain names (Virgin Enterprises plc, British Telecommunications plc, Marks & Spencer plc, Ladbroke Group plc and J Sainsbury plc) and then tried to make money by selling the names back to them.[68]

16.35   Damage might be done to the pursuer's business in a variety of ways. The issue might be damage to goodwill because an inferior product has been put on the market which existing or potential customers of the pursuer confuse with the pursuer's product. This might lead to permanent loss of existing customers who are dissat-

---

[61] [1961] 1 WLR 277.
[62] [1994] 4 All ER 75.
[63] Reg 110/2008.
[64] SI 2009/2890.
[65] *Times* 1 April 1997.
[66] [1999] RPC 826.
[67] [1999] 1 WLR 903.
[68] See also *Smith Kline Beecham Ltd* v *GSKline Ltd* [2011] EWHC 169 (Ch).

isfied with the goods. In other cases, passing off by the introduction of infringing goods which are of good quality but which dilute the market may lead to a reduction in numbers of customers. In some cases, as evidenced by the *One in a Million* case, damage has not actually taken place at the time of the action, but there is evidence that damage is likely to take place if the passing off is allowed to continue.

This kind of passing off has recently been even further developed, in a manner **16.36** similar to the form seen in the *One in a Million* case. In *Lifestyle Management Ltd* v *Frater*,[69] a disgruntled agent registered various domain names identical apart from the suffix to those of the claimant, and put potentially defamatory material on the websites about the claimant, to use as a lever to secure payment in a contractual dispute. The court held that as the requirements of the classic trinity for a passing off action were shown, an interim injunction would be granted.

DEFENCES TO AN ACTION OF PASSING OFF

DEFENCE ON THE FACTS

Questions of fact are very important in actions of passing off, and the defender may be **16.37** able to prove that there was no misrepresentation, or no damage, or that the pursuer did not have any goodwill, or that his goodwill was not harmed by the defender, or that the act was done with permission.

DEFENCE OF ILLEGALITY

As in all areas of delict, the defence of illegality applies – *ex turpi causa non oritur* **16.38** *actio* (a legal action does not arise out of an illegality). In *Bile Beans Manufacturing Co Ltd* v *Davidson*,[70] the pursuer had claimed that their product, "bile beans", contained a vegetable product from Australia, known to the Aborigines to have curative properties, which they said had been discovered by Charles Forde, an eminent scientist. The defenders began to sell a rival product under the name "bile beans" and the pursuers sought an interdict against them on the ground of passing off. However, it was discovered that there was no scientist called Charles Forde, and that the product was not an Australian plant extract, but was made in a chemical laboratory in the United States. In fact, the pursuers were perpetrating a fraud on the public. The court applied the principle *ex turpi causa non oritur actio*, and refused to grant the interdict.

PERSONAL BAR

If the pursuer can be shown to have acquiesced in the face of the defender's passing **16.39** off – for example, by inordinate delay in bringing a case to court – the pursuer may be personally barred from pursuing the matter because of *mora* and taciturnity. However, in *William Grant & Sons Ltd* v *Glen Catrine Bonded Warehouse Ltd (No 3)*,[71] the Inner House of the Court of Session held that a delay of 8 years, while the pursuers waited to

---

[69] [2010] EWHC 3258.
[70] (1906) 8 F 1181.
[71] 2001 SC 901.

see how things would develop before going to court, was not too long so as to amount to acquiescence. However, this is dependent on the facts of the individual case.

INNOCENCE

16.40 Innocent misrepresentation can be a defence to a claim of damages, but not to an action for interdict or interim interdict.[72]

EU LAW

16.41 In theory it would be a defence to a passing off action to prove that enforcement of the pursuer's rights would infringe EU competition law. The relevant provisions are Arts 101 and 102 of the Consolidated version of the Treaty on the Functioning of the European Union.[73] However, in practice, as the delict demands proof of a misrepresentation, and the courts are careful not to allow passing off actions to be used as a means of restriction of competition,[74] cases are unlikely to arise where this is successfully pleaded.[75]

16.42 Chapter 21 on Defences in Delict should also be referred to.

REMEDIES

16.43 The principal remedy is interdict but damages are also available, and, in appropriate cases, an action of accounting for profits as an alternative to damages. Declarator may also be sought.

INTERDICT

16.44 This discretionary remedy will be covered in more detail in Chapter 22 on Remedies. It is sought in almost every passing off action. The defender may be ordered to refrain from passing off, and may be required to change the name of a product, or change its get-up, or change the way in which a business or product is marketed. All of these changes will result in disruption of business to the defender and considerable expense. Breach of an interdict is punishable as contempt of court.

16.45 Interim interdict is often sought on the dependence of the action, which is a request for an interdict to take effect right away, before the action has been heard in full. A case has to be made out for interim interdict and the court must decide on the "balance of convenience" whether to grant it. Lord President Inglis explained this concept in *Tennant & Co v Thomson*,[76] thus:

---

[72] *GNS Railway v Mann* (1892) 19 R 1035.
[73] [2010] OJ C83/47.
[74] Eg the requirement that there be goodwill within the jurisdiction, as shown in *Alain Bernardin et Compagnie v Pavilion Properties Ltd* [1967] RPC 581, and the steps taken to ensure that a pursuer cannot prevent others from using generic names or words in the English language, as in *Cellular Clothing Company Ltd v Maxton & Murray* (1899) 1 F (HL) 29.
[75] *Clerk & Lindsell on Torts* (20th edn, 2010), para 25–18.
[76] (1870) 8 SLR 15.

"The object is to regulate interim possession in such a way as to do least damage in the meantime to either party, at the same time to provide sufficiently for proper restitution being made for any damage suffered by the party who shall be found to have been in the right when the case is over. The question always comes to be a balance of advantages and disadvantages on the two sides."

The economic position of both parties is assessed. In *Pebble Beach Co* v *Lombard Brands Ltd*,[77] the pursuer owned a golf course in California and had various European Community trade marks in the name "Pebble Beach" for software, games and sporting activities, while the defenders, a whisky marketing company based in Scotland, had a UK trade mark for the name "Pebble Beach" for alcoholic beverages (Pebble Beach malt whisky). In an action for breach of trade mark and passing off, interim interdict was refused on the basis that the two operated in different areas of activity, there had not been misrepresentation and hence no passing off, and there was little likelihood of confusion. By contrast, in *Gleneagles Hotels Ltd* v *Quillco 100 Ltd*,[78] an interim interdict was awarded to protect the proprietor of the famous Gleneagles Hotel against a proposed development of a film studio with five-star hotel and golf course a few miles away under the name "Gleneagles". The court surmised from the evidence that the name had been chosen deliberately, and held that the balance of convenience favoured the protection of the long-established business against the new one, which at the stage of the action was only a "vision" rather than a reality. In *Wise Property Care Ltd* v *White Thomson Preservation Ltd*,[79] the Inner House confirmed the Lord Ordinary's decision to award interim interdict in a case in which, after the sale of a timber preservation business which had been a family business, one of the family members set up a rival business under a very similar name operating from the same street in Dunfermline. The evidence showed that there had been a deliberate attempt to mislead customers of the original company on the telephone into thinking it was one and the same business. **16.46**

In many cases, for practical reasons, there may be no need to return to court later to make out a case for a permanent interdict, and interim interdict may be sufficient. If interim interdict is granted, the defender will often have to make major and costly changes to his/her business operation. An interdict can require the delivery up or destruction of infringing products or marketing materials, and can require the change of a company or business name. **16.47**

DAMAGES

The remedy of damages will be discussed in full in Chapter 22. Hector MacQueen, in *Stair Memorial Encyclopaedia: The Laws of Scotland* states that there is no modern authority in Scotland on the award of damages in a passing off action.[80] In England, nominal damages were awarded for passing off in *Procea Products Ltd* v *Evans*.[81] Damages may, potentially, be awarded for loss of profits by the pursuer, for damage to his/her goodwill, and generally for harm to the pursuer's business reputation. In any event, damages would be extremely difficult to quantify, as it would be hard to **16.48**

---

[77] 2002 SLT 1312.
[78] 2003 SLT 812.
[79] 2008 CSIH 44.
[80] See vol 18, Pt II, Chap 7, para 1400 at n 28.
[81] (1951) 68 RPC 210.

determine whether all the lost customers would have gone to the pursuer if they had not been poached, and the defender's accounting system may make it hard to identify which sales actually result from the passing off.

ACCOUNTING

16.49 An alternative remedy to damages is an action for accounting for the profits obtained from passing off. The pursuer must choose between this remedy and an action of damages, as shown in *Treadwells Drifters Inc v RCL Ltd*.[82]

THE DIFFERENCES BETWEEN A PASSING OFF ACTION AND AN ACTION FOR TRADE MARK INFRINGEMENT OR BREACH OF OTHER INTELLECTUAL PROPERTY RIGHTS

16.50 When a passing off action is brought, the facts will often also support an action for infringement of a trade mark, or of a patent, or registered trade mark, or breach of copyright or design right or registered design. Acts that may give rise to an action for infringement of trade mark are probably the most likely also to give rise to a passing off action.[83] However, there are significant differences between the two.

16.51 First, the principal objective of a passing off action is to protect goodwill. As was stated by Lord Diplock in *Star Industrial Co Ltd v Yap Kwee Kor*:[84] "A passing off action is a remedy for the invasion of a right of property not in the mark, name or get up improperly used, but in the business or goodwill likely to be injured by the misrepresentation made by passing off one person's goods as the goods of another." It followed, therefore, in that case, that where there was no longer any business in the supply of toothbrushes carried out in Singapore, there was no goodwill and hence there could be no passing off action. The court held that it was not competent to use a passing off action to protect a trade mark. The purpose of the remedies for infringement of trade mark is to protect the property rights in the mark and goodwill would be irrelevant.[85]

16.52 Second, s 56 of the Trade Marks Act 1994 provides that, in relation to a well-known mark, it does not matter whether the pursuer has any goodwill in the United Kingdom. In relation to a passing off action, this factor is essential, as shown in *Alain Bernardin et Compagnie v Pavilion Properties Ltd*,[86] the "Crazy Horse" case.

16.53 Third, in a passing off action, there should usually be a "common field of activity", as discussed earlier in this chapter. The courts will not normally allow a pursuer to restrict the use of a word or a name or the get-up of a product where the two products

---

[82] 1996 SLT 1048.
[83] An action for trade mark infringement under ss 14–21 of the Trade Marks Act 1994 would be competent where the defender is using an identical or similar mark to refer to identical or similar goods, and also where the goods or services are *not* identical or similar. An action can also be raised for infringement of a well-known but unregistered mark under s 56 of the same Act, where the pursuer is a national of a country which is a signatory to the Paris Convention for the Protection of Industrial Property 1883.
[84] [1976] FSR 256 (PC).
[85] Trade Marks Act 1994, s 10(2) and (3).
[86] [1967] RPC 581 (Ch D).

are entirely different, or the two businesses trade in entirely different markets, and confusion is unlikely to arise. However, under s 10(3) of the Trade Marks Act 1994, a mark can be infringed even where the goods or services of the defender are not similar to those of the holder of the registered trade mark.

Fourth, in a passing off action, there must always be a misrepresentation. A **16.54** misrepresentation is not one of the requirements for infringement of a registered trade mark, or for infringement of a well-known mark which is protected by the Paris Convention.[87]

An action to enforce a trade mark will be easier to win than a passing off action **16.55** at common law, because the registered mark in the name of the pursuer is already a strong piece of evidence for the pursuer. In a passing off action, the classic trinity has to be proved. The unregistered property rights may be harder to enforce because of the need to establish that the pursuer has the right.

Although trade marks can be renewed, most intellectual property rights give **16.56** protection for a limited time only. While intellectual property rights may be easier to enforce than goodwill in a passing off action, if the time period of the intellectual property right has expired, a passing off action may offer the most suitable remedy. In *Numatic International Ltd* v *Qualtex (UK) Ltd*,[88] the design rights for Henry the vaccuum cleaner with the face had expired, but Numatic won a passing off action against Qualtex to protect the shape and get-up. In this case the defendant gave an undertaking to alter its design and the court made a declaration without the need to make an injunction.

See also Chapter 22 on Remedies.   **16.57**

---

[87] See ss 10 and 56 of the Trade Marks Act 1994.
[88] [2010] RPC 26.

17 BREACH OF CONFIDENCE

In this chapter we turn our attention to the obligation of confidence which is now well **17.1**
recognised in the law of Scotland. Bankton stated that: "Advocates are bound by their
office not to reveal the secrets of their clients' causes."[1] He went on to state that clerks
to the Signet were sworn at their admission not to reveal what they write or do for
their employers.[2]

There are a number of 19th-century cases where the courts have recognised the **17.2**
existence of an obligation on the part of the defender not to impart confidential information. For example, the courts recognised the principle that a former employee was
under a duty not to disclose to others trade secrets which his employer had imparted
to him during his period of employment.[3] Again, a doctor was held to owe a duty of
confidence to his patient.[4]

In essence, the delict of breach of confidence provides a remedy for the unauthorised **17.3**
use of information which relates to the pursuer. For example, if I submitted the
manuscript for a book I had written to a potential publisher (B) in order for him to
peruse, and B gave the manuscript to an academic (C) for his appraisal, and C in turn
read out extracts of the work during lectures to his students, would the law of delict
provide me with a remedy? If, indeed, there was liability, who would be liable? Would
the law provide me (ie the original confider) with a remedy against either B or C, or
both? These are the important issues which we will be discussing in this chapter.

Whereas the law relating to breach of confidence probably does not owe its origin **17.4**
to the law of England, the law of Scotland does draw heavily on the jurisprudence of
the law developed by the Courts of Chancery over the 18th and 19th centuries.[5]

An early example of the principle of breach of confidence being applied by the **17.5**
courts is seen in *Pollard* v *Photographic Co.*[6] In that case, a photographer who had
taken a negative likeness of a lady in order to supply her with copies for money
was restrained by the court from selling or exhibiting copies of the photographs,
not only on the ground that there was an implied contract not to use the negative
for such purposes, but also because such a use constituted a breach of confidence.
More recently, in *Duchess of Argyll* v *Duke of Argyll*,[7] the plaintiff sought to restrain the
defendant, from whom she had been divorced, from communicating to a newspaper,
information about her which was of an intimate nature. She also sought to restrain the

---

[1] *Institute* 4, 3, 27.
[2] *Ibid*, 4, 4, 10.
[3] *Roxburgh* v *McArthur* (1841) 3 D 556.
[4] *AB* v *CD* (1851) 14 D 177.
[5] For a useful discussion of the role played by the Courts of Chancery in the development of the action for
breach of confidence, see *Imerman* v *Tchenguiz* [2010] EWCA Civ 908, per Lord Neuberger MR at paras 54–61.
[6] (1889) 40 ChD 345.
[7] [1967] 1 Ch 302.

newspaper from publishing the information. The plaintiff succeeded in her action. The court held that a breach of confidence can arise quite independently of any right of property or contract. As far as the protection of confidential information which existed within the context of the relationship of husband and wife was concerned, Ungoed-Thomas J stated:[8] "[there] could hardly be anything more intimate or confidential than is involved in that relationship or than in the mutual trust and confidences which are shared between husband and wife." His Lordship stated that it was up to the court to decide whether the communications were confidential.[9] The learned judge went on to state that in order to protect a breach of confidence in such a relationship an injunction would be granted not simply to restrain the publication of the information by the person who was party to the confidence, but also to restrain publication by other persons into whose hands the confidential information had come.[10]

17.6   There need be no contract between the person who imparts the relevant information and the person who receives such information for the obligation of confidence to exist. In other words, the obligation of confidence is imposed solely by operation of law. Indeed, in *Coco v A N Clark*,[11] Megarry J stated that that the obligation of confidence was a "pure equitable doctrine" which was unaffected by contract.[12] In *Coco*, the manufacturer of a moped engine designed by Coco disclosed details of the workings of his engine to a number of potential manufacturers, including the defendant company, in order to ascertain the commercial viability of his product. The negotiations with the defendant were unsuccessful. Allegedly, the defendant made commercial use of the information which had been acquired during the discussion period with the plaintiff. It was held that the defendant was liable for a breach of confidence. His Lordship stated[13] that there were three elements which were required if, apart from contract, a case of breach of confidence is to succeed: first, the information must have the necessary quality of confidence about it; second, the information must have been imparted in circumstances which imported an obligation of confidence;[14] and, third, there must be an unauthorised use of that information to the detriment of the party who communicates the information (ie the original confider as opposed to the person who subsequently divulges it in breach of confidence).

---

[8] [1967] 1 Ch 302 at 322.

[9] *Ibid* at 330.

[10] *Ibid* at 333. In *Lord Advocate v The Scotsman Publications Ltd* [1990] 1 AC 812, the majority of the House of Lords held that the law of confidentiality in Scotland was the same as that of England, particularly in relation to a situation where a person comes into possession of confidential information, knowing it to be such, but not having received it directly from the original confider. See also *Mosley v News Group Newspapers Ltd* [2008] EMLR 679 where it was held at first instance that the action for breach of confidence protected information which related to sexual conduct between unmarried individuals.

[11] [1968] FSR 415.

[12] *Ibid* at 419.

[13] *Ibid*.

[14] See also *Vestergaard Frandsen A/S v Bestnet Europe Ltd* [2009] EWHC 657. In that case the court held that there was an actionable breach of confidence in relation to a manufacturer where confidential recommendations had been used in the development of a product by a former consultant of the manufacturer and those recommendations amounted to trade secrets. The court had to consider whether the information had been communicated in circumstances which imported an obligation of confidence. It was an express term of the consultant's contract of employment that he would keep information arising out of his work for the claimants confidential. Once the defendant ceased to work for the manufacturer, the scope of the obligation of confidence was confined to the protection of trade secrets. See also *Vestergaard Frandsen A/S v Bestnet Europe* [2009] EWHC 1456.

As far as the first requirement was concerned, Megarry J stated that if the infor- **17.7**
mation was already common knowledge, the information could not be regarded as
confidential.[15]

In relation to the second point, there could be no binding obligation of confidence **17.8**
if the information was blurted out in public or was communicated in other circumstances which negated any duty of holding the information confidential. His Lordship
suggested[16] that in order to ascertain whether the information was confidential, one
should ask whether the relevant circumstances were such that any man who stood in
the shoes of the recipient of the information would realise that the information was
being given in confidence. His Lordship went on to decide that, in the instant case, the
relevant disclosure seemed to be redolent of trust and confidence.[17] The basis of the
obligation was explained in *Stephens v Avery*.[18]

Sir Nicolas Browne-Wilkinson V-C stated:[19] **17.9**

> "The basis of equitable intervention to protect confidentiality is that it is unconscionable
> for a person who has received information on the basis that it is confidential to reveal that
> information. Although the relationship between the parties is often important in cases where
> it is said there is an implied as opposed to express obligation of confidence, the relationship
> between the parties is not the determining factor. It is the acceptance of the information
> on the basis that it will be kept secret that affects the conscience of the recipient of the
> information."

As far as the unauthorised disclosure of information was concerned, Megarry J, in **17.10**
Coco, was of the view that in certain circumstances the court possibly could intervene
on behalf of the plaintiff, notwithstanding the fact that the plaintiff had suffered no
detriment by such disclosure.[20] An example of such a circumstance would be one
where the relevant confidential information shows the plaintiff in a favourable light
but, at the same time, gravely injures some relation or friend of his, whom he wishes
to protect.

An interesting example of the application of the first requirement of confidentiality **17.11**
identified by Megarry J in *Coco* is seen in *The Author of a Blog v Times Newspapers Ltd*.[21]
In that case, the author of a blog who was known as "Night Jack" sought an interim
injunction to restrain the defendants from publishing any information which either
would or might lead to his identification as the person responsible for the blog. Eady J
held that the relevant information did not have the necessary quality of confidentiality
about it in order to warrant protection by the law.[22]

An example of both the first and second principles identified in *Coco* are illus- **17.12**
trated in the Court of Appeal case of *Napier v Pressdram Ltd*.[23] In that case, the court

---

[15] [1968] FSR 415 at 420.
[16] *Ibid* at 421.
[17] *Ibid*.
[18] [1988] Ch 449.
[19] *Ibid* at 455.
[20] [1968] FSR 415 at 421.
[21] [2009] EWHC 1358.
[22] His Lordship also held (*ibid* at [11]) that the claimant had failed to prove that he had an expectation of
privacy in terms of Art 8 of the ECHR, since blogging was essentially a public rather than a private activity.
For a useful discussion of this case, see K Brimsted, "The anonymous police blogger, the newspaper and the
unmasking of the Night Jack" (2009) 25(6) *CLS Rev* 583.
[23] [2009] EWCA Civ 443.

held that the judge at first instance had been entitled to refuse to grant an injunction preventing a publisher of a magazine from publishing information about the outcome of a complaint made to the Law Society against a solicitor and also about an ombudsman's report regarding the handling of the complaint. The court held that for a duty of confidentiality to be owed to the claimant the information in question had to be of such a nature and also obtained in such circumstances that any reasonable person in the position of the recipient of the information (in the instant case the complainant) ought to have recognised that the information should be treated as confidential. This was not so in the instant case. Furthermore, the complainant did not owe the solicitor a duty of confidentiality simply by reason of the fact that the former had invoked the Law Society's extra-statutory scheme for investigating complaints against solicitors.[24]

17.13 In *Imerman* v *Tchenquiz*,[25] Eady J was of the view that there was a powerful case for saying that *any* information stored on a computer to which access was password protected should, by virtue of that fact alone, be regarded as confidential, irrespective of its actual content.

17.14 It is not necessary for liability to lie for breach of confidence that the defender is not conscious of the fact that what he is doing amounts to misuse of the relevant information.[26]

17.15 In *JN Dairies Ltd* v *Johal Dairies Ltd*,[27] it was held that information contained in invoices which had been prepared by a wholesaler for its customers had the necessary degree of confidentiality for the claimant wholesaler (X) to bring an action for breach of confidence against the person who was responsible for their misappropriation (S), and also against the person who was responsible for using that information to his advantage. The learning in *Coco* applied to the facts of the case. The information was not in the public domain, such information being ascertainable either from customer records or from the knowledge of its employees or from the customers themselves. However, it was not necessary for the claimant to establish that the content of the documents met the stringent test of confidentiality (ie the first two tests in *Coco*) or potential to cause commercial harm. It was clear when the appropriating employee, S, took the invoices that he knew that they contained commercially valuable information and that he had no right either to obtain that information or to pass it on without X's authority. That was sufficient, in itself, for the court to impose on him a duty of confidentiality. Finally, there had been an unauthorised use of the information following the approaches that had been made to X's customers. This was to the detriment of X. The learning in *Coco* therefore applied.

17.16 The law of breach of confidence was discussed again in the House of Lords case of *AG* v *Observer Ltd (No 2)*[28] (the "Spycatcher" case). This case involved one Peter Wright who was a retired MI5 agent who had moved to Australia and written an account of his career (in a book which was entitled *Spycatcher*) in the secret service despite the fact that former members of MI5 owe a lifelong duty of confidence to the Crown. By the time the case came before the House of Lords, the book had already been published in several countries including the USA and Canada. Furthermore,

---

[24] [2009] EWCA Civ 443 at [49]. See also *Burrows* v *Smith* [2010] EWHC 22.
[25] [2009] EWHC 2024. Upheld by the Court of Appeal: see [2010] EWCA Civ 908.
[26] *Vestergaard Frandsen A/S* v *Bestnet Europe Ltd* [2009] EWHC 657 at [24].
[27] [2009] EWHC 1331.
[28] [1990] 1 AC 109.

many copies of the book had been imported into the UK. The House of Lords refused to grant an injunction against the defendant newspapers (namely the *Observer* and the *Guardian*) preventing them from reproducing extracts from the book since the information contained in *Spycatcher* was in the public domain and, therefore, no longer confidential. Therefore, no further damage could be done to the public interest than that which had already been done.[29]

Lord Keith stated[30] that the law had long recognised that an obligation of confidence could arise out of particular relationships such as those between doctor and patient, priest and penitent, solicitor and client, and banker and customer. Whereas the obligation of confidence could be imposed by an express or an implied term in a contract, such an obligation could exist quite independently of any contract on the basis of an independent equitable principle of confidence. His Lordship went on to state[31] that the majority of cases had arisen in circumstances where there had been a threatened or an actual breach of confidence by either an employee or an ex-employee or where information about the plaintiff's business affairs had been given in confidence to someone who had proceeded to exploit it for his own benefit.[32] However, there were other cases where there was no financial detriment to the plaintiff, in that the relevant breach comprised no more than a breach of personal privacy as in *Duchess of Argyll* v *Duke of Argyll*.[33] Indeed, such a right was one which the law relating to breach of confidence should seek to protect. It was of sufficient detriment to the confider of the information that the information which was given in confidence was to be disclosed to persons whom he would prefer not to know of such information even though the disclosure would not be harmful to him in any positive way. Importantly, Lord Keith went on to hold that a third party who comes into possession of confidential information, which he knows to be such, may come under a duty not to pass it on to anyone else.[34] Lord Griffiths addressed the situation where the confidential information had already entered the public domain when the case was brought before the court. His Lordship expressed[35] the view that a third party (who was in no way connected or tainted with the original breach of confidence) into whose hands the confidential information had come would not be restrained from making use of the information, even though he may have realised that the information must have been leaked in breach of confidence. It was not practicable for the courts to attempt to restrain everyone with access to the relevant knowledge from making use of it. That was not to say that the original confidant, or even a third party in the direct chain from the confidant, might not be restrained. Each case would depend on its own facts.

For Lord Goff, as far as restraining further publication of *Spycatcher* was concerned, the fact that the contents of the book in question were no longer confidential was all

17.17

17.18

---

[29] See also *Vestergaard Frandsen A/S* v *Bestnet Europe Ltd* [2009] EWHC 1456. See also *Barclays Bank* v *Guardian News and Media Ltd* [2009] EWHC 591, where an application for the continuation of injunctive relief until trial was granted to a bank in order to prevent, in particular, the publication by a media company of certain documents which related to financial transactions. As to whether confidentiality continued to exist in view of the dissemination of the documents, *AG* v *Observer Ltd (No 2)* applied. General availability of material on the internet would mean that it would be likely that such material would lose its confidential character. However, it was observed that only partial dissemination, perhaps in some remote or expert site which was not generally available, might not result in a loss of confidentiality.

[30] [1990] 1 AC 109 at 255.

[31] *Ibid* at 256.

[32] Eg *Seager* v *Copydex Ltd* [1967] 1 WLR 923.

[33] [1967] 1 Ch 302.

[34] [1990] 1 AC 109 at 260.

[35] *Ibid* at 272.

important. The subject-matter of the action was gone, and, with it, the obligation of confidence.[36] However, his Lordship did reserve the question as to whether, in a case similar to that which was before him, some limited obligation continued to rest upon the confidant.[37] According to Baroness Hale in *Douglas* v *Hello Ltd (No 3)*,[38] *Spycatcher* expanded liability for failing to keep a secret beyond the person to whom it had originally been confided to the person who knowingly took advantage of it.

17.19   More recently, both the nature and extent of the scope of the concept of breach of confidence were discussed in *Campbell* v *Mirror News Group Newspapers*.[39] Here the claimant was an internationally famous fashion model. She gave information to the media about her private life. She claimed, untruthfully, that she did not take drugs. The defendant newspaper published articles which disclosed both her drug addiction and the fact that she was having therapy by means of a self-help group. The articles gave details of the group meeting which the claimant was attending and also showed photographs of her in a street as she was leaving the meeting. The claimant accepted the fact that the newspaper was entitled to publish the fact of her drug addiction, and also the fact that she was receiving treatment. However, she claimed that the newspaper had acted in breach of confidence both by obtaining and also by publishing both details of her therapy and also the photographs of her which had been taken covertly. The newspaper denied the claim on the ground that it was entitled, in the public interest, to publish the information in order to correct the claimant's misleading statements. The newspaper also asserted that the information it had published was both peripheral and not sufficiently significant in order to amount to a breach of confidence. However, the House of Lords, by a majority, ruled in favour of the claimant.

17.20   Lord Nicholls (dissenting) was of the view that information about an individual's private life would not, in ordinary usage, be called "confidential". The essence of the tort of breach of confidence would better now be encapsulated as misuse of private information.[40] His Lordship endorsed the opinion of Lord Goff in *AG* v *Guardian Newspapers Ltd (No 2)*[41] to the effect that a duty of confidence arises when confidential information comes to the knowledge of a person in circumstances where he has notice, or is held to have agreed, that the information is confidential, with the effect that it would be just in all the circumstances that he should be precluded from disclosing the information to others. His Lordship then went on to address the impact of human rights jurisprudence on the tort of breach of confidence.[42] In his Lordship's view, by virtue of human rights law identifying private information as something worth protecting, this had resulted in a shift in the centre of gravity of the action for breach of confidence when it is used as a remedy for the unjustified publication of personal information. In essence, in his Lordship's view, human rights law had transformed the tort of breach of confidence from one based on a prior relationship of confidence, to one where a duty was placed on a wider range of people.

---

[36] [1990] 1 AC 109 at 287.
[37] *Ibid* at 288.
[38] [2008] 1 AC 1 (at 87). See para 17.30 below. See also *Imerman* v *Tchenguiz* [2010] EWCA Civ 908, per Lord Neuberger MR at [64].
[39] [2004] 2 AC 457.
[40] [2004] 2 AC 457 at 465. In *Imerman* v *Tchenguiz* [2010] EWCA Civ 908 at [65], Lord Neuberger MR (with whom the court agreed) expressed the view that *Campbell* established that English law recognised a tort of misuse of private information.
[41] [1990] 1 AC 109 at 281.
[42] [2004] 2 AC 457 at 473.

For Lord Hope, the fact that the claimant had not only lied about her addiction but had **17.21** also sought to benefit from this by comparing herself with others in the fashion business meant that the press had not breached any confidence simply by "putting the record straight". However, for his Lordship the real issue in the appeal was whether the details of the claimant's treatment which had been published amounted to a breach of confidence. In order to decide this, one had to ascertain whether the information was private and not public. In the instant case, the details of the claimant's attendance at a Narcotics Anonymous meeting was private information which imported a duty of confidence.[43] In deciding whether information was private and, therefore, warranted protection in terms of the law of breach of confidence, one had to ascertain how a reasonable person of ordinary sensibilities would feel if she were placed in the same position as the claimant and also faced with the same publicity.[44] The test propounded by Lord Hope in order to ascertain whether any given information ranked as private was, therefore, objective-subjective.

The next question which had to be answered was whether the publication of **17.22** the relevant private information was justified. A balance had to be struck between Art 8 (which protects the right to respect for private and family life) and Art 10 (which protects freedom of expression but, at the same time, recognises the need to protect the rights and freedom of others).[45] In this context, Lord Hope equated the rights under Art 8 as being at the heart of the action for breach of confidence. This approach constituted a huge leap forward, in effect.

As far as the Art 10 right was concerned, the details of the claimant's treatment **17.23** were private and of sufficient importance to justify limiting the defendant's rights of expression under Art 10.[46]

The next question which had to be answered was whether the means by which the **17.24** court chooses to limit the rights enshrined in Art 10 impair those rights as minimally as

---

[43] [2004] 2 AC 457 at 483.
[44] *Ibid* at 484.
[45] *Ibid* at 486.
[46] *Ibid* at 489. See also the European Court of Human Rights case of *Financial Times Ltd v UK* (C-821/03) 50 EHRR 46 where an order which mandated that the complainant newspapers disclose certain documents to a brewing company in order that anonymous journalistic sources might be identified was held to contravene the Art 10 right to freedom of expression of the complainants. Moreover, the interference was not justified under Art 10(2). Although the legal basis for the disclosure (*Norwich Pharmacal Co v Customs and Excise Commissioners* [1974] AC 133 and the Contempt of Court Act 1981, s 10) pursued legitimate aims (protection of confidentiality), there was also a public interest in the protection of journalistic sources. This was vital to press freedom and also to the ability of the press to provide accurate and reliable information to the public. See also *Mosley v News Group Newspapers Ltd* [2008] EMLR 679 where the interrelationship between Convention rights and those comprised in an action for breach of confidence were discussed. In that case it was held that the exposure by a national newspaper of sado-masochist sexual activities between the claimant and other consenting adult participants could not be justified on grounds of public interest and had constituted a breach of confidence and also a breach of the claimant's rights under the Convention. The law now afforded protection in relation to information in respect of which there was a reasonable expectation of privacy, even in circumstances where there was no pre-existing relationship which gave rise to an enforceable duty of confidence. *Campbell v Mirror Group Newspapers* therefore applied. There was a reasonable expectation of privacy in relation to sexual activities carried on between consenting adults on private property and the participants thus owed each other a duty of confidence. The clandestine recording of sexual activities carried on between consenting adults on private property engaged the rights which were protected by the Convention and serious reasons had to exist before interferences with it could be justified: *Dudgeon v UK* (A/45) (1982) 4 EHRR 149 applied. In the light of modern rights-based jurisprudence, the unconventional nature of the activities could not provide justification for the intrusion on the personal privacy of the claimant. Hewson regards *Mosley* as a landmark ruling because of the acceptance by the High Court of the maxim that the private conduct of adults is essentially no one else's business: see B Hewson, "Privacy at Last" (2008) 152 *SJ* 10.

possible. In this context, the right of the public to receive information about the details of the claimant's treatment was of a much lower order than the right of the public to be informed about the fact that the claimant was lying.[47] However, in the last analysis, the claimant, who had been photographed surreptitiously outside the place where she had been receiving therapy, would have been distressed by seeing the photographs, and also by reading the article which revealed what she had been doing. This meant that a gross interference with her private life had taken place. This factor outweighed the right to freedom of expression which the defendants enjoyed under Art 10.[48]

17.25   Baroness Hale emphasised that the Human Rights Act 1998 did not create any new cause of action between private parties.[49] However, the court, as a public authority, was obliged to act in accordance with the European Convention on Human Rights. Baroness Hale went on to consider when the balancing exercise required under Arts 8 and 10 should commence. For Baroness Hale such an exercise should commence when the person who publishes the information either knows or ought to know that there is a reasonable expectation that the information in question will be kept confidential.[50] The "reasonable expectation" test was a threshold test which brought the balancing exercise into play.[51] As far as such an exercise was concerned, it centred round balancing the interests of a *prima donna* celebrity against a celebrity-exploiting newspaper.[52] In the last analysis, the claimant's right to privacy outweighed the defendant's right to publish. An important factor in reaching this conclusion was the potential harm which the publication of the story could do to the claimant.[53]

17.26   For Lord Carswell, who agreed with Lord Hope and Baroness Hale, an important factor in deciding in favour of the claimant was the potential detrimental effect the publication of the details of the claimant's medical treatment would have on her.[54]

17.27   In the authors' view, the House of Lords decision in *Campbell* seems to stretch the tort of breach of confidence to breaking point[55] in order to accommodate the facts. Indeed, in the eye of the cynic, the decision could be regarded as result oriented. That is to say, the publication of details of the nature of the treatment the claimant was receiving was, to all intents and purposes, a breach of privacy, pure and simple, in

---

[47] [2004] 2 AC 457 at 490.

[48] The common law of England had developed a doctrine to the effect that the law did not protect obligations of confidence in cases where the enforcement of the obligation would prevent the disclosure of misconduct. There was no confidence in inequity. The precise ambit of the doctrine was not wholly clear and there was some controversy as to whether it extended beyond the disclosure of a crime or civil wrong. The doctrine clearly included matters which were carried out or in contemplation in breach of the country's security, or in breach of law, including statutory duty, fraud, or otherwise destructive of the country or its people, including matters medically dangerous to the public; Report of the Scottish Law Commission on *Breach of Confidence* (Scot Law Com No 90 (Cmnd 9385, 1984) at para 38. The rule seems to have its origin in *Gartside* v *Outram* (1857) 26 LJ Ch 113 at 114 where Wood VC stated that there was no confidence in inequity. However, Professor Rogers points out that English law has not yet reached a stage where conduct must be unlawful in order to justify its disclosure; W V H Rogers (ed), *Winfield & Jolowicz on Tort* (18th edn, 2010) at p 679.

[49] [2004] 2 AC 457 at 494.

[50] *Ibid* at 495.

[51] *Ibid* at 496.

[52] *Ibid* at 497.

[53] *Ibid* at 502.

[54] *Ibid* at 503.

[55] This view is also shared by Mulheron. See R Mulheron, "A Potential Framework for Privacy? A Reply to Hello!" (2006) 69 *MLR* 679 at 686.

contradistinction to a breach of confidence. However, the House of Lords was not bold enough to recognise the existence of a new tort in the form of an invasion of privacy. That would probably have been a step too far.[56] In the last analysis, the subject-matter of the action in *Campbell* concerned the disclosure of that which Ms Campbell preferred the world not to know about. The case was, therefore, to all intents and purposes, about the protection of the claimant's privacy. Indeed, Moreham argues that in *Campbell* the House was not really applying the concept of confidence at all. The learned author goes on to state that their Lordships tended to use the words "private" and "confidential" interchangeably, and the tests which were devised in order to determine what was private in other jurisdictions were used by the House in order to determine whether there was an obligation of confidence in *Campbell*.[57] Indeed, Moreham opines that, in the wake of *Campbell*, the tort of breach of confidence now constitutes two separate actions: one action which applies in the traditional context, and one which applies where the disclosure of "private" information (which the learned author equates with privacy)[58] is concerned.[59] Phillipson, in turn, argues that if the need for a prior relationship of trust and confidence is dispensed with, then it can be fairly said that, at the conceptual level, the action for breach of confidence would be transformed into a privacy tort.[60] In the same vein, Sims argues that privacy and confidentiality are two distinct and separate concepts.[61] Privacy is concerned with the ability to control the dissemination of information about a person, regardless of how the information came to be known by the disseminator. Confidentiality, on the other hand, is concerned with both the nature of the information and also the circumstances under which that information was communicated. The learned author goes on to argue that the creation of an extended breach of confidence has done violence to the principles upon which breach of confidence is founded.[62] Sims concludes by stating that the creation of a tort of privacy is a better option than attempting to shoehorn[63] privacy into an action for breach of confidence. Mulheron, in turn, has argued that, in the wake of *Campbell*, information which is regarded as private may not need to satisfy the traditional first

---

[56] In *Kaye* v *Robertson* [1991] FSR 62 the claimant, a well-known actor, was seriously injured and was hospitalised. A press reporter gained access to his room and photographed him against his will. The claimant sought an injunction, *inter alia*, on the grounds that such an invasion of his privacy amounted to a tort. However, the Court of Appeal denied the existence of a such a tort. For a useful discussion of how the courts have treated privacy in the United States, see D Bedingfield, "Privacy or Publicity? The Enduring Confusion Surrounding the American Tort of Invasion of Privacy" (1992) 55 *MLR* 111.

[57] N Moreham, "Privacy in the common law: a doctrinal and theoretical analysis" (2005) 123 *LQR* 628 at 629. See also Sir Brian Neill, "Privacy: A Challenge for the Next Century" in B Markesinis, *Protecting Privacy* (1999) at p 1.

[58] (2005) 123 LQR 628 at 636.

[59] *Ibid* at 629.

[60] G Phillipson, "Towards a common law right of privacy" (2003) 66 *MLR* 726 at 744.

[61] See n 62 below. See also E Reid, "Protection for rights of personality in Scots law: a comparative evaluation" (2007) 11(4) *EJCL* at 20 who argues that the terms "private" and "confidential" may overlap but are not synonymous. For an interesting discussion on how the law of delict can address privacy issues, see K Middleton, "A right to privacy" 1963 *JR* 178. See also M Hogg, "The very private life of the right to privacy' in *Privacy and Property* (Hume Papers on Public Policy), vol 2, no 3 (1994), p 1 for a general discussion of privacy in Scots law prior to the advent of the Human Rights Act 1998.

[62] A Sims, "A shift in the centre of gravity: the dangers of protecting privacy through breach of confidence" [2005] *IPLQ* 27 at 51.

[63] In *McKennitt* v *Ash* [2008] QB 73 at 80, Eady J emphatically denied the existence of the tort of the invasion of privacy in English law.

limb test in *Coco* as being confidential information with the necessary quality of confidence about it.[64]

17.28   Baroness Hale's approach to the effect of the Convention on the action for breach of confidence is, perhaps, slightly more traditional by deciding that, by virtue of being a public body, the court, perforce, must apply the Convention. Therefore, there was no need to recognise a new tort in the form of an invasion of privacy. For Baroness Hale, the concept of privacy was simply one factor which was to be weighed in the judicial scales in balancing the competing rights enshrined in both Arts 8 and 10 of the ECHR. In the last analysis, the issue as to whether the claimant's privacy had been invaded was not to be considered when one was determining whether there had been a breach of confidence but, rather, at the stage at which one was considering whether publication of the information was justified.[65]

17.29   Reid argues that whereas there is Scots authority for the extension of confidentiality to a third party receiving information in such circumstances that the information is known to be confidential, there is no clear Scots authority to extend it in the rather more open-ended way as posited by the House of Lords in *AG v Guardian Newspapers (No 2) Ltd* and *Campbell* to the effect that the courts will protect private information as such. The learned author suggests that if the Scottish courts were minded to follow the English courts in developing the law of confidentiality as a general means of protecting private information, a significant point of principle would require to be confronted.[66]

17.30   The issue of tortious liability for breach of confidence came before the House of Lords again in *Douglas v Hello! Ltd (No 3)*.[67] The facts of the case were simple and straightforward. The first and second claimants (the Douglases) were well-known film actors. They had entered into an agreement with the third claimant who was the publisher of an English celebrity magazine called *OK!* The Douglases granted *OK!* exclusive rights to publish photographs of their wedding. Wedding guests were informed that no photographs were to be taken. Also, tight security measures were put in place. However, despite those measures, the wedding reception was infiltrated by a freelance photographer who surreptitiously took photographs. He then sold the exclusive right to publish the unauthorised photographs to the first defendant, Hello! Ltd, the publisher of a celebrity magazine which was in competition with the third claimant. The House of Lords held that whereas information about the wedding was information which anyone was free to communicate, the photographic images of the wedding were not publicly available and were, therefore, confidential information which warranted protection in law. Therefore, a duty of confidence was owed both to the Douglases and also to the publishers of *OK!* magazine.

17.31   According to Lord Hoffmann, the fact that the information in question happened to have been about the personal life of the Douglases was irrelevant as far as the action for breach of confidence was concerned. The subject-matter of the action was not about protection of privacy. The relevant information could have been anything which a newspaper was willing to pay for. What was significant was the fact that the

---

[64] (2006) 69 MLR 679 at 693.
[65] In *Mosley v News Group Newspapers Ltd* [2008] EMLR 679 at 726, Eady J, referring to *Campbell v Mirror Group Newspapers Ltd* (above), expressed his uncertainty as to whether a future House of Lords would recognise an invasion of privacy as a tort in its own right.
[66] (2007) 11(4) EJCL 20 at 23.
[67] [2008] 1 AC 1.

Douglases, by the way in which they arranged their wedding, were in a position to impose an obligation of confidence. They were in control of the information.[68] His Lordship went on to state[69] that there was no policy reason why the law of confidence should not protect information which took the form of a photograph. There was no question of creating an "image right" or any other form of intellectual property. The information in the instant case was capable of being protected simply because it was information of commercial value over which the Douglases had sufficient control to enable them to impose an obligation of confidence. Black has argued that relying on commercial value to determine whether information warrants protection in terms of an action for breach of confidence may create considerable legal uncertainty.[70] She postulates whether the law would still have decided in favour of the claimants in *Douglas* if the Douglases had not charged a fee at all, or if they had charged a lesser sum, or if they had donated their fee to charity.

The action for breach of confidence is not confined to media intrusion. It extends to **17.32** the misuse of private information by private individuals. *McKennitt* v *Ash*[71] illustrates this point neatly. In that case, the claimant who was, *inter alia*, a famous musician, raised an action against the defendant, who had written a book which contained intimate details of the personal relationship which the latter had had with the claimant. At first instance, an injunction was granted to prevent further publication of a significant part of the work which was complained of, on the ground that such information constituted private information, the misuse of which fell within the ambit of both the tort of breach of confidence and also Art 8 of the ECHR.

The law relating to the misuse of private information was neatly summarised in **17.33** the English Court of Appeal case of *Murray* v *Express Newspapers Ltd*[72] (which was a striking-out action). The facts of the case were simple and straightforward. The claimant (an infant) was the son of the famous author Joanne Murray (J K Rowling). One day, when the claimant and his parents were out walking in an Edinburgh street, the defendant took a colour photograph of the family group. The photograph was subsequently published in a popular newspaper. The newspaper publisher settled the proceedings against it. On an application by the photographic agency, the judge struck out a claim against it on the basis that innocuous conduct in a public place or routine activities such as a simple walk down the street or a visit to the shops, as distinct from engagement in family or sporting activities, did not attract any reasonable expectation of privacy. The claimant appealed successfully. The Court of Appeal endorsed the decision in *McKennitt*[73] to the effect that both Art 8 and Art 10 of the Convention constituted the substance of the action for breach of confidence.[74]

According to Sir Anthony Clarke MR, the questions which fell to be answered in **17.34** relation to a case where the subject-matter was the misuse of private information were, first, whether the information was private in the sense that it is in principle protected by Art 8, and, if so, second, whether, in all the circumstances, the interest of the owner of the information must yield to the right of freedom of expression conferred on the

---

[68] [2008] 1 AC 1 at 48.
[69] *Ibid* at 49.
[70] G Black, "OK for some: *Douglas* v *Hello!* in the House of Lords" (2007) *Edin LR* 402 at 404.
[71] [2008] QB 73.
[72] [2009] Ch 481.
[73] See n 71, above.
[74] [2009] Ch 481 at 500.

publisher by Art 10.[75] In order to answer the first question it was necessary at the outset to ascertain whether the claimant had a reasonable expectation of privacy.[76] That was an objective question. The approach which was taken by the House of Lords in *Campbell* was endorsed. For his Lordship, the question as to whether there was a reasonable expectation of privacy was a broad one which took into account all the circumstances of the case. Such circumstances included the attributes of the claimant, the nature of the activity in which the claimant was engaged, the place at which it was happening, the nature and purpose of the intrusion, the absence of consent, and whether such absence of consent was known or could be inferred, the effect on the claimant and also the circumstances in which and the purposes for which the information came into the hands of the publisher. In the instant case, as to whether the claimant had a reasonable expectation of privacy, one was required to ask how a reasonable person in the position of the claimant would feel if the photograph were published.[77] The question as to whether a reasonable person in the position of the claimant would regard such publication as highly offensive fell to be determined not when one was considering whether Art 8 was engaged but, rather, when one was balancing the rights enshrined in that Article with those in Art 10. At each stage, the questions which fell to be determined were essentially questions of fact.[78] The question as to whether there was a reasonable expectation of privacy was a question of fact. If there was, indeed, an expectation of privacy on the part of the claimant one had next to determine the relevant factors which fell to be taken into account and to balance them.

17.35   In the last analysis, it was at least arguable that the claimant had a reasonable expectation of privacy.[79] In the view of the Master of the Rolls, the fact that the claimant was a child was of greater significance than the trial judge had thought. In the instant case, the claimant had a reasonable expectation not to have his photograph taken. The test which was to be applied by the court was what a reasonable person of ordinary sensibilities would feel if he or she was placed in the same position as the claimant and also faced with the same publicity.[80] However, in applying this test, the focus should not be on the taking of the photograph but, rather, on its publication. The Master of the Rolls went on to state that he could not endorse the opinion of the trial judge to the effect that routine visits, such as one to the shops or a ride on a bus, should not attract any reasonable expectation of privacy.[81] Finally, his Lordship held that the claimant had an arguable case in that, first, Art 8 was engaged, and, second, in a subsequent balancing exercise between Art 8 and Art 10, the court would find in his favour.[82]

---

[75] [2009] Ch 481 at 500.

[76] *Ibid* at 502.

[77] *Ibid* at 503.

[78] *Ibid* at 504.

[79] *Ibid* at 507.

[80] *Ibid* at 510.

[81] *Ibid* at 511. Brimstead argues, *inter alia*, that, given the role which is played by technology in making it easier to make and also widely disseminate images, a lower threshold for privacy claims is perhaps desirable: K Brimstead, "Privacy: greater expectations of protection" (2008) 19 *PLC* 9.

[82] For a discussion of both *Murray* and *Mosley* v *News Group Newspapers Ltd* (n 46, above), see R Keenan, "Image rights and privacy law: a summary of the UK position" (2009) 30 *BusLR* 110. The learned author argues that, while the press believe that that they are becoming less "free", privacy campaigners believe that protection of privacy in the UK does not go far enough. The author argues that legislation would probably be required to introduce a specific law of privacy in the UK. The author notes that the right to one's image in itself is not protected by UK law. The court in *Murray* focused on the misuse of an image, that is to say the

However, Professor Rogers points out that of importance in *Murray* was the fact **17.36** that the claimant was a very young child. The learned author notes that the court refrained from opining whether the outcome would have been the same if the claimant's famous mother had been photographed in similar circumstances.[83] Second, *Murray* was not a case of a single photograph which was taken by random chance. Rather, it was the product of sustained "papparazzo" interest in his mother. In short, according to the learned author, *Murray* is not inconsistent with the decision in *Campbell* where Baroness Hale expressed the view that if the claimant in that case had been photographed simply going out to the shops in order to purchase a bottle of milk, she would have been unable to argue that the publication of such a photograph would have damaged her private life.[84]

Therefore, as far as the protection of privacy is concerned, whereas the law does not **17.37** expressly recognise a free-standing delictual wrong for the invasion of one's privacy,[85] the action for breach of confidence, most richly embellished by human rights jurisprudence, has, in effect, given us such a form of delictual action.

We have seen how the courts have expanded, at times rather artificially, the "old" **17.38** action for breach of confidence in order to embrace the protection of private information in circumstances where the action is not based on a prior confidential relationship. *Campbell*, as we have seen above, serves as a good example of such an extension of the law. However, the important question remains as to the extent, if any, of the impact of human rights jurisprudence on the "old" action for breach of confidence, that is to say, in a situation where the action is prefaced on a prior confidential relationship.

This issue fell to be discussed in the Court of Appeal case of *HRH Prince of Wales* **17.39** v *Associated Newspapers Ltd*.[86] The facts of the case were simple and straightforward. The claimant, the Prince of Wales, kept handwritten travel journals which recorded his views and impressions of overseas visits. The journals were photocopied by a member of his private office and then circulated to chosen individuals in envelopes which were marked "private and confidential". Someone who was employed in the

---

subsequent publication of the photograph rather than the simple fact that the photograph was taken. This contrasts with the approach in other jurisdictions, for example in France. See also R Bunn and M Sannie, "How image conscious are you? Protecting rights in UK law" (2008) 178 *Copyright World* 19, where the authors discuss the extent to which the courts will protect an individual's control over their photographic image which is taken in a public place. In respect of breach of confidence, it is opined that the interpretation of the ECHR in *Campbell v Mirror Group Newspapers* and *Murray* [2007] EWHC 1908 (Ch) leaves little room for such protection, the courts being unwilling to hold that activities which are conducted in public could become either "private" or "confidential". Melville-Brown, who summarises recent case law relating to the protection of privacy, comments that it is often difficult to draw a boundary between public and private activities, particularly in the case of public figures: see A Melville-Brown, "Camera Shy – the interaction between the camera and the law of privacy in the UK" (2008) 22 *IRLCT* 209.

See also T Brookes *et al*, "Australia: breach of confidence applied to protect privacy rights" (2009) 25 *CLS Rev* 202, where the authors discuss the Victorian Court of Appeal decision in *Giller* v *Procopets* [2008] VSCA 236 (CA Vic), which awarded the plaintiff damages for breach of confidence after her former partner attempted to distribute pornographic images of her to her friends, family and employers following the breakdown of their relationship. The authors suggest that this case represents another step towards the recognition of a common law right to privacy in Australia.

[83] W V H Rogers (ed), *Winfield & Jolowicz on Tort* (18th edn, 2010) at p 680.
[84] *Campbell* v *MGN Ltd* [2004] 2 AC 457 at 501.
[85] MacQueen, referring to the conservative approach of the English judiciary to the invasion of privacy, suggests that such a judicial stance stems from the traditional English suspicion of general principles and the preference for regulating specific problems piecemeal: H MacQueen, "Protecting privacy" (2004) 8 *Edin LR* 249 at 251.
[86] [2007] 3 WLR 222.

claimant's private office removed the journals from the claimant's office and supplied the defendant newspaper with copies of eight of the claimant's journals. The employee was employed under a contract which provided that any information she acquired during the course of her employment was subject to an undertaking of confidence and was not to be disclosed to any unauthorised person. The defendant newspaper published substantial extracts from the journal which related to a visit by the Prince to Hong Kong in 1997 when the colony was handed over to the Republic of China. The claimant contended, *inter alia*, that such publication contravened his rights under Art 8 of the Convention, and also constituted a breach of confidence. The trial judge[87] ruled in favour of the claimant. The defendant appealed.

17.40   As one can see from the facts of the case, the action stemmed from a breach of confidence which had been imposed on the person who had obtained the information in question. Lord Phillips MR, in the Court of Appeal, stated that the action was not concerned with a claim for breach of confidence which involved an extension of the old law of breach of confidence. Rather, the information was disclosed in breach of a well-recognised relationship of confidence, namely that which existed between master and servant. The disclosure was in breach of an express contractual duty of confidentiality. Furthermore, the newspaper was aware that the journals were disclosed in breach of confidence. Therefore, all the elements existed for a claim for breach of confidence.[88] Lords Phillips then went on to discuss the relevance of Arts 8 and 10 to the facts of the case. As far as the former Article was concerned, the documents were paradigm examples of confidential documents.[89] Notwithstanding this fact, his Lordship went on to state that, by reason of both the form and the content of the documents, the information they contained ranked as private information which warranted protection in terms of Art 8. As far as such protection was concerned, a distinction fell to be made between, first, whether a claimant could reasonably expect those in a confidential relationship with him to keep information confidential and, second, whether a claimant could reasonably expect the media not to publish such information if the duty of confidence was breached. The second issue fell to be addressed solely when one was considering the application of Art 10.[90] Lord Phillips then went on to address Art 10 in terms of an action for breach of confidence. His Lordship drew attention to the fact that, prior to the coming into force of the Human Rights Act 1998, it was well recognised by English courts that the public interest could justify the publication of information which was known to have been disclosed in breach of confidence.[91] His Lordship then went on to state that when one is considering whether publication involves a breach of a relationship of confidence or an interference of privacy or both, it is necessary to consider whether these matters justify the interference with the Art 10 rights that will be involved if the publication is made the subject of judicial sanction. A balance had to be struck.[92] Where no breach of a confidential relationship is involved, that balance would be between Art 8 and Art 10 of the Convention, and such a balance would normally involve weighing the nature and consequences of the breach of privacy against the public interest, if any, in the disclosure of the information.

---

[87] Blackburne J.
[88] [2007] 3 WLR 222 at 275.
[89] *Ibid* at 277.
[90] *Ibid* at 278.
[91] *Ibid* at 281.
[92] *Ibid* at 284.

Furthermore, if the disclosure relates to information which is received in confidence, this is also a factor capable of justifying restrictions on the freedom of expression. Lord Phillips went on to state that, before the coming into force of the Human Rights Act 1998, the circumstances in which the public interest defence in publication overrode a duty of confidence were very limited. However, according to His Lordship, the test was different today. The appropriate test which fell to be applied was whether a fetter of the right to freedom of expression was, in the particular circumstances, necessary in a democratic society. It was a test of proportionality. But a significant element to be weighed in the balance was the importance in a democratic society of upholding duties of confidence that are created between individuals. Lord Phillips went on to state that it was not enough to justify publication that the information in question was a matter of public interest.[93] The test to be applied when considering whether it was necessary to restrict the freedom of expression in order to prevent disclosure of information which was received in confidence was whether in all the circumstances it was in the public interest that *the duty of confidence should be breached*. In other words, for Lord Phillips, in order to ascertain whether publication was justified in the public interest, one should not confine oneself simply to the nature and content of the publication in question and so regard it as a free-standing factor. Rather, the restriction right embedded in Art 10 derived some of its hue from the rights embedded in Art 8. In the last analysis, the trial judge was correct in deciding that the interference with Art 8 rights effected by the newspaper's publication of information of the journal outweighed the significance of the interference with Art 10 rights that would have been involved had the newspaper been prevented from publishing that information.[94]

REMEDIES

The subject of remedies is dealt with in more detail elsewhere in this work. However, it is appropriate here simply to mention briefly the subject of remedies in the context of breach of confidence.   **17.41**

Interdict is the primary remedy for breach of confidence.[95] Damages are also available where a breach of confidence has taken place. In *Seager v Copydex (No 2)*,[96] Lord Denning MR stated: **17.42**

> "The value of confidential information depends on the nature of it. If there was nothing very special about it, that is, if it involved no particular inventive step, but was the sort of information which could be obtained by employing any competent consultant, then the value of it was the fee which a consultant would charge for it. But, on the other hand, if the information was something special, as, for instance, if it involved an inventive step or something so unusual that it could not be obtained by just going to a consultant, then the value of it is much higher. It is not merely a consultant's fee, but the price which a willing buyer – desirous of obtaining it – would pay for it."

---

[93] [2007] 3 WLR 222 at 285.
[94] *Ibid* at 286.
[95] Bell, *Commentaries*, vol 1, 111–112 incl.
[96] [1969] 1 WLR 809 at 813.

Seager was followed in the Outer House in *Levin* v *Caledonian Produce (Holdings) Ltd.*[97] In that case the pursuer claimed recompense on the ground that the defenders allegedly benefited from certain investigations and actings of the pursuer. Lord Robertson stated[98] that the measure of damages is either the market value of the information as between a willing buyer and a willing seller, or a consultant's fee for the information, depending upon the nature and quality of the information.

17.43   As an alternative to claiming damages for breach of confidence it is possible that the pursuer may elect to require the defender to account for any profits which the person who has used the information has made from such use.[99] The remedy is a notoriously difficult concept to apply. There is little Scottish authority on this point.[100]

17.44   Finally, it is possible that the court may make an order for the delivery up and destruction of materials which were either made or obtained in breach of confidence. There is little recent authority on this remedy in Scots law.[101]

---

[97] 1975 SLT (Notes) 69.
[98] *Ibid* at 70.
[99] For an example of the application of this remedy in English law, see *Peter Pan Manufacturing Corporation* v *Corsets Silhouette* [1964] 1 WLR 96. In the *Spycatcher* litigation, the *Sunday Times* was ordered to account for its profits from publishing Peter Wright's serialised memoirs: *AG* v *Guardian Newspapers (No 2)* [1990] 1 AC 109.
[100] In *Levin* v *Caledonian Produce (Holdings) Ltd*, above, this remedy was not accorded much discussion.
[101] In *Liverpool Victoria Legal Friendly Society* v *Houston* (1890) 3 F 42, *inter alia*, lists of members of the pursuer's friendly society were ordered to be delivered up. The Scottish law Commission recommended that the court should have the power to order the delivery up or destruction of relevant documents: Scot Law Com No 90, 1984, para 4.99.

18 PRODUCT LIABILITY

In this chapter we turn our attention to harm which is caused by defective products. **18.1**
We consider liability under the common law of negligence and then go on to look at
liability in terms of the Consumer Protection Act 1987.

LIABILITY UNDER THE COMMON LAW

We have already discussed the famous case of *Donoghue* v *Stevenson*[1] in terms of **18.2**
liability in general in the law of negligence.[2] We now go on to discuss the "narrow"
rule in that case in terms of liability for defective products.

In *Donoghue*, Lord Atkin stated:[3]

> "a *manufacturer* of *products* which he *sells* in such a form as to show that he intends them to
> reach the *ultimate consumer* in the form in which they left him with no reasonable *possibility*
> *of intermediate examination* and with the *knowledge that the absence of reasonable care in the prepa-*
> *ration or putting up of the products* will result in an *injury to the consumer's life or property owes*
> *a duty of care to the consumer to take that reasonable care*" (emphasis added).

We shall now consider how the narrow rule in *Donoghue* has been extended by judicial **18.3**
decision over the years. However, at the very outset of our discussion, attention should
be drawn to the fact that in some of the cases which are discussed it is difficult to
ascertain whether the courts are simply applying the "narrow" rule in *Donoghue* or, on
the other hand, applying the "broad" rule.

"MANUFACTURER"

In *Donoghue*, the case revolved around the potential liability of a manufacturer. **18.4**
However, it is now no longer necessary that the defender produces the relevant
product. For example, liability has been extended since 1932 to include those who
repair and also supply products,[4] erectors of tombstones,[5] installers of electrical

---

[1] [1932] AC 562.
[2] See para 2.4.
[3] [1932] AC 562 at 599.
[4] *Herschal* v *Stewart and Ardern Ltd* [1940] 1 KB 155 and *Marschler* v *G Masser's Garage* [1956] OR 328.
[5] *Brown* v *Cotterrill* (1934) 51 TLR 21.

equipment,[6] those who supply water,[7] those who simply lend products,[8] and also a lift repairer.[9]

PRODUCTS

18.5 As far as the interpretation of the term "product" is concerned, the expression is no longer confined to food. The courts have extended the expression "product" to include underwear,[10] lifts,[11] hair dye[12] and cars.[13]

SELLS

18.6 It is probably good law that the product in question does not require to be sold by the defender for liability to lie.[14] Furthermore, it is not necessary that the product in question is used immediately by the consumer who sustains harm.[15]

ULTIMATE CONSUMER

18.7 The term *ultimate consumer* has been widely extended to include the ultimate user of the article,[16] or anyone into whose hands the article might pass,[17] and even anyone in close proximity to the article in question.[18]

"WITH NO REASONABLE POSSIBILITY OF INTERMEDIATE EXAMINATION"

18.8 Whereas, in *Donoghue*, Lord Atkin stated that the liability of a manufacturer in relation to harm caused by a defective product depended on there being no reasonable possibility of intermediate examination of that product, the courts have subsequently adopted a different approach. In *Grant* v *Australian Knitting Mills Ltd*,[19] the plaintiff contracted dermatitis as a result of wearing a woollen undergarment which he had purchased from retailers. This occurred because the garment contained an excess of sulphites which the manufacturers had negligently allowed to remain in the garment. The manufacturers were held liable. The Privy Council was of the view that, as far as liability of the manufacturer of the garments was concerned, it was simply necessary that the defect in question could not be detected by any examination which could

---

[6] *Eccles* v *Cross and McIlwham* 1938 SC 697.
[7] *Barnes* v *Irwell Valley Water Board* [1939] 1 KB 21.
[8] *Pivovaroff* v *Chernabaet* (1978) 21 SASR 1.
[9] *Haseldine* v *Daw* [1941] 2 KB 343.
[10] *Grant* v *Australian Knitting Mills Ltd* [1936] AC 85.
[11] *Haseldine* v *Daw* [1941] 2 KB 343.
[12] *Watson* v *Buckley* [1940] 1 All ER 174.
[13] *Andrews* v *Hopkinson* [1957] 1 QB 229.
[14] See Denning LJ in *Hawkins* v *Coulsdon and Purley UDC* [1954] 1 QB 319 at 333.
[15] *Daley* v *Gypsy Caravan Co Pty Ltd* [1966] 2 NSWR 22 at 25.
[16] *Grant* v *Australian Knitting Mills* [1936] AC 85.
[17] *Barnett* v *Packer* [1940] 3 All ER 575.
[18] *Brown* v *Cotterill* (1934) 51 TLR 21.
[19] [1936] AC 85.

reasonably be made.[20] Again, in the English Court of Appeal case of *Haseldine* v *Daw*,[21] a lift mechanism was negligently repaired by the defendants, with the result that the lift fell to the bottom of the lift well in the premises which the plaintiff was visiting. The plaintiff sustained injuries. In holding the repairer liable, the court expressed the view that it was preferable to interpret Lord Atkin's expression "reasonable possibility" in relation to intermediate inspection of the product in question as meaning "reasonable probability" of inspection.

"PREPARATION OR PUTTING UP OF THE PRODUCTS"

In addition to defects caused by the manufacturing process, the relevant product **18.9** defect may consist of a defect in design,[22] the inadequacy in the container of the product in question,[23] and the inadequacy of a label on a container or advert which pertains to the product and which fails to warn of the dangers of the product.[24] The relevant defect may also consist of a defect caused by the wear and tear of the product after the product has been put to use by the consumer in contradistinction to the state of the product on leaving the manufacturer,[25] or the negligent repair of the article.[26]

"INJURY TO THE CONSUMER'S LIFE OR PROPERTY"

Life

Liability will lie in relation to a product defect which causes the person who uses or **18.10** consumes the product to become ill,[27] or injured.[28] However, there is no liability if the harm derives from the fact that the product has been used in a manner which is unforeseeable.[29]

Property

As far as injury to property is concerned, no liability will lie in respect of damage **18.11** which is restricted to the defective product itself.[30] In the eyes of the law such loss ranks as pure economic loss and is, as we have already seen, generally speaking, not recoverable in the law of delict.[31] For example, if in *Donoghue* v *Stevenson* the pursuer had, on discovering that the ginger beer was defective, poured the offensive liquid into a sink, she would simply have sustained pure economic loss and, therefore, would

---

[20] [1936] AC 85 at 106.
[21] [1941] 2 KB 343.
[22] *Hindustan SS Co* v *Siemens & Co Ltd* [1955] Lloyd's Rep 167.
[23] *Bates* v *Batey* [1913] 3 KB 351.
[24] *Buchan* v *Ortho Pharmaceutical (Canada) Ltd* (1986) 25 DLR (4th ed.) 658.
[25] *Andrews* v *Hopkinson* [1957] 1 QB 229.
[26] *Herschtal* v *Stewart and Ardern Ltd* [1940] 1 KB 155 and *Malfroot* v *Noxal Ltd* (1935) 51 TLR 551.
[27] *Donoghue* v *Stevenson* [1932] AC 562; *Grant* v *Australian Knitting Mills Ltd* [1936] AC 85. See also *Fillmores Valley Nurseries Ltd* v *North American Cyanamid Ltd* (1958) 14 DLR (2d) 297.
[28] *Brown* v *Cotterill* (1934) 51 TLR 21; *Williams* v *Eady* (1893) 10 TLR 41; *Malfroot* v *Noxal Ltd* (1935) 51 TLR 551; and *Jull* v *Wilson and Horton* [1968] NZLR 88.
[29] See *Aswan Engineering Est Co* v *Lupdine Ltd* [1987] 1 All ER 135, per Lloyd LJ at 153.
[30] *D & F Estates Ltd* v *Church Commissioners* [1989] AC 177 (defective premises). In *Rivtow Marine Ltd* v *Washington Iron Works* [1972] 6 WWW 692 it was held that the manufacturer of a crane was not liable to the hirers of the crane for the cost of the repair to the crane, which was found to be dangerously defective.
[31] See Chapter 4.

have been unable to recover. However, in exceptional circumstances where there is close proximity between the pursuer and the defender, and the former has relied on the latter, who, in turn, has assumed responsibility for the effectiveness of the product, liability may lie for pure economic loss which results from the use of the product.[32] However, such proximity does not exist between the ultimate purchaser of a product and the manufacturer in relation to goods which have been supplied under a chain of ordinary contracts.[33]

18.12   An interesting issue in the context of damage to the actual product itself concerns the so-called "complex" product, that is to say one which is made up of component parts. For example, would the manufacturer of a defective wire installed in a television during its manufacture be liable if the wire causes a short-circuit in the television, which then explodes and is destroyed? There seems little doubt that the manufacturer of a defective component, which is installed in a product (after the latter has been manufactured) and damages that product, would be liable.[34] For example, if a new car radio is installed in a motor car after the car is purchased, and the radio then catches fire and the fire destroys the car, the radio and the car would be regarded as separate property and, therefore, the damage which was caused by the former to the latter would be recoverable. That is to say, the manufacturer of the radio would be liable for such loss in terms of the "narrow" rule in *Donoghue.*

18.13   The issue of complex products is analogous to the so-called "complex structure theory" in relation to buildings. The theory, which had attracted some academic support during the 1980s, was discussed by the House of Lords in *Murphy v Brentwood District Council.*[35] In that case, a local authority carried out its building inspection duties negligently, by reason of failing to notice that a building in the course of construction had been erected on foundations which were too shallow. The upshot of this was that the walls of the building began to crack. The plaintiff sustained financial loss since his house could only be sold at a reduced price. The House held, *inter alia,* that the building was not to be regarded as comprising separate parts, but, rather, was to be regarded as an entity, or indivisible unit. The loss in question, therefore, ranked as pure economic loss. However, Lord Keith stated *obiter* that an electrical contractor could be liable for a defect which destroys a whole building.[36]

"OWES A DUTY … TO TAKE THAT REASONABLE CARE"

18.14   It is the latency of the defect in the product, in contrast to the potential harm posed by the product, which is covered by the narrow rule in *Donoghue v Stevenson.* This point was graphically illustrated in *McTear v Imperial Tobacco Ltd.*[37] In that case the pursuer claimed that her deceased husband had died from lung cancer caused by his consuming cigarettes which had been manufactured by the defenders. In the Outer House, Lord Nimmo Smith held that the cigarettes in question were not defective products within the meaning of the "narrow" rule in *Donoghue* in that the cigarettes

---

[32] *Muirhead* v *Industrial Tank Specialities Ltd* [1986] QB 507 and *Bacardi Martini Beverages Ltd* v *Thomas Hardy Packaging Ltd* [2002] All ER (Comm) 335.
[33] *Muirhead* v *Industrial Tank Specialities Ltd* [1986] QB 507.
[34] *Nitrigin Eireann Teoranta* v *Inco Alloys Ltd* [1992] 1 WLR 498.
[35] [1991] 1 AC 398, per Lord Bridge at 478.
[36] *Ibid* at 465.
[37] 2005 2 SC 1.

did not contain some extraneous substance as a result of a manufacturing error.[38] In short, the defender intended to manufacture the cigarettes in the very form and state in which they reached the deceased. The latter, in turn, received the very product he desired to purchase, and proceeded to consume them in the manner in which cigarettes are intended to be consumed. The cigarettes also met public expectation.[39] Furthermore, a person who is injured by either consuming or using a product, the defective nature of which he is well aware, has no remedy against the manufacturer.[40]

The pursuer is required to prove on a balance of probabilities that the defect in question was due to the negligent act of the defender.[41] The court is at liberty to set a higher standard of care than that which is set by relevant legislation.[42] However, the fact that the product does not comply with relevant legislation is evidence against liability at common law.[43]

WARNINGS

The duty of care the law imposes on manufacturers under the "narrow" rule may **18.15** extend to the duty to warn of potential danger which the product may pose to the consumer.[44] The required explicitness of the warning varies with the danger which is likely to be encountered by the ordinary use of the product.[45] However, the duty to warn arises only if there is a foreseeable risk that a person will be led into believing that something is safe when it is not.[46] Provided that the ordinary consumer is in a position to make an informed choice about the safety of the product, there is no duty to warn of any dangers associated with the use of the product. That is to say, there is no duty to warn of risks of which it would be reasonable to expect an ordinary consumer to be aware.[47] The duty of care the law imposes on the manufacturer to warn of the relevant dangers in the product extends not only to that which is known at the time of the sale of the product but also to dangers discovered after the product has been sold and delivered.[48] However, where the product is of a highly technical nature and is intended or expected to be used only under the supervision of experts, a warning to such experts will suffice in order to discharge the duty the law imposes.[49] Finally, if the manufacturer discovers a defect after the product is put into general circulation, and there is serious risk of injury to the user of the product, the warning requires to consist of an obligation to recall the product in question.[50]

---

[38] [1991] 1 AC 398 at 537, 548 and 549.
[39] In *Reyes v Wyeth Laboratories* 498 F 2d 1264 at 1273, it was held that a product is unreasonably dangerous only when it is dangerous to an extent beyond that contemplated by an ordinary consumer. See also *Maguire v Pabst Brewing Co* 387 NW 2d 565.
[40] *Grant v Australian Knitting Mills* [1936] AC 85.
[41] *Evans v Triplex Safety Glass Ltd* [1936] 1 All ER 283.
[42] *Best v Wellcome Foundation* [1992] ILRM 609.
[43] *Hamilton v Papakura DC* [2002] 2 NZLR 308.
[44] *Lewis v University of Bristol* [1999] EWCA Civ 1569.
[45] *Lambert v Lastoplex Chemical Co Ltd* (1972) 25 DLR (3d) 121.
[46] *Graham Barclay v Ryan* (2002) 211 CLR 540.
[47] *McTear v Imperial Tobacco Ltd* 2005 2 SC 1 at 515.
[48] *Buchan v Ortho Pharmaceutical (Canada) Ltd* (1986) 25 DLR (4th) 658, per Robins J A at 667.
[49] *Ibid* at 668.
[50] *Loveday v Renton* [1990] 1 MedLR 117; *Walton & Walton v British Leyland UK Ltd*, *The Times*, 13 July 1978; and *Wright v Dunlop Rubber Co Ltd* (1972) KIR 255.

CONCLUSIONS ON PRODUCT DEFECTS AND THE LAW OF NEGLIGENCE

18.16   This section of the chapter can be concluded by drawing the attention of the reader to certain pronounced limitations the law of negligence possesses in providing a remedy for harm caused by dangerous products. In addition to requiring to prove that the manufacturer owes the pursuer a duty of care in law, which may be problematic, a formidable obstacle in the path of the potential pursuer is the requirement to prove that the defender has failed to attain the standard of care which the law demands of the latter. Indeed, the limitations of the law of negligence were cruelly exposed in the Thalidomide disaster. The drug Thalidomide was manufactured in the 1950s in Germany by Chemie Grunenthal which allowed others, including Distillers (Biochemicals) Ltd in the United Kingdom, to manufacture the drug under licence. The drug was used as a sedative and also to ease the symptoms of morning sickness in pregnancy, and was widely prescribed. Unfortunately, the drug caused severe birth defects and deformities. It was estimated that some 8,000–10,000 children in the world were born with deformities because their mothers took Thalidomide. Of these children, 400 were born in the United Kingdom.[51] A total of 62 actions in negligence were brought against Distillers, which denied negligence. The claims were all settled out of court. It should be emphasised, however, that Distillers may not have been negligent on the basis that they could not reasonably have been expected to know that the drug would have such devastating side-effects.

18.17   A Royal Commission was appointed in 1973 to inquire into the basis of civil liability in the United Kingdom for causing death and personal injury. Indeed, the Thalidomide tragedy was a major factor in the Government's decision to do this.[52] As far as liability for defective products was concerned, the Commission recommended that producers be strictly liable (subject to certain limited defences) in tort for death and personal injury caused by defective products.[53] In 1977, the Law Commission and the Scottish Law Commission published a joint report on the subject of product liability.[54] The report advocated a change in the law whereby strict liability would apply to producers in relation to personal injury which was caused by defective products.[55] While these initiatives were taking place in the United Kingdom, liability for defective products was taking its place on the European stage. The Convention on product liability in regard to personal injury and death (the Strasbourg Convention) was issued by the Council for Europe in 1977.[56] One of the main recommendations in the Convention was the imposition of strict liability on producers for injuries or death caused by defective products.[57] However, the importance of this Convention was, in effect, eclipsed in 1985 by the EEC Product Liability Directive.[58] The Directive was implemented in the United Kingdom by the Consumer Protection Act 1987, Pt 1 of which relates to product

---

[51] Royal Commission on Civil Liability and Compensation for Personal Injury (Cmnd 7054–1, 1978), ch 26, para 1414.
[52] C Newdick, "The future of negligence in product liability" (1987) 103 LQR 288 at 288.
[53] Cmnd 7054–1, para 1236.
[54] *Liability for Defective Products* (Law Com No 82/Scot Law Com No 45, Cmnd 6831, 1977).
[55] *Ibid*, para 125.
[56] ETS no 91(1977).
[57] *Ibid*, Art 3(1).
[58] EC Directive 85/374.

liability and came into force in March 1988. We now turn our attention to the provisions of that Act.

CONSUMER PROTECTION ACT 1987

WHAT IS A PRODUCT?

The Consumer Protection Act 1987 defines the expression "product" widely. A product **18.18** is defined as any goods[59] or electricity and includes a product which is comprised in another product whether by virtue of being a component part or raw material or otherwise.[60] Therefore, in a complex product such as a computer, a defective microchip would rank as a product as well as the computer itself. The Act also provides that, as far as Scotland is concerned, reference to things which are comprised in land by virtue of being attached to it is a reference to moveables which have become heritable by accession to heritable property.[61] Furthermore, the Act provides that the performance of any contract, by the erection of any building or structure on any land, or by the carrying out of any other building works, requires to be treated for the purposes of the Act as the supply of goods insofar as it involves the provision of any goods to any person by means of their incorporation into the building, structure or works.[62] However, the supply of goods does not include references to supplying goods which are comprised in land where the supply is effected by the creation or disposal of a real right in the land.[63] The consequence of these provisions is that, for example, an electrician who installs defective wires in an existing house which results in the house being damaged by fire would be liable under the Act,[64] whereas a builder who sells a house he has constructed and which has the same defective wires would not be liable, on the basis that the conveyance of the house involves the creation or disposal of a real right in land.[65]

Originally, game and agricultural products were excluded from the scope of the Act **18.19** unless they had undergone an industrial process.[66] However, the Act was amended,[67] the result being that agricultural products fall within the scope of the Act. Therefore, a farmer who sells fresh duck eggs contaminated with salmonella micro-organisms would be liable under the Act. The Act appears to be confined to harm which derives from the physical characteristics of the product. It is suggested, therefore, that informational defects contained in computer software do not fall within the scope of the Act.

---

[59] Under s 45(1) "goods" includes substances, growing crops and things comprised in land by virtue of being attached to it, and any ship, aircraft or vehicle. "Substance" means any natural or artificial substance whether in solid, liquid or gaseous form or in the form of a vapour, and includes substances that are comprised in or mixed with other goods.
[60] Consumer Protection Act 1987, s 1(2).
[61] *Ibid*, s 45(5).
[62] *Ibid*, s 45(3).
[63] *Ibid*, s 46(4).
[64] Provided that he failed to give the name of the producer of the product in terms of s 2(3) of the Act (see below).
[65] See J Blaikie, "Product liability: the Consumer Protection Act 1987, Part 1" (1987) 32 JLSS 325 at 326.
[66] Section 2(4) repealed.
[67] See Consumer Protection Act 1987 (Product Liability) (Modification) (Scotland) Order 2001 (SSI 2001/265), art 2(3).

LIABILITY UNDER THE ACT

18.20   Under s 2(1) and (2) of the Act it is provided that where any damage is caused wholly or partly by a defect in a product, the following persons are liable for the damage:

  (a)   the producer of the product;
  (b)   any person who, by putting his name on the product or using a trade mark or other distinguishing mark in relation to the product, has held himself out to be the producer of the product;
  (c)   any person who has imported the product into a Member State from a place outside the Member State in order, in the course of any business of his, to supply it to another.

Liability under the Act is strict but not absolute.[68] That is to say, unlike the position which obtains under the common law, there is no need for the pursuer to prove negligence in order to succeed.[69] The purpose of the Directive and also the Act is, therefore, to achieve a higher and consistent level of consumer protection throughout the Community, and also to render the recovery of compensation easier and uncomplicated by the need to prove negligence.[70]

Producers

18.21   The expression "producer" of the product is defined in s 1(2) as:

  (a)   the person who manufactured it;
  (b)   in the case of a substance which has not been manufactured but has been won or abstracted, the person who won or abstracted it;
  (c)   in the case of a product which has not been manufactured, won or abstracted but essential characteristics of which are attributable to an industrial or other process having been carried out (for example, in relation to agricultural produce), the person who carried out that process.

18.22   Paragraph (a) calls for little comment. As far as paragraph (b) is concerned, examples would include those who abstract mineral water from an underground source. Under (c), the processor who cures and smokes salmon would rank as a producer and so would be liable for any damage caused by the relevant defect. However, it is not necessary that the relevant defect derives from the relevant process. For example, in the example which has just been given, the processor of the salmon would be liable

---

[68] *A v National Blood Authority* [2001] 3 All ER 289. See J Williams, "Product liability: hepatitis C litigation" (2001) 3 JPIL 238.
[69] For a useful discussion of the merits of a strict liability regime for products, see J Henderson, "Coping with the time dimension in product liability" (1981) 69 Calif L Rev 919 at 931–941. The learned author argues that strict liability is thought to be preferable to negligence because it better enhances social utility by reducing the costs associated with accidents and also because strict liability promotes fairness. Strict liability is believed to increase utility by satisfying four major objectives: (a) encouraging investment in product safety; (b) discouraging consumption of hazardous products; (c) reducing transaction costs; and (d) promoting loss spreading.
[70] Per Burton J in *A v National Blood Authority* [2001] 3 All ER 289 at 310.

for any damage caused by a fish-hook which had become embedded in the flesh of the fish prior to the processing of the salmon.

Those holding themselves out to be producers

The rationale for placing liability on those who hold themselves out as producers is **18.23** that consumers tend to rely on the reputation of certain companies and organisations. Such bodies invariably carry out rigorous checks of the premises where the relevant product is manufactured. It is, therefore, appropriate that "own branders" should bear the responsibility for any damage caused by such products.[71] It is the very act of the "brander" putting his name or mark on the relevant product that makes him liable under the Act.[72] As far as liability under the Act is concerned, it is quite irrelevant that consumers as a body are under any impression that a so-called "own brander" actually produced the product.[73]

Importers

Any person who imports a product into a Member State from a place which is outside **18.24** the EU is also liable under the Act. Therefore, even if the non-EU producer cannot be sued, the importer of the product into the EU can. Under the provisions of the Civil Jurisdiction and Judgments Act 1982,[74] Scottish courts have jurisdiction over the importer even if the importer is not normally resident in Scotland, provided that the damage occurred in Scotland.

LIABILITY OF SUPPLIERS

Under the Act, primary liability for defective products lies with the producer, as we **18.25** have seen. It may, however, sometimes be difficult to identify the producer. The Act, therefore, provides that where any damage is caused wholly or partly by a defect in a product, any person who supplied[75] the product is liable if the person who suffered the damage requests[76] the supplier to identify either the producer, own brander or importer, and the supplier fails to comply with the request within a reasonable period.[77] A condition precedent to liability is the supply of the defective product to a person, who need not be the pursuer. As far as goods supplied under a hire-purchase

---

[71] See Miller and Goldberg, *Product Liability* (2nd edn, 2004), para 8.17.
[72] In *Swift and Co* v *Blackwell* 84 F 2d 130, a consumer was injured by a broken glass in a can of condensed milk which bore the wholesaler's label. The wholesaler had his name printed in bold type on the label. The name was repeated eight times on the label although it also bore the word "distributor". The wholesaler was held liable.
[73] Stapleton argues that buyers of Ford motor vehicles are not duped into believing that Ford made every component, and few are misled by a "St Michael" wine label into thinking that Marks and Spencer runs the relevant vineyards: J Stapleton, *Product Liability* (1994) at p 298.
[74] Schedule 8.
[75] Under the Consumer Protection Act 1987, s 46, the supply of goods includes: selling, hiring out or lending the goods; entering into a hire-purchase agreement to furnish the goods; the performance of any contract for work and materials to furnish the goods; the performance of any contract for work and materials to furnish the goods; providing the goods in exchange for any consideration other than money (including trading stamps); providing the goods in, or in connection with, the performance of any statutory function; or the giving of goods as a prize or otherwise making a gift of the goods. In relation to gas or water the provision of the relevant service constitutes a supply of the gas or water.
[76] The request must be made within a reasonable period after the damage occurs.
[77] Section 2(3).

agreement are concerned, the person who actually supplied the product is potentially liable as opposed to the finance company with whom the agreement is made.[78] Furthermore, the performance of any contract by the erection of any building or structure on land by the carrying out of building works, ranks as the supply of goods, but only insofar as it involves the provision of any goods to any person by means of their incorporation into the building, etc.[79] For example, an electrician who installs an extraction fan in a bathroom would be deemed, under the Act, to have supplied the fan.

MEANING OF "DEFECT"

18.26   There is a defect in a product for the purposes of Pt 1 of the Act[80] if the safety of the product is not such as persons generally are entitled to expect,[81] and for those purposes "safety" in relation to a product includes safety with respect to products comprised in that product and safety in the context of risks of damage to property, as well as in the context of risks of personal injury or death.

18.27   In determining what persons generally are entitled to expect in relation to a product, all the circumstances are required to be taken into account, including:

"(a) the manner in which and the purposes for which the product has been marketed, its get up, the use of any mark in relation to the product and any instructions for, or warnings with respect to, doing or refraining from doing anything with or in relation to the product;
(b) what might reasonably be expected to be done with or in relation to the product;
(c) the time when the product was supplied by its producer to another."[82]

Nothing in s 3 requires a defect to be inferred merely from the fact that the safety of the product which is supplied later is greater than the safety of the product in question.[83] For example, the fact that the producer of a mountain bike has developed a superior braking system from that which was installed in the relevant product does not, of itself, mean that the product was defective at the time it was supplied.

18.28   The test as to whether the product is defective is objective.[84] The burden of proof that the product is defective rests with the pursuer.[85] The pursuer also requires to prove that the product is defective on a balance of probabilities.[86] In other words, the onus is on the pursuer to establish some shortcoming in the design or the manufacture of the product. While there is no need for the pursuer to establish fault on the part of the defender, the pursuer must show that the relevant injury or damage was caused

---

[78] Section 46(2).
[79] Section 46(3).
[80] Section 3(1).
[81] Stapleton has criticised the definition of defect as being inherently circular: "[What] a person is entitled to expect is the very question which a definition of defect should be answering" (Stapleton, *Product Liability* at p 234). See also *Richardson* v *LRC Products* [2000] PIQR 164.
[82] Section 3(2).
[83] *Ibid.*
[84] *Worsley* v *Tambrands Ltd* [2000] PIQR 95 at 98; and *Sam B* v *McDonald's Restaurants Ltd* [2002] EWHC 490.
[85] *Sam B* v *McDonald's Restaurants Ltd* [2002] EWHC 490 at [73]; and *A* v *National Blood Authority* [2001] 3 All ER 289 at 311.
[86] *Foster* v *Biosil* (2001) 59 BMLR 178.

by the defect in question.[87] Whereas there is little authority on the point, in the absence of authority, it is suggested that the rules of causation which apply in the law of negligence would apply to damage caused by dangerous products.[88] The relevant damage may be caused in whole or in part by the defect in question.[89] In ascertaining whether the product is defective it is irrelevant that the harm which emanated from the risk in question could have been avoided.[90] That is to say, the emphasis is upon the safety of the relevant product, rather than upon the reasonableness of the producer's conduct.[91] However, a product is not defective because its common attributes are such that a risk of injury is posed to persons who use the items improperly.[92] For example, simply because a kitchen knife is sharp and can, therefore, inflict injury does not render the knife defective within the meaning of s 3(2). Accordingly, it has been held that a disposable cup which contained a hot beverage securely covered by a lid that could, nonetheless, be dislodged if the cup fell and struck a hard surface was not a defective product: since people generally know that if a hot drink is spilled, a serious scalding injury may result, the risk is obvious and the cup is not defective.[93] The safety of the product is what the public in general are entitled to expect, in contrast to what the public actually do expect. In the last analysis, the test the court uses to decide whether a given product meets public expectation is objective. The court decides what the public is entitled to expect.[94] The court decides whether that expectation is fulfilled in respect of the actual product which has injured in contrast to the potential defectiveness of products of the appropriate genus or type of product.[95] In determining what the public can legitimately expect, appropriate warnings can be taken into account. In other words, lack of appropriate warnings can render an otherwise safe product defective in terms of the Act.[96] Conversely, the addition of a suitable warning can render an otherwise unsafe product safe. Therefore, if it is impossible that tests can establish the purity of blood intended to be used for blood transfusions, the public require to be suitably informed before the product meets public expectation.[97] However, a warning will not always be sufficient in order to deflect the producer's liability under the Act. For example, a computer supplied with an un-insulated power connection would not be made duly safe by attaching a warning for potential users to beware of an electric

---

[87] *Richardson v LRC Products Ltd* [2000] PIQR 164. See R Freeman, "Strict product liability laws" (2001) 1 JPIL 26; D Strang and M Wing, "Unlucky for Some – Or the Son, the Wife and the Mother" (2001) 22 Bus L Rev 84 at 86. See also *Mei v San Pellegrino SpA* [1999] ECC 550.

[88] Reimann states that the majority of jurisdictions which have a product liability regime require that the harm would not have occurred without the defect and that the link between the two is close enough to justify holding the defendant responsible: M Reimann, "Liability for defective products at the beginning of the twenty-first century: emergence of a worldwide standard? (2003) 51 *American Journal of Comparative Law* 751 at 772.

[89] *Worsley v Tambrands Ltd* [2000] PIQR 95 at 98.

[90] *Sam B v McDonald's Restaurants Ltd* [2002] EWHC 490 at [73]. For a general discussion of this case, see E Deards and C Twigg-Flesner, "The Consumer Protection Act 1987: proof at last that it is protecting consumers" (2001) 10 Nott LJ 1 at 12, 13.

[91] *Feldman v Lederle Laboratories* 479 A 2d 374.

[92] *A v National Blood Authority* [2001] 3 All ER 289 at 311.

[93] *Sam B v McDonald's Restaurants Ltd* [2002] EWHC 490.

[94] *A v National Blood Authority* [2001] 3 All ER 289 at 311. See also J Henderson, "Judicial review of the manufacturers' design choices: the limits of adjudication" (1973) ColLR 1531 at 1565 where the author argues that the courts are inherently ill suited to establishing product safety standards.

[95] *A v National Blood Authority* [2001] 3 All ER 289 at 318.

[96] *Worsley v Tambrands Ltd* [2000] PIQR 95.

[97] *A v National Blood Authority* [2003] 3 All ER 289 at 339.

shock. Indeed, some products may be so inherently dangerous that they should not be marketed at all, either with or without a warning.[98]

18.29   Since liability under the Directive is strict, it is irrelevant whether the defect in question could have been avoided by the defender.[99] It is also irrelevant that the defender was not aware of the relevant defect.[100] Similarly, the impracticability of precautions, the cost and difficulty of taking such measures, and the benefit to society, or utility of the product, are irrelevant considerations.[101] In the absence of an appropriate warning, a product may be defective within the meaning of the Act if the product is of such a design that it may pose a risk of injury if it is used in a certain way.[102] In deciding whether a product is defective, the nature of the potential injury the product is capable of inflicting is also taken into account. For example, if the product can pose a potential threat to delicate parts of the body, such as the eye, appropriate measures require to be taken.[103] Knowledge of previous accidents which occur with the use of the product is not relevant.[104]

18.30   The Act requires the court to take into account what may reasonably be expected to be done with or in relation to the product.[105] For example, the fact that someone cuts his mouth with a sharp knife while eating meat does not render the knife defective in terms of the Act, since it is not expected that a person will place a sharp knife in his mouth.[106] However, the misuse of the product may be relevant, especially where the product is of a sophisticated nature and the relevant dangers are not readily apparent. In such a case the court would consider whether any relevant warnings have been given in relation to the product. Therefore, if someone has failed to use (say) a tree-stump shredder in the manner the manufacturer intended, thereby causing injury, the shredder would be defective in the absence of any relevant instructions or warnings. In determining what may be expected to be done with the product, account would be taken of possible misuse by children, the elderly and also the disabled. For example, it is reasonable to expect children to play with and consume household disinfectants and cleaning fluids, unless the relevant containers are provided with tamper-proof tops.

18.31   As far as food products are concerned, in some US jurisdictions no liability will attach to the manufacturer for harm caused by a substance which is considered to be natural to that product. For example, in *Shapiro v Hotel Statler Corporation*,[107] a restaurateur was found not to be liable when the plaintiff was injured after a fish bone (which was in a seafood mornay) lodged in her throat. It was held that the fish bone was not a foreign substance (ie it was natural to the product) and, therefore, the food was not defective. However, even if the substance is deemed to be natural to the product in question, the manufacturer may be held liable for any injury which is sustained if

---

[98] See J Wade, "On the nature of strict tort liability for products" (1973) 44 Miss LJ 825 at 842.
[99] *A v National Blood Authority* [2001] 3 All ER 289 at 340.
[100] *Carrecter v Colson Equipment Co* 499 A 2d 326.
[101] Except in the context of whether with full information and proper knowledge the public does and also ought to accept that risk: *A v National Blood Authority* [2001] 2 All ER 289 at 340.
[102] *Abouzaid v Mothercare Ltd* [2000] 1918530 at [27].
[103] *Ibid* at [27].
[104] *Ibid* at [29].
[105] Consumer Protection Act 1987, s 3(2)(b).
[106] W V H Rogers (ed) in *Winfield and Jolowicz Tort* (18th edn, 2010) para 10–22 mentions an American case (which he does not cite) of someone who attempted to dry her dog in a microwave oven, the result being that the dog was injured. Here, the microwave would not be defective.
[107] 132 F Supp 891(DC Cal, 1955).

the consumer would not reasonably expect to find the substance in the product. For example, if the style and/or get-up of the food would lead to the expectation that the substance in question will not be present, the manufacturer will be held liable for damage caused by the product. For example, in the US case of *Bryer v Rath Packing Co*,[108] it was held that a chicken bone should not have appeared in a chicken chow mein where the defendant had advertised the product as containing boned chicken (ie boneless).

Product design

Brief mention should be made at this juncture of the design in a product which makes **18.32** the product defective in terms of the Act. For example, if the tyres of a car are prone to being easily punctured while the car is being driven on normal roads, are the tyres defective in terms of s 3(1) of the Act on the basis that they fail to meet public expectation? There is no doubt that design defects do fall within the scope of the Act.[109] However, notwithstanding this fact, what sets an immediate problem for the court is that there is no objective standard to assist the court in deciding whether a product is defective by reason of its design.[110] Another problem in this context is that safety is not an absolute concept. In other words, no product, irrespective of its design, can be perfectly safe all of the time and under any circumstances. To take the example just given, all car tyres are capable of being punctured. Most tyres will become more prone to being punctured through wear and tear. However, some tyres are more resilient than others. In *A v National Blood Authority*,[111] Burton J expressed the view that in relation to standard products (that is, a product which presents a potential risk to consumers by virtue, *inter alia*, of the design of the product), no account should be taken of what the producer could have done differently and, of greater importance in the present context, whether the producer in question could or could not have done the same as others. Therefore, whether another manufacturer could have designed a better product was quite irrelevant.

In the authors' view, the fundamental problem with design defects in relation to **18.33** the "consumer expectation" test in s 3(1) is that it may be difficult to gauge accurately what the public expects of a product in terms of safety by reason of the shortcomings which are inherent in the design of the product. Some authors have argued that in some cases consumer expectations simply do not exist.[112] This is particularly so if the product in question is of a complex or technical nature.[113]

---

[108] 156 A 2d 442.
[109] *A v National Blood Authority* [2001] 3 All ER 289 at 339.
[110] Stoppa argues that design defect cases are undoubtedly at the very core of product liability's conceptual structure and constitute also the most problematical category in terms of adjudication. Another fundamental difficulty in applying the consumer expectation test is that it does not provide the interpreter with an objective standard against which the safety of a product can be assessed: A Stoppa, "The concept of defectiveness in the Consumer Protection Act 1987: A Critical analysis" (1992) 12 LS 210 at 225.
[111] [2001] 3 All ER 289 at 341.
[112] A Stoppa (n 110, above) at 214.
[113] For an interesting discussion of design defects in terms of the consumer expectation test in the US, see Miller and Goldberg, *Product Liability*, paras 11.10–11.14.

DEFENCES

18.34 In common with other statutes which make provision for strict liability, the Consumer Protection Act 1987 contains defences.

18.35 Under s 4(1) of the Act, it is a defence for D to show that:

(a) The defect in question was attributable to compliance with any statutory requirement imposed by or under any enactment or with any Community obligation

For this defence to succeed it must be proved that the existence of the defect in the product was the direct and inevitable consequence of the defender complying with the relevant legal requirement. An example of the application of this defence would be if legislation which governed the construction of motorbikes prescribed the diameter of the bike cable brakes for bikes over a certain engine capacity. If a motorbike brake were to be manufactured in accordance with such legislation but, nonetheless, the brake was not able to perform its intended task and the motorbike were to crash and cause someone to be injured, the manufacturer would have a complete defence under the Act. It should be emphasised that it is not sufficient for the defence to succeed that the product in question simply complies with relevant legislation.[114] In other words, in the example given, the statutory defence would not apply if the legislation merely prescribed the minimum diameter of the brake.

(b) The defender did not supply the product in question

18.36 It is a defence if the defender did not supply the product to another. The Act[115] defines the expression "supply" broadly and includes the selling, hiring out or lending of the goods and the giving of the goods as a prize or otherwise making a gift of the goods. The defence would also apply if the product in question had been stolen from the defender's premises. However, the defence would not apply if the defender was a food manufacturer who distributed free samples of his product.

(c) The only supply of the product to another by the defender was otherwise than in the course of the defender's business

18.37 Thus, a person would not be liable under the Act if he brewed defective beer in his house and dispensed the beer to his friends at a party. Nor does the Act apply to persons by virtue of things done otherwise than with a view to a profit.

(d) The defect did not exist in the product at the relevant time

18.38 It is a defence that the defect did not exist in the product at the relevant time. In relation to producers, own branders and importers the relevant time is the time when the product was supplied by them.[116] For example, if a sausage manufacturer sold perfectly sound sausages to a retailer who, in turn, sold the sausages to the consumer

---

[114] This may, however, provide evidence that the product is not defective.
[115] Consumer Protection Act 1987, s 46.
[116] *Ibid*, s 4(2)(a).

who failed to keep the sausages in a hygienic condition and became ill, the manufacturer of the sausages would not be liable under the Act.[117]

In relation to the liability of others (retailers), the relevant time is the time when the product was last supplied by a producer, own brander or importer.[118] Therefore, if the sausages had left the meat factory in a perfectly sound condition but had become contaminated and harmful to health by virtue of being conveyed to the retailer's premises in a vehicle which was not sufficiently cool, the retailer would not be liable under the Act.

(e) The state of scientific and technical knowledge at the relevant time was not such that a producer of products of the same description as the product in question might be expected to have discovered the defect[119]

This defence is commonly known in the United States as the "state of the art"   **18.39**
defence[120] or, in the United Kingdom, as the "development risk" defence.[121] It is the most controversial of the defences which are permitted both under the Directive and under the Act.[122]

Some authors have argued that the inclusion of a development risk defence in a system which purports to introduce strict liability is a contradiction in terms.[123] The phrase "scientific and technical knowledge" is not a term of art. Rather, the phrase bears its everyday meaning. The words "scientific" and 'technical' should be construed disjunctively, that is to say, the words have different meanings. In order to come within the ambit of scientific and technical knowledge the knowledge must be, to some extent, esoteric. In other words, that which is merely general knowledge would not fall within the ambit of the defence. For example, it is commonly known, of course, that products such as sharp knives can cut one if care is not taken in their use. However, the existence or absence of such knowledge would be irrelevant as far as the defence is concerned.[124]

The state of knowledge must be construed so as to include all the data in the infor-   **18.40**
mation circuit of the scientific community as a whole, taking into account the actual

---

[117] Nor would the retailers, notwithstanding the fact that they failed to supply the consumer with details of the person who supplied the meat to them in terms of s 2(3) of the Act.

[118] *Ibid*, s 4(2)(b).

[119] See (1997) 42 JLSS 416.

[120] In *Smith* v *Minster Machine Co* 669 F 2d 628 it was stated that "state of the art" meant the custom and practice of the industry. In *Lohrmann* v *Pittsburgh Corning Corp* 782 F 2d 1156 at 1164 it was held that "state of the art" includes all of the available knowledge on a subject at a given time and this includes scientific, medical, engineering, and other knowledge that may be available. The expression also includes the element of time, what is known and when this was knowledge available. In *Potter* v *Chicago Pneumatic Tool Co* 694 A 2d 1319 it was stated that the majority of courts have defined the state of the art defence as the level of relevant scientific, technological and safety knowledge existing, and reasonably feasible, at the time of design.

[121] Miller and Goldberg argue that the expression "development risk" defence is a term which is preferable to the "state of the art" defence since development risk refers to undiscoverable defects, whereas state of the art is associated with the most up-to-date technology and safety standards in a particular industry against which a product can be judged, the latter term (state of the art) being relevant to ascertaining whether a product is defective: (n 113, above), para 13.36.

[122] D Powles, "Product Liability: A novel dimension in Scotland' in *Essays in Honour of David Walker* (A Gamble ed.) 1990. at p 59.

[123] See, eg, C Newdick, "Risk, uncertainty and 'knowledge' in the development risk defence" (1991) 20 Anglo-Am LR 309 at 310.

[124] In *Abouzaid* v *Mothercare (UK) Ltd* [2000] WL 1918530 at [29], Pill LJ doubted that a record of accidents came within the category of scientific and technical knowledge.

opportunities for the information to circulate.[125] The defence is not concerned with either the conduct or the knowledge of individual producers. The test is objective[126] and includes constructive knowledge: that is, what the producer ought to know.[127] The producer must establish that the knowledge, at the time when the product was put into circulation, was not such as to enable the existence of the defect to be discovered.[128] However, once the risk is known, if the product is supplied, and if the defect recurs by then, it is a known risk and, even if the defect is undiscoverable in a particular example of the product, the defence provided under s 4(1)(e) is inapplicable.[129]

18.41 **(f) The relevant defect consisted of a defect in a complex product in which the product in question had been comprised and the defect was wholly attributable to the design of the complex product, or the producer of the component complied with the instructions of the producer of the complex product**

Thus, for example, the manufacturer of car windscreens could avail himself of the defence if the windscreens had become defective because they were unsuited to the type of car in which they were installed.

18.42 The Act also makes provision for the defence of contributory negligence.[130]

DAMAGE

18.43 The defender is liable for damage which is caused wholly or partly by a defect in a product.[131] "Damage" is defined as death or personal injury[132] or any loss of, or damage to, any property including land.[133] However, "damage" does not extend to loss or damage to the product itself nor to damage to the whole or any part of any product which has been supplied with the product in question comprised in it.[134]

18.44 Economic loss is therefore excluded. Therefore, if a microwave bursts into flames and burns a hole in my kitchen table, damages could be recovered for the table but not for the microwave itself. In order to avoid liability, the relevant defective product must have been supplied with the product which is damaged. Therefore, in the instant case, if a defective fuse had been inserted into the microwave by a repairer after the microwave had been purchased, liability would lie for damage to the microwave.

18.45 Furthermore, there is no liability in respect of any loss of, or damage to, any property which at the time it is lost or damaged:

(a) is not of a kind ordinarily intended for private use, occupation or consumption; and

---

[125] *A v National Blood Authority* [2001] 3 All ER 289 at 326.
[126] *Commission of European Communities v UK*, Case C–300/95 at [36].
[127] S Whittaker, "The EEC Directive on Product Liability" (1995) 5 *Yearbook of European Law* 233 at 258.
[128] *A v National Blood Authority* [2001] 3 All ER 289 at 328.
[129] *Ibid* at 328.
[130] Consumer Protection Act 1987, s 6(4).
[131] *Ibid* s 2(1).
[132] "Personal injury" includes any disease and any other impairment of a person's physical or mental condition; Consumer Protection Act 1987, s 45(1).
[133] *Ibid*, s 5(1).
[134] *Ibid*, s 5(2).

(b) is not intended by the person suffering the loss or damage mainly for his own private use, occupation or consumption.[135]

Damage to commercial property is, therefore, not actionable.   **18.46**

Under the Act, claims for damage are limited to damage to any property (including   **18.47** land) exceeding the sum of £275.[136] Any person who has suffered actionable damage can raise an action under the Act. Therefore, if a guest in my house was injured by the burning microwave, he would be able to recover damages under the Act. Liability cannot be excluded by any contract, notice or other provision.[137] Furthermore, the Act does not abrogate the existing common law on product liability.[138]

PRESCRIPTION AND LIMITATION OF ACTIONS

The Consumer Protection Act 1987 amends the Prescription and Limitation (Scotland)   **18.48** Act 1973 as it relates to prescription and limitation of actions in respect of claims brought under the former Act.

As far as the law relating to prescription is concerned, an obligation to make   **18.49** reparation for damage[139] which has been caused wholly or partly by a defect in a product extinguishes after 10 years unless a relevant claim is made within that period.[140] The relevant period commences at the time when the product was supplied.[141] The upshot of this is that where a person is either injured or made ill by a defective product and the injury or illness is not discovered until 10 years after the supply of the product, that person may not sue under the Consumer Protection Act 1987. It would, therefore, be necessary for the pursuer to bring a claim at common law.

As far as the law relating to limitation of actions is concerned, an action which   **18.50** relates to damage caused by a defective product ceases to be competent after a period of 3 years after the earliest date on which the pursuer was aware that there was a defect in the product, and that the damage was caused by such a defect.[142] The 1973 Act makes similar provisions in relation to actions concerning death caused by a defective product.[143]

---

[135] Consumer Protection Act 1987, s 5(3).
[136] *Ibid*, s 5(4).
[137] *Ibid*, s 7.
[138] *Ibid*, s 2(6).
[139] The Consumer Protection Act 1987, s 5(1) defines "damage" as death or personal injury or any loss or damage to property including land.
[140] Prescription and Limitation (Scotland) Act 1973, s 22A(1).
[141] *Ibid*, s 22A(3).
[142] *Ibid*, s 22B(1) and (2).
[143] *Ibid*, s 22C.

19 OCCUPIERS' LIABILITY

INTRODUCTION

Land may present a danger to those who enter the land by virtue of its physical **19.1** state. For example, land may be undermined and, therefore, prone to subsidence, the upshot of which is that the land may contain deep pits. Land may also pose a danger by virtue of an activity which takes place there. For example, land may pose a danger by virtue of its being crossed by a railway line or electricity pylons, or because it is being used as a go-cart racing circuit. The question to be answered here is to what extent, if any, the law imposes a duty of care on the occupier of the relevant land to those who enter the premises and sustain injury.

HISTORY OF THE LAW PRIOR TO 1960

By the end of the 19th century it had been established by case law that the occupier of **19.2** land owed a duty of care in certain circumstances to those who were present on the land.[1] Under the English common law, the obligations of the occupier towards a person who entered the relevant premises depended upon the class into which the person entering fell. He could be invited by the occupier to visit the premises, in which case he would have the status of an invitee. Alternatively, he could be merely permitted by the occupier to enter the premises and, therefore, be a licensee. Finally, he could be there without any permission at all, and fall to be categorised as a trespasser.[2] The highest standard of care was owed to an invitee.[3] A lower standard of care was owed to a licensee.[4] The lowest standard of care was owed to trespassers. Here, the law simply placed a duty on the occupier not to deliberately injure the trespasser. In *Dumbreck* v *Robert Addie and Sons (Collieries) Ltd*,[5] the House of Lords held that the aforementioned rigid categories which governed those who entered premises also represented the law of Scotland. The law was rather confusing, not least because judges north and south of the Border did not always agree as to where the demarcations between the three categories lay. For example, in *Plank* v *Magistrates of Stirling*[6] it was held that a child who was playing in a public park was an invitee, whereas in a series of previous

---

[1] See, eg, *Beveridge* v *Kinnear* (1883) 11 R 387; *Cormack* v *School Board of Wick* (1889) 16 R 812.
[2] P North, *Occupiers' Liability* (1971) at p 1.
[3] The duty was to "use reasonable care to prevent damage from unusual danger, which he ought to have known": per Willes J in *Indermaur* v *Dames* (1866) LR 1 CP 274 at 288.
[4] *Fairman* v *Perpetual Investment Building Society* [1923] AC 74. The duty owed to licensees was to warn them of concealed dangers (or traps) of which the occupier was aware.
[5] 1929 SC (HL) 51.
[6] 1956 SC 92.

English decisions in similar circumstances a child was held to be a licensee. There was also some doubt as to whether the rigid categories simply applied to land as opposed to moveable structures such as mobile shops.[7]

19.3   The liability of occupiers was reviewed by the Law Reform Committee for Scotland in 1957.[8] The Committee recommended that legislation be enacted to abolish the categories of invitee, licensee and trespasser. The Committee also recommended that the law should be reformed in order to include liability in respect of moveables as well as land and buildings. A further recommendation was that legislation should make a landlord of tenanted premises liable to parties who were not the tenant for injury or loss which resulted from the state of the premises. The Committee's recommendations were implemented by the Occupiers' Liability (Scotland) Act 1960 which will now be discussed.

OCCUPIERS' LIABILITY (SCOTLAND) ACT 1960

19.4   Under s 2(1) of the Occupiers' Liability (Scotland) Act 1960 (generally, hereinafter referred to as the "Act"), an occupier of land or other premises is placed under a duty to show care towards persons who enter the premises in respect of the dangers which are due to the state of the premises or to anything done or omitted to be done on them and for which he is in law responsible. The duty of care the Act imposes on occupiers extends not only to heritable property but also in relation to fixed and moveable structures, including any vessel, vehicle or aircraft in relation to persons entering such property.[9]

WHO IS AN "OCCUPIER" OF LAND?

19.5   The Act does not define the expression "occupier" in relation to land. Therefore, it has been left up to the courts to fill the legislative gap. In *Telfer* v *Glasgow Corporation*,[10] the pursuer (aged 10) fell through the roof of a vacant building. At the time the accident occurred, the Co-operative Wholesale Society Ltd was retaining the keys of the building, notwithstanding the fact that the Co-operative had negotiated a sale of the premises to the Corporation. It was held in the Outer House that, by reason of the fact that the Co-operative had the *de facto* power to exclude others, the Co-operative was to be regarded as the occupier of the premises in terms of the Act. However, one need not have exclusive occupation of the land in question in order to fall within the scope of the Act. For example, a contractor who is working on land or other premises owned or leased by someone else may be classed as the occupier of relevant land.[11]

19.6   A mere administrative act by a local authority may not be sufficient to make the authority an occupier in terms of the Act. For example, in *Feely* v *Co-operative Wholesale Society Ltd*,[12] the making of a control order under the Housing (Scotland) Act 1974 by

---

[7] See, eg, *Carney* v *Smith* 1953 SC 19.
[8] *First Report of the Law Reform Committee for Scotland* (Cmnd 88, 1957).
[9] Section 1(3)(a).
[10] 1974 SLT (Notes) 51.
[11] See, eg, *Duncan* v *Cammell Laird and Co Ltd* [1947] KB 901.
[12] 1990 SLT 547.

a local authority in relation to premises was not sufficient to bring the authority into a position of control in terms of the Occupiers' Liability (Scotland) Act 1960.

Where the owner of the common parts of a tenement is under a legal duty to **19.7** maintain such parts (such as a stairway) in a safe condition, the owner may be in control of such parts in the eye of the law.[13]

In *Johnstone* v *Sweeney*[14] it was held that a landowner remains in possession and **19.8** control of a public right of way over his land, even if he lacks the legal right to exclude access to that land. It has been argued that the duty owed to users of rights of way is analogous, though probably not identical, to the duty owed by landowners to members of the public exercising the rights of access to the countryside conferred by the Land Reform (Scotland) Act 2003 (LR (S)A 2003).[15] The duty owed by landowners in terms of the 1960 Act to those who exercise rights of access under the LR(S)A 2003 therefore requires to be clarified by the courts.

WHAT IS "LAND"?

The expression "land or other premises" is not defined in the Act. The expression **19.9** "land" would, however, clearly cover all heritable property. As far as the meaning of "premises" is concerned, it could be argued that the words "land" and "premises" should be construed conjunctively, that is to say, that the words mean the same. Indeed, a grandstand,[16] a football stadium,[17] a lift,[18] a swimming pool,[19] an open-air market,[20] a private road[21] and a pond[22] have all fallen to be described as premises.

The scope of the Act is wide and includes not simply heritable property but also **19.10** fixed or moveable structures, including any vessel, vehicle or aircraft.[23] The expression "fixed or moveable structures" has been held to include scaffolding,[24] a ladder,[25] staging,[26] an oil rig[27] and a stall in a market.[28]

Public roads and streets probably do not come within the ambit of the Act.[29] **19.11** However, some authors have argued that it is not immediately obvious why roads and streets should be precluded from the Act, on the basis that "other statutory liability appears to sit alongside it and frequently to be pleaded as an alternative ground".[30]

---

[13] *Mellon* v *Henderson* 1913 SC 1207.
[14] 1985 SLT (Sh Ct) 2.
[15] J M Thomson (ed), *Delict* (2007) at para 17.30.
[16] *Francis* v *Cockrell* (1870) LR 5 QB 501.
[17] *Hosie* v *Arbroath Football Club Ltd* 1978 SLT 122.
[18] *Haseldine* v *C A Daw and Son Ltd* [1941] 2 KB 343.
[19] *Ratcliff* v *McConnell* [1999] 1 WLR 670.
[20] *Mallon* v *Spook Erections Ltd* 1993 SCLR 845.
[21] *Beggs* v *Motherwell Bridge Fabricators Ltd* 1998 SLT 1215. See also *Lewis* v *National Assembly of Wales*, 2008, unreported.
[22] *Darby* v *National Trust, The Times*, 23 February 2001.
[23] Section 1(1).
[24] *Morton* v *Glasgow City Council* 2007 SLT (Sh Ct) 81; *Poliskie* v *Lane* 1981 SLT 282.
[25] *Woodman* v *Richardson and Concrete Ltd* [1937] 3 All ER 866.
[26] *London Graving Dock Co Ltd* v *Horton* [1951] AC 737.
[27] *Clark* v *Maersk Co Ltd* 2000 SLT (Sh Ct) 9.
[28] *Mallon* v *Spook Erections Ltd* 1993 SCLR 845.
[29] *Kirkpatrick* v *Dumfries and Galloway Council* 2001 SCLR 261.
[30] Thomson (ed), *Delict* at para 17.29.

NUMBER OF OCCUPIERS

19.12 There can be more than one occupier of land for the purposes of the Act.[31]

WHAT DUTY IS OWED?

19.13 The Act provides as follows:

> "The care which an occupier of premises is required, by reason of his occupation or control of the premises, to show towards a person entering thereon in respect of dangers which are due to the state of the premises or to anything done or omitted to be done on them and for which the occupier is in law responsible shall, except in so far as he is entitled to and does extend, restrict, modify or exclude by agreement his obligations towards that person, be such care as in all the circumstances of the case is reasonable to see that that person will not suffer injury or damage by reason of any such danger."[32]

Parties can, therefore, vary the duty which the law imposes as far as the occupation of land is concerned, solely by *agreement*. Notices, signs, etc are therefore insufficient to exclude liability.[33]

Injury requires to be due to the state of the premises

19.14 In order to come within the scope of the Act, the injury which is sustained by the pursuer must be caused by the physical state of the premises in contradistinction to that which the pursuer wishes to do on the relevant premises. This point is neatly illustrated in *Lewis* v *National Assembly of Wales*.[34] In that case the claimant, L (aged 14), was injured while riding a motorcycle on land occupied by the defendant. He sustained injury while trying to negotiate a small hillock and ditch situated at the end of a road on land which the defendants occupied. L claimed that the land was inherently dangerous and that he had sustained injury by reason of the state of the premises. It was held that L's injury was not caused by the state of the premises. Rather, his injury had been caused by the use which L chose to make of the premises. However, it may, indeed, be difficult to distinguish between injury caused by the very state of the relevant premises, on the one hand, and injury simply caused by the use the pursuer wishes to make of the premises. For example, in the sheriff court case of *Morton* v *Glasgow City Council*,[35] the pursuer (aged 14) entered a plot of ground occupied by the defender, by means of an unlocked gate, on which ground a block of flats was situated and around which the defenders had erected scaffolding. The pursuer climbed up the scaffolding, fell to the ground and was injured. It was held that the presence of the scaffold constituted an allurement to young persons. Therefore, effective measures ought to have been taken in order to protect them from associated dangers. However, one could have plausibly argued, as it was in *Lewis*, that the pursuer had sustained injury simply by virtue of the use he chose to make of the premises.

---

[31] Thomson (ed), *Delict* at para 17.29.
[32] Section 2(1).
[33] See also s 16 of the Unfair Contract Terms Act 1977 in relation to business premises.
[34] 2008, unreported.
[35] 2007 SLT (Sh Ct) 81.

Occupier required to do only that which is reasonable in the circumstances

The Act requires the occupier of the relevant premises to do only that which is **19.15** reasonable in the circumstances. In order to ascertain whether the standard of care the law demands of the defender has been attained, the court takes into account such things as the likelihood of harm, the probability of injury and the possibility of severe injury.[36] The fact that the law simply demands the occupier of the land to do that which is reasonable in the circumstances is neatly illustrated in the Court of Appeal case of *Lewis* v *Six Continents plc*.[37] In that case, a hotel was held not liable for injuries sustained by a guest who fell out of a hotel window, since the window did not present any obvious danger to an adult. Furthermore, no accident had previously occurred and it was not reasonably foreseeable that an adult would lean out of the window in such a way to prompt the occupier to limit the way in which the window opened. *Hill* v *Lovett*[38] provides another interesting example of the nature of the duty imposed on the relevant occupier of land under the Act. In *Hill*, a veterinary surgeon's receptionist was given permission by her employers to enter a private garden (which belonged to her employer) in order to clean the surgery windows. While she was in the garden she was bitten on the leg by a dog belonging to her employer. It was held that her employer owed her a duty of care in terms of s 2 of the Act. Lord Weir was of the view[39] that liability was to be determined by reference to the foreseeability of injury by the defenders. Furthermore, the learning in *Bolton* v *Stone*[40] was to be followed, that is to say, one had to ascertain whether the risk of damage to the pursuer was sufficiently probable as to lead the defenders to anticipate it.

Again, in *McGlone* v *British Railways Board*,[41] a boy who was aged 12 climbed up an **19.16** electricity transformer which belonged to the British Railways Board. The transformer was situated at the foot of a railway bank which arose from a vertical wall. The transformer was surrounded on three sides by a large fence and, on the other side, by the railway. There was no fence on the side nearest the railway. Furthermore, there were gaps between the fence and the wall. However, the gaps were closed by five strands of barbed wire. There were signs which bore the words "Danger – Overhead live wires". The pursuer managed to get through the barbed wire and climbed up the transformer. He was electrocuted when he came into contact with wires situated high up in the transformer. The House of Lords held that the defenders had done all that could reasonably have been demanded of them in the circumstances and were not, therefore, liable in terms of the Act. Lord Pearce stated: "In a case like this an occupier does, in my view, act reasonably if he erects an obstacle which a boy must take some trouble to overcome."[42]

However, *McGlone* should be contrasted with the English Court of Appeal case of **19.17** *Adams* v *Southern Electricity Board*,[43] where the plaintiff (aged 14) was electrocuted after climbing a pole-mounted transformer situated in a copse near his home. The plaintiff and his friends had frequently gone to play there. The climbing of the transformer

---

[36] See, eg, *Jolley* v *Sutton LBC* [2000] 3 All ER 409. See also *Pannett* v *McGuinness* [1972] 2 QB 599.
[37] [2005] EWCA Civ 1805.
[38] 1992 SLT 994.
[39] *Ibid* at 995.
[40] [1951] AC 850.
[41] 1966 SLT 2.
[42] *Ibid* at 12.
[43] *The Times*, 21 October 1993.

structure often played a part in their games. Originally, the transformer had been provided with an anti-climbing device, but, when the accident occurred, the device was in a defective state of repair. It was held that the defendants owed a duty to the plaintiff.[44] It is worth remembering, at this juncture, that many of the cases we are discussing are fact-sensitive[45] and, therefore, the courts are wary about laying down hard and fast rules about what particular kind of precautions an occupier of land should take.[46]

19.18   The duty of care which the Act imposes on an occupier of land may extend to the provision and enforcement of a proper system of work.[47]

19.19   It must be emphasised here that the duty in question is owed to the very person who enters the relevant premises, in contradistinction to that which is owed to a notional or "ordinary" person. This point was emphasised in *Titchener* v *British Railways Board*.[48] In that case the pursuer, a girl who was aged 15, was struck by a train on a busy railway line. The pursuer averred that the Board was under a duty to maintain the fence which protected the railway line in such a condition as to prevent access to the railway line. The House of Lords held that the duty owed by the defenders to the pursuer under s 2(1) of the Act was towards the particular person who entered the premises in question. Since the girl was well aware of the danger from the trains, she was deemed to have been *volenti*, in that she was deemed to have consented to assume the risk of being injured by a passing train. As far as the duty of care the defenders owed to the pursuer was concerned, Lord Fraser stated:

> "The existence and extent of a duty of care to fence will depend on all the facts of the case, including the age and the intelligence of the particular person entering the premises. The duty will tend to be higher in a question with a very young or very old person than in the question with a normally active and intelligent adult or adolescent."[49]

Lord Fraser went on to state[50] that the nature of the *locus* in question was also important in determining the extent of the duty which was owed under the Act.

Allurements

19.20   If the premises or part of the premises on which a young pursuer sustains injury constitute an allurement or trap it is incumbent on the occupier of the premises to take appropriate prophylactic measures. A good illustration of this principle is seen in *Glasgow Corporation* v *Taylor*.[51] In that case the pursuer, a child aged 7, was in the

---

[44] However, the amount of damages which fell to be awarded were reduced by reason of contributory negligence on the part of the plaintiff.

[45] *Jolley* v *Sutton LBC* [2000] 3 All ER 409, per Lord Steyn at 416.

[46] See also *Davie* v *Edinburgh Corporation* 1977 SLT (Notes) 5 at 6. In that case, the pursuer sustained injury by falling down an unlit stair occupied by the defenders. Lord Kincraig stated that it could not be affirmed as a question of law that an ordinary stair in a building was not in all circumstances a danger to persons using it in darkness. It was a question to be determined in all the circumstances.

[47] *McGuffie* v *Forth Valley Health Board* 1991 SLT 231. See also *Porter* v *Strathclyde RC* 1991 SLT 446, which did not concern potential liability under the Occupiers' Liability (Scotland) Act 1960 but, rather, the common law duty of care the law imposes on an employer to his employee. However, it is suggested that the learning in *Porter* is applicable to the interpretation of s 2 of the Act.

[48] 1984 SLT 192.

[49] *Ibid* at 195.

[50] 1984 SLT 192 at 195.

[51] [1922] AC 44.

Botanic Gardens in Glasgow. He ate some berries which had the appearance of grapes. However, the berries were poisonous, the result being that the pursuer died. The House of Lords held the occupiers of the gardens liable. The basis of the decision was that the presence of the berries constituted an allurement and, therefore, a potential danger to the young. In the view of Lord Atkinson, the relevant plant and the deadly berries which it bore was something in the nature of a trap.[52]

In the more recent case of *Telfer* v *Glasgow Corporation*,[53] the pursuer (aged 10) fell **19.21** through the roof of a derelict building. The building was situated in a working-class area which was "prolific with children". Indeed, the premises in question afforded every possible allurement to children. The building was provided with, *inter alia*, sliding doors that had come off their runners, inspection pits full of water, and rubbish, tyres, glass partitions to be broken, a roof with pigeons and with pigeons' eggs, "wee round spiral stairs", and even, for a time, a derelict motor van. The premises, in effect, had become a glorified playground. The defender occupiers were held liable to the pursuer in terms of s 2 of the Act.[54]

Again, in *Morton* v *Glasgow City Council*[55] the pursuer entered, by means of an **19.22** unlocked gate, a plot of ground in which a block of tenement houses was situated and, around which the defenders had erected scaffolding. The pursuer (aged 14) climbed up the scaffolding and fell to the ground. He sustained injury as a consequence. The sheriff held that the presence of the scaffolding constituted an allurement to young persons. Therefore, effective measures ought to have been taken to protect them from associated dangers.

As far as young children are concerned, virtually any object or activity can present **19.23** a potential danger. What is the position as far as the potential liability of occupiers of premises is concerned in relation to such young children? In the Inner House case of *Hastie* v *Magistrates of Edinburgh*,[56] a father brought an action arising from the death of his son (a child aged 4) against Edinburgh Town Council, as it was then known. The child, who was unaccompanied at the time, had drowned after he fell into an artificial pond situated in a public park owned by the defenders. It was held that the defenders did not owe the child a duty of care in law. In short, responsibility for the child's safety rested with his parents, not the local authority.[57] In the modern English case of *Phipps* v *Rochester Corporation*,[58] a child (aged 5), who lived in the vicinity with his parents, was walking across a large open space of grassland which was part of a building site on which a housing estate was being developed by the defendants. A long, deep trench had been dug in the grassland. The boy fell into the trench and was injured. The plaintiff claimed that the occupiers of the land in question owed him a

---

[52] [1922] AC 44 at 52. See also *Cooke* v *Midland Great Western Railway of Ireland* [1909] AC 229, where a railway turntable situated on land to which children had access constituted an allurement. See also *Buckland* v *Guildford Gas and Light Coke Co* [1949] 1 KB 410, where live wires which were accessible from an easily climbable tree but were obscured by foliage were held to constitute a trap in relation to children.

[53] 1974 SLT (Notes) 51.

[54] However, the damages awarded to the pursuer were reduced by 50% on account of his contributory negligence.

[55] 2007 SLT (Sh Ct) 81.

[56] 1907 SC 1102.

[57] See also *Stevenson* v *Glasgow Corporation* 1908 SC 1034. In that case, the defenders, who were occupiers of a public park which bordered the River Kelvin, were held not to be under a duty of care to prevent children from falling into the river and drowning.

[58] [1955] 1 QB 450.

duty of care. However, it was held, at first instance, that the defendants were entitled to take into account that reasonable parents would not permit their children to be sent to the place where the child was injured without protection. In the last analysis, in the eye of the law, responsibility for the safety of young children rested with their parents or guardians as opposed to the occupiers of the land in question. Devlin J (as he then was) stated:[59]

> "[The] responsibility for the safety of little children must rest primarily upon the parents; it is their duty to see that such children are not allowed to wander about by themselves, or at least to satisfy themselves that the places to which they do allow their children to go unaccompanied are safe for them to go to. It would not be socially desirable if parents were, as a matter of course, able to shift the burden of looking after their children from their own shoulders to those of persons who happen to have accessible bits of land."

19.24 The Court of Appeal recently had to address the question of liability of occupiers of land in relation to young children in *Bourne Leisure Ltd* v *Marsden*.[60] In that case, a child, aged 2½, drowned in a pond situated in a holiday park where he was holidaying with his parents and younger brother. The child and his brother had wandered away from the caravan in which they were staying, while his mother was talking to someone who was occupying another caravan. The learning in *Phipps* was followed and the court held that the occupiers of the land concerned were not under a duty to fence off the pond. The occupiers could assume that young children would not be allowed to approach the pond unaccompanied.

Dangers required to emanate from occupier's land

19.25 The duty which the Act imposes on the occupier of the premises concerned is simply confined to protecting the person who enters the premises from any dangers which arise from the state of the particular premises. The duty does not extend to ensuring that the land is not used as a base from which the person entering the land can gain access to other land or premises which poses a danger. This point was neatly illustrated in *McCluskey* v *Lord Advocate*.[61] In that case, the pursuer fell from a path into a river and was injured. The path was not situated on land occupied by the Forestry Commission. However, access to the path could be obtained from Forestry Commission paths. It was held that the Commission was under no obligation in terms of the Act to prevent the pursuer from gaining access to the path from which she fell.

Foreseeable acts of others

19.26 The duty imposed on an occupier of land towards those who enter the land extends to protecting them from the foreseeable actions of third parties. This point was illustrated in the Outer House case of *Hosie* v *Arbroath Football Club Ltd*.[62] In that case, the pursuer sustained serious injury when he was knocked down and trampled upon by a crowd at a football ground occupied by the defenders. The crowd had gained access to the ground by breaking down a security gate. It was alleged on the part of the pursuer

---

[59] [1955] 1 QB 450 at 472.
[60] [2009] EWCA Civ 671.
[61] 1994 SLT 452.
[62] 1978 SLT 122.

that the defenders ought to have known that the gate could be lifted off its runners by the pressure of a crowd, with the result that someone could be injured. The defenders were held liable in terms of the Act for the injury the pursuer sustained, on the basis that they had failed to reasonably maintain the gate. Furthermore, the actions of the crowd on the day in question were reasonably foreseeable and, therefore, did not break the chain of causation between the negligent inaction on the part of the defenders and the injury sustained by the pursuer.

Obvious dangers

19.27 The occupier of land is not required to guard those who enter the premises from obvious dangers. For example, the Act does not require the occupier of land which includes natural features such as cliffs or lochs[63] to provide effective measures to protect those entering the land concerned from obvious dangers which are inherent in the land.[64] Similarly, there is no duty to provide protection from obvious dangers which arise from man-made features of the land.[65]

STATUS OF THE PURSUER

19.28 The Act places the occupier of land under a duty in respect of dangers which are on the relevant land, not only to those who are lawfully on the relevant land, but also to trespassers. However, the standard of care owed by the occupier to a trespasser is lower than that which is owed by the occupier to someone who is lawfully on the premises.[66] For example, if, one night, a burglar broke into my garden tool shed and tripped on a rake lying on the floor, thereby injuring himself, I would not be liable in terms of the Act.

DEFENCES

19.29 The Act preserves the common law defence of *volenti non fit injuria*, that is to say that the occupier of land is not liable for any injury caused to someone who enters the land if that person has willingly accepted the relevant risk of so entering.[67] For example, in *Forbes* v *Aberdeen Harbour Commissioners*,[68] the pursuer (aged 16), for his own amusement, was standing on a raft which was floating on a patch of water situated on land owned by the defenders. The raft capsized and the pursuer was drowned. It was held by the Inner House that the defenders were not liable. The pursuer had consented to the risk of drowning by using the raft on the water.[69] The leading modern case on the application of the *volenti* defence is *Titchener* v *British Railways Board*,[70] which has

---

[63] *Graham* v *East of Scotland Water Authority* 2002 SCLR 340.
[64] *Tomlinson* v *Congleton BC* [2004] 1 AC 46. For a discussion of this case, see J Elvin, "Occupiers' liability, free will, and the dangers of a compensation culture" (2004) 8 EdinLR 127. See also *Forbes* v *Aberdeen Harbour Comrs* (1888) 15 R 323 and *Kelly* v *State Line Steamships Co Ltd* (1890) 27 SLR 707.
[65] *Evans* v *Kosmar Villa Holidays* [2008] 1 WLR 297. See also *Titchener* v *British Railways Board* 1984 SLT 192.
[66] See, eg, *McGlone* v *British Railways Board* 1966 SLT 2. See also *Pannett* v *McGuiness* [1972] 2 QB 599.
[67] Occupiers' Liability (Scotland) Act 1960, s 2(3). For a discussion of the defence of *volenti*, see Chapter 21.
[68] (1888) 15 R 323.
[69] See also *Kelly* v *State Line Steamship Co Ltd* (1890) 27 SLR 707.
[70] 1984 SLT 192.

been discussed above.[71] It will be recalled that the pursuer, who sustained injury while trespassing on a railway line, was deemed to have fully consented to the risk of being struck by a train.

LIABILITY OF LANDLORDS

19.30   Under the Act, primary responsibility for injury which is caused by the defective state of the premises, falls on the occupier. However, in certain circumstances the Act makes the landlord of premises liable. The Act[72] provides:

> "Where premises are occupied or used by virtue of a tenancy under which the landlord is responsible for the maintenance or repair of the premises, it shall be the duty of the landlord to show towards any persons who, or whose property, may from time to time be on the premises the same care in respect of dangers arising from any failure on his part in carrying out his responsibility aforesaid as is required by virtue of the foregoing provisions of this Act to be shown by an occupier of premises towards persons entering on them."

19.31   In essence, therefore, the landlord is made liable for dangers which manifest themselves on the relevant premises by virtue of the landlord flouting a repairing obligation imposed on him either by common law, or statute, or by the terms of the lease.[73]

19.32   The Act applies to tenancies created before the commencement of the Act as well as to tenancies created after its commencement.[74]

19.33   Finally, the Act binds the Crown.[75]

---

[71] See para 19.19.
[72] Section 3(1).
[73] For a detailed account of landlords' obligations to maintain and repair premises, see Thomson, *Delict*, paras 17.58–17.85.
[74] Section 3(5).
[75] Section 4.

20 VICARIOUS LIABILITY

In this chapter we shall consider the extent, if any, to which one is liable in law for the **20.1** actions of others. Whereas the vast majority of vicarious liability cases concern liability for the negligent conduct of others, the concept of vicarious liability is not confined to negligent conduct. Rather, vicarious liability embraces all forms of wrongful act.[1] Vicarious liability is of importance from a practical as well as an academic viewpoint, in that, generally, pursuers are inclined to sue only those who are able to compensate them. For example, if I am negligently injured, while riding my bicycle, by an army private who is driving a military vehicle, it is preferable that I should sue the Crown which has more money, of course, than the person who actually injured me. Similarly, if I am defamed by a newspaper, it would normally be more prudent to sue the relevant newspaper than the author of the offending article.

Commonly, cases relating to vicarious liability concern the liability of employers **20.2** for the conduct of their servants. However, we will see later that it is not simply employers who are vicariously liable for the conduct of their employees. Employers are occasionally liable for the conduct of independent contractors. The concept of vicarious liability was well engrained in Scots law by the early 19th century.[2] Indeed, the concept of vicarious liability has its roots firmly embedded in public policy.[3] A number of reasons have been advanced as to the legal policy which underlies vicarious liability. In the authors' view, the underlying policy of the law was succinctly expressed by Lord Nicholls in the House of Lords in *Dubai Aluminium Co Ltd* v *Salaam*.[4] His Lordship stated:

> "The underlying legal policy is based on the recognition that carrying on a business enterprise necessarily involves risks to others. It involves the risk that others will be harmed by wrongful acts committed by the agents through whom the business is carried on. When those risks ripen into loss, it is just that the business should be responsible for compensating the person who has been wronged ... It is fair to allocate risk of losses [which arise from the wrongful acts of employees] to the businesses rather than leave those wronged with the sole remedy, of doubtful value, against the individual employee who committed the wrong."

Whereas vicarious liability is not confined to the liability of employers for the conduct **20.3** of their employees, the vast majority of decided cases comprise such a form of liability. It is, therefore, important, at the very outset, to distinguish an employee from an

---

[1] In *Majrowski* v *Guy's and St Thomas's NHS Trust* [2007] 1 AC 224 the defendants were held vicariously liable for breach of the Protection from Harassment Act 1997, s 3 which creates the civil wrong of harassment.
[2] *Baird* v *Hamilton* (1826) 4 S 790.
[3] *Rose* v *Plenty* [1976] 1 All ER 97, per Scarman LJ at 103.
[4] [2003] 2 AC 366 at 377. This case concerned vicarious liability on the part of a firm for the alleged dishonest conduct of one of its partners.

independent contractor, since, generally speaking, subject to the exceptions we discuss below, an employer is vicariously liable only for those acts of his employee which are committed within the scope of employment of the latter.

DISTINCTION BETWEEN EMPLOYEE AND INDEPENDENT CONTRACTOR

20.4 Whereas an employee is employed under a contract of service, an independent contractor is employed under a contact for services, that is to say that one employs an independent contractor to perform a particular task or tasks. It is often easy to recognise a contract of service when one sees it, but it is difficult to say wherein the distinction lies between contract of service and contract for services. A ship's master, a chauffeur and a reporter of a newspaper are all employed under a contract of service, whereas a taxi-driver and a newspaper contributor are employed under a contract for services. That is to say, the last two are independent contractors in the eyes of the law.

THE "INTEGRATION" TEST

20.5 A crude distinction[5] between an employee and an independent contractor is that, whereas the former's work is integrated in the employer's business, the latter's work is not. For example, in *Inglefield* v *Macey*,[6] the plaintiff, who was self-employed, began to work with the defendant who was a timberman. The arrangement between the two parties was that the plaintiff should retain his self-employed status. The defendant instructed the plaintiff as to what work he wanted done. The defendant also supplied the necessary equipment. However, the defendant did not tell the plaintiff how to perform the work because the former knew that the latter possessed the requisite experience. One day, the plaintiff was injured while felling a tree. Ashworth J adopted the "integration" test and held that the plaintiff was an independent contractor since, while his work was done for the business, it was accessory to the business and was not integrated in it. However, while the "integration" test is superficially attractive, the test may be difficult to apply in practice.

20.6 In the English Court of Appeal case of *O'Kelly* v *Trusthouse Forte*,[7] it was held that whether the relevant relationship between the relevant parties falls to be categorised either as one of service or as one for services is a question of law. However, it is up to the court not only to ascertain the relevant facts, but also to assess them qualitatively. It is only if the weight given by the trial court to a particular factor shows that the court has misdirected itself in law that an appellate court can interfere with the decision.

---

[5] This distinction was made by Denning LJ (as he then was) in *Stevenson, Jordan and Harrison Ltd* v *MacDonald* [1952] 1 TLR 101 at 111.
[6] (1967) 2 KIR 146.
[7] [1984] QB 90.

FACTORS TAKEN INTO ACCOUNT

In the House of Lords case of *Short v J & W Henderson Ltd*,[8] Lord Thankerton endorsed **20.7** the opinion of the Inner House and laid down the following tests in order to distinguish an employee from an independent contractor:

(1) the power of selection of employee;
(2) the payment of wages or remuneration;
(3) the control which is exercised by the employer;
(4) the employer's right of dismissal.

We now discuss each test in turn. **20.8**

Power of selection of individual

The fact that the employer can select the very individual who is to carry out the relevant tasks for him is indicative that the relevant contract is one of service. However, simply because I have the right to select the person who carries out a particular task does not, automatically, make the person who performs the task my employee. For example, the fact that I, a householder, can select which heating engineer should repair my gas boiler does not make the latter my employee.

Payment of wage

The fact that the individual is in receipt of regular payment from the employer is more **20.9** in keeping with a contract of service or employment than one for services.

Control exercised by the employer over the employee

In order to ascertain whether the individual in question is an employee or independent **20.10** contractor, the court considers the extent, if any, to which the employer is in a position to control the person whom he employs in the performance of his duties. The greater the degree of control exercised by the employer over the person whom he employs, the more likely the relationship between the parties will be regarded as that of employer and employee. This point is illustrated in *Woodhead v Gartness Mineral Company*.[9] In that case a docker was injured by a fellow docker while unloading a ship. The work was paid for on a tonnage basis. The defenders, who were purchasers and also shippers of a quantity of cement in bags, were responsible for their discharge at a port. It was held that the defenders exercised a sufficient degree of control over the operation to make them vicariously liable for the negligence of the docker.

In the current context, the concept of control means a situation where the employer **20.11** can not only order or require what is to be done, but also dictate how the work is to be done.[10] However, while the "control" test fitted quite comfortably into the work practices of the Victorian era where the concept had its roots,[11] modern work practices are often of such a nature that an employer simply does not possess the requisite

---

[8] 1946 SC (HL) 24 at 33.
[9] (1877) 4 R 469.
[10] Per Hilbery J in *Collins v Hertfordshire County Council* [1947] KB 598 at 615.
[11] See, eg, *Yewens v Noakes* (1880) 6 QBD 530.

technical knowledge to control his employees effectively. For example, it would be very difficult, if not impossible, for either a hospital authority to instruct a surgeon (whom it employs) on how to remove an appendix, or a local authority to direct a building inspector as to how he should carry out his professional duties. However, both the surgeon and the building inspector would fall to be regarded as employees of their respective organisations.

The right of dismissal

20.12 If the employer has the right to dismiss the employee during the period when the work is being carried out, such power is more consistent with a contract of service.

20.13   However, the above "tests" laid down in *Short* were criticised by MacKenna J in *Ready Mixed Concrete (South East) Ltd* v *Minister of Pensions and National Insurance*,[12] who expressed the view that (1) and (4) are simply indicative of a contract of *any* (emphasis added) nature between the supposed master and servant. Generally speaking, the same could also be said of (2). His Lordship laid[13] down the following tests in order to distinguish between a servant and an independent contractor. According to his Lordship:

- the servant agrees that he will provide his own work and skill in return for wages;
- the servant agrees that he will be subject to the other's control;
- the other provisions of the contract are consistent with the contract being a contract of service.

STATUS OF CONTRACT

20.14 It is not conclusive that the parties have categorised the relationship between themselves as being either a contract for services or a contract of service. For example, in *Ferguson* v *Dawson Partners (Contractors) Ltd*,[14] the relevant contract between the parties (ie a labourer and a construction firm) described the relationship as a contract for services, that is to say that the labourer was self-employed. However, the Court of Appeal held that the contract was one of service. Indeed, the relevant contract was a mere sham, calculated to circumvent legal requirements which related to both tax and national insurance. Public policy in this case, therefore, decreed that the parties should not have the right to determine the status of the relevant agreement. However, notwithstanding the fact that the parties do not enjoy such a right, the court does attach some weight as to how the parties have categorised the relevant contract. For example, in *Calder* v *H Kitson Vickers Ltd*,[15] a worker had worked for the defendants sometimes as an employee and at other times as an independent contractor. It was held that the terms of the contract between the parties should be taken into account by the court.

---

[12] [1968] 2 QB 497 at 524.
[13] *Ibid* at 515.
[14] [1976] 1 WLR 676.
[15] [1988] ICR 232.

FINANCIAL RISK, INVESTMENT

To what extent the employer has taken a financial risk in the project in question; what **20.15** degree of responsibility for management he enjoys; to what extent he can profit from the relevant work, as well as whether he provides his own equipment and hires his own helpers are all taken into account.[16] In the authors' view, these factors provide one of the most comprehensive tests for determining whether an individual is an employee or an independent contractor.

FOR WHICH ACTS OF THE EMPLOYEE IS THE EMPLOYER LIABLE?[17]

According to Salmond and Heuston, "A master is not responsible for a wrongful act **20.16** done by his servant unless it is done in the course of his employment. It is deemed to be so done if it is either (1) a wrongful act authorised by the master, or (2) a wrongful and unauthorised mode of doing some act authorised by the master."[18] There is no problem in dealing with (1). Indeed, it is arguable that (1) is not really a form of vicarious liability but, rather, a situation where the employer would be directly liable for the harm caused to the pursuer.[19]

We are, therefore, left with the task of ascertaining what conduct of the employee **20.17** falls within the scope of his employment. That question is one of law as opposed to one of fact.[20] However, the question as to whether a particular act on the part of the employee was performed within the scope of his employment is one of fact.[21] In the House of Lords case of *Kirby* v *National Coal Board*,[22] Lord Clyde expressed the view that, whereas it was not advisable to lay down an exhaustive definition of what falls within the scope of employment, there were four different types of situation which served as guides. First, if the master authorised the act in question, he is liable for it. Second, if the workman does some act which he is appointed to do but does it in a way which his master has not authorised, the master would still be liable since the servant's act would still be within the scope of his employment. Third, if the servant is employed only to do a particular piece of work or a particular class of work and the servant does something outside the scope of that work, the master is not responsible for any mischief the servant may do. Fourth, if the servant uses his master's time or his master's place or his master's tools for his own purposes, the master is not responsible.

---

[16] *Lee* v *Chung* [1990] 2 AC 374.
[17] For a general discussion of employers' vicarious liability, see S Arnell, "Employers' vicarious liability – where are we now?" 2010 J R 243.
[18] R Heuston and R Buckley (eds), *Law of Torts* (21st edn, 1996) at p 443. Approved by the Lord President (Lord Hamilton) in *Wilson* v *Exel UK Ltd* 2010 SLT 671 at 672.
[19] The Lord President expressed a similar view in *Wilson*, above, at 672.
[20] Per Lord Neuberger MR in *Maga* v *Archbishop of Birmingham* [2010] 1 WLR 1441 at 1454.
[21] *Dubai Aluminium Co Ltd* v *Salaam* [2003] AC 366, per Lord Millett at 397.
[22] 1958 SC 514 at 532–533.

SCOPE OR COURSE OF EMPLOYMENT

20.18   The courts take a variety of factors into account in ascertaining whether the conduct in question falls within the employee's scope of employment.

Limits of time

20.19   An employer is liable for the conduct of his employees at the relevant place of employment, and also during the hours the employee is employed, as long as the employee is on the premises concerned, within reasonable limits of time of the commencement and the conclusion of the shift. In the English case of *Ruddiman and Co v Smith*,[23] a clerk who was employed by the defendants used a washroom which was provided by the latter. However, the clerk left a tap running in the washroom. The water from the overflowing sink flooded the adjoining premises. It was held that he was acting within the scope of his employment. Again, in *Bell v Blackwood, Morton & Sons*,[24] a woman, who was in the employment of a firm of carpet manufacturers, was jostled by a fellow employee while travelling down a stair, after the hooter had sounded for the end of the shift. The defenders (the pursuer's employers) were held vicariously liable for the conduct of the negligent employee.

20.20   An employee is not, usually, at work if he is simply travelling to and from work. However, in certain circumstances, the courts are prepared to accept that an employee is at work when the latter is simply travelling to work. In the Outer House case of *Thomson v British Steel Corp.*[25] X and T, who were employed by the defenders, were sent by the latter to work at Laconby. X and T were normally employed at Motherwell. They completed their work one evening at Laconby and set off for Motherwell at around 0930 hrs by car, which was driven by X. At around 1430 hrs the car was involved in a collision with another car. T was killed. It was held that, at the time of the accident, X was acting within the scope of his employment. It was held to be significant, as far as the outcome of the case was concerned, that the defenders had made arrangements that both X and T should make the two-way journey within the employers' time, and, furthermore, a decision had also been made by the defenders as to how many cars should be used for the journey.

Deviation from authorised route

20.21   The employer is not vicariously liable for the conduct of his employee if the latter is "on a frolic of his own" when the accident takes place. That is to say, no liability will lie if the employee deviates from his authorised route to such an extent that it can be said that he is no longer acting within the scope of his employment. In the leading case of *Joel v Morrison*,[26] Baron B stated: "If [the employee] was going out of his way, against his master's implied commands when driving on his master's business, he will make his master liable, but if he was going on a frolic of his own without being at all on his master's business, the master will not be liable."

20.22   A number of the so-called "frolic" cases concern the use of vehicles in a manner which has not been authorised by the relevant employer. For example, in *Storey* v

---

[23] (1889) 60 LT 708.
[24] 1960 SC 11.
[25] 1977 SLT 26.
[26] (1834) 6 C & P 501 at 503.

Ashton[27] a cart driver completed his employer's work and then went to visit a relative. During the course of the journey the carter injured the plaintiff. It was held that the employer was not liable for this tort. In the eyes of the law, the deviation from the employee's authorised route ranked as an independent journey. The employee was, therefore, on a frolic of his own. Similarly, in *Hilton v Burton*,[28] X, H and Y were building workers who were employed at a building site. H drove X and Y to a café 7 miles away to get tea. X was killed by H's negligent driving. It was held that H was not acting within the scope of his employment. Again, in *Williams v Hemphill*,[29] a bus driver, while carrying children, made a substantial detour at the request of some of the children. The bus was involved in a collision. The pursuer was injured. The House of Lords held that the driver was acting within the scope of his employment. Lord Pearce stated:[30] "[when] there are passengers whom the servants on his master's behalf has taken aboard for transport to Glasgow, their transport and safety does not cease at a certain stage of the journey to be the master's business, or part of his enterprise, merely because the servant has, for his own purposes chosen some route which is contrary to his instructions".

Similarly, in *Smith v Stages*[31] the defendant and another employee were travelling **20.23** to their homes in the Midlands after working in South Wales. During the course of the journey they were involved in an accident. The employer paid them travelling expenses, but the former did not stipulate the means by which the employees were to travel. It was held by the House of Lords that the men were acting within the scope of their employment when the accident occurred.

Whether the degree of deviation from the intended route takes the employee out **20.24** of the course of his employment is a question of both fact and degree. The case law, therefore, is not particularly helpful since each case depends on its own particular facts. However, two contrasting cases can be used to illustrate that there is a fine line between conduct which is within the scope of employment and that which is not.

In *Whatman v Pearson*,[32] a carter was in charge of a horse and cart. Without **20.25** permission, he drove them home, a quarter of a mile out of his way, in order that he could eat a meal. He left his horse unattended outside his home. His horse ran away and damaged property which belonged to the plaintiff. It was held that the employers of the car were not liable to the plaintiff.

In *Crook v Derbyshire Stone*,[33] a lorry driver stopped his vehicle at the side of a **20.26** road and then crossed the road in order to get a cup of tea in a café. While walking across the road he caused an accident. It was held that he was not acting within the course of his employment since obtaining a refreshment was outwith the scope of his employment.

However, notwithstanding the fact that an employee has gone on a frolic of his **20.27** own, he may return to his employment. Exactly when such resumption takes place, however, is difficult to ascertain. Case law indicates that once the employee has gone outwith the scope of his employment, some clear unequivocal act on the part of the

---

[27] (1869) LR 4 QB 476.
[28] [1961] 1 All ER 74.
[29] 1966 SC (HL) 31.
[30] *Ibid* at 46.
[31] [1989] 2 WLR 529.
[32] (1868) LR 3 CP 422.
[33] [1956] 2 All ER 447.

employee is required before the court would be prepared to accept the proposition that he had resumed employment. For example, in *Rayner* v *Mitchell*[34] a carter was employed to deliver beer and also to pick up empty bottles. He used the cart on an unauthorised trip and, on his return, he picked up some empty bottles. The carter injured the plaintiff while the former was returning to his place of work with the empty bottles. It was held that the carter had not resumed his employment at the time when the accident took place. Therefore, his employer was not vicariously liable for his conduct.

Other conduct

20.28   We now ask what other forms of wrongful conduct (that is, apart from a situation where the employee has deviated from a given route) can take the employee outside the scope of his employment. However, before we proceed to do this it is salutary to have regard to the *dictum* of Lord Nicholls in the House of Lords case of *Dubai Aluminium Co Ltd* v *Salaam*[35] to the effect that the question as to whether or not a given act of the employee falls within the scope of his employment falls to be answered by the courts making an evaluative judgment in each case, having regard to all the circumstances, and, importantly, having regard also to the assistance provided by previous court decisions. One should also bear in mind the fact that, whereas the forms of wrongful conduct on the part of the employee are discussed under separate subheadings, the authors have done this both for the sake of convenience and also as a concession to convention. In the last analysis, there is often an overlap between each category.

The effect of express prohibitions and other unauthorised conduct

20.29   Often employees are expressly prohibited from engaging in certain activities during the course of their employment. For example, it is not uncommon for employers to prohibit factory workers to consume alcohol during working hours. The question which we have to answer now, of course, is to what extent, if any, the courts set store by a prohibition which has been issued by an employer to an employee. For example, if someone who is employed at a slaughterhouse were, contrary to the instructions of his employer, to consume large quantities of alcohol during working hours, become drunk and, as a result of this, inadvertently stab a colleague while they are both dressing a carcass, would the employer be vicariously liable for the conduct of his employee? Does the employee's failure to obey his employer's instructions automatically take the employee outwith the scope of his employment?

20.30   The general rule is that if an express prohibition sets a limit to the work which the employee is authorised to do, the employee acts outwith the scope of his employment if he flouts the relevant instructions. However, if the employee simply does what he is authorised to do in an unauthorised way, he remains within the scope of his employment. In the House of Lords case of *Plumb* v *Cobden Flour Mills Co Ltd*,[36] Lord Dunedin stated: "[There] are prohibitions which limit the sphere of employment and prohibitions which only deal with conduct within the sphere of employment. A trans-

---

[34] (1877) 2 CPD 357.
[35] [2003] 2 AC 366 at 378.
[36] [1914] AC 62 at 67.

gression of a prohibition of the latter class leaves the sphere of employment where it was, and consequently will not prevent recovery of compensation. A transgression of the former class carries with it the result that [the employee] has gone outside the sphere." The rationale for this approach was succinctly expressed by Willes J in *Limpus v London General Omnibus Co.*[37] His Lordship stated: "The law casts upon the master a liability for the act of his servant in the course of his employment; and the law is not so futile as to allow a master, by giving secret instructions to his servant, to discharge himself from liability." An application of this principle is seen in *McKean v Raynor Bros Ltd*.[38] There, a workman was employed by the defendants. He was instructed by the defendants to take a lorry and meet and give a message to a convoy which was coming by road. He proceeded on his journey, but, instead of taking the firm's lorry, he used his father's car. He drove that car negligently and collided with and killed the plaintiff's husband. It was held that the workman was doing, in an unauthorised way, that which he was authorised to do. His employer was, therefore, vicariously liable for his conduct.

Again, in *Hamlyn v John Houston and Co*,[39] one aspect of the business of the **20.31** defendant firm of grain merchants was to obtain, by lawful means, information about its competitors' activities. H, who was a partner in the firm, obtained confidential information on the plaintiff Hamlyn's business by bribing one of Hamlyn's employees. The Court of Appeal held that the firm was liable for the loss suffered by Hamlyn. Sir Richard Henn Collins MR stated[40] that if it was within the scope of H's authority to obtain the information by legitimate means, then for the purposes of vicarious liability it was within the scope of his authority to obtain it by illegitimate means, and the firm was liable accordingly.

Acts intended to benefit employer

If the employee's conduct is, at the time the relevant accident takes place, motivated **20.32** by a desire to assist his employer, the courts will more readily lean towards the view that the conduct in question falls within the scope of his employment provided that the employee's act is incidental to the work the employee is employed to perform. For example, in *Bayley v Manchester & Sheffield Railway*,[41] a railway porter mistakenly thought that the plaintiff was boarding the wrong train. As a result, the porter violently pulled the plaintiff out of the train. The plaintiff was injured as a result. The defendant railway company was held vicariously liable for the conduct of the porter since he was held to have been acting within the scope of his employment. Similarly, in *Polland v Parr*,[42] a carter hit a boy he thought was stealing from his master's lorry. It was held that the master was vicariously liable for this assault. Again, in *Century Insurance Co Ltd v Northern Ireland Road Transport Board*,[43] the driver of a petrol lorry struck a match in order to light a cigarette while filling a tank at a petrol station. There was an explosion which resulted in extensive damage. It was held that the employer

---

[37] (1862) 1 H &C 526 at 539.
[38] [1942] 2 All ER 650.
[39] [1903] 1 KB 81.
[40] *Ibid* at 85.
[41] (1873) LR 8 CP 148.
[42] [1927] 1 KB 286.
[43] [1942] AC 509.

was liable, since the servant was doing, albeit in an incompetent way, something he was authorised to do.

20.33   The master may be liable even if the servant has usurped the job of another provided that his temporary new role is closely connected with the master's business and also not too remote from his own permanent work. For example, in *Mulholland* v *William Reid and Leys Ltd*,[44] the pursuer was killed at work by one of his employer's vans which was being driven by an apprentice who possessed no driving licence and was also not an authorised driver. Prior to driving it, he and another apprentice had been assisting a tradesman to move a piece of equipment into a workshop by hand. The way had been blocked by the van which collided with the pursuer. The apprentice had not been authorised to drive the van. The Inner House held that whereas the conduct of the apprentice had not been authorised, it was sufficiently incidental to the work he was employed to do in order to bring the negligent conduct within the scope of his employment. In short, the apprentice was simply doing what he was employed to do.[45]

20.34   However, there are cases where the pursuer has ostensibly acted with a desire to benefit his employer but, at the same time, the courts have held that the employee has acted outwith the scope of his employment. For example, in *Riddell* v *Glasgow Corporation*,[46] a local government tax collector, in the course of collecting tax, accused the pursuer of having fraudulently altered a tax receipt. The pursuer, in turn, raised an action for defamation against the defenders. The House of Lords held that the collector had acted outwith the scope of his employment and, therefore, the defenders were not liable. Again, in *Martin* v *Wards*,[47] a shopkeeper instructed his salesman to remove certain articles from one of his shops to another. The salesman borrowed a van from a friend who came with it in order to drive it. Owing to the salesman's careless driving, the pursuer was injured. It was held that the salesman was not acting within the scope of his employment since he was not authorised to drive.

Assaults by employees

20.35   As a general rule an employer is not liable for an assault which is perpetrated by an employee if the latter is solely motivated by personal spite towards the person who is assaulted. For example, in *Warren* v *Henlys Ltd*,[48] a garage attendant, B, erroneously believed that the plaintiff had tried to drive away from the defenders' garage without paying for petrol which he had put in the tank of his car. The plaintiff and B became involved in an altercation which ended with B assaulting the plaintiff. It was held that the assault in question was simply an act of personal vengeance on the part of B and was not done within the scope of his employment. Again, in *Daniels* v *Whetstone Entertainments*,[49] a dance hall steward struck the plaintiff in a dance hall. The plaintiff then went outside and, while talking to friends, was struck again by the steward. Shortly before the second assault, the dance hall manager had told the steward to go

---

[44] 1958 SC 290.
[45] See also the Court of Appeal case of *Kay* v *ITW* [1967] 3 All ER 22 where the facts of the case resemble those in *Mulholland.*
[46] 1911 SC (HL) 35.
[47] (1887) 14 R 814.
[48] [1948] 2 All ER 935.
[49] [1962] 2 Lloyd's Rep 1.

back inside. It was held that the steward's employers were liable for the first but not for the second assault.

However, if the assault is carried out in furtherance of the business of the employer, **20.36** there is less likelihood of the court categorising the conduct in question as falling outwith the scope of the employment of the employee. For example, in *Hanlon* v *Glasgow and SW Railway Co*,[50] a guard, who was under the impression that a boy had got on to the wrong train, pushed the boy between the space which separated the train from the platform, as a result of which the boy died. It was held that the guard was doing what he was authorised to do, albeit in a negligent way. Therefore, the employer was liable.

Again, in *Dyer* v *Munday*,[51] the defendant was a hire-purchase dealer. He sent **20.37** his manager to recover furniture in respect of which instalments were unpaid. The furniture had been pledged by the person in possession of the furniture to the landlord of the premises, as security for rent. The wife of the landlord attempted to prevent the manager from removing the furniture, whereupon the manager assaulted her. The manager's employer was held vicariously liable for the assault. Again, in *Knight* v *Inverness District Board of Control*,[52] the attendants of a lunatic asylum used undue force in order to restrain a patient, as a result of which the patient died. It was held that the defendants had been acting within the scope of their employment. The defendant board was, therefore, vicariously liable for the conduct of the attendants.

More recently, in the Court of Appeal case of *Fennelly* v *Connex South Eastern* **20.38** *Ltd*,[53] the claimant alleged that one of the defendants' employees, S, who was a ticket inspector, had assaulted him at a railway station in the course of S's employment. The claimant had purchased a ticket and had passed through a ticket barrier. As he made his way down steps towards the platform, S called after him and asked to see his ticket. However, the claimant did not stop. An altercation broke out. During the altercation S put the claimant in a headlock. It was held that when deciding whether an act was carried out in the course of employment, it was necessary to look at the job in question. One should not divide out each step and task carried out by the employee in order to decide whether each step or task was authorised by the employer. The initial altercation occurred as a result of S's job as a ticket inspector. The assault followed from the altercation. It was artificial to say that, because the claimant was walking away when the assault took place, what happened during the assault was divorced from that which preceded it.

The leading case concerning liability for assaults perpetrated by employees is now **20.39** *Lister* v *Hesley Hall Ltd*.[54] The claimant was resident in a boarding house attached to a school which was owned and managed by the defendants. The warden of the boarding house, who was employed by the defendants, without their knowledge systematically sexually abused the claimant. The claimant sued the defendants on the basis that the harm inflicted on him was so inflicted during the course of the warden's employment, and, therefore, the defendants were vicariously liable for his conduct. The House of Lords held that there was sufficient connection between the work the warden had been

---

[50] (1898–99) 1 F 559.
[51] [1895] 1 QB 742.
[52] 1920 2 SLT 157.
[53] [2001] IRLR 390.
[54] [2001] 2 WLR 1311. For an interesting discussion of *Lister*, see P Giliker, "Rough justice in an unjust world" (2002) 65 MLR 269.

employed to do and the acts of abuse he had committed against the claimant, for those acts of abuse to fall within the scope of his employment. It was quite irrelevant that the warden had acted both illegally and also for his own personal gratification. According to Lord Clyde:[55] "[His] position as warden and the close contact with the boys which that work involved created a sufficient connection between the acts of abuse which he committed and the work which he had been employed to do." In the last analysis, the House of Lords in *Lister* adopted a "broad brush" approach as to what falls within the scope of employment. Indeed, Lord Steyn expressed the view that when one was considering whether the conduct of an employee fell within the scope of his employment, a broad approach should be adopted and one should not concentrate too closely on the particular act complained of.[56]

20.40   An employer's liability for the assaults of his employee fell to be determined by the Court of Appeal in *Mattis* v *Pollock*.[57] In that case, the defendant owned a nightclub. He employed X as a doorman. X was expected to act aggressively towards customers so as to maintain order among them. One night X grabbed a member of a group of people who were about to enter the nightclub. A fracas broke out. X was struck several times. He was also assaulted by a bottle. He then escaped to his flat, from which he emerged carrying a knife. X then stabbed and inflicted serious injuries on the claimant while he was standing outside the nightclub. The Court of Appeal held that the employer of X was vicariously liable for the assault on the basis that X's act was so closely connected with what the employer had either authorised or had expected of X, that it was fair, just and reasonable to make the employer vicariously liable for the assault which had been perpetrated by X.[58] We can see, of course, that the illegal conduct on the part of the employee which was the subject-matter of the action was an independent act of retribution on the part of the employee. However, the court did not regard this as a hurdle in the way of the claimant. According to Judge LJ:[59] "[*Lister*] demonstrated the heresy of the proposition that an employer cannot be vicariously liable for an independent act of 'self-indulgence or self-gratification' by his employee."

20.41   The Court of Appeal recently had to consider the concept of vicarious liability in terms of child abuse in *Maga* v *Archbishop of Birmingham*.[60] Here the claimant, who had learning difficulties, brought an action against a Roman Catholic diocese. The claimant alleged that he had been sexually abused as a child by a priest, who both lived and worked in the diocese. The claimant was not a Roman Catholic. However, he had met the priest who had special responsibility for youth work through church discos. The claimant had also done jobs for the priest, including work in the presbytery where the priest lived. Reversing the decision of the trial judge, the court held the diocese

---

[55] [2001] 2 WLR 1311 at 1330.
[56] *Ibid* at 1327.
[57] [2003] 1 WLR 2158. For an interesting discussion of this case, see R Weekes, "Vicarious liability for violent employees" [2004] CLJ 53.
[58] See also the Court of Appeal case of *Vasey* v *Surrey Free Inns* [1996] PIQR P373. There, V visited a nightclub which was owned by S. V was refused entry. He thereupon kicked the door of the premises and broke its glass. V was pursued into the car park of the premises by two doormen and the manager of the premises. V was assaulted and injured. S was held vicariously liable for the assault since the conduct of the staff was a reaction to damage to S's property. The assault, therefore, fell to be categorised as an authorised act, which took place within the scope of the doormen's employment. The doormen were not, therefore, at the time of the assault, taking part in a frolic of their own.
[59] [2003] 1 WLR 2158 at 2164.
[60] [2010] 1 WLR 1441. For a useful discussion of *Maga*, see J Bell, "Vicarious liability for child abuse" [2010] CLJ 440.

vicariously liable for the conduct of the priest. Lord Neuberger MR advanced the following reasons for holding the Catholic Church vicariously liable for the conduct of the priest:[61]

(1) The priest was usually dressed in clerical garb, and was so dressed when he had met the claimant.
(2) The priest's duties included a duty to evangelise or bring the gospel to both Catholics and non-Catholics.
(3) At the time the abuse took place the priest was carrying out one of his specifically assigned functions in the church.
(4) The priest was both able to develop and did develop his relationship with the claimant by inviting him to a disco which was held on church premises and which was organised by the priest.
(5) The relationship between the priest and the claimant was further developed by the priest getting the claimant to help clear up after discos.
(6) The claimant worked at the request of the priest on premises which were owned by the priest's archdiocese. The premises also adjoined the church where the priest worked.
(7) The opportunity to spend time alone with the claimant, especially in the presbytery, arose from the priest's role in the archdiocese.

For Longmore LJ, the fact that the priest had both the status and the authority **20.42** associated with that role, meaning that no one would question his being alone with the claimant, provided the close connection between the abuse and what the priest was authorised to do.[62]

In the last analysis, in the authors' view, the "close connection" test which was **20.43** used by both the House of Lords and the Court of Appeal in *Lister*, *Mattis* and *Maga* to ascertain whether an employee was acting within the course of his employment may be over-glib. Such a test can, at best, serve simply as a factor for the court to take into account, rather than assume the status of a definitive test. Indeed, in *Dubai Aluminium Co Ltd v Salaam*,[63] Lord Nicholls observed that the "close connection test provides no guidance on the type or degree of connection which will usually be regarded as sufficiently close to prompt the legal conclusion that the employer should be vicariously liable for the conduct of his employee", nor did the test provide assistance on when an incident was to be regarded as sufficiently work related, as distinct from personal.

Giliker, in turn, argues that a preferable test would be to focus on the nature of the **20.44** duties given to the employee, rather than the facts of each case, and whether these duties include an express or implied duty to protect or care for certain individuals or property belonging to the employer.[64] While this approach has the virtue of some clarity in relation to the facts in the above trilogy of cases, it is suggested that this test would be incapable of providing a universal test to determine vicarious liability. For example, to parody the example given by the learned author[65] herself, would the test

---

[61] [2010] 1 WLR 1441 at 1455–1456.
[62] *Ibid* at 1463.
[63] [2003] 2 AC 366 at 377–378.
[64] P Giliker, "Lister revisited: vicarious liability, distributive justice and the course of employment" [2010] LQR 521.
[65] *Ibid* at 524.

which she posits yield a satisfactory answer to determine the vicarious liability of the employer of a Bible tract distributor who rapes a woman who answers his door call? It is suggested that it would not.

Theft of goods by employees

20.45   To what extent, if any, is an employer vicariously liable for his employee stealing goods which the pursuer has deposited with the former? One could argue that, in the eyes of the law, such conduct on the part of the employee could not come within the course of his employment simply because the employee is not employed to steal goods. Indeed, it could be said in this context, as it could, indeed, have been said in *Lister*, that such conduct would constitute the very antithesis of what the employee is employed to do. In the Court of Appeal case of *Morris v C W Martin and Sons Ltd*,[66] the plaintiff sent her mink coat to a furrier to be cleaned. However, the furrier did not carry out cleaning so he sent the coat to be cleaned by the defendants. While the coat was with the defendants it was stolen by one of their employees. The coat was never recovered. The court held that the defendants were liable for the loss of the coat on the basis that they were bailees for reward (that is, the coat had been deposited with them for reward) of the coat. The employers were, therefore, under a non-delegable duty to return the coat to the person who had bailed (deposited) the coat with them.[67]

20.46   Whereas *Morris* was decided on the somewhat narrow ground of the duties which a bailee owes to the bailor of goods, the decision in that case was treated as one of general application in the law relating to vicarious liability by the House of Lords in *Lister*.[68]

20.47   However, the leading case on the subject of vicarious liability for thefts committed by employees is now *Brink's Global Services Inc v Igrox Ltd*.[69] In that case the claimants provided a worldwide door-to-door service for the carriage of goods. They entered into a contract with a London bank to convey bars of silver to India. The bars of silver were packed on wooden pallets which were required to be fumigated in order to reduce the risk of infestation. The claimants, therefore, entered into a contract with the defendants, whereby the latter undertook to fumigate the pallets. An employee of the defendants was charged with the task of fumigating the pallets which were stored in a container. He entered the container and stole some bars of silver, which were never returned. The Court of Appeal held the defendants vicariously liable for the theft. Moore-Bick LJ expressed the view that in order to establish liability for vicarious liability there must be some greater connection between the tortious act of the employee and the circumstances of his employment than the mere opportunity to commit the act which has been provided by the access to the premises which the employment has afforded.[70] The correct approach is to concentrate on the relative closeness of the connection between the nature of the employment and the particular tort, and to ask whether, looking at the matter in the round, it is just and reasonable to hold the employers vicariously liable. In deciding this question, a relevant factor is the risk to others which is created by an employer who entrusts duties, tasks and functions

---

[66] [1966] 1 QB 716.
[67] See also *Central Motors (Glasgow) Ltd v Cessnock Garage and Motor Co* 1925 SC 796.
[68] [2001] 2 WLR 1311, per Lord Steyn at 1318, per Lord Clyde at 1328 and per Lord Hobhouse at 1333.
[69] [2010] EWCA Civ 1207.
[70] *Ibid* at [19].

to an employee.[71] In the instant case there was a sufficiently close connection between the employee's theft of the silver and the purpose of his employment to make it fair and just that the defendants should be vicariously liable for his actions. The theft by an employee from the very container which he was instructed to fumigate, was a risk which was reasonably incidental to the purpose for which he was employed.[72]

Fraud of the employee

Before discussing vicarious liability in relation to fraud it is necessary briefly to **20.48** describe the elements of fraud. Fraud is a delict in Scots law. The gist of the wrong is that the defender has, by his dishonest word or deed, deliberately persuaded the pursuer to act to his detriment.[73] Falsity is the very foundation of the delict. In the House of Lords case of *Derry* v *Peek*,[74] Lord Herschell stated:

> "[F]raud is proved when it is shown that a false representation has been made—
> (1) knowingly, or
> (2) without belief in its truth, or
> (3) recklessly, careless whether it be true or false."

His Lordship went on to state[75] that making a false statement through want of care falls **20.49** far short of, and is a very different thing from, fraud. This point was re-emphasised by the House of Lords in *Boyd and Forrest* v *Glasgow and South Western Railway Co*,[76] where it was held that an honest belief on the part of the defender in his representations vitiated fraud. We can see, therefore, that, given the very nature of the delict, *prima facie*, an act of fraud on the part of an employee would automatically fall outwith the scope of employment of the employee who perpetrated the relevant fraud.

Furthermore, historically, the courts have been less ready to find vicarious liability **20.50** in cases of an employee's dishonesty than in cases of his acts of negligence.[77] Indeed, this area of vicarious liability largely travels in a compartment of its own.

The House of Lords had an opportunity to decide on the vicarious liability of **20.51** an employer in the leading case of *Lloyd* v *Grace Smith and Co Ltd*.[78] In that case, the defendant solicitor's clerk fraudulently persuaded the plaintiff to transfer her property to him. The employer was held liable for this act of fraud. The House held that his fraudulent act fell within the scope of his employment. Furthermore, it was quite irrelevant that the employee had simply acted for his own benefit in contradistinction to that of his employer. The latter was, therefore, held liable for this fraud. Again, in the Court of Appeal case of *Uxbridge Permanent Benefit Building Society* v *Pickard*,[79] a solicitor's clerk had full authority to conduct the business of a solicitor's office on the part of his employer. The clerk fraudulently persuaded the plaintiff building society to lend money to a third party by way of a mortgage loan on a property. The

---

[71] [2010] EWCA Civ 1207 at [23].
[72] *Ibid* at [30].
[73] *Bradford Third Equitable Benefit Society* v *Borders* [1941] 2 All ER 205.
[74] (1889) 14 App Cas 337 at 374.
[75] *Ibid* at 375.
[76] 1912 SC (HL) 93.
[77] *Dubai Aluminium* v *Saleem* [2003] 2 AC 366, per Lord Nicholls at 378.
[78] [1912] AC 716.
[79] [1939] 2 KB 238.

relevant title deeds were a forgery. In holding the employer liable for the fraud, the court expressed the view that *Lloyd* was not authority for the proposition that the employer in that case was simply vicariously liable for the employee abusing his right to enter into contractual negotiations with a third party. Rather, liability extended to a fraudulent act of the employee which fell within the ostensible authority of the employee, whereby a third party was induced to act to his detriment on the basis that the business being offered by the employee was genuine business.[80] Whether the employee has ostensible authority to perform the very act which defrauds the pursuer falls to be judged objectively and also in the light of all the circumstances of the case. Of prime importance is the conduct of the employer in the relevant circumstances: that is to say, it is not sufficient that the act of fraud has been achieved solely by the pursuer relying on a misrepresentation by the employee to the effect that the latter has the requisite authority to carry out the act in question. This point was neatly illustrated in the House of Lords case of *Armagas* v *Mundogas SA*.[81] In that case, the employee of the defendants had authority to sell a vessel which belonged to the defendants. As part of a fraudulent scheme, he induced the plaintiffs, the purchasers, to believe that the contract involved a 36-month charter back. An employee, in the position of that of the defendants, was not entitled to make such a transaction. The plaintiff sustained loss by relying on this fraudulent representation. The House held that, since the plaintiffs' beliefs rested solely on the representation of the employee, the defendants were not vicariously liable. Lord Keith stated:[82]

> "The essential feature for creating liability in the employer is that the party contracting with the fraudulent servant should have altered his position to his detriment in reliance on the belief that the servant's activities were within his authority, or to put it another way, were part of his job, this belief having been induced by the *master's representations by way of words or conduct* [emphasis added]."

20.52   There need be no contract between the fraudster and the person who has been duped.[83] The House of Lords had an opportunity to consider liability for the fraudulent act of an employee in *Dubai Aluminium Co Ltd* v *Salaam*.[84] In that case, a partner in a firm of solicitors dishonestly drafted an agreement, the result of which was that the claimants were defrauded. The House held that the acts of fraud were so closely connected with what the partner was authorised to do that such acts could fairly be regarded as done by him in the ordinary course of the firm's business.[85]

Lending a servant

20.53   It sometimes happens that X, who is an employee of A, is hired by B in order to perform some task for him and, during the time when X is working for B, X negligently injures P. In such a scenario, would either A or B, or both A and B, be vicariously liable for the conduct of X?

---

[80] [1939] 2 KB 238, per Sir Wilfred Greene MR at 253.
[81] [1986] AC 717.
[82] *Ibid* at 781.
[83] See, eg, *Uxbridge Permanent Benefit Building Society* v *Pickard* [1939] 2 KB 238 and *Taylor* v *City of Glasgow DC* 1997 SC 183.
[84] [2003] 2 AC 366.
[85] *Ibid* per Lord Nicholls at 379.

In the Inner House case of *Malley* v *LMS Railway Co*,[86] a railway company lent both **20.54**
a railway engine and a crew to the owners of certain works. A workman who was
employed at the works was knocked down and injured on the railway track by the
engine. It was held that the railway company was vicariously liable for the accident,
on the ground that the engine had been operated by the crew in accordance with the
general directions which had been given by its officials to the crew. In the last analysis,
the degree of control which was being exercised by the railway company over its crew
at the time the accident took place was sufficiently strong to warrant the conclusion
that there had been no transfer of employment to the owner of the works.

Of importance, Lord Cooper expressed the view that the law imposes a strong **20.55**
presumption against the person who borrows a servant being held vicariously liable
for the conduct of the servant while he is performing tasks for the hirer.[87]

The leading case on this subject is now *Mersey Docks and Harbour Board* v *Coggins* **20.56**
and Griffith.[88] In that case, a harbour authority lent a mobile crane to a firm of stevedores, Coggins and Griffith, for loading a ship. A craneman was also lent. He was paid
by the Mersey Docks and was also liable to be dismissed by it. The contract between
Mersey Docks and the stevedores stipulated that cranemen who were hired should
be deemed to be employees of the hirers. While the craneman was carrying out work
for the stevedores he injured the plaintiff, who sued the harbour authority and the
stevedores for damages. The House of Lords held the harbour authority liable since,
in the eyes of the law, it had continued to employ him throughout the duration of the
period while he was working for the stevedores. The House expressed the view that,
in circumstances where an employee is borrowed by another party, there is a strong
presumption that the employee remains the employee of the lender. Furthermore, the
provisions of the contract between the parties which governed who was to be regarded
as the employer of the worker concerned, were not to be regarded as conclusive as to
who was to be liable for any injury caused to a third party. In reaching its decision, the
House set much store by the fact that the right to control the cranedriver remained with
the harbour authority as opposed to the stevedores. According to Lord Macmillan:[89]

> "The stevedores were entitled to tell him (the stevedore) where to go, what parcels to lift
> and where to take them, that is to say they could direct him as to what they wanted him to
> do; but they had no authority to tell him how he was to handle the crane in doing his work.
> In driving the crane, which was the appellant board's property confided to his charge, he
> was acting as the servant of the appellant board, not as the servant of the stevedores. Here
> the driver became the servant of the stevedores only to the extent and effect of his taking
> directions from them as to the utilization of the crane in assisting their work, not as to how
> he should drive it."

For Lord Porter,[90] in addition to the factor as to who had the right to control the crane- **20.57**
driver, it was relevant to consider who was his paymaster, who could dismiss the
cranedriver and also how long the alternative period lasted.

---

[86] 1944 SC 129.
[87] *Ibid* at 137.
[88] [1947] AC 1.
[89] *Ibid* at 13–14.
[90] *Ibid* at 17.

Unauthorised lifts

20.58 Consider the case where an employee is forbidden from giving a lift to others in a vehicle which belongs to his employer. However, if, in the face of such a prohibition, the employee does give someone a lift and drives negligently, the result being that the vehicle is involved in an accident and the passenger is injured, would the driver's employer be vicariously liable for the conduct of the employee? In *Peebles* v *Cowan and Co*,[91] a driver allowed a boy to ride on a horse-driven lorry. The boy fell off and was injured. It was held that, by giving the boy permission to ride on the lorry, the employee was acting outwith the scope of his employment. His employers were, therefore, not vicariously liable for the injury which the boy had sustained. Again, in *Twine* v *Beans Express Ltd*,[92] a vehicle driver gave a lift against the master's instructions to X. X was injured. At first instance it was held that the employer was not vicariously liable for the conduct of the driver since, vis-à-vis the employer, X was a trespasser.[93] Again, in the Court of Appeal case of *Conway* v *George Wimpey and Co Ltd*,[94] the defendants had a lorry which was used to transport their workers. The defendants' driver was forbidden to carry anyone other than the defendants' men. However, the driver proceeded to give a lift to the plaintiff, who was not employed by the defendants. The plaintiff fell off the lorry on account of the driver's negligence. It was held that, in the absence of the fact that the defendants knew that the driver was giving a lift to an unauthorised person, such a person ranked simply as a trespasser to the defendants and, therefore, the defendants were not vicariously liable for the conduct of their driver.[95]

The potential liability of employers in relation to accidents which are based on unauthorised lifts fell to be considered again in the Court of Appeal case of *Rose* v *Plenty*.[96] There, the employers of a milk-float driver had prohibited him from allowing boys to assist him in delivering milk. However, he flouted this instruction and allowed the plaintiff to assist him one day. On account of the driver's negligence, the plaintiff was injured. He sued the driver's employers. It was held that since the boy had been allowed to ride on the float in order to assist the driver in delivering milk, the driver was simply doing what he was authorised to do but in an unauthorised way. The employers' instructions which prohibited the driver from enlisting the aid of others did not limit the scope of the employment of the driver. The boy was assisting the driver in furthering his employers' interests. The driver's employers were, therefore, vicariously liable for his conduct. *Twine* and *Conway* were distinguished.

LIABILITY FOR THE ACTS OF AN INDEPENDENT CONTRACTOR

20.59 We now have to consider the liability of the employer, not in relation to the delictual acts of his employee, but in relation to the acts of an independent contractor. For

[91] 1915 1 SLT 363.
[92] [1946] 1 All ER 202.
[93] The decision was affirmed by the Court of Appeal: (1946) 62 TLR 458.
[94] [1951] 1 All ER 363.
[95] However, in *Young* v *Edward Box* [1951] 1 TLR 789 the defendants' foreman consented to the driver's inviting a third party into a vehicle. He was injured on account of the driver's negligence. It was held that, by reason of such consent being within the ostensible authority of the foreman, his employer was vicariously liable for the negligence of the driver.
[96] [1976] 1 All ER 97.

example, if I commission a plumber to repair the burst water pipes in my garage and the plumber proceeds to uses his blowlamp negligently, the upshot of which is that he causes a which fire spreads to the property of my next-door neighbour, would I be vicariously liable for the negligent conduct of the plumber? Again, if I pay a taxi-driver to drive me to the airport and he negligently collides with a vehicle during the course of the journey, would I be vicariously liable for his conduct in the law of delict? The general rule is that I, the employer, would not be liable in either case, since the law sets its face against holding an employer vicariously liable for the acts of an independent contractor. However, there are certain situations when an employer will be held liable for the acts of an independent contractor. We now look at various categories of activities where the courts have held an employer vicariously liable for the conduct of an independent contractor. The list of such categories is not closed.

EMPLOYER AT FAULT

If the employer is at fault in some way for the injury in question, he would be liable. **20.60** For example, if I employ a contractor who was patently unsuited to carrying out the duties which I have commissioned him to perform, and he injures the pursuer, I would be vicariously liable in law for his conduct.[97] Therefore, if I employ an incompetent builder to construct a garage which adjoins a street and the garage collapses and injures a pedestrian, I would be liable to the pedestrian in the law of delict.

The employer would also be liable if he fails to give the independent contractor **20.61** proper instructions as to how the latter should carry out his duties. For example, in *Robinson* v *Beaconsfield Rural District Council*,[98] the defendant local authority employed contractors to clean out cesspools in its district. However, the defendant failed to make any arrangements for the safe disposal of the sewage which had been extracted from the cesspools. The contractors proceeded to deposit the offensive material on the plaintiff's land. It was held that the defendant was liable in tort for the actions of its contractor since it had failed to take proper precautions to dispose of the sewage.

THE PERFORMANCE OF NON-DELEGABLE DUTIES

The law places an employer under a non-delegable duty in a number of situations. In **20.62** other words, the law will not allow the employer to transfer any duty which the law imposes on him, to the person whom he has commissioned to carry out the relevant task. The law has developed piecemeal. The following comprise situations where liability has been imposed on employers for the acts of independent contractors. The list of categories where liability has been imposed by the courts is not exhaustive.

Acts which derogate from the right of support of land

If A employs an independent contractor, X, who, in the course of carrying out work on **20.63** A's land, causes subsidence or loss of support on the adjoining premises which belongs to B, who is entitled to the support afforded by A's premises, then A is liable for the

---

[97] See, eg, *Stennett* v *Hancock* [1939] 2 All ER 578.
[98] [1911] 2 Ch 188.

harm caused to B's property.[99] In the Inner House case of *Stewart* v *Malik*,[100] the proprietors of a flat which was situated in a tenement brought an action for damages against the defenders, who were proprietors of a shop situated immediately below the flat, in respect of damage to the flat which had been caused by the removal of a load-bearing wall as a result of works being carried out in the shop. The court decided that since, in Scotland, the law of the tenement casts on the servient proprietor a positive duty, in carrying out works which may affect support, to avoid endangering the "dominant" property,[101] such a duty could not be displaced by commissioning an independent contractor to carry out the works in question. The defenders were, therefore, liable for the damage which had been caused by the independent contractor.

Extra-hazardous acts

20.64   If A commissions an independent contractor to carry out works which are intrinsically hazardous, the law will impose strict liability on A for any damage which is caused by the contractor. For example, in *Holliday* v *National Telephone Co*,[102] the defendants, who were laying telephone wires along a street, employed an independent contractor to solder the tubes in which the wires were carried. He used a blowlamp negligently. A passer-by was injured. The Court of Appeal held that the defendants were liable since the operations the contractor was employed to carry out were extra-hazardous in the eye of the law. Again, in *Honeywill and Stein* v *Larkin Brothers Ltd*,[103] an independent contractor was employed to take flashlight photographs in a cinema. During the course of taking photographs, curtains in the cinema caught fire, and damage was caused to the cinema. The Court of Appeal held that, since the activity in question was intrinsically dangerous, the party which had commissioned him to take the photographs was vicariously liable for the damage the contractor had caused. More recently, in the Court of Appeal case of *Alcock* v *Wraith*,[104] S, the owners of a house, contracted with W to carry out re-roofing work on their terraced house. W carried out the work in an incompetent manner, in that he filled the void between the top of the party wall which separated S's house from that of A, with newspaper, the upshot of which was that damp penetrated A's premises. It was held that S was liable in nuisance and negligence for the acts of W on the ground that the activity which was undertaken by W was, by its very nature, likely to cause damage. The court was assisted in reaching this conclusion by drawing an analogy, on the facts of the case, with the strict liability which the law imposes on the owners of land who withdraw support from neighbouring land.

20.65   In the recent Court of Appeal case of *Biffa Waste Services Ltd* v *Maschininenfrabrok Ernst Hese GmbH*,[105] Stanley Burnton LJ expressed the view that the doctrine of vicarious liability for the performance of extra-hazardous activities was so unsatisfactory that it should be kept within narrow limits.

20.66   The fundamental question which requires to be answered at this juncture, of course, is to what extent, if any, does the above learning apply to the law of Scotland? In

---

[99]   See, eg, *Bower* v *Peate* [1876] 1 QBD 321.
[100]   2009 SC 265.
[101]   *Ibid*, per the Lord President (Lord Hamilton) at 275.
[102]   [1899] 2 QB 392.
[103]   [1934] 1 KB 191.
[104]   *The Times*, 23 December 1991.
[105]   [2009] QB 725 at 952. For a discussion of this case, see S Tofaris, "Who pays for the sub-contractor's negligence? Vicarious liability and liability for extra-hazardous activities re-examined" [2010] CLJ 13.

Stewart v *Malik*,[106] the Lord President reserved his opinion as to whether an employer was liable for harm which had been caused by an independent contractor while he was carrying out extra-hazardous operations. However, in the authors' view such learning does, indeed, apply in Scots law and is, therefore, good authority.

Employer retains full control over independent contractor

There is authority for the proposition that an employer is liable for the negligence of **20.67** an independent contractor if the former continues to exercise a significant degree of control over the latter at the time the accident takes place. For example, in the Inner House case of *Steven* v *Thurso Commissioners of Police*,[107] the pursuer raised an action against the Commission (in effect, a local authority) for injuries he sustained when he fell over a heap of rubbish which had been left on a street after nightfall. It was held that the defender was liable since it had retained complete control over the execution of the operations. This case should be contrasted with *Anderson* v *Glasgow Tramway and Omnibuses Co Ltd*.[108] In that case a tramway company was employed by the Post Office to deliver the Royal Mail. The pursuer was injured when she was hit by a tram. It was held that the tramway company, and not the Post Office, was liable since the latter did not enjoy sufficient control over the former to make it vicariously liable for the former's negligence.

Non-delegable legal duties

The common law duty which is imposed on an employer to ensure the safety of his **20.68** employees cannot be delegated to an agent. For example, in *Wilsons and Clyde Coal Co* v *English*,[109] the House of Lords held that the duty which the common law imposed on an employer to maintain a safe system of work could not be delegated to an agent. The employer was, therefore, liable for the injury which a miner sustained as a result of such a system not being maintained by its agent.

Furthermore, if statute, in contradistinction to the common law, imposes an **20.69** absolute duty on an employer to perform a particular task (that is the employer is solely responsible for discharging the relevant duty), the employer remains liable if the duty is negligently discharged by an independent contractor. For example, in the Court of Appeal case of *Robinson* v *Beaconsfield Rural District Council*,[110] which was mentioned above, the Public Health Act 1875[111] imposed a duty upon the authority to empty cesspools in its area. The authority was held liable when its contractor deposited sewage which had been extracted from cesspools on the plaintiff's land. Finally, in *Farraj* v *Kings Healthcare NHS Trust*,[112] the Court of Appeal accepted the proposition that there was persuasive authority to the effect that hospitals owe a non-delegable duty to their patients to ensure they are treated with skill and care.

---

[106] 2009 SC 265 at 274.
[107] (1876) 3 R 535.
[108] (1893) 21 R 318.
[109] [1938] AC 57.
[110] [1911] 2 Ch 188.
[111] Repealed.
[112] [2010] 1 WLR 2139.

Operations affecting the highway

20.70 Where an employer commissions an independent contractor to carry out work either on or adjoining a highway, such work being of a potentially dangerous nature, the employer remains liable should the contractor carry out the work negligently. For example, in *Tarry* v *Ashton*[113] the defendant employed an independent contractor to repair a lamp which was attached to his house. The lamp, which overhung a highway footpath, was not securely fastened and fell on and injured the plaintiff. It was held that the employer was liable for the contractor's negligence.[114]

NO LIABILITY FOR COLLATERAL ACTS OF NEGLIGENCE

20.71 An employer is not liable for the collateral acts of negligence of an independent contractor. This means that there is no liability for acts which are extrinsic to the task the contractor has been commissioned to perform. For example, if I employ a builder to lay a drain near the foundations of my neighbour's house and he decides to dispose of the waste material (which he has extracted in the course of excavating) by burning the waste on site, with the result that the fire spreads to my neighbour's house, which is damaged, I would not be vicariously liable for the damage, simply because the creation of the fire was extrinsic to the prime function of the builder of laying a drain. However, it would be otherwise if the operations which I had commissioned caused my neighbour's house to collapse because its foundations were undermined during the course of the excavations taking place, since, here, the damage caused emanates from the risk which is inherent in the very work I have instructed to be carried out.

20.72   The leading case on the subject is *Padbury* v *Halliday and Greenwood Ltd*.[115] In that case, an independent contractor was employed to fit casement windows in certain premises. A workman negligently put a tool on the sill of the window on which he was working at the time. The wind blew the window open. The tool was knocked off the window sill. A passer-by was injured as a consequence. The Court of Appeal held that the employer was not liable for this injury since the tool in question was not placed on the sill in the ordinary course of work. There was nothing inherently dangerous in the work which the contractor was employed to perform. Rather, it was the *way* in which the work was carried out which created the danger.

LENDING A CAR

20.73 To what extent, if any, is the owner of a vehicle liable for the injury caused by someone else driving that vehicle in a negligent manner? For example, if I were to lend my car to my son in order that he can visit his friend who lives several miles away, and, in the course of driving to his house, my son negligently collides with X, would I be liable to him?

20.74   The leading case is *Morgans* v *Launchbury*.[116] In that case, the defendant owned a car. She lent it to her husband, who took it on a pub crawl. He drank too much alcohol with

---

[113] (1876) 1 QBD 314.
[114] See also *Holliday* v *National Telephone Co* [1899] 2 QB 392.
[115] (1912) 28 TLR 494.
[116] [1973] AC 127.

the result that he could not drive safely. Therefore, he asked his drinking companion to drive the car. He drove the car negligently and injured the plaintiff. The House of Lords held that the defendant was not liable on the basis that the owner of a vehicle could only be liable in respect of the negligent driving of a vehicle if either the driver is the owner's employee or the driver is the owner's authorised agent, that is to say, the driver is driving for, and also on behalf of, the owner. In the instant case, therefore, it was insufficient that the car was simply being used with the consent of the owner. Rather, it was essential that it was being used for the purposes of the owner, under delegation of a task or duty. For Lord Wilberforce,[117] the expression "agent", as far as the facts of the instant case were concerned, was, in effect, simply a shorthand way of stating that the owner of the car was vicariously liable for the negligence of the driver. His Lordship stated:

> "I accept entirely that 'agency' in contexts such as these is merely a concept, the meaning and purpose of which is to say, 'is vicariously liable', and that either expression reflects a judgement of value–*respondeat superior* is the law saying that the owner ought to pay. It is this imperative which the common law has endeavoured to work out through the cases. The owner ought to pay, it says, because he has authorised the act, or requested it, or because the actor is carrying out a task or duty delegated, or because he is in control of the actor's conduct."

Whereas it is essential, for liability to lie, that the driver of the vehicle is acting in the **20.75** interests of the owner, it is not necessary that the driver acts in the sole interest of the owner. For example, in the Court of Appeal case of *Ormrod v Crossville Motor Services Ltd*,[118] the plaintiff, who was the friend of the owner of a car, was driving it from Birkenhead to Monte Carlo to meet the owner of the car, who was taking part in the Monte Carlo Rally. The intention was that after the race the owner and the plaintiff should go on holiday to Switzerland. The plaintiff agreed that, before meeting the owner of the car, the plaintiff should visit a friend in Normandy. The plaintiff collided with an omnibus while the plaintiff was on his way to Dover. In third-party proceedings, brought by the first defendants, it was held that the owner of the car was vicariously liable for the damage done to the omnibus since, at the time of the accident, the plaintiff was driving the car in the joint interest of the owner and himself. The plaintiff was, therefore, the agent of the car owner who was vicariously liable to the driver of the omnibus.

However, for the vehicle owner to be vicariously liable for the negligence of the **20.76** driver of the vehicle, it is necessary that the driver is using the vehicle for a specific purpose on behalf of the owner. This point is illustrated in the Court of Appeal case of *Norwood v Navan*.[119] The facts of the case were homely, indeed. A husband allowed his wife to use his car. She would often use the car in order to go shopping. One day the wife went on a shopping expedition with friends. She drove the car negligently. The plaintiff was injured. It was held that the husband was not vicariously liable for his wife's negligence since, at the time the accident took place, she was not executing a particular task at the behest of her husband. It was insufficient that he simply knew that the car could be used for family shopping when the wife chose to do so.

---

[117] [1973] AC 127 at 135.
[118] [1953] 1 WLR 1120.
[119] [1981] RTR 457.

21 DEFENCES IN DELICT

INTRODUCTION

Even where the pursuer proves all the material facts which are necessary to succeed **21.1** in his action, he may nevertheless be defeated if the defender is able to rely on a substantive defence. In this chapter, we will examine the various defences which may be invoked by a defender in a delictual action. Certain defences are specifically applicable to certain delicts.[1] The defences of self-defence in an assault action[2] and *veritas* in a defamation action are examples of such defences. It is not the purpose of this chapter to examine such defences. They are considered in context. Instead, we will consider defences which are more generally available.

COMMON LAW AUTHORITY

The common law sometimes authorises acts which would otherwise attract civil **21.2** liability. Where there is such common law authority for the defender's actions, this will provide him with a defence to a subsequent delictual action. Thus, a police officer is justified in using reasonable force in the exercise of his duties.[3] The common law also entitles parents to exercise reasonable corporal chastisement over their children. Thus, the defence of reasonable chastisement may be open to a parent in an action of assault at the instance of his child. It is for the appropriate court to determine what is *reasonable* in the circumstances. In *B v Harris*,[4] the court stressed that the key issue was whether the force was reasonable. It was not considered to be relevant that the parent had lost his or her temper at the time. In *Harris*, a 9-year-old girl had slapped her 4-year-old neighbour and as a result was slapped by her own mother. The girl then swore at her mother, who hit her with a leather belt on the thigh, although the mother had aimed the belt at her bottom. The court *at the time* held that such action fell within the bounds of reasonable force. However, subsequent developments lead to the conclusion that *Harris* would now be decided differently. In *A v UK*,[5] a 9-year-old child was beaten with a garden cane by his stepfather. The stepfather invoked the defence of reasonable chastisement and was acquitted of assault on that basis. The

---

[1] See, eg, s 8(4) of the Protection from Harassment Act 1997 which provides: "It shall be a defence to any action of harassment to show that the course of conduct complained of—(a) was authorised by, under or by virtue of any enactment or rule of law; (b) was pursued for the purpose of preventing or detecting crime; or (c) was, in the particular circumstances, reasonable."

[2] See, eg, *Ashmore v Rock Steady Security Ltd* 2006 SLT 207 (defender's plea of self-defence failed).

[3] See *Mason v Orr* (1901) 4 F 220.

[4] 1990 SLT 208.

[5] (1999) 27 EHRR 611.

child applied to the European Court of Human Rights, asserting a violation of Art 3 of the European Convention on Human Rights (prohibition of torture or inhuman and degrading treatment or punishment). The court held that to fall within the scope of Art 3, the ill treatment had to attain a certain level of severity which would depend upon an assessment of the particular circumstances. In the circumstances, the ill treatment did offend Art 3. The Government's failure to provide adequate protection for children against inhuman or degrading treatment or punishment constituted a violation of Art 3. The matter has now been addressed, as far as Scotland is concerned, by the Criminal Justice (Scotland) Act 2003. The Act provides that if the assault involves a blow to the head, shaking or the use of an implement it will not be capable of being justified.[6] It follows that if the circumstances of *Harris* were to come before the Scottish courts today, the defence of reasonable chastisement would be excluded given that the mother's actions involved the use of an implement. The 2003 Act also provides that in considering whether the assault is justifiable the court must have regard to "(a) the nature of what was done, the reason for it and the circumstances in which it took place; (b) its duration and frequency; (c) any effect (whether physical or mental) which it has been shown to have had on the child; (d) the child's age; and (e) the child's personal characteristics (including, without prejudice to the generality of this paragraph, sex and state of health) at the time the thing was done".[7]

It is provided that "[t]he court may also have regard to such other factors as it considers appropriate in the circumstances of the case".[8] If the physical chastisement cannot be justified the child can sue the parent for assault. The defence of reasonable chastisement is available not only to parents but also to those *in loco parentis*, that is, those standing in the position of parents. Thus step-parents and cohabitants would also be able to avail themselves of the defence of common law authority in the event of being sued in assault by a child of their partner, provided, of course that the force used was reasonable in the circumstances. It is also permissible for parents to delegate the right to chastise.[9]

21.3   At common law, schoolteachers, like parents, were entitled to exercise reasonable corporal chastisement over their pupils. There has, however, been statutory intervention in relation to the position of schoolteachers, with the result that corporal punishment in schools cannot now be justified.[10]

STATUTORY AUTHORITY

21.4   Statute may permit the doing of something which would otherwise be actionable.[11] With the recent increase in government regulation, a great many powers have been vested in government officials and public bodies to carry out acts which would be unlawful if done by others. In *X* v *Bedfordshire County Council*,[12] Lord Browne-Wilkinson stated:[13]

---

[6] Criminal Justice (Scotland) Act 2003, s 51(3).
[7] *Ibid*, s 51(1).
[8] *Ibid*, s 51(2).
[9] *Stewart* v *Thain* 1981 SLT (Notes) 2.
[10] See Standards in Scotland's Schools etc Act 2000, s 16.
[11] See, eg, *Bell* v *McGlennan* 1992 SC 41.
[12] [1995] 3 WLR 152.
[13] *Ibid* at 170.

"[M]ost statutes which impose a statutory duty on local authorities confer on the authority a discretion as to the extent to which, and the methods by which such statutory duty is to be performed. It is clear both in principle and from the decided cases that the local authority cannot be liable in damages for doing that which Parliament has authorised. Therefore, if the decisions complained of fall within the ambit of such statutory discretion they cannot be actionable in common law."

Although the defence of statutory (or legislative) authority has, potentially, a very **21.5** wide application, it is most commonly seen in cases of nuisance. Immunity may be expressly granted, but it is more often implied from the terms of the statute. It is a matter of interpretation what powers are conferred by a particular statute. It is also a matter of interpretation whether authority to do something is absolute, irrespective of what damage is caused; or whether the authority is conditional, with damages or interdict being competent in certain circumstances.[14] Two cases serve to illustrate the distinction. In *Managers of the Metropolitan Asylum District v Hill*[15] a local authority was authorised by statute to erect a hospital for infectious diseases. The Metropolitan Poor Act 1867[16] allowed the defendants to "purchase or hire, or to build ... buildings for [hospitals], of such nature and size, and according to such plan, and in such manner, as [they] think fit". The hospital was built near the plaintiff's house. He brought an action on the ground of nuisance as the hospital caused the risk of infection from smallpox. The action was met by the defence of statutory authority. The defence failed, however, as it was held that the local authority had no authority to site the hospital where it would constitute a nuisance, namely in a residential area. Clearly, the statutory authority in question was not absolute. Rather, it was conditional on the hospital being located in a reasonable location.

Vaughan v Taff Vale Railway[17] can be contrasted with the *Metropolitan Asylum* case. **21.6** A railway company was authorised by statute to use locomotive engines. Despite the fact that the engine in question had been carefully constructed, sparks escaped and set fire to the surrounding verge. Eight acres of the plaintiff's plantation were burned and he brought an action for the damage which he had sustained. It was held that the statutory authority conferred an implied use of the surrounding area and thus was a defence to the action. Blackburn J stated:[18] "[W]hen the legislature has sanctioned the use of a locomotive engine, there is no liability for injury caused by using it, so long as every precaution is taken consistent with its use."

The immunity conferred by statutory authority will extend only to the necessary **21.7** and inevitable consequences of the authorised conduct. The onus rests on the defender to show that no more harm was done than was inevitable or really necessary. In *Allen v Gulf Oil Refining Ltd*[19] the defendants set up and began to operate an oil refinery on land which they had compulsorily acquired at Milford Haven. The acquisition of the land was authorised by the Gulf Oil Refining Act 1965. The plaintiffs complained that the smell, noise and vibration which emanated from the refinery constituted a nuisance. The House of Lords held that the 1965 Act conferred statutory immunity

---

[14] See *Lord Advocate v North British Railways* (1894) 2 SLT 71.
[15] (1880–81) LR 6 App Cas 193, HL.
[16] 30 & 31 Vict c 6.
[17] (1860) 5 H & N 679.
[18] *Ibid* at 688.
[19] [1981] AC 1001.

from proceedings where nuisance was the inevitable result of the construction and operation of the oil refinery but the onus was on Gulf Oil to establish that the nuisance was an inevitable result of a refinery on that site.

21.8   It should be noted that the defence of statutory authority does not give the defender free rein to act negligently. In *Geddis v Proprietors of the Bann Reservoir*[20] Lord Blackburn stated[21] that "it is now thoroughly well established that no action will lie for doing that which the legislature has authorised, if it is done without negligence, although it does occasion damage to anyone; but an action does lie for doing that which the legislature has authorised, if it be done negligently".

DAMNUM FATALE

21.9   This defence, which is sometimes known as Act of God or *vis major*, is very rarely invoked in Scots law. There is little modern authority on it. For such a defence to apply, the circumstances giving rise to the action must arise from natural causes without human intervention and they must go beyond anything which is reasonably foreseeable or preventable. Stewart[22] gives the examples of an earthquake in Edinburgh or a volcanic eruption in Thurso. Rodger has observed that the limited Scottish case law has focused on fires[23] and floods.[24] A happening will not amount to *damnum fatale* simply because it rarely happens. This is clear from *Caledonian Railway Co v Greenock Corporation*.[25] There, the Corporation altered the channel of a burn. During an exceptionally heavy rainfall, the burn overflowed and damaged property belonging to the pursuer. The burn, in its natural state, would have carried off all the water which came down the burn on the day of the flood. It was held that an extraordinary rainfall did not amount to *damnum fatale*. The Corporation was held liable.

21.10   Whether a particular happening can be characterised as *damnum fatale* is a question of fact.[26] The defence is applicable in appropriate circumstances in cases of strict liability.[27]

INEVITABLE ACCIDENT

21.11   The defence of inevitable accident is similar to that of *damnum fatale*. The defence can be relied upon where the happening in question could not have been avoided by a reasonable man at the moment at which it happened. It might, for example, apply in the case of a driver who, having had no previous symptoms and who appears to be in

---

[20] (1877–78) LR 3 App Cas 430.
[21] *Ibid* at 455–456.
[22] W J Stewart, *Delict* (4th edn, 2004), p 309.
[23] See, eg, *Burns v Royal Hotel (St Andrews) Ltd* 1958 SC 354 (defender failed to establish that a fire which originated in a hotel boiler room and which damaged the pursuer's car was *damnum fatale*).
[24] B J Rodger in *Delict* (J M Thomson (ed)) (SULI, 2007) at para 8–51.
[25] 1917 SC (HL) 56.
[26] *Caledonian Railway Co v Greenock Corporation* 1917 SC (HL) 56, per Lord Dunedin at 65.
[27] *Burns v Royal Hotel (St Andrews) Ltd* 1958 SC 354.

good health, suddenly has a heart attack at the wheel of the car and another road user is injured as a result.[28]

NECESSITY

In certain circumstances, the defence of necessity may succeed as a defence to a delictual action,[29] although there is little authority on it. This defence is applicable only in cases of emergency. There must be present what a reasonable man would regard as actual danger and the action taken by the defender must also be reasonable[30] (for example, inflicting damage on property in order to save life). In these circumstances, the defender would be able to rely on the defence of necessity. "[T]he safety of human lives belongs to a different scale of values from the safety of property. The two are beyond comparison and the necessity for saving life has at all times been considered a proper ground for inflicting such damage as may be necessary upon another's property."[31] The essence of the defence is that greater injury would have resulted had the defender not acted as he did. Thus, it would be a defence to an action of trespass and damage to another's property that the acts of trespass and infliction of damage were necessary in order to escape from, say, a gang of thugs wielding knives. In *Cope v Sharpe (No 2)*,[32] the defendant successfully relied on the defence of necessity. He had trespassed and set fire to heather on the plaintiff's land in an effort to prevent a fire spreading onto land over which his master had shooting rights.

21.12

If a patient is suffering from a temporary incapacity, say, following an accident, the law permits doctors to do what is necessary to save his life and avoid permanent damage to health. Thus, a doctor clearing the airways of a patient choking to death would be able to rely on the defence of necessity in the event of being sued for assault. In the Canadian case of *Marshall v Curry*,[33] a surgeon, during the course of a hernia operation, discovered that the patient's testicle was diseased. He removed the testicle during the operation and was later sued in battery in respect of that part of the operation to which the patient had not consented, ie the removal of the testicle. The surgeon relied successfully on the defence of necessity because the patient's life would have been endangered had the surgeon not acted as he did. The procedure was held to have been necessary in the circumstances. A Scottish court is likely to take a similar view. It should be noted that in *Marshall v Curry* the patient was unconscious at the time of the discovery of the life-threatening condition. However, if the patient is capable of giving or withholding consent to a particular course of treatment and

21.13

---

[28] Note, however, that Rodger (under reference to *Stanley v Powell* [1891] 1 QB 86) has stated that the defence "appears to be redundant as it predates the modern law of negligence, and is derived from a speciality of English law" (B J Rodger in *Delict* (J M Thomson (ed)) (SULI, 2007) at para 8–51). Similar views have been expressed by English commentators. Thus, W V H Rogers states: "It ... seems that the conception of inevitable accident has no longer any useful function and it is doubtful whether much advantage is gained by the continued use of the phrase" (Winfield and Jolowicz, *Tort* (18th edn, 2010) at p 1164).

[29] The defence may also operate in a criminal context – see the discussion in *Moss v Howdle* 1997 JC 123 (defence failed in the context of a speeding charge where the driver was carrying a passenger whom he thought to be seriously ill).

[30] See *Cope v Sharpe (No 2)* [1912] 1 KB 496.

[31] Per Devlin J in *Southport Corporation v Esso Petroleum Ltd* [1953] 3 WLR 773 at 779.

[32] [1912] 1 KB 496.

[33] [1933] 3 DLR 260.

refuses to consent, the doctor could not proceed in the face of that objection. If he did, he would be liable for assault and he could not rely on the defence of necessity in those circumstances. Nor would the doctor be entitled to take advantage of unconsciousness to carry out a procedure which is not "necessary", albeit that it might be *convenient* to perform the procedure on the spot.[34]

EXCLUSION OF DELICTUAL REMEDIES BY CONTRACT

21.14   At common law it was possible to exclude delictual liability by way of contractual agreement or notice.[35] Account must now be taken of the provisions of the Unfair Contract Terms Act 1977. Section 16 of the Act, which deals with liability for breach of duty, provides that any such attempt to exclude liability for death or personal injury arising from breach of duty in the course of business is void. Any other attempt to exclude liability will be ineffective unless it is fair and reasonable in the circumstances.

RES JUDICATA[36]

21.15   This defence is to the effect that the issue has already been litigated between the same parties and has been determined by a competent court.[37] It is a complete defence and has long been recognised as such.

> "It has been accepted for good reason that in individual disputes a single action and one final judgment is sufficient, lest otherwise the ambit of suits be greatly increased and cause very great and insurmountable difficulty, especially if different judgments are pronounced. To be subject to a defence of *res judicata* is therefore frequent."[38]

21.16   The defence was invoked, albeit unsuccessfully, in *Edinburgh & District Water Trs v Clippens Oil Co.*[39] The Trustees had laid pipes to carry water. By the Waterworks Clauses Act 1847, owners of adjacent minerals were precluded from working the minerals within 40 yards of the pipe track until they had given statutory notice to the undertaker of their intention to work them. The Trustees sought interdict against Clippens to prevent them working the minerals within 40 yards of the pipe on the grounds that they had failed to comply with the provisions as to notice and that, if they did have the right to work them, their manner of work violated the 1847 Act. The court

---

[34] See *Re F* [1990] 2 AC 1, per Lord Goff at 74–77. For a fuller discussion of the position of the unconscious patient and the principle of necessity, see J K Mason and G T Laurie, *Mason and McCall Smith's Law and Medical Ethics* (8th edn, 2011), paras 4.09–4.13.

[35] At common law, the *contra proferentem* rule applied with the result that a contract attempting to exclude liability, if ambiguous, would be construed against the *proferens*, that is, against the person seeking to rely on the exclusion. See, eg, *North of Scotland Hydro Electric Board v D & R Taylor* 1956 SC 1; *Smith v UMB Chrysler (Scotland) Ltd* 1978 SC (HL) 1.

[36] For a more detailed discussion, see I D Macphail, *Sheriff Court Practice* (Sheriff Welsh, QC (ed), (SULI, 3rd edn, 2006), vol 1, paras 2.104–2.109.

[37] For an interesting discussion of the cases in which insurance companies and their insured have brought separate actions against the same defender in respect of different heads of loss stemming from the same incident, see A A Summers, "Res judicata and excess clauses in insurance contracts" 1996 SLT 189.

[38] Digest, 44, 2, 6.

[39] (1899) 1 F 899.

refused interdict. A subsequent common law action was raised, seeking declarator to the effect that the Trustees had a right to have their pipe supported. In the second action, the Trustees also sought interdict against the defenders working the minerals adjacent to or under the pipe so as to injure or bring the pipe down. The defenders argued that the matter was *res judicata*. However, the plea of *res judicata* was repelled. The question of the common law right of support had not been raised in the former action and was a new ground of action. Accordingly, the pursuers were held entitled to bring a new action based on different grounds.

The defence of *res judicata* is often invoked when a claim is brought first at common **21.17** law and is later brought averring breach of a statutory provision. In *Matuszczyk v NCB*,[40] a miner raised an action against the National Coal Board (NCB), averring (a) that the NCB had failed to provide a safe system of work and (b) that a shotfirer had breached various common law duties. The defender was assoilzied. The miner proceeded to raise a second action for the same injuries based on breach of statute, namely the Coal Mines (Training) General Regulations 1945. The Lord Ordinary (Strachan) held that, in the circumstances, the common law and statutory actions were based on the same ground and the plea of *res judicata* was upheld. The question to be answered in the second action was the same as the question raised in the first action which had already been answered. In both instances, the pursuer's case was dependent on his establishing that the accident was caused by the fault of the defender.

A plea of *res judicata* will be upheld where there is identity as to the following **21.18** matters:

(1) the parties;
(2) the subject-matter;
(3) the *media concludendi* – the two suits must present one and the same ground of action so that the specific point raised in the second suit must have been directly raised and concluded by the judgment of the first.

VOLENTI NON FIT INJURIA

The defence of *volenti non fit injuria* can be literally translated as "a wrongful act is not **21.19** done to one who is willing". It is sometimes referred to as the pursuer's voluntary assumption of risk.[41] This defence is one of considerable antiquity and its origins can be traced back to the time of Aristotle.[42] Essentially, what the defence means is that where a person consents to run the risk of injury caused by another, he cannot thereafter claim damages in respect of an injury caused by the risk which he accepted.[43] According to Lord Herschell, "[t]he maxim is founded on good sense and justice. One

---

[40] 1955 SC 418.
[41] See the discussion by Lord Nimmo Smith in *McTear v Imperial Tobacco Ltd* 2005 2 SC 1 as to the various ways in which the defence might be articulated (at para 7.205).
[42] See T Ingham, "A history of the defence of *volenti non fit injuria*" 1981 JR 1.
[43] See *Frost v E K Cole Ltd* 1949 SLT (Notes) 41 where Lord Guthrie observed (at 41): "The maxim is appropriate to a case where [the pursuer] suffers by the act of another, but is held to have voluntarily accepted the risk of that act."

who has invited or assented to an act being done towards him cannot, when he suffers from it, complain of it as a wrong".[44]

21.20　　*Volenti* operates as a complete defence to an action. The onus of proving that the pursuer was *volens* rests on the defender.[45] The defence must be specifically pled if it is to be relied upon at proof.

21.21　　In *Morris* v *Murray*[46] the plaintiff had spent an afternoon drinking with the defendant. The defendant consumed the equivalent of 17 whiskies. The defendant had a pilot's licence and following the drinking session both men went for a flight in the defendant's light aircraft. The defendant took off downwind in poor flying conditions. The aircraft crashed soon after take-off and the pilot was killed. The plaintiff was injured. He raised an action against the pilot's representatives. They successfully relied on the defence of *volenti*. The Court of Appeal held that the plaintiff had willingly boarded the aircraft in the knowledge that the pilot was drunk and that he therefore would not be capable of exercising reasonable care. The court concluded that the plaintiff was not so insensible that he could not appreciate the nature and extent of the risk inherent in the expedition.

21.22　　For the defence to apply, the defender requires to show that the pursuer, with full knowledge of the nature and extent of the risk he ran, freely and voluntarily agreed to incur it. The pursuer must be both *sciens et volens*,[47] that is, there must be both knowledge of the risk *and* evidence of acceptance of the risk. Thus, in *White* v *Blackmore and Ors*[48] an action in respect of the death of a spectator at a "jalopy" (ie old car) racing event was not defeated by the defence of *volenti*. The deceased had no knowledge of the risk caused by the defendants' failure to take proper precautions at the event.[49] Where the pursuer does have the requisite knowledge of the risk, that, in itself, is insufficient to establish the defence. There must also be evidence of acceptance of the risk.[50] Although the pursuer's consent can be either express or inferred from the whole circumstances,[51] it must be real and freely given. The pursuer must have acted voluntarily, that is, he must have been able to exercise a free choice. Consent extracted by violence, or threats thereof, is not a real consent.

21.23　　The agreement to run the risk is construed narrowly, against the defender. *Slater* v *Clay Cross Co Ltd* [52] illustrates this point. A woman was struck by a train while walking along a narrow railway tunnel. She and other villagers had been in the habit of using the tunnel as a shortcut. The train driver was found to have been negligent in failing to sound the train's whistle and slow down when entering the tunnel. The woman was found to have been contributorily negligent, ie partly to blame for her injuries, but

---

[44] *Smith* v *Baker & Sons* [1891] AC 325 at 360.
[45] See, eg, *McTear* v *Imperial Tobacco Ltd* 2005 2 SC 1, per Lord Nimmo Smith at para 7.204.
[46] [1991] 2 WLR 195.
[47] See *Merrington* v *Ironbridge Metal Works Ltd* [1952] 2 All ER 1101. (*Volenti* did not apply to a claim by a part-time fireman who went to deal with a fire at a factory. He was injured in a subsequent explosion which had been caused by the presence of aluminium and carbon particles, of which he was unaware.)
[48] [1972] 2 QB 651.
[49] It is not enough that the pursuer *ought to have known* of the risk to which he was exposing himself. He must in fact have known of the risk which he was running: see *Toms* v *Royal Mail Group plc* 2006 SLT 431, per Lord Glennie at para 37.
[50] See *Smith* v *Baker & Sons* [1891] AC 325 (discussed below).
[51] See, eg, *ICI* v *Shatwell* [1965] AC 656. See, also, the observations of Lord Nimmo Smith in *McTear* v *Imperial Tobacco Ltd* 2005 2 SC 1 at para 7.205.
[52] [1956] 2 QB 264.

she was held not to have been *volens*. Denning LJ stated:[53] "It seems to me that when this lady walked in the tunnel, although it may be said that she voluntarily took the risk of danger from the running of the railway in the ordinary and accustomed way, nevertheless she did not take the risk of negligence by the driver."

It has been said that "[i]n Scotland the plea of *volenti* has never been regarded as being a denial of the duty, but rather as a consent to accept the consequences of a breach of the duty".[54] The basis of the *volenti* defence is not therefore that there was no negligence, rather it is that the pursuer waives his right to an action of negligence. Lord Denning MR stated in *Nettleship* v *Weston*:[55]   **21.24**

"Knowledge of the risk of injury is not enough. Nor is a willingness to take the risk of injury. Nothing will suffice short of an agreement to waive any claim for negligence. The plaintiff must agree either expressly or impliedly, to waive any claim for any injury that may befall him due to the lack of reasonable care by the defendant, or more accurately, due to the failure of the defendant to measure up to the standard of care that the law requires of him."   **21.25**

In *Nettleship*, the defendant had been receiving driving lessons from the plaintiff and on one occasion the plaintiff was injured when the defendant struck a lamp-post. The instructor sued his pupil. The defence of *volenti* was unsuccessful. The plaintiff had asked for and had obtained an assurance that there was a policy of insurance in force which covered injury to a passenger. By checking as to his position under the car insurance before agreeing to instruct the defendant, the plaintiff had shown expressly that he did not consent to run the risk of injury.

The consent, whether express or inferred, must be to the *particular* risk involved in the accident. Professor Walker has observed:[56] "If the plea is to succeed it must be shown not that the pursuer consented to take the risk of *some* harm befalling him, but that he consented to take the risk of *the particular kind* of harm which in fact befell him." This point is illustrated in *Fowler* v *Tierney*.[57] A girl was injured while riding pillion on a motor scooter, the accident having been caused by the driver. It was established that the defender was initially unwilling to give the pursuer a lift because he was only a provisional licence holder and, as such, was not permitted to take pillion passengers. The court held that the girl was willing to take the risk of trouble with the police but was not waiving her rights with regard to injury caused by the driver's negligence. The *volenti* defence did not succeed.   **21.26**

The defence of *volenti* can be excluded by statute. Thus s 149 of the Road Traffic Act 1988 excludes the defence of *volenti* in an action brought by a passenger in a negligently driven vehicle in circumstances where insurance is necessary by law.[58] The provision is designed to prevent passengers being denied the benefits of third party liability insurance which users of motor vehicles are obliged to hold. The statutory   **21.27**

---

[53] [1956] 2 QB 264 at 271.
[54] *Bankhead* v *McCarthy* 1963 SC 263, per Lord Walker at 265 (under reference to *Stewart's Exrx* v *Clyde Navigation Trs* 1946 SC 317). For the English approach, see the discussion by Rodger in *Delict* (Thomson (ed)) at para 8–39.
[55] [1971] 2 QB 691 at 701.
[56] D M Walker, *The Law of Delict in Scotland* (2nd edn, 1981), p 347.
[57] 1974 SLT (Notes) 23.
[58] At one time, the defence could succeed in these circumstances – see the observations of Lord Kilbrandon in *McCaig* v *Langan* 1964 SLT 121 at 124.

exclusion of the defence is illustrated in the Inner House decision of *Winnik v Dick*.[59] In that case, which was decided under the analogous provision in the earlier Road Traffic Act 1972, the parties to the action had been drinking together in a public house. The pursuer then took a lift in the defender's car and was injured. The defender attempted to rely on the defence of *volenti* but the court held that the defence was barred by statute.[60]

21.28   It has been noted above that *volenti* is a complete defence to an action. The effect of a successful plea of *volenti* is therefore that the pursuer's claim fails completely. The court has no power to award a lesser amount of damages, as it does where a successful plea of contributory negligence is made.

21.29   It appears that the defence of *volenti* is applicable only to a case of *future* negligence, it having been judicially stated that "[w]here the negligence has already occurred, and the pursuer steps into the situation created thereby, with his eyes open, the proper analysis may be not *volenti* but *novus actus interveniens*".[61] In *Sabri-Tabrizi v Lothian Health Board*,[62] the pursuer underwent a sterilisation procedure but, as a result of negligence, it failed and the pursuer subsequently became pregnant. Following a termination, she became pregnant again and gave birth to a stillborn child. She sought damages from the Health Board. The Board argued that the real cause of the pursuer's pregnancy was her decision to have intercourse in the knowledge that the sterilisation had failed. Such action, the Health Board argued, amounted to a *novus actus interveniens*. The Lord Ordinary (Nimmo Smith) accepted that argument. The Health Board also argued that the pursuer had taken the risk of pregnancy on herself and that the maxim *volenti non fit injuria* applied. The Lord Ordinary held, however, that the acceptance of risk necessary for the application of the maxim must occur either before or at the same time as the negligent act or omission. That was clearly not so in the instant case.

21.30   We will now look at the application of the defence in relation to particular areas of activity.

OCCUPIERS

21.31   The defence of *volenti* may be available to the occupier of premises on which the pursuer is injured. In *Titchener v British Railways Board*[63] a railway line was bordered by a dilapidated fence. The pursuer, who was aged 15, went through one of the gaps in the fence in order to cross the railway line. She was struck by a train and was severely injured as a result. She sued the defenders, averring that they were in breach of their duty to take reasonable care in terms of the Occupiers' Liability (Scotland) Act 1960. The girl had admitted that she was aware of the railway line's existence and of the danger of going onto it. In these circumstances, had a breach of duty been made out (which

---

[59] 1984 SLT 185.
[60] *Winnik* was subsequently approved and applied in *Pitts v Hunt* [1991] 1 QB 24 (discussed below) where the court took the view that the *volenti* defence would have applied on the facts of the case had it not been for the statutory exclusion in the Road Traffic Act 1972.
[61] *Toms v Royal Mail Group plc* 2006 SLT 431, per Lord Glennie at para 37. See, also, *McTear v Imperial Tobacco Ltd* 2005 2 SC 1, per Lord Nimmo Smith at 7.206.
[62] 1998 SC 373.
[63] 1984 SC (HL) 34.

it was not), the House of Lords held that the defence of *volenti* would have applied as the pursuer had willingly accepted the risk of walking onto the line.[64] Unlike the case of *Slater* v *Clay Cross Co Ltd*[65] (discussed above), there was no suggestion in *Titchener* that the train was being driven in a negligent manner.

The position of the pursuer in *Titchener* can be contrasted with the position of the **21.32** injured party in *McGlone* v *British Railways Board*.[66] There, a 12-year-old boy suffered injury when he climbed a transformer on premises occupied by the defenders. The transformer was surrounded on three sides by a strongly constructed mesh fence. There was no fence on the side nearest the railway line. Warning notices bearing the words "Danger – Overhead live wires" had been attached to the fence. The boy, having got through some barbed wire and having climbed the transformer, sustained severe burning from electric shock when his arm came into contact with the live wires. His father raised an action against the defenders under the Occupiers' Liability (Scotland) Act 1960. The defenders sought to rely on the defence of *volenti non fit injuria* but the House of Lords took the view that the boy did not have a proper appreciation of the danger from live wires.[67] (In the event, the defenders were found not to have been in breach of duty.)

LANDLORDS

Where a tenant continues in occupation of property in the knowledge of a specific risk, **21.33** such continued occupation does not demonstrate that the tenant willingly accepts the risk. In *Hughes' Tutrix* v *Glasgow District Council*[68] a tenant raised an action as tutrix of a child who had been injured when she caught her hand on a broken toilet bowl. The action was raised against the landlords, it being averred that they were in breach of s 3(1) of the Occupiers' Liability (Scotland) Act 1960 in respect of their failure to repair the bowl despite several complaints having been made to them in respect of the bowl's condition. The defender pled *volenti*, contending that by continuing to reside in the premises while aware of the condition of the toilet bowl, the pursuer had accepted the danger and was thereby barred from asserting her claim. The sheriff held that the defender had failed to demonstrate that the pursuer had "willingly" accepted the danger and even if the defender had shown such willing acceptance on the pursuer's

---

[64] Specific provision for the *volenti* defence is made under s 2(3) of the Occupiers' Liability (Scotland) Act 1960. See, also, *Devlin* v *Strathclyde RC* 1993 SLT 699. Lord Coulsfield held that, had there been a breach of duty (which there was not), the defence of *volenti* would have applied against a 14-year-old boy who was killed when he fell through a skylight on a school roof. The deceased had jumped on the skylight during a game of tig, whereupon the skylight shattered and he fell to his death. Lord Coulsfield expressed his agreement (at 703) with Lord Hailsham LC in *Titchener* to the effect that the different pleas of sole fault and *volenti* "may involve little more than different ways of formulating the same result". See, also, *Ratcliff* v *McConnell and Ors* [1999] 1 WLR 670 (19-year-old college student was aware of and accepted the risk of diving into an open-air college swimming pool; he sustained severe injuries when he hit his head on the bottom).

[65] [1956] 2 QB 264.

[66] 1966 SC 1.

[67] See *ibid*, per Lord Reid at 13. See, also, the observations of Lord Pearce at 18: "Had the intruder been a young man of, say, 18 years, such an inference [of acceptance of the risk] would have been wholly justified on the facts of this case … If an invader with appreciation of the possible consequences defies the exclusion and the warning, the reasonable inference is that he is accepting the risk and taking the consequences on his own head. But since this was a boy of twelve years, who was believed when he said that he did not appreciate the danger, it was, in my opinion, right to reject the inference."

[68] 1982 SLT (Sh Ct) 70.

part, it was impossible to suggest that the child herself had willingly accepted the risk of the state of the bowl. Accordingly, the defender's plea of *volenti* was rejected.

SPORTING EVENTS[69]

Spectators

21.34 The plea of *volenti* is often raised successfully where the injury occurs to a spectator at a sporting event. By attending, the spectator takes the risk of an error of judgment by a participant, but he does not consent to a reckless disregard for his own safety. This is illustrated in *Wooldridge* v *Sumner*.[70] There was a competition at a horse show. A horse rounded a bend at considerable speed, apparently out of control. A photographer fell into the horse's path in fright and was injured. Diplock LJ concluded that the defendant was guilty of an error of judgement only. The defence of *volenti* would not prevail against a spectator where there was evidence of a reckless disregard for the spectator's safety but there was no suggestion of such a reckless disregard here. The defence of *volenti* was accordingly upheld. Diplock LJ stated the position in the following terms:[71]

> "A person attending a game or competition takes the risk of any damage caused to him by any act of a participant done in the course of and for the purposes of the game or competition, notwithstanding that such an act may involve an error of judgment or lapse of skill, unless the participant's conduct is such as to evince a reckless disregard of the spectator's safety."[72]

Participants

21.35 Where, in a sporting activity, an injury is inflicted by one participant on another participant, the availability of the defence of *volenti* will depend on the particular circumstances. Participants are deemed to impliedly consent to the risk of injury which is incidental to the sport in question. They are not considered to have consented to the use of unnecessary force.[73] Thus a rugby or football player would be considered to have consented to a fair tackle upon him but he would certainly not be *volens* in relation to a deliberate punch on the nose.[74] In *Smoldon* v *Whitworth*,[75] the plaintiff was seriously injured when his neck was broken after a scrum collapsed during a rugby match. It was held that the referee had failed to ensure that the standard sequence of engagement was used and that the standard of refereeing had fallen below an acceptable standard. The referee was not entitled to argue that the plaintiff had consented to the risk of injury by participating voluntarily in the scrum. While the plaintiff might have consented to the ordinary risks of the game, he could not be said to have agreed to the referee's breach of duty in failing to apply the rules intended to protect players from injury.

---

[69] See, generally, B Gardiner, "Liability for Sporting Injuries" 2008 JPIL 16.
[70] [1962] 2 All ER 978.
[71] *Ibid* at 989–990.
[72] Compare *White* v *Blackmore and Ors* [1972] 2 QB 651.
[73] See *ibid*.
[74] For an interesting discussion, see A Duff, "Civil actions and sporting injuries sustained by professional footballers" 1994 SLT 175.
[75] 1997 PIQR P133.

The defence of *volenti* was again rejected in *Lewis* v *Buckpool Golf Club*.[76] There, a **21.36** golfer who was putting on the fourth green of a golf course was struck by a golf ball which had been mis-hit by the second defender who was teeing off on the fifth hole. The second defender attempted to rely on the defence of *volenti non fit injuria*. He argued that the pursuer had assumed the risk of injury in going on to the green in the knowledge that he could not be relied on to drive down the fairway, but could put his ball anywhere. That argument was rejected. The sheriff principal stated:[77]

> "[T]he lack of care on which the pursuer founds in this case is not the bad stroke which the second defender made when he hit the ball with the toe instead of with the face of the club, but the fact that, knowing that he might make such a mis-hit and injure the pursuer if he did so, he nevertheless drove off. There is nothing in the act of the pursuer in approaching the fourth green while the second defender was on the fifth tee which can be construed as a consent to the second defender's driving off before the pursuer and his party had finished putting and left the green. The pursuer may have known that the second defender was a golfer of limited skill, and therefore more likely than a good golfer to mis-hit the ball when he drove it. But it does not follow that he knew that the second defender would drive off when there was a real risk that the ball might hit someone on the fourth green, or that he consented to run that risk. There is therefore no basis for the plea of *volenti non fit injuria*."

EMPLOYMENT SITUATIONS

In an employment context, the defence of *volenti* very rarely succeeds.[78] This is because **21.37** it is difficult to establish that an employee has any real freedom of choice in relation to acceptance of the risk of injury because he works under economic pressure. It has been stated that "[v]olenti, as a defence has, perhaps, been in retreat during this century – certainly in relation to master and servant cases".[79] In *Bowater* v *Rowley Regis Corporation*,[80] Goddard LJ pointed out that, in an employment context, the courts should apply the *volenti* defence with "extreme caution".[81] There, a carter, despite his protests, was ordered by his employer to take out a horse which was known to be unsafe. He was injured when he was thrown from the cart when the horse bolted. Scott LJ observed:[82] "[A] man cannot be said to be truly willing unless he is in a position to choose freely and freedom of choice predicates, not only full knowledge of the circumstances ... but the absence of any feeling of constraint so that nothing shall interfere with the freedom of his will."

In *Smith* v *Baker & Sons*[83] the plaintiff was employed by the defendant to drill holes **21.38** in rocks. The plaintiff was aware that a crane regularly swung loads of stones over his head. A stone fell and injured him and the employer defendant relied on the defence of *volenti*, namely that the plaintiff had consented to run the risk of injury from falling stones. The court held, however, that the plaintiff had continued to work *knowing* the

---

[76] 1993 SLT (Sh Ct) 43.
[77] *Ibid* at 46.
[78] *Baddeley* v *Earl Granville* (1887) 19 QBD 423 (see, in particular, the observations of Wills J at 426–427); *Wheeler* v *New Merton Board Mills* [1933] 2 KB 669.
[79] *Morris* v *Murray* [1991] 2 WLR 195, per Fox LJ at 204.
[80] [1944] KB 476.
[81] *Ibid* at 480–481.
[82] *Ibid* at 479.
[83] [1891] AC 325.

risk, but he had not voluntarily *accepted* the risk. Indeed, several complaints had been made to management raising concerns about the danger. Therefore, the plaintiff may have been *sciens* (knowing) but he was not *volens* (willing). To continue working did not indicate that the plaintiff was *volens*.[84] In *Stewart's Exrx* v *Clyde Navigation Tr*,[85] a docker was injured by a crane which was being operated without a signaller. It was held that the defence of *volenti* had not been established. There was no proof that the docker knew that there was no signaller and, in any event, the mere fact that he had continued at his work was insufficient to establish that he had accepted the risk of working without a signaller.

21.39 The reluctance of the courts to hold an employee to be *volens* is also illustrated in *Monaghan* v *W H Rhodes & Son*.[86] There, iron ladders, which were normally used when loading a ship, were blocked. The plaintiff therefore attempted to use a Jacob's ladder which was a type of rope ladder, which was fastened at the top to the coamings of the hatch and which swung loose some feet from the bottom of the hold. Going up the ladder, the plaintiff's hand caught between the ladder and the coamings and, trying to free himself, the plaintiff fell to the bottom of the hold and was severely injured. He was held not to be *volens*, there being no sufficient evidence that he undertook the risk of this dangerous ladder.

21.40 If, in an employment context, there is an express contract term to the effect that an employee will accept a certain risk of injury, that will, of course, be governed by the Unfair Contract Terms Act 1977. A contractual term which attempts to exclude or limit liability for death or personal injury arising from breach of duty in the course of business is void.[87]

RESCUERS

21.41 A person will not be considered to be *volens* if he tries to save life or rescue valuable property. This is because he is not held to have freely and voluntarily assumed the risk of injury where he is acting under a social or moral duty. No doubt, considerations of policy lie behind the law's concession to rescuers in this area. In other words, the law clearly wishes to encourage people to rescue rather than deter them. The leading case is that of *Baker* v *T E Hopkins & Son Ltd*.[88] The defendants operated a petrol-driven pump to clear out a well. The pump released carbon monoxide fumes. Realising the danger, the employer instructed his employees not to go down the well until he arrived. However, two employees did go down the well and were overcome by fumes. A doctor was summoned to give medical aid and he too was advised not to go down the well. However, in an effort to save the two men who were in difficulty, the doctor tied a rope around himself and went down the well, leaving instructions that he should be hauled up in the event of his getting into difficulty. However, the rope caught on an obstruction and all three men perished. The executors of the doctor sued the men's employer. Wilmer LJ pointed out:[89] "Bearing in mind that danger invites rescue, the court should not be astute to accept criticism of the rescuer's conduct from

---

[84] See, also, *Jeffrey* v *Donald* (1901) 9 SLT 199.
[85] 1946 SC 317.
[86] [1920] 1 KB 487.
[87] Section 16, as amended by the Law Reform (Miscellaneous Provisions) (Scotland) Act 1990, s 68.
[88] [1959] 1 WLR 966.
[89] *Ibid* at 984.

the wrongdoer who created the danger." The court concluded that the doctor had not been *volens*.

In *Cutler* v *United Dairies (London) Ltd*,[90] on the other hand, the defence of *volenti* **21.42** served to defeat the claim of the plaintiff who was injured while attempting to restrain a horse which had bolted. Slesser LJ stated:[91] "The appellants can ... properly say that the respondent agreed to accept freely and voluntarily, with full knowledge of the risk he ran, the chances of the injury he suffered. The case is one where the maxim *volenti non fit injuria* applies."

There is no special principle which prevents firemen from claiming damages for **21.43** injuries sustained as a result of fighting a negligently started fire.[92]

SELF-HARM

In *Reeves* v *Commissioner of Police of the Metropolis*,[93] a prisoner in police custody **21.44** committed suicide by hanging himself, using his shirt as a ligature. He was able to do this because a hatch on his cell door had been left open. The police owed the deceased a duty to prevent him from harming himself. It was held that the defence of *volenti* could not be relied upon where the act of suicide was the very act which the defendant had a duty to prevent. The very existence of the duty foreclosed the *volenti* argument. Lord Jauncey of Tullichettle rationalised the decision in the following manner:[94] "If the defence were available in circumstances such as the present where a deceased was known to have suicidal tendencies it would effectively negative the effect of any duty of care in respect of such suicide."[95]

VOLENTI AND BREACH OF STATUTORY DUTY

The plea of *volenti* is not normally available in breach of statutory duty cases,[96] it being **21.45** considered contrary to public policy to allow persons to assume a risk against which statute has provided protection. However, it can succeed in limited circumstances if public policy points the other way. The leading case is *ICI Ltd* v *Shatwell*.[97] There, two experienced shotfirers, who were aware of the statutory regulations incumbent upon them, decided to act in breach of those regulations. Both men were injured. One raised an action against the employer, ICI, seeking to hold the latter vicariously liable in respect of his fellow worker's breach. The employers in the instant case were not themselves in breach of statutory duty. The workmen had combined *deliberately* to disobey an order although they were aware of the risk involved in so doing. In

---

[90] [1933] 2 KB 297.
[91] *Ibid* at 306.
[92] *Ogwo* v *Taylor* [1988] AC 431. See, also, *Flannigan* v *British Dyewood Co Ltd* 1970 SC 110.
[93] [2000] 1 AC 360.
[94] *Ibid* at 375.
[95] See, also, *Kirkham* v *Chief Constable of the Greater Manchester Police* [1990] 2 QB 283. The defence of *volenti* in respect of an act of suicide was "inappropriate where the act of the deceased relied on is the very act which the duty cast upon the defendant required him to prevent" (per Farquharson LJ at 295). See, also, *Corr* v *IBC Vehicles Ltd* [2008] 1 AC 884. (A worker who committed suicide while in a state of depression induced by an industrial accident was not *volens*. Lord Bingham stated (at para 18): "[His suicide] was not something to which [the deceased] consented voluntarily and with his eyes open but an act performed because of the psychological condition which the employer's breach of duty had induced.")
[96] See, *eg*, *Baddeley* v *Earl Granville* (1887) 19 QBD 423; *Wheeler* v *New Merton Board Mills* [1933] 2 KB 669.
[97] [1965] AC 656.

the court's view, it was necessary to distinguish deliberate disobedience from mere carelessness. In a deliberate breach, as was the case here, both men were to blame. The employer therefore could not be held vicariously liable. The House of Lords did support the general principle that assumption of risk will not usually exclude a claim by an employee against his employer. However, in the case of a flagrant disregard of a safety rule by fellow employees, their Lordships were not prepared to allow recovery through the application of vicarious liability. ICI's defence of *volenti* was therefore upheld.[98]

21.46   A similar case is that of *Hugh v National Coal Board*.[99] There, an apprentice and other colliery workers were travelling on a train towards a lift cage after their shift. While the train was still in motion, the apprentice and others alighted and raced towards the cage. In the rush, the apprentice was knocked over and his foot was injured by a moving wheel of the train. The practice of jumping from a moving train was prohibited by statute (as well as by the employers) and the men were aware of the attendant risk of injury. The apprentice sought damages from his employers. He contended that his fellow employees were in breach of statutory duty and that his employers were vicariously liable in respect of that breach. In the circumstances, the Lord Ordinary (Keith) held that the employers were entitled to rely on the defence of *volenti non fit injuria*.

21.47   Certain statutes make provision for a statutory form of the *volenti* defence.[100]

21.48   The defence of *volenti* has a more limited application than the defence of contributory negligence, to which we now turn our attention.

CONTRIBUTORY NEGLIGENCE

21.49   Contributory negligence is a defence which is frequently invoked by the defender in a delictual action. In fact, in personal injury cases it is invoked almost as a matter of routine. Contributory negligence is fault on the part of the pursuer which is jointly causative of his loss or injury along with the fault of the defender. In other words, the pursuer is partly to blame for his own loss or injury. The pursuer need not have breached a duty of care to the defender for the defence to apply.[101]

THE COMMON LAW POSITION

21.50   At common law, contributory negligence (like *volenti*) was a complete defence to an action for damages.[102] If the pursuer had contributed to his loss by his own negligent acts or omissions, he was regarded as being solely responsible for the harm caused. Even if the pursuer was only one-tenth to blame for his injuries, he recovered nothing under the common law doctrine. The law became very convoluted as a result of this

---

[98] See, also, *McMullen v National Coal Board* [1982] ICR 148.
[99] 1972 SC 252.
[100] The Occupiers' Liability (Scotland) Act 1960, s 2(3). See *McGlone v British Railways Board* 1966 SC (HL) 1; *Titchener v British Railways Board* 1984 SC (HL) 34; the Animals (Scotland) Act 1987, s 2(1)(b).
[101] See *Nance v British Columbia Electric Ry* [1951] AC 601, per Viscount Simon at 611: "[W]hen contributory negligence is set up as a defence, its existence does not depend on any duty owed by the injured party to the party sued, and all that is necessary to establish such a defence is to prove … that the injured party did not in his own interest take reasonable care of himself and contributed, by this want of care, to his own injury."
[102] See *Butterfield v Forrester* (1809) 11 East 70.

"all or nothing" rule and a great deal of judicial juggling took place in an attempt to evade the effects of the rule which were often considered to work an injustice. The judges began to develop various rules such as the "last opportunity" rule[103] in an effort to circumvent the consequences of the common law rule. The effect of the "last opportunity" rule was that the person who had the last opportunity of avoiding the accident was treated as having caused it. In *Davies* v *Mann*,[104] the plaintiff negligently left his donkey on the highway. The defendant, travelling too fast on his wagon, drove into the donkey and killed it. The plaintiff was allowed to recover because the defendant had the last opportunity of avoiding the accident. However, the "last opportunity" rule was also open to criticism as it resulted in the person whose negligence came last being held wholly responsible for the damage. Sometimes, rather than focusing on the chronological sequence of events, the courts would instead attempt to isolate what was the "decisive and immediate cause" of the pursuer's loss. In *Taylor* v *Dumbarton Tramways Co*,[105] a 2-year-old child playing on a roadway suffered injury when a car drove off without it first being established that there was no child to the south side of the car. Recovery was permitted. The Lord Chancellor (Finlay) stated:[106]

> "Even granting that there was some negligence in leaving a child of such tender years in the street without more efficient guidance, yet that negligence was not part of the transaction itself in which the accident occurred. Historically it led up to it, but the accident was really ... entirely caused by the omission of those in charge of the car to look out to see whether there was any child about on the south side as well as on the north side of the car."

Viscount Haldane made the following observations:[107]   **21.51**

> "[I]n order that contributory negligence may be an answer to the plaintiff's action, the negligence which has contributed must have been shown to be negligence which actually and directly led in itself to the accident; it must not be a negligence independent of the act which caused the accident. The question always is, Which was the decisive and immediate cause? and, if the decisive and immediate cause was the negligence of the defender, then it does not matter that there was negligence on the part of the pursuer apart from which he would not have been in the position which brought about the injury by the accident."

The common law inevitably involved a degree of artifice as the judiciary, by means   **21.52** of various rules and subtle devices, attempted to avoid a finding of a small degree of contributory negligence, given that such a finding would defeat the claim altogether. The common law, however, was altered by the Law Reform (Contributory Negligence) Act 1945 and a fairer and more realistic[108] approach emerged.

---

[103] See *Carse* v *NB Steam Packet Co* (1895) 2 SLT 577.
[104] (1842) 10 M & W 546.
[105] 1918 SC (HL) 96.
[106] *Ibid* at 103–104.
[107] *Ibid* at 105–106.
[108] This point was acknowledged by Lord Porter in *Stapley* v *Gypsum Mines Ltd* [1953] AC 663 at 677: "It [the 1945 Act] enables the court ... to seek less strenuously to find some ground for holding the plaintiff free from blame."

THE LAW REFORM (CONTRIBUTORY NEGLIGENCE) ACT 1945

21.53 The subtleties and complexity of the law of contributory negligence, discussed above, were largely removed by the Law Reform (Contributory Negligence) Act 1945. The Act provides that a claim should not fail completely because a pursuer is in some way to blame for his loss or injury. Instead, the damages should be reduced accordingly.

21.54 Section 1(1) of the 1945 Act states:

> "Where any person suffers damage as the result partly of his own fault and partly of the fault of any other person, or persons, a claim in respect of that damage shall not be defeated by reason of the fault of the person suffering the damage, but the damages recoverable in respect thereof shall be reduced to such extent as the court thinks just and equitable having regard to the claimant's share in the responsibility for the damage."

21.55 Section 4 of the Act states that "damage includes loss of life and personal injury". It is safe to assume that the term also includes property damage as that was the case prior to the Act. Economic loss is also covered.[109] "Fault" is defined for Scotland in s 5(a) as "wrongful act, breach of statutory duty or negligent act or omission which gives rise to liability in damages, or would apart from this Act, give rise to the defence of contributory negligence". Fault appears to embrace deliberate acts of the pursuer as well as negligent acts. Certainly, there is English authority to that effect.[110]

21.56 The 1945 Act applies, by virtue of s 5(c), to claims brought by dependants of a deceased person where that person has died partly as a result of his own fault. In other words, provision is made for the apportionment of damages in an action brought in respect of a person's death.[111]

21.57 The standard of care required of the pursuer for his own safety is that which is reasonable in the circumstances.[112] As well as proving that the pursuer failed to take reasonable care for his own safety, the defender must prove that the pursuer's failure to take reasonable care was a cause of his damage. Sometimes the defender's failure to take care will be a cause of the accident itself. However, it is not necessary for contributory negligence to operate that the pursuer's want of care has contributed to the accident itself. It is sufficient for the defence to operate that the defender's failure was a cause of his damage.[113] The seatbelt cases illustrate this point. A is driving carefully but without wearing his seatbelt. B, driving negligently, collides with him and A is injured. It is obvious that A's failure to wear his seatbelt did not cause *the accident* but his failure to do so may well have contributed to *his injuries* and thus he

---

[109] See, eg, *Platform Home Loans Ltd* v *Oyston Shipways Ltd* [2000] 2 AC 190.

[110] See *Reeves* v *Commissioner of Police of the Metropolis* [2000] 1 AC 360. There, a prisoner committed suicide by hanging himself while in police custody. The defendant was subject to a duty to prevent deliberate self-harm by the prisoner. Responsibility for the suicide was apportioned equally between the deceased and the defendant and damages to the prisoner's estate were therefore reduced by 50%. Lord Hoffmann stated (at 370): "Because the police were under a duty to take reasonable care not to give [the deceased] the opportunity to kill himself, the common sense answer to the question whether their carelessness caused his death is 'Yes'. Because [the deceased] also had responsibility for his own life, the common sense answer to the question whether he caused his own death is 'Yes'. Therefore both causes contributed to his death and the Act of 1945 provides the means of reflecting this division of responsibility in the award of damages." Cf *Corr* v *IBC Vehicles Ltd* [2008] 1 AC 884.

[111] See, eg, *Campbell* v *Gillespie* 1996 SLT 503.

[112] See *Porter* v *Strathclyde RC* 1991 SLT 446.

[113] The failure of pursuers to wear seatbelts or helmets offers a ready example. See the *dicta* of Lord Denning MR in *Froom* v *Butcher* [1976] QB 286. See, also, *O'Connell* v *Jackson* [1972] 1 QB 270.

will be contributorily negligent. If, however, something crushes the car in which A is travelling from above (for example, a falling tree), then A's failure to wear the seatbelt does not exacerbate his injuries and he would not be contributorily negligent in those circumstances. His failure to wear the seatbelt did not cause his injuries (in whole or in part) and is therefore legally irrelevant.[114]

In the event of an accident, failure on the part of a motorcyclist/cyclist to wear a **21.58** crash helmet/cycling helmet may result in greater injuries than otherwise would have been the case. The cyclist would therefore be contributorily negligent.[115] One could not say, however, that failure to wear a helmet contributed to the accident; rather, it contributes to the injuries.

It is important to note that the defence does not depend on the pursuer owing the **21.59** defender a duty of care. It does, however, depend on the concept of foreseeability, a point which was made by Denning LJ in *Jones* v *Livox Quarries Ltd*:[116]

"Although contributory negligence does not depend on a duty of care, it does depend on foreseeability. Just as actionable negligence requires the foreseeability of harm to others, so contributory negligence requires the foreseeability of harm to oneself. A person is guilty of contributory negligence if he ought reasonably to have foreseen that, if he did not act as a reasonable, prudent man, he might be hurt himself; and in his reckonings he must take into account the possibility of others being careless."

In that case the plaintiff was riding on the back of a traxcavator. He was injured when **21.60** another vehicle was negligently driven into the back of the traxcavator. His damages were reduced on the basis of his contributory negligence although Denning LJ pointed out that the result would have been different had he been hit in the eye by a shot fired by a negligent sportsman.

The defence of contributory negligence must be specifically pled if it is to be relied **21.61** upon at proof. The court cannot of its own motion take it into account. Where the defence of contributory negligence is raised, the onus of proof thereof rests on the defender.[117] In *Anderson* v *Scottish Ministers*,[118] a cycling accident occurred on a path occupied and controlled by Historic Scotland (for whom the defenders were legally responsible). It was alleged that the siting of a drain and gulley immediately adjacent to the cycling track was an obvious danger and that Historic Scotland was in breach of duties both at common law and under the Occupiers' Liability (Scotland) Act 1960. The defenders relied on the defence of contributory negligence, averring that it could be inferred that the pursuer had lost control of his bicycle. However, the defenders failed to discharge the onus of proving that the pursuer was contributorily negligent in the circumstances.

---

[114] See *Caswell* v *Powell Duffryn Associated Collieries Ltd* [1940] AC 152, where Lord Atkin stated (at 165): "[I]f the plaintiff were negligent but his negligence was not a cause operating to produce the damage there would be no defence."

[115] See *O'Connell* v *Jackson* [1972] 1 QB 270. See, also, *Capps* v *Miller* [1989] 2 All ER 333, where the plaintiff had worn his crash helmet but had failed to fasten the chinstrap. The helmet came off following the plaintiff's impact with a motor vehicle driven by a drunk driver and before the motorcyclist hit the ground. He suffered brain injuries and was adjudged to be 10% contributorily negligent.

[116] [1952] 2 QB 608 at 615. See, also, *Westwood* v *Post Office* [1974] AC 1, per Lord Kilbrandon at 16–17.

[117] *Caswell* v *Powell Duffryn Associated Collieries Ltd* [1940] AC 152; *Grant* v *Sun Shipping Co Ltd* 1948 SC (HL) 73; *Porter* v *Strathclyde RC* 1991 SLT 446.

[118] 2009 Rep LR 122.

21.62   Contributory negligence is not available as a defence in relation to intentional delicts such as deceit or fraudulent misrepresentation.[119]

21.63   There is no definitive test for determining the level of the reduction in damages. It depends on the circumstances of the particular case.[120] The court treats each case on its own merits. The Act simply requires that the reduction be "just and equitable". It has been judicially stated that "[t]his involves a consideration, not only of the causative potency[121] of a particular factor, but also of its blameworthiness".[122] It is a broad question of common sense, not a matter for complex arithmetical calculations, and the judge must use his discretion.

21.64   If the judge finds that the pursuer's fault contributed to his injuries, the wording of the legislation would appear to suggest that he or she *must* make an apportionment. The Act directs the judge to do so in the following terms: "the damages … *shall* be reduced". Thus, in several cases, the view has been expressed that the court is obliged to reduce the damages in circumstances where the pursuer's fault has contributed to his injuries.[123] However, the contrary view has also found favour.[124] It is respectfully submitted that, given the statutory wording, the former view is to be preferred and that the judge should not ignore the pursuer's fault on the basis that such a course would be just and equitable.

21.65   At the opposite end of the spectrum, is it possible for a finding of 100 per cent contributory negligence to be made against a pursuer? Such a conclusion has been described as "logically unsupportable"[125] in view of the wording of s 1 of the 1945 Act. It is submitted that such a view is correct and that if the pursuer is totally to blame the correct decision is one of sole fault on the part of the pursuer.[126] If, on the other hand, both pursuer and defender are equally to blame, the correct apportionment is 50/50.

21.66   In contributory negligence cases, the court determines what the total amount of damages would be if the pursuer had not been at fault and then it apportions liability

---

[119] *Standard Chartered Bank* v *Pakistan National Shipping Corporation* [2003] 1 AC 959. See, also, the views of the Scottish Law Commission in its Report on *Civil Liability – Contribution* (Scot Law Com No 115, 1988) (at para 4.25): "We are not … convinced that extension of the plea into the field of intentional wrongdoing is warranted."

[120] See *Blackhall* v *Macinnes* 1997 SLT 649, per Lord Hamilton (at 650–651): "In my view citation of decided cases on the extent of contributory negligence is of limited value. While they may assist in indicating broadly an appropriate range, each case turns on its own particular circumstances."

[121] On the issue of causal potency, see *St George* v *Home Office* [2009] 1 WLR 1670. A prisoner who was a drug addict and alcoholic fell from a top bunk following a withdrawal seizure. He sustained brain damage as a result. He was found not to be contributorily negligent. His addiction was not a potent cause of the injury.

[122] *Davies* v *Swan Motor Co (Swansea) Ltd* [1949] 2 KB 291, per Denning LJ at 326. See, also, *McCluskey* v *Wallace* 1998 SC 711, per Lord Marnoch at 717: "[I]t is not merely a question of asking whether or not each contributed causally to the accident. The concept of … blameworthiness is inherent in sec 1(1) itself."

[123] See *Boothman* v *British Northrop* [1972] 13 KIR 112; *Badger* v *Ministry of Defence* [2006] All ER 173, per Burnton J at para 15 ("Once relevant fault on the part of the claimant has been established, a reduction on account of his fault in the damages recoverable is obligatory.") See, also, J F Clerk and W H B Lindsell, *Torts* (A Dugdale and M Jones (eds)) (20th rev edn, 2010) at para 3–83.

[124] See, eg, *Hawkins* v *Ian Ross Castings Ltd* [1970] 1 All ER 180; *St George* v *Home Office* [2009] 1 WLR 1670. See, also, the observations of Lord Emslie in *McEwan* v *Lothian Buses plc* 2006 RepLR 134 at para 31: "It is not unknown for the degree of carelessness or inattention established against a pursuer to be held insufficient to warrant the making of any finding of contributory negligence under the 1945 Act."

[125] Per Balcombe LJ in *Pitts* v *Hunt* [1991] 1 QB 24 at 51. See, also, Beldam LJ at 48. See, also, *Anderson* v *Newham College of Further Education* [2003] ICR 212: "If there is liability, contributory negligence can reduce its monetary quantification but it cannot legally or logically nullify it" (per Sedley LJ at para 19).

[126] Note, however, that in *McEwan* v *Lothian Buses plc* 2006 Rep LR 134, Lord Emslie suggested (at para 31) that a finding of 100% contributory negligence may be competent: "[T]he degree of fault on the part of the defenders [may] be regarded as too small to warrant an apportionment."

as a percentage of that total. Thus, if a blameless pursuer would have recovered £5,000 in respect of his injuries, then the pursuer who is, say, two-fifths to blame for his injuries will recover only £3,000. If there is more than one defender, then liability will be apportioned between or among them depending on their respective blame-worthiness. Such a scenario is neatly illustrated by the leading case on contributory negligence, *Davies v Swan Motor Co (Swansea) Ltd*.[127] In that case, which was decided shortly after the 1945 Act came into force, Denning LJ explained the effect of contributory negligence. His Lordship stated[128] that: "Previously in order to mitigate the harshness of the doctrine of contributory negligence, the courts, in practice, sought to select, from a number of competing causes, which was *the* cause – the effective or predominant cause of the damage and to reject the rest. Now the courts have regard to all the causes and apportion the damages accordingly." Davies had been standing on the sidestep of a lorry in contravention of instructions given to him. A bus ran into the lorry. Davies was killed. It was held that both the bus driver and the lorry driver were at fault. It was also held that Davies himself had been partly to blame in that he should have known that it was dangerous to stand on the sidestep of a lorry and, accordingly, his own negligence had contributed to his death. Damages to his widow were reduced by 20 per cent. Thereafter, liability was apportioned on a two-thirds to one-third basis between the bus driver and lorry driver.

Let us now examine the operation of the defence in specific contexts.   **21.67**

SLIPPING/TRIPPING CASES

In slipping and tripping cases it is almost routine for the defender to raise the defence   **21.68**
of contributory negligence. The pursuer is expected to keep a reasonable lookout and to avoid hazards. In *Porter v Strathclyde Regional Council*,[129] a nursery assistant slipped on some food which had been spilled on the floor of a room in which young children were eating. She sued her employers, the Regional Council, in respect of her injuries but she was found to have been contributorily negligent and her damages were reduced by 50 per cent.[130] It was held that the pursuer should have looked out for food on the floor, as spillage was a common occurrence. The apportionment might seem unduly harsh given that the pursuer was carrying a distraught child at the time. Nevertheless, the appeal court refused to interfere with the apportionment. In *Ellis v Bristol City Council*,[131] the claimant slipped on a pool of urine on a care home floor. The claimant's lack of concentration on the risk to be expected went beyond inadvertence and resulted in a finding of contributory negligence to the extent of one-third.

---

[127] [1949] 2 KB 291.
[128] *Ibid* at 322.
[129] 1991 SLT 446.
[130] The court would have made a similar apportionment (ie 50%) in *McClafferty v British Telecommunications plc* 1987 SLT 327 had liability been established (pedestrian tripped on a raised manhole cover). See, also, *McMillan v Lord Advocate* 1991 SLT 150; *Porter v Scottish Borders Council* 2009 RepLR 46; *Brown v Edinburgh City Council* 1999 SLT (Sh Ct) 43.
[131] [2007] ICR 1614.

ROAD TRAFFIC ACCIDENT CASES

21.69 The defence of contributory negligence is frequently invoked in road accident cases. In *Campbell* v *Gillespie*,[132] the pursuer sought damages in respect of the death of her husband. He had been travelling north when he collided with the rear of a stationary lorry which was blocking the northbound carriageway. At the time of the collision, no lights were operating on the lorry. The lorry had broken down and was being worked on by the third defender, a mechanic. Although the lorry had previously been displaying its hazard lights, the lights went out when the existing battery was disconnected. It was during this time that the accident occurred. It was averred that, if it was necessary to switch off the hazard lights, then an alternative means of warning should have been given. It was also averred that a Transit van (which had been parked at the front of the lorry) should have been placed, with its hazard lights on, at the *rear* of the lorry so that it could be seen by traffic travelling towards the lorry on the northbound carriageway. There was, however, a police warning sign some 150 yards to the rear of the lorry. The temporary judge, while accepting that the third defender was at fault, also concluded that the deceased was at fault. If he had been keeping a good lookout, he would have seen the police sign. He also failed to observe the unlit rear of the lorry in his own lights in time. The judge concluded:[133]

> "The actings and omissions of the [deceased] and of the third defender are both causes of this accident. In my opinion this accident was due partly to the presence of an inadequately lit obstruction which was not sufficiently flagged given the circumstances, and partly due to the deceased's failure to take reasonable care to keep a proper lookout and keep proper control as he proceeded along the roadway ... It has been said more than once that these questions should be approached broadly and judged as a matter of common sense, looking at the whole circumstances ... Every case depends upon its own peculiar circumstances ... I have concluded that fault should be shared on the basis of 60 per cent fault to the [deceased] and 40 per cent to the third defender."

21.70 In *Malcolm* v *Fair*,[134] a drunken pedestrian who was crossing a road was struck by an approaching car, the driver of which had failed to see him. The pedestrian was held to be contributorily negligent to the extent of 50 per cent. Again, in *Kemp* v *Secretary of State for Scotland*,[135] a drunken pedestrian tripped on a raised kerb and fell into the path of a van. He was found to be contributorily negligent to the extent of one-third.

21.71 In *Dolby* v *Milner*,[136] D had been turning right into a major road when he collided with M, a motorcyclist. The motorcyclist had been travelling at excessive speed and had failed to take evasive action. D raised an action against the motorcyclist in respect of the damage to his car and the motorcyclist counterclaimed for personal injuries. The trial judge apportioned liability as 75 per cent against the motorcyclist and 25 per cent against D. The motorcyclist appealed. The appeal court reversed the trial judge's apportionment. The appeal court held that D was under a continuing obligation to

---

[132] 1996 SLT 503.
[133] *Ibid* at 510.
[134] 1993 SLT 342.
[135] 2000 SLT 471.
[136] [1996] CLY 4430.

give way and, as the motorcycle had been visible from 95 yards, D ought to have seen it.

In *Blackhall v Macinnes*,[137] the pursuer was struck by a car when, following a puncture, she was attempting to change the wheel on her car. Rather than driving her car onto the verge, the pursuer attempted to change the wheel at the side of the dual carriageway. She was found to be contributorily negligent to the extent of 20 per cent, the Lord Ordinary stating[138] that "the course of action adopted by the pursuer, namely to attempt to change the offside wheel while on the carriageway, was particularly hazardous".

The defence of contributory negligence has also been raised against passengers in **21.72** cars driven by intoxicated drivers. In *Owens v Brimmell*,[139] the plaintiff, knowing that the defendant was under the influence of alcohol, took a lift from him and was held to be contributorily negligent to the extent of 20 per cent for his resulting injuries when the car collided with a lamp-post. In *Currie v Clamp's Executor*,[140] the pursuer was injured in a car accident in which the driver died. However, the pursuer knew or ought to have known that the deceased had been drinking heavily and was unfit to drive. In those circumstances the pursuer was found to be contributorily negligent to the extent of one-third.[141]

The defence of contributory negligence has also been invoked against drivers or **21.73** passengers who have failed to wear their seatbelts and have thus sustained more serious injuries than would otherwise have been the case. It is now recognised by statute[142] that it is an offence for those travelling in a car not to wear a seatbelt. From a delictual point of view, where injuries are sustained or aggravated because of a failure to wear a seatbelt, the award of damages will be reduced proportionately.[143] In *Froom v Butcher*,[144] the plaintiff would not have suffered head and chest injuries had he been wearing his seatbelt but the seatbelt would have made no difference to his broken finger. Lord Denning MR suggested that the appropriate reduction was 25 per cent where the injuries would have been prevented by wearing the seatbelt and 15 per cent where the injuries would have been less severe had the belt been worn. In *Froom*, the plaintiff's damages were reduced by 20 per cent. *Froom* was an English case. Scottish case law tends to support a 10 per cent to 20 per cent reduction in damages where no seatbelt has been worn.[145] In the Scottish case of *Mitchell v Swanson's Executor*,[146] an 18-year-old man, who was a front-seat passenger in a motor vehicle, sustained injuries which would have been lessened, but not avoided, had he worn his seatbelt. It was observed in that case, that where damage would have been prevented by wearing a seatbelt, the appropriate reduction was 20 per cent. However, in *Mackay v Borthwick*,[147]

---

[137] 1997 SLT 649.
[138] *Ibid* at 650.
[139] [1977] QB 859.
[140] 2002 SLT 196.
[141] See, also, *Sloan v Triplett* 1985 SLT 294; *McCaig v Langan* 1964 SLT 121; *Hill v Chivers* 1987 SLT 323.
[142] Road Traffic Act 1988, s 14(3) and associated regulations.
[143] Such findings were made by the courts even prior to the introduction of legislation requiring the wearing of seatbelts. Indeed, the *Froom* decision (discussed below) pre-dates the relevant legislation.
[144] [1976] QB 286.
[145] See *Hanlon v Cuthbertson* 1981 SLT (Notes) 5 (10% deduction); *Sloan v Triplett* 1985 SLT 294 (20% deduction suggested); *Hill v Chivers* 1987 SLT 323 (30% deduction but that related to *both* failure to wear a seatbelt and the pursuer's allowing himself to be driven by an intoxicated driver).
[146] 1980 SLT (Notes) 41.
[147] 1982 SLT 265.

the pursuer was held not to be contributorily negligent for failing to wear a seatbelt as it was uncomfortable for her to do so as she was suffering from a hiatus hernia.[148] In *Pace* v *Culley*,[149] the pursuer, a taxi driver, failed to wear a seatbelt. He had been advised by the police not to do so in the event that he might be attacked by passengers. While accepting that failure to wear a seatbelt could amount to contributory negligence, the Lord Ordinary (Weir) was of the opinion that the driver's conduct in this case was a misjudgement as opposed to a failure to take care for his own safety.

21.74   In *Taylor* v *Leslie*,[150] a passenger in a car was killed on the Orkney island of Shapinsay. He was being driven by an underaged, unlicensed and uninsured driver at the time. The car had been on a grass farm track which led down to a road. The driver was revving the engine so that the wheels of the car began to spin. The deceased opened the front passenger door in order to observe the spinning wheels. He was not wearing a seatbelt and encouraged the driver to rev up the engine even more. The car sped forward onto the road and collided with another vehicle, causing the deceased's death. The deceased was held to be 50 per cent contributorily negligent in the circumstances.

WORKPLACE ACCIDENTS

21.75   Contributory negligence is often raised as a defence in actions arising from injuries sustained in the workplace.[151] In *Beggs* v *Motherwell Bridge Fabricators Ltd*,[152] a factory worker was killed following an accident which occurred when he was driving a forklift truck along a road situated within factory grounds. The truck had come to a sudden halt when the forks stuck in the road surface which was very uneven. The deceased had, however, failed to set the forks at an appropriate level. The Lord Ordinary (Eassie), holding the deceased to be 20 per cent contributorily negligent, made the following observations:[153]

> "In my view … a driver in the position of the deceased ought reasonably to have appreciated the need to give some consideration to changes in the type of surface over which he was about to drive and to adjust the forks setting so as to avoid obstacles if he were to embark upon a rougher and more undulating surface … the deceased did not apply properly his mind to the condition of the surface of the perimeter roadway and did not reach a proper decision that the forks be set at the higher level necessary to clear the obstacles which were presented. In the circumstances I find therefore that the deceased did not wholly fulfil his obligation to take reasonable care for his own safety and thus contributed to the accident."

21.76   In *McLellan* v *Dundee City Council*,[154] the pursuer, who was employed as a gardener by the defenders, worked as a driver of a triple mower. He suffered significant injury to his right hand when attempting to clear a blockage in the central cutter of the mower. A subsequent action proceeded on both breach of statutory duty and common law negligence. Contributory negligence was assessed at 20 per cent.

---

[148] It may be that pregnant women would receive a similar concession. See the *dictum* of Lord Denning MR in *Froom* v *Butcher* [1976] QB 286 at 295.
[149] 1992 SLT 1073.
[150] 1998 SLT 1248.
[151] See, eg, *Wallace* v *Glasgow City Council* [2011] CSIH 57.
[152] 1998 SLT 1215.
[153] *Ibid* at 1221.
[154] 2009 RepLR 61.

In *MacDonald* v *Wood Group Engineering (North Sea) Ltd*,[155] the pursuer, an experi- **21.77** enced deck crew rigger, placed his fingers in a pinch point (a place of danger) when transferring a container. This resulted in the loss of the tip of his middle finger. Although his employer was in breach of common law duty and statutory duty, the pursuer was held to be 50 per cent contributorily negligent.

In *Robb* v *Salamis (M And I) Ltd*,[156] the pursuer was employed at an offshore instal- **21.78** lation. He was injured when using a removeable ladder to descend from his bunk. He had failed to check whether it had been properly secured (which it had not been). His action against his employers proceeded on the basis of breach of the Provision and Use of Work Equipment Regulations 1998.[157] The House of Lords held that a breach of the Regulations was established but that the pursuer was contributorily negligent to the extent of one-half. Lord Rodger observed[158] that "[b]efore putting his weight on the ladder, it would have been only sensible for the pursuer to check that it was stable".

Many accidents arising from accidents in the workplace proceed (as in *Robb* above) **21.79** on the basis of breach of statutory duty. While the defence of contributory negligence can apply in cases of breach of statutory duty, the courts have displayed a certain circumspection as regards the defence in breach of statutory duty cases,[159] especially in circumstances where an absolute duty is imposed on the employer.[160] This matter is returned to below.

APPEALS

Appeal courts are not generally overzealous to interfere with apportionments made **21.80** by the trial judge unless there has been an obvious mistake made by the latter.[161] Thus, in *Porter* v *Strathclyde Regional Council*,[162] the Inner House refused to interfere with the apportionment made by the Lord Ordinary. Lord Dunpark, who delivered the opinion of the Second Division, stated:[163]

"It has been laid down in *McCusker* v *Saveheat Cavity Wall Insulation Ltd*,[164] and in *MacIntosh* v *National Coal Board*[165] that the Inner House will not interfere with the Lord Ordinary's apportionment of negligence except in exceptional circumstances which must demonstrate

---

155 2011 GWD 1–50.
156 2007 SC (HL) 71.
157 SI 1998/2306.
158 2007 SC (HL) 71 at para 54.
159 See, eg, *Westwood* v *Post Office* [1974] AC 1 where Lord Kilbrandon stated (at 16–17): "[T]he defence of contributory negligence as an answer, even as nowadays, only a partial answer, to a claim arising out of breach of statutory duty is one which it must always be difficult to establish. The very existence of statutory safety provisions must be relevant to the consequences which a man may reasonably be expected to foresee as arising from his own conduct." See, also, the comments of Lawrence J in *Flower* v *Ebbw Vale Steel, Iron and Coal Co Ltd* [1934] 2 KB 132 at 140 to the effect that "it is not for every risky thing which a workman in a factory may do in his familiarity with the machinery that a plaintiff ought to be held guilty of contributory negligence".
160 See *McGowan* v *W & J R Watson Ltd* 2007 SC 272, per Lord Nimmo Smith (at para 14) to the effect that a momentary lapse by an employee would not fall below the standard of reasonable care where the employer was subject to an absolute statutory obligation.
161 See, eg, *McCluskey* v *Wallace* 1998 SC 711.
162 1991 SLT 446.
163 *Ibid* at 449.
164 1987 SLT 24.
165 1988 SLT 348.

that 'he has manifestly and to a substantial degree gone wrong.' Even if the Inner House would have expected a different apportionment, it will not interfere."

The Second Division concluded that the Lord Ordinary had been entitled to make the apportionment which he did.

21.81   In *McFarlane v Scottish Borders Council*,[166] on the other hand, the appeal court was prepared to interfere with the apportionment made by the lower court.[167] The pursuer was constructing a passing place on a single-track road in the Borders. He sustained injuries when the roadroller on which he was sitting tipped over and he tumbled down the bank. The temporary judge had held that, had the defenders been at fault, the pursuer would have been 75 per cent contributorily negligent. The Inner House took the view that the employers could not be held less than 50 per cent to blame in the circumstances, it being stated that "[e]ven if [the pursuer] was careless of his own safety, the defenders had a duty to protect him against the consequences of his carelessness".[168]

CONTRIBUTORY NEGLIGENCE AND THE "AGONY OF THE MOMENT" RULE

21.82   The agony of the moment rule means that if the pursuer is put into a dangerous situation by virtue of the defender's negligence, the defender is liable for the damage which accrues by virtue of the pursuer trying to extricate himself, ie there is no contributory negligence. It has been said that "it is not in the mouth of those who have created the danger of the situation to be minutely critical of what is done by those whom they have by their fault involved in the danger".[169]

21.83   In *Jones v Boyce*,[170] the plaintiff was a passenger on the top of the defendant's coach. There was a defective coupling rein on the coach which created a danger of the coach being overturned. The plaintiff jumped from the coach and broke his leg. Although the coach did not overturn, the plaintiff was held not to have been contributorily negligent as his conduct had been reasonable in the face of danger presented by the defendant's negligence.

CONTRIBUTORY NEGLIGENCE AND THE "DILEMMA" RULE

21.84   Another exception from the defence is available under the "dilemma" rule. Where the pursuer chooses the wrong course of action of two options open to him in a situation created by the defender, the pursuer will not be contributorily negligent. This rule is illustrated in *Wallace v Bergius*.[171] A driver travelling on his own side of the road saw a vehicle approaching him also on his side of the road. He swerved to the other side of

---

[166] 2005 SLT 359.
[167] The trial judge was held, on appeal, to have erred in both *Pitts v Hunt* [1991] 1 QB 24 and *Capps v Miller* [1989] 2 All ER 333. The trial judge's apportionment was also reversed in *Dolby v Milner* [1996] CLY 4430. The appeal court also reduced the plaintiff's share of responsibility from one-half to one-third in *Mullard v Ben Line Steamers Ltd* [1970] 1 WLR 1414.
[168] 2005 SLT 359 at para 29 (per Temporary Judge Sir David Edward, QC).
[169] *Laird Line v United States Shipping Board* 1924 SC (HL) 37, per Lord Dunedin at 40.
[170] (1816) 1 Stark 493.
[171] 1915 SC 205.

the road but so too did the other vehicle and a collision resulted. The first driver was held not to have been contributorily negligent in those circumstances.[172]

We will now look at the operation of the defence of contributory negligence in relation to particular pursuers, namely children and those with a physical or mental disability. **21.85**

CHILDREN

Children may be held to be contributorily negligent. There is no fixed age below which a child is absolved from taking reasonable care for his own safety. Whether a child will be deemed to have been contributorily negligent is a question of circumstances and degree.[173] It will depend on the age of the child and the nature of the accident whether a child will be expected at law to have some regard for his own safety. In *Galbraith's Curator ad Litem* v *Stewart (No 2),*[174] the defender had been involved in construction work and left a number of concrete pipes unsecured overnight. A group of children gained access to the pipework and one of them (an 8-year-old boy) sustained head injuries when he fell off a rolling pipe. It was held to be reasonably foreseeable that children would be attracted to the pipes which were capable of moving and that personal injury would result. The injured child was held not to have been contributorily negligent. Lord Nimmo Smith stated that no hard and fast rule could be derived from the cases and "the question of a child's contributory negligence must depend on the nature of the particular danger and the particular child's capacity to appreciate it".[175] **21.86**

In *Yachuk* v *Oliver Blais,*[176] a 9-year-old child bought petrol from the defendant after falsely stating that his mother required it for her car. The child used the petrol for a game and was burned. The court held that the defendant was negligent in supplying petrol to such a young child. The child was held not to be contributorily negligent because he could not be expected to know the qualities of petrol. In *Gough* v *Thorne,*[177] the plaintiff, who was 13 years of age, was injured while crossing the road after having been signalled to do so by a lorry driver. The plaintiff was knocked down by a car which was being driven too fast. It was held that the plaintiff would only be contributorily negligent if she did not act with all the prudence expected of a child of a similar age. In *McKinnel* v *White,*[178] a 5-year-old child was held to be contributorily negligent to the extent of 50 per cent when he let go of his brother's hand and ran in front of a car and was injured. Lord Fraser, in accepting that a child of 5 years of age can, as a matter of law, be contributorily negligent, pointed out that the danger of running across a main road was very obvious and must have been within the child's understanding. **21.87**

---

[172] It should be noted that *Jones* v *Boyce* and *Wallace* v *Bergius* pre-date the 1945 Act and the court's ability to apportion blame. It has been said that "[t]he agony rule [and] the dilemma principle … have limited significance since the 1945 Act". (See Rodger, *Delict* (SULI) at para 8–15.)

[173] "A child is not expected to meet the standard of care of a reasonable adult. He need only show the degree of care to be expected from a child of the same age, intelligence and experience in the circumstancess." (Report on *Civil Liability – Contribution* (Scot Law Com No 115) at para 4.5.) See, also, *Frasers* v *Edinburgh Street Tramways Co* (1882) 10 R 264, per Lord Fraser at 269.

[174] 1998 SLT 1305.

[175] *Ibid* at 1307.

[176] [1949] AC 386.

[177] [1966] 1 WLR 1387.

[178] 1971 SLT (Notes) 61.

He had been told of the danger of traffic and of the need to look out for traffic before crossing the road. Indeed, Lord Fraser inclined to the view that any child aged 5 living in an urban area would be bound to be aware of the danger of traffic.[179] In *Banner's Tutor v Kennedy's Trs*,[180] a girl, aged 5, alighted from the rear of a minibus and ran into a lorry. She was held to be one-fifth responsible and her damages were reduced accordingly. The girl, who was found by the court to be of normal intelligence and who had prior experience of heavy traffic, had been specifically warned by the bus driver not to get out until he had opened the door. In *O'Connor v Matthews*,[181] a 12-year-old boy suffered severe brain injury when he was knocked down by a van in a road accident. He raised an action of damages against the driver of the van and against the driver's employers. The Lord Ordinary (Marnoch) found the pursuer and the first defender equally to blame for the accident. He therefore awarded damages subject to a 50 per cent reduction in respect of the pursuer's contributory negligence.

21.88   In *Dawson v Scottish Power plc*,[182] an 11-year-old child was held to be one-third contributorily negligent in respect of injuries sustained when scaling a spiked fence surrounding an electricity substation in order to retrieve a football. In *McCluskey v Wallace*,[183] a 4-year-old child was held to be 20 per cent contributorily negligent when she was knocked off her bicycle by a car driven by the defender. Neither party had noticed the other.

21.89   A child will not necessarily be contributorily negligent merely because any adult he is with is negligent. This is demonstrated in *Oliver v Birmingham & Midlands Omnibus Co Ltd*.[184] A child was struck by an omnibus and injured while crossing the road with his grandfather. The grandfather had been negligent in letting go of the child's hand. Nevertheless, the child's claim was not reduced. In *Brogan's Tutors v Glasgow District Council*,[185] Lord Wylie repeated the view that contributory negligence by a parent cannot be pleaded against the child.[186] There, a 2-year-old child was left on his own for a short time while his mother ran his bath. There was an electric fire in the room in which the child had been left. It was switched on. It had a guard over it which had missing retaining screws. When his mother investigated the noise in the room, she discovered the child being thrown backwards and forwards. The child had succeeded in gripping hold of the uppermost of two elements, which was live at the time. When the child's mother switched the fire off, the child was thrown into the middle of the room. As a result, the child suffered burning injuries. The Lord Ordinary held that the guard had been insecure from installation by the landlords and found them 20 per cent to blame. The remaining 80 per cent of blame he apportioned to the child's mother, having regard to the fact that the fire had been obviously unsafe for some length of time. Counsel for the defenders submitted that in the case of a very young child, too young to be capable of contributory negligence, a doctrine of identification fell to be

---

[179] 1971 SLT (Notes) 61 at 62. See, also, *Harvey v Cairns* 1989 SLT 107 (6-year-old child was contributorily negligent to the extent of two-thirds when she stepped from a pavement into the path of an oncoming vehicle which was being driven at an excessive speed); *Barnes v Flucker* 1985 SLT 142.
[180] 1978 SLT (Notes) 83.
[181] 1996 SLT 408.
[182] 1999 SLT 672.
[183] 1998 SC 711.
[184] [1933] 1 KB 35.
[185] 1978 SLT (Notes) 47.
[186] In *Hughes' Tutrix v Glasgow DC* 1982 SLT (Sh Ct) 70, the sheriff endorsed the decision in *Brogan's Tutors*.

applied and the child's claim should be cut down to the extent to which the parent contributed to the accident. Lord Wylie rejected that argument, stating[187] that "it would be contrary to principle that, as a matter of law, a child's claim should be cut down in the way suggested".

Interestingly, in 1978, the Royal Commission on Civil Liability and Compensation   **21.90** for Personal Injury (the "Pearson Commission") recommended that contributory negligence should not be available as a defence in road accident cases where the person injured is under 12 years of age.[188]

THE PHYSICALLY AND MENTALLY DISABLED

Although a person who is physically or mentally disabled is less likely to be held to   **21.91** be contributorily negligent, he will be expected to take the care which a person with his disabilities normally takes. In *Cork* v *Kirby Maclean Ltd*,[189] Cork, unknown to his employers, was subject to epilepsy and had been forbidden to work at heights. He fell from a platform which should have had a guardrail and the fall, which resulted in his death, proved to have been the result of an epileptic seizure. He was held in those circumstances to have been contributorily negligent and damages to his representatives were reduced by 50 per cent. However, a person of unsound mind who is unable to appreciate the danger of a given course of action will not be contributorily negligent as it will not be just and equitable to attribute responsibility to such a person.[190]

BREACH OF STATUTORY DUTY AND CONTRIBUTORY NEGLIGENCE

Contributory negligence can apply in cases arising from breach of statutory duty just   **21.92** as it does in claims arising from common law negligence.[191] In *Caswell* v *Powell Duffryn Associated Collieries Ltd*,[192] the House of Lords held the defendants to be in breach of statutory duty in respect of a fatal injury sustained by a colliery worker. An argument to the effect that contributory negligence could not operate as a defence in an action based on breach of statutory duty was rejected by the House of Lords. Lord Atkin stated:[193]

> "I cannot ... accept the view that the action for injuries caused by breach of statutory duty differs from an action for injuries caused by any other wrong. I think that the defendant will succeed if he proves that the injury was caused solely or in part by the omission of the plaintiff to take the ordinary care that would be expected of him in the circumstances."[194]

---

[187] 1978 SLT (Notes) 47 at 47.
[188] *Royal Commission on Civil Liability and Compensation for Personal Injury* (Cmnd 7054, 1978) vol 1, para 1077.
[189] [1952] 2 All ER 402.
[190] See *Kirkham* v *Chief Constable, Greater Manchester Police* [1990] 2 QB 283; *Reeves* v *Commissioner of Police of the Metropolis* [2000] 1 AC 360, per Lord Hoffmann at 371.
[191] Indeed, this was recognised even before the Law Reform (Contributory Negligence) Act 1945. See *Gibb* v *Crombie* (1875) 2 R 886.
[192] [1940] AC 152.
[193] *Ibid* at 166.
[194] See, also, the *dictum* of Lord Wright (at 178): "I am not prepared to agree that the defence of contributory negligence should be excluded in such cases simply on the technical ground that the cause of action is not negligence in the strict sense ..."

21.93   His Lordship did lend his support,[195] however to the following *dictum* of Lawrence J in *Flower* v *Ebbw Vale Steel Iron and Coal Co Ltd*:[196]

"in considering whether an ordinary prudent workman would have taken more care than the injured man, the tribunal of fact has to take into account all the circumstances of work in a factory, and that it is not for every risky thing which a workman in a factory may do in his familiarity with the machinery that a plaintiff ought to be held guilty of contributory negligence".

21.94   Of course, *Caswell* was decided before the Law Reform (Contributory Negligence) Act 1945 was enacted. Section 5 of the 1945 Act now defines "fault" as "wrongful act, breach of statutory duty or negligent act or omission which gives rise to liability in damages". The Act therefore makes clear that the operation of the defence extends to actions for breach of statutory duty, a position which is consistent with that of the common law as illustrated in *Caswell*. Under the 1945 Act, fault is now apportioned according to the relative blameworthiness of the injured party and the defender. Accordingly, an action for breach of statutory duty no longer fails on account of the injured party's contributory negligence; rather, the damages are reduced by what the court considers to be an appropriate amount.[197]

21.95   In *Smith* v *Chesterfield Co-operative Society*,[198] the plaintiff had been operating a dough-making machine in a bakery. She disregarded instructions which had been given to her not to put her hand under the guard to put through pieces of dough which the machine had missed. Her hand was injured by the rollers. She raised an action against her employers on the basis that the machine had not been securely fenced as was required by statute. The court held that there had been a statutory breach in that the machine had not been securely fenced but the plaintiff was contributorily negligent to the extent of 60 per cent because she was guilty of doing a deliberate act against which she had been warned.

21.96   In *Westwood* v *Post Office*,[199] disobedience by an employee was in issue once again but, there, no finding of contributory negligence was made.[200] A number of Post Office workers who were employed at a telephone exchange went to the flat roof of the building for a "breather". The normal access route was blocked, so they went through the lift motor room, the door to which was ajar. A notice on the door declared "Notice. Only the authorised attendant is permitted to enter." On returning from the roof through the lift motor room, a worker stood on a trap door, which gave way under

---

[195] [1940] AC 152 at 166.

[196] [1934] 2 KB 132 at 140.

[197] *Cakebread* v *Hopping Bros (Whetstone) Ltd* [1947] KB 641; *Boyle* v *Kodak Ltd* [1969] 1 WLR 661; *King* v *RCO Support Services Ltd and Yorkshire Traction Co Ltd* [2001] ICR 608. (The claimants in all three cases were found to be 50% contributorily negligent.) See, also, *Tasci* v *Pekalp of London Ltd* [2001] ICR 633.

[198] [1953] 1 WLR 370.

[199] [1974] AC 1.

[200] For other cases proceeding on breach of statutory duty where no finding of contributory negligence was made, see *John Summers & Son Ltd* v *Frost* [1955] AC 740 ("At most there was a mere error of judgment by the plaintiff as to how the work on which he was engaged could best be carried out, and possibly only a mere momentary inadvertence" (per Lord Keith of Avonholm at 777)); *McNeill* v *Roche Products Ltd* 1989 SLT 498 (The court must "draw the line between mere thoughtlessness or inadvertence on the one hand and real negligence on the other and ... give due regard to the actual conditions under which men work, to the fatigue, to the slackening of attention which naturally comes from constant repetition of the same operation and other such factors" (per Lord McCluskey at 504)).

his weight. He fell to the floor beneath, sustaining fatal injuries. His estate brought an action against the Post Office, alleging breach of a statutory duty to provide floors of sound construction. The Post Office asserted that the deceased had been contributorily negligent. The House of Lords rejected the defence. The terms of the notice had not been such as to suggest that there was any danger in the room. Rather, its terms implied that the room was safe enough for the authorised attendant. Lord Kilbrandon stated:[201]

> "Any fault on the part of the deceased was a fault of disobedience, not a fault of negligence, because he had no reason to foresee that disregard of the order to keep out of the lift motor room would expose him to danger. It would indeed not have done so, had it not been that, unknown to him, the defendants were in breach of their duty to take care for the safety of those employed in the premises."

It has been stated that "[i]t is not usual for there to be marked findings of contributory negligence in a breach of statutory duty case".[202] This is especially so in cases involving mere momentary inattention.[203] In *Mullard* v *Ben Line Steamers Ltd*,[204] the plaintiff fell down an open, unfenced hatch in complete darkness while working on board a ship. In a subsequent action, the plaintiff asserted a breach of certain statutory regulations. The defendants maintained that the plaintiff had been contributorily negligent. Sachs LJ commented[205] that the plaintiff's conduct in entering a dark compartment without a torch amounted to   **21.97**

> "a momentary error, not to be judged too harshly when balanced against the defendants' flagrant and continuous breach of statutory duty. What happened was indeed exactly of the nature intended to be guarded against by the precautions prescribed by the regulations; and when a defendant's liability stems from such a breach the courts must be careful not to emasculate those regulations by the side-wind of apportionment."[206]

The courts appear especially reluctant to make findings of contributory negligence in relation to regulations of an *absolute* nature. It has been judicially asserted[207] that "[i]n Factory Act cases the purpose of imposing the absolute obligation is to protect the workmen against those very acts of inattention which are sometimes relied upon as constituting contributory negligence so that too strict a standard would defeat the object of the statute".[208]   **21.98**

---

[201] [1974] AC 1 at 17.
[202] *Toole* v *Bolton MBC* [2002] EWCA Civ 588, per Buxton LJ at para 13.
[203] Where, however, a risk has been consciously accepted by an employee, different considerations may arise, particularly where the employee is skilled and could readily adopt suitable precautions: see *Sherlock* v *Chester City Council* [2004] EWCA Civ 201, per Latham LJ at para 32.
[204] [1970] 1 WLR 1414.
[205] *Ibid* at 1418.
[206] See, also, the observations of Goddard LJ in *Hutchinson* v *London and North Eastern Railway Co* [1942] 1 KB 481 at 488.
[207] *Staveley Iron and Chemical Co Ltd* v *Jones* [1956] AC 627, per Lord Tucker at 648.
[208] See, also, *Quintas* v *National Smelting Co Ltd* [1961] 1 WLR 401, where Sellars LJ said at 408: "It has often been held that there is a high responsibility on a defendant who fails to comply with his statutory duty, which is absolute and has penal sanctions. A workman is not to be judged so severely."

21.99   In *Reeves* v *Commissioner of Metropolitan Police*,[209] Lord Hoffmann, having referred to
the above *dictum*, stated:[210]

> "[W]hat section 1 [of the 1945 Act] requires the court to apportion is not merely degrees
> of carelessness but 'responsibility' and ... an assessment of responsibility must take into
> account the policy of the rule, such as that of the Factories Acts, by which liability is imposed.
> A person may be responsible although he has not been careless at all, as in the case of breach
> of an absolute statutory duty. And he may have been careless without being responsible, as
> in the case of 'acts of inattention' by workmen."

WHAT IS THE POSITION WHERE THERE ARE TWO OR MORE WRONGDOERS AND CONTRIBUTORY NEGLIGENCE IS RAISED AS A DEFENCE?

21.100   Sometimes the defence of contributory negligence arises in cases which involve two
or more defenders. In *Fitzgerald* v *Lane*,[211] the House of Lords provided guidance as to
how the courts should approach such cases. Their Lordships stressed that such cases
involved two distinct stages, those being, first, the extent of contributory negligence
and, second, the question of contribution between the defenders. The facts of the
case were that the plaintiff had walked across a pelican crossing when the light was
showing red for pedestrians. He was struck by a car driven by the first defendant
and propelled into the road where he was struck by another car driven by the second
defendant. The trial judge had held that each party was one-third to blame. The House
of Lords held that the trial judge had erred in telescoping the two issues into one. The
matters of contributory negligence, on the one hand, and apportionment of contribution between joint wrongdoers, on the other hand, required to be kept separate.[212]
The House of Lords took the view that the plaintiff was substantially the author of
his own misfortune and found him to be 50 per cent contributorily negligent. Each
defendant was thereafter to contribute equally.[213]

A CAUTIONARY NOTE

21.101   Pre-1945 cases involving the defence of contributory negligence should be read with
caution as, under the common law, contributory negligence was a complete defence.
Because, under the common law, the effects of contributory negligence and *volenti*
were the same (ie the defender was not liable at all), some of the older authorities do
not distinguish very clearly between the two defences as there was no practical need
to do so.

---

[209] [2000] 1 AC 360.
[210] *Ibid* at 371.
[211] [1989] AC 328.
[212] In view of the principle of joint and several liability (which enables the pursuer to recover the whole of
his damages from any one of the defenders found liable) it has been said that "the logic of the approach
adopted by the House of Lords is unavoidable" (Report on *Civil Liability – Contribution* (Scot Law Com No
115) at para 4.45).
[213] The House approved the *dictum* of Denning LJ in *Davies* v *Swan Motor Co (Swansea) Ltd* [1949] 2 KB 291
at 325.

SOME REFLECTIONS ON CONTRIBUTORY NEGLIGENCE

It would be quite misleading to view contributory negligence as simply a mirror image **21.102** of negligence. There are several reasons for this. First, as we have noted, a finding of contributory negligence is not dependent on the pursuer owing the defender a duty of care (although he may do so). For a finding of negligence to be made against a defender, however, the defender must owe the pursuer a duty of care.

Second, the economic consequences of the two findings differ. A finding of contrib- **21.103** utory negligence impacts directly on the pursuer's pocket – if he is found to have been contributorily negligent he is awarded less by way of damages. On the other hand, a finding of negligence very rarely impacts on the defender's pocket because he will usually be insured against the loss. Cane sums up the position as follows: "In practice, negligent people do not pay for the consequences of their negligence; but contributorily negligent people do pay for the consequences of their contributory negligence."[214]

PRACTICAL MATTERS

As stated at the outset, contributory negligence is frequently encountered in practice. **21.104** In fact, the defence is often included in pleadings simply as a matter of course where there is no real basis for it. Where the pursuer believes this to be the case, he should, as a matter of pleading, place a call on the defender to further specify in his pleadings details of the conduct which is alleged to amount to contributory negligence.

The defender is required to give fair notice to the pursuer of the case of contrib- **21.105** utory negligence which he intends to advance. In *McGowan v W & J R Watson Ltd*,[215] Lord Nimmo Smith stated:[216]

> "There is … a requirement, which is imposed on defenders as much as on pursuers, to give at least fair notice of a case which it is proposed to make. Thus, defenders could not secure a finding of contributory negligence if they had not at the very least made some reference to it in their pleadings. How much beyond that is required depends very much on the circumstances of each case. It may be that the pursuer's own pleadings would support a plea of contributory negligence, in which case very little need be said. But if defenders choose to give notice of a specific case of contributory negligence, as was done here … they may be precluded from seeking to argue for a finding of contributory negligence on any other ground because they have not given fair notice of it …"

Although there is no rule of law to this effect, it is rare in practice to encounter appor- **21.106** tionments of less than 10 per cent.[217]

---

[214] P Cane, *Atiyah's Accidents, Compensation and the Law* (7th edn, 2008), p 56.
[215] 2007 SC 272. See, also, *Weir v Robertson Group (Construction) Ltd* [2006] CSOH 107, where Lord Glennie observed (at para 7): "The defences should aver the facts which the defender regards as necessary to support his defence or plea of contributory negligence. Otherwise how is the pursuer to know what investigations to make and what evidence to lead."
[216] 2007 SC 272 at para 13.
[217] See the comments of Croom Johnson LJ in *Capps v Miller* [1989] 1 WLR 839 at 848–849. A finding of 5% contributory negligence, as was made in *Pasternack v Poulton* [1973] 1 WLR 476, is unusual.

21.107   Finally, it should be noted that certain Acts make express provision for the operation of the defence of contributory negligence.[218]

DIFFERENCES BETWEEN CONTRIBUTORY NEGLIGENCE AND *VOLENTI NON FIT INJURIA*

21.108 It should be noted, as a practical point, that the defences of contributory negligence and *volenti non fit injuria* are not mutually exclusive and in fact often arise together in the same case. The defences, however, have different outcomes. *Volenti* is a complete defence and, if the defence succeeds, the pursuer's case will fail. Contributory negligence, on the other hand, is a partial defence. It is open to the court to find the pursuer to blame to a small or greater degree, with a corresponding reduction in damages. It has been stated that it is illogical to make a finding of 100 per cent contributory negligence.[219] This is because s 1 of the 1945 Act refers to a person suffering damage as a result *partly* of his own fault and *partly* of the fault of another person.

21.109   A person may take the requisite care for his own safety, but may nonetheless be held to have been *volenti*. However, to be held contributorily negligent a pursuer must in some respect have disregarded his own safety.

21.110   Finally, for the defence of *volenti non fit injuria* to apply the pursuer must be *sciens et volens* – he must know and consent to the risk: that is a subjective test. The defence will fail where the pursuer was not aware of the risk even although he should have been.[220] On the other hand, a pursuer may be contributorily negligent if he failed to exercise the care of the reasonable man: that is an objective and impersonal standard.

THE DEFENCE OF ILLEGALITY (OR PUBLIC POLICY)

21.111 If the defender was engaged in criminal activity at the time at which his injuries were sustained, he may be prevented from recovering damages. In other words, the criminality of the pursuer may constitute a defence. The maxim *ex turpi causa non oritur actio*, which has its origins in the sphere of contract law,[221] can also operate as a defence in delict. With the increase in litigation consciousness generally, more and more people have resort to the law when they feel aggrieved. Even those involved in nefarious activities have shown themselves willing to seek legal redress as a result of injuries arising from such activities. The development of the illegality defence is based on public policy considerations.[222] The courts quite simply are not prepared to allow a person engaged in serious criminal activities successfully to sue in respect of injuries sustained during the course of those illegal activities. Not only would there be a moral

---

[218] See Animals (Scotland) Act 1987, ss 1(6), 2(1)(a) and (3)(a); Consumer Protection Act 1987, s 6(4).
[219] *Pitts v Hunt* [1991] 1 QB 24. Compare, however, *McEwan v Lothian Buses plc* 2006 RepLR 134.
[220] See, eg, *Smith v Austin Lifts Ltd* [1959] 1 WLR 100; *Toms v Royal Mail Group plc* 2006 SLT 431, per Lord Glennie at 439.
[221] See the observations of Buxton LJ in *Reeves v Commissioner of Police of the Metropolis* [1999] QB 169 at 184.
[222] See *Hewison v Meridian Shipping Pte Ltd* [2003] ICR 766, per Ward LJ at 794: "It is an inherent aspect of the public policy which informs the whole doctrine." It has also been said that "[t]he court ought not to allow itself to be made an instrument to enforce obligations alleged to arise out of the plaintiff's own criminal act" (per Beldam LJ in *Clunis v Camden & Islington Health Authority* [1998] QB 978 at 990).

objection to the recovery of compensation[223] in such circumstances, but it would also be demeaning for the courts to engage in a consideration of what would constitute reasonable care in the context of an illegal enterprise. Thus, a safeblower who blows up his partner in crime, which partner was acting as a lookout, would be able to rely on this defence should his fellow wrongdoer attempt to seek legal redress from his.[224] While the criminal enterprise may be joint[225] in nature, this is not an essential requirement. Thus, the defence may be invoked against a pursuer who acted alone in the course of criminal activity.[226] It will be obvious to the reader that there is a very wide range of criminal activities. It is, however, only in cases of serious crime that the defence is likely to succeed. For example, over the years, many people have recovered damages in respect of injuries sustained in motor accidents notwithstanding that they had been exceeding the speed limit at the time.[227]

Duncan v *Ross Harper & Murphy*[228] illustrates the operation of the defence. There, a **21.112** 19-year-old man was injured while a passenger in a negligently driven Ford Escort. He had participated in the theft of the vehicle. The action raised by the pursuer was not against the driver of the car but rather against the solicitors whom he had instructed to deal with his personal injury claim. The solicitors had failed to raise the action for personal injuries against the driver within the statutory limitation period. The pursuer therefore sought to recover damages from his solicitors in respect of professional negligence. The Lord Ordinary (Kirkwood) held that the solicitors had been negligent but he assoilzied the defenders on the basis that, even if the personal injuries action had been raised timeously, the defence of illegality would have prevented the pursuer from recovering any damages against his fellow wrongdoer. The pursuer had been involved in the theft of the car and accordingly was not entitled to recover damages from his co-participant in crime. Similarly, in *Sloan* v *Triplett*,[229] the pursuer, a passenger in a car, was held disentitled to recover damages from the driver in respect of injuries sustained in a road traffic accident. The pursuer, the defender and another person had stolen the car from outside a bar and were all acting together in pursuance

---

[223] Cane has observed that, in this area, "the compensatory aim of the law is subordinated to other values": *Atiyah's Accidents, Compensation and the Law*, p 67.

[224] See the *dictum* of Lord Asquith in *NCB* v *England* [1954] AC 403 at 429.

[225] See *Pitts* v *Hunt* [1991] 1 QB 24; *Sloan* v *Triplett* 1985 SLT 294; *Ashcroft's Curator Bonis* v *Stewart* 1988 SLT 163; *Wilson* v *Price* 1989 SLT 484; *Weir* v *Wyper* 1992 SLT 579; *Taylor* v *Leslie* 1998 SLT 1248; *Currie* v *Clamp's Exr* 2002 SLT 196.

[226] See *Revill* v *Newberry* [1996] QB 567. (There, the owner of an allotment was sleeping in his shed when a trespasser attempted to break into it. The owner poked his shotgun through a hole in the shed door and fired. The shot hit the trespasser and the owner was found liable in negligence. The mere fact that the plaintiff was engaged in criminal conduct upon the premises when he suffered injury was held not sufficient of itself to debar him from claiming damages for those injuries.) See, also, *Clunis* v *Camden and Islington Health Authority* [1998] QB 978. *Gray* v *Thames Trains Ltd* [2009] 1 AC 1339.

[227] The defender would almost certainly attempt to rely on the defence of contributory negligence in such a situation.

[228] 1993 SLT 105.

[229] 1985 SLT 294.

of a criminal enterprise.[230] *Weir* v *Wyper*[231] can be contrasted with *Duncan* and *Sloan*. In *Weir*, a 16-year-old girl went on a trip with another girl and two men. One of the men and the other girl left the car. Thus, the girl was left with the defender in the car in the dark in an unfamiliar place. She knew that the defender held only a provisional licence but nevertheless asked him for a lift home. The defender began to drive at high speed, braking violently when he required to stop. The car left the road and overturned and the pursuer was injured. Lord Coulsfield concluded that the illegality defence should not apply in these circumstances.[232] His Lordship was of the view that each case had to be decided on its own merits and it seems that the defence will therefore only prevent recovery in cases which involve serious illegality. The element of criminality in *Duncan* and *Sloan* was clearly of a more serious nature[233] than in *Weir*, hence the failure of the pursuer to recover in the former cases.

21.113   In *Ashmore* v *Rock Steady Security Ltd*,[234] a nightclub doorman punched the pursuer, causing him to fall backwards and strike his head on the pavement. In a subsequent action, it was held that the pursuer's persistent annoyance and verbal abuse of the doorman did not operate to defeat his claim on the basis of *ex turpi causa non oritur actio*. Indeed, the pursuer stood exonerated of any unlawful act.

21.114   In *Kirkham* v *Chief Constable of Greater Manchester*,[235] the police knew that a prisoner was a suicide risk but failed to pass this information on to the prison authorities. The prisoner, who was suffering from clinical depression, committed suicide. The defendant argued that the defence of *ex turpi causa non oritur actio* was applicable. The Court of Appeal held that as suicide was not a criminal act and as it could not be said that a claim arising from the suicide of a clinically depressed person would affront the public conscience, the defence of *ex turpi causa non oritur actio* could not succeed.

---

[230] See, also, *Lindsay* v *Poole* 1984 SLT 269 (the pursuer, who was associated with the defender in the theft of a car and was injured when it struck a lamp-post, failed to recover damages); *Wilson* v *Price* 1989 SLT 484 (the pursuer failed to recover damages in respect of injuries sustained when the car in which he was a passenger collided with a tree. The defender, the driver of the car, was under age and had taken the car without the owner's permission. The Lord Ordinary (Milligan) held on the evidence that the car had been taken by the defender without the consent of the owner and that the pursuer, in that knowledge, had allowed himself to be carried in it. Accordingly, the defence of joint criminal enterprise succeeded); *Andersen* v *Hameed* 2010 RepLR 132.

[231] 1992 SLT 579.

[232] See, also, *Currie* v *Clamp's Exr* 2002 SLT 196 (the degree of criminality, being a minor statutory breach, was not serious enough to disable the injured party from recovering. He had allowed himself to be carried in a car which had been taken and was being driven without the owner's consent. Lord Clarke expressed the view that a pragmatic approach to the facts ought to be taken); *Toms* v *Royal Mail Group plc* 2006 SLT 431 (a man was killed when he fell asleep at the wheel of a lorry which he was driving for the Post Office. It was alleged that the deceased's driving hours exceeded those permitted by statute. The defender argued that the pursuer's action was defeated by the defence of *ex turpi causa*. The defence failed, Lord Glennie stating (at para 38): "Even if it were shown that the deceased was in breach of a legal limit in the hours driven or worked, and even if he was aware of such contravention of the law, it seems to me that that illegality is properly to be described as collateral to the claim and is insufficient to defeat the claim"); *Taylor* v *Leslie* 1998 SLT 1248 (the facts are discussed above in relation to contributory negligence. The driver's illegal conduct would not have been considered particularly reprehensible on the Orkney island in question and it would be wrong to deny recovery on the ground that the deceased was engaged in the course of a common criminal enterprise with the defender).

[233] For further cases where the actions in question were found to be sufficiently serious for the defence to operate, see *Clunis* v *Camden and Islington Health Authority* [1998] QB 978; *Vellino* v *Chief Constable of Greater Manchester* [2002] 1 WLR 218 (escaping from custody was a sufficiently serious criminal offence to justify the invocation of the defence); *Gray* v *Thames Trains Ltd* [2009] 1 AC 1339 (the claimant committed manslaughter as a result of psychological problems caused by the negligence of the defendant; he was held disentitled to recover losses which were the consequence of the sentence imposed on him).

[234] 2006 SLT 207.

[235] [1990] 2 QB 283.

However, the illegality defence was successfully invoked in *Pitts* v *Hunt*.[236] The **21.115** plaintiff and his friend, Hunt, were at a disco, drinking. They set off home on Hunt's motorcycle. The plaintiff was aware that Hunt was neither licensed nor insured to drive. The plaintiff rode pillion on the way home and actively encouraged Hunt to drive in a fast, reckless and hazardous manner deliberately intended to frighten other members of the public using the highway. The motorcycle collided with a car. The plaintiff was seriously injured and Hunt was killed. Hunt's blood alcohol level was found to have been over twice the legal limit. It was held that the plaintiff had encouraged Hunt to commit offences. Therefore, on the grounds of *ex turpi causa non oritur actio* and public policy, the plaintiff would not be allowed to recover. The Court of Appeal also held that s 148 of the Road Traffic Act 1972 prevented Hunt's executor from pleading *volenti*. The court thus approved the Scottish decision in *Winnik* v *Dick*.[237] The court also pointed out that while s 148(3) of the 1972 Act precluded a defence of *volenti*, it was not concerned with and did not therefore preclude the defence of illegality.

Although the illegality defence is not often encountered in practice, it will be **21.116** evident from *Pitts* v *Hunt*[238] that the defence plays a crucial role in road traffic cases where the court's disapproval of the pursuer's conduct is so great that it feels no damages should be awarded. The operation of the Road Traffic Act 1988, as we have already noted, excludes the defence of *volenti* and it would appear that a finding of 100 per cent contributory negligence is illogical.[239] The illegality defence therefore achieves the desired outcome.

The illegality defence can be employed in an action for breach of statutory duty. In **21.117** *Clunis* v *Camden & Islington Health Authority*,[240] the plaintiff was released from hospital following a period of detention under the mental health legislation. Following his release, he killed a person in an unprovoked attack and was convicted of manslaughter on the ground of diminished responsibility. This resulted in his being detained in a secure hospital. The plaintiff raised an action in which he contended that the district health authority had failed to discharge its statutory duty to arrange after-care for him following his initial release from hospital. The Court of Appeal rejected the plaintiff's claim on the basis of *ex turpi causa non oritur actio*. The plaintiff was attempting to found on his own illegal conduct in advancing his case and, although his culpability was reduced by reason of mental disorder, his mental state did not justify a verdict of not guilty by reason of insanity. Accordingly, he must be assumed to have known what he was doing and that it was wrong and he was therefore debarred from recovering damages. The case does indicate, however, that the plea of *ex turpi causa* may fail where the pursuer does *not* know the nature and quality of his act or that his actions are wrong.[241]

A defender who attempts to rely on the defence of illegality may also try to invoke **21.118** the defence of contributory negligence.[242] Often, when the illegality defence is rejected on the facts, the defence of contributory negligence succeeds.[243]

---

[236] [1991] 1 QB 24.
[237] 1984 SLT 185.
[238] [1990] 3 All ER 344.
[239] See, however, *McEwan* v *Lothian Buses plc* 2006 RepLR 134.
[240] [1998] QB 978.
[241] *Ibid* per Beldam LJ at 989.
[242] See, eg, *Pitts* v *Hunt* [1991] 1 QB 24.
[243] ee, eg, *Taylor* v *Leslie* 1998 SLT 1248; *Currie* v *Clamp's Exr* 2002 SLT 196.

22 REMEDIES

INTRODUCTION

"[T]he rule of public policy which has first claim on the loyalty of the law [is] that **22.1** wrongs should be remedied."[1] Many years before Sir Thomas Bingham MR said these words, Erskine had stated the position thus:

> "[E]veryone who has the exercise of reason, and so can distinguish between right and wrong is naturally obliged to make up the damage befalling his neighbour from a wrong committed by himself. Wherefore every fraudulent contrivance, or unwarrantable act by which another suffers damage, or runs the hazards of it, subjects the delinquent to reparation."[2]

It is important to note, at the outset, that an individual does not necessarily have a **22.2** remedy merely because he has suffered a loss.[3] There are cases where loss has been occasioned but the law will not afford the aggrieved individual a remedy. The pure economic loss cases discussed in Chapter 4 provide an obvious example of instances where loss has been suffered but the pursuer is without a remedy. As a matter of public policy, the courts will not generally permit recovery in such cases owing to their fear of a flood of claims.

As delict forms part of the civil law of Scotland, the pursuer should seek his **22.3** remedy in a civil court, namely the appropriate sheriff court or the Court of Session.[4] (The UK Supreme Court does, of course, have an appellate jurisdiction in relation to Scottish civil matters.) From a practical point of view, it may be preferable to raise the action in the sheriff court as it is a local court whereas the Court of Session sits only in Edinburgh. Moreover, it is not necessary to instruct counsel (an advocate) if one proceeds in the sheriff court – the pursuer's solicitor can conduct the case on his behalf whereas solicitors do not have rights of audience in the Court of Session.[5]

Where the delictual conduct also constitutes a crime – for example, an assault – the **22.4** victim may recover compensation from the Criminal Injuries Compensation Authority.[6] Although this chapter is concerned with civil remedies, it is interesting to note that a

---

[1] X (Minors) v Bedfordshire CC [1994] 2 WLR 554, per Sir Thomas Bingham MR at 572.
[2] Erskine, Inst III, i,13.
[3] See, eg, Caparo Industries plc v Dickman [1990] 2 AC 605, discussed in Chapter 2.
[4] For a detailed discussion of the factors which might inform the pursuer's decision as to choice of court, see C Hennessy, Civil Procedure and Practice (3rd edn, 2008), pp 30–33. Note, however, that the sheriff court has privative (ie exclusive) jurisdiction in actions where the sum sued for does not exceed £5,000 (exclusive of interest and expenses).
[5] However, solicitor-advocates do have rights of audience in the Court of Session: see s 24 of the Law Reform (Miscellaneous Provisions) (Scotland) Act 1990.
[6] This is a non-departmental public body in the UK which administers a scheme of compensation for the victims of violent crime. The scheme was originally set up in 1964, at which time it was administered by

criminal court is empowered, in certain circumstances, to make what is known as a *compensation order*. Such an order directs a person found guilty of a crime or offence to pay to the victim a sum of money by way of compensation. This is in addition to any term of imprisonment or fine which the criminal court may impose on the offender.

22.5   Where an employee is injured in the workplace he may be eligible for industrial injuries disablement benefit. However, there are certain rules, which are discussed in more detail below, which prevent the injured party being overcompensated and which allow the state to recover state benefits from the person who makes an award of compensation.

22.6   In many of the reported cases the term "reparation" is used in the context of delictual remedies. If the pursuer seeks reparation it simply means that he is seeking compensation for his loss. It has been said that "[r]eparation is the pecuniary remedy afforded by law for loss caused by a wrong".[7]

22.7   Let us now turn to the various remedies available to the pursuer. The most common remedies in delict are damages and interdict and in some cases the pursuer may seek both damages *and* interdict. However, we will deal first with the less common remedies of self-help and declarator.

SELF-HELP

22.8   In certain limited circumstances it is permissible for an individual to take steps to prevent a wrong occurring without seeking sanction from the civil courts. A landowner, for example, might erect a wall around his property in an effort to keep trespassers off his land. Similarly, a landowner can cut off branches of a tree which overhang his land but he must not cause unnecessary damage. In *Lemmon* v *Webb*[8] the defendant cut off branches from a tree belonging to the adjoining landowner. The branches overhung the defendant's own property. He gave no notice of his intention to cut the branches and he did not require to trespass on his neighbour's land to do so. In concluding that the defendant had not exceeded his legal right, Lord Macnaghten pointed out:[9]

> "[A] man is not bound to permit a neighbour's tree to overhang the surface of his land ...
> Nor can it, I think, be doubted that if he can get rid of the interference or encroachment
> without committing a trespass or entering upon the land of his neighbour he may do so
> whenever he pleases, and that no notice or communication is required by law."

22.9   The law allows the use of reasonable force to prevent a wrong being committed against one's property. Thus, a farmer may shoot a dog which is about to attack his livestock provided that such action is reasonable in the circumstances.[10] It would appear that an occupier may turn a trespasser off his land so long as he does not overstep the bounds of reasonable force in so doing.[11] A landowner is not permitted to set a trap or set dogs

---

the Authority's predecessor, the Criminal Injuries Compensation Board. In Scotland, the criminal injuries compensation scheme is funded by the Scottish Government.

[7] *A* v *Glasgow City Council* 2010 SC 411, per the Lord President (Lord Hamilton) at para 10 (under reference to A T Glegg, *The Law of Reparation in Scotland* (4th edn, 1955), p 3).

[8] [1895] AC 1.

[9] *Ibid* at 7.

[10] The matter is now regulated by statute: see Animals (Scotland) Act 1987, s 4.

[11] See, eg, *Wood* v *NB Railway* (1899) 2 F 1. There, a cabman, having deposited a passenger at Waverley Station, was asked to leave but failed to do so. Railway employees were held entitled to remove him. Lord Young,

upon a trespasser, or indeed to shoot him,[12] such acts being considered to go beyond reasonable force.

Self-defence is permissible in order to resist an assault[13] as long as the steps taken **22.10** to defend oneself are reasonable in the circumstances.[14]

DECLARATOR

Sometimes declarator may be sought as a delictual remedy. If a person seeks declarator, **22.11** he is, in essence, asking the court to make a statement as to *his* legal position. Declarator is not competent in order to obtain a *general statement of the law* on a particular issue. Rather, it must settle a live practical question between the litigants. Lord Dundas provided guidance as to the province of declarator and the circumstances in which it might competently be sought in *Rothfield* v *North British Railway Co*:[15]

> "[A] declarator 'cannot be used for the mere purpose of declaring legal propositions, where no practical question or dispute lies beneath' (*per* Lord Dunedin in Birrell's Trustees, 1918 SC (HL), at p 47); and a declarator 'not with reference to any particular case, but in general,' is incompetent (*per* Lord Adam in Callender, (1900) 2 F, at p 401)."[16]

In *Webster* v *Lord Advocate*[17] the petitioner obtained declarator to the effect that a **22.12** nuisance existed in relation to the noise created by the erection of the metal grandstand for the Edinburgh Military Tattoo. The remedy of declarator is rarely sought alone – it is usually combined with a plea for damages or interdict. Indeed, in *Webster*, both declarator and interdict were sought.[18]

INTERDICT[19]

It is convenient to commence a discussion of the remedy of interdict by reference to **22.13** *dicta* of Lord Gifford in *Hay's Trs* v *Young*:[20] "The remedy of judicial interdict is a most

---

endorsing the direction which had been given to the jury by the Lord Justice-Clerk, stated (at 3): "[A] cabman with a carriage and horse, must obey the orders of a railway company's authorised servants as to leaving the station, and when he is ordered to leave it he must leave it, and if he refuses and persists may be turned out. He is not to remain there until it has been settled by some disinterested tribunal whether he had right to remain, and whether the servant of the railway company was wrong in ordering him out."

[12] In *Revill* v *Newberry* [1996] QB 567 the owner of an allotment was sleeping in his shed when a trespasser attempted to break into it. The owner poked his shotgun through a hole in the shed door and fired. The shot injured the trespasser and the owner was found liable in negligence. Self-help which is considered to be "excessive" in nature is therefore impermissible and may result in a finding of assault or (as in this case) negligence.

[13] See *Hallowell* v *Niven* (1843) 5 D 759.

[14] See *Moore* v *MacDougall* 1989 SCCR 659. See, also, *Ashmore* v *Rock Steady Security Ltd* 2006 SLT 207 (where the plea of self-defence was rejected on the evidence).

[15] 1920 SC 805 at 830.

[16] The full citations of the two cases mentioned in this *dictum* are as follows: *North British Railway* v *Birrell's Trs* 1918 SC (HL) 33; *Callender's Cable and Construction Co* v *Corporation of Glasgow* (1900) 2 F 397.

[17] 1985 SC 173.

[18] See, also, *Edinburgh & District Water Trs* v *Clippens Oil Co* (1899) 1 F 899.

[19] For a detailed exposition of the law of interdict in Scotland, see S Scott Robinson, *The Law of Interdict* (2nd edn, 1994).

[20] (1877) 4 R 398 at 402.

important one, for it proceeds on the principle that prevention is better than cure, and that in many cases it is more expedient to prevent a wrong from being done than merely to attempt to give subsequent redress." Interdict, therefore, is the appropriate remedy to prevent someone committing a threatened wrong or continuing to commit a wrong. Interdict is a preventive process: that is, it is designed to prevent something being done. The remedy of interdict is not appropriate where a wrong has been completed and there is no threat of repetition.

22.14   The pursuer may seek interdict on its own or he may seek interdict in conjunction with damages[21] or declarator.[22]

TITLE AND INTEREST TO SUE

22.15   A person seeking interdict must have both title and interest to sue. In other words, he must have the right to bring the court proceedings in question. In *Dundee District Council* v *Cook*[23] it was held that a local authority had neither title nor interest to obtain interim interdict against a house proprietor who was allegedly abusing and frightening the Council's tenants in nearby premises owned by the Council.

INTERDICT WILL BE GRANTED ONLY ON REASONABLE GROUNDS

22.16   Interdict will never be granted as a matter of course. It will be granted only on strong, or, at least, reasonable grounds.[24] Thus, there must be reasonable fear that delictual conduct will take place. Therefore, in a case where interdict is sought against trespass, there would need to be evidence of a course of actual trespass (ie a continuing wrong) or a clear threat to trespass (a threatened wrong) before the court will grant interdict. *Hay's Trs* v *Young*[25] neatly illustrates this point. Young and another, without permission, went on to the trustees' lands with a view to obtaining evidence for a trial which was pending. In the course of their investigations, they opened drains at several points to determine the flow of a sewer. One month later, the trustees presented a petition to have Young interdicted from trespassing on the land. In the Court of Session, Lord Ormidale[26] quoted with approval from the sheriff-substitute's judgment: "Interdict is a remedy, by decree of Court, either against a wrong in course of being done, or against an apprehended violation of a party's rights, only to be awarded on evidence of the wrong, or on reasonable grounds of apprehension that such violation is intended." Lord Ormidale concluded that not only was there no wrong in the course of being done, but there was not even an averment that there was a threat or apprehension of a future wrong. The court concluded that the action was ill founded and refused to apply "a process of law, which was intended for protection, to a case which looks more like persecution".[27]

---

[21] See D Walker, *The Law of Delict in Scotland* (2nd edn, 1981), p 449.
[22] See *Edinburgh & District Water Trs* v *Clippens Oil Co* (1899) 1 F 899.
[23] 1995 SCLR 559 (Sh Ct).
[24] See *Hay's Trs* v *Young* (1877) 4 R 398, per Lord Gifford at 402.
[25] (1877) 4 R 398.
[26] *Ibid* at 401.
[27] *Ibid*, per the Lord Justice-Clerk at 400.

PERMANENT INTERDICT AND INTERIM INTERDICT

Permanent interdict, that is to say, an interdict applying without limit of time, is an order preventing a defender from doing an illegal act. It is a discretionary remedy and will be granted only if there are cogent reasons to support its grant.[28] **22.17**

Alternatively, interdict may be interim, ie intended to preserve the *status quo* or prevent the occurrence of an imminent wrong. This was the case in *McMurdo* v *Ferguson*,[29] where interim interdict was used to prevent the imminent publication of material which was *prima facie* defamatory. **22.18**

Interim interdict is an immediate and temporary remedy and may be sought at any stage of proceedings for permanent interdict pending final determination of the issue. An interim interdict is without prejudice to the parties and remains in force until such time as it is recalled.[30] A decree of perpetual interdict, however, will supersede an earlier interim interdict in identical terms.[31] **22.19**

Interim interdict is a discretionary remedy – it is at the court's discretion whether to grant or refuse interdict.[32] In *Deane* v *Lothian Regional Council*[33] the Lord Justice-Clerk (Lord Wheatley), quoting from *Burn Murdoch on Interdict* (at p 128), explained:[34] "The test at the stage of interim interdict is not so much the absolute relevancy of the case as the seeming cogency of the need for interim interdict." In other words, the test to be applied in determining whether interim interdict should be granted is whether a *prima facie* title to sue exists and whether a case has been made warranting the granting of an interim order. **22.20**

The basic requirements for grant of interim interdict are therefore: **22.21**

(1) a prima facie case;
(2) a favourable balance of convenience – in other words, the court will weigh up the relative inconvenience resulting to either party from the grant or refusal of interdict and will choose the course of action which will do least damage to either party in the meantime. In *McMurdo* v *Ferguson*[35] the petitioner claimed that a defamatory article, which threatened his reputation and means of livelihood, was about to be published. The respondents claimed that public interest favoured publication. The court, in granting interim interdict, concluded that the loss of reputation, and its consequences, could be immediate and irreparable and the balance of convenience therefore favoured the petitioner.[36]

---

[28] See, eg, *Kelso School Board* v *Hunter* (1874) 2 R 228.
[29] 1993 SLT 193.
[30] See, eg, *Home Drummond* v *McLachlan* 1908 SC 12.
[31] See, eg, *Stewart* v *Stallard* 1995 SCLR 167 (Sh Ct).
[32] See, eg, *Kelso School Board* v *Hunter* (1874) 2 R 228.
[33] 1986 SLT 22.
[34] *Ibid* at 23.
[35] 1993 SLT 193.
[36] Note, however, that s 12 of the Human Rights Act 1998 must now be taken into account "if a court is considering whether to grant any relief which, if granted, might affect the exercise of the Convention right to freedom of expression" (ie Art 10 of the ECHR). The court may not restrain publication before trial unless it is "satisfied that the applicant is likely to establish that publication should not be allowed". In effect, this imposes a third hurdle for the petitioner to overcome when seeking interim interdict in such cases in addition to a *prima facie* case and a favourable balance of convenience. See *Dickson Minto WS* v *Bonnier Media Ltd* 2002 SLT 776 (the third hurdle was held not to have been overcome). See, also, the guidance provided by Lord Nicholls of Birkenhead in *Cream Holdings Ltd* v *Banerjee* [2005] 1 AC 253 (HL) (at para 22) and the

PERSONAL LIABILITY TO INTERDICT

22.22 Liability to interdict is personal to the wrongdoer and does not, therefore, transmit with property. It follows that the current owner of a property cannot be interdicted in respect of a nuisance perpetrated by a previous owner.[37] In *Lord Advocate* v *Scotsman Publications Ltd*[38] the Inner House considered the point that liability to interdict is personal to the wrongdoer. Anthony Cavendish, a former member of M16, wrote a book called *Inside Intelligence* containing his memoirs about his service with the British security service. Although authority to publish the book was refused by the Government, Cavendish published a number of copies privately. After representations were made to him by the Crown, he undertook not to publish further copies without first giving notice of his intention to do so. However, copies of the book had come into the hands of the *Sunday Times* and the *Scotsman*. In England, the Attorney-General sought and obtained an injunction against the publishers of *The Sunday Times*. The publishers of *The Scotsman*, having refused to give any undertakings not to publish any material from the book, were then faced with a petition for interdict to prevent further publication of the contents of the book. The petition for interdict, which was sought by the Lord Advocate, on behalf of the Crown, was against *The Scotsman* "and any other person having notice of the interlocutor" (the court order). In the Inner House, the Lord Justice-Clerk (Lord Ross) took exception to the form of interdict sought. His Lordship observed:[39] "[I]n Scots law, there is no justification for courts pronouncing an order of interdict against a named respondent 'and any other person having notice of the interlocutor'." To do so, the Lord Justice-Clerk observed, "would conflict with the recognised practice and procedure in Scotland". Although the case was subsequently appealed to the House of Lords on other grounds, their Lordships did not disturb the decision of the Inner House insofar as it related to the personal nature of interdict.

QUASI-CRIMINAL NATURE OF INTERDICT

22.23 The process of interdict is, by its nature, quasi-criminal. Therefore, if the party interdicted fails to obtemper (ie obey) the terms of the interdict he is liable to summary punishment by way of fine or imprisonment.[40]

NEED FOR CLARITY AND PRECISION IN FRAMING OF INTERDICT

22.24 In view of these draconian penalties for failure to observe the terms of an interdict, it is imperative that the petition for interdict is framed in clear, precise and definite terms. The petition, and indeed the decree granting it, must specify precisely what conduct is objected to so that the person interdicted is left in no doubt about what he is not permitted to do. The case of *British Motor Trade Association* v *Gray*[41] illustrates this

---

application of that guidance in *Ntuli* v *Donald* [2011] 1 WLR 294. See, also, R M M McInnes, "Section 12(3) of the Human Rights Act 1998 in Scotland – the short story so far" 2005 HR & UK P 14.

[37] *Bankier Distillery Co* v *Youngs Collieries Ltd* (1899) 2 F 89.

[38] 1988 SLT 490.

[39] *Ibid* at 506.

[40] See Scott Robinson, *The Law of Interdict*, Chapter 16.

[41] 1951 SC 586.

point. The facts of the case are stated in more detail in the chapter on economic delicts. An interim interdict was sought against Gray. He was engaged in trade as a car dealer and routinely induced others to breach valid and subsisting contracts. It was against such conduct that the interdict was directed. In the Inner House, the Lord President (Lord Cooper) held that the wording in the petition for interdict was inspecific. His Lordship stated that because grave consequences follow non-compliance with an interdict, the petitioners should be afforded an opportunity to amend the terms of the petition to make them more precise.

The interdict sought must therefore be precise in its wording. Fear of some **22.25** nebulous and unspecified injury would not constitute adequate grounds for interdict. A petition for interdict which is too undefined and speculative will be refused by the court. Although stated in the context of a matrimonial case, the words of Lord President Emslie in *Murdoch* v *Murdoch*[42] are of general application to the law of interdict: "Where interdict is granted by the court the terms of the interdict must be no wider than are necessary to curb the illegal actings complained of and so precise and clear that the person interdicted is left in no doubt what he is forbidden to do."[43]

Webster v *Lord Advocate*[44] also illustrates the need for precision in the framing of the **22.26** terms of the interdict. In 1977, the petitioner moved into a flat which was adjacent to Edinburgh Castle esplanade. She sought interdict in respect of the noise occasioned by the Edinburgh Military Tattoo and the noise of erecting the steel scaffolding to provide the seating. The Lord Ordinary concluded that the Tattoo did not constitute a nuisance but that the noise from the erection of the scaffolding did. His Lordship's interlocutor interdicted the Tattoo Policy Committee "from making preparations for the Edinburgh Military Tattoo on the esplanade at Edinburgh Castle in such manner as by reason of noise to create a nuisance to the pursuer ...". The defenders reclaimed on the basis that the terms of the Lord Ordinary's interlocutor were insufficiently precise. They argued that they had been left in doubt as to what they were forbidden to do. The Inner House agreed with the defenders' assertion, taking the view that the words "metallic construction" should be inserted before the word "noise". Lord Robertson stated the position as follows:[45]

> "It was argued on behalf of the second defenders in the appeal that the Lord Ordinary had erred in granting interdict in these terms. It was a cardinal principle of the law of interdict that 'in all cases ... where interdict is granted by the court the terms of the interdict must be no wider than are necessary to curb the illegal actings complained of, and so precise and clear that the person interdicted is left in no doubt what he is forbidden to do'. (*Murdoch* v *Murdoch* (at 13), per Lord President Emslie).
>
> In my opinion the interdict granted by the Lord Ordinary offended against this principle in both particulars: viz. – (a) it was in terms far wider than was necessary to curb the actings found to be a nuisance and illegal; and (b) it was not in terms so clear and precise that the second defenders were left in no doubt as to what they were forbidden to do. They might, for instance, be in doubt as to whether the interdict might cover the activities of motor vehicles, or cranes, or even of individual workmen communicating with each other: and they would

---

[42] 1973 SLT (Notes) 13.
[43] *Ibid* at 13.
[44] 1985 SC 173.
[45] *Ibid* at 188.

be hampered in their legitimate preparations and activities by reason of the terms of such an interdict."

INJURY MUST BE APPRECIABLE

22.27 In general, interdict will be granted to restrain an injury only if it is appreciable.[46] The court is unlikely to grant interdict in the case of trivial injury[47] on the basis of *de minimis non curat lex* (the law does not concern itself with trifles). It may also be important to ascertain whether the wrong was intentional or merely inadvertent. Inadvertent wrongs are generally less amenable to the remedy of interdict as they are less likely to be repeated. In *Hay's Trs v Young*[48] the single act of trespass which had occurred was carried out innocently and in good faith. Lord Ormidale therefore refused to grant interdict in that situation.

RELEVANCE OF PUBLIC INTEREST

22.28 It is no defence to a petition for *permanent* interdict that the respondent's actions are in the public interest.[49] In *Webster* v *Lord Advocate*[50] an argument was presented to the effect that the public interest in the continuance of the Tattoo outweighed the interest of neighbouring proprietors in its cessation. That argument did not prevail. The fact that the Tattoo was a spectacle enjoyed by citizens and ratepayers of Edinburgh as well as visitors to the city did not serve to permit the nuisance to continue. Lord Stott, in the Outer House, stated:[51] "while [the public interest] consideration would no doubt be all-important at the stage of interim interdict when balance of convenience is the main consideration, the situation is different once it is established that what the defenders have done and propose to do is an infringement of an occupier's rights."

A REMEDY OF LAST RESORT

22.29 It has been judicially stated that interdict is a remedy of last resort.[52] Where an *interim* interdict would cause great public inconvenience the court may make a declaratory finding and suspend the operation of that finding pending the taking of remedial measures.[53]

---

[46] *Russell v Cowper* (1882) 9 R 660.
[47] "[A]n interdict against a thing which would cause such material discomfort and annoyance is proper to be granted. The word 'material' is of great importance there—it excludes any sentimental, speculative, trivial discomfort or personal annoyance of that kind, a thing which the law may be said to take no notice of and to have no care for." (Per the Earl of Selborne LC in *Fleming v Hislop* (1886) 13 R (HL) 43 at 45.)
[48] (1877) 4 R 398.
[49] An *interim* interdict may be refused, however, if it is in the public interest to do so: see the discussion by J Chalmers in *Delict* (J M Thomson (ed) (2007) at para 10–13.
[50] 1985 SC 173.
[51] *Ibid* at 179.
[52] See *Duke of Richmond v Burgh of Lossiemouth* (1904) 12 SLT 166, per Lord Kyllachy at 169.
[53] See *Clippens Oil Co v Edinburgh and District Water Trs* (1897) 25 R 370, per Lord McLaren at 383–384. That opinion was quoted with approval by LP Cooper in *Ben Nevis Distillery (Fort William) Ltd v North British Aluminium Co* 1948 SC 592 at 598.

EXAMPLES OF INTERDICT

Having considered these general points in relation to interdict, let us now turn to **22.30** consider the types of delictual conduct which are capable of being restrained by interdict.

Wrongs to reputation

Wrongs to reputation, for example a *particular* statement of a defamatory character, **22.31** may be restrained by interdict. However, a petition for interdict against publishing "defamatory statements" about the pursuer would be too vague and general to be amenable to interdict. This follows from *British Motor Trade Association* v *Gray*,[54] which makes it clear that the wording of the petition must be precise and specific.

Wrongs in respect of the pursuer's rights in heritable property

Wrongs in respect of the pursuer's rights in heritable property are amenable to **22.32** interdict. For example, interdict would be competent to prevent trespass on one's land, subject, of course, to what is said in *Hay's Trs* v *Young* [55] above.[56] Land is owned *a coelo usque ad centrum* (from the heavens to the centre of the earth). Thus, a landowner whose property was adjacent to a building development was able to obtain an interdict against contractors to prevent their crane invading the airspace over his land.[57]

There is, however, a statutory exception to the rules regarding trespass in another's **22.33** airspace. The Civil Aviation Act 1982 sanctions trespass by aircraft flying over another person's property subject, of course, to certain height and other restrictions.[58]

Nuisance

Interdict is an apposite remedy in the event of nuisance.[59] Interdict will be granted **22.34** to prevent a nuisance being continued or repeated and damages will be awarded in respect of any loss occasioned by the nuisance. One of the most celebrated cases on nuisance is *Webster* v *Lord Advocate*,[60] the facts of which are narrated above. The defender there alleged that even if there was a nuisance, interdict should not, in the public interest, be granted. The court did not accept that argument and interdict was granted restricting the times at which work could be carried out.

Harassment

Section 8(1) of the Protection from Harassment Act 1997 confers an enforceable right **22.35** not to be harassed. Section 8(2) provides that "[a]n actual or apprehended breach of subsection (1) may be the subject of a claim in civil proceedings by the person who is

---

[54] 1951 SC 586.
[55] (1877) 4 R 398.
[56] Damages also may be sought in some cases where trespass has occurred but only where *actual* damage has been occasioned.
[57] *Brown* v *Lee Constructions Ltd* 1977 SLT (Notes) 61.
[58] See s 76 of the 1982 Act.
[59] It is not necessary to prove fault in order to obtain an interdict against a nuisance. However, in order to recover damages in respect of a nuisance it is necessary to prove fault: see *RHM Bakeries (Scotland) Ltd* v *Strathclyde RC* 1985 SC (HL) 17. On nuisance, generally, see Chapter 11.
[60] 1985 SC 173.

or may be the victim of the course of conduct in question; and any such claim shall be known as an action of harassment". Section 8(5)(b)(i) of the 1997 Act goes on to provide that, in an action of harassment, the court may grant interdict or interim interdict (without prejudice to any other remedies which it may grant).[61]

Breach of confidence

22.36   Interdict is an appropriate remedy in respect of breach of confidence.[62]

Passing off

22.37   Passing off[63] at common law is amenable to interdict. The gist of this wrong is that one party has falsely represented his wares as being those of another in a way which was designed to mislead the general public, redirect trade in his own direction and thus cause loss to the pursuer. The *locus classicus* is *Haig* v *Forth Blending Co.*[64] There, an action was raised by a whisky company against blenders and retailers. The petitioners wished to restrain the use by the respondents of a triangular-shaped bottle similar to their own Dimple bottle which had been in use for some time. Evidence produced in court indicated that barmen and customers had been confused and had thought that the respondents' product was in fact the petitioners' Dimple brand. Interdict was accordingly granted.

Use of land *in aemulationem vicini*

22.38   Use of land *in aemulationem vicini* may be restrained by way of interdict. This wrong involves the use of one's land in such a way as to harm one's neighbour in the use of his land. The prime purpose of the behaviour in question must be to cause harm, and loss must result. In *Campbell* v *Muir*[65] an owner of salmon fisheries acted in such a way as to interfere with an angler fishing from the opposite bank. The First Division held that such conduct amounted to use of land *in aemulationem vicini* and the petitioner would have been entitled to interdict had she insisted upon it.

Economic delicts

22.39   Interdict is often appropriate in relation to the economic delicts, as is evident from *British Motor Trade Association* v *Gray*[66] where the remedy was invoked to prevent the defendant from inducing breaches of further contracts.

---

[61] As well as the power to award damages in respect of harassment, the court may also (under s 8(5)(b)(ii) of the Act) grant a "non-harassment order" requiring the defender to refrain from such conduct in relation to the pursuer as may be specified in the order for a specified (and possibly indeterminate) period. However, a person may not be subjected to the same prohibitions in an interdict or interim interdict and a non-harassment order at the same time.

[62] See *Waste Systems International Inc* v *Eurocare Environmental Services Ltd* 1999 SLT 198. (In the circumstances of that case, the balance of convenience favoured the interdict being refused.) See, also, *Osborne* v *BBC* 2000 SC 29.

[63] See Chapter 16.

[64] 1954 SC 35.

[65] 1908 SC 387.

[66] 1951 SC 586.

DAMAGES

The award of damages is the most common remedy in delict. It was said in one case **22.40** that "[m]oney is the universal solvent".[67] Damages are therefore monetary compensation paid by the defender to the pursuer. The purpose of an award of damages is to effect *restitutio in integrum*, that is to restore the pursuer as far as possible to the position he was in before the delictual conduct took place.[68] The award of damages is designed to compensate, not to punish.[69] Therefore, the amount of compensation which a negligent defender is required to pay bears no relation to his degree of fault. A minor act of negligence may have catastrophic consequences for the pursuer and in such a case a large award of damages would be appropriate. Conversely, a gross act of negligence may result in only slight injury and in such a case the award of damages will be small. Damages are designed to compensate the injured party, not to reflect the degree of opprobrium with which the court views the defender's conduct. The concept of punitive damages plays no part in Scots law.[70] The law of delict in Scotland is not concerned with punishing the wrongdoer – it is concerned with compensating the victim.[71]

The law lays down the various heads of damages which the pursuer may incor- **22.41** porate in his claim. For example, *solatium* (which represents the pursuer's pain and suffering) and patrimonial loss (that is, financial or pecuniary loss) are heads of damage which Scots law recognises. However, in order to recover damages under these heads, the pursuer requires to bring evidence of his loss to court. In other words, the *actual* losses sustained are questions of fact which, failing admission by the defender, require proof.[72]

It is a well-established common law rule that only one action is competent in **22.42** respect of a single wrong. Accordingly, damages for *all* losses, both past and future, must be claimed in that one action.[73] (This, however, is subject to what is said below in relation to provisional damages.) The damages are assessed as at the date of proof. However, the pursuer may find that his losses increase before the date of final

---

[67] See *Auld* v *Shairp* (1874) 2 R 191, per Lord Neaves at 199.

[68] Stair I, 9, 2; *Livingstone* v *Rawyards Coal Co* (1880) 7 R (HL) 1, per Lord Blackburn at 7. See, also, *Cantwell* v *Criminal Injuries Compensation Board* 2002 SC (HL) 1: "The guiding principle in Scots Law ... is that damages for personal injury are intended to be compensatory. The principle is that the compensation which the injured party receives by way of the sum of money as damages should as nearly as possible put him in the same position as he would have been in if he had not sustained the wrong for which he is to be compensated." (Per Lord Hope of Craighead at para 22.)

[69] See *Gibson* v *Anderson* (1846) 9 D 1; *Black* v *North British Railway Co* 1908 SC 444.

[70] Note, however, that the English courts can make an award of exemplary (or penal) damages. Such awards are rare, however. See, generally, J F Clerk and W H B Lindsell, *Torts* (A Dugdale and M Jones (eds)) (20th rev edn, 2010), paras 28–139–28–151.

[71] See *Gibson* v *Anderson* (1846) 9 D 1.

[72] See, eg, *Smith* v *Opportunus Fishing Co Ltd* 2011 RepLR 34 (liability was admitted by the second of three defenders and proof was restricted to quantum).

[73] *Stevenson* v *Pontifex & Wood* (1887) 15 R 125 (per LP Inglis at 129); *Dunlop* v *McGowans* 1980 SC (HL) 73, per Lord Keith at 81: "An obligation to make reparation for ... loss, injury and damage is a single and indivisible obligation, and one action only may be prosecuted for enforcing it." See, however, *Duke of Abercorn* v *Merry & Cunninghame Ltd* 1909 SC 750 where a new action was permitted in respect of what was said to be "substantially a new claim". It is significant, however, that the context there was not personal injury but rather damage to real property. Lord McLaren stated (at 753): "I do not think that the rule which governs claims for personal injury can be applied without discrimination to actions for injury to real property. The person is an indivisible unit, and the damages obtained cover all heads of injury whether known or apprehended."

judgment. In such cases, it is possible for the pleadings to be amended even if that has the effect of opening up a concluded proof. In *Rieley* v *Kingslaw Riding School*[74] an additional proof was allowed in circumstances where, pending an appeal on liability, the pursuer's leg required to be amputated below the knee. At the original proof, the Lord Ordinary, in his assessment of damages, had considered the future risk of amputation of the pursuer's leg to be a very remote one and had discounted it. Cases such as *Rieley* are rare. The principle that damages are assessed upon evidence led at proof is an important one and the court will exercise its discretionary power to depart from it only in exceptional circumstances.[75]

22.43 Where the claim is in respect of damage to property[76] the damages should be reasonably straightforward to quantify – namely diminution in market value or the cost of repair or replacement of the property.[77] Such damages would fall under the umbrella of patrimonial loss. In *Hutchison* v *Davidson*[78] liability was established in respect of a fire which damaged a building. The court held that the damages should be calculated by reference to the selling value of the subjects as at the date of destruction rather than the reinstatement cost which would yield a much larger sum. There were no special circumstances which required to be taken into account. The court observed that where damage is caused to property, the award of damages "while it will compensate the claimant for all the direct and natural consequences of the wrongful act, it will neither enrich nor impoverish him beyond the position in which he would have been if the wrongful act had not occurred".[79]

22.44 As well as claiming in respect of the damaged property itself, the pursuer may have a claim in respect of derivative economic loss, namely loss which flows from the physical damage to his property. Such a claim was made in *Scottish Eastern Omnibuses Ltd* v *Leslie*.[80] There, the pursuers raised an action of damages relating to a road traffic accident. They claimed, *inter alia*, for loss of use of their vehicle while it was undergoing repair. This figure was based on a formula by which the operating costs were deducted from the total expenses for a year. This produced a "standing cost" which was then divided by the average number of vehicles multiplied by the number of days in the year. The resultant figure was said to represent the cost per day of having a substitute vehicle, or the cost of the loss of the vehicle. The defender argued that the basis of the pursuer's claim was incorrect. The sheriff court held that the prime consideration was that the pursuers were fairly compensated for their loss. There was no special sanctity about any particular method and the pursuers were therefore entitled to claim on a standing cost per day basis. Damages were awarded accordingly.

---

[74] 1975 SC 28.
[75] See the observations of the Lord Justice-Clerk (Lord Wheatley) in *Dalgleish* v *Glasgow Corporation* 1976 SC 32 at 50.
[76] For a more detailed discussion in relation to damage to property, see D M Walker, *The Law of Civil Remedies in Scotland* (1974), Chapter 57. See, also, J Chalmers in *Delict* (Thomson (ed)) (2007) at para 10–50.
[77] If the cost of repair of a damaged item is less than the replacement cost, then repair would be the appropriate course to follow in view of the general duty on the pursuer to mitigate his loss. On mitigation, generally, see the discussion below. For a more detailed discussion of damages for destruction of or damage to property, see Chalmers, *Delict* (SULI) at para 10.50.
[78] 1945 SC 395.
[79] *Ibid* per Lord Russell at 408.
[80] 1996 SLT (Sh Ct) 53.

In *McIver* v *Judge*[81] it was held that where the victim of negligence was impecunious and his car had been damaged beyond economic repair, he was entitled to recover the full cost of hiring a car until he received an interim award of damages[82] which enabled him, within a week, to replace his car.

An interesting issue arose in *Dimond* v *Lovell*.[83] The plaintiff's car was damaged as a **22.45** result of an accident caused by the defendant. The plaintiff hired a substitute car from a credit hire company but it subsequently transpired that the credit hire agreement was unenforceable (having not been properly executed under the Consumer Credit Act 1974). Accordingly, the plaintiff could not recover damages from the defendant for the notional cost of hiring the car as this would have led, in effect, to double recovery.

The discussion above has focused on the question of *derivative* economic losses. **22.46** Where the case is one of *pure* economic loss which the law will recognise (and, of course, it is only in limited cases that the law will allow recovery of a pure economic loss), the loss should again be reasonably straightforward to quantify. Therefore, in a negligent survey case, the damages will be either the cost of repair or the difference between the value of the property with the undetected faults and the value without the undetected faults.[84] Similarly, where an intended beneficiary does not receive his legacy owing to a solicitor's negligence, the relevant loss is the amount of the intended legacy.[85]

DAMAGES IN RESPECT OF PERSONAL INJURY CASES

More difficulty is encountered in calculating damages in personal injury cases. The **22.47** pursuer in a personal injury action is entitled to reparation in respect of his physical injury (known as *solatium*)[86] and any derivative economic loss (known as patrimonial loss).[87] Therefore, in personal injury actions, the claim will usually incorporate a number of heads of damages.[88] For example, in *Hodge* v *British Coal Corporation (No 2)*[89] the pursuer sought damages from his former employees in respect of a crush injury to his finger. Three amputations were required to his finger which led to a reduction in manual grip and dexterity. The pursuer returned to work but later became unfit for work. However, had he been able to continue working, he would, in any event, have become redundant on closure of the colliery. Damages were recovered in respect of

---

[81] 1994 SCLR 735 (Sh Ct). See, also, *Carson* v *McDonald* 1987 SCLR 415 (Sh Ct) (an impecunious victim of fault, whose car had been damaged beyond economic repair, was held entitled to recover the cost of hiring a cheap car in addition to the net value of the damaged vehicle). See also *Lagden* v *O'Connor* [2004] 1 AC 1067.
[82] For a discussion of interim damages, see below.
[83] [2000] 1 AC 384.
[84] See, eg, *Martin* v *Bell Ingram* 1986 SLT 575.
[85] *White* v *Jones* [1995] 2 AC 207; *Holmes* v *Bank of Scotland* 2002 SLT 544.
[86] Such an award has been made in respect of the discomfort, inconvenience, stress and pain of pregnancy: see *McFarlane* v *Tayside Health Board* 2000 SC (HL) 1. The case involved a negligent misstatement as regards a husband's sterility. He was not, in fact, sterile and an unwanted pregnancy resulted. (Interestingly, and somewhat controversially, the *economic costs of childrearing* were rejected as being irrecoverable: see J Thomson, "Abandoning the law of delict" 2000 SLT 43.)
[87] The inability of an injured fisherman to retrieve his creels – which were subsequently lost at sea during high tides – would thus be recoverable as derivative economic losses (if liability were established): see *Bremner* v *Bartlett* 2008 SCLR 258. (In the event, the degenerative changes to the pursuer's spine were held to have resulted from natural processes rather than from the defender's wrongdoing.)
[88] These heads of damages do not constitute separate claims. Rather, they form part of the *one* claim: see *Irving* v *Hiddleston* 1998 SLT 912.
[89] 1992 SLT 913.

(1) his pain and suffering; (2) loss of wages up until the date of closure of the colliery; and (3) the reduction in his prospects of securing employment in the future owing to his disability.

22.48   Claims in respect of personal injuries have, in recent times, become much more complex. This can be demonstrated by means of a simple comparison. In *McCallum v Paterson*[90] the only head of damages sought by the paraplegic pursuer was *solatium*, ie damages for pain and suffering. This case can be contrasted with *McMillan v McDowall*[91] (decided some 25 years later) where an award of £356,000 was made to the pursuer in respect of eight heads of loss. Some recent cases are discussed in more detail at the end of this chapter.

SOLATIUM

22.49 The *solatium* award represents compensation for pain and suffering. The Latin word *solatium* simply means "solace". Essentially, the award of *solatium* represents compensation in respect of a non-pecuniary loss and therefore the sum awarded is somewhat artificial. The artificial nature of the assessment of non-pecuniary losses was commented upon in *The Mediana*.[92] The Earl of Halsbury, LC, made the following observations in relation to non-pecuniary losses:[93]

> "[Y]ou very often cannot even lay down any principle upon which you can give damages. How is anybody to measure pain and suffering in monies counted? Nobody can suggest that you can, by any arithmetical calculation, establish what is the exact sum of money which would represent such a thing as pain and suffering which a person has undergone by reason of accident."

22.50 Certainly, it is obvious that no monetary sum can adequately compensate for physical injury. If a doctor mistakenly carries out a hysterectomy instead of a tonsillectomy, then, clearly, money cannot restore the patient's womb. This is a fact which has been judicially acknowledged. Thus, Lord Dunedin in *Admiralty Commissioners v SS Valeria*[94] observed: "If by somebody's fault I lose my leg and am paid damages, can any one in his senses say I have had restitutio in integrum?"[95] More recently, at the Court of Appeal stage of *X (Minors) v Bedfordshire County Council*,[96] Sir Thomas Bingham MR, dealing with a claim for damages in respect of psychiatric injury suffered by a child, pointed out:[97] "I agree that money is an inadequate remedy for the injury which the child claims to have suffered. So it is for the loss of a leg, or an eye, or a life. But it is usually the best the law can do. If plaintiffs do not want financial recompense they need not claim. It may be assumed that those representing the child regard it as better than nothing."

22.51   Despite criticism (most notably by the Royal Commission on Civil Liability and Compensation for Personal Injury) (the "Pearson Report"),[98] the current system has

---

[90] 1968 SC 280.
[91] 1993 SLT 311.
[92] [1900] AC 113.
[93] *Ibid* at 116.
[94] [1922] 2 AC 242.
[95] *Ibid* at 248.
[96] [1994] 2 WLR 554.
[97] *Ibid* at 572.
[98] Cmnd 7054–1, 1978, paras 359–398.

been in operation for many years and a large body of case law has built up in relation to the pain and suffering consequent upon injury involving the various body regions. Solatium is calculated as at the date of proof[99] (as opposed to the date of injury). Awards made in similar cases are often cited in court as evidence of *quantum* of damages[100] but these can be no better than guidelines as no two cases will be identical. In *McMillan v McDowall*[101] the temporary judge (TG Coutts QC) stated: "While the assessment of solatium is not a precise science … the view of Lord McDonald in a similar case must be treated with respect." As far as older cases are concerned, where they are cited as authority, the effects of inflation should be taken into account.[102] In assessing solatium, reference is sometimes made to the Judicial Studies Board's Guidelines.[103] The objective of the Guidelines is to bring consistency to the level of awards.

Damages in respect of solatium vary according to the extent of the injury, its permanence or otherwise and in serious cases very substantial damages will be awarded. Medical evidence should, of course, be adduced in relation to the injury or disability.[104] Solatium may be awarded in respect of psychiatric injury arising from delictual conduct.[105] Again, expert evidence should be adduced in such cases.[106] **22.52**

In *Dalgleish v Glasgow Corporation*[107] the Lord Justice-Clerk (Lord Wheatley) stated:[108] "There are three heads of damages in a solatium claim: (a) pain and suffering; (b) loss of faculties and amenities; and (c) loss of expectation of life." The award in respect of pain and suffering may embrace both pain and suffering already experienced and future pain and suffering but *awareness* of pain and suffering is required before an award will be made. It follows that a person rendered unconscious as a result of another's wrongdoing will not recover damages for pain and suffering.[109] *Dalgleish* makes clear that the solatium award also includes damages in respect of loss of faculties and amenities.[110] The pursuer's loss of amenity[111] simply means everything which reduces his enjoyment of life – for example, if he is no longer able to pursue certain hobbies as a result of his injury then an award could be made **22.53**

---

[99] See *Purryag v Greater Glasgow Health Board* 1996 SLT 794; *J v Fife Council* 2009 SC 163 at para 33.

[100] The use of English authority is competent and appropriate: (see *Allan v Scott* 1972 SC 59) but awards made in the Republic of Ireland (which are among the highest in Europe) have been said to be "not helpful" (see *J v Fife Council* 2009 SC 163 at para 20 (per the Lord President (Lord Hamilton))).

[101] 1993 SLT 311 at 312.

[102] Inflation tables can be found in McEwan and Paton on *Damages for Personal Injuries in Scotland* (2nd edn, 1989). This looseleaf publication (with two releases annually) aims to provide practical information on the assessment of damages for personal injuries and death.

[103] Judicial Studies Board, *Guidelines for the Assessment of General Damages in Personal Injury Cases* (10th edn, 2010). See, eg, *Logan v Logan* 2010 RepLR 135; *Smith v Opportunus Fishing Co Ltd* 2011 RepLR 34; *MacDonald v Wood Group Engineering (North Sea) Ltd* 2011 GWD 1–50 at para 31.

[104] See, eg, *McKinnel v White* 1971 SLT 61.

[105] A claim arising out of mere anxiety would not normally sound in damages: see *G v S* 2006 SLT 795, per Lord Turnbull at para 18.

[106] Thus, in *J v Fife Council* 2007 SLT 85 where no expert evidence was led to support an averment of psychiatric injury, the Lord Ordinary declined to make an award in respect of any such loss.

[107] 1976 SC 32.

[108] *Ibid* at 53.

[109] See *Lim Poh Choo v Camden and Islington AHA* [1980] AC 174; *Dalgleish v Glasgow Corporation* 1976 SC 32 at 54.

[110] Where the injured party is rendered unconscious, he can recover for loss of amenity and faculties but *not* for awareness of such loss: see *Dalgleish v Glasgow Corporation* 1976 SC 32.

[111] *Haining v Babcock Energy Ltd* 1994 SLT 107. There, the pursuer, who had suffered a crush injury to his left hand, was no longer able to carry out his pre-accident hobby of rowing and his hobby of breeding and racing pigeons was also interfered with as a result.

for loss of amenity.[112] Damages can also be sought in respect of the pursuer's loss of expectation of life but only where he is *aware* that his life expectancy has been diminished.[113] The solatium award may be apportioned between past and future solatium.[114] The portion attributable to the past will attract interest.[115] Two further points can usefully be extracted from the Inner House decision in *Dalgleish*. First, it is irrelevant that the victim may derive no personal or financial benefit from the award.[116] Second, appeal courts are reluctant to alter assessments of damages made by the court of first instance, unless a clear error has been made. In *Dalgleish*, the Lord Justice-Clerk stated in the Inner House[117] that "[t]his Court is always slow to interfere with a Lord Ordinary's assessment of damages unless he has made a substantial error one way or another". The test appears to be whether the award made by the lower court is out of all proportion to what ought to have been awarded[118] or whether the amount awarded was wholly unreasonable.[119]

22.54   The reluctance of appeal courts to interfere with awards made by the court of first instance is illustrated in *Henry v Rentokil Initial plc*.[120] There, the pursuer was injured while working as a nurse. She raised an action against the defenders, who admitted liability. The injuries involved an injury to the hip and further injury to a network of nerves which materially impaired the quality of the pursuer's day-to-day existence. The sheriff awarded £30,000 by way of solatium, £17,500 of which was attributable to the past. The defenders appealed and argued that the range of appropriate awards for solatium was between £6,500 and £25,000. The Inner House held that the sum awarded by way of solatium was not out of all proportion to the sum which ought to have been awarded. Delivering the opinion of an Extra Division, temporary judge Sir David Edward, QC stated:[121]

> "It is not in dispute that the appropriate test to be applied in this case is whether the sum awarded by the sheriff is 'out of all proportion to the true sum which ought in the opinion of the appeal Court to have been awarded' (*Purdie v William Allan & Sons* 1949 SC 477 per Lord Justice-Clerk Thomson, p 480). Standing the range of figures suggested by the Judicial Studies Board for injuries of the type sustained by the pursuer, the suggestion that the sum awarded by the sheriff was 'out of all proportion' to the sum

---

[112] Lord Scarman in *Lim Poh Choo v Camden and Islington AHA* [1980] AC 174 (at 188) drew "a distinction between damages for pain and suffering and damages for loss of amenities. The former depend upon the plaintiff's personal awareness of pain, her capacity for suffering. But the latter are awarded for the fact of deprivation – a substantial loss, whether the plaintiff is aware of it or not".

[113] Damages (Scotland) Act 2011, s 1(2) and (3).

[114] See, eg, *McGarrigle v Babcock Energy Ltd* 1996 SLT 471 (two-thirds of the solatium award were attributed to the past); *Henry v Rentokil Initial plc* 2008 SC 447. (There, the sheriff awarded £30,000 by way of solatium in respect of neck and shoulder injuries: £17,500 of that figure was attributable to the past. The Inner House refused to disturb that award.)

[115] *Smith v Middleton* 1972 SC 30; *J v Fife Council* 2009 SLT 160.

[116] *Dalgleish v Glasgow Corporation* 1976 SC 32, per LJ-C Wheatley at 54. There, the injured girl "was virtually unconscious throughout" but that fact did not serve to prevent an award for loss of faculties or amenity.

[117] 1976 SC 32 at 54.

[118] *Purdie v William Allan & Sons* 1949 SC 477, per LJ-C Thomson at 480. See, also, *Barker v Murdoch and Ors* 1979 SLT 145 at 146–147.

[119] *Inglis v London, Midland and Scottish Rly* 1941 SC 551, per LP Normand at 560.

[120] 2008 SC 447.

[121] *Ibid* at paras 13–14.

that ought to have been awarded is wholly untenable. The appeal under this head must fail."[122]

Let us now consider some recent solatium awards made by the Scottish courts. In **22.55** *Smith* v *Opportunus Fishing Co Ltd*,[123] the pursuer, a share fisherman, was working as a deckhand on a boat when a heavy metal plate fell from a gallast frame and struck him on the head. He sustained a head injury resulting in permanent neuropsychological deficits and mild brain injury. He suffered an intense period of incapacity for about 8 months, which included severe and frequent headaches. Solatium was assessed at £17,500, of which 60 per cent was attributable to the past. (The other heads of loss are discussed further below.)

In *MacDonald* v *Wood Group Engineering (North Sea) Ltd*,[124] the pursuer (who was **22.56** right-handed) lost the top of his left middle finger in the course of a manual handling operation while at work on an offshore oil platform. At proof, the finger remained sensitive both to touch and to the cold and there was a 20 per cent reduction in grip in the left hand and 5 per cent impairment of function. The temporary judge (M G Thomson, QC) concluded that an appropriate figure for solatium was £5,500 (of which £3,500 was attributed to the past and £2,000 to the future.)

Pleural plaques

In *Rothwell* v *Chemical & Insulating Co Ltd*[125] the claimants had been exposed to asbestos **22.57** and had developed pleural plaques. Although pleural plaques are an asymptomatic condition, they do indicate that asbestos fibres have penetrated the lungs. The House of Lords held, however, that symptomless pleural plaques do not sound in damages. Lord Hoffmann gave the leading speech, stating:[126] "Proof of damage is an essential element in a claim in negligence ... in my opinion the development of pleural plaques, whether or not associated with the risk of future disease and anxiety about the future, is not actionable injury." The *Rothwell* decision does not, however, apply in Scotland. The Damages (Asbestos-related Conditions) (Scotland) Act 2009 provides that pleural plaques and other related conditions continue to constitute actionable injury for the purposes of Scots law.[127]

Historic child abuse

Before leaving the issue of solatium, some mention should be made of the level **22.58** of award which is appropriate in cases of historic child abuse. There have been a number of cases before the Scottish courts in recent years arising from abuse allegedly suffered by children in care. Many such actions have been raised only many years

---

[122] See, also, *J* v *Fife Council* 2009 SC 163 where a challenge to the Lord Ordinary's award of solatium failed in the Inner House, the Lord President (Lord Hamilton) saying (at para 19) that the "award cannot, in our view, be said to be so low as to be wholly unreasonable or out of all proportion to the sum which should have been awarded".
[123] 2011 Rep LR 34.
[124] 2011 GWD 1–50.
[125] [2008] 1 AC 281.
[126] *Ibid* at para 2.
[127] Judicial review of the 2009 Act was sought by various insurers but Lord Emslie ruled against them: see *Axa General Insurance Ltd, Petrs* 2010 SLT 179. That decision was subsequently upheld by the Inner House: 2011 SLT 439 and by the UK Supreme Court: [2011] UKSC 46. See, also, T Mullen, "The Axa Insurance case: challenging Acts of the Scottish Parliament for irrationality" 2010 SLT 39.

after the events in question and, as a result, many such actions have been thwarted by the rules of prescription or, more usually, limitation.[128] However, in *J* v *Fife Council*,[129] the defender did not state a plea of limitation and the court proceeded to consider the issue of quantum. During his childhood, the pursuer resided in a children's home where he became the victim of abuse by an employee over a 5- to 6-year period. He was subjected to repeated sodomy, violent non-sexual assaults and punishment which was designed to humiliate him in front of other children. The abuse occurred on a daily, or almost daily, basis. As a result, the pursuer claimed to have suffered serious psychological and social sequelae. These consequences caused him to have difficulties in relationships with his wife, children and others. In a subsequent action, the pursuer sought an award of solatium. The Lord Ordinary (Menzies) indicated what factors ought to be taken into account in such cases:[130]

"There are several factors which may be relevant in the assessment of an award of solatium in circumstances such as this. The following is not intended to be an exhaustive list, nor is it listed in order of importance, but it appears to me that the following factors may affect the amount of an award of solatium:

(1) The nature and severity of the abuse, and its character – whether sexual, non-sexual but violent, or mental/emotional.
(2) The frequency of the abuse.
(3) The duration of the abuse.
(4) The age of the pursuer at the time of the abuse.
(5) The immediate effects of the abuse on the pursuer.
(6) Whether any apportionment is required to reflect abuse by others, or other causes of the pursuer's problems.
(7) The emotional and social consequences of the abuse for the pursuer.
(8) Any psychiatric illness or psychological condition suffered by the pursuer as a consequence of the abuse."

22.59 Stating[131] that it was "difficult to imagine a worse case of child abuse", Lord Menzies held that £75,000 was an appropriate award in the circumstances. This sum was referable to the past. The horrific nature, character and severity of the abuse taken together with its frequency and duration, the age of the pursuer at the time (from the age of 8 to 14) and its immediate effects on him (physical pain and loss of self-esteem, and helplessness), justified an award at that level.[132] The Inner House subsequently affirmed that award.[133]

---

[128] See Chapter 24.
[129] 2007 SLT 85. For further discussion, see E Russell, "Historic abuse – Limitation leaves the frame and quantum comes into focus" 2007 SLT 181.
[130] 2007 SLT 85 at para 44.
[131] *Ibid* at para 45.
[132] Had expert psychiatric testimony been led (and accepted) in support of the pursuer's psychiatric difficulties and had the pursuer not coped so well with life, Lord Menzies would have considered an even higher award.
[133] 2009 SC 163.

PATRIMONIAL LOSS

Patrimonial loss covers all pecuniary losses which the pursuer has suffered as a result **22.60** of the defender's wrong. It will therefore embrace such matters as loss of earnings, outlays and expenses, cost of services, etc. The court must calculate both past and future patrimonial loss.[134] Past patrimonial loss covers losses sustained between the date of the delictual conduct and the date of proof. The award in respect of future patrimonial loss, on the other hand, compensates the pursuer for losses which he will suffer subsequent to the proof. Future patrimonial loss is an important head of claim and the award can be substantial,[135] especially if the pursuer is young and no longer able to work as a result of his injuries. It has been said that "[a]ssessment of future loss, where there are ... many imponderables ... is not an exact science".[136]

Generally speaking, in personal injury cases, the younger the pursuer, the more **22.61** matters which have to be taken into account: for example, loss of career advancement opportunities. In *Stark* v *Lothian and Borders Fire Board*[137] a 26-year-old fireman sued his employers in respect of injuries sustained in the course of employment. He suffered extensive burn injuries and thereafter developed post-traumatic stress disorder. He was unable to return to work as a fireman but obtained work in the defender's community education department where his job was less secure and there were no prospects of promotion. The Lord Ordinary held that, had the pursuer continued in employment as a fireman, he would have had reasonable prospects of promotion to leading fireman by 1991. This was therefore taken into account in the assessment of his patrimonial loss.[138] Clearly, loss of promotion prospects is less likely to be an issue with an older pursuer. Similarly, if the pursuer was reaching retirement age, the figure for future wage loss would generally be low, whereas it may be substantial in the case of a young pursuer.

Let us now look at the most important elements of the patrimonial loss claim. **22.62**

Loss of earnings

If the pursuer has been unable to work as a result of his injuries, he will wish to **22.63** claim for loss of earnings in his action for damages. The first step is to establish loss of earnings in respect of the period from date of injury until the date of proof. In calculating loss of earnings, tax,[139] national insurance contributions[140] and pension contributions[141] are taken into consideration, with the result that it is the pursuer's net earnings which are used for this calculation. In *Clark* v *Chief Constable of Lothian and*

---

[134] *Robertson's CB* v *Anderson* 1996 SLT 215; 1996 SLT 828.
[135] *McMillan* v *McDowall* 1993 SLT 311.
[136] *Henry* v *Rentokil Initial plc* 2008 SC 447, per temporary judge Sir David Edward, QC at para 36.
[137] 1993 SLT 652.
[138] See, also, *Henry* v *Rentokil Initial plc* 2008 SC 447 where the Inner House concluded that it was more likely than not that the pursuer, who had been devoted to her work as a nurse, would have been promoted to a higher grade prior to the date of proof (see para 29).
[139] See *British Transport Commission* v *Gourley* [1956] AC 185; *Smith* v *Opportunus Fishing Co Ltd* 2011 RepLR 34 at para 27.
[140] See *Cooper* v *Firth Brown* [1963] 1 WLR 418; *Gibney* v *Eric Johnson Stubbs (Scotland) Ltd* 1987 SLT 132; *Smith* v *Opportunus Fishing Co Ltd* 2011 RepLR 34 at para 27.
[141] See *Dews* v *NCB* [1987] 3 WLR 38 (HL); *Anderson* v *Gerrard* 1994 SLT 1326.

Borders[142] the defenders reclaimed against an award which included an assessment of loss of earnings to the injured person. The Inner House held that the evidence as to past wage loss was deficient, as it failed to reveal the net amounts the pursuer would have earned during the relevant period. There was, however, sufficient evidence for the court to have a basis for assessing the minimum amount of gross earnings which the pursuer would have lost. Such a minimum should be a figure which reflected the lowest amount which the pursuer hoped to have earned on resuming work and which would allow for increases which would have occurred thereafter. Although no evidence of tax, insurance contributions and other deductions from that gross salary was led, it was reasonable to make a deduction of one-third from that figure as it represented a deduction which was unlikely to have been exceeded. In other words, because of the deficiencies in the evidence, it was the *lowest* figure extracted from the evidence which was to form the basis of the assessment of wage loss.

22.64   In *Smith* v *Opportunus Fishing Co Ltd*[143] the pursuer, a share fisherman, suffered a head injury at work. He was absent from work and suffered loss of earnings for about 8 months. Taking as a starting point the gross earnings of a comparable deckhand, and making the appropriate deductions for income tax and national insurance, the court assessed the pursuer's net earnings' loss during the period of his absence at £22,836.50. The court concluded that neither receipt of a loan made by the first defenders from their share of the profits of each fishing trip during the pursuer's absence[144] nor payments made under a personal accident insurance policy fell to be deducted from the net earnings loss figure.[145]

22.65   To assess future loss of earnings, the court must establish the net annual earnings of the pursuer as at the date of proof.[146] This figure is known as the multiplicand. The next step is to find a multiplier, which, when applied to the multiplicand, will produce a lump sum. That lump sum is intended to provide a fund in lieu of the pursuer's income until his death. The theory is that, by the date of death, both the capital sum and the investment income which it generates will be exhausted. It has been said that finding a multiplier "is a more subtle exercise than simply estimating the number of years over which the future loss will be incurred"[147] as clearly the lump sum payment is capable of being invested to produce a return.[148] The Ogden actuarial tables[149] should be used as the appropriate starting point in determining the multiplier.[150] A deduction will then usually be made in

---

[142] 1993 SC 320.

[143] 2011 RepLR 34.

[144] "Receipt of a loan does not mitigate losses which the injured person would otherwise sustain. The loan remains repayable. It is not a payment to account of damages." (Per the Lord Ordinary (Doherty) at para 32.) The loan payments were not payments of a benevolent character within the meaning of s 10(iv) of the Administration of Justice Act 1982 (see discussion below). They therefore did not fall to be taken into account. In any event, the payments had not been made by the "responsible" person (ie the second defender who had lodged a minute of admission). Rather, they had been made by the first defender against whom the action was no longer proceeding.

[145] 2011 RepLR 34 at paras 28–39.

[146] See, eg, *McGarrigle* v *Babcock Energy Ltd* 1996 SLT 471.

[147] See Chalmers, *Delict* (SULI) at para 10.31.

[148] See *O'Brien's CB* v *British Steel plc* 1991 SC 315, per the Lord President (Lord Hope) at 319.

[149] *Actuarial Tables with Explanatory Notes for Use in Personal Injury and Fatal Accident Cases* ("*The Ogden Tables*") (6th edn, 2007). These are actuarial tables prepared by the Government Actuary's Department for use in personal injury and fatal accident cases. The tables were named after Sir Michael Ogden who chaired the 1982 working party which first produced them.

[150] See *Wells* v *Wells* [1999] 1 AC 345; *McNulty* v *Marshalls Food Group Ltd* 1999 SC 195; *McManus' Exrx* v *Babcock Energy Ltd* 1999 SC 569; *Wilson* v *Pyeroy Ltd* 2000 SLT 1087; *Robertson* v *Smith* 2000 SC 591. The earlier

respect of contingencies, ie to take account of the possibility of early retirement or redundancy. (The risk of mortality is taken account of in the Tables themselves.) In professions where the normal age of retirement is lower than 65, the multiplier will be lower. This would be the case with, say, professional footballers or divers. The case of *Howard* v *Comex Houlder Diving Ltd*[151] concerned an action by a professional diver who was aged 25 at the date of accident and aged 30 at the date of proof. As divers normally retire at about the age of 40, a multiplier of only 3 was applied in that case.

Once the multiplier and multiplicand have been established, they are simply multi- **22.66**
plied to give a lump-sum figure. Therefore if the net annual salary as at the date of proof was £30,000 and the multiplier was 10, the lump sum awarded for future loss of earnings will be £300,000. This example assumes that the pursuer will not work after the accident. More usually, the pursuer will be able to continue working in some capacity, albeit in a less remunerative position owing to his disabilities. In such a case, the court must establish the difference between likely future earnings and earnings had the pursuer not been disabled (the multiplicand) and then apply the appropriate multiplier. Such an approach was taken in *Stark* v *Lothian and Borders Fire Board*[152] which was discussed above.

Damages may be awarded in respect of earnings and relevant benefits lost as a result **22.67**
of reduced life expectancy in consequence of the accident.[153] Living expenses which would have been incurred during the period are deducted from the figure. The Damages (Scotland) Act 2011, s 1(6)(c) sets the living expenses at 25 per cent of the total earnings and benefits, although, in terms of s 1(7) of the Act, a different percentage may be applied if "necessary to do so for the purpose of avoiding a manifestly and materially unfair result".

Evidence requires to be led to substantiate the pursuer's claim for future loss. In **22.68**
MacDonald v *Wood Group Engineering (North Sea) Ltd*[154] the pursuer lost the end of a finger in his non-dominant hand in an industrial accident. The medical evidence indicated that he would not be prevented from continuing his current type of work up until the age at which he wished to retire. Past wage loss was agreed between the parties. Counsel for the pursuer sought an award in respect of future loss of earnings to reflect an 8-week absence from employment during further operative treatment to which reference had been made in the medical prognosis. The temporary judge refused to make an award under this head because the pursuer's own evidence indicated that he was unlikely to have such an operation in view of the pain and disruption which it would occasion.

Damages may be reduced on account of the pursuer's contributory negligence. **22.69**
Thus, in *MacDonald* (above), where the pursuer was held to have been contributorily negligent to the extent of 50 per cent, decree was granted for payment by the defenders for half of the sum which would have been awarded on a full liability basis.[155]

Occasionally, instead of using the multiplier/multiplicand method for assessing **22.70**
future loss of earnings, the court will award a lump sum in respect of loss of

case law had disclosed a somewhat sceptical approach to the Ogden Tables (see *O'Brien's CB* v *British Steel plc* 1991 SC 315). See, generally, R Milligan, "Multipliers for future wage loss: Wells, O'Brien and the Ogden tables" 1998 SLT 291.

[151] 1987 SLT 344.
[152] 1993 SLT 652.
[153] Damages (Scotland) Act 2011, s 1(5) and (6).
[154] 2011 GWD 1–50.
[155] In *Campbell* v *Gillespie* 1996 SLT 503, a 60% reduction in damages was made in respect of the deceased's contributory negligence. In *Beggs* v *Motherwell Bridge Fabricators* 1998 SLT 1215, a 20% reduction in damages was made in respect of the deceased's contributory negligence.

employability,[156] general disadvantage on the labour market or a loss of earning capacity. For example, in *Robertson's CB* v *Anderson*,[157] the judge at first instance made an award in respect of loss of employability, although on a reclaiming motion to an Extra Division, it was held that, in the circumstances of the case, such an approach was unfounded and an award for loss of earnings was substituted.

22.71   An award in respect of disadvantage on the employment market was sought (unsuccessfully) in *MacDonald* v *Wood Group Engineering (North Sea) Ltd*.[158] It will be remembered that the pursuer lost the tip of his left middle finger in an industrial accident. An award was sought to compensate the pursuer for disadvantage on the employment market. The temporary judge found no evidence to justify the making of such an award. The pursuer had been in secure employment for 21 years and was regarded as "supervisor material". The judge concluded:[159] "In the absence of any expert evidence on the subject, it was not self-evident to me that the pursuer would be at any disadvantage on the labour market if he ever found himself there."

22.72   An award in respect of "loss of earning capacity" was made, however, in *Smith* v *Opportunus Fishing Co Ltd*[160] (in addition to the past loss of earnings noted above). Evidence was given to the effect that the pursuer (a share fisherman) was slower and less helpful as a crew member following a head injury and that another skipper would be unlikely to put up with his problems. Lord Doherty observed:[161]

> "[The pursuer] is in a demanding occupation, where he often needs to work in adverse conditions. He depends upon the goodwill of others to obtain work, and to keep that work. His disabilities do create noticeable difficulties. In those circumstances it appears to me that he is at significantly greater risk of having periods of unemployment in the future than would have been the case but for the accident. I accept that the pursuer ought to be compensated for this disadvantage."

An award of £7,500 was made under this head.

22.73   In personal injuries cases, the multiplier is applied as at the date of proof. In fatal accident cases, the multiplier was previously applied as at the date of death[162] but the Damages (Scotland) Act 2011 now provides in s 7(1)(d) that it is to apply from the date of the interlocutor.

Loss of pension rights

22.74   Loss of pension *rights*[163] is also an important element of many claims in respect of future patrimonial loss. It is, perhaps, surprising that it has been recognised only relatively recently that an inability to work, owing to injury, results not only in a loss of earnings but also in a loss of pension rights.[164] It is usual to obtain detailed actuarial evidence

---

[156] See *Smith* v *Manchester* [1974] KIR 1.
[157] 1996 SLT 215 (OH); 1996 SLT 828.
[158] 2011 GWD 1–50.
[159] *Ibid* at para 33.
[160] 2011 RepLR 34. See also *Hill* v *Wilson* 1998 SC 81.
[161] 2011 RepLR 34 at para 44.
[162] See, eg, *Campbell* v *Gillespie* 1996 SLT 503.
[163] See *Barratt* v *Strathclyde Fire Brigade* 1984 SLT 325; *Cantwell* v *Criminal Injuries Compensation Board* 2002 SC (HL) 1.
[164] For a more detailed exposition of this subject, see J Blaikie, "Assessment of Pension Rights in Personal Injuries Claims" 1995 JR 40.

in respect of this head of claim.[165] In *Henry v Rentokil plc*[166] parties had agreed a sum in respect of pension loss in order to avoid the necessity of leading the evidence of an actuary who had produced a report in this regard. The Inner House held that there was no reason to deny the pursuer the sum agreed by way of pension loss. It was not in dispute that the pursuer was making pension contributions at the time of the accident.

Outlays and expenses

Reasonable outlays and expenses may also be recovered by the pursuer. Damages can **22.75** thus be claimed in respect of maintenance costs,[167] reasonable medical expenses,[168] nursing costs,[169] prescription charges,[170] and the cost of a curatory.[171] The cost of wheelchairs, crutches, etc is also recoverable in appropriate circumstances, as is additional expenditure incurred in respect of adaptations to a car and various household items.[172] It is no answer to a claim in respect of private medical expenses that comparable treatment was available on the NHS. The Law Reform (Personal Injuries) Act 1948, s 2(4) provides that, in determining the reasonableness of medical expenses, the possibility of avoiding or reducing them by taking advantage of NHS facilities shall be disregarded. Therefore, a pursuer may claim for the full cost of private treatment even where identical facilities are available free on the NHS. Expenses which have been incurred in good faith are recoverable even where they are subsequently discovered to have been unnecessary.[173] Again, past and future outlays require to be assessed. In relation to future outlays, the method outlined above is normally used: a multiplicand representing the annual cost for maintenance etc is taken and is multiplied by a multiplier extracted from the Ogden actuarial tables.

Compensation in respect of the cost of "services"

Where a person has sustained personal injuries[174] as a result of another's wrong, the **22.76** responsible person may be liable to pay damages in accordance with ss 8 and 9 of the Administration of Justice Act 1982. These two provisions enable the pursuer to seek a sum in respect of:

(a) necessary services rendered to him by his relatives (s 8), and/or
(b) services which, owing to his injuries, he is no longer able to render to his relatives (s 9).

Section 8 claims: necessary services rendered to the injured person by a relative

Section 8(1) of the 1982 Act provides: **22.77**

---

[165] See, eg, *Beggs v Motherwell Bridge Fabricators* 1998 SLT 1215.
[166] 2008 SC 447.
[167] See *McMillan v McDowall* 1993 SLT 311.
[168] See *Lewis v Laird Line* 1925 SLT 316.
[169] See *MacIntosh v NCB* 1988 SLT 348.
[170] See *Bonar v Trafalgar House Offshore Fabrication Ltd* 1996 SLT 548.
[171] See *Robertson's CB v Anderson* 1996 SLT 215 (OH); 1996 SLT 828.
[172] See *Henry v Rentokil Initial plc* 2008 SC 447 where the sheriff's award of £3,500 in respect of such adaptations was not disturbed by the Inner House on appeal.
[173] See *Clippens Oil Co v Edinburgh and District Water Trs* 1907 SC (HL) 9.
[174] "Personal injuries" means any disease and any impairment of a person's physical or mental condition: Administration of Justice Act 1982, s 13(1).

"Where necessary services have been rendered to the injured person by a relative in conse-quence of the injuries in question, then, unless the relative has expressly agreed in the knowledge that an action for damages has been raised or is in contemplation that no payment should be made in respect of those services, the responsible person shall be liable to pay to the injured person by way of damages such sum as represents reasonable remuneration for those services and repayment of reasonable expenses incurred in connection therewith."[175]

22.78 In other words, the pursuer can recover damages which amount to "reasonable remuneration" for necessary[176] services rendered to him by a *relative*. This provision enables the injured person to recompense the relative and remuneration is due provided the relative did not agree that no payment should be made.[177] The injured party is under a duty to account to the caring relative for the money received under s 8(1) in respect of past services.[178] Necessary services might include various household tasks such as washing, ironing, shopping and cooking. It has been held not to include the provision of bone marrow to the injured party who would have died without the donation.[179]

22.79 As originally enacted, the 1982 Act did not give a right to claim remuneration for services which might be rendered by a relative in the future.[180] The Law Reform (Miscellaneous Provisions) (Scotland) Act 1990, s 69(1) amended the 1982 Act in this regard, with the result that s 8(3) of the 1982 Act, as amended, now permits recovery of the cost of necessary services likely to be rendered by a relative *after* the date of an award of damages. (The multiplier/multiplicand method of calculation outlined above will be used in respect of the assessment of any future services award.) Although the injured party is under a duty to account to the caring relative for the money received in respect of *past* services, he is under no such duty in respect of *future* services.[181] The relative has no direct right of action against the wrongdoer in respect of any services or expenses referred to in s 8.[182]

22.80 The word "relative" (in relation to the injured person) is defined in s 13(1) of the 1982 Act, as amended, and it is important to note than no one other than a relative can be the subject of a claim under s 8. If the services are rendered by a friend or a neighbour, a claim under s 8 is not competent. Relatives include the following:

- the spouse or divorced spouse;
- the civil partner or former civil partner;

---

[175] This provision represents an innovation on the position at common law under which a pursuer could not recover damages for economic losses suffered by a relative as a result of the pursuer's injuries, eg where a wife stopped working/reduced her working hours in order to care for her injured husband: see *Edgar* v *Lord Advocate* 1965 SC 67. The position had been subject to adverse comment by the Scottish Law Commission: see *Damages for Personal Injuries: Report on (1)Admissibility of Claims for Services (2) Admissible Deductions* (Scot Law Com No 51, 1978) at para 18.

[176] In practice this seems to have been interpreted as reasonable services: see the discussion in R M White and W J Fletcher, *Delictual Damages* (2000) at p 20.

[177] In *Campbell* v *City of Glasgow District Council* 1991 SLT 616 the pursuer's sister asserted that she would not accept payment for services even if the sum was recovered from a third party. In those circumstances, the court declined to make an award.

[178] Section 8(2).

[179] *Duffy* v *Lanarkshire Health Board* 1998 SCLR 1142. See, also, *Sturgeon* v *Gallagher* 2003 SLT 67: services rendered to a *partnership* (a farming business run by the pursuer and his wife) as opposed to the pursuer personally were not compensatable under s 8 of the Act.

[180] See *Forsyth's CB* v *Govan Shipbuilders Ltd* 1988 SC 421.

[181] Section 8(2) and (3).

[182] Section 8(4).

- any person, not being the spouse or civil partner of the injured person, who was, at the time of the wrong, living with the injured person as spouse or civil partner;
- any ascendant or descendant;
- any brother, sister, uncle or aunt; or any issue of any such person;
- any person accepted by the injured person as a child of his family.

For the purposes of the foregoing definition, any relationship by affinity shall be **22.81** treated as a relationship by consanguinity, any relationship of the half blood shall be treated as a relationship of the whole blood and the stepchild of any person shall be treated as his child. Furthermore, s 1(1) of the Law Reform (Parent and Child) (Scotland) Act 1986 shall apply (in other words, the fact that a person's parents are or were not married to each other is irrelevant).

The rationale behind s 8 is essentially a desire to avoid a multiplicity of actions. **22.82** Thus, in *Gripper* v *British Railways Board*[183] a man was able to recover compensation in respect of services rendered to him by his wife, which included assisting him with shaving, washing and dressing for a period of 8 weeks while his wrist was in plaster. In *Williamson* v *GB Papers plc*[184] the pursuer suffered injuries to her ankle and neck when she slipped and fell on a factory floor. She claimed damages, *inter alia*, for services rendered to her by her husband and son, which services included washing, ironing and shopping.[185]

In *Forsyth's Curator Bonis* v *Govan Shipbuilders*,[186] Lord Clyde observed[187] that **22.83** evidence should be led to enable the court to assess accurately what in all the circumstances a reasonable remuneration would be. That *dictum* was approved in *Clark* v *Chief Constable of Lothian and Borders*.[188] In *Clark*, the defenders reclaimed against an award which included an assessment of necessary services rendered to the injured person where the evidence as to the extent of the necessary services provided was deficient. The Second Division held that, although evidence should have been led for the s 8 claim so that the court could assess accurately what in all the circumstances a reasonable remuneration would be, the effect of a failure to lead precise evidence was not to exclude altogether consideration of the claim, but to restrict the court's assessment to an amount, if any, which represented the *minimum* that could reasonably be inferred as appropriate on the basis of such evidence as there was.

An interesting situation arose in *Kozikowska* v *Kozikowski*.[189] The pursuer sued both **22.84** her husband and a roads authority in respect of injuries sustained when her husband's car skidded on an icy road. Her claim included a s 8 claim for necessary services rendered to her by her husband. Clearly, the net result of a successful claim would have been the recovery by the pursuer of the cost of services rendered to her by the

---

[183] 1991 SLT 659.
[184] 1994 SLT 173.
[185] For recent cases providing guidance as to the appropriate level of the s 8 award, see *Wallace* v *Glasgow City Council* 2011 RepLR 96; *Burgess* v *Napier University* 2009 RepLR 55; *Brookes* v *First Aberdeen Ltd* 2010 RepLR 42 (although liability was not ultimately established in *Burgess* or *Brookes*); *Stuart* v *Advocate General for Scotland* 2009 SCLR 737; *Smith* v *Opportunus Fishing Co Ltd* 2011 RepLR 34; *McEwan* v *Ayrshire and Arran Acute Hospitals NHS Trust* 2009 GWD 13–208; *MacDonald* v *Wood Group Engineering (North Sea) Ltd* 2011 GWD 1–50; *Logan* v *Logan* 2010 RepLR 135.
[186] 1988 SC 421.
[187] *Ibid* at 430. His Lordship also stated that the court "cannot pluck figures from the air in this matter".
[188] 1993 SC 320.
[189] 1996 SLT 386.

defender. She would then be under a duty to account to the defender in respect of the costs recovered. The Lord Ordinary (Coulsfield) held that it was incompetent for the wife to recover from the husband remuneration in respect of his own services.[190]

22.85   Where the injured person dies before the action is concluded, his executor can recover damages for necessary services rendered to him by a relative before he died.[191]

22.86   "Reasonable expenses" incurred in connection with the services are also recoverable. This might embrace items such as travel costs and costs of temporary accommodation near a hospital.

22.87   Although the courts have often taken a broad approach to the issue of services,[192] increasingly they have had resort to hourly rates which might have been paid to a carer.

Section 9 claims: necessary services rendered by the injured party to a relative

22.88   Section 9 of the 1982 Act enables a claim to be made where the injured person is unable to render necessary services to a relative. In such a situation, the wrongdoer will have to pay a reasonable sum by way of damages. Again, no one other than a relative can be the subject of a claim under s 9 of the 1982 Act. For the definition of "relative", see the discussion above.[193] Where the victim of the delict is merely injured (as opposed to being killed) the relative has no direct claim – it must be channelled through the victim.[194] Section 9 can form an important head of claim where a housewife is severely injured and is no longer able to render housekeeping and childrearing services. Professor Thomson[195] observes that the Act, by providing for the payment of compensation in this respect, recognises the "economic value" of work in the home.

22.89   Where the victim of the delict has died then any person who is entitled to an award for loss of support under s 4(3)(a) of the Damages (Scotland) Act 2011 (see below) will be entitled to seek compensation for loss of personal services within his claim.[196] Such fatal cases are no longer subject to the provisions of the 1982 Act but are now governed instead by s 6 of the Damages (Scotland) Act 2011. The relative's right to damages in respect of loss of personal services, if vested, transmits upon his own death to his executor in terms of s 9 of the 2011 Act.

22.90   "Personal services" are defined in s 9(3) as services: "(a) which were or might have been expected to have been rendered by the injured person before the occurrence of the act or omission giving rise to liability, (b) of a kind which, when rendered by a person other than a relative, would ordinarily be obtainable on payment, and (c) which the injured person but for the injuries in question might have been expected to render gratuitously to a relative".

22.91   In *Campbell* v *Gillespie*[197] the widow of a man who had been killed in a road accident at the age of 37 sought damages for herself and her two children. Her action included a claim in respect of services formerly provided by her late husband. The deceased had done much of the decoration and general maintenance at the family home in

---

[190] The Outer House thus followed the House of Lords' decision in the English appeal of *Hunt* v *Severs* [1994] 2 AC 350.
[191] Section 2(1) of the Damages (Scotland) Act 2011. See *McManus's Exrx* v *Babcock Energy Ltd* 1999 SC 569; *Murray's Exrx* v *Greenock Dockyard Co Ltd* 2004 SLT 346.
[192] See, eg, *Miller* v *Sabre Insurance Co Ltd* 2010 GWD 38–774; *Kerr* v *Stiell Facilities Ltd* 2009 SLT 851.
[193] Section 13(1) of the Administration of Justice Act 1982 provides the definition.
[194] Section 9(4) of the 1982 Act.
[195] J M Thomson, *Delictual Liability* (4th edn, 2009), p 255.
[196] See, eg, *Campbell* v *Gillespie* 1996 SLT 503.
[197] 1996 SLT 503.

Portree. He also provided substantial services of a DIY nature and assisted with the domestic chores. His widow estimated the domestic assistance at 2–3 hours per week. The deceased had also inherited a house in Sutherland where he was doing much of the renovation work himself. The temporary judge (DB Robertson, QC), recognising that "one cannot be too precise in these matters ... and taking a broad approach", concluded that an average rate for the services should be £4.50 per hour and that 1 hour per day would be appropriate in respect of all the services rendered by the deceased. This gave an annual sum of £1,620. Taking a multiplier of 13, the judge awarded a total of £21,060 in respect of the claim for loss of services.

In *Ingham v John G Russell (Transport) Ltd*[198] the deceased had carried out a variety **22.92** of domestic chores including DIY, babysitting, gardening, electrical work, plumbing, joinery and general house maintenance. Lord McCluskey emphasised that the determination of a "reasonable sum" should be approached broadly. The effect of any other approach would, in his Lordship's view, be to overcomplicate the pleadings.[199]

Cases involving s 8 and s 9 claims

Often a pursuer will seek an award under both s 8 and s 9 of the 1982 Act. A first point **22.93** to note is that where damages are sought under both sections, it is essential to distinguish the two heads of loss. In *Henry v Rentokil Initial plc*[200] the pursuer was injured while working as a nurse. She raised an action against the defenders in which she sought damages under a number of heads, including awards under s 8 and s 9 of the 1982 Act. In making an award of damages, the sheriff failed to distinguish between s 8 and s 9 services, and in relation to s 8 he failed to identify the individuals and the amount attributable to each relative. On appeal, an Extra Division held that the total award in respect of services was very modest and there was no reason to disturb it. However, the Division observed that the sheriff should have made separate awards under s 8 and s 9 and accordingly the relevant finding in fact was amended to distinguish between the s 8 and s 9 services. Moreover, in the case of the s 8 services it was necessary to identify the individuals who had provided the services and the amount attributable to each of them.[201]

In *Smith v Opportunus Fishing Co Ltd*[202] damages were sought under both s 8 **22.94** and s 9 of the 1982 Act. The pursuer was unable to work over an 8-month period, having sustained a head injury at work. During this period he was unable to do the household cooking or other domestic chores (such as cleaning and gardening) which he normally did when at home. He was unable to drive, and was unable to take his mother shopping or his son to college. In addition, the pursuer's wife had to render services to the pursuer, which, she estimated, took approximately 2–3 hours each day. The pursuer suggested that the services award be based on an average of 2.5 hours per day. The defenders submitted that 1 hour per day was more appropriate, and that account should be taken of the fact that, but for the accident, the pursuer would have been at sea for part of the 8-month period (and therefore not rendering the services

---

[198] 1991 SLT 739.
[199] For recent cases providing guidance as to the appropriate level of the s 9 award, see *Wallace v Glasgow City Council* [2011] CSIH 57; *Burgess v Napier University* 2009 RepLR 55, although liability was not ultimately established in *Burgess*; *McEwan v Ayrshire and Arran Acute Hospitals NHS Trust* 2009 GWD 13–208.
[200] 2008 SC 447.
[201] Given the duty of the injured person to account to the relative who has provided past services (s 8(2) of the 1982 Act), the importance of making such a distinction is self-evident.
[202] 2011 RepLR 34.

claimed to have been lost). Lord Doherty accepted that the pursuer would have been at sea for a significant part of the 8-month period. Accordingly, the s 9 claim was diminished to that extent. However, the s 8 services which the pursuer's wife rendered (such as cooking and cleaning) were rendered to the pursuer for the entire period. Lord Doherty allowed 2 hours a day for half of the period and 1 hour per day for the remainder. Using the pursuer's suggested net rate of £5 per hour, the resultant figure for services (on the basis of about 250 days' absence from work) was £1,875.

22.95 In *MacDonald* v *Wood Group Engineering (North Sea) Ltd*[203] the pursuer suffered a traumatic partial amputation of his left middle finger in the course of his employment. At the time of the accident he was living at Portree with his wife and two sons, then aged 14 and 17. His younger son suffered from cerebral palsy and required constant attention. The pursuer's normal routine was to work offshore for 2 weeks and then spend 2 weeks at home. During his 2 weeks offshore his wife acted as the younger son's principal carer with some support from her parents. When the pursuer was at home he became the principal carer and provided respite for his wife's parents. The younger son attended school, but at the time of the accident was on his Easter holidays. When the pursuer returned home on the day following the accident, his wife required to care for him too and the pursuer's ability to assist with the care of their son was seriously impaired. The pursuer required help to bathe and to dress and was unable to drive. His wife required to drive him to numerous GP and hospital appointments. During this period the pursuer was also unable to carry out his normal share of the household tasks.

22.96 The pursuer sought damages in respect of services under ss 8 and 9 of the 1982 Act. The s 9 claim related to a period of approximately 3 months when the pursuer was unable to undertake the practical care required by his younger son. If the accident had not occurred, the pursuer would have been working offshore for half of that time, and during a substantial part of it the child would have been at school. The claim under s 8 related to the services rendered by the pursuer's wife over a period of approximately 4 weeks. The temporary judge awarded a total of £1,200 in respect of the combined ss 8 and 9 claims, that figure being apportioned two-thirds in respect of the claim under s 9 and one-third for the claim under s 8.

22.97 As far as patrimonial losses are concerned, appeal courts are disinclined to interfere with awards made by the court of first instance if the award made falls within the range of reasonable assessment.[204] This mirrors their approach to awards of solatium (as discussed above).

INTEREST[205]

22.98 After calculating the damages payable under the various heads of damage, the court then considers the question of interest. Interest is payable in terms of the Interest on

[203] 2011 GWD 1–50.
[204] See *Henry* v *Rentokil Initial plc* 2008 SC 447. See, also, *Blair* v *FJC Lilley (Marine) Ltd* 1981 SLT 90 where the Lord Justice-Clerk (Lord Wheatley) observed (at 92): "It is only when the assessment has been reached through the use of wrong facts or the application of wrong principles or a manifestly unfair assessment has been reached that a court of appeal will interfere with the finding of the judge at first instance."
[205] In 2005, the Scottish Law Commission published a Discussion Paper on *Interest on Debt and Damages* (Scot Law Com DP No 127, 2005). This provides a comprehensive account of the current law (see, in particular, paras 2.34 and 2.35).

Damages (Scotland) Act 1958 as amended by the Interest on Damages (Scotland) Act 1971. "The primary purpose of an award of interest is to acknowledge the fact that by being deprived of the use of money, a creditor has either lost an opportunity to benefit from the use of the money or, alternatively, has suffered a further loss as a consequence of not having it to hand."[206] The rate of interest is a matter for the court's discretion[207] and an appeal court should not interfere save in exceptional circumstances. Different rates of interest are often applied to different parts of the award. The court generally awards interest at either the full judicial rate or half the judicial rate. The court rates are stipulated in various Acts of Sederunt.[208]

Interest on solatium

The court generally makes clear in its judgment how much of the solatium award **22.99** is referable to the past and how much is referable to the future. The past solatium award refers to the period from the date of injury until the date of proof, or the date of cessation of suffering, if earlier. The future solatium award applies to the period after the proof until such time as the court determines the pain and suffering will cease.

Where the pain and suffering is continuing as at the date of proof, the court will **22.100** apportion the solatium award between past and future solatium and will generally award interest at one-half of the current judicial rate on the past solatium.[209] Where the pain and suffering has ceased prior to the proof, the whole solatium award is allocated to the past and the courts generally award the full rate of interest on the past solatium[210] from the date of the accident.

In *Purryag v Greater Glasgow Health Board*[211] a proof in a medical negligence action **22.101** took place some 18 years after the alleged omission. The pain and suffering was continuing as at the date of proof. The defender submitted that the usual practice of awarding interest should not be followed. If it were followed, the pursuer would be "getting her cake and eating it". The figure for solatium had been brought up to date and the pursuer, if the usual practice were followed, would also receive the full rate of interest on the updated figure. The defender therefore submitted that a rate of only 2 per cent interest should apply in the circumstances to the element of solatium attributable to the past. In the event, liability was not established. However, Lord Abernethy stated:[212]

> "I see the force of counsel for the defenders' submission but in the circumstances of this case I do not think it is either appropriate or desirable that I should express a concluded view on it. It is perhaps sufficient to say that given the longstanding Scottish practice I would have felt obliged, sitting in the Outer House, to follow it. I would have apportioned half of the amount of solatium to the past and allowed interest at that sum at half the court rate as it has been from time to time for the whole period from 1 February 1978 to date."

---

[206] Scot Law Com DP No 127 at para 3.1.
[207] *MacIntosh v National Coal Board* 1988 SLT 348. The exercise of the discretion in respect of interest requires a selective and discriminating approach: see *Macrae v Reed and Malik Ltd* 1961 SC 68; *Smith v Middleton (No 2)* 1972 SC 30.
[208] See, eg, Act of Sederunt (Interest in Sheriff Court Decrees and Extracts) (SI 1993/769). The judicial rate is currently set at 8%. The rate applies to court decrees granted after 1 April 1993.
[209] See, eg, *Purryag v Greater Glasgow Health Board* 1996 SLT 794; *Bonar v Trafalgar House Offshore Fabrication Ltd* 1996 SLT 548; *McGarrigle v Babcock Energy Ltd* 1996 SLT 471.
[210] See, eg, *McKinnon v British Telecommunications Ltd* 1996 SLT 798.
[211] 1996 SLT 794.
[212] *Ibid* at 795.

22.102   The matter of interest in relation to "historic" wrongs came before the Inner House in
J v *Fife Council*.[213] The pursuer alleged that he had been seriously abused while resident
in a children's home from June 1961 to September 1966. The Lord Ordinary[214] made a
solatium award of £75,000 and attributed the whole amount to the past. However, in
view of the delay of some 35 years from the end of the abuse until the raising of the
action, the Lord Ordinary awarded interest on that sum *from the date of citation* only.
The pursuer reclaimed, asserting that (a) the solatium award was derisory and wholly
unreasonable, and (b) the approach taken to interest had been unduly restrictive. It
has already been noted that the challenge to the solatium award failed. The Inner
House considered, however, that the Lord Ordinary's decision on interest was open
to review. The Inner House was critical of the Lord Ordinary's view that there was
no satisfactory explanation for the delay. The pursuer would have been mounting an
allegation of gross criminal conduct against an individual who was highly regarded in
the local community. The pursuer did not think that he would be believed. Moreover,
the Lord Ordinary had considered only what was fair or unfair to the respondents
without having regard (at least expressly) to what was fair to the reclaimer. Delivering
the opinion of the First Division, the Lord President (Lord Hamilton) stated:[215]

> "Usually the nature of the pain and suffering to be compensated will be of a sufficiently
> homogenous nature that it will not be necessary, for the purposes of making an award of
> interest, to divide past solatium into constituent elements. Unusually, in the present case,
> there are, it seems to us, two discrete elements, namely (1) the pain, affront and humiliation
> experienced by the reclaimer while resident at the home and (2) the emotional and social
> consequences which he experienced after leaving the home."

22.103   In respect of the first element (to which the Inner House allocated £50,000 of the award)
interest was awarded at half the judicial rate and in respect of the second element (ie
£25,000) the Inner House awarded interest at one-quarter of the judicial rate.

Interest on patrimonial loss

22.104   In relation to patrimonial loss, no interest is payable on future loss.[216] In relation to past
patrimonial loss (ie from date of injury to date of proof) interest is generally awarded
at one-half of the average court rate.[217]

22.105   The above rules are in addition to the usual rules which require interest to run from
the date of decree until payment is made by the defender.

22.106   In its Report on *Interest on Debt and Damages*[218] the Scottish Law Commission
outlined a number of difficulties with the existing law. Foremost among these difficulties is that the provisons of the 1958 Act, as amended by the 1971 Act, are reliant on
judicial discretion and provide no express guidance as to how they are to be applied.

---

213 2009 SC 163.
214 2007 SLT 85.
215 2009 SC 163 at para 25.
216 *Hill* v *Wilson* 1998 SC 81 at 85.
217 See the calculation, eg, in *Campbell* v *Gillespie* 1996 SLT 503.
218 Scot Law Com No 203, 2006.

The Commission recommended[219] that "interest should run on each head of loss from the date on which the loss in question was sustained".[220]

CALCULATING DAMAGES IN RESPECT OF CHILDREN

The quantification of damages is likely to be more difficult in reparation cases **22.107** involving children because of the degree of speculation involved in assessing their future earnings. The court will usually consider how well the child is performing at school, his intelligence, the occupation of parents, etc. In *McKinnel* v *White*[221] a child aged 5 was severely injured as a result of a road accident which rendered him incapable of normal life. He would almost certainly have to spend his whole life in an institution. Lord Fraser concluded that the child would never be able to earn a living or live an independent life. In assessing damages in respect of lost earning capacity, his Lordship considered both the intelligence of the child prior to the accident (he "was an alert and intelligent child who had got into a small school under the age of five")[222] and his father's occupation (he was in business as a building contractor).

In *O'Connor* v *Matthews*[223] the pursuer suffered a very severe brain injury at the **22.108** age of 12 as a result of a road accident. He was aged 17 at the date of proof. He had been rendered physically disabled as a result of the accident with a tremor affecting all four limbs. His short-term memory and his ability to concentrate were limited. An expert in rehabilitation gave evidence that there was no real prospect of the pursuer obtaining profitable employment in the future. The pursuer gave evidence that prior to the accident he had hoped to become a professional boxer, which failing, a manual labourer. It was common ground that the latter was more probable. Damages were assessed using a multiplicand of £9,734 in respect of loss of earnings (with the exception of £2,600 which it was agreed would have been the net earnings for the first year of any employment.) A multiplier of 12 was applied in respect of future wage loss and a lump sum of £15,000 was awarded in respect of wage loss to date of proof.

DEDUCTIONS FROM AWARDS[224]

An accident victim may be entitled to certain state benefits (eg sickness benefit, invalidity **22.109** benefit, mobility allowance) and the courts have recognised that this may lead to double recovery in circumstances where compensation is also paid by the wrongdoer.[225] A statutory scheme allowing for recoupment of certain state benefits in such circumstances was introduced by the Social Security Act 1989. The Compensation Recovery Unit

---

[219] Scot Law Com No 203 at para 4.6.
[220] The Scottish Government subsequently issued a consultation document and draft Interest (Scotland) Bill in January 2008.
[221] 1971 SLT (Notes) 61.
[222] *Ibid* at 62.
[223] 1996 SLT 408.
[224] For a comprehensive account of this area of law, including the historical background, see R Lewis, *Deducting Benefits from Damages for Personal Injury* (1999).
[225] See *Hodgson* v *Trapp* [1989] AC 807: "The underlying principle is, of course, that damages are compensatory. They are not designed to put [the injured party] ... in a better financial position than that in which he would otherwise have been if the accident had not occurred." (Per Lord Oliver at 826.) See, also, Lord Bridge at 819. The House of Lords held in *Hodgson* that the full value of attendance and mobility allowance should be deducted from the damages award.

was set up to administer the scheme. The reasoning behind compensation recovery is twofold: namely that the taxpayer should not bear the burden of compensating an accident victim where the courts would hold someone else legally responsible and that an accident victim should not be compensated twice in respect of the same injury. It was stated in the Beveridge Report[226] in 1942: "An injured person should not have the same need met twice over. He should get benefit at once without prejudice to any alternative remedy, but if the remedy in fact proves to be available, he should not in the end get more from the two sources together than he would have got from the one source alone."

22.110   The 1989 scheme provided that where a person suffered an injury in consequence of which he received state benefits, then in the event of him successfully pursuing a claim for damages, the compensator required to repay to the Secretary of State the benefits which the injured party had received as a result of his injury. The scheme attracted considerable criticism on a number of fronts[227] and was significantly revised in 1997. The current law is found in the Social Security (Recovery of Benefits) Act 1997.

22.111   Under s 1(1) of the Act, the recovery scheme applies where:

"(a) a person makes a payment (whether on his own behalf or not) to or in respect of any other person in consequence of any accident, injury or disease suffered by the other, and

(b) any listed benefits have been, or are likely to be, paid to or for the other during the relevant period in respect of the accident, injury or disease."

22.112   The compensator is "liable to pay to the Secretary of State an amount equal to the total amount of the recoverable benefits".[228]

22.113   Under the 1997 scheme, benefit recovery is now effected on a like-for-like basis.[229] The deductions to be made in respect of certain benefits are deducted from one of the following three heads of loss:[230]

(1) compensation in respect of earnings lost (and interest thereon) during the relevant period;[231]

(2) compensation for care costs incurred over the relevant period;[232]

(3) compensation for loss of mobility over the relevant period.[233]

---

[226] *Social Insurance and Allied Services*, Report by Sir William Beveridge, November 1942 (Cmnd 6404), para 260.
[227] Perhaps the most significant criticism was that clawback was permitted from the whole award including the solatium element. Thus recoupment of benefits which were paid in order to replace lost earnings could serve to diminish the solatium award! Moreover, under the 1989 scheme, recoupment was excluded where the damages were £2,500 or less with the result that many settlements were effected at or below that level, thus circumventing the recoupment provisions.
[228] Section 6(1) of the 1997 Act.
[229] Lewis explains the position as follows: "This principle of equivalence means, for example, that a benefit listed as being paid in respect of lost earnings can only be deducted against damages for lost earnings and not against damages paid for the cost of care." (*Deducting Benefits from Damages for Personal Injury* at para 13.03.)
[230] See s 8 of and Sch 2, col 1 to the 1997 Act.
[231] From this head the following benefits are deducted: disability working allowance; disablement pension; incapacity benefit; income support; invalidity pension and allowance; jobseeker's allowance; reduced earnings allowance; severe disablement allowance; sickness benefit; statutory sick pay; unemployability supplement; unemployment benefit.
[232] From this head the following benefits are deducted: attendance allowance; the care component of disability living allowance; any disablement benefit increase.
[233] From this head the following benefits are deducted: mobility allowance; the mobility component of disability living allowance.

Importantly, the solatium element of an award of damages is now ringfenced: ie there **22.114** can be no deduction from damages awarded for solatium. (This had not been the case under the 1989 scheme.)

The recoverable benefits are listed in Sch 2, column 2 to the Act. Any benefits not **22.115** listed are not recoverable. The benefits are only recouped in relation to the "relevant period", which is the period of 5 years immediately following the day on which the accident or injury occurred (or, in disease cases, the period of 5 years beginning with the date on which the victim first claimed a listed benefit in consequence of his disease).[234] However, the relevant period ends when the final compensation payment is made, irrespective of whether the 5-year period has elapsed. There is, thus, an incentive to pursuers' agents to prosecute the claim speedily in an effort to reduce the amount of benefits to be repaid.[235] If a claim settles in 1 year as opposed to 5, it follows that a much smaller amount is repaid to the Compensation Recovery Unit. Because the state benefits are only recouped for a maximum 5-year period, any benefits received after the expiry of the 5-year period are not taken into account.

The benefits are deducted by the compensator, ie the defender in the action. He **22.116** obtains a certificate from the Compensation Recovery Unit which specifies the amount of recoverable benefits. He then deducts the benefits as appropriate from each head of compensation.[236] It may be that in some cases the recoverable benefits exceed the award of compensation under a given head, in which case the payment to the injured party under that head is reduced to nil. The excess of benefit cannot be carried over to another head of compensation. It is important to note that the *recovery* scheme applies irrespective of whether the compensator is able to offset the recoverable benefit against the damages award.

Under the 1989 recoupment scheme, recoupment took place only where the **22.117** damages award exceeded £2,500. Although the 1997 Act envisages the possibility of regulations being made to introduce a prescribed threshold below which no benefit would be recovered,[237] this power has not been invoked. It follows that, at present, benefits can be recovered against *any* level of damages.

Section 11 of the Administration of Justice Act 1982 provides that in an action for **22.118** damages for personal injuries any saving to the injured person which is attributable to his maintenance wholly or partly at public expense in (a) a hospital or other institution, or (b) accommodation provided by a care home service (as defined by s 2(3) of the Regulation of Care (Scotland) Act 2001), shall be set off against any income lost by him as a result of the injuries.

However, certain payments are not taken into account to reduce the amount **22.119** of damages. These are listed in s 10 of the Administration of Justice Act 1982 and include: (a) any contractual pension or benefit (including any payment by a friendly society or trade union); (b) any pension or retirement benefit payable from public funds other than any pension or benefit to which s 2(1) of the Law Reform (Personal Injuries) Act 1948 applies; (c) any benefit payable from public funds in respect of any period after the date of the damages award which is designed to secure for the

---

[234] Section 3 of the 1997 Act.
[235] Lewis states the position in the following terms: "[S]ettle today and keep tomorrow's benefits; settle tomorrow and you will lose them."(*Deducting Benefits from Damages for Personal Injury* at para 13.20.)
[236] Social Security (Recovery of Benefits) Act 1997, s 6.
[237] Schedule 1 to the Act, paras 1 and 9.

injured person or any relative a minimum level of subsistence; (d) any redundancy payment under the Employment Rights Act 1996, or any payment made in circumstances corresponding to those in which a right to a redundancy payment would have accrued if s 135 of that Act had applied; (e) any payment made to the injured person (or any relative) by his employer following upon the injuries where the recipient is under an obligation to repay the employer in the event of damages being recovered; and (f) subject to paragraph (iv), any payment of a benevolent character made to the injured person or to any relative of his by any person following upon the injuries in question.

22.120   Section 10 continues that the following *shall* be taken into account to reduce the amount of damages:

> "(i) any remuneration or earnings from employment;
> (ii) any contribution-based jobseeker's allowance (payable under the Jobseekers Act 1995);
> (iii) any benefit referred to in paragraph (c) above payable in respect of any period prior to the date of the award of damages;
> (iv) any payment of a benevolent character made to the injured person or to any relative of his by the responsible person following on the injuries in question,[238] where such a payment is made directly and not through a trust or other fund from which the injured person or his relatives have benefited or may benefit."

DAMAGES WHERE DEATH HAS OCCURRED

22.121   Where the injured person has died either as a result of his injuries or from an unrelated cause prior to proof there are a number of important provisions which apply in relation to a claim for damages. The question of transmissibility of the injured party's claim to his executor on death is discussed in Chapter 24 (Transfer and Extinction of Liability) and is not therefore considered here. However, the potential claims by relatives will be considered.

Non-patrimonial award for "immediate family" of deceased[239]

22.122   It has been said that "a death arising from personal injuries is not merely a wrong against the deceased but also a wrong against those who have been closest to the deceased".[240] Accordingly, s 4(3)(b) of the Damages (Scotland) Act 2011 provides for a non-patrimonial award in such circumstances. Such an award can be claimed by the "immediate family".

22.123   The award provides for compensation in respect of the following:

---

[238] See *Smith v Opportunus Fishing Co Ltd* 2011 RepLR 34. "Loan" payments made to the pursuer by the first defender did not fall under this head and accordingly did not fall to be deducted from the damages award.
[239] The Scottish Law Commission has recently proposed that this award should be renamed as a "grief and companionship award". See Report on *Damages for Wrongful Death* (Scot Law Com No 213, 2008), recommendation 13(b).
[240] Scottish Law Commission in its Report on *Title to Sue for Non-Patrimonial Loss* (Scot Law Com No 187, 2002) at para 2.8.

(a) distress and anxiety endured in contemplation of the suffering of the deceased before death; (s 4(3)(b)(i) of the 2011 Act);[241]

(b) grief and sorrow caused by the deceased's death (s 4(3)(b)(ii) of the 2011 Act); and

(c) loss of such non-patrimonial benefit as the immediate family member might have expected to derive from the deceased's society and guidance if the deceased had not died (s 4(3)(b)(iii) of the 2011 Act).

All three heads may apply in appropriate circumstances.[242] The court need not ascribe any part of the award specifically to (a), (b) or (c).

The non-patrimonial award can be claimed only by the "immediate family".[243] **22.124** "Immediate family" is defined as a relative falling within paras (a)–(d) of the definition of "relative" in s 14(1) of the 2011 Act. Immediate family includes the following:

(1) a spouse or civil partner;

(2) any person living with the deceased as spouse or civil partner;

(3) a parent or any person who accepted the deceased as a child of his or her family;

(4) a child[244] or someone accepted by the deceased as a child of the family;

(5) a brother or sister (or anyone brought up in the same household as the deceased and who was accepted as a child of the family in which the deceased was a child);

(6) a grandparent or someone who accepted the deceased as a grandchild;

(7) a grandchild or someone who was accepted by the deceased as a grandchild.

Section 14(2)(a)(ii) of the 2011 Act provides that, for the purposes of the non-patri- **22.125** monial award, any relationship of the half blood is to be treated as a relationship of the full blood. For the purposes of the non-patrimonial award, however, relationships of affinity (ie in-laws) are not treated as a relationship by consanguinity and a stepchild of a person is not treated as a person's child (s 4(5)(b) of the 2011 Act).

Given the nature of the award, the evidence provided by the relative in relation **22.126** to the nature and quality of his/her relationship with the deceased may be of crucial importance in the court's assessment under this head,[245] although differing judicial views have been expressed on this issue.[246]

---

[241] While this head will not be relevant in cases of instantaneous death, it will be relevant in cases of lingering death, eg death resulting from mesothelioma. See, also, *Wells v Hay* 1999 RepLR 44 (A 19-year-old man sustained 60% burns when his car exploded and he was trapped inside. He died 16 days later. A non-patrimonial award in the region of £37,000 was made (by a jury) to the deceased's mother.)

[242] See *Murray's Exrx v Greenock Dockyard Co Ltd* 2004 SLT 1104; *McLean v William Denny & Bros Ltd* 2004 SC 656; *Cruikshank v Fairfield Rowan Ltd* 2005 SLT 462 (all mesothelioma cases).

[243] This is a smaller group than "relatives" who can claim loss of support: see below.

[244] This includes a posthumous child: see *Cohen v Shaw* 1992 SLT 1022.

[245] See *Campbell v Gillespie* 1996 SLT 503 (at 511). Hajducki has observed that where one is dealing wth the death of a child "[t]he strength of relationship between parent and child is not explored, presumably on an application of the widely-held view that the greatest human tragedy is to outlive one's own children although possibly estranged children would merit a lesser award." See A M Hajducki, "Changing values: bereavement awards in a post Shaher world" 2003 SLT 189 at 192.

[246] In *Cruikshank v Fairfield Rowan Ltd* 2005 SLT 462 Lord Brodie confessed (at para 26) "to some difficulty with the notion that it is possible to discern in the circumstances of one family, bonds of affection that are stronger or a degree of emotional investment in the future of a child that is more profound, than in

22.127   Awards to spouses tend to be higher than those made to children and parents,[247] although in *Shaher* v *British Aerospace Flying College Ltd*[248] an award of £20,000 was made (in 2003) to each parent of a 19-year-old man (who had died in a flying accident). At the time, this was considered to be a very generous award. The Extra Division which heard the reclaiming motion[249] remarked upon the huge gulf between the level of judicial awards and the level of recent jury awards so far as bereavement generally was concerned. The Division stated that the court is encouraged to look for guidance to jury as well as judicial awards of damages and that the philosophy that the assessment of damages is first and foremost a matter for a jury gave awards of damages their essential legitimacy, and these awards should reflect the expectations of society rather than be simply an invention of the legal profession.

22.128   In *Murray's Executrix* v *Greenock Dockyard Co Ltd*,[250] the Inner House significantly increased non-patrimonial awards made by the temporary judge to a widow and daughter of a man who had died as a result of mesothelioma. The Inner House took the view that the awards made by the temporary judge were "unreasonably low". Delivering the opinion of the First Division, Lord President Cullen stated:[251]

> "It is plainly right for us to have regard both to judicial awards and to jury awards. As we explained in our opinion in *McLean* [v *William Denny & Bros Ltd* 2004 SLT 1099], while the jury awards provide evidence that judicial awards have been on the low side, it is extremely difficult, in view of the paucity of the latter awards, to see clearly to what extent judicial awards require to be increased. While an award for one class of relative may be of some value in considering what would be an appropriate award in respect of another class, it cannot be assumed that what holds good for one will necessarily apply to the other. There is a long standing and continuing tendency for awards to create a hierarchy between different classes of relative."

22.129   That awards to spouses tend to be higher than those made to children is evident from *Campbell* v *Gillespie*.[252] There, a 37-year-old man was killed in a road traffic accident. The death occurred before the new non-patrimonial award was introduced and so it was the former "loss of society" awards which were sought. The court awarded £13,500 for the widow, £8,000 for a child aged 4½ and £9,000 for a child aged almost 3. (There was evidence of a happy, stable marriage and that the deceased was a "family man".) *Campbell* v *Gillespie* also illustrates the general rule that, upon the death of a parent, a younger child will receive a higher non-patrimonial award than will an older child. The same general trend is evident in awards to parents in cases involving the loss of a child: the younger the child, the greater the award.[253]

22.130   Awards will be apportioned between past and future losses to reflect suffering of the immediate family member both before and after the date of proof[254] and to enable

---

the circumstances of another family". While acknowledging that there "was clearly a close, loving and supportive relationship" between the deceased son and his elderly mother in this case, his Lordship continued: "It was a good relationship between mother and son but I cannot see any basis upon which I could conclude that it did not fall within the generality of such relationships."

[247] See, eg, the awards made in *Bellingham* v *Todd* 2011 RepLR 68.
[248] 2003 SC 540.
[249] The Lord Ordinary had awarded £35,000 to each parent under this head.
[250] 2004 SLT 1104.
[251] *Ibid* at para 13.
[252] 1996 SLT 503.
[253] See *Cruikshank* v *Fairfield Rowan Ltd* 2005 SLT 462, per Lord Brodie at para 29.
[254] See *McAllister* v *Abram* 1981 SLT 85.

interest to be applied to the former. The right to damages under s 4(3)(b) of the 2011 Act, once vested, is transmissible to the family member's executor upon death.[255]

Section 4(2) of the Damages (Scotland) Act 2011 prevents the deceased's immediate **22.131** family from claiming damages for distress, grief and loss of non-patrimonial benefit where liability to the deceased has been discharged during his lifetime. Section 4(2) is disapplied, however, where the personal injury in consequence of which the deceased died was mesothelioma and where the discharge and the death each occurred on or after 20 December 2006.[256] This allows the immediate family of a mesothelioma victim to seek a non-patrimonial award from the wrongdoer following the sufferer's death even where the victim had settled his claim or recovers damages while alive.[257]

Loss of support award for "relatives" of deceased

A broader group of relatives can make what is known as a loss of support claim in **22.132** terms of s 4(3)(a) of the 2011 Act. The award covers loss of support since the date of the deceased's death, future loss of support and any reasonable expense incurred in connection with the deceased's funeral.[258] This head of loss can result in the payment of substantial damages. The definition of "relative" is provided in s 14(1) of the Damages (Scotland) Act 2011. Where the deceased died in consequence of personal injuries sustained by him, a loss of support award can be sought by the following relatives:

(1) immediate family (those who fall within this category are enumerated above);
(2) ascendants and descendants (other than a parent or grandparent or a child or grandchild);
(3) an uncle or aunt of the deceased or a child or other issue of such a person;
(4) a child or other issue of a brother or sister;
(5) a divorced spouse or former civil partner of the deceased but not a former cohabitee.

Section 14(2) of the 2011 Act provides that, for the purposes of the definition of **22.133** "relative", any relationship by affinity is to be treated as a relationship by consanguinity, any relationship of the half blood is to be treated as a relationship of the whole blood and a stepchild of a person is to be treated as the person's child.

In *Phillips* v *Grampian Health Board*[259] a woman married a man after a delict had taken place and in the knowledge that he was dying as a result of personal injuries sustained by him. She was held entitled to claim in respect of loss of support.

A significant change to the law as regards loss of support claims was introduced by the Damages (Scotland) Act 2011. The Act applies to cases in which proceedings are raised after the date of commencement of the Act (ie 7 July 2011). Section 7(1) of the Act fixes the total amount to be available to support the relatives of the deceased at an amount equivalent to 75 per cent of the deceased's net income. (In other words, the deceased would have spent 25 per cent on himself.) The court does, however, have

---

[255] Section 2 of the Damages (Scotland) Act 2011.
[256] See now Damages (Scotland) Act 2011, s 5.
[257] The matter is discussed in more detail in Chapter 24.
[258] In *Prentice* v *Chalmers* 1985 SLT 168 the cost of a headstone erected some months after the deceased's funeral was held to be recoverable.
[259] 1988 SLT 628.

discretion to depart from the fixed percentage approach "if satisfied that it is necessary to do so for the purposes of avoiding a manifestly and materially unfair result" (s 7(2)).

The relative for whom the fixed award is available is a spouse, civil partner, cohabiting partner or a dependent child. A dependent child is defined in s 7(3) of the Act as one who has not attained the age of 18 years and who is owed an obligation of aliment by the deceased. If any other relative makes a claim for loss of support, such a claim has to be met from the 75 per cent figure (s 7(1)(c)(ii)). However, if a relative (other than spouse, civil partner, cohabiting partner or dependent child) makes a claim, he or she is required to prove the *actual* loss of support (s 7(1)). It is for the court to apportion damages among the relatives where there is more than one claimant.

The loss of support claim is transmissible to the relative's executor, should the relative die before an award of damages is made.[260] To assess the future loss of support, recourse is had to the multiplicand/multiplier method outlined above. The multiplier applies from the date of the count's interlocutor. In determining loss of support, no account is taken of any patrimonial gain by virtue of succession or settlement or any insurance money, benefit, pension or gratuity payable as a result of the death.[261]

General points regarding relatives' claims

22.134 The relative will not recover damages if it is established that the deceased was not owed a duty of care or if it is established that there has been no breach of the duty or, of course, if there was no causal link between the breach of duty and the loss.[262] Similarly, the relative will not recover if the deceased is proved to have been *volens* to the risk. In other words, the defender will only be liable to pay damages to the relatives if he would have been liable to pay damages to the deceased. The relative's damages will be reduced if it is proved that the deceased had been contributorily negligent.[263] Finally, it should be noted that the relative's various claims can arise only if the deceased died "in consequence of suffering personal injuries".[264]

PROVISIONAL DAMAGES

22.135 The "once and for all" principle in relation to recovery of damages demands that damages for all losses arising from a delict must be claimed and recovered in the one action.[265] This rule has the potential to leave in an invidious position an injured person whose condition might deteriorate in the future. Section 12 of the Administration of

---

[260] Section 9 of the Damages (Scotland) Act 2011.

[261] Section 8(1) of the 2011 Act.

[262] See *McWilliams* v *Sir Wm Arrol* 1962 SC (HL) 70.

[263] See *Campbell* v *Gillespie* 1996 SLT 503.

[264] Section 3 of the Damages (Scotland) Act 2011. A baby wrongfully injured *in utero* will have a right of action if subsequently born alive: *Hamilton* v *Fife Health Board* 1993 SC 369. Once the baby is born, there is a concurrence of *injuria* and *damnum*, giving the baby the right to sue. The relatives will have dependant claims, should the baby (having been born alive) subsequently die. However, if the child is not born alive, no such rights arise.

[265] *Stevenson* v *Pontifex & Wood* (1887) 15 R 125 per LP Inglis at 129: "[T]hough the delict ... be of such a nature that it will necessarily be followed by injurious consequences in the future, and though it may for this reason be impossible to ascertain with precise accuracy at the date of the action or of the verdict the amount of loss which will result, yet the whole damage must be recovered in one action, because there is but one cause of action." See, also, *Dunlop* v *McGowans* 1979 SC 22 per LJ-C Wheatley at 33. See, also, *Potter* v *McCulloch* 1987 SLT 308, per Lord Weir. at 310.

Justice Act 1982 addresses this issue. Section 12 entitles the court in certain circumstances to make an award of provisional damages in respect of personal injuries. Such an award can be made where it is admitted or proved that there is a risk that, at a definite or indefinite time in the future, the pursuer will develop some *serious* disease or *serious* deterioration[266] in his physical or mental condition as a result of the defender's delict. Provisional damages are awarded only where the defender was at the time of the accident a public authority or an insured person.

Section 12 enables the pursuer to claim damages where he is unable to quantify his **22.136** loss fully because his condition will take some time to deteriorate, and to apply for further damages should the feared serious deterioration transpire. It has been said that "[p]rovisional damages ... may enable a claimant to avoid the worry that his condition may suddenly become much worse and that he will be left with insufficient compensation for his new-found circumstances".[267] Thus in *Lappin* v *Brittania Airways*[268] an award of provisional damages was made where there was a serious risk of the injured person developing epilepsy.

The court is not obliged to defer an award of damages and will have some regard to **22.137** the interests of the defender in not being called upon to pay further damages at some indefinite time in the future.[269] The court, therefore, is empowered to place a time limit after which the pursuer is no longer able to make a further application for damages. For example, in *McColl* v *Barnes*[270] there was a risk of epilepsy developing within 7 years of an accident. The Lord Ordinary (Morrison) imposed a time limit of 7 years on the application for further damages.

For an award of provisional damages to be made, there must be a clear threshold **22.138** when the pursuer could apply for damages in the future on the basis that such a serious deterioration has occurred.[271]

The Outer House had occasion to consider the question of provisional damages **22.139** in *Bonar* v *Trafalgar House Offshore Fabrication Ltd.*[272] A spray painter, aged 36 at proof, contracted industrial asthma as a result of his working conditions. In his action of damages he sought an award of provisional damages under s 12 of the 1982 Act. Lord Gill considered in some detail the circumstances in which such an award would be competent:[273]

> "[T]he court in applying this section must first consider what the apprehended deterioration is. If provisional damages are awarded it is essential, in my opinion, that the court's determination should make clear to the parties the nature of the deterioration on the occurrence of which the pursuer's right to final damages will emerge. Such a determination will also make clear what is being left out of account in the assessment of provisional damages. In my view the court should not impose upon a defender or his insurers a contingent liability for final damages unless the nature and extent of that liability are clear. That principle will serve to

---

[266] On the meaning of serious, see *White* v *Inveresk Paper Co Ltd (No 2)* 1988 SLT 2. See, also, *Meek* v *Burton's Gold Medal Biscuits Ltd* 1989 SLT 338.
[267] Lewis, *Deducting Benefits from Damages for Personal Injury* at para 15.22.
[268] 1989 SLT 181.
[269] See *Bonar* v *Trafalgar House Offshore Fabrication Ltd* 1996 SLT 548.
[270] 1992 SLT 1188.
[271] See *Prentice* v *William Thyne Ltd* 1989 SLT 336; *Robertson* v *British Bakeries Ltd* 1991 SLT 434.
[272] 1996 SLT 548.
[273] *Ibid* at 550.

minimise the risk of future litigation on the question whether some alleged deterioration is of a kind contemplated by the court in its earlier assessment."

His Lordship continued:[274]

"Section 12 may be easier to apply when the apprehended deterioration is, for example, an amputation of a damaged limb or the onset of post-traumatic osteo-arthritis – or post-traumatic epilepsy ... The section will ... be difficult to apply in cases where the deterioration may take several forms, of varying severity ... or where it may progress gradually."

22.140   Lord Gill could not, in the instant case, identify a future event against which a claim for final damages could be preserved. His Lordship went on to say that even if he was wrong on this point, the risk in the instant case did not justify an award of provisional damages. His Lordship stated:[275]

"In applying s 12 the court has to consider seriousness in relation to the deterioration and not the risk ... Nevertheless, the court is entitled to consider the degree of risk as a relevant factor in the exercise of its discretion ... In the present case the risk of a serious deterioration in the pursuer's condition is agreed to be small. In my opinion, it is not reasonable that the defenders and their insurers should be exposed to a contingent liability in respect of such a minor risk. For that reason too I consider it more appropriate that I should assess damages once and for all."

22.141   His Lordship also expressed the opinion that an order under s 12 should not be granted without limit of time unless in exceptional circumstances.

22.142   Although the 1982 Act does not state *in express terms* that actions in which provisional damages are sought are unsuitable for jury trial, it has been judicially stated that Parliament has *by implication* removed such actions from the list of those appropriate for jury trial.[276] This followed, *inter alia*, from the need for the court to which further application is made to have precise knowledge of how the earlier award was arrived at.

22.143   Where an award of provisional damages has been made to a pursuer who subsequently dies ("A"), A's relatives are not thereby prevented from making claims in respect of loss of support (or indeed for the non-patrimonial award) but in assessing damages for loss of support and loss of personal services, the court must take into account "such part of the provisional award relating to future patrimonial loss as was intended to compensate A for a period beyond the date on which A died".[277] This is designed to prevent double recovery.

22.144   Although the court's power to award provisional damages is sometimes said to constitute an exception to the "once and for all" rule, the better view would appear to be that stated by Lord Weir in *Potter v McCulloch*:[278] "The general principle of the common law ... is ... not essentially affected. The claim is for a single award of

---

[274] 1996 SLT 548 at 551.
[275] *Ibid.*
[276] See *Potter v McCulloch* 1987 SLT 308.
[277] Damages (Scotland) Act 2011, s 8(3).
[278] 1987 SLT 308 at 310.

damages which may be met in two stages and, if the second stage arises, it is dealt with by the revival of the process in the original action."

INTERIM DAMAGES

The court can award interim damages in certain circumstances. The procedure is available **22.145** in both the Court of Session[279] and the sheriff court.[280] The rules apply only in personal injury (or fatal cases). They do not apply to any other type of claim.[281] An application for interim damages can be made by the pursuer after lodging of defences. In *McNeill* v *Roche Products Ltd*,[282] Lord Coulsfield stated that "the purpose of the rule, must, I think, be to benefit pursuers who are almost certainly going to be awarded damages, by allowing them to obtain partial payment without suffering the inevitable delays of litigation". Although it is often said that the purpose of an interim damages award is to mitigate the hardship which might be suffered by the injured party pending final resolution of the action, it is not strictly necessary for the pursuer to demonstrate that he is suffering actual hardship.[283] The court can award interim damages if satisfied that (a) the defender has admitted liability *or* (b) if the case proceeded to proof, the pursuer would succeed in a question of liability[284] without any substantial[285] finding of contributory negligence.

Interim damages were awarded in *Cleland* v *Campbell*.[286] There, the pursuer was **22.146** injured in a road traffic accident when the defender's vehicle crossed to her side of the carriageway. Photographs were lodged in process which showed that there was mud on the road. The defender admitted that he had lost control of the car, but that this had resulted from the presence of the mud, of which there was no warning. Lord McCluskey held that the court was entitled to consider the photographs to be an admission that there was mud on the road which was visible from some distance from the scene of the accident and, failing an explanation in the defender's pleadings as to why he had not seen the mud, the pursuer would almost certainly succeed in an action against the defender on the question of liability.

---

[279] As far as the Court of Session is concerned, the rules in respect of interim damages were originally introduced by statutory instrument in 1974. The procedure is now governed by Act of Sederunt (Rules of the Court of Session Amendment No 2) (Personal Injuries Actions) 2002 (SSI 2002/570). (See Rules of the Court of Session (RCS), rr 43.11 and 43.12.)

[280] See Act of Sederunt (Amendment of Sheriff Court Ordinary Cause, and Summary Cause, Rules) 1988 (SI 1988/1978). (See Ordinary Cause Rules (OCR), rr 36.8–36.10.) Note, however, that there are no rules relating to interim damages in summary causes.

[281] Thus in *Mackenzie* v *Digby Brown* 1992 SLT 891 a motion for interim damages was refused in a professional negligence action, this not being "an action of damages for personal injury".

[282] 1988 SC 77.

[283] See *McNeill* v *Roche Products Ltd* 1988 SC 77, per Lord Coulsfield at 81.

[284] The test would seem to be that the pursuer would almost certainly succeed on the question of liability. See *Herbertson* v *Ascosamit Co Ltd* 1992 SLT 1115. (The employers of the pursuer (a diver) had been convicted of an offence under the Health and Safety at Work etc Act 1974 and, having regard to that conviction, the pursuer was almost certain to succeed against them. An interim award of £100,000 was made against the employers. (No interim award was made against the second defender, however, as a substantial question remained about his fault.)) See, also, *Douglas' CB* v *Douglas* 1974 SLT (Notes) 67; *Walker* v *Infabco Diving Services Ltd* 1983 SLT 633; *Nelson* v *Duraplex Industries Ltd* 1975 SLT (Notes) 31; *Reid* v *Planet Welding Equipment Ltd* 1980 SLT (Notes) 7.

[285] In *McNeill* v *Roche Products Ltd* 1988 SC 77, Lord Coulsfield (at 80) took the word "substantial" to mean "considerable or big" and in so doing approved the approach of Lord Ross in *Reid* v *Planet Welding Equipment Ltd* 1980 SLT (Notes) 7.

[286] 1998 SLT 642.

22.147   In *Calder* v *Simpson* [287] the pursuer averred that he had been crossing a dual carriageway and was struck by a car which had been travelling at excessive speed. He sought interim damages. The defender argued that he had been travelling at a lower speed and that the pursuer had run into his path and had failed to use a pedestrian crossing nearby. The sheriff found the pursuer entitled to interim damages. The defender appealed to the sheriff principal. In allowing the appeal, the sheriff principal held that "substantial" meant "of considerable amount" and it could not be said that the pursuer would almost certainly succeed on the question of liability without any substantial finding of contributory negligence.

22.148   In *Cowie* v *Atlantic Drilling Co Ltd*,[288] on the other hand, the First Division upheld an award of interim damages to a workman who had been injured on an oil rig. The court was satisfied that he would succeeed on a question of liability and that he would do so without any substantial finding of contributory negligence. Delivering the opinion of the First Division, the Lord President (Hope) stated:[289]

> "It appears to us that in this context the word 'substantial' means something which is of real importance of the point at issue, which is the assessment of the extent of the defenders' liability to the pursuer in damages ... What the Lord Ordinary has to be satisfied about, to the required standard, is that the finding of contributory negligence will not be so large as to have a material effect on his assessment of the amount which the pursuer is likely to recover as damages."

22.149 In *Walker* v *Dunn*[290] the pursuer, who was travelling as a rear-seat passenger in the defender's car, was injured as a result of the defender's careless driving. The pursuer, however, had failed to wear her seatbelt and would thus be 10–15 per cent contributorily negligent. This was held not to amount to a substantial finding of contributory negligence and thus interim damages were competent. In that case, the pursuer's claim was thought to be worth £1 million. The amount sought (and awarded) by way of interim damages was £350,000, being the amount required to build and equip suitable home care accommodation for the pursuer.[291]

22.150   Interim damages should be of such an amount as the court thinks fit but the award is to be restricted to a "reasonable proportion" of the damages which might ultimately be awarded.[292] It has been suggested that, in some cases, 75 per cent or more could be such a reasonable proportion, especially where a minimum figure of likely damages was accepted by the defender.[293] The court can have regard to future losses in its determination of an appropriate interim award.[294] Interim damages are taken into account in making the final award. An interim award will be made only if the defender is insured in respect of the pursuer's claim, if the defender is a public authority, if the

---

[287] 1994 SLT (Sh Ct) 32.
[288] 1995 SC 288.
[289] *Ibid* at 294.
[290] 1995 SCLR 588.
[291] See, also, *Hogg* v *Carrigan* 2001 RepLR 60 where, again, the pursuer failed to wear a seatbelt and an interim award was made in circumstances where the projected deduction was 25%.
[292] See *Fletcher (A guardian)* v *Lunan* 2008 RepLR 72.
[293] *D's Parent and Guardian* v *Argyll and Clyde Acute Hospitals NHS Trust* 2003 SLT 511 (per Lord Carloway at para 5).
[294] *Moodie* v *Maclean* 1981 SLT (Notes) 53; *Nisbet* v *Marley Rooftile Co Ltd* 1988 SC 29; *Thompson's CB* v *Burnett* 1989 SLT 264.

defender's means are such as to enable him to make such an interim payment or if the defender is a person who is not insured but in respect of whose liability the Motor Insurers' Bureau will be liable to make payment. [295]

DAMAGES FOR HARASSMENT

It will be remembered that s 8(1) of the Protection from Harassment Act 1997 confers **22.151** an enforceable right not to be harassed and that s 8(2) goes on to provide that "[a]n actual or apprehended breach of subsection (1) may be the subject of a claim in civil proceedings by the person who is or may be the victim of the course of conduct in question; and any such claim shall be known as an action of harassment". Section 8(5)(a) of the 1997 Act provides that in an action of harassment the court may award damages (without prejudice to any other remedies which it may grant (ie interdict or a non-harassment order)). Section 8(6) of the 1997 Act provides that "[t]he damages which may be awarded in an action of harassment include damages for any anxiety caused by the harassment and any financial loss resulting from it".[296]

DAMAGES FOR DEFAMATION

Only a brief account is offered here in relation to damages for defamation.[297] Damages **22.152** for defamation are likely in the main to comprise solatium for hurt feelings, although patrimonial losses may be claimed in appropriate cases.[298] "[I]t is well established that the principle of making an award of punitive or exemplary damages in defamation cases does not form part of the law of Scotland."[299]

The Inner House has said that it is inappropriate to compare an award of solatium **22.153** made in respect of physical injury with an award of solatium for injury to feelings and reputation in a defamation action.[300] While a Scottish court may take account of awards in other Scottish defamation cases, the potential benefit of such an exercise has been doubted.[301] A higher award may be justified in the case of a particularly sensitive individual.[302] Regard is not had to English decisions where awards are based on different principles.[303] The Inner House has held that a court of appeal should be even

---

[295] See RCS r 43.11(5); OCR r 36.9(5).
[296] Note that mere anxiety does not sound in damages in personal injury cases but, in *G v S* 2006 SLT 795, Lord Turnbull observed that in ordinary parlance, it could not be said that an action of harassment was one concerned with personal injuries. *Tudhope v Finlay Park (t/a Park Hutchison Solicitors)* 2004 SLT 795 was applied.
[297] For a more detailed exposition, the reader is referred to K M Norrie, *Defamation and Related Actions in Scots Law* (1995), Chapter 12.
[298] See *Capital Life Assurance Society Ltd v Scottish Daily Record and Sunday Mail (The Scotsman,* 6 January 1979) (£327,000 awarded primarily in respect of lost business).
[299] *Winter v News Scotland Ltd* 1991 SLT 828, per Lord Morison at 829.
[300] *Ibid.* The point was repeated in *Baigent v British Broadcasting Corporation* 2001 SC 281 at para 22: such comparisons were not "helpful or useful".
[301] *Baigent v British Broadcasting Corporation* 2001 SC 281, per Lord Johnston at para 22: "Every case of defamation is unique in respect of both the content of the slander and its effect upon the victims and it therefore follows in our view that even comparison with other decided cases in that area is of very limited value."
[302] *Winter v News Scotland Ltd* 1991 SLT 828 at 831.
[303] *Ibid.*

more reluctant to interfere with a jury's award in cases of defamation than in cases of physical injury.[304]

AGREEING OF LOSSES

22.154   It is common practice for parties to an action of damages to agree some of the losses in advance as this will restrict the matters on which evidence has to be led at proof. Parties may therefore enter into joint minutes in relation to items which are not contested. For example, loss of earnings prior to proof is often agreed[305] by the respective agents. Of course, there are frequently other matters which will be fiercely contested at proof.

JURY TRIALS

22.155   Personal injury actions in the Court of Session may be tried by jury.[306] Juries appear to be somewhat more generous in their awards of damages than are judges.[307] However, while a new trial may be ordered where the damages awarded by the jury are excessive, that power will not be exercised unless the damages awarded are beyond what a reasonable jury would award. The mere fact that a judge would have made a lower award is insufficient reason to order a new trial.[308] Under s 9(2) of the Court of Session Act 1988, a case may be withheld from a jury if special cause exists. The potential complexity of any damages award may constitute such special cause. In *O'Neill* v *Dowding & Mills plc*[309] the defenders and third party in the action maintained that, on account of the complexity of assessing future losses, special cause existed for withholding jury trial under s 9(2) of the Court of Session Act 1988. Lord Emslie agreed. The application of the Ogden Tables would be a source of real difficulty in the context of a jury trial, although the fact that the Tables would require to be applied was not in itself sufficient reason to deny trial by jury. Complex actuarial evidence might be difficult for a jury to follow; a multiplicity of calculations would need to be attempted. There would, in addition, be the difficulty of identifying appropriate multipliers and the difficulty of dealing with contingencies, as yet unidentified, for which allowance would have to be made. Lord Emslie observed:[310]

> "[I]t seems to me that even a personal damages action may involve such a degree of complexity that only a proof in front of an experienced judge would be appropriate. At a proof the judge would have the benefit of full submissions on both legal and factual issues, including the proper application of different parts of the Tables and the treatment of matters which these Tables do not directly address. A judge would also be in a position to derive the fullest assistance from the explanatory notes in the Tables themselves, and would have the

---

[304] *Winter* v *News Scotland Ltd* 1991 SLT 828. (The defender argued that a jury award of £50,000 was excessive but a motion for a new trial was refused.)

[305] Wage loss down to date of proof was agreed in *McGarrigle* v *Babcock Energy Ltd* 1996 SLT 471.

[306] RCS 1994, Chapter 37. See, generally, A Hajducki, *Civil Jury Trials* (2nd edn, 2006).

[307] It had been observed judicially that it might be that the levels fixed by judges in respect of personal injury claims were lower than they should be (*Baigent* v *British Broadcasting Corporation* 2001 SC 281, per Lord Johnston at para 24). Because jury awards help to inform judicial awards, an increase in awards generally is discernable: see See Hajducki, "Changing values: bereavement awards in a post Shaher world" 2003 SLT 189.

[308] See *Girvan* v *Inverness Dairy Farmers (No 2)* 1998 SC (HL) 1.

[309] 2008 RepLR 40.

[310] *Ibid* at para 13.

facility of taking time to consider all issues carefully before pronouncing a reasoned, and thus reviewable, decision. Trial by jury would, I think, have none of these advantages."[311]

On the other hand, in *Robertson v Smith*[312] the Inner House allowed a personal damages **22.156** claim to go to jury trial notwithstanding the involvement of the Ogden Tables. There, however, the decision proceeded on the basis that the pursuer would never work again and thus the future loss calculation would be relatively straightforward.[313]

In *Mykoliw v Botterill*[314] it was argued that special cause existed to withhold the **22.157** case from trial by jury. There, a stepfather was suing along with other relatives of the deceased, who had died in a traffic accident. It was submitted by the defender and third party that the multiplicity of pursuers and their respective claims would only cause difficulty for a jury in assessing damages. Lord Pentland rejected that argument and allowed a jury trial. None of the difficulties was sufficient to justify the pursuers being denied their statutory right to jury trial and none of the issues likely to arise on damages seemed of such complexity as to render quantification of the various claims unduly difficult for a properly directed jury.

SOME RECENT SCOTTISH DECISIONS ON DAMAGES

In *Henry v Rentokil Initial plc*[315] a nurse sustained injury in the course of her employment. **22.158** An injury to her hip resolved within 6 months but the principal injury to the network of nerves in the area of her neck and shoulder resulted in loss of function of her left hand and arm. These conditions were likely to be permanent and the pursuer would never again be able to work as a nurse. (Indeed, her employers had terminated her contract of employment.) She was unable to perform any task requiring the use of two hands. As a result of her injury, the pursuer suffered severe pain for about 2 years. The quality of her day-to-day existence had been materially impaired and she had incurred and would incur costs in respect of modifying a car and purchasing modified articles for everyday use. At the date of proof, the pursuer was studying at university with a view to qualifying as a primary teacher. The sheriff found that the pursuer would lose 3 years' earnings before qualifying for remunerative employment as a teacher and on qualifying it would take her approximately 10 years before her earnings matched those she could reasonably have expected to receive in her previous career as a nurse.

The defenders admitted liability and proof was restricted to quantum. Following **22.159** proof, the sheriff (I D Dunlop) awarded the sum of £315,306.45 under various heads as follows:

(1)	Past solatium (including interest)	£22,146.85
(2)	Future solatium	£12,500.00
(3)	Loss of past earnings (including interest)	£165,131.93
(4)	Loss of future earnings to 31/08/2009	£76,950.00

[311] Issues (ie jury trials) were also refused in *MacDonald v Mallan* [2008] CSOH 01, *Slessor v Vetco Gray UK Ltd and Ors* 2007 SLT 400 and *Potts v McNulty* 2000 SLT 1269 on account of the potential complexities in calculating damages. See, also, J Casey, "Ogden six and the civil jury" 2008 SLT 249.
[312] 2000 SC 591.
[313] See, also, *Reid and Ors v BP Oil Grangemouth Refinery Ltd* 2001 GWD 16–589.
[314] 2010 SLT 1219.
[315] 2008 SC 447.

    (5) Loss of earnings from 01/09/2002   £23,750.00
    (6) Services from others (past including interest)   £6,327.67
    (7) Services from others (future)   £5,000.00
    (8) Additional expenses   £3,500.00.

22.160   On appeal, every head of award was challenged by the defenders. It was contended that the pursuer had failed to prove that she would have been promoted and that, therefore, future wage loss should be calculated on the basis of her grade at the time of the accident. The Inner House observed that the pursuer was devoted to her work and it was more probable than not that she would have been promoted at some time between 2000 and 2006. The sums awarded by the sheriff were well within the range of any reasonable assessment. The Inner House also held that the sums awarded by the sheriff in respect of *future* loss of earnings were well within the range of any reasonable assessment. The appeal ultimately failed on all points except as regards apportionment of the sum awarded under the head of past and future services. (See the discussion of this aspect of the case under services, above.) A cross appeal in relation to pension loss was allowed with the result that the principal sum awarded by the sheriff was increased by the amount of the agreed pension loss figure, producing a total of £339,497.45, with interest from the date of the sheriff's interlocutor.

22.161   In *Smith* v *Opportunus Fishing Co Ltd*[316] the pursuer was a share fisherman who sustained a head injury resulting in permanent neuropsychological deficits and mild brain injury. An appropriate *total* award of damages was £56,694, the award of damages being made up as follows:

    (1) Solatium, including interest   £18,849.
    (2) Past wage loss, including interest   £28,043.
    (3) Loss of earning capacity   £7,500.
    (4) Section 8 and s 9 services, including interest   £2,302.

In *D's Guardian* v *Greater Glasgow Health Board*[317] the Lord Ordinary (Stewart) recommended that part of the settlement should be made in periodical payments. The case concerned a boy who was left paralysed following catastrophic neurological trauma sustained during a forceps-assisted delivery. The child could not breathe unaided and required 24-hour care costing hundreds of thousands of pounds every year. Although structured settlements are not uncommon in England, they are rare in Scotland. Medical negligence cases are usually settled on a lump sum basis but the Lord Ordinary in *D's Guardian* suggested (at para 3) that the settlement represents "new thinking" about the resolution of certain catastrophic injury cases in Scotland.

MITIGATION

22.162   The general duty which is incumbent on a pursuer to mitigate his loss applies in the law of delict.[318] As noted above, if repair of an item of property is less costly than replacement that is the course which should be followed. If, on the other hand, it

---

[316] 2011 RepLR 34.
[317] [2011] CSOH 99.
[318] *Barry* v *Sutherland* 2002 SCLR 427, per Lord Eassie at para 22.

would be cheaper to treat a damaged vehicle as a write-off, but the pursuer elects the more expensive alternative of repair, damages will be calculated on the basis of treating the vehicle as a total loss.[319] In relation to personal injuries cases, the same rule as regards mitigation applies.[320] Therefore, it might be argued that an injured person could have returned to work earlier than he did and that, by not doing so, he failed to mitigate his losses. Similarly, it might be argued that an injured person whose injuries prevent him from working in his previous employment, has failed to seek alternative employment.[321] It might similarly be argued that in failing to attend medical appointments and accept advice as to treatment, the pursuer has failed to mitigate his losses.[322]

---

[319] *Rolls-Royce (1971) Ltd* v *Hutchison* 1976 SLT (Notes) 15. See, also, *Pomphrey* v *James A Cuthbertson Ltd* 1951 SC 147, per the Lord Justice-Clerk (Lord Thomson): at 152 "It is a pursuer's duty to take reasonable steps to minimise a defender's loss. When a thing is so severely damaged that to repair it and hire a substitute during the period of repair is more costly than to treat it as a total loss, a pursuer must prefer that course which is less costly to the defender."

[320] Stewart has observed, however, that "[i]n practice, [the principle of mitigation] is found very seldom in personal injuries cases, where the plea is usually that the sum sued for is excessive, and the pursuer is put to proof of his losses" (W J Stewart, *Delict* (4th edn, 2004) at p 325).

[321] An argument to that effect was proferred (but was rejected on the facts) in *Anderson* v *Jas B Fraser & Co Ltd* 1992 SLT 1129.

[322] See *Davidson* v *Lothian and Borders Fire Board* 2003 SLT 363, per Lord Dawson at para 89. (Although a reclaiming motion on the issue of liability under the statutory ground of action was subsequently allowed, there was no challenge to the Lord Ordinary's assessment of damages.)

23 EVIDENTIAL[1] AND PRACTICAL MATTERS

INTRODUCTION

In order to succeed at proof, the pursuer in a delictual action must adduce evidence **23.1** of the facts which he requires to prove.[2] Although evidential matters are intimately connected with the substantive law of delict, they do require to be distinguished. The difference between substantive law and matters of evidence can be illustrated by means of a simple example. It is a matter of *law* that an employer is vicariously liable for the negligent acts of his employee, provided that those acts are carried out within the scope of the employment. However, in a vicarious liability case, evidence has to be led to show that the employee was, *in fact*, acting within the scope of his employment.

GENERAL MATTERS

ADMISSIONS

If the defender in an action admits certain facts,[3] then those facts do not require **23.2** evidence or proof. In other words, the admission is conclusive against the defender on the matters covered. Facts which are averred by the pursuer which are within the knowledge of the defender and which are not denied by him fall to be held as admitted. Ross and Chalmers[4] state: "Both in the Court of Session and in the sheriff court an averment made by one party of a fact within the knowledge of the other party is held by implication to be admitted if it is not denied by the other party."[5]

Sometimes, rather than admitting a certain fact, a party to an action may answer **23.3** an averment with the words "believed to be true". The question therefore arises as to

---

[1] This chapter deals only with the key elements of the law of evidence as it applies in civil cases. For a more detailed account of the law of evidence, see F P Davidson, *Evidence* (SULI, 2007); FE Raitt, *Evidence – Principles, Policy and Practice* (4th edn, 2008); M Ross and J Chalmers, *Walker and Walker: The Law of Evidence in Scotland* (3rd rev edn, 2009).

[2] Certain facts may be within "judicial knowledge", in which case evidence does not require to be led on that matter. The mischievous habits of children is one such example: see *Taylor* v *Glasgow Corporation* 1922 SC (HL) 1.

[3] This may be done in one of four ways: (1) an admission in the closed record (ie written pleadings); (2) a minute of admissions; (3) an uncontradicted notice to admit; or (4) an oral admission. For further discussion, see Ross and Chalmers, *Walker and Walker: The Law of Evidence in Scotland*, paras 11.21–11.26.

[4] *Ibid* at para 11.2.5.

[5] The sheriff court Ordinary Cause Rules 1993 (SI 1993/1956) contain a specific provision to this effect: see r 9.7.

whether evidence is required in relation to that point. It was observed in the case of *Binnie* v *Rederij Theodoro BV*[6] that a party, whose averment was met by a reply of "believed to be true", together with a denial of other averments, was entitled to assume that the matter believed to be true was not disputed and was not one on which evidence was necessary.

TYPES OF EVIDENCE

23.4   Evidence can be broadly categorised in one of three ways: real, documentary or oral. Real evidence is a thing which is not a document: for example, a piece of work equipment in a personal injury case. Documentary evidence might include a sketch of an accident scene or a medical report. Oral evidence is simply verbal testimony given in court: for example, the pursuer's account of a road traffic accident in which he sustained injury.

WHAT REQUIRES EVIDENCE

23.5   Failing admission by the defender, the pursuer would require to lead evidence of, for example, the defender's conduct which is alleged to amount to a breach of duty, the causal connection between the breach of duty and the injury, and the extent of his loss. The court, obviously, requires evidence of loss to enable it to assess damages. Therefore, in a personal injuries case, evidence should be produced as to loss of earnings, the degree of disability suffered by the pursuer (this, of course, will usually be spoken to by medical witnesses)[7] and, if appropriate, evidence as to loss of pension rights (actuarial evidence is usually obtained in respect of this head of loss).[8]

AGREEING EVIDENCE

23.6   It is usual for the parties to the action to agree some of the evidence before proof. This is a convenient thing to do because it will have the effect of shortening the subsequent court proceedings in that the proof will be limited to contentious matters only. Thus, matters such as pre-accident earnings[9] are often agreed because they are very rarely in dispute. Sometimes the nature and extent of the pursuer's injuries will be agreed, thus dispensing with the need to call medical experts, as witnesses, to court. However, this is a matter which is not always agreed and it may, in fact, be hotly disputed[10] where, for example, the defender is of the view that the pursuer is exaggerating his injuries with a view to inflating the award of damages.

PROOFS RESTRICTED TO QUANTUM

23.7   It is not unusual for the defender to admit liability and contest the action only on the amount of damages. In other words, the proof is restricted to quantum.[11] In *Taggart* v

---

[6] 1993 SC 71.

[7] See, eg *McKinnell* v *White* 1971 SLT (Notes) 61.

[8] See *Higgins* v *Tayside Health Board* 1996 SLT 288.

[9] See, eg, *McGarrigle* v *Babcock Energy Ltd* 1996 SLT 471 where parties had agreed the wage loss which had occurred prior to the date of proof.

[10] See *Taggart* v *Shell (UK) Ltd* 1996 SLT 795.

[11] See *Clark* v *Chief Constable of Lothian and Borders* 1993 SC 320; *J* v *Fife Council* 2007 SLT 85; *Henry* v *Rentokil Initial plc* 2008 SC 447; *Smith* v *Opportunus Fishing Co Ltd* 2011 RepLR 34.

Shell (UK) Ltd[12] the pursuer suffered a serious fracture to his foot when it was caught between a step on a stairway and a piece of equipment when a loose grating on the step moved. The pursuer's employers admitted liability and the proof was restricted to quantum. A clear divergence in opinion emerged between the two medical witnesses, both of whom were consultant surgeons. The defender's medical expert took a more optimistic view of the pursuer's prognosis. In the event, the Lord Ordinary preferred the evidence of the pursuer's expert on the basis that the defender's expert consistently underestimated the pursuer's disability.

Alternatively, damages are sometimes agreed[13] but liability is disputed. For **23.8** example, in *Smith* v *Bush; Harris* v *Wyre Forest DC*,[14] two cases of alleged surveyor's negligence, the damages in the second appeal were agreed at £12,000 although liability was disputed. More recently, in *Todd* v *Clapperton*,[15] damages in respect of a hand injury were agreed at £25,000 and proof was restricted to liability, which, in the event, was not established.

APPEALS

Generally speaking, appeal courts are reluctant to interfere with findings of fact which **23.9** have been made by the court of first instance.[16] This is because the judge in the lower court actually hears and sees the witnesses and is, therefore, in a better position to assess their credibility and reliability. Thus, Lord Hope in *Thomson* v *Kvaerner Govan Ltd* observed:[17] "An appellate court should be slow to interfere with a decision based on a view of the reliability of witnesses of whom the Lord Ordinary was able to make a personal assessment."

The appeal court will more readily interfere where what is at issue is an *inference* **23.10** from the facts. This point was made by Lord Bridge in *Whitehouse* v *Jordan*:[18]

"[I]n the realm of fact, as the authorities repeatedly emphasise, the advantages which the judge derives from seeing and hearing the witnesses must always be respected by an appellate court. At the same time the importance of the part played by those advantages in assisting the judge to any particular conclusion of fact varies through a wide spectrum from, at one end, a straight conflict of primary fact between witnesses, where credibility is crucial and the appellate court can hardly ever interfere, to, at the other end, an inference from undisputed primary facts, where the appellate court is in just as good a position as the trial judge to make the decision."[19]

---

[12] 1996 SLT 795.

[13] See *Ruddy* v *Marco* [2008] CSOH 40; 2008 SC 667 (IH) where damages on the basis of full liability had been agreed at £450,000 in a situation where the pursuer alleged that he had fallen from scaffolding in the course of his employment. See, also, *McGovern* v *Glasgow City Council* 2010 RepLR 2.

[14] [1990] 1 AC 831.

[15] 2009 SLT 837.

[16] See the guidance offered by Lord Thankerton in *Thomas* v *Thomas* 1947 SC (HL) 45 at 54. See, also, *Hamilton* v *Allied Domecq plc* 2006 SC 221, per Lord Hamilton at paras 84–85.

[17] 2004 SC (HL) 1 at para 20.

[18] [1981] 1 WLR 246 at 269–270.

[19] For a recent attempt to challenge inferences drawn from primary facts by the judge at first instance, see *Clegg* v *Rogerson and Network Rail* 2008 SLT 345. The challenge proved unsuccessful.

REQUIREMENT OF FAIR NOTICE[20]

23.11   Evidence is competent only to substantiate averments made on record.[21] The purpose of pleadings is to give fair notice of one's case and it is considered to be unfair for a party to adduce evidence in the course of a proof of which no notice has been given and thus, in effect, "ambush" the other side. This point was well expressed by the Lord Justice-Clerk (Hope) in the case of *Neilson* v *Househill Coal & Iron Co*:[22] "The beauty of the Scotch system is, that, without disclosing what is properly called evidence, you must at least state the line of defence, and the main facts and points in the enquiry on which you rest, so that the other party shall be fully able previously to investigate, the case, and be prepared for it." Therefore, if a fact is to be proved there must be an averment of that fact in the written pleadings. If there is no such averment, the evidence may be objected to and disallowed by the court. The pleadings should therefore be drafted with care, as failure to do so may lead to crucial evidence being excluded. For example, let us say that an action is raised against a local authority by a member of the public. The pursuer sustained injury when he tripped in a pothole on a footpath maintained by the authority. Numerous complaints concerning the pothole had been intimated to the authority but the authority had failed to repair the area of ground in question. Unfortunately, the pursuer's solicitor has omitted to put an averment in the written pleadings to the effect that complaints had been made. A and B are cited to attend court as witnesses as they had made complaints to the local authority in respect of the footpath. When these witnesses are called to give evidence as to their complaints, the authority's solicitor would be quite entitled to object to the evidence on the ground that there is no record for it, ie that there is no basis for it in the written pleadings. Without that vital evidence, the pursuer may be unable to establish a failure to take reasonable care and may therefore be forced to abandon the case.

23.12   The pleadings, therefore, may play a crucial role in the conduct of the case and, indeed, in the outcome of the whole litigation. Indeed, the pleadings proved to be of crucial importance in *Parker* v *Lanarkshire Health Board*.[23] There, the pursuer sought damages from her employers in respect of a back injury which she claimed to have sustained while lifting a male patient into the bath in his home. During the course of the proof, the defenders sought to lead evidence about a "pivot lift". Counsel for the pursuer objected to this line of evidence on the ground that it might "be designed to demonstrate that some other method could or should have been used by the pursuer". There were no express averments in the pleadings in relation to the use of a "pivot lift". Thus, no notice had been given in the written pleadings of an intention to lead such evidence. The Inner House, affirming the decision of the Lord Ordinary, excluded the evidence about a pivot lift. Lord McCluskey, who delivered the opinion of the court, observed:[24] "We regret very much that the court has been put in the situation of having to exclude evidence … but the responsibility, in our view, lies with the defenders if their intention was to suggest that the pursuer and her colleague should have

---

[20] See C Hennessy, *Civil Procedure and Practice* (3rd edn, 2008) at p 39.
[21] See *Campbell* v *Gillespie* 1996 SLT 503 at 509; *Ruddy* v *Marco* [2008] CSOH 40 at paras 21 and 59; *Weir* v *Robertson Group (Construction) Ltd* 2006 RepLR 114 at para 7; *McGowan* v *W & JR Watson* 2007 SC 272 at para 13.
[22] (1842) 4 D 1187 at 1193.
[23] 1996 SCLR 57.
[24] *Ibid* at 65.

employed a pivot lift ... If that was their intention, they totally failed to give effect to it in the drafting of the pleadings."

In *Campbell* v *Gillespie*[25] the pursuer raised an action in respect of her husband's **23.13** death. She averred that her husband's death had resulted from his collision with the rear of a broken down lorry, which was inadequately lit. The hazard warning lights on the lorry had gone out when the battery was disconnected by the mechanic who was working on the lorry. A Transit van had been placed, with its lights on, at the *front* of the lorry. The pursuer averred that it should have been placed at the rear of the lorry where it could have been observed by drivers on the side of the road on which the lorry was sitting, as opposed to drivers on the other side of the road. At proof, the pursuer's counsel raised the issue of portable warning signs with the mechanic who had been working on the lorry. These questions were objected to by the defender's counsel on the ground that there was no case on record based on a failure to place portable lights at the locus. Temporary Judge Robertson, QC, observed:[26] "The defender's objection on the matter of pleading was well founded and I consider that the case of fault is confined to a failure to park the Transit at the rear in the event of the hazard lights of the lorry being off. That is the only case on record and it is quite specific."[27]

In *Weir* v *Robertson Group (Construction) Ltd*[28] a workman died when he fell through **23.14** a hole in a roof during the course of his employment. An action of damages was subsequently raised. At proof, at which the matter of contributory negligence was in issue, counsel for the defender sought to advance a case that the deceased ought to have known that a safety net had been removed. Objection was taken to that line of cross-examination on the basis that there was no record for it. Lord Glennie upheld the objection and stated:[29]

"Although the new personal damages rules contained in Rule of Court 43 encourage abbreviated pleadings, they do not dispense with the requirements of fair notice. Rule of Court 43.2 requires the summons to contain averments 'relating only to those facts necessary to establish the claim.' The same approach, in my view, applies *mutatis mutandis* to the defences, though there is no specific rule about defences. The defences should aver the facts which the defender regards as necessary to support his defence or plea of contributory negligence. Otherwise how is the pursuer to know what investigations to make and what evidence to lead?"

The approach taken in *Weir* was endorsed by the Inner House in *McGowan* v **23.15** *W & JR Watson Ltd*.[30] There, Lord Nimmo Smith (who delivered the opinion of an Extra

---

[25] 1996 SLT 503.
[26] *Ibid* at 509.
[27] See, also, Lord President Clyde in *Morrison's Associated Companies Ltd* v *James Rome & Sons Ltd* 1964 SC 160 at 182: "It is a well-settled rule of our practice in pleading in Scotland that where a duty in general terms is averred, followed by a particularisation of the specific way or ways in which it is alleged that that duty has been breached, the enquiry on the facts is restricted to the specific breach or breaches of which notice has been given, and evidence directed to some other unspecified way in which the general duty may have been breached is excluded. The pursuer stands or falls on his establishing his averments of the specific breach or breaches."
[28] 2006 RepLR 114.
[29] *Ibid* at para 7.
[30] 2007 SC 272.

Division) stated[31] that the requirement to give at least fair notice of a case which it is proposed to make is incumbent on defenders as much as on pursuers.

ONUS OR BURDEN OF PROOF

23.16   The onus or burden of proof determines which party must prove the case and ensures that there will always be a winner in any litigation. Thus, where matters are evenly balanced, the burden of proof will acquire a crucial significance in the outcome of the case. The question of who bears the persuasive burden is determined by law and such a burden never moves. The persuasive burden[32] of proof in a civil case is on the pursuer. In *Brown* v *Rolls Royce Ltd*[33] Lord Cohen observed:[34] "It seems to me that the authorities clearly show that it is for the pursuer in an action founded on negligence to show that the defenders have been negligent, and that their negligence has caused the injury of which the pursuer complains." It follows that it is for the pursuer to aver (by means of written pleadings) and prove (by means of evidence brought to court) a sufficient case. If he does not do so he will not succeed. It is for the pursuer to prove fault and not for the defender to rebut it. In *Wilsher* v *Essex Area Health Authority*[35] the question of the onus of proof arose in the context of a medical negligence action. A baby was born prematurely and was admitted to a neonatal unit managed by the defenders. The baby required extra oxygen. However, a junior doctor inserted the catheter into a vein instead of an artery with the result that the monitor gave an incorrect oxygen reading. The baby was "supersaturated" with oxygen as a result. The child developed a condition called retrolental fibroplasia (RLF) which rendered him almost blind. A possible cause of RLF was excess oxygen but it was not the only possible cause. Indeed, the child was afflicted with four other conditions, all common in premature infants, which could also have caused RLF. The trial judge, Peter Pain J, held that because negligence had been proved, the burden of disproving the causal connection between that negligence and the injuries moved to the defendants. In other words, in the judge's view, it was for the defendant Health Authority to establish that the child's RLF resulted from one of the other possible causes. The House of Lords condemned this approach and emphasised that the burden of proving causation rests on the plaintiff[36] and does not shift to the defendant simply because a breach of duty is established.

23.17   In *Robinson* v *Midlothian Council*[37] the pursuer raised an action of damages against his former employers in which he alleged that he had suffered noise-induced deafness resulting from his work as an arts and craft teacher. The medical evidence adduced was to the effect that while hearing loss may be caused by exposure to noise, it could also be caused by the ageing process and there could be other causes. The council was

---

[31] 2007 SC 272 at para 13.
[32] The persuasive burden is undoubtedly the most important type of burden but, in certain circumstances, a provisional burden can arise. See discussion below.
[33] 1960 SC (HL) 22.
[34] *Ibid* at 25.
[35] [1988] AC 1074.
[36] Note, however, that where the defender contends that the causal chain has been broken as a result of a *novus actus interveniens*, the burden of proving that rests with him: see *Kelvin Shipping Co* v *Canadian Pacific Railway (The Metagama)* 1928 SC (HL) 21 at 25.
[37] [2009] CSOH 109.

granted decree of absolvitor. The pursuer had failed to establish – the onus being on him – that the cause of his hearing loss was exposure to noise.

Again, in *McTear v Imperial Tobacco Ltd*[38] the pursuer sought damages from a **23.18** cigarette manufacturer in respect of the death of her husband from lung cancer. She claimed that her husband's death was caused to a material extent by his smoking from 1964 to 1992 cigarettes which were manufactured by the defender and that throughout that period the defender was negligent in selling cigarettes, or, in any event, in selling them without appropriate warnings. The burden was on the pursuer, the smoker's widow, to prove on the balance of probabilities that, as a matter of fact, smoking can cause lung cancer. This she failed to do in the particular circumstances of the case given that she had failed to present any of the relevant primary literature on which her experts had relied.[39]

What is therefore required of the defender in a civil action? The case of *Johnstone* **23.19** *v City of Glasgow District Council*[40] illustrates that the defender need do nothing other than lodge appropriately framed defences. He is not required to offer an alternative explanation for the occurrence of an accident.[41] A lack of candour on the defender's part is not sufficient to make his defences legally irrelevant. In *Ganley v Scottish Boatowners Mutual Insurance Association*,[42] a case arising from alleged professional negligence, Lord Thomson stated:[43] "I am not aware of any rule of practice nor is there I think any principle that requires a defender as a matter of relevancy to state more than a general denial of the factual averments on any issue raised between the parties."

CIRCUMSTANCES IN WHICH THE DEFENDER BEARS THE BURDEN OF PROOF

There are certain circumstances in which the burden rests upon the defender. If the **23.20** pursuer has made a *prima facie* case and the defender relies on a substantive defence (eg the defence of *veritas* or truth in a defamation action), then the onus to establish that defence is on the defender. Similarly, if the defender alleges that the pursuer voluntarily assumed the risk of injury or was contributorily negligent then the burden of proof in respect of these substantive defences will rest on the defender.[44] In *Anderson v Scottish Ministers*[45] a cyclist was thrown from his bicycle while cycling on a path which was occupied and controlled by Historic Scotland for whom the defenders were legally responsible. The pursuer averred that he had ridden into a sunken drain immediately adjacent to the cycling path. The defenders contended that the pursuer was contributorily negligent. The onus of establishing that the pursuer was contributorily negligent was imposed on the defenders and, in the event, they failed to discharge that onus.

---

[38] 2005 2 SC 1.
[39] It is therefore not within judicial knowledge that smoking causes lung cancer. For further discussion of *McTear*, see B Pillans, "Smoking Kills – Not Proven" 2005 SLT 113.
[40] 1986 SLT 50.
[41] See the observations of Lord Hope in *Thomson v Kvaerner Govan Ltd* 2004 SC (HL) 1 at para 26. (This is subject, however, to what is said below on *res ipsa loquitur* where the evidence raises a presumption that the defender is to blame for the accident and an explanation is called for in such circumstances.)
[42] 1967 SLT (Notes) 45.
[43] *Ibid* at 46.
[44] See, eg, *Porter v Strathclyde RC* 1991 SLT 446.
[45] 2009 RepLR 122.

23.21   Similarly, if the defender contends that the pursuer's conduct amounts to a *novus actus interveniens*, with the result that the subsequent harm was caused by the pursuer himself, the onus of proof in respect of that matter rests on the defender.

EFFECT OF STATUTE ON BURDEN OF PROOF

23.22   Statutory provisions can affect the burden of proof. For example, statutory provisions may require that a workplace is kept safe "so far as is reasonably practicable". In such circumstances, the burden of proving that a particular step was not reasonably practicable rests on the defender. This was made clear by the House of Lords in *Nimmo v Alexander Cowan & Sons*.[46] The pursuer was unloading bales of pulp during the course of his employment. He stood on one of the bales in order to unload others. He fell due to the tipping of the bale and sustained injury. He sued his employers averring breach of s 29(1) of the Factories Act 1961, which provided that there "shall, so far as is reasonably practicable, be provided and maintained safe means of access" to working places and "every such place shall, so far as is reasonably practicable, be made and kept safe for any person working there". The House of Lords held that, on the true construction of s 29, the burden of proving that it was not reasonably practicable to make the working place safer than it was lay on the defenders. Lord Pearson observed:[47] "How is the injured workman to know, and how is the widow of a deceased workman to know, what steps would have been practicable? These matters are within the province of the defenders ..."[48]

THE DISTINCTION BETWEEN THE PERSUASIVE AND PROVISIONAL BURDEN OF PROOF

23.23   A distinction has been drawn between the *persuasive* burden (sometimes called the legal burden) of proof and the *provisional* burden of proof. The persuasive or legal burden of proof is imposed by the law itself and is normally on the pursuer. The provisional burden, however, is raised by the state of the evidence and may be raised by any cogent piece of evidence, such as that a precaution normally taken was omitted. If that evidence is not answered, then the court might infer that the defenders were at fault. In *Brown v Rolls Royce Ltd*[49] Lord Denning pointed out:[50]

> "how important it is to distinguish between a *legal* burden, properly so called, which is imposed by the law itself, and a *provisional* burden which is raised by the state of the evidence. The legal burden in this case was imposed by law on the pursuer. In order to succeed, he had to prove that the defenders were negligent, and that their negligence caused the disease."

---

[46] 1967 SC (HL) 79.
[47] *Ibid* at 111.
[48] For further illustrations of the inversion of onus, see *Gibson v British Insulated Callenders Construction Co Ltd* 1973 SC (HL) 15; *Bowes v Sedgefield District Council* [1981] ICR 234; *Larner v British Steel plc* [1993] ICR 551; and *Bilton v Fastnet Highlands Ltd* 1998 SLT 1323.
[49] 1960 SC (HL) 22.
[50] *Ibid* at 27.

His Lordship went on to say:[51] **23.24**

> "[A] provisional burden may shift from one party to the other as the case proceeds or may remain suspended between them. But it has no compelling force. At the end of the day, the Court has to ask itself – not whether the provisional burden is discharged – but whether the legal burden has been discharged, that is to say: Has the pursuer proved that the defenders were negligent?"

THE STANDARD OF PROOF

The burden of proof must be distinguished from the standard of proof. The standard **23.25** of proof in delictual actions, as in all civil actions, is "the balance of probabilities". In criminal cases, on the other hand, the Crown requires to establish guilt "beyond reasonable doubt", which is a higher standard than the civil standard (and, therefore, more difficult to achieve). Where an allegation of criminal conduct is made in the course of a civil proof, however, the appropriate standard of proof is the balance of probabilities. This is illustrated in *Mullan v Anderson*,[52] which concerned a civil action for damages for a death which had been caused deliberately or recklessly with a knife. The Lord Justice-Clerk (Ross) observed[53] that the standard of proof was on the balance of probabilities and he did not consider the matter to be open to doubt. Indeed, the other four judges sitting in that case (Lords Morison, Penrose, Prosser and Brand) agreed. Therefore, their Lordships were unanimous on that point. This principle is important because certain actions may give rise to both civil and criminal consequences. An assault,[54] for example, is both a crime and a civil wrong. In relation to the civil action the pursuer only has to prove the essential facts on the balance of probabilities, whereas in the criminal proceedings, the Crown requires to prove its case beyond reasonable doubt.

THE BALANCE OF PROBABILITIES

What then is meant by the pursuer having to establish his case on "the balance of **23.26** probabilities"? Consideration was given to the meaning of the phrase in *Brown v Rolls Royce Ltd*.[55] The case concerned an employee who worked with oil and who contracted dermatitis. He alleged negligence against his employers for failing to provide a safe system of work. He claimed that his employers should have provided him with barrier cream. Lord Denning stated:[56] "It is sufficient if there is a greater probability on one side or the other, but if at the end of the case the evidence is so evenly balanced that the court cannot come to a determinate conclusion, the legal burden comes into play and requires the court to reject the case of negligence alleged ..." The defenders argued that they did provide an effective precaution against dermatitis in that adequate washing

---

[51] 1960 SC (HL) 22 at 28.
[52] 1993 SLT 835. *Mullan* was followed in *L v L* 1996 SLT 767 where allegations of child sexual abuse (which would amount to criminal conduct) were made in the course of a civil case.
[53] 1993 SLT 835 at 840.
[54] See Chapter 13.
[55] 1960 SC (HL) 22.
[56] *Ibid* at 28.

facilities were made available. The court concluded that the employers had not failed in their duty.

23.27 Lord Simon in *Davies* v *Taylor*[57] offered further guidance as to the meaning of the phrase:[58] "[T]he concept of proof on a balance of probabilities ... can be restated as the burden of showing odds of at least 51 to 49 that such-and-such has taken place or will do so."

23.28 In *Rhesa Shipping Co SA* v *Edmunds*[59] Lord Brandon stated:[60]

> "[T]he legal concept of proof of a case on a balance of probabilities must be applied with common sense. It requires a judge of first instance, before he finds that a particular event occurred, to be satisfied on the evidence that it is more likely to have occurred than not. If such a judge concludes, on a whole series of cogent grounds, that the occurrence of an event is extremely improbable, a finding by him that it is nevertheless more likely to have occurred than not, does not accord with common sense."

23.29 In *Hodge* v *British Coal Corporation (No 2)*[61] the pursuer recovered damages under a number of heads from his previous employer in respect of an injury to his finger. However, Lord Marnoch denied recovery in respect of recurrent swelling to the pursuer's hand and forearm which had occurred subsequent to the injury. The pursuer had not satisfied the court on a balance of probabilities that the swelling resulted from the industrial injury. Lord Marnoch stated the position thus:[62]

> "I am unable to conclude that the pursuer has discharged the onus of demonstrating that the episodes of swelling to which he has been subject have been a consequence either of the accident or of any of the operations which followed it ... The most that can be said is that the swelling is a result of vascular disturbance which may or may not have been a development of the pursuer's condition as it appeared to be in September 1988. I therefore exclude this element of the pursuer's present condition from my assessment of damages."

23.30 An interesting point arose in relation to the standard of proof in the context of causation in *Hotson* v *East Berkshire AHA*.[63] The plaintiff fell from a swing rope and injured his hip. At hospital, his condition was not properly diagnosed. It was only some 5 days later that the nature of his injuries was discovered. There was thus a delay in treatment. The plaintiff developed avascular necrosis which left him with a permanent disability. He sued the Health Authority. The Health Authority admitted a breach of duty but denied that its delay in treatment had caused the avascular necrosis. It was proved that the fall itself produced a 75 per cent likelihood of the onset of avascular necrosis. The delay in treatment made its onset inevitable. The trial judge awarded 25 per cent of full damages, which decision was affirmed by the Court of Appeal. The House of Lords, however, on further appeal, condemned this approach. Their Lordships observed that the crucial question was whether the fall or the negligent delay in treatment had caused the disability. The question of causation was

---

[57] [1974] AC 207.
[58] *Ibid* at 219.
[59] [1985] 1 WLR 948.
[60] *Ibid* at 956.
[61] 1992 SLT 913.
[62] *Ibid* at 914.
[63] [1987] 2 AC 750 (HL).

to be determined on a balance of probabilities. As the fall itself resulted in a 75 per cent likelihood of the onset of avascular necrosis, the court concluded that it was the fall, on the balance of probabilities, which had caused the disease. The plaintiff, therefore, did not recover damages from the defendants in respect of the onset of avascular necrosis. Lord Mackay of Clashfern quoted[64] with approval from the judgment of Lord Diplock in *Mallett* v *McMonagle*:[65] "In determining what did happen in the past a court decides on the balance of probabilities. Anything that is more probable than not it treats as certain."[66]

RES IPSA LOQUITUR

Res ipsa loquitur is an evidential device[67] which, on occasion, is of great assistance to the pursuer. Literally translated, the phrase means "the thing speaks for itself": in other words, an occurrence sometimes tells its own story. The very happening of the incident will itself create an inference of fault on the defender's part. The exact cause of the accident must be unexplained for the maxim to operate. If the pursuer knows what caused the accident, he should aver and lead evidence as to the cause. In *Roe* v *Ministry of Health*[68] Morris LJ provided some guidance as to the meaning of the maxim:[69] **23.31**

"… this convenient and succinct formula possesses no magic qualities: nor has it any added virtue, other than that of brevity, merely because it is expressed in Latin. When used on behalf of a plaintiff it is generally a short way of saying: 'I submit that the facts and circumstances which I have proved establish a *prima facie* case of negligence against the defendant.'"[70]

It is important to note at the outset that it is only in certain limited circumstances that the maxim can operate. **23.32**

The leading case is *Scott* v *London and St Katherine Docks Co.*[71] Scott was a customs officer who was lawfully walking past a warehouse when he was hit by six bags of sugar. The bags were being lowered from the warehouse to the ground by means of a crane. The area in which the officer was walking had not been fenced off and no warning had been given. Erle CJ set out[72] what is now regarded as the classic exposition of the maxim as follows: **23.33**

"There must be reasonable evidence of negligence. But where the thing is shown to be under the management of the defendant or his servants, and the accident is such as in the ordinary course of things does not happen if those who have the management use proper

---

[64] [1987] 2 AC 750 at 785.
[65] [1969] 2 All ER 178 at 191.
[66] See also, *Gregg* v *Scott* [2005] 2 AC 176 where the House of Lords affirmed (in the context of a medical negligence action) that causation was to be established on a balance of probabilities.
[67] Although *res ipsa loquitur* is sometimes referred to as a "doctrine", that terminology has attracted adverse comment: see *Lloyde* v *West Midlands Gas Board* [1971] 1 WLR 749, per Megaw LJ at 755.
[68] [1954] 2 QB 66.
[69] *Ibid* at 87.
[70] See, also, the observations of Hobhouse LJ in *Ratcliffe* v *Plymouth and Torbay HA* 1998 PIQR p 170 at p 189.
[71] (1865) 3 H & C 596.
[72] *Ibid* at 667.

care, it affords reasonable evidence, in the absence of explanation by the defendants, that the accident arose from want of care."

23.34   Accordingly, there are three conditions which have to be met before the maxim of *res ipsa loquitur* can apply:

(1) there must be reasonable evidence of negligence;

(2) the circumstances must be under the control of the defender or his servants;

(3) the accident must be of such a type that it does not happen in the absence of negligence.

23.35 In the instant case the maxim did in fact operate to assist Scott. The bags of sugar were in the control of the dock company or its servants. An accident of this nature would not normally happen unless there was a failure to exercise proper care. The presumption was, therefore, that the accident arose from lack of care by the defendants.

23.36   In *Milne v Townsend* [73] Lord Adam observed[74] that "the *res* can only speak so as to throw the inference of fault upon the defender in some cases where the exact cause of the accident is unexplained". However, if the defender can demonstrate a way in which the accident may have occurred without fault on his part, the pursuer is put back into his original position and must demonstrate negligence.[75] This point was articulated by Lord Dunedin in *Ballard v North British Railway Co*,[76] where his Lordship observed[77] that the question was whether "the mere fact of the occurrence which caused hurt or damage is a piece of evidence relevant to infer negligence". His Lordship continued:[78] "But what is the next step? I think that, if the defenders can show a way in which the accident may have occurred without negligence, the cogency of the fact of the accident by itself disappears, and the pursuer is left as he began, namely, that he has to show negligence."

23.37   In *Devine v Colvilles Ltd*[79] the maxim *res ipsa loquitur* was successfully invoked by the pursuer, who was employed by the defenders at their Ravenscraig steelworks. The pursuer had jumped from a platform and injured himself following a violent explosion. The explosion had occurred in a hose which carried oxygen. The pursuer relied on *res ipsa loquitur*. The necessary requirements for the application of the *res ipsa loquitur* rule were present. Such explosions do not usually occur in the absence of negligence. The hose (the *res*) in which the explosion had occurred was under the control of the defenders. Nobody knew the exact cause of the explosion. The defenders were able to demonstrate that the likely cause of the explosion was the presence of dust particles in the flow of oxygen. That explanation, however, did not establish that they were not negligent as the defenders had failed to demonstrate that they had exercised due care to prevent such particles gaining access to their plant. The defenders thus failed to displace the inference of negligence and, accordingly, were found liable.

---

[73] (1892) 19 R 830.
[74] *Ibid* at 836.
[75] See *O'Hara v Central SMT* 1941 SC 363.
[76] 1923 SC (HL) 43.
[77] *Ibid* at 53.
[78] *Ibid* at 54.
[79] 1969 SC (HL) 67.

An attempt to rely on the *res ipsa loquitur* maxim was made in *McQueen* v *Glasgow*   **23.38**
Garden Festival.[80] A spectator at a fireworks display was injured when she was hit by
part of a steel launching tube which fragmented when a firework exploded inside
it. She raised an action against the company responsible for the management of the
display. It was agreed that the explosion had been caused by a defect which had caused
the firework to explode while on the ground rather than when airborne. The pursuer
attempted to establish fault against the defenders on the basis of *res ipsa loquitur*. She
alleged that the explosion of the firework under the management of the company was
the *res* demonstrating fault. The Outer House held that the defect in the firework was
latent. There were no facts showing that the company knew or ought to have known
that there was a risk of the device for the lifting charge or the delay mechanism being
defective. The fact of the explosion was not, therefore, indicative of fault on the part
of the company. Rather it was indicative of fault on the part of the manufacturer.
Accordingly, *Devine* v *Colvilles Ltd* was distinguished.

In *Cassidy* v *Ministry of Health*[81] the plaintiff went into hospital to undergo surgery   **23.39**
on two stiff fingers. He was suffering from a condition known as Dupuytren's
contraction. When he emerged from surgery he had four useless fingers. He relied
successfully on the *res ipsa loquitur* rule. Denning LJ said[82] that the plaintiff was entitled
to say: "I went into hospital to be cured of two stiff fingers. I have come out with four
stiff fingers and my hand is useless. That should not have happened if due care had
been used. Explain it, if you can."

Although *Cassidy* arose in a medical context, the maxim is rarely successful in   **23.40**
medical cases. Where a person claims to have been injured as a result of medical negligence, it is seldom obvious that it was medical negligence as opposed to an inherent
risk of the therapy which caused the injury. In other words, the thing will rarely speak
for itself in a medical context. In *Roe* v *Ministry of Health*[83] the plaintiffs submitted that
the doctrine of *res ipsa loquitur* applied. The case concerned two patients who were
paralysed following the injection of a contaminated spinal anaesthetic. The judges
were alert to the dangers of treating the unfortunate outcomes of medical intervention
as a case of *res ipsa loquitur*. In the event, the inference of negligence was rebutted.
A somewhat cautious approach to the doctrine can also be detected in *Whitehouse* v
Jordan.[84] It was alleged that an attempted forceps delivery of a child had been carried
out with too much vigour. The child, who was eventually delivered by Caesarean
section, was brain damaged. Lord Fraser, in the House of Lords,[85] referred to passages
in the trial judge's judgment containing a "caution that such damage may be caused
by the violent event of birth itself ... and may occur without professional fault". Lord
Fraser observed that the trial judge "was evidently on his guard against treating this
case as a case of res ipsa loquitur".

On occasion, however, the maxim has succeeded in a medical context. Thus,   **23.41**
in *Mahon* v *Osborne*,[86] where a swab was left behind in a patient's body, with the

---

[80] 1995 SLT 211.
[81] [1951] 2 KB 343.
[82] *Ibid* at 365.
[83] [1954] 2 QB 66.
[84] [1981] 1 WLR 246.
[85] *Ibid* at 264.
[86] [1939] 2 KB 14.

result that he died 3 months later, the Court of Appeal held that *res ipsa loquitur* did apply.[87]

23.42   *Res ipsa loquitur* does not apply where the cause of the accident is known. In *Black v LB Richard Ellis Management Services Ltd*[88] the pursuer slipped on a puddle of water on a tiled floor in a shopping centre. The puddle was caused by rainwater which had leaked through the roof. *Res ipsa loquitur* did not apply in these circumstances as the cause of the event was known, namely water on the tiles caused by a leak in the roof.

23.43   More recently, the maxim was successfully invoked in the Privy Council in *George v Eagle Air Services Ltd and Ors*.[89] The claimant sought damages from the owners and operators of an aircraft in respect of the death of her common law husband in an air crash. She alleged that her husband was travelling in the course of his employment and that his death was caused by pilot negligence. The defendants alleged that the aircraft had been serviced by the deceased (who was a mechanic working for the first defendants) and was airworthy for the flight. The defendants denied the allegations of negligence but advanced no positive case to explain the crash. The Privy Council held that *res ipsa loquitur* applied in the circumstances. Lord Mance made the following observations:[90]

> "This was the defendants' aircraft, their flight and their pilot. Aircraft, even small aircraft, do not usually crash, and certainly should not do so. And, if they do, then, especially where the crash is on land as here, it is not unreasonable to suppose that their owner/operators will inform themselves of any unusual causes and not unreasonable to place on them the burden of producing an explanation which is at least consistent with absence of fault on their part. The defendants have in fact never suggested or attempted to suggest any explanation of the accident or any reason preventing them giving an explanation. In the Board's opinion, they have in the result failed to displace the inference of negligence which in the circumstances results from the crash itself."

The claim succeeded.

INFERENCE

23.44   Inference may also be of assistance to the pursuer in the proof of his case. The pursuer is likely to rely on inference where one of the necessary ingredients for *res ipsa loquitur* is missing: for example, control. The court is entitled to draw inferences from facts which are proved or admitted and if the facts, on balance, suggest to a reasonable person that the inference that the pursuer's story rather than the defender's is correct then a finding for the pursuer is justified.

23.45   *Inglis v London, Midland and Scottish Railway Co*[91] illustrates the use of inference in a negligence case. A boy aged 8 fell to his death from the door of a railway carriage after the train had travelled some 26 miles. The defenders proved that the door had

---

[87] For a useful discussion of the operation of *res ipsa loquitur* in a medical context, see *Ratcliffe v Plymouth and Torbay HA* 1998 PIQR P170.
[88] 2006 Rep LR 36.
[89] [2009] 1 WLR 2133.
[90] *Ibid* at para 13.
[91] 1941 SC 551.

been checked before the train had left the station and gave evidence to the effect that even if the door had not been properly closed it should have opened of its own accord earlier in the journey. The basic contention of the defenders was that a passenger had interfered with the door. Witnesses, however, were able to give evidence to the effect that neither the child himself nor any other passenger had interfered with the door. Clearly, the *res ipsa loquitur* rule could not apply as one of the basic elements for its application was missing, namely control. The door was not within the exclusive control of the railway company because there was obviously some possibility of inter-ference by others. The Inner House held that the accident was *prima facie* evidence of negligence which only had to be brought home to the railway company. The court held that the pursuer had succeeded in excluding any interference with the door (whether intentional or inadvertent) by the passengers in the compartment at any stage in the journey. Accordingly, the inference was that the door had not been properly secured by the defenders' servants owing to their negligence. The railway company was therefore found liable.

The operation of inference also assisted the plaintiff in *Grant* v *Australian Knitting*   **23.46**
Mills Ltd.[92] A doctor bought a pair of long woollen underpants. There was a manufac-turing defect in the pants. They contained the residue of a chemical which should have been washed out during the manufacturing process. As a result, the doctor suffered very severe dermatitis. In his subsequent action, the doctor alleged, *inter alia*, negli-gence against the manufacturer. The court held that the negligence arose by inference from the facts. Lord Wright made the following observation:[93]

> "According to the evidence, the method of manufacture was correct: the danger of excess sulphites being left was recognised and was guarded against: the process was intended to be foolproof. If excess sulphites were left in the garment, that could only be because someone was at fault. The appellant is not required to lay his finger on the exact person in all the chain who was responsible, or to specify what he did wrong. Negligence is found as a matter of inference from the existence of the defects taken in connection with all the known circum-stances: even if the manufacturers could by apt evidence have rebutted that inference they have not done so."

The distinction between cases where there is insufficient evidence and those where   **23.47**
there is sufficient evidence to permit the drawing of an inference, is a very narrow one. Indeed, *Johnstone* v *City of Glasgow District Council*[94] demonstrates that the operation of inference can only avail a pursuer within certain well-defined parameters. The pursuer fell and was injured when descending a common stairway. The District Council was both owner and occupier of the building. The property was in an extremely run down state but there was no proof that the Council knew of the missing step which had allegedly caused the pursuer to fall. The Lord Ordinary had found that the broken step had existed for about 3 months. No evidence was adduced, however, as to the usual practice of inspection of common stairs by landlords. Counsel for the defenders argued that there was no evidence from which it could be affirmed that a reasonably prudent proprietor would have made an inspection within a shorter period than 3 months and that the 3-month period itself was not sufficient to allow an inference

---

[92] [1936] AC 85.
[93] *Ibid* at 101.
[94] 1986 SLT 50.

of lack of care to be drawn. The Inner House, on appeal, agreed that the evidence was deficient. It held that there was no proof that the defenders had failed to act as a reasonable occupier or landlord and, in such circumstances, no inference of negligence could be drawn. All that could be done in the circumstances would be to speculate as to what a reasonable landlord would have done and that was an insufficient basis on which to make a finding of liability.

23.48   In *Maroney* v *Hugman*[95] a refuse collector was injured when he lifted a bag of refuse outside the house of a married couple. He averred that the load, which contained garden refuse as well as household refuse, was exceptionally heavy (approximately 2.5 to 3 stones in weight). He sued the couple, averring that the rubbish had been placed in the sack "by the defenders or either of them" and that they knew or ought to have known of the risk of injury. The defenders argued that there were insufficient averments to justify an inference that the act complained of was done by both defenders or one or other of them. The pursuer, on the other hand, argued that as the refuse had been collected from within the curtilage of the defenders' house, the natural inference was that one or other of them had filled it and placed it there. Lord Gill, in dismissing the action, observed that there were no averments as to the actings of either defender from which either could be identified with the negligent act. His Lordship stated:[96]

> "The case begins and ends with the lifting of the sack at the rear door of the defenders' house. There is no foundation in the pursuer's factual averments for proof, by a process of elimination or otherwise, that the act complained of was done by either the first or the second defender or by both of them. Any inquiry on the pursuer's record could be no more than an expedition based on hope."

23.49   On occasion, the drawing of an inference will assist the *defender* in an action as opposed to the pursuer. For example, in *McWilliams* v *Sir Wm Arrol & Co Ltd*,[97] McWilliams was killed when he fell from a lattice tower. His employers had not provided him with a safety belt and had thus breached their duty of care towards the deceased. His widow raised an action for damages. She was unsuccessful as she failed to establish a causal link between the breach of duty and her husband's death. The court concluded that, even if the belt had been provided, the deceased would not have worn it. Clearly, the deceased was not able to give direct evidence as to what he would have done had the belt been available. Their Lordships held, however, that what the deceased would have done could be a matter of inference. There was evidence (a) that the deceased did not normally wear a belt, (b) that he had failed to wear a belt when working at greater heights than that from which he fell, and (c) that at times when safety belts were available, he had not worn or asked for a safety belt. In those circumstances, the irrebuttable inference was that the deceased would not have worn the belt on the occasion in question.

---

[95] 1997 SLT 240.
[96] *Ibid* at 242.
[97] [1962] 1 WLR 295.

THE CIVIL EVIDENCE (SCOTLAND) ACT 1988[98]

The Civil Evidence (Scotland) Act 1988 made a number of important amendments to **23.50** the law of civil evidence in Scotland relating, *inter alia*, to the rules on:

(1) corroboration,
(2) hearsay statements, and
(3) prior consistent statements.

The Act followed a number of recommendations which had been made by the Scottish **23.51** Law Commission in its 100th Report.[99] One of the guiding principles which was followed by the Commission was that, "[a]s a general rule all evidence should be admissible unless there is good reason for it to be treated as inadmissible".[100]

CORROBORATION

At one time, the law of evidence required that a pursuer prove all material or crucial **23.52** facts[101] by corroborated evidence, that is, evidence from two separate sources. Quite often, two eyewitnesses would give evidence but, as one might expect, an injured person might not always be able to produce another person who had witnessed his injury. This had the unfortunate effect of precluding recovery in certain circumstances, such as a worker being injured in a quiet corner of a factory or a pedestrian being run down on an isolated country road.

Considerable assistance was given to such pursuers by the Law Reform **23.53** (Miscellaneous Provisions) (Scotland) Act 1968, s 9(2). That section provided that *in personal injury cases* the court was entitled to find a fact proved by evidence even though that evidence was not corroborated.[102] It should be noted that that section merely entitled the court to treat uncorroborated evidence as being sufficient in personal injury cases. It did not oblige the court to do so. The section therefore made uncorroborated evidence sufficient, if accepted. It did not make it conclusive. Section 9(2) of the 1968 Act was applied in *Thomson* v *Tough Rope*.[103] There, the pursuer raised an action of damages against her employers. She averred that she had been injured at work when a removable plate came off a rope-making machine and fell on her foot. The pursuer herself gave evidence as to how the accident had occurred but the only other eyewitness to the accident was found to be unreliable. Nonetheless, the pursuer was held entitled to succeed. The Lord Ordinary (Ross) said:

> "Once it appears that the pursuer's account of the accident is a possible one, there is no reason to reject the pursuer's evidence. I felt that she gave her evidence frankly and in all the

---

[98] See, generally, D Field, "Civil Evidence: A Quantum Leap" 1988 SLT (News) 349.
[99] *Evidence: Report on Corroboration, Hearsay and Related Matters in Civil Proceedings* (Scot Law Com No 100, 1986).
[100] *Ibid*, para 1.3.
[101] Such facts are known as the *facta probanda*. "In a civil cause they are the facts which a party must, or ought to, aver in order to make a case relevant to be sent to proof." (Ross and Chalmers, *Walker and Walker: The Law of Evidence in Scotland*, para 5.31.)
[102] See, eg, *Ward* v *Upper Clyde Shipbuilders Ltd* 1973 SLT 182.
[103] 1978 SLT (Notes) 5.

circumstances I accept her evidence. The defenders asked me to conclude that the pursuer had dropped the removable plate on her foot, but there was no evidence to support such a conclusion, and I believe the pursuer when she states that the removable plate sprung out and fell on her foot. I have already explained that I cannot accept the evidence of [the eye-witness] ... I am satisfied that the pursuer's own evidence establishes that the accident occurred as she has stated, notwithstanding that her evidence is not corroborated ... In my opinion, I am entitled to apply s 9 where the accident occurred in the absence of any credible eye-witness other than the pursuer herself. The fact that there was evidence from an unreliable eye-witness who purported to corroborate the pursuer, should not deprive the pursuer of the assistance of s 9."

23.54   However, a note of caution was sounded as to the application of the statutory provision in *McLaren* v *Caldwell's Paper Mill Co Ltd*.[104] There, Lord Kissen opined:[105] "[I]n a case where s 9(2) has to be applied, that is, in a case where a pursuer is not corroborated on crucial facts, the evaluation and assessment of a pursuer's evidence requires special care and attention because of the absence of corroborative evidence. A trial judge should, I think, be more hesitant in accepting such evidence as credible and reliable in the absence of supporting evidence from other sources."

23.55   Early authorities seemed to indicate that the statutory provision was aimed at situations where no corroboration was available[106] and cautioned that, where corroborative evidence was available, it should be led (or an explanation provided for failure to do so), failing which an adverse inference might be drawn by the court. Failure to lead apparently available corroboration was a ground of judgment in *McGowan* v *Lord Advocate*.[107] There, the pursuer suffered injury at work when he was unloading boxes of ammunition from a trailer on to a platform. He claimed damages from his employers, alleging that there was a defective system of "slinging" in operation. The First Division observed that there were at least three other witnesses to the accident and their evidence might have corroborated the evidence of the pursuer. However, no material part of the pursuer's account of the accident was corroborated. Evidence was led from only one of those three witnesses and his evidence, rather than corroborating the pursuer, directly contradicted his account in every material respect. That witness's evidence was not challenged as false or inaccurate. In that situation, the court concluded that s 9 of the Act could not assist the pursuer. The court concluded that the pursuer had not established his case.

23.56   The 1968 Act applied only to personal injuries cases. Therefore, the requirement for corroboration in respect of property damage and economic loss cases remained. Therefore, if an individual had deliberately vandalised my car in a quiet street, I would be unable to recover damages unless corroborated evidence was produced in court. Reporting on the issue in 1986, the Scottish Law Commission observed that "[i]t ... may be inconsistent with justice that a party, though he may have an honest and credible case, must nevertheless necessarily fail if, through circumstances over which he perhaps has no control, corroboration is not available".[108] Noting that s 9 of the 1968 Act had been "generally satisfactory in its operation" and that there had been,

---

[104] 1973 SLT 158.
[105] *Ibid* at 165.
[106] See the opinion of Lord President Clyde in *Morrison* v *Kelly* 1970 SC 65 at 79.
[107] 1972 SLT 188.
[108] Scot Law Com No 100, para 2.8.

as far as the Commission was aware, "no evidence that section 9 [had] led to a flood of weak claims",[109] the Commission recommended that the requirement of corroboration in civil proceedings (insofar as it still applied) should be abolished.[110]

That recommendation was duly implemented by the Civil Evidence (Scotland) Act 1988. Section 1 of the Act provides that *all* civil actions can now be proved without the need for corroboration. Section 9(2) of the 1968 Act has now been repealed under the Schedule to the 1988 Act. **23.57**

Section 1(1) of the 1988 Act provides: **23.58**

> "In any civil proceedings the court or, as the case may be, the jury, if satisfied that any fact has been established by evidence in those proceedings, shall be entitled to find that fact proved by that evidence notwithstanding that the evidence is not corroborated."

In *L* v *L*[111] the Lord Ordinary (Hamilton) took the view that authorities in relation to s 9 of the 1968 Act could be relied upon in relation to s 1 of the 1988 Act to allow an adverse inference to be drawn from failure to lead corroborative evidence where such evidence was available. In *L* v *L*, it was held that, notwithstanding the abolition of the rule that corroboration was required for legal sufficiency by s 1(1), failure to lead other evidence which might support a single witness speaking to crucial facts might be material as to whether a court was satisfied that that fact had been proved by the evidence led. **23.59**

In view of cases such as *McLaren* v *Caldwell's Paper Mill Co Ltd*[112] and *L* v *L*,[113] the safest course, it is suggested, is to lead corroborative evidence where it is available. Indeed, in *L* v *L*, Lord Hamilton observed:[114] "Even where the single witness's evidence is or appears to be credible, corroborative evidence may still constitute a valuable check on the accuracy of the witness's evidence."[115] **23.60**

It has, however, been said in the Inner House that "it is going far too far to say that a pursuer must bring into the witness box every person who was in the vicinity of an accident who might have seen it, even if only for the purpose of giving evidence to the effect that he or she knew nothing whatsoever about the accident."[116] **23.61**

In *Airnes* v *Chief Constable of Strathclyde*[117] the pursuer sought damages in an action against the Chief Constable. She averred that a punch to her face by a police officer had knocked her to the ground, causing her to suffer a seizure. At proof, the sheriff **23.62**

---

[109] Scot Law Com No 100, para 2.10.

[110] The Commission stated (at para 2.10): "We ourselves can find no good reason either on principle or on practical grounds for preserving the situation where corroboration remains a general requirement in civil litigation, but is not required in what is numerically one of the most important classes of case where, moreover, the abolition of the requirement has not, we believe, had any adverse effect on the administration of justice."

[111] 1996 SLT 767.

[112] 1973 SLT 158.

[113] 1996 SLT 767.

[114] *Ibid* at 773.

[115] One commentator has observed that "the failure to call available witnesses without good explanation will always leave the court with the lingering suspicion that something adverse to the pursuer's case is being held back". See D Field, "Going it Alone" 1989 SLT (News) 216 at 217.

[116] *McCallum* v *British Railways Board* 1991 SLT 5, per Lord Sutherland at 8. See, also, *McLaren* v *Caldwell's Paper Mill Co Ltd* 1973 SLT 158, per Lord Milligan at 164: "There were apparently other persons in the vicinity at the time but in the absence of any evidence that they must have seen what happened I cannot attach much importance to their absence."

[117] 1998 SLT (Sh Ct) 15.

accepted the uncorroborated evidence of the pursuer and awarded her damages. The Chief Constable appealed, arguing that, as there had been a number of witnesses present who might have been expected to give evidence on the pursuer's behalf, the sheriff had been wrong to accept the uncorroborated evidence of the pursuer. The sheriff principal observed that there were only two direct witnesses to the assault: the pursuer and the police officer. Accordingly, the sheriff had only to reach a judgment as to the credibility of the two witnesses. The sheriff principal, in refusing the appeal, stated:[118]

"In my opinion this is not at all the sort of case in which it may be ill advised to reach a conclusion without being provided with the assurance of corroboration. Rather is it an example of a case justifying the alteration to the law that was effected by the 1988 Act. It is a reparation claim based upon an assault consisting of a single blow. The issue was one turning entirely on credibility. In support of the claim the sheriff was provided with evidence that was inherently probable. She accepted that evidence as truthful and she had good reason for rejecting the evidence that conflicted with it. This court is therefore bound to acknowledge that the sheriff was justified in proceeding upon the evidence which she accepted."

23.63　Given that the rule requiring corroboration has been abolished in civil cases, it follows that corroboration is not required of expert opinion but the court is not bound to accept the conclusion of an expert witness even if it is not contested.[119]

HEARSAY STATEMENTS

23.64　The abolition of the rule requiring corroboration was not the only significant change made by the 1988 Act to the rules of civil evidence. There was also a significant change made to the rules on hearsay evidence in civil cases. The rule against hearsay was to the effect that statements made other than by a witness giving evidence were not admissible. Many arguments have been used to justify the former rule excluding hearsay evidence in civil cases and include the following :

(1) Hearsay evidence was not the best evidence.
(2) Hearsay statements were not delivered under oath.
(3) The truthfulness of the person, whose words are spoken to by another witness, could not be tested by cross-examination.
(4) The demeanour of the person who had made the statement could not be tested.
(5) A danger of inaccuracy emerges through the repetition of the statement.[120]

23.65　When it reported on the matter in 1986, the Scottish Law Commission stated:[121]
"We consider that the rule against hearsay ... operates unreasonably to exclude potentially valuable evidence. We have therefore concluded that reform of the rule is required in the interests of justice."

---

[118] 1998 SLT (Sh Ct) 15 at 19.
[119] See *Sidaway* v *Board of Governors of Bethlem Royal Hospital* [1985] AC 871.
[120] Some of these reasons for the exclusion of hearsay evidence were summarised by Lord Normand in the English criminal case of *Teper* v *R* [1952] AC 480.
[121] Scot Law Com No 100, para 3.22.

Section 2 of the Civil Evidence (Scotland) Act 1988 abolished the rule against **23.66** hearsay statements in all civil proceedings. Section 2(1) provides:

"In any civil proceedings – (a) evidence shall not be excluded solely on the ground that it is hearsay; (b) a statement made by a person otherwise than in the course of the proof shall be admissible as evidence of any matter contained in the statement of which direct oral evidence by that person would be admissible; and (c) the court or as the case may be the jury, if satisfied that any fact has been established by evidence in those proceedings shall be entitled to find that fact proved by the evidence notwithstanding that the evidence is hearsay ..."

It should be noted that the provision states that the court is *entitled* to find a fact proved **23.67** by hearsay evidence. In other words, the court is not *obliged* to hold the fact proved. The weight to be given to a hearsay statement, as indeed to any evidence, is at the court's discretion.[122] If the maker of a statement is available to come to court to give evidence, but is not called as a witness, the court may well draw an adverse inference. Admissibility is not to be equated with acceptability. Indeed, in *Gould* v *Glasgow District Council*[123] it was argued that one of the facts in dispute was established by evidence of a statement made by the pursuer to a witness at the time of his accident. Lord Allanbridge, in rejecting that argument, commented: "[T]hat is not how I read the section, and it would be surprising if it were so."

A statement is defined in s 9 of the 1988 Act as "any representation (however made **23.68** or expressed) of fact or opinion but does not include a statement in a precognition". The wording of s 9 makes it clear that documentary hearsay is now admissible. However, the rule prohibiting precognitions in evidence is retained, the justification being that a precognition is "filtered through the mind of another".[124]

It is important, however, to distinguish what is said to a precognoscer from what is **23.69** recorded in the precognition. The former will be admissible in evidence whereas the latter will not be. In *Anderson* v *Jas B Fraser & Co Ltd*[125] Lord Morton of Shuna said:[126]

"It appears to me that in civil proceedings the only reason for the exclusion of a precognition is that what is stated in the precognition is or may be coloured by the mind of the precognoscer who produces in the precognition an edited version of what the witness has said. This would exclude the actual document prepared by the precognoscer but would not exclude evidence of what the witness actually said to the precognoscer prior to the preparation of the document. I am of opinion that the exception in the definition of 'statement' in the Civil Evidence (Scotland) Act excluding 'a statement in a precognition' means what is recorded in a document prepared by the precognoscer and does not exclude evidence of what the person said to the precognoscer in interview."

McAvoy v *City of Glasgow District Council*[127] illustrates the inadmissibility of precog- **23.70** nition statements as evidence. A visitor to a flat, which was owned by the defender,

---

[122] See, eg, *L* v *L* 1996 SLT 767 where the Lord Ordinary stated (at 773): "having regard to the nature and source of the allegations, I should have been slow to hold them proved on the basis of hearsay evidence alone". See, also, *Cavanagh* v *BP Chemicals* 1995 SLT 1287 and *Davies* v *McGuire* 1995 SLT 755.
[123] OH, 17 May 1990, unreported.
[124] See *Kerr* v *HM Advocate* 1958 JC 14 at 19.
[125] 1992 SLT 1129.
[126] *Ibid* at 1130.
[127] 1993 SLT 859.

fell and was injured at a close doorway. He sought damages from the District Council, alleging that a large hole had caused his fall. The person whom the pursuer had visited died before the date of proof. The pursuer led hearsay evidence of what the deceased had told his (the deceased's) family. This was held to be admissible evidence in terms of the 1988 Act. However, the pursuer also attempted to lead evidence based on statements taken from the deceased by the pursuer's solicitor. The statements prepared by the solicitor were held to be inadmissible because they were precognitions.

23.71   *McAvoy* can be contrasted with *Ellison* v *Inspirations East Ltd.*[128] There, an action of damages was raised in respect of injuries suffered in a coach crash in Turkey. The defenders led evidence at proof from a solicitor who had taken a statement from the coach driver to the effect that a lorry travelling in the opposite direction had crossed into the wrong lane on two occasions prior to the point of impact. The pursuer argued that the solicitor's evidence was inadmissible as her notes were not a statement for the purposes of the Civil Evidence (Scotland) Act 1988 and she had required to work through an interpreter. The Lord Ordinary (Hardie) noted that the pursuer had conceded that the solicitor's notes were not a precognition "in the traditional form". Accordingly, Lord Hardie concluded[129] that there was "no justifiable reason for excluding the evidence on the basis that it [was] anything other than a statement by the driver to the solicitor for the insurers". It was also held that to exclude the statement because the services of an interpreter had been utilised would be contrary to public policy and would discriminate against those whose first language was not English.

23.72   The 1988 Act states that the hearsay evidence is admissible only if "direct oral evidence by that person would be admissible". Originally, it was thought that this provision embraced a competence test[130] with the result that, where a child's competence had not been determined, any hearsay evidence of the child would be inadmissible.[131] It is now clear, however, that this is not the correct interpretation. In a five-bench decision in *T* v *T*[132] (a family law case, the facts of which do not concern us here), the Inner House held that the admissibility of a hearsay statement depended not on the competence of the person who made the statement, but on the admissibility of the evidence itself.[133] Accordingly, s 2(1)(b) of the 1988 Act did not embody a competence test.[134]

23.73   "Hearsay" is defined in s 9 of the Act as including hearsay of whatever degree. The definition thus includes both simple hearsay and multiple hearsay. Thus if A enters

---

[128] 2003 SLT 291.

[129] 1992 SLT 1129 at 291.

[130] Thus, in *L* v *L* 1996 SLT 767 the Lord Ordinary (Hamilton) concluded that direct oral evidence of a statement made extrajudicially by a child was not admissible within the meaning of s 2(1) because the child had not been tendered as a witness, nor had the child undergone a preliminary examination by the judge to determine competency. See, also, *F* v *Kennedy (No 1)* 1992 SC 28.

[131] This interpretation of the statutory provision had the unfortunate result that the child would have to be brought to court in order to allow the sheriff or Lord Ordinary to determine his competence. "Not only could this examination be long and painful for all concerned, and especially for the child, but in addition the procedure could seem like a ritual and somewhat disconnected indeed from reality, since there was no actual intention to take the child's evidence, even if he or she proved to be competent." (*T* v *T* 2001 SC 337, per the Lord President (Rodger) at 340.)

[132] 2001 SC 337.

[133] The Lord President gave as an example (at 355) the situation where evidence by the maker of a statement would be inadmissible because it would be in breach of an obligation of confidentiality.

[134] The competence test (under which a child would be judicially examined to determine whether he knew the difference between truth and lies and then admonished to tell the truth) was abolished by the Vulnerable Witnesses (Scotland) Act 2004, s 24.

the witness box and states that B told him that C made a certain statement, then that is admissible evidence of what C said. Of course, the evidence need not be accepted and it seems self-evident that the further back in the hearsay chain one goes, the less likely the evidence is to be accepted by the court.

PRIOR CONSISTENT STATEMENTS

Before the 1988 Act, prior consistent statements of a witness were not generally admis- **23.74** sible to bolster his credibility.[135] However, a previous statement of a witness which was *inconsistent* with his oral testimony in court could be used to attack his credibility.[136] The Scottish Law Commission when it reported in 1986 found "difficulty in appreciating the logic and principle of this".[137] The 1988 Act made certain changes in that a witness's prior consistent statements are now admissible to support his credibility.

Section 3 of the 1988 Act provides: "In any civil proceedings a statement made **23.75** otherwise than in the course of the proof by a person who at the proof is examined as to the statement shall be admissible as evidence in so far as it tends to reflect favourably or unfavourably on that person's credibility."

IRREGULARLY OBTAINED EVIDENCE

Although the issue of irregularly obtained evidence is more likely to arise in criminal **23.76** trials than in civil proofs, it is not unknown in the civil context.[138] As far as the law of delict is concerned, the issue was raised in the case of *Martin v McGuiness*.[139] There, the pursuer sought damages in respect of injuries allegedly sustained in a road accident. The defender instructed private investigators and formed the view that the pursuer was exaggerating his injuries. The pursuer sought declarator that the conduct of the private investigators was unlawful and damages for the infringement of his right to privacy under Art 8 of the European Convention on Human Rights. The pursuer averred that the investigator had come to his house and spoken to his wife under the pretence of being a former army colleague of the pursuer. The pursuer's wife had become anxious, interpreting these events as being carried out with a view to a burglary and she and the pursuer had decided to install a burglar alarm. The pursuer also alleged that the investigator had carried out surveillance of him via a telephoto lens which had been installed in an adjacent property and which had followed his movements within the curtilage of his own property. The pursuer sought to have the private investigator's evidence excluded, asserting that if the court admitted the evidence, it would be in breach of s 6(1) of the Human Rights Act 1998. Lord Bonomy held that the pursuer's averments had identified conduct which was *capable* of amounting to an infringement of Art 8 in the absence of other considerations. However, the pursuer was bound to anticipate that his conduct might be scrutinised. Such inquiries and surveillance could

---

[135] See the discussion in Scot Law Com No 100 at paras 3.5 and 3.55.
[136] This was an exception to the hearsay rule.
[137] Scot Law Com No 100, para 3.55.
[138] In the civil context, the matter is most usually encountered in divorce actions involving allegations of adultery, with which this book is not concerned.
[139] 2003 SLT 1424.

conceivably be proved as having been reasonable and proportionate steps to be taken on the defender's behalf to protect his rights in terms of Art 8(2) and as a contribution to the protection of the wider rights of the community. Accordingly, the court would not be acting incompatibly with the pursuer's Art 8 right in admitting the evidence gathered by these inquiries and surveillance.

EXPERT EVIDENCE

23.77   Generally speaking, a witness can give evidence only as to matters of fact and must not offer an opinion. Expert or skilled witnesses may, however, give opinion evidence and, indeed, expert evidence is often adduced in the course of proof. Thus, for example, in a personal injury case, a medical consultant may give opinion evidence as to the likely prognosis of a person's condition. In an industrial injury case, a safety expert may give opinion evidence relating to a piece of work equipment. In *Clegg* v *Rogerson and Network Rail*,[140] which involved a fatal accident on a level crossing, evidence was led from a former Head of the Ergonomics Section at the Health and Safety Laboratory in Sheffield and from a professor at the Centre of Applied Social Psychology at the University of Strathclyde.[141]

23.78   It is important to note that an expert witness cannot usurp the function of the judge or jury. The classic statement as to the proper role of the expert witness is found in the judgment of the Lord President (Cooper) in *Davie* v *The Magistrates of Edinburgh*:[142]

> "Expert witnesses, however skilled or eminent, can give no more than evidence. They cannot usurp the functions of the jury or Judge … Their duty is to furnish the Judge or jury with the necessary scientific criteria for testing the accuracy of their conclusions, so as to enable the Judge or jury to form their own independent judgment by the application of these criteria to the facts proved in evidence. The scientific opinion evidence, if intelligible, convincing and tested, becomes a factor (and often an important factor) for consideration along with the whole other evidence in the case, but the decision is for the Judge or jury."

23.79   No formal qualifications are required in order to qualify as a skilled or expert witness – what matters is the knowledge and experience of the witness. This will be established at the outset of his testimony when the expert will be questioned as to his knowledge and experience of the issue at hand. In *Bremner* v *Bartlett*[143] an issue arose

---

140 2008 SLT 345.
141 See, also, *McGovern* v *Glasgow City Council* 2010 RepLR 2 (civil engineer called as expert witness in respect of road defects); *Lees* v *North Lanarkshire Council* [2008] CSOH 8 (expert evidence adduced from civil engineer in relation to defective footpath); *Robinson* v *Midlothian Council* [2009] CSOH 109 (medical evidence adduced as to possible causes of hearing loss); *Anderson* v *The Scottish Ministers* 2009 RepLR 122 (evidence led from an expert as to cycling skills and safety in the context of a cycling accident); *Ruddy* v *Marco* [2008] CSOH 40, 2008 SC 667 (IH) (evidence led from an expert in construction practice in context of a worker's fall from scaffolding); *Bremner* v *Bartlett* 2008 SCLR 258 (evidence led from medical experts in relation to degenerative changes to the pursuer's spine and evidence of accountant led as to future loss of income); *Todd* v *Clapperton* 2009 SLT 837 (evidence led from chartered building surveyor who specialised in fenestration following an incident involving a glass door); *McLellan* v *Dundee City Council* 2009 RepLR 61 (expert evidence led from chartered mechanical engineer and occupational health and safety consultant following gardener's injury sustained when attempting to clear blockage in a mower).
142 1953 SC 34 at 40.
143 2008 SCLR 258.

as to whether whiplash injuries sustained in a road traffic accident had caused degenerative changes in the pursuer's spine. Medical experts were at odds as to whether the pursuer's spine problems were attributable to natural degeneration or to the accident. In deciding to prefer the evidence of the defender's expert witness, the court took account of the authority and qualifications of the experts.

Although an expert will be called as a witness for a particular party in the litigation, **23.80** he has a duty to be independent and to offer unbiased assistance to the court.[144] In *Whitehouse* v *Jordan*[145] Lord Wilberforce stated[146] that "expert evidence presented to the court should be, and should be seen to be, the independent product of the expert, uninfluenced as to form or content by the exigencies of litigation." In *McTear* v *Imperial Tobacco Ltd*[147] (the facts of which are narrated above), Lord Nimmo Smith again emphasised the need for expert witnesses to be independent. His Lordship stated:[148]

> "As I understand it, all the expert witnesses for the pursuer provided their services without remuneration. Three of them ... were or had been connected in one way or another with ASH, and were clearly committed to the anti-smoking cause; and no doubt for this reason were prepared to give evidence gratis. This is not in itself a criticism of any of them, but it does in my opinion justify scrutiny of each of their evidence, so as to see to what extent they complied with their obligations as independent expert witnesses and how soundly based their views were."

His Lordship continued:[149] "I am bound to say that none of [the three witnesses] **23.81** seemed to me to be mindful of the need to be independent ... and each appeared to me to engage in advocacy to a greater or lesser extent."

Failure to lead expert testimony where it is appropriate to do so can have a deleterious **23.82** effect on the pursuer's case. That this is so is clear from *J* v *Fife Council*.[150] The pursuer sought damages from a local authority in respect of abuse inflicted upon him in the 1960s by an employee in a children's home. The abuse was alleged to be of a psychological as well as a sexual and non-sexual physical nature and was alleged to have resulted in psychological and social sequelae which had caused the pursuer difficulties in his relationships with his wife, children and others. However, no expert testimony was given in relation to any psychiatric or psychological condition suffered by the pursuer as a consequence of the abuse. Lord Menzies observed that the pursuer himself had given evidence to the effect that he had attended two or three sessions of psychiatric treatment and that he had consistently received treatment for depression. His Lordship continued:[151]

> "The onus of proving the pursuer's loss, injury and damage rests with the pursuer himself. An important element of that loss, injury and damage may be psychiatric illness or psycho-

---

[144] See *National Justice Compania Naviera SA* v *Prudential Assurance Co Ltd (The Ikarian Reefer) (No 1)* [1993] 2 Lloyd's Rep 68. See, also, *Jones* v *Kaney* [2011] UKSC 13, per Lord Phillips at para 50: "The expert witness must give his evidence honestly, even if this involves concessions that are contrary to his client's interests." See, also the observations of Lord Hope at para 156.

[145] [1981] 1 WLR 246.

[146] *Ibid* at 256–257.

[147] 2005 2 SC 1.

[148] *Ibid* at para 5.18.

[149] *Ibid* at 6.149.

[150] 2007 SLT 85. The case was reversed in part (in relation to the issue of interest) by the Inner House: see 2009 SC 163.

[151] 2007 SLT 85 at para 52.

logical consequences. The court is not in a position to assess the cause, nature, extent or prognosis of such illness or condition on its own, without the assistance of expert evidence. The pursuer himself is neither a psychiatrist nor a psychologist, and is not in a position to assist the court in this regard."

23.83 Had there been such evidence, Lord Menzies would have considered a higher award than that which he ultimately determined to be appropriate. The judgment emphasises that in circumstances where the pursuer contends that he has suffered psychiatric or psychological injury as a result of the defender's wrongful conduct it is imperative that expert evidence is adduced in support of that element of the claim. It is clearly insufficient to simply have the pursuer give evidence of his various difficulties in this respect.

23.84 It should be noted that medical textbooks in themselves have no evidential value. Rather, their contents require to be spoken to by a witness. In *Gerrard v Edinburgh NHS Trust Royal Infirmary*[152] a medical negligence action brought in respect of the death of a baby, Lord Osborne, delivering the opinion of the Inner House, stated:[153]

> "In the course of the hearing before us much use was made by counsel for the pursuers of extracts from textbooks on medical practice ... it has to be recognised that a medical textbook, dealing with accepted medical practice, however authoritative it may be and however distinguished the author or authors may be, of itself, possesses no evidential value. Its subject-matter will not be within judicial knowledge. However, a passage from such a book may acquire evidential value to the extent that it is adopted by a witness as representing his opinion, or otherwise dealt with in the evidence of a witness."

23.85 Finally, an expert witness should not speak to the "ultimate issue" before the court. Determination of the actual issue on which the case centres is a matter for the court itself. "The function of the expert witness is to assist the trier of fact to come to a decision on the ultimate issue in the case but not to offer the court a view on the ultimate issue."[154]

VULNERABLE WITNESSES[155]

23.86 Under the Vulnerable Witnesses (Scotland) Act 2004, vulnerable witnesses[156] may be entitled to "special measures" when giving evidence in the course of civil proceedings. Such measures are designed to make the giving of evidence easier and less traumatic. The special measures are set out in s 18 of the Act and include the use of screens, live TV link, the use of supporters and evidence being taken on commission.

23.87 The competence test (which was previously applied in respect of child witnesses)[157] has now been abolished by the 2004 Act. Section 24 of the Act provides as follows:

---

[152] 2005 1 SC 192.
[153] *Ibid* at para 81.
[154] Raitt, *Evidence – Principles, Policy and Practice* at para 4–38.
[155] For a more detailed examination of this issue, see L Sharp and M Ross, *The Vulnerable Witnesses (Scotland) Act 2004: Text and Commentary* (2008).
[156] A person is a vulnerable witness if he (a) is under the age of 16 on the date of commencement of proceedings or (b) is an adult where there is a significant risk of the quality of his evidence being diminished by reason of mental disorder or because of fear or distress in connection with the giving of evidence (s 11).
[157] Under this test, the sheriff or judge would examine the child to determine whether he knew the difference between truth and lies and then admonish the child to tell the truth.

"(1) The evidence of any person called as a witness (referred to in this section as 'the witness' in ... civil proceedings is not inadmissible solely because the witness does not understand –
  (a) the nature of the duty of a witness to give truthful evidence, or
  (b) the difference between truth and lies.
(2) Accordingly, the court must not, at any time before the witness gives evidence, take any step intended to establish whether the witness understands those matters."

24 TRANSFER AND EXTINCTION OF LIABILITY

INTRODUCTION

This chapter examines the various ways in which a delictual claim may be transferred **24.1** or extinguished. Particular attention will be given to the rules on prescription and limitation[1] which are extremely important from a practical point of view.

ASSIGNATION

A claim may be assigned at any time to another person[2] but, if this is done, any **24.2** defences which might have been invoked against the original party will be available against the assignee.[3]

SUBROGATION

Where an insurer has indemnified (ie paid out to) an insured person in respect of a **24.3** loss for which another person is legally liable then the insurer is entitled to proceed against the wrongdoer without the need for an assignation. In this situation, we say that the insurer is "subrogated to" the injured party's right to recover damages from the wrongdoer. In other words, the insurer is entitled to stand in the shoes of the victim of the delict and recover the damages which the injured party would have recovered from the wrongdoer. In those circumstances, the insurer's right under subrogation is only to recoup the payment which he has made to the insured. The insurer cannot retain any damages in excess of the sum insured.

Section 1 of the Third Parties (Rights against Insurers) Act 2010[*] provides that if **24.4** an insured person becomes insolvent (and in certain other specified circumstances), anyone who has incurred a loss which is covered by the insurance can proceed

---

[1] Limitation, unlike prescription, is not a mode of extinction. Rather, it renders a right of action unenforceable. The concepts are normally considered together, however, and such an approach is adopted here.
[2] See, eg, *Cole Hamilton* v *Boyd* 1963 SC (HL) 1, where Lord Reid based his decision in favour of assignability *inter vivos* "both on authority and on practical grounds" (at 13).
[3] See *Cole Hamilton* v *Boyd* 1963 SC (HL) 1, per Lord Reid at 14: "An assignee can have no greater right against the debtor than the cedant had when the assignation was intimated to the debtor. Any defence which the debtor then had against the cedant is available to him against the assignee." It follows that an assignee's right to sue is subject to prescription from the date of the original liability to the injured party and not from the date of assignation.
[*] The Act received Royal Assent on 25 March 2010 but, as at the date of writing, is not yet in force.

directly against the insurer.[4] In other words, the insured's rights against the insurer are transferred to and vest in the third party to whom the liability has been incurred.[5] This ensures that the pursuer receives the full benefit of the insurance proceeds which might otherwise become part of the funds available to general creditors in the insolvency.

CONTRIBUTION AND RELIEF

24.5   Where two persons are in breach of duty and both breaches are causative of the pursuer's loss, the wrongdoers will be jointly and severally liable.[6] This simply means that the wrongdoers are liable jointly and each of them is also liable individually to the injured party for the full amount of the damage. The holder of a joint and several decree is entitled to enforce the decree against any one of the wrongdoers, ie he can obtain all the damages from any one of them.[7] The party who satisfies the decree (ie makes payment under the decree) is then left to recover the relevant proportion from his fellow wrongdoer(s). In so doing, he is said to exercise his right of relief. In *Palmer v Wick & Pultneytown Steam Shipping Co Ltd*,[8] a joint and several decree was obtained against two co-delinquents and payment was exacted from one of them. The payer sought half of what he had paid from his fellow wrongdoer. The fellow wrongdoer maintained that the action was incompetent on the ground that there was no contribution between wrongdoers. The House of Lords rejected that argument, holding that each wrongdoer was liable for a pro rata share of the damages awarded. Lord Watson stated:[9] "[T]he claim of relief rests ... upon the fact, as Lord Bankton puts it, that by the use of [the claimant's] money the rest [that is, "the other obligants"] have been freed

---

[4] The 2010 Act aims, *inter alia*, to ensure that the two crucial issues (whether the insured is liable to the third party and whether the insurance policy covers that liability) can be resolved simultaneously in a single set of legal proceedings against the insurer. Under the previous legislation (Third Parties (Rights against Insurers) Act 1930) the third party was only entitled to issue proceedings against the insurer once the insured's liability had been established. Thus, it was possible for a third party to spend time and money establishing a claim against, say, an insolvent employer, only to find that the insurer did not accept that the employer's policy of insurance covered that particular claim. The 2010 reforms obviate the need for multiple legal proceedings and allow all issues to be resolved in the same proceedings. However, s 1(3) provides that before the third party can *enforce* rights transferred against the insurer, he must establish the liability of the relevant person.

[5] Section 1(2) of the 2010 Act.

[6] Joint and several liability does not apply where the wrongs are entirely separate and disconnected – see *Hook* v *McCallum* (1905) 7 F 528 (two separate slanders by husband and wife). There, the Lord Justice-Clerk (Lord MacDonald) stated at 532: "If two men attack a third, one hitting him on the head and another on the shins, they may both be jointly and severally liable for the whole injuries ... but if A is assaulted by B and is subsequently assaulted by C then plainly there are two separate wrongs, for one of which B is alone responsible, and for the other of which C is alone responsible."

[7] Clearly, a wrongdoer who is solvent and/or insured will be of more interest to the holder of such a decree than one who is impecunious and uninsured!

[8] [1894] AC 318.

[9] *Ibid* at 329.

from their obligation – a circumstance which, in ordinary cases, is sufficient according to the law of Scotland to raise a right of relief."[10] His Lordship continued:[11]

> "[W]here the injured party's claim is liquidated by a joint and several decree against all the delinquents ... the sum decreed is simply a civil debt, and the meaning which the law attaches to a decree constituting a debt in these terms is, that each debtor under the decree is liable *in solidum* to the pursuer, and that *inter se*, each is liable only *pro rata*, or, in other words, for an equal share with the rest."

Under the common law, as stated in *Palmer*'s case, joint delinquents were liable pro **24.6** rata according to their number – whatever their respective degrees of fault. "[C]ontribution by co-delinquents [was] proportionate to their numbers, not to their degree of guilt."[12] The law relating to contribution among joint wrongdoers is now statutory and is governed by the Law Reform (Miscellaneous Provisions) (Scotland) Act 1940. In a development from the common law, the contribution may now vary with the court's estimate of the wrongdoer's degree of blame. Section 3(1) of the Act provides:

> "Where in any action of damages in respect of loss or damage arising from any wrongful acts or negligent acts or omissions two or more persons are, in pursuance of the verdict of a jury or the judgment of a court, found jointly and severally liable in damages or expenses, they shall be liable *inter se* to contribute to such damages or expenses in such proportions as the jury or the court, as the case may be, may deem just: Provided that nothing in this subsection shall affect the right of the person to whom such damages or expenses have been awarded to obtain a joint and several decree therefor against the persons so found liable."[13]

Under s 3(1) of the Act, the wrongdoer who pays the damages is entitled to recover a **24.7** contribution from the other wrongdoer in proportion to what the court considers just. Thus, where the pursuer elects to sue all the alleged wrongdoers, the defenders may be found jointly and severally liable to pay damages in proportions which are judicially assessed to reflect their respective liability (say, 40 per cent to A and 60 per cent to B). The pursuer is entitled to execute his decree against the wrongdoer of his choosing, but the wrongdoer who pays the damages retains his right of relief against his fellow wrongdoer(s) as quantified by the court.

Section 3(1) of the 1940 Act therefore allows the court to assess the relative fault of **24.8** wrongdoers who have been sued jointly and severally and apportion liability between or among them accordingly. The operation of the statutory section is neatly illustrated in *Drew* v *Western SMT Co*.[14] On a dark December morning, a bread van was delivering

---

[10] More recently, it has been said that "[t]he principle underlying one person's right to claim relief from another is that he has discharged the proper debt or liability of that other person" (Report on *Civil Liability – Contribution* (Scot Law Com No 115, 1988), para 1.1 – under reference to *Glasgow Corporation* v *John Turnbull & Co* 1932 SLT 457, per Lord Murray at 459). It has also been observed that "the law on rights of relief is designed to complete the loss shifting process which often starts with a delictual action. Indeed, rights of relief are expected to carry out the fine tuning aspect of the loss shifting process" (A R W Young, "Rights of relief on assignation in settlements" 1992 SLT (News) 225 at 228).
[11] [1894] AC 318 at 332.
[12] *National Coal Board* v *Thomson* 1959 SC 353, per L J-C Thomson at 366.
[13] For a judicial discussion of this provision, see *Comex Houlder Diving* v *Colne Fishing Co Ltd* 1987 SC (HL) 85, per Lord Keith at 120–121 and *Farstad Supply AS* v *Enviroco Ltd and Asco UK Ltd* 2010 SC (UKSC) 87, per Lord Clarke at paras 7–9.
[14] 1947 SC 222.

bread to a shop in Ardrossan. Although the van's rear lamp was lit, it was obscured by the lower half of the open back door which folded downwards to allow the bread to be unloaded. An omnibus ran into the back of the bread van, fatally injuring a boy who was unloading bread. The boy's father sued both the owners of the omnibus and the owners of the bread van. Both defenders were found to be at fault, the former in respect of their driver's failure to maintain a proper lookout and the latter in respect of allowing their vehicle to be on the road during "lighting up time" with a rear light which was invisible. The Second Division held that the faults of both defenders were causes which led to the accident and awarded a joint and several decree against them. Applying s 3 of the 1940 Act, the court held the two defenders equally to blame and, accordingly, they were liable *inter se* to contribute in equal portions.

24.9   In *Grant* v *Sun Shipping Co Ltd*,[15] the pursuer, a dock labourer, fell through an open and unlit hatch on a ship and sustained injury. He sought damages from both the shipowners (the first defenders) and the ship repairers (the second defenders). The latter had been carrying out operations on the ship on the day of the accident and had left the hatch uncovered. The shipowners had failed to ensure that the place where the labourer was to work was reasonably safe. Both defenders were found liable in negligence (and both were also in breach of certain statutory duties). In the House of Lords, Lord du Parcq, applying s 3 of the 1940 Act, took the view[16] that 75 per cent of the damages award should be contributed by the second defenders and 25 per cent by the first defenders. Lord Porter and Lord Uthwatt agreed with that apportionment.

24.10   More recently, contribution was sought – albeit unsuccessfully – in *Clegg* v *Rogerson and Network Rail*.[17] There, a child was injured when the car in which she was travelling was struck by a train at a level crossing. The child's parents sued the driver of the car, R. R, in turn, pled that the accident was caused by the rail operator in having designed and constructed an inherently dangerous crossing. R brought the rail operator into the action by third-party notice and the rail operator was thereafter convened as a second defender in the action. The Lord Ordinary found that the vehicle had been driven across the crossing while the red stop light was showing and a klaxon was sounding and awarded damages on the basis that R (the first defender) had failed to exercise reasonable care. Although the rail operator could be criticised for failing to repeat operating instructions beside the driver's side controls, that failure had not caused or materially contributed to the accident. On R's reclaiming motion, an Extra Division refused to displace that finding on causation. Accordingly, the first defender's claim for a contribution from the rail operator was unsuccessful.

24.11   Section 3(1) provides for the situation where two or more wrongdoers are, in the same action, found jointly and severally liable. In other words, the pursuer has elected to sue two or more wrongdoers in the one action. The pursuer may, however, choose to sue only one of several wrongdoers. It has been judicially observed that "[i]t would obviously be unjust to limit contribution to the one case where the injured party elects to sue all the co-delinquents".[18] Accordingly, s 3(2) of the 1940 Act provides as follows: "Where any person has paid any damages or expenses in which he has been

---

[15] 1948 SC (HL) 73.
[16] *Ibid* at 98.
[17] 2008 SLT 345. For further discussion of this case, see E Russell, "No causation – no contribution – *Clegg* v *Rogerson* considered" 2008 SLT (News) 83.
[18] *NCB* v *Thomson* 1959 SC 353, per L J-C Thomson at 363.

found liable[19] in any such action as aforesaid,[20] he shall be entitled to recover from any other person who, if sued, might also have been held liable in respect of the loss or damage on which the action was founded, such contribution, if any, as the court may deem just."[21] This provision might apply where the pursuer sues only one alleged wrongdoer. The person sued may assert that another party who was not sued is liable and he may seek contribution or total relief from that person. An action of relief might take the form of third party procedure[22] or separate cause by the wrongdoer who has paid the damages awarded in respect of the first action.

The statutory section was considered in *Farstad Supply AS v Enviroco Ltd and Asco* **24.12**
UK Ltd.[23] Farstad owned an oil rig supply vessel which was damaged by fire while at harbour. They sued Enviroco, a service company, for damages, averring that the fire resulted from the negligence of Enviroco's employees during a cleaning operation. Enviroco, in turn, alleged that Asco, the charterer of the vessel, was at fault in *inter alia* failing to direct and supervise the cleaning operations. Enviroco accordingly brought Asco into the proceedings as a third party[24] and asserted that in the event that they (Enviroco) were found liable in damages to the pursuers, they ought to recover a contribution from Asco in terms of s 3(2) of the Law Reform (Miscellaneous Provisions) (Scotland) Act 1940. In terms of their charterparty with Asco, Farstad had granted Asco an indemnity against liabilities resulting from damage to the vessel irrespective of whether such damage was caused, or contributed to, by the negligence of the charterer. Farstad argued that Enviroco could not recover a contribution from Asco under s 3(2) of the 1940 Act, submitting that, by virtue of the contractual indemnity, Asco was not a person from whom the pursuers could recover damages, if sued. The Supreme Court held that the charterparty, properly construed, excluded Asco's liability to Farstad in

---

[19] The provision does not apply to a person who has made a wholly *extrajudicial* settlement. Rather, it requires that the defender has been sued "to judgment", ie damages must have been awarded against him: see *National Coal Board v Thomson* 1959 SC 353, per L J-C Thomson at 367. It is not necessary, however, that the judgment follows a *contested* action. It is sufficient that there has been a formal decree of the court giving effect to an agreed settlement: see *Comex Houlder Diving v Colne Fishing Co Ltd* 1987 SC (HL) 85. For further discussion, see D McNaughtan, "When is a liability not a liability? Third party procedure: traps for the unwary" 2003 SLT (News) 113.

[20] These words refer back to the kind of action described in s 3(1), namely "any action of damages in respect of loss or damage arising from any wrongful acts or negligent acts or omissions". Section 3(1) and (2) apply only to actions which have been raised and decided upon in the *Scottish* courts: see *Comex Houlder Diving v Colne Fishing Co Ltd* 1987 SC (HL) 85, per Lord Keith at 122–123.

[21] As with s 3(1), contribution under s 3(2) is according to the proportion in which the faults of the co-delinquents contributed to the injury, not pro rata according to their number. See *Davis v Catto and CIS General Insurance Ltd* 2010 GWD 26–512, where a third party was held to be 20% responsible for a car accident in which the pursuer was injured, while the driver of the car in which the pursuer was a passenger bore 80% of the responsibility. For discussion of the operation of the statutory provision, see *Central SMT Co v Lanark CC* 1949 SC 450 at 460; *Comex Houlder Diving Ltd v Colne Fishing Co Ltd* 1987 SC (HL) 85 at 121.

[22] The use of third-party procedure allows a defender to call any party who might be liable to contribute or indemnify as a third party to the existing action. The procedure is available both in the Court of Session (RCS 1994 (SI 1994/1443), Chapter 26) and in the sheriff court (OCR 1993 (SI 1993/1956), Chapter 20). See C Hennessy, *Civil Procedure and Practice* (3rd edn, 2008), paras 15–05 to 15–10 for a fuller discussion. It has been judicially observed that third-party procedure "is a procedure which enables a right of relief to be claimed at an early stage although, of course, it will not be exercisable unless and until the defenders are found liable" (per Lord Kissen in *Findlay v National Coal Board* 1965 SLT 328 at 330). See, also, the observations of L P Clyde in *Beedie v Norrie* 1966 SC 207 at 210.

[23] 2010 SC (UKSC) 87. For further discussion of this case, see E Russell, "Contribution causes confusion" 2010 SLT (News) 169.

[24] Farstad did not, however, adopt the case of fault against Asco, with the result that Enviroco remained sole defenders.

respect of damage to the vessel caused by Asco's negligence. Lord Clarke observed[25] that "if Asco is not liable to the owner, the whole basis of its liability to contribution is removed". Accordingly, Enviroco was not entitled to a contribution under s 3(2) from Asco.

24.13 Where the pursuer abandons an action against one of several defenders, this does not prevent the remaining defenders from pursuing a right of relief under s 3(2) against the person released from the action.[26] This is because the words "if sued" in the statutory section have been held to mean "if sued to judgment" and the party released from the action has not been sued to judgment.

24.14 Another interesting point as regards contribution arose in *Dormer* v *Melville Dundas & Whitson Ltd*.[27] A personal injuries action was raised against defenders shortly before the expiry of the 3-year limitation period (discussed below). The defenders brought a third party into the proceedings. The pursuer thereafter sought to convene the third party as an additional defender but, insofar as directed against the third party, the action was held to be time barred. The First Division held that the fact that the pursuer's action against the third party was time barred did not defeat the defenders' right of relief against the third party. This was because the words "if sued" assume that the third party has been "relevantly, competently and timeously sued" by the pursuer, ie that all the essential preliminaries to a determination of the other party's liability have been satisfied.[28]

24.15 Before leaving the issue of contribution and relief, mention should be made of the employer's right of relief in the context of vicarious liability. Vicarious liability is, of course, a species of joint and several liability and, accordingly, comes within the scope of the 1940 Act. An employer who has been held to be vicariously liable for his employee's negligence therefore has a right of relief under s 3 of the 1940 Act against that employee.[29] In other words, the employer can recoup the damages he has paid to the injured party from the employee. It is rare, however (although not unknown)[30] for an employer to seek relief or contribution from a negligent employee.[31] Clearly, such a practice would have a deleterious effect on industrial relations. The employee may not have sufficient funds from which to reimburse his employer in any event and it is only because of the employment relationship that the employee was put in the position from which the negligence arose.

24.16 Finally, it should be noted that obligations to make contribution by virtue of s 3(2) of the 1940 Act are subject to a 2-year prescriptive period.[32] Where a defender has been found jointly and severally liable with other joint wrongdoers and has paid more than

---

[25] 2010 SC (UKSC) 87 at para 17.

[26] *Singer* v *Gray Tool Co (Europe)* 1984 SLT 149.

[27] 1989 SC 288.

[28] See, also, *Central SMT Co Ltd* v *Lanarkshire CC* 1949 SC 450, per Lord Keith at 461.

[29] See the discussion in G J Junor, "The employer solicitor's right of relief?" 1998 SLT (News) 275.

[30] See, eg, *Lister* v *Romford Ice and Cold Storage Co Ltd* [1957] 1 All ER 125. L, during the course of his employment, negligently injured his father. The father recovered damages from his son's employers on the basis of their vicarious liability. The employers sought to recover a contribution from the son under the English legislation which applied at the time (s 6 of the Law Reform (Married Women and Tortfeasors) Act 1935). (Proceedings were in fact brought by an insurance company under rights of subrogation. The employers were therefore nominal plaintiffs only.)

[31] See the discussion in the Report on *Civil Liability – Contribution* (Scot Law Com No 115, 1988), para 3.69.

[32] Prescription and Limitation (Scotland) Act 1973, s 8A. The 2 years run from "the date on which the right to recover contribution became enforceable".

his proportion of the damages (ie where s 3(1) applies), his claim for contribution is subject to the long negative prescription.[33]

TRANSMISSION ON DEATH

The subject of damages is discussed in detail in Chapter 22. Here we consider the **24.17** extent to which a person's claim to damages transmits on death to his executor. Where the claim does transmit, the damages recovered by the executor will form part of the deceased's estate and will be distributed to beneficiaries under the deceased's will or according to the law of intestate succession, as appropriate.

It is important to distinguish between two main heads of damages for this purpose **24.18** – solatium and patrimonial losses. Solatium is compensation for pain and suffering and may be awarded for physical pain, psychological damage, loss of limbs, loss of faculties and amenities, disease and disfigurement, and awareness of loss of expectation of life. Patrimonial losses are pecuniary losses such as loss of earnings, loss of employability, and outlays and expenses.

We will deal first with any claim to solatium. At common law, where an injured **24.19** party died without having instituted proceedings, his executor could not *commence* proceedings to recover damages in respect of solatium. In *Bern's Executor v Montrose Asylum*,[34] the pursuer, as executor dative of his wife, sought to recover damages for maltreatment of his wife while in the asylum. By a majority of five to two, a Court of Seven Judges held that he had no title to sue.

On the other hand, where, prior to his death, the deceased had commenced an **24.20** action in which he sought damages for solatium, the executor could *continue* with that action.[35] Lord Young in *Bern's Executor* made reference to the "rule of our law and practice that the raising of an action by the sufferer from the wrong changes the situation altogether".[36]

The decision in *Bern's Executor* was affirmed by the House of Lords in *Stewart's* **24.21** *Executrix v London, Midland and Scottish Railway Co*.[37] There, two sisters were injured while travelling on the defender's railway. One of them died the same evening. The surviving sister raised an action, as executrix nominate of the deceased, seeking damages for her late sister's pain and suffering. Viscount Simon LC, in discussing the right to institute proceedings for damages for personal injuries due to negligence, stated:[38]

"Such a cause of action survives against the representative of the wrongdoer, but it does not transmit to the representative of the party injured. This is due to the essentially personal character of such a claim, and follows the treatment in Roman law of the *actio injuriarum*. No one but the individual who has suffered can complain of his sufferings by instituting proceedings ... If, however, the sufferer from personal injuries has instituted

---

[33] See *Davidson v Sinclair* (1877–78) LR 3 App Cas 765, per Lord Blackburn at 788.
[34] (1893) 20 R 859.
[35] See *Neilson v Rodger* (1853) 16 D 325.
[36] (1893) 20 R 859 at 873. It was subsequently held by a Court of Seven Judges in *Smith v Stewart* 1960 SC 329 that the mere intimation of a claim for solatium by the injured person before death did not result in the transmission of the claim to the representatives (overruling *Leigh's Exrx v Caledonian Railway Co* 1913 SC 838).
[37] 1943 SC (HL) 19. See, also, *Dick v Burgh of Falkirk* 1976 SC (HL) 1, per Lord Kilbrandon at 26.
[38] 1943 SC (HL) 19 at 25.

legal proceedings in his lifetime and then dies, his executor or other personal representative can carry on these proceedings, and can recover, for the benefit of the deceased's estate, the damages which the sufferer could himself have recovered."

24.22 In 1973, however, the Scottish Law Commission in its Report on *The Law relating to Damages for Injuries Causing Death* (Scot Law Com No 31) proposed that a solatium claim should not transmit to an executor *in any circumstances*.[39] That recommendation was subsequently enacted in the Damages (Scotland) Act 1976.[40] Accordingly, under the 1976 Act, as originally enacted, no right to *solatium* for personal injuries transmitted on death to the executor of the deceased person. The deceased's right to solatium died with him *even where he had raised proceedings prior to his death*. Concern soon arose, however, that the law provided an incentive to defenders to delay making settlement or reaching proof until after the pursuer's death in order to minimise the amount of damages to be paid. The claim for solatium might be substantial, particularly in occupational disease cases involving mesothelioma or asbestosis.[41] The Secretary of State therefore referred the matter to the Scottish Law Commission which, in March 1992, issued its Report on *The Effect of Death on Damages* (Scot Law Com No 134). The Commission observed that "under the present rules actual suffering may go unacknowledged, if the injured person dies before the claim is resolved. We find that difficult to justify on ordinary principles of justice".[42] It continued: "There are of course counter-arguments about the personal nature of solatium, but we do not regard them as conclusive. Whether a right to claim solatium should be transmissible is a matter of policy on which a decision could be taken either way."[43] The Commission recommended that the solatium claim should transmit to the executor[44] but that account should be taken only of pain and suffering ending immediately before death.[45]

24.23 The position is now governed by s 2(1) of the Damages (Scotland) Act 2011 which provides that there are transmissible to a deceased person's executor the like rights to damages for non-patrimonial loss in respect of personal injuries suffered by the deceased and vested in the deceased immediately before his death.[46]

24.24 Section 2(2) of the 2011 Act provides that, in determining the amount of damages for non-patrimonial loss payable to the deceased person's executor, the only period to which the court is to have regard is that ending immediately before the deceased's death.[47]

24.25 The Scottish Law Commission has observed that "the shorter the period between injury and death, the smaller the claim for solatium is likely to be".[48] In *Beggs* v

---

[39] The Commission asserted (at para 23) that "it is artificial to allow compensation for a person's suffering after his death".
[40] See *Allison* v *British Rail Engineering Ltd* 1978 SLT (Notes) 34.
[41] See Report on *The Effect of Death on Damages* (Scot Law Com No 134, 1992), para 2.14.
[42] *Ibid* at para 3.13.
[43] *Ibid* at para 4.7.
[44] *Ibid* at para 4.10.
[45] *Ibid* at para 4.12.
[46] The right transmits even where death is from a cause unrelated to the accident or disease which forms the basis of the claim.
[47] It has been observed that "[l]ogically, an instantaneous death in a plane crash would not trigger a solatium payment. However, evidence of conscious survival for a definite period would" (S Forsyth, "Transmissible solatium after death: a reappraisal" 1999 SLT (News) 45 at 47).
[48] Report on *The Effect of Death on Damages* (Scot Law Com No 134, 1992), para 4.11.

Motherwell Bridge Fabricators Ltd,[49] a widow sought to recover damages following the death of her husband who had been involved in an accident while driving a forklift truck at work. The interval of time between the occurrence of the accident and death was about half an hour. Lord Eassie stated:[50] "Mr Beggs was in considerable pain and distress for a short period before he lost consciousness. But despite the intensity of that pain and distress, the brevity of its suffering dictates that the award be of modest proportions." Solatium for the deceased's pain and suffering was valued at £250 (in 1998) and this transmitted to the widow as executrix of her late husband (subject to a deduction in respect of the deceased's contributory negligence).

Wells v *Hay*[51] stands in stark contrast to *Beggs*. In *Wells*, a 19-year-old man was **24.26** involved in a road traffic accident in which he sustained full-thickness burns to 60 per cent of his body. He also suffered fractures to his legs and skull as well as chest injuries and a partial lung collapse. He was trapped in a car for 40 minutes and was conscious until transferred to hospital 1 hour after the accident. He was admitted to intensive care in hospital and died 16 days later, having regained consciousness on at least one occasion and thereby experiencing some pain and discomfort. The sum of £50,000 was awarded (in 1998) by a jury by way of transmissible solatium to the deceased's mother as executrix dative.[52]

In *McManus' Executrix* v *Babcock Energy Ltd,*[53] McManus was diagnosed with **24.27** mesothelioma at Easter 1996. Prior to his diagnosis he had been a keen walker and gardener. He frequently played golf and went swimming. Following his diagnosis, he agreed to major surgery but the operation was not the success that had been hoped for. He underwent chemotherapy sessions in June and September 1996. He began to suffer progressive pain from his condition, particularly after the second dose of chemotherapy. Painkilling drugs had only a limited effect. The chemotherapy produced unpleasant side effects and McManus suffered substantial loss of weight. His breathing was very bad. He died in December 1996 (aged 55). The defenders admitted liability and proof was restricted to quantum. The Lord Ordinary (Kingarth) took the view that £50,000 was a reasonable award in respect of solatium (in 1999) and this transmitted to the widow as executrix dative.

A claim in respect of injury to name or reputation transmits to the executor but **24.28** insofar as it relates to non-patrimonial losses, the claim transmits *only* if the deceased brought an action while alive.[54] Injuries resulting from harassment actionable under s 8 or s 8A of the Protection from Harassment Act 1997 are transmissible to the deceased person's executor in terms of s 2(1)(b)(ii) of the Damages (Scotland) Act 2011.

We will now consider the question of transmissibility of claims in respect of patrimonial **24.29** losses. Although at common law a claim for solatium was not transmissible (subject to the exception where an action had already been instituted by the deceased person), claims in respect of property damage or other patrimonial loss did transmit to the executor, even if the deceased had died without taking action. This was acknowledged

---

[49] 1998 SLT 1215.
[50] *Ibid* at 1224.
[51] 1999 RepLR 44.
[52] For a more detailed discussion, see S Forsyth, "Transmissible solatium after death: a reappraisal" 1999 SLT (News) 45.
[53] 1999 SC 569.
[54] Section 2(1)(b)(i) and s 2(3) of the Damages (Scotland) Act 2011.

in *Stewart's Executrix* v *London, Midland and Scottish Railway Co.*[55] There, Viscount Simon LC, having indicated that the solatium claim did not transmit to an executor, went on:[56] "If, on the other hand, the defender's negligence, besides causing personal injuries, damaged the sufferer's property or caused him other patrimonial loss, the claim to recover this loss would survive in the deceased sufferer's representative."[57]

24.30   It was held in *Smith* v *Stewart & Co*[58] that this extended not only to damage to property (eg damage to the deceased's motor car in a collision) but also to wages which the deceased lost by reason of the injuries which he sustained. In *Smith*, an employee was injured in the course of his employment. He intimated a claim against his employers but no court action had been raised at the time of his death. His executor sought damages *inter alia* in respect of loss of wages suffered by the deceased as a result of the accident. Lord Mackintosh, having quoted the Lord Chancellor's *dictum* from *Stewart's Executrix* (above), observed: "I am quite unable to see why a loss of wages resulting from an accident caused by a defender's negligence does not fall under the Lord Chancellor's words 'other patrimonial loss' caused by the negligence."[59]

24.31   It remains the case that patrimonial losses are transmissible[60] but compensation in respect of patrimonial losses suffered by the deceased can only be claimed by the executor *up until the date of death*.[61] Accordingly, future patrimonial losses (eg loss of future earnings) do not transmit to the executor.[62] In *Mackintosh* v *Morrice's Executrices*,[63] a man and his wife were killed in a road traffic accident in 2001. During their lifetime they had made substantial gifts to their two daughters which were expected to become exempt transfers for the purpose of inheritance tax in 2002 and 2004. Because of their untimely deaths in 2001, the transfers became chargeable, resulting in a substantial increase in inheritance tax payable on their estates. Affirming the decision of the Lord Ordinary, the Inner House held that the loss to the estates of the deceased caused by the payment of inheritance tax was attributable to a period *after* death and, as such, did not transmit to the pursuers as executrices.

24.32   A relative's loss of support claim in terms of s 4(3)(a) of the Damages (Scotland) Act 2011 is transmissible to that relative's executor.[64] Similarly, a non-patrimonial award which may be made to a member of the deceased's immediate family[65] (in terms of s 4(3)(b) of the 2011 Act), once vested, transmits to the executor of that family member.[66] In determining the amount of damages payable, the court shall

---

[55] 1943 SC (HL) 19.
[56] *Ibid* at 25.
[57] Some years earlier, in *Neilson* v *Rodger* (1853) 16 D 325, the right of the executor to recover the deceased's loss of wages was considered to be a matter that was too clear to admit of dispute and was a matter of concession by counsel for the defender (see L J-C Hope at 326).
[58] 1961 SC 91.
[59] *Ibid* at 99.
[60] Damages (Scotland) Act 2011, s 2(1).
[61] *Ibid*, s 2(2).
[62] Where the deceased has died in consequence of personal injuries, relatives of the deceased may, however, be able to claim for loss of support in terms of s 4(3)(a) of the Damages (Scotland) Act 2011. See Chapter 22 for a fuller discussion.
[63] 2007 SC 6.
[64] Damages (Scotland) Act 2011, s 9.
[65] For a definition of "immediate family", see Damages (Scotland) Act 2011, s 4(5).
[66] Damages (Scotland) Act 2011, s 9. The Scottish Law Commission observed that "since we take the view that a right to claim solatium should transmit, we think that the relative's right to claim non-patrimonial damages should likewise transmit" (Report on *The Effect of Death on Damages* (Scot Law Com No 134, 1992), para 4.42).

have regard only to the period ending immediately before the relative's death (s 9(2) of the 2011 Act). The nature of the loss of support and non-patrimonial claims is discussed in more detail in Chapter 22.

DECREE AND PAYMENT

If a pursuer has obtained a decree in his favour against the defender and the decree **24.33** is satisfied (ie the defender has made payment of the whole sum for which decree has passed, together with any interest and expenses thereon), the obligation to make reparation is extinguished. Any attempt to raise the action again would most probably be met by the defence of *res judicata*.[67] This is a plea to the effect that the merits of the case have already been decided by a competent court.[68]

A decree in favour of the defender may take the form of a decree of dismissal or **24.34** a decree of absolvitor.[69] The difference between the two decrees has been described in the following terms: "Scots law makes an important distinction between an order that puts an end to a pending action while preserving the right of action (dismissal) and an order that extinguishes the right of action and the underlying rights and obligations (absolvitor)."[70] A decree of absolvitor is clearly preferable from the defender's point of view as it completely extinguishes the pursuer's claim in the action. A decree of dismissal, on the other hand, leaves it open to the pursuer to raise a fresh action.[71] In other words, a decree of dismissal[72] does not render a case *res judicata*[73] whereas a decree of absolvitor does do so. Absolvitor is usually granted after the court has heard evidence – in other words, the merits have been considered. It has been described as "the only sure way of bringing litigation to an end once and for all".[74]

COMPROMISE (OR SETTLEMENT) AND DISCHARGE

Compromise is simply an out-of-court settlement by agreement between the parties to **24.35** the action.[75] There is no requirement to seek leave or permission of the court to settle an action. The settlement terms are matters for the parties to the action. Settlement of the case can take two forms. First, it may take the form of extrajudicial offer of compromise

---

[67] See Chapter 21.
[68] See the discussion in I D Macphail, *Sheriff Court Practice* (Sheriff Welsh QC (ed)) (3rd edn, 2006), vol 1, paras 2.104–2.109.
[69] See Hennessy, *Civil Procedure and Practice* at pp 295–296 for further discussion.
[70] *Tonner v Reiach and Hall* 2008 SC 1, per Lord Abernethy at para 143.
[71] See *ibid*, at para 144.
[72] A decree of dismissal may follow a debate where a plea to the relevancy of the action has been sustained.
[73] See *Cunningham v Skinner* (1902) 4 F 1124.
[74] See *Tonner v Reiach and Hall* 2008 SC 1 at para 144.
[75] For a case in which a dispute arose as to whether a settlement had discharged *all* aspects of the pursuer's claim, see *Irving v Hiddleston* 1998 SC 759. It was held there that the burden of proving that the defender's liability to the pursuer has been wholly discharged rests on the defender. The case held further that the scope of the settlement and of any discharge is a matter to be judged by objective inference from the whole circumstances including the course and terms of the negotiations.

and acceptance thereof.[76] The parties agree the terms of settlement. Usually a joint minute is prepared and lodged in court. The parties record in that joint minute that the action has been settled extrajudicially and request that the court interpones its authority to the joint minute and grants decree accordingly. Alternatively, settlement may take the form of judicial offer (or tender)[77] and judicial acceptance thereof. In the latter case the offer of settlement is made by minute in the process. If a tender is acceptable to the pursuer, the normal practice is to lodge a minute of acceptance of tender in response to the defender's minute of tender. From a practical point of view, it is important to consider the terms of the tender carefully. If the pursuer does not accept the defender's tender and is subsequently awarded a decree for an amount less than the sum tendered, he will normally be required to bear the expenses of the action from the date of tender.[78] A settlement reached by the parties is binding upon them even although the court's authority has not been interponed thereto.

24.36　　Discharge of an action once a claim has been settled prevents the pursuer from bringing a subsequent action even if he finds his loss is greater than he had at first appreciated. The terms of the discharge are matters for the parties to the action.[79] Where there are several wrongdoers, a discharge may be effective as against one of them but not as against the others.[80] It is only the party in whose favour the discharge is granted who is entitled to found on the discharge.

24.37　　Before leaving the issue of settlement and discharge, mention should be made of the special position of mesothelioma victims. The general rule is that a deceased's immediate family is prevented from claiming damages for non-patrimonial loss where the deceased had settled his or her own claim while still alive (s 4(2) of the Damages (Scotland) Act 2011). If this rule was applied to mesothelioma sufferers, they would face the dilemma of either pursuing their damages claim while still alive or not pursuing their claim so that their immediate family could claim damages after their death. Accordingly, an exception to the general rule is provided in s 5 of the 2011 Act which states that where a *mesothelioma* sufferer has both died and discharged his claim on or after 20 December 2006, members of the immediate family have a right to damages under s 4(3)(b) of the 2011 Act following his death. It has been judicially stated that "[this] amendment now prevents the invidious choice faced by a person who is gravely ill".[81] It should be stressed, however, that the general rule is that damages in respect of the non-patrimonial award are irrecoverable where liability to the deceased has been discharged during his lifetime. Section 5 of the 2011 Act provides an exception to that rule but *only* in relation to mesothelioma sufferers.[82]

---

[76] The purpose of extrajudicial settlement has been said to be "to get rid of the uncertainty and the expense, and the risks of litigation on the one side and on the other" (*North British Railway Co v Wood* (1891) 18 R (HL) 27, per Earl of Selborne at 33). For further discussion of extrajudicial settlements, see Macphail, *Sheriff Court Practice*, vol 1, paras 14.67–14.74.

[77] For a detailed discussion of tenders, see Macphail, *Sheriff Court Practice*, paras 14.36–14.66.

[78] See Hennessy, *Civil Procedure and Practice*, paras 15–16 to 15–20 for a fuller discussion of tenders.

[79] Many claims are settled without a formal written discharge but there are risks attached to such an approach: see the discussion in *Irving v Hiddleston* 1998 SC 759, per Lord Macfadyen at 773.

[80] See *Dillon v Napier, Shanks & Bell* (1893) 30 SLR 685.

[81] *McLeod v Crawford & Ors* 2010 SLT 1035, per Lord Woolman at para 32.

[82] For commentary on the legislation, see J Chalmers, "Legislative comment – The Rights of Relatives to Damages (Mesothelioma) (Scotland) Act 2007" 2007 Edin LR 407.

PRESCRIPTION AND LIMITATION[83]

A creditor is required to exercise his rights within certain time limits in order that the **24.38** wrongdoer is not exposed to a permanent threat of legal action. The law takes the view that there should be a cut-off point beyond which the rights of the injured party are extinguished or rendered unenforceable. If actions could be raised without limit of time, vital evidence would probably be lost before the case reached proof. Witnesses might have died in the intervening period. Rules of prescription and limitation seek to avoid the problems created by stale litigation.

In practice, the rules of prescription and limitation are vitally important. The rules **24.39** require civil proceedings to be brought within certain specified time limits, failing which the pursuer's right of action will be extinguished or rendered unenforceable. From the pursuer's point of view, therefore, these rules are very important. Moreover, these rules are often the cause of much anxiety to the pursuer's solicitor. Indeed, if a solicitor fails to raise civil proceedings within the statutory time limits (at least where it is his fault), that is good evidence of professional negligence. Indeed, that was the basis of the pursuer's claim in *Duncan v Ross, Harper & Murphy*,[84] where negligence was proved against the solicitors who had failed to raise their client's personal injuries action within the statutory time limit. The pursuer failed to recover damages, however, as his injuries had resulted from an illegal enterprise in which he had participated. Accordingly, even if the civil action had been raised timeously, the illegality defence would have prevailed against the pursuer.[85]

The rules governing prescription and limitation are found in the Prescription and **24.40** Limitation (Scotland) Act 1973 (the "1973 Act") (as amended by the Law Reform (Miscellaneous Provisions) (Scotland) Act 1980, the Prescription and Limitation (Scotland) Act 1984, the Law Reform (Miscellaneous Provisions) (Scotland) Act 1985, the Consumer Protection Act 1987 and the Protection from Harassment Act 1997).[86]

The concepts of prescription and limitation require to be distinguished. Prescription **24.41** operates to extinguish the obligation in question completely, whereas limitation simply renders the obligation unenforceable.[87] In the former case, the defender does not require to state a plea because the court will automatically take note of the fact that prescription has extinguished the obligation. In the latter case, however, the defender does require to state a plea to the effect that the claim is no longer enforceable as a result of the operation of limitation. He may choose not to do so,[88] in which case any decree which passes against him will be valid and enforceable.

---

[83] For a detailed analysis, see DM Walker, *The Law of Prescription and Limitation of Actions in Scotland* (6th edn, 2002); Johnston, *Prescription and Limitation* (1999). See, also, E Russell, "Prescription and Limitation of Actions" in J M Thomson (ed), *Delict* (2007).

[84] 1993 SLT (Notes)105.

[85] See Chapter 21.

[86] Following a review of the provisions of the 1973 Act, the Scottish Law Commission has made a number of proposals for change in the law: see Report on *Personal Injury Actions: Limitation and Prescribed Claims* (Scot Law Com No 207, 2007). These proposals are discussed in E Russell, "Reform of limitation in personal injury actions" 2008 Edin LR 262. The Scottish Government began a consultation process on 15 February 2011, *Civil Law of Damages: Issues in Personal Injury*, one of the aims of which is to further explore the key recommendations made by the Scottish Law Commission in its 2007 Report.

[87] "Prescription extinguishes the right, while limitation merely cuts off the right of action": per Lord Abernethy in *Tonner v Reiach and Hall* 2008 SC 1 at para 51.

[88] See *J v Fife Council* 2007 SLT 85; 2009 SC 163 where no limitation plea was taken in respect of abuse perpetrated between 1961 and 1966. Liability was admitted and a proof on quantum took place.

PRESCRIPTION

24.42 The general concept of prescription is that rights are extinguished after a certain period. The concept, which originated in Roman law, is now governed by the 1973 Act.

Short negative prescription

24.43 The 1973 Act introduced a new short negative prescription of 5 years (the quinquennium) which extinguishes the obligations to which it applies. Section 6(1) of the 1973 Act provides that:

> "If, after the appropriate date, an obligation to which this section applies has subsisted for a continuous period of five years – (a) without any relevant claim having been made in relation to the obligation, and (b) without the subsistence of the obligation having been relevantly acknowledged, then as from the expiration of that period the obligation shall be extinguished."

24.44 By virtue of Sch 1, para 1(d), s 6 applies to any obligation "arising from liability (whether arising from any enactment or from any rule of law) to make reparation". The general rule is therefore that obligations *to make reparation*[89] for a delict are extinguished after 5 years provided that the creditor has not made a relevant claim nor has the debtor made a relevant acknowledgement. Therefore, if I leave my car in the university car park and then I see someone negligently driving into it, causing damage, I will have a period of 5 years to raise my action, failing which the obligation to make reparation is extinguished.

24.45   Certain obligations are excluded from the operation of the short negative prescription. These are stated in Sch 1, para 2 to the Act and include obligations arising from personal injury or death, obligations to make reparation in respect of defamation within the meaning of s 18A of the Act, obligations arising from liability under the Consumer Protection Act 1987 and obligations which are specified in Sch 3 as being imprescriptible.

24.46   The 5-year period runs from the date on which the obligation becomes enforceable.[90] In terms of s 11 of the 1973 Act, that will be one of three possible dates:

(a) the date on which the loss, injury or damage occurred;[91]

(b) if it is a continuing wrong, the date on which the wrong ceased (if that date is later than the date on which the loss occurred)[92] (an obvious example would be where the damage results from a continuing delict such as a nuisance);

(c) if the creditor was not aware and could not with reasonable diligence have been aware that loss, injury or damage had occurred, the date on which the creditor became or could with reasonable diligence have become so aware.[93]

---

[89] Where a remedy other than reparation is sought, eg interdict or specific implement, the obligation is excluded from the operation of the short negative prescription.

[90] Section 6(3) of the 1973 Act.

[91] Section 11(1).

[92] Section 11(2). For an interesting discussion as to whether this provision applied, see *Johnston* v *Scottish Ministers* 2006 SCLR 5.

[93] Section 11(3). See *Adams* v *Thorntons WS (No 3)* 2005 1 SC 30.

There must be a concurrence of *damnum* and *injuria* before the prescriptive period **24.47**
begins to run.[94] Quite often in delictual cases there will be a time lapse between the
breach of legal duty (the *injuria*) and the loss or injury (the *damnum*). If this is the
case then the period runs from the date on which the damage occurs. The position is
articulated by Lord Keith of Kinkel in *Dunlop v McGowans*,[95] where his Lordship, in
considering s 11(1), stated:[96] "The right to raise such an action accrues when *injuria*
concurs with *damnum*. Some interval of time may elapse between the two ... and ...
in such circumstances time is to run from the date when *damnum* results, not from the
earlier date of *injuria*."

Dunlop v McGowans was cited with approval in *Renfrew Golf Club v Ravenstone* **24.48**
Securities Ltd.[97] There, a golf club raised an action against a building company in
connection with the faulty construction of a golf course. The greens on the new golf
course were affected by flooding by reason of defects in design and construction. It
was held that, although the defects in question may have been present for a period in
excess of 5 years, the prescriptive period commenced on the date on which the damage
occurred. In other words, a concurrence of *damnum* and *injuria* was required to activate
the running of the prescriptive period.

Difficulties can be encountered in determining the date on which loss or damage **24.49**
actually occurred.[98] In *Osborne & Hunter Ltd v Hardie Caldwell*[99] the pursuers lent
money to and became guarantors for a company. They did so on the advice of their
accountants. The company defaulted on the loan and the pursuers were called upon to
make payment to a bank in terms of the guarantee. They sued their accountants. The
defenders argued that any obligation to make reparation had prescribed as the loan
monies had been advanced more than 5 years prior to the raising of the action. The
issue for the Inner House was whether *damnum* occurred as at the date of the loan or
as at the later date of default. The Lord Justice-Clerk (Cullen) emphasised[100] that each
case depends on its particular circumstances but in the instant case it was clear that the
company was already in financial difficulties as at the date of the loan. It was therefore
inadvisable for the pursuers to have lent money to the company and *damnum* accordingly occurred as at the date of the loan.

In *Kusz v Buchanan Burton*[101] the pursuers raised an action against a firm of solicitors. **24.50**
They alleged that a partner in the firm had been instructed to raise proceedings against
a builder and to arrest and inhibit on the dependence of the action. At that time, the
builder was the sole proprietor of a dwelling house. Some months later, on 26 July 1995,
the builder conveyed the dwelling house to his wife. At that date, no proceedings had
been raised and no inhibition was in place. By the time an initial writ was warranted

---

[94] See, eg, *Pelagic Freezing Ltd v Lovie Construction Ltd* 2010 GWD 37–763. It has been judicially stated that "[a]s
soon as any form of loss, injury or damage occurs following a breach of legal duty or obligation (the *injuria*) the
concurrence takes place. There can only be one point of concurrence and this is it" (per L J-C Wheatley in *Dunlop
v McGowans* 1979 SC 22 at 33). See, also, *K v Gilmartin's Exrx* 2004 SC 784, where the First Division held that for
the purposes of prescription, time runs from the *first* conjunction of *injuria* and *damnum* and is not postponed
by the emergence of a later, separate loss or injury caused by the same act, neglect or default.
[95] 1980 SC (HL) 73.
[96] *Ibid* at 81.
[97] 1984 SLT 170.
[98] See E Russell, "Determining the date of damnum" 2009 SLT (News) 197. See, also, *J G Martin Plant Hire
Ltd v Bannatyne, Kirkwood, France & Co* 1996 SC 105; *Jackson v Clydesdale Bank plc* 2003 SLT 273.
[99] 1999 SLT 153.
[100] *Ibid* at 156.
[101] 2010 SCLR 27.

and an inhibition registered, the builder was no longer the proprietor of any heritable property in Scotland. Decree by default was subsequently obtained against the builder but the decree remained unsatisfied. The action against the solicitors was commenced on 14 May 2004. The defenders tabled a plea of prescription, arguing that the starting point for prescription was 26 July 1995. The pursuers contended that there was no concurrence of *damnum* and *injuria* until at least 17 May 2001 when decree had been obtained against the builder and the pursuers had been unable to obtain satisfaction of it. The Inner House held that in the absence of any averments that the claim against the builder had a value as at July 1995, there was no proper basis for the contention that damage was sustained either by the loss of security or by the loss of any opportunity. Rather, "[t]he 'fatal blow' or 'disaster' occurred ... only on perfection of the contingency by the obtaining of decree for a substantial sum". Accordingly, the plea of prescription was repelled.

24.51   Of course, the pursuer may be unaware that he has suffered *damnum*, as, for example, in the case of latent damage. An obvious example might be progressive damage to the pursuer's property caused by the defender's delictual conduct but which is not discovered by the pursuer until sometime after its commencement.[102] In such cases, s 11(3) of the 1973 Act alleviates the pursuer's difficulties by incorporating what is sometimes referred to as the "discoverability formula". Accordingly, the short negative prescription does not run against the pursuer until he was aware or could with reasonable diligence[103] have become aware that loss, injury or damage had occurred.[104]

24.52   Section 11(3) may be invoked in cases of professional negligence where the loss remains latent or undiscovered for some time. In *Glasper* v *Rodger*,[105] the pursuers raised an action of professional negligence on 16 August 1990 against their former solicitor. The pursuers' losses were actually sustained on 20 March 1984, when, contrary to their instructions, title to a hotel which they were purchasing was taken in the name of their son alone. The pursuers argued that they had been unaware that they had sustained loss until 21 August 1985 when their son disappeared and a heritable creditor commenced proceedings to enforce its security over the hotel. Accordingly, they argued that the action was timeously raised. The defender argued that the claim had prescribed in terms of s 6 of the 1973 Act. The First Division observed that s 11(3) required not only an awareness of loss but also an awareness that negligence had caused that loss. The court went on to say that in a case such as this, where the pursuers argued that they were unaware that they had sustained a loss at all, the question was whether they had exercised reasonable diligence in order to discover whether a loss had occurred. The Lord President (Hope) stated:[106]

---

[102] See *Watt* v *Jamieson* 1954 SC 56.

[103] "Reasonable diligence requires the taking of those steps that a person of ordinary prudence would have taken if placed in the circumstances in which the pursuer found himself": per Lord Penrose in *Adams* v *Thorntons (WS) (No 3)* 2005 1 SC 30 at 41. His Lordship continued (at 41): "prescription will not run against a creditor who does not know that he has suffered loss if he establishes that a person of ordinary prudence in his position would have had no reason to exercise reasonable diligence in order to discover whether a loss had occurred".

[104] Note, however, that lack of awareness does not prevent the running of the long negative prescription, discussed below. Rather, the 20-year prescription runs from the date on which the loss or damage occurred or the date on which a continuing wrong ceased.

[105] 1996 SLT 44.

[106] *Ibid* at 47.

"In the present case the pursuers' lack of awareness ... relates not to the question of causation but to the fact that they had sustained a loss in the first place. A party who is aware that he has sustained loss, injury or damage may reasonably be expected to take some steps to find out what has caused that loss. Failure to do this will call for an explanation, if the test of reasonable diligence to which s 11(3) refers is to be capable of being satisfied. But a lack of awareness that loss, injury or damage has been sustained at all gives rise to a different question ... It is whether, in all the circumstances, the pursuer had any reason to exercise reasonable diligence in order to discover whether a loss had occurred."

24.53 The court concluded that the pursuers' averments disclosed no reason for them to suspect that anything had gone wrong with the purchase and those averments were sufficient to entitle them to a proof before answer.[107]

24.54 As *Glasper* v *Rodger* indicates, in interpreting s 11(3), the courts take the view that time does not run against the creditor until he is aware (or could with reasonable diligence have become aware) that he has suffered loss *and* that the loss was caused by wrongdoing. In *Kirk Care Housing Association Ltd* v *Crerar and Partners*,[108] certain housing suffered a failure in the roughcast. The Association, for which the housing had been built, had become aware of this failure in the roughcast more than 5 years before it raised its action against the architects and building contractors involved. The defenders argued that the claim had prescribed as the Association had been aware that it had suffered loss for more than 5 years before raising the action. The Association argued that it had not been aware more than 5 years before raising the action and could not with reasonable diligence have become aware that the failure in the roughcast *had been the result of any act, neglect or default*. Lord Clyde was of the opinion that the fact that the Association was not aware and could not reasonably have become aware that its loss had been caused by act, neglect or default was sufficient to prevent prescription of the Association's right.[109]

24.55 The 5-year prescriptive period does not run during any period when the creditor is under legal disability.[110] The term "legal disability" embraces both nonage and unsoundness of mind.[111] It follows that the quinquennium does not run against a creditor who is under the age of 16.[112] Similarly, any period of unsoundness of mind[113] is disregarded for the purposes of computing the 5-year prescriptive period. If the pursuer refrains for a certain period from raising proceedings as a result of being induced by fraud or error of the debtor (or his representative), that period is disregarded[114] (although any period occurring after the creditor could with reasonable diligence have discovered the fraud or error will not be disregarded).

---

[107] See, also, *Legal Services Centre Ltd* v *Miller Samuel LLP* [2009] CSOH 141.

[108] 1996 SLT 150.

[109] Compare *McDougal Inglis* v *Scottish Borders Council* [2007] CSOH 147.

[110] Section 6(4)(b) of the 1973 Act.

[111] Section 15(1) of the 1973 Act.

[112] See s 1(2) of the Age of Legal Capacity (Scotland) Act 1991.

[113] For a discussion of what amounts to "unsoundness of mind", see *Bogan's Curator Bonis* v *Graham* 1992 SCLR 920.

[114] Section 6(4)(a) of the 1973 Act. See *BP Exploration Operation Co Ltd* v *Chevron Transport (Scotland)* 2002 SC (HL) 19; *Legal Services Centre Ltd* v *Miller Samuel LLP* [2009] CSOH 141; *Pelagic Freezing Ltd* v *Lovie Construction Ltd* 2010 GWD 37–763 (no evidence to the effect that the pursuer was in error).

24.56   The 5-year period will be interrupted in the event of a "relevant claim"[115] being made by or on behalf of the creditor. The raising of court proceedings thus serves to interrupt the prescriptive period.[116] In *Boyle v Glasgow Corporation*,[117] Lord Justice-Clerk Wheatley observed[118] that the exact point at which an action is brought is when the summons has passed signet and it has been served on the defender. In *Beveridge & Kellas, WS v Abercromby*,[119] the Sheriff Principal (Nicholson) observed[120] that "for a claim to amount to a relevant claim such as to interrupt a period of prescription or limitation, two requirements must be fulfilled. They are first, that the claim should have been made in appropriate proceedings,[121] and secondly, that the claim should have been brought to the notice of the other party". Thus, before a minute of amendment or counterclaim can interrupt the prescriptive period, it must have been both lodged in process and intimated to the other party.

24.57   The quinquennium will also be interrupted in the event of a "relevant acknowledgement"[122] being made by or on behalf of the debtor (eg a payment to account or unequivocal written admission that the obligation subsists). The prescriptive period must then recommence from the date of the interruption.

Long negative prescription

24.58   Section 7 of the 1973 Act makes provision for a long negative prescription of 20 years. This vicennial prescription applies to obligations of any kind[123] including those to which s 6 applies. It is possible for an obligation to be extinguished through the operation of the long negative prescription before it would be extinguished through the operation of the short negative prescription. This is because lack of awareness of loss, induced error and fraud and legal disability do not prevent the running of time in relation to the long negative prescription (although all of these factors do prevent time running in the context of the short negative prescription). It is important to note that the long negative prescription (unlike the 5-year prescription) operates irrespective of whether liability was discoverable.[124] Because the awareness provision is inapplicable in relation to the long negative prescription, it follows that the starting date for the running of the 20-year prescription will be one of two possible dates. These starting dates are provided for in s 7(1) and s 11 of the 1973 Act. In most cases the starting

---

[115] The term "relevant claim" is defined in s 9(1) of the 1973 Act. As well as claims made in "appropriate proceedings" (ie court or arbitration proceedings) the term also embraces claims made in the debtor's insolvency or bankruptcy and diligence. See *Clark v Argyle Consulting Ltd* 2011 SLT 180 (a complaint to a Financial Ombudsman was not an arbitration process and therefore did not constitute a relevant claim for the purposes of interrupting the prescriptive period).

[116] For further discussion, see *British Railways Board v Strathclyde RC* 1981 SC 90.

[117] 1975 SC 238.

[118] *Ibid* at 250.

[119] 1997 SLT (Sh Ct) 5.

[120] *Ibid* at 8.

[121] For an interesting discussion on this point, see *Clark v Argyle Consulting Ltd* 2011 SLT 180.

[122] The term "relevant acknowledgement" is defined in s 10(1) of the 1973 Act.

[123] The long negative prescription applies to obligations arising both from statute and the common law. It is not confined to obligations *to make reparation* (ie pay damages).

[124] The rationale behind this was articulated by the Scottish Law Commission in its Report on *Reform of the Law Relating to Prescription and Limitation of Actions* (Scot Law Com No 15, 1970), para 34(2), wherein it was stated that: "The law should not give countenance to latent and antiquated claims which may affect even the successors of the person responsible and, if revived after many years, may disturb the basis on which they have arranged their lives."

date will be the date on which the loss, injury or damage occurred.[125] In the same way as with the short negative prescription, there must be a concurrence of *damnum* and *injuria* before time begins to run. There can be only one point of concurrence.[126] A second possible starting date for the running of the long negative prescription applies in the case of a continuing wrong, where the starting date will be the date on which the wrong ceased, if that is later than the date on which the loss occurred.[127]

Relevant claims and relevant acknowledgements serve to interrupt the long negative prescription. These concepts have been discussed above in the context of the short negative prescription. The prescriptive period must start again after the interruption. The long negative prescription does not apply to obligations arising under the Consumer Protection Act 1987,[128] to obligations which are specified in Sch 3 as being imprescriptible and to obligations to make reparation in respect of personal injuries within the meaning of Pt II of the Act or death resulting therefrom. **24.59**

Contracting out

Any attempt to contract out of the prescription provisions in ss 6 and 7 of the 1973 Act, as amended, is null.[129] **24.60**

Amendment of pleadings and prescription

It has been observed[130] that "[a]mendment powers are wide in the sheriff court and the Court of Session[131].... one of the considerations in allowing a minute of amendment is whether it raises a new matter after the prescriptive period".[132] **24.61**

In *Pompa's Trs* v *Edinburgh Magistrates*,[133] the Lord Justice-Clerk (Cooper) stated:[134] **24.62**

"[O]ur reports contain many decisions showing that the court will not in general allow a pursuer by amendment to substitute the right defender for the wrong defender, or to cure a radical incompetence in his action, or to change the basis of his case if he seeks to make such amendments only after the expiry of a time limit which would have prevented him at that stage from raising proceedings afresh."

An amendment which seeks to substitute the correct defender for the wrong defender after the expiry of the prescriptive period is, therefore, unlikely to be **24.63**

---

[125] Determining the date of loss for the purposes of the long negative prescription can be contentious: see *Beard* v *Beveridge, Herd & Sandilands* 1990 SLT 609; *MacDonald-Haig* v *MacNeill & Critchley and Ors* 2004 SLT (Sh Ct) 75.

[126] See *K* v *Gilmartin's Exrx* 2004 SC 784.

[127] *Ibid*.

[128] Such obligations are subject to a 10-year prescriptive period: s 22A of the 1973 Act. That period runs, not from the date of *damnum*, but from the date of supply (ie the date on which the product was placed on the market).

[129] Section 13 of the 1973 Act.

[130] W J Stewart, "Reparation – prescription and limitation" (1994) 39 JLSS 374 at 376.

[131] See Ordinary Cause Rules 1993, Ch 18 and Rules of the Court of Session 1994, Ch 24.

[132] See *J G Martin Plant Hire Ltd* v *Bannatyne, Kirkwood, France & Co* 1996 SC 105; *Milnbank Housing Association Ltd* v *Page and Park and Anor*, OH, 4 December 2001, unreported, where Lord Carloway took the view that the new averments contained in the amendment did not make out a fundamentally different claim. On the contrary, "in relation to both the defects averred and the duties breached, the case against the defenders remains fundamentally the same" (at para 32).

[133] 1942 SC 119.

[134] *Ibid* at 125.

allowed. However, the court will consider whether the amendment is one of form or of substance. In *Orkney Islands Council v S & JD Robertson*,[135] an amendment to the defender's designation was allowed, it being regarded in the circumstances as a matter of form rather than substance. Although the designation of the defender had contained an error (the use of the former company name), the company had a distinctive number and had been in continuous existence despite a change in name. There was no question of convening an additional defender or substituting a different defender.[136]

Personal injury and fatal cases

24.64   Obligations to make reparation in respect of personal injuries or death do not prescribe.[137] Although, under the 1973 Act, as originally enacted, such obligations were subject to a 20-year prescriptive period, the Scottish Law Commission recommended that such obligations be excluded from the long negative prescription of 20 years.[138] The law was amended by the Prescription and Limitation (Scotland) Act 1984 (the "1984 Act")[139] and such obligations are now imprescriptible[140] (although they are subject to the rules on limitation discussed below).

Imprescriptible obligations

24.65   It should be noted that certain obligations do not prescribe:[141] for example, any obligation of a trustee to make reparation in respect of any fraudulent breach of trust to which the trustee was a party or was privy.

Defamation cases

24.66   Obligations to make reparation in respect of defamation are also subject to special rules by virtue of the Law Reform (Miscellaneous Provisions) (Scotland) Act 1985. Such obligations prescribe after 20 years,[142] although they are not affected by the short negative prescription.[143]

---

[135] 2003 SLT 775.
[136] See, also, *Stewart v Highlands and Islands Development Board* 1991 SLT 787.
[137] Obligations arising under the Consumer Protection Act 1987 are an exception: they are subject to a 10-year prescriptive period.
[138] *Prescription and the Limitation of Actions; Report on Personal Injuries Actions and Private International Law Questions* (Scot Law Com No 74, 1983), para 2.6.
[139] Section 6(1) of and Sch 1, para 2 to the 1984 Act.
[140] However, the disapplication of the 20-year prescription to obligations arising from death and personal injuries was not retrospective: see *K v Gilmartin's Exrx* 2004 SC 784. Accordingly, obligations which had already prescribed before 1984 by operation of the long negative prescription remain extinguished. Because of concern for the victims of historic child abuse, the Scottish Ministers made a reference to the Scottish Law Commission to consider whether obligations which had already prescribed before 1984 ought to be revived. The Scottish Law Commission's recommendation was that they ought not to be revived. (See Report on *Personal Injury Actions: Limitation and Prescribed Claims* (Scot Law Com No 207, 2007), para 5.24.)
[141] See Sch 3 to the 1973 Act.
[142] Section 7(1) and (2) of the 1973 Act.
[143] Section 6(2) of and Sch 1, para 2(gg) to the 1973 Act.

Obligations arising under the Consumer Protection Act 1987

Obligations to make reparation in respect of damage[144] caused by breach of the Consumer Protection Act 1987 (ie defective products) are subject to a 10-year prescriptive period.[145] **24.67**

Application to the Crown

The various prescriptive periods provided for in the 1973 Act are binding upon the Crown.[146] **24.68**

LIMITATION

Introduction

Statutes sometimes provide that certain actions must be brought within stated periods of time known as limitation periods. The lapse of a period of limitation does not extinguish an obligation; rather, it renders the obligation unenforceable.[147] The distinction between prescription and limitation was clearly articulated by Lord Justice-Clerk Cooper in *Macdonald v North of Scotland Bank*.[148] His Lordship stated[149] that "non-enforcement ... for the prescriptive period infers an irrebuttable presumption that the right has been abandoned and therefore that the correlative obligation has been extinguished ... the doctrine of limitation ... merely denies certain rights of action after a certain lapse of time". **24.69**

The court will not take account of limitation *ex proprio motu* (of its own motion); rather, it is for the defender to plead the fact of limitation.[150] If a plea of limitation is not taken timeously by the defender then any decree which passes against him will be valid and enforceable. The concept of limitation is, therefore, a procedural concept. Its purpose is to counteract the long delay in the raising of actions. In other words, limitation protects the defender from being vexed by stale claims many years after the occurrence in question, by which time evidence may well have been forgotten or lost.[151] **24.70**

---

[144] "Damage" is defined as "death or personal injury or any loss of or damage to any property (including land)" (s 5 of the 1987 Act).

[145] Section 22A of the 1973 Act. This section does not affect product liability cases arising at common law.

[146] Section 24 of the 1973 Act.

[147] "The effect of limitation in Scotland is not to extinguish the relative obligation but to provide to the alleged wrongdoer a right, which he may or may not choose to exercise, to have the action dismissed where it has been raised against him out of time": per the Lord President (Lord Hamilton) in *A v Glasgow City Council* 2010 SC 411 at para 12.

[148] 1942 SC 369.

[149] *Ibid* at 373.

[150] See *A v Glasgow City Council* 2010 SC 411, per the Lord President (Lord Hamilton) at para 12. In *J v Fife Council* 2007 SLT 85; 2009 SC 163 no plea of limitation was taken despite the historic nature of the allegations in question.

[151] The rationales for rules of limitation have frequently been asserted: see, eg, *B v Murray (No 2)* 2005 SLT 982 (per Lord Drummond Young at para 21) and 2008 SC (HL) 146 (per Lord Hope at para 5); *Tonner v Reiach and Hall* 2008 SC 1 (per Lord Abernethy at paras 120–121). Similar examples can readily be found from other jurisdictions: see *Brisbane Regional Health Authority v Taylor* [1996] 186 CLR 541 (per McHugh J at 551–554); *Yew Bon Tew v Kenderaan Bas Maria* [1982] 3 All ER 833 (per Lord Brightman at 839).

Actions in respect of personal injury

24.71 Although obligations in respect of personal injury are imprescriptible (except for product liability cases proceeding under the Consumer Protection Act 1987), personal injury actions *are* subject to the rules on limitation. Actions for damages in respect of personal injuries[152] are governed by s 17 of the 1973 Act and must be brought within a 3-year period (usually referred to as the "triennium").[153] There are a number of possible starting dates for that 3-year period. The starting dates are set out in s 17(2) of the Act. In the most straightforward case, time begins to run from the date on which the injuries were sustained.[154] That date may be later than the date of the breach of duty. In *Watson v Fram Reinforced Concrete Co & Winget Ltd*,[155] a workman was injured in August 1956 because of defective machinery which had been supplied to his employer in 1955. The workman sued his employer, who convened the manufacturers of the machinery into the action as second defenders in March 1959. The manufacturers pled that this was too late because a period in excess of 3 years had elapsed since the manufacture of the machinery. The House of Lords, however, held that the triennium ran from the date on which the workman suffered the injury and accordingly the manufacturers were sued timeously.

24.72 What is the position where separate injuries result from the one wrong? This might happen where a person suffers physical injury in an accident and these injuries are followed some time later by psychological damage. For some years the view was taken that where the subsequent injury was distinct, a separate triennium could apply in respect of it.[156] Accordingly, even if proceedings in respect of the first injury were time barred, an action could proceed within 3 years of the emergence of the subsequent injury. This view has now been firmly rejected by the Inner House in *A v Glasgow City Council*.[157] There, the pursuer raised an action in August 2003. He alleged that he had been sexually abused in a children's home when he was 9 (in 1974) and thereafter physically punished for revealing the abuse. He further alleged that he now suffered from post-traumatic stress disorder. The defenders pled that the action was time barred. The Lord Ordinary (McEwan) accepted that the claim was simply for psychiatric damage and not for physical injury. The psychiatric harm arose in 2001 and his Lordship held the action was not time barred and allowed a proof before answer. The council reclaimed. In the Inner House, five judges held unanimously that the "separate triennium" approach was misconceived. Indeed, it had been subject to criticism by the Scottish Law Commission.[158] The Inner House concluded that Parliament intended that time should run from the date on which a right of action emerged by reason of the concurrence of *injuria* and *damnum* (see *Watson v Fram Reinforced Concrete Co (Scotland)*

---

[152] "Personal injuries" include any disease and any impairment of a person's physical or mental condition (s 22(1) of the 1973 Act).

[153] The Scottish Law Commission recommends an extension of the limitation period from 3 to 5 years in respect of personal injury actions. See Report on *Personal Injury Actions: Limitation and Prescribed Claims* (2007), para 2.59.

[154] Section 17(2)(a).

[155] 1960 SC (HL) 92.

[156] *Shuttleton v Duncan Stewart & Co Ltd* 1996 SLT 517; *Carnegie v Lord Advocate* 2001 SC 802; *Hill v McAlpine* 2004 SLT 736. These cases are discussed in E Russell, "The separate triennium – destined to die?" 2007 SLT (News) 205.

[157] 2010 SC 411. For a discussion of this case, see E Russell, "Cheerio Carnegie" 2010 SLT (News) 81.

[158] See Report on *Personal Injury Actions: Limitation and Prescribed Claims* (2007), para 2.24.

Ltd,[159] above). In other words, time runs from when there is a conjunction between wrongdoing on the part of the defender and the *beginning* of the damage to the pursuer as a result thereof. The running of time is not delayed on account of a later emerging injury.

A further possible starting date for the triennium applies in relation to continuing **24.73** wrongs. Section 17(2)(a) provides that, where the act or omission was of a continuing nature, time begins to run from the date on which the injuries were sustained or the date on which the act or omission ceased, whichever is the later. Thus, as far as an injured employee wrongfully exposed to a noxious substance over a period of time is concerned, time runs from the date on which the wrongful exposure ceased.

A final possible starting date relates to the pursuer's awareness of certain facts.[160] **24.74** This starting date may be relevant in cases involving latent disease.[161] It may be that the pursuer is initially unaware that he has been injured. Imagine, for example, that a person receives a slight knock for which he would not consider seeking legal redress. A few years later that slight knock results in the onset of arthritis for which the person would wish to seek compensation. Alternatively, the pursuer may know that he has been injured but may not know that his injury is attributable to wrongdoing on the part of the defender. He may, for example, have put his injury down to natural causes. Section 17(2)(b) governs such situations. The 3-year period will run from the date on which the pursuer became aware, or the date on which the court deems it would have been reasonably practicable for him to become aware, of each of the following:

(i) that the injuries were sufficiently serious to justify bringing an action of damages on the assumption that the defender did not dispute liability and was able to satisfy a decree;

(ii) that the injuries were attributable, in whole or in part, to an act or omission; and

(iii) that the defender (or his employer or principal) was a person to whose act or omission the injuries were attributable.[162]

In *Blake v Lothian Health Board*,[163] the pursuer suffered a back injury at work in **24.75** September 1986, although his symptoms soon improved. His back pain re-emerged a year later, resulting in him taking time off work in October 1987. He raised an action in August 1990. A dispute arose between the pursuer and the defender as to the commencement date of the triennium. The defender argued that because the pursuer had been diagnosed as suffering from acute lumbar pain after the accident, the triennium had now expired and the action was time barred. The pursuer argued that the triennium did not commence until October 1987 and, accordingly, the action had not suffered limitation. The court repelled the defender's limitation plea. The court observed that the correct test was based on the reasonable claimant. In the instant case,

---

[159] 1960 SC (HL) 92.
[160] See *Chinn v Cyclacel Ltd* 2010 GWD 14–268.
[161] An example is provided by Lord Carswell in *A v Hoare* [2008] 1 AC 844 at para 67 (albeit in the context of the English statutory provisions).
[162] The pursuer must be aware (actually or constructively) of *all* three statutory facts before time begins to run. However, knowledge that any act or omission was or was not as a matter of law actionable is irrelevant: s 22(3) of the 1973 Act, as amended.
[163] 1993 SLT 1248.

the earlier incident of back pain (which would have attracted an award of no more than £200) was not *sufficiently serious* to trigger the limitation period.[164]

24.76   The first statutory fact – as to sufficient seriousness of the injuries – is directed at the issue of quantum of injury. That this is so is clear from *B v Murray (No 2)*,[165] where the Inner House rejected an argument that the correct approach to s 17(2)(b)(i) might also involve consideration of whether a pursuer (a victim of historic child abuse) would realise that the injury called for resort to litigation. The Lord President (Hamilton) observed:[166]

> "subhead (i) of section 17(2)(b) ... is concerned only with the extent of the injury, in terms of quantum of damages ... Whether the likely amount of damages would justify taking proceedings no doubt involves some element of judgment, particularly in marginal cases ... It will also be the case that ... some subjective, or perhaps more properly, individual personal features may enter into the assessment of quantum in that ... injury to a finger may be of much greater consequence to a concert pianist than to someone whose work and hobbies do not involve fine finger movements. But subject to those observations we consider that the statute can only be construed as intending subhead (i) to be concerned with quantum, an objective assessment having to be made whether the gravity of the injury to the pursuer in question was such that it would have justified proceedings on the statutory assumptions of undisputed liability and a solvent defender. The subhead is concerned with a single fact, namely the severity of the injury in so far as the pursuer was aware of it or could reasonably practicably have become aware of it."[167]

24.77   In *McE v de la Salle Brothers*,[168] the pursuer alleged that he had suffered abuse in a residential school between 1963 and 1966. His action was commenced in May 2000. The defenders stated a plea of time bar. The issue of repressed memory featured in the pursuer's pleadings, it being averred that until the victim underwent therapy the consequences of the abuse were such that the victim did not possess the awareness required by s 17(2). The Inner House held that the case was time barred under s 17(2)(b). The pursuer's pleadings indicated that he *was* aware that he had been subject to very serious assaults and "it would be absurd if a claimant could avoid the consequences of s 17(2)(b) by saying that he had put to the back of his mind his actual awareness of the statutory facts".[169] In the court's view, the running of time could not be interrupted by the development of suppressed memory or induced reticence.[170]

24.78   In *Ferla v Secretary of State for Scotland*,[171] a prison works officer suffered injury to his shoulder and back in March 1988. He attended hospital and was absent from work for 3 months before returning to lighter duties. He later submitted a claim to the Criminal Injuries Compensation Board, which awarded him compensation of £2,000 in November 1990. He continued to suffer back pain and underwent surgery in June 1991

---

[164] For a contrasting case, see *Mackie v Currie* 1991 SCLR 640 (Notes).
[165] 2007 SC 688.
[166] *Ibid* at paras 25–26.
[167] That construction of the statutory provisions was not questioned when the case came before the House of Lords. See also *G v Glasgow City Council* 2011 SC 1 where Lord Eassie quoted the Lord President's observations with approval (at para 18).
[168] 2007 SC 556. The case is also known as *M v Hendron*.
[169] *Ibid*, per Lord Osborne at 620.
[170] For other cases involving awareness of the statutory facts in the context of historic abuse, see *M v O'Neill* 2006 SLT 823; *W v Glasgow City Council* 2011 SC 15.
[171] 1995 SLT 662.

in respect of a protruding disc. An action was raised in June 1992. The defender took a plea of time bar. The pursuer responded that, until he was aware of his disc problems, the injuries were not sufficiently serious to justify raising an action. The Lord Ordinary (Johnston) rejected the pursuer's argument and held the action to be time barred. His Lordship stated:[172] "I do not consider a claim that was valued in conjunction with a solicitor at £2,000 under reference to the CICB offer can properly be categorised as trivial or de minimis." The court concluded that as the CICB settlement was achieved within the 3-year period, the pursuer had been aware that his injuries were sufficiently serious to warrant raising an action.

The second statutory fact of which the pursuer must be actually or constructively **24.79** aware before time starts to run is that the injuries were attributable, in whole or in part, to an act or omission.[173] The pursuer may think, for example, that his condition is due to natural causes rather than wrongdoing by another.[174] This statutory fact was considered in *Minshull* v *Advocate General for Scotland*.[175] The pursuer alleged that while engaged as a Royal Air Force engineer with the Ministry of Defence he was sprayed in the face with a toxic fluid (Coolanol 25R), which he inhaled. This event allegedly occurred in August 1997. The pursuer went on to develop chronic asthma. An action was commenced against the defender (as representing the Ministry of Defence) on 14 February 2004. The defender contended that the action was time barred. The pursuer's position was that he was unaware – and it was not reasonably practicable for him to have been aware – of the cause of his injuries until after a CT scan on 14 February 2001, when he was advised that he had asthma and that this could have been caused by inhaling Coolanol 25R. At a preliminary proof on the issue of time bar, Lord Macphail rejected the pursuer's argument. The pursuer's breathing difficulties had commenced within a few days of the Coolanol incident. Although the pursuer had also been in contact with bird droppings around the same time, investigation shortly after the incident excluded exposure to birds as a cause of the pursuer's complaint. Yet, despite various testing over a 3-year period, it was not until a consultation in November 2000 that the pursuer imparted details of the Coolanol incident to his medical advisers. An investigation as to whether Coolanol was responsible for the pursuer's condition would have led to a conclusion within about 4 months. Accordingly, it would have been reasonably practicable for the pursuer to ascertain whether his condition was attributable to the Coolanol incident long before 14 February 2001.

The third statutory fact of which the pursuer must have actual or constructive **24.80** awareness before time begins to run is that the defender was a person to whose act or omission the injuries were attributable. Thus, time will not run against the victim of a hit-and-run driver where he was unaware of the identity of the driver and it was not reasonably practicable for him to have become aware of the driver's identity.

In relation to any of the above statutory facts, the court may well determine a date **24.81** of constructive awareness which pre-dates the date of actual awareness.[176] As far as constructive awareness is concerned, it has been held that it is reasonably practicable for a pursuer to become aware of a fact if he would be able to do so without excessive

---

[172] 1995 SLT 662 at 665.
[173] For a discussion of this statutory fact, see *Agnew* v *Scott Lithgow Ltd (No 2)* 2003 SC 448.
[174] See *Clark* v *Scott Lithgow Ltd*, OH, 30 July 2004, unreported.
[175] [2008] CSOH 38. The case is discussed in greater detail in E Russell, "Time bar – an update" 2008 SLG 32.
[176] *Agnew* v *Scott Lithgow (No 2)* 2003 SC 448; *Little* v *East Ayrshire Council* 1998 SCLR 520; *Minshull* v *Advocate General for Scotland* [2008] CSOH 38; *Elliot* v *J & C Finney* 1989 SLT 208.

expenditure of time, effort or money.[177] The fact that he had a reasonable excuse for not taking steps is irrelevant.[178] Thus, it was held to have been reasonably practicable for a hospitalised road traffic accident victim to enquire of an attending police officer as to the identity of the other driver, notwithstanding that the patient's main concern at the time was for his own recovery![179]

24.82   In *Webb v BP Petroleum Development Ltd*[180] it was emphasised[181] that the pursuer must explain in his averments why it was not reasonably practicable for him to know the crucial fact 3 years before the date of the action.[182]

Periods to be disregarded

24.83   For the purposes of limitation, any time during which the injured party is under a legal disability by reason of nonage or unsoundness of mind[183] falls to be disregarded in terms of s 17(3) of the 1973 Act. The Age of Legal Capacity (Scotland) Act 1991 (the "1991 Act"), which came into force on 25 September 1991, provides that a child attains legal capacity at the age of 16.[184] Accordingly, time does not begin to run against a child until he attains the age of 16.[185]

24.84   Mention should also be made of actions in which damages are sought in respect of asbestos-related pleural plaques, pleural thickening or asbestosis. *Rothwell v Chemical & Insulating Co Ltd*[186] held that asbestos-related pleural plaques were not actionable injury. The effect of that decision was subsequently reversed by the Damages (Asbestos-related Conditions) (Scotland) Act 2009 in Scotland. The 2009 Act now provides that asbestos-related pleural plaques, pleural thickening and asbestosis do constitute actionable injury. For the purposes of limitation of such actions, s 3 of the 2009 Act provides that the period between the date of decision in *Rothwell* (that being 17 October 2007) and the coming into force of the Act (17 June 2009) shall be disregarded. The Act thus ensures that such claims do not become time barred during the period between the date of the judgment in *Rothwell* and the date on which the 2009 Act came into force.

Death from an unrelated cause

24.85   Where a person has died before the expiry of the triennium from a cause *unrelated to the personal injuries*, his executor can raise or continue the action. Section 17 determines

---

[177] *Elliot v J & C Finney* 1989 SLT 208; *Mackay v Lothian Health Board* 2001 SLT 581.
[178] *Elliot v J & C Finney* 1989 SLT 208 at 210–211; *Agnew v Scott Lithgow (No 2)* 2003 SC 448 at 454; *M v O'Neill* 2006 SLT 823 at 832. The Scottish Law Commission has expressed the view that the current test is unduly harsh and has proposed that time should not run while the pursuer is, in the court's opinion, excusably unaware of one or more of the statutory facts: see Scot Law Com No 207 (2007), paras 2.52–2.53.
[179] *Elliot v J & C Finney* 1989 SLT 208.
[180] 1988 SLT 775.
[181] *Ibid*, per Lord Weir at 776.
[182] See, also, *McArthur v Strathclyde RC* 1995 SLT 1129; *Cowan v Toffolo Jackson & Co Ltd* 1998 SLT 1000; *Nimmo v British Railways Board* 1999 SLT 778.
[183] See *Bogan's Curator Bonis v Graham* 1992 SCLR 920 for guidance as to the meaning of this term. The Scottish Law Commission considers the term "unsoundness of mind" to be outdated. It recommends that the statutory reference be replaced by a reference to the pursuer's being incapable for the purposes of the Adults with Incapacity (Scotland) Act 2000 by virtue of s 1(6) of that Act. See Scot Law Com No 207 (2007), para 2.71.
[184] Section 1(2) of the 1991 Act.
[185] Prior to the Age of Legal Capacity (Scotland) Act 1991, nonage ceased at age 18.
[186] [2008] 1 AC 281.

the starting date of the triennium because the action relates to "personal injuries not resulting in death" (the death is unrelated to the injuries). For the purposes of s 17(2)(b) of the Act, an executor is regarded as *eadem persona cum defuncto*, with the result that it is the date of the deceased's awareness of the statutory facts which is crucial.[187]

Actions in respect of death[188]

Limitation of actions where death has *resulted* from personal injuries is governed by s 18 of the 1973 Act.[189] Where damages are claimed by a relative or executor in respect of death, the action must be commenced within 3 years from the date of death[190] or within 3 years from the date on which the pursuer (note not the deceased) became or on which it would have been reasonably practicable for him to have become aware of both of the following facts: (1) that the injuries of the deceased were attributable in whole or in part to an act or omission and (2) that the defender was a person to whose act or omission the injuries were attributable in whole or in part or the employer or principal of such a person.[191]   **24.86**

Time does not run against a relative who is subject to disability by reason of nonage or unsoundness of mind.[192]   **24.87**

It should also be noted that s 3 of the Damages (Asbestos-related Conditions) (Scotland) Act 2009 (discussed above in the context of personal injury actions) also applies in fatal cases (under s 18), with the result that the period between the *Rothwell* decision and the coming into force of the 2009 Act is left out of account in computing the limitation period.   **24.88**

Where an injured party has not raised proceedings within the time specified in s 17(2) and death from those injuries occurs after the expiry of the triennium, no action can be brought by a relative or executor.[193]   **24.89**

Actions for defamation

A limitation period of 3 years applies to defamation actions.[194] It runs from the date of accrual of the action, that being the date on which the allegedly defamatory publication or communication came to the pursuer's notice.[195] Periods of legal disability by reason of nonage or unsoundness of mind are disregarded.[196]   **24.90**

---

[187] *Mackie's Exrx* v *AB 2000 Ltd* 2004 SC 334.
[188] It will be remembered that obligations in respect of death (other than those arising under the Consumer Protection Act 1987) are imprescriptible.
[189] Section 18 does not apply where the death results from an independent cause. Thus, it would not apply to an occupational disease case where death has subsequently occurred but the death resulted not from the disease but from an unrelated accident. Instead, s 17 ("Actions in respect of personal injuries not resulting in death") would govern such a case.
[190] Section 18(2)(a).
[191] Section 18(2)(b).
[192] Section 18(3).
[193] Section 18(4).
[194] Section 18A of the 1973 Act.
[195] Section 18A(4)(b) of the 1973 Act.
[196] Section 18A(2).

Product liability cases proceeding under the Consumer Protection Act 1987

24.91 A limitation period of 3 years applies to such actions. By virtue of s 22B of the 1973 Act, as amended, that period applies to actions of reparation in respect of personal injuries (not resulting in death) and damage to property caused by a defect in a product. Section 22C applies a 3-year limitation period in respect of actions where death has resulted from personal injuries caused by a defective product. Provision is made to disregard any period of legal disability by reason of nonage or unsoundness of mind.[197]

Actions of harassment

24.92 Actions of harassment *in which a claim for damages is included*[198] are subject to a 3-year limitation period.[199] The limitation period runs from the date on which the harassment ceased.[200] In *Marinello* v *City of Edinburgh Council*,[201] the pursuer sought damages from his employers in respect of an alleged breach by his superiors of s 8 of the Protection from Harassment Act 1997. The pursuer alleged that he had been subject to verbal abuse and criticism in the workplace on an almost daily basis, the last specified act having occurred on 24 September 2005. The pursuer stopped working on the following day. The pursuer asserted that some 17 months later, in March 2007, he was walking on a public road when one of the perpetrators had driven a van towards him and gesticulated with a clenched fist. The pursuer raised an action on 30 September 2008. He sought to rely on the March 2007 incident to defeat the defender's plea of time bar. The Lord Ordinary, Lord Uist, took the view that the 2007 incident was so removed in time, place and circumstances from the other incidents that it was not part of the same course of conduct. The Inner House disagreed, however, and concluded that the 2007 incident could not be excluded at this stage. A proof before answer was allowed.

24.93 Provision is also made in the 1973 Act for a later starting date which relates to the date of the pursuer's actual or constructive awareness that the defender was a person responsible for the alleged harassment, or the employer or principal of such a person. Periods of legal disability by reason of nonage or unsoundness of mind are disregarded.[202]

Limitation and the Crown

24.94 Section 24 of the 1973 Act provides that the Act is binding upon the Crown. It follows that all of the limitation periods discussed above run against the Crown.

---

[197] Section 22B(4) and, as regards a relative (in fatal cases), s 22C(3).
[198] If no such claim for damages is made, the statutory provision is inapplicable. Thus the section would not apply where the victim of harassment seeks only interdict.
[199] Section 18B – inserted into the 1973 Act by the Protection from Harassment Act 1997, s 10.
[200] Section 18B(2)(a).
[201] 2011 SLT 615.
[202] Section 18B(3).

The equitable extension[203]

In terms of s 19A of the 1973 Act, the court has a discretion to allow an action[204] to **24.95** proceed outwith the triennium if it deems it equitable to do so. The court's jurisdiction is based upon equity.[205] In considering whether equitable grounds exist, the court should have regard to all factors which are relevant and to the interests of the parties to the action.[206] The court's discretion must be exercised on the basis of the material placed before it[207] but is otherwise unfettered.[208] In *Forsyth v A F Stoddard & Co Ltd*,[209] the Lord Justice-Clerk (Wheatley) stated:[210] "The judge's unfettered discretion has to be exercised on all the relevant circumstances placed before him. That means that there is no restrictive table of considerations. Each case has to be decided on its own facts ..."

The onus is on the pursuer to satisfy the court that it is equitable to allow the action **24.96** to proceed.[211] The defender is likely to argue that the action should not be allowed to proceed and will usually advance arguments to the effect that investigation of the matter becomes harder with the lapse of time and that he will be prejudiced by the delay.[212] In *Carson v Howard Doris Ltd*,[213] Lord Ross suggested that the following points should be taken into consideration:

(i) the conduct of the pursuer since the date of injury, including the reason why the action was not brought timeously;

(ii) any prejudice which might be caused to the pursuer[214] if the extension were not granted; and

(iii) any prejudice which might be caused to the other party by the grant of the extension.[215]

However, these three considerations are not to be seen as necessarily applicable in all **24.97** cases nor as representing an exhaustive list.[216] The court must have regard to all the

---

[203] See E Russell, "Limitation of personal injury actions and the equitable extension – the case for reform" 2008 JR 33; E Russell, "The equitable extension of the three-year limitation period in personal injury cases" 1998 SLG 5; E Russell, "The law of limitation revisited – 'awareness' and the s 19A equitable extension" 1997 SLPQ 328.

[204] The statutory provision applies to actions for personal injury, death, defamation and harassment which would otherwise be time barred under ss 17, 18, 18A and 18B of the 1973 Act.

[205] In *Donald v Rutherford* 1984 SLT 70, Lord Cameron stated (at 75): "[E]quity requires that an equitable decision should be one which proceeds on a fair balancing of the interests and conduct of the parties and their advisers, as well as the nature and circumstances and prospects of success in pursuit of the time-barred claim itself."

[206] *Ibid*, per Lord Cameron at 77; *Anderson v City of Glasgow DC* 1987 SC 11, per L J-C Ross at 24; *Thomson v Newey & Eyre Ltd* 2005 SC 373, per Lord Macfadyen at para 22. The legislation itself does not list the factors to which the court should have regard, although the Scottish Law Commission has recommended the introduction of statutory guidelines in relation to the exercise of the s 19A discretion. See Report on *Personal Injury Actions: Limitation and Prescribed Claims* (2007), para 3.37.

[207] See the observations of Lord Glennie in *Quigley v Hart Builders (Edinburgh) Ltd* [2006] CSOH 118 at para 15.

[208] *Donald v Rutherford* 1984 SLT 70, per Lord Cameron at 75.

[209] 1985 SLT 51.

[210] *Ibid* at 53.

[211] *Forsyth v A F Stoddard & Co Ltd* 1985 SLT 51, per L J-C Wheatley at 53; *Clark v McLean* 1994 SC 410, per Lord MacLean at 413.

[212] See, eg, *Shuttleton v Duncan Stewart & Co Ltd* 1995 SCLR 1137; *Kane v Argyll and Clyde Health Board* 1999 SLT 823 (IH); *B v Murray (No 2)* 2008 SC (HL) 146.

[213] 1981 SC 278.

[214] See, eg, *Ferla v Secretary of State for Scotland* 1995 SLT 662.

[215] See, eg, *Johnston v Thomson* 1995 SCLR 554.

[216] See *Forsyth v A F Stoddard & Co Ltd* 1985 SLT 51, per Lord Hunter at 55.

circumstances of the particular case in deciding whether to grant[217] or refuse[218] the equitable extension. It is instructive to analyse some decided cases to ascertain how the courts have approached the question in particular situations.

24.98   In *B v Murray (No 2)*,[219] an extension of time was denied to pursuers who alleged that they had been abused in the 1960s and 1970s while resident in Nazareth House children's home. The matter of the s 19A discretion came to preliminary proof before the Lord Ordinary (Lord Drummond Young). For the pursuers, it was submitted that lack of knowledge, psychological disruption and "blocking out" were all relevant to the s 19A issue. Lord Drummond Young refused to exercise the s 19A discretion in the pursuers' favour and dismissed the action. The 21-year delay (since the last allegation) was sufficient in itself to make it inequitable to allow the action to proceed.[220] Both the Inner House[221] and the House of Lords subsequently endorsed that decision. The House of Lords held that the Lord Ordinary had been entitled to conclude that the prejudice caused to the defender by the lapse of time in raising the proceedings (including the loss of evidence that resulted from it) was, by itself, a sufficient reason for not allowing the actions to proceed under s 19A.[222]

24.99   In *McLaren v Harland & Wolff Ltd*,[223] McLaren had been employed by the defender as a plumber between 1953 and 1960. He was diagnosed as suffering from asbestosis in 1983 but did not raise a civil action against his former employer. It was only after his death, in 1988, that his widow and children raised proceedings averring that his death had been caused by asbestosis which, in turn, had resulted from his employment with the defender. In considering whether to allow the action to proceed under s 19A of the 1973 Act, Lord Milligan pointed out that, had McLaren raised the action timeously, the defender would have had an opportunity to have him medically examined prior to his death. There might also have been a *post mortem*. However, McLaren's medical condition had been closely monitored during the 7 years prior to his death and Lord Milligan regarded it "as at best ... speculative"[224] as to whether the defenders were prejudiced on the medical aspects. His Lordship further observed that the loss of McLaren's own evidence would probably disadvantage the pursuers' case rather than the defender's. Moreover, the case concerned regular exposure to asbestos over

---

[217] For cases where the action was allowed to proceed in terms of the statutory provision, see *Webb v BP Petroleum Development Ltd* 1988 SLT 775; *Comber v Greater Glasgow Health Board* 1989 SLT 639; *McCluskey v Sir Robert McAlpine* 1994 SCLR 650; *Sinclair v Morrison and Ors* [2009] CSOH 81; *McFarlane v Breen* 1994 SLT 1320; *Ferla v Secretary of State for Scotland* 1995 SLT 662; *Anderson v Glasgow DC* 1987 SC 11; *Carson v Howard Doris* 1981 SC 278; *Hill v McAlpine* 2004 SLT 736; *Kinross v Sterling Precast Ltd* 2002 SCLR 397.

[218] For cases where the discretion was not exercised, see *Craw v Gallagher* 1987 SC 230; *Bell v Greenland* 1981 SC 278; *Harrison v West of Scotland Kart Club and Ors and Royal Automobile Club Motor Sport Association Ltd* [2008] CSOH 33; *Minshull v Advocate General for Scotland* [2008] CSOH 38; *Fleming v Keiller* [2006] CSOH 163; *Cowan v Toffolo Jackson & Co Ltd* 1998 SLT 1000; *Forsyth v A F Stoddard & Co Ltd* 1985 SLT 51; *Morrice v Martin Retail Group Ltd* 2003 SCLR 289; *Leith v Grampian University Hospital NHS Trust* [2005] CSOH 20; *Whyte v Walker* 1983 SLT 441; *M v O'Neill* 2006 SLT 823; *Kane v Argyll & Clyde Health Board* 1997 SLT 965; 1999 SLT 823.

[219] 2008 SC (HL) 146.

[220] The Outer House decision is reported at 2005 SLT 982.

[221] The Inner House decision is reported at 2007 SC 688.

[222] For a similar case involving allegations of historic institutional abuse, see *M v O'Neill* 2006 SLT 823 Again, the court refused to exercise the s 19A discretion. Its exercise would have resulted in considerable prejudice to the defenders who would have been required to defend an action in respect of events which were alleged to have occurred some 35 years earlier. It was said that such a lengthy delay leads inevitably to loss of evidence and a decline in its quality. A fair trial was no longer possible. The action was dismissed.

[223] 1991 SLT 85.

[224] *Ibid* at 89.

a lengthy period rather than "a single transient event on which a witness no longer available could prospectively have provided evidence". His Lordship concluded that it would be equitable to allow the action to proceed. The deceased was unaware that he had a prospective right of action and his lack of awareness was not unreasonable. McLaren had been away from employment in the shipyards for 28 years prior to his death and in his subsequent work as a driver would not have received warnings about asbestosis, nor did he have contacts with people who might have alerted him to the possibility of an action. There was no fault on the deceased's part in failing to raise an action, nor was there a material delay by his widow and children in raising the action after his death.[225]

In *Donald* v *Rutherford*,[226] a man sustained personal injuries on 3 November 1975. **24.100** He did not commence his action until some 5 years later. The defender took a plea of limitation but the pursuer argued that the action should proceed in terms of s 19A of the 1973 Act. The Inner House, in holding that it was not equitable for the action to proceed, was heavily influenced by the fact that the pursuer had a claim against his solicitors who had failed to raise the action timeously. It has been observed[227] that *Donald* v *Rutherford* is an important case which provides informal guidance that a strong case against solicitors means that the discretion is not required.[228]

In *Forsyth* v *A F Stoddard & Co Ltd*,[229] an employee who had been injured in the **24.101** course of his employment sought damages from his employer. The action was raised 48 days after the expiry of the triennium owing to an oversight by an assistant solicitor. The sheriff refused to allow the action to proceed. The sheriff principal, on appeal, allowed an extension under s 19A. The defenders appealed against that decision. The Second Division, allowing the appeal, held that the pursuer had to bear the responsibility for his agent's fault. He had a right of action against his agents and the burden of expenses would fall on the defenders whether they succeeded or failed as the pursuer was legally aided. The balance of equities therefore lay with the defenders and an extension of time was refused.

The fact that the triennium has expired only days before the raising of the court **24.102** action will not of itself lead to the court exercising its s 19A discretion. In *Wilson* v *Telling (Northern) Ltd*,[230] a personal injuries action was raised in September 1991, 3 days after the expiry of the triennium. The defenders argued that, as the action was time barred, it should be dismissed. The pursuer argued that the court should exercise its discretion under s 19A and allow the action to proceed as the delay was of 3 days only. The pursuer also argued that the defenders had not been prejudiced as the claim had been intimated to them well before the expiry of the triennium and the delay had resulted from administrative oversight on the part of his agents. Lord McCluskey

---

[225] See, also, *Elliot* v *J & C Finney* 1989 SLT 605.
[226] 1984 SLT 70.
[227] W J Stewart, "Reparation – prescription and limitation" (1994) 39 JLSS 374.
[228] See, also, *Clark* v *McLean* 1994 SC 410. Note, however, that in *Johnston* v *Thomson* 1995 SCLR 554, it was held to be equitable to allow the pursuer to raise her action outwith the triennium as she had taken all necessary steps to prosecute her claim and the inevitable delay in pursuing another action against her solicitors would be detrimental to her health, which was deteriorating. Also, in *McFarlane* v *Breen* 1994 SLT 1320, it was held that although the pursuer would be entitled to proceed against the solicitor, who had raised the action in the wrong forum, this would result in further substantial delay and further litigation. It was therefore equitable to allow the action to proceed outwith the triennium.
[229] 1985 SLT 51.
[230] 1966 SLT 380. See, also, *Fleming* v *Keiller* [2006] CSOH 163 (where the action was raised only 1 day late!).

observed[231] that, "as has been pointed out in the Scottish cases, a defender is entitled to found upon his statutory rights even after the lapse of one day". The Lord Ordinary also observed that the fact that no prejudice had been occasioned to the defenders was of no great significance in the instant case. He went on to state that a pursuer acts through his agents and must thus be responsible for their actings. In any event, the pursuer had a possible alternative remedy against both his local and Edinburgh agents (and conceivably his counsel) in respect of the delay in raising proceedings. His Lordship accordingly refused to grant the s 19A extension.

24.103   As a result of the application of the equitable discretion being a matter for the discretion of the court, appeal courts are disinclined to interfere with decisions made by the court below. If, however, the court below has misdirected itself or a clear error has been made, the appeal court will, in those circumstances, consider the matter afresh.[232]

Late amendment and limitation

24.104   Where an action is raised timeously, limitation may nonetheless become an issue where the pursuer seeks to amend his case after the 3-year period has expired.[233] Walker has observed that "[t]he leading principle is that a pursuer is not entitled to change the basis of his case by amendment at a time when he would have been time-barred from raising an action".[234] In other words, if the effect of the amendment is to change the basis of the pursuer's case, it will be disallowed,[235] whereas if the basis of the action is unaltered by the amendment, it will generally be allowed.[236]

24.105   What is the position where a pursuer seeks by amendment to introduce a new defender to the action after the limitation period has expired? It will be recalled that in *Pompa's Trs* v *Edinburgh Magistrates*,[237] Lord Justice-Clerk Cooper observed:[238] "[O]ur reports contain many decisions showing that the Court will not in general allow a pursuer by amendment to substitute the right defender for the wrong defender … if he seeks to make such amendments only after the expiry of a time limit which would have prevented him at that stage from raising proceedings afresh."

24.106   In *McCullough* v *Norwest Socea*,[239] the proposed amendment sought, after the expiry of the triennium, to substitute a partnership for a limited company. This was held to be a difference of such substance that it ought not to be allowed (although in the event the court exercised its discretion under s 19A of the Act to allow the action to proceed).

24.107   In *Harrison* v *West of Scotland Kart Club and Ors and Royal Automobile Club Motor Sport Association Ltd*,[240] an action arising from injuries sustained in a go-kart accident was originally raised against the club and five office bearers as representing the club and as individuals. The action insofar as directed against the club and the five

---

[231] 1966 SLT 380 at 381.
[232] See *Donald* v *Rutherford* 1984 SLT 70; *McCabe* v *McLellan* 1994 SC 87; *Clark* v *McLean* 1994 SC 410; *Forsyth* v *A F Stoddard & Co Ltd* 1985 SLT 51.
[233] See, E Russell, "Amendment and time bar – a review" 2008 SLT (News) 5.
[234] Walker, *Prescription and Limitation of Actions in Scotland* at p 129.
[235] See *Pratt* v *Scottish Ministers* [2005] CSOH 59; *Greenhorn* v *J Smart & Co (Contractors) Ltd* 1979 SC 427.
[236] See *Cork* v *Greater Glasgow Health Board* 1997 SLT 740.
[237] 1942 SC 119.
[238] *Ibid* at 125.
[239] 1981 SLT 201.
[240] [2008] CSOH 33.

members in their *representative* capacity was subsequently dismissed and the case against the five members as *individuals* was remitted to proof before answer. After the expiry of the triennium, the pursuer sought by amendment to introduce 16 persons as additional defenders. These persons were the office bearers and committee members of the club but there was nothing in the original summons to suggest that they were individually at fault. The amendment, however, sought to ascribe personal liability to the 16 new individuals. As these individuals had never previously been named in the action, Lord Menzies took the view that this change was both radical and fundamental and held that the action as directed against the 16 new defenders was time barred.

General points

Where a claim arises from both personal injury and some other loss, such as economic loss or damage to property, the combined claim is subject to limitation. **24.108**

Where a claim does not involve personal injury, the rules on limitation do not apply, although prescription will operate in the usual way. **24.109**

The running of the limitation period is stopped by the raising of court proceedings. **24.110**

MORA (DELAY), TACITURNITY AND ACQUIESCENCE[241]

If the pursuer delays in bringing his action (but such delay does not amount to the prescriptive period) that delay, *in itself*, does not prevent the pursuer's claim from proceeding. In *Mackenzie v Catton's Trs*,[242] Lord Deas stated:[243] "*Mora* is not a good *nomen juris*. There must either be prescription or not. We are not to rear up new kinds of prescription under different names." More recently, it has been stated: **24.111**

> "In Scotland, for centuries past, the decision whether, and if so when, a right – and the corresponding right of action – should be cut off by passage of time has been taken by the legislature rather than the courts … The Scottish courts have therefore been unwilling to treat delay in itself as a ground for cutting off the right of action where the underlying right has not prescribed."[244]

While the Scottish courts have recognised the plea known as *mora* (delay), it is clear that factors additional to delay must be present before the plea can be successfully invoked. It has been stated judicially that "[t]he term *mora* is a short hand form of referring to a defence which encompasses the elements of *mora*, taciturnity and acquiescence".[245] **24.112**

One of the most helpful discussions of the plea of *mora* is to be found in the judgment of the Lord President (Lord Kinross) in *Assets Co Ltd v Bain's Trs*:[246] **24.113**

---

[241] For a more detailed analysis of this issue, see Johnston, *Prescription and Limitation* (Chapter 19); Reid and Blackie, *Personal Bar* (SULI, 2006) (Chapter 3); Walker, *The Law of Prescription and Limitation of Actions in Scotland*, (Chapter 11).

[242] (1877) 5 R 313.

[243] *Ibid* at 317.

[244] *Tonner v Reiach and Hall* 2008 SC 1, per Lord Abernethy at para 52.

[245] *D's Curator Bonis v Lothian Health Board* 2010 SLT 725, per Lady Clark at para 38.

[246] (1904) 6 F 692 at 705 (reversed on the facts (1905) 7 F (HL) 104).

"[I]t appears to me ... that the plea of *mora* cannot be successfully maintained merely on account of the lapse of time, but that the person stating it must also be able to shew that his position has been materially altered, or that he has been materially prejudiced, by the delay alleged. In other words, mere lapse of time will not, in my judgment, found an effective plea of *mora*. The law of Scotland provides for cases in which it is considered that lapse of time alone should form a sufficient answer to a claim, or lead to the mode of proof being restricted, in the various prescriptions and limitations ... I think we should be slow to add, by decision, a plea of bar or discharge resulting from mere lapse of time, which the Legislature has not thought fit to sanction by statute. At the same time, I do not doubt that where, coupled with lapse of time, there have been actings or conduct fitted to mislead, or to alter the position of the other party to the worse, the plea of *mora* may be sustained. But in order to lead to such a plea receiving effect, there must, in my judgment, have been excessive or unreasonable delay in asserting a known right, coupled with a material alteration of circumstances, to the detriment of the other party."

24.114 More recently, Johnston has explained the nature of the plea of *mora* in the following terms:[247]

"[T]he statutory provisions [on prescription] do not guarantee that a right or obligation will remain enforceable until the statutory period has run. All they postulate is that, once that period has run, it shall not be. It is therefore consistent with the statutory rules that there should be some common law doctrine of delay. But what is essential is that this should not undermine the statutory provisions. What this means is that it is not the mere passage of some period of time short of the prescriptive period which gives rise to a plea of delay. Instead it is the passage of time combined with other factors, namely taciturnity and acquiescence."[248]

24.115 Further guidance is given in *Somerville* v *Scottish Ministers*,[249] where the Lord President (Lord Hamilton), delivering the opinion of the Inner House, stated:[250]

"[M]ora, or delay, is a general term applicable to all undue delay ... taciturnity connotes a failure to speak out in assertion of one's right or claim. Acquiescence is silence or passive assent to what has taken place ... By its nature, acquiescence is almost always to be inferred from the whole circumstances, which must therefore be the subject of averments to support the plea."[251]

24.116 The plea of *mora* is essentially an aspect of the doctrine of personal bar. It is a plea on the merits as opposed to a preliminary plea.[252] If the plea is upheld, decree of absolvitor is the appropriate disposal.[253] It is clear from the case law that a plea of *mora* can be

---

[247] *Prescription and Limitation*, at para 19.02.
[248] Johnston expresses the view (*Prescription and Limitation* at para 19.12) that "of the three elements of the plea it is acquiescence which is significant, but as a rule only when coupled with reliance by or prejudice to others".
[249] 2007 SC 140.
[250] *Ibid* at para 94.
[251] See also the comments of Lady Clark in *D's Curator Bonis* v *Lothian Health Board* 2010 SLT 725 at para 44.
[252] Maclaren, *Court of Session Practice*, p 403; *Halley* v *Watt* 1956 SC 370 at 374; *Tonner* v *Reiach and Hall* 2008 SC 1 at para 52. See, also, Walker, *The Law of Prescription and Limitation of Actions in Scotland*, at p 158: "It is not ... a matter which, if established excludes the pursuer's claim; it is rather a matter which if established must be weighed and may be held to be sufficiently strong to justify the view that the claim has been departed from and cannot now be given effect to."
[253] *D's Curator Bonis* v *Lothian Health Board* 2010 SLT 725 at para 51; *Tonner* v *Reiach and Hall* 2008 SC 1 at para 145.

successfully invoked only if there is delay in prosecuting a *known* claim – that is, a claim known to the pursuer to exist.[254]

It is a question of circumstances whether a plea of *mora* is likely to succeed. In *Assets* **24.117** *Co Ltd* v *Bain's Trs* [255] Lord Trayner stated:[256] "As to Mora—On this matter many authorities were cited to us, which I am glad to say do not call for any detailed consideration. The decisions upon this question of *mora* and its effects, depend so much upon the special facts of each case that scarcely one can be cited as an exact precedent for another."

How, then, have the courts responded to a plea of *mora* in given circumstances? In **24.118** *Cunningham* v *Skinner*,[257] there had been considerable delay in bringing an action for defamation based on a document issued some 10 years earlier. The delay was held not to bar the action as the reason for the delay was that the pursuer had become bankrupt while the former suit had been pending. The original action (which had been raised 2 months after the alleged defamatory statements had been uttered) had been dismissed because the pursuer had been unable to obey an order to find caution for expenses. Similarly, in *Cassidy* v *Connochie*,[258] a retired police sergeant brought an action of damages against a publican in respect of slanderous statements made 3½ years prior to the raising of the action. The defender's plea of *mora* was repelled on the ground that, for 3 years after the alleged slander, the pursuer had remained a member of the police force and that by the rules of the force he was debarred from raising an action without the consent of the Chief Constable, which consent had been withheld. The fact that the pursuer was "under inhibition from his superior officer" for most of the relevant period was "a decisive consideration".[259]

In *Bethune* v *A Stevenson & Co Ltd*,[260] the Lord Ordinary (Lord Johnston) refused **24.119** to sustain a plea of *mora* where a workman sued his employers more than 15 years after sustaining injury. His Lordship found it impossible to draw an inference of prejudice or acquiescence in the circumstances. The pursuer had denied the defender's averments of prejudice and had made averments of the availability of evidence, of efforts to have his claim pressed, of instructions to his then solicitors to press the claim some 5 years after the accident and further averments that he had attempted to interest other solicitors in his claim and had not abandoned it.

There are no recent examples of the plea of *mora* being successfully invoked in a **24.120** personal injury case. This is no doubt because in most cases of delay the defender will seek to rely instead on the statutory limitation provisions. However, an attempt to invoke the plea of *mora* was made in *D's Curator Bonis* v *Lothian Health Board*.[261] There, an action was raised against the Health Board in 2006 arising from alleged negligence in relation to the birth of a child (D) in 1980. The action was raised by D's curator bonis. The child suffered from cerebral palsy and was *incapax* and remained so as an adult. Accordingly, D's right of action would never be subject to limitation.[262] Nor

---

[254] See *Assets Co Ltd* v *Bain's Trs* (1904) 6F 692, per Lord Trayner at 740 and per the Lord President (Lord Kinross) at 705; *D's Curator Bonis* v *Lothian Health Board* 2010 SLT 725 at paras 42–43.
[255] (1904) 6 F 692.
[256] *Ibid* at 739.
[257] (1902) 4 F 1124.
[258] 1907 SC 1112.
[259] *Ibid*, per Lord Stormonth Darling at 1116.
[260] 1969 SLT (Notes) 12.
[261] 2010 SLT 725.
[262] For the purposes of limitation, any time during which the injured party is under a legal disability by reason of nonage or unsoundness of mind falls to be disregarded in terms of s 17(3) of the 1973 Act.

would the obligation be subject to prescription. The Board stated a plea of *mora*. The Lord Ordinary (Lady Clark) observed that the defence of *mora* was capable of being applied to circumstances prior to and post the raising of an action. Under reference to the Lord President's *dictum* in *Assets Co Ltd*, Lady Clark stated that mere lapse of time would not found an effective plea of *mora*. There must in addition be "actings or conduct fitted to mislead, or to alter the position of the other party to the worse".[263] Moreover, Lord Trayner in *Assets Co Ltd* had stated that for the plea to succeed the delay in question must be delay in asserting a *known* claim. Her Ladyship continued:[264]

> "[I]t is for the defenders to plead averments relevant to found the defence. The plea refers specifically to the concept of acquiescence. It is difficult to understand how there could be any inference of acquiescence in a situation where there was no knowledge at all ... If knowledge is relevant to the defence of *mora*, it is difficult to understand how the knowledge (actual or implied) might arise in this case. It could only arise if the common law defence fixed the *incapax* with the knowledge of a parent. I would be very slow to reach that conclusion without binding authority because such a result might result in injustice and unfairness to the *incapax*."

Her Ladyship concluded that the defender had not pled a relevant case to support the plea of *mora*.

COURT'S INHERENT POWER TO PUT AN END TO PENDING ACTION

24.121   What is the position where the *institution* of an action is not delayed but there has been inordinate and inexcusable delay thereafter? This was the issue which Lord Glennie was required to address in *McKie v MacRae*.[265] An action was raised by the children of a woman who had been killed in a road traffic accident. They sued the widow of the driver of the car and the owner of the car. The accident had occurred in 1986 and the action was raised in 1996. (This was within the triennium as the period of nonage of the pursuers required to be disregarded for the purposes of limitation.) The action was sisted in 1997 and the sist was recalled in 2003. In 2005, the pursuers sought to amend. The defenders argued that the action should be dismissed owing to the unwarrantable delay in prosecuting the action which resulted in a substantial risk that a fair trial would not be possible and their ability to defend the action would be prejudiced. Dismissing the action, Lord Glennie held there had been inordinate and inexcusable delay on the pursuers' part in progressing the action. The court had an inherent jurisdiction to control actions and where a party, through no fault of his own, had been denied a hearing within a reasonable time the court could not allow a hearing to take place.

24.122   The power of the Scottish courts to dismiss an action involving inexcusable and inordinate delay was confirmed by the Inner House in *Tonner v Reiach and Hall*[266] and

---

[263] *Assets Co Ltd v Bain's Trs* (1904) 6 F 692, per the Lord President (Lord Kinross) at 705.
[264] 2010 SLT 725 at paras 42–43.
[265] 2006 SLT 43.
[266] 2008 SC 1.

again in *Hepburn* v *Royal Alexandria Hospital NHS Trust*.[267] In *Tonner* (a professional negligence action against a firm of architects), the Inner House held that the prior existence of a rule of court was unnecessary in order for the Scottish courts to exercise such a power.[268] Lord Abernethy, delivering the opinion of an Extra Division, stated:[269] "While Scottish ... civil procedure remains substantially party driven ... it does not follow that parties to civil litigation have an unqualified right, once an action has been raised, to proceed with it in as leisurely a manner as they think fit." His Lordship continued:[270] "[T]he Court has the power to bring an action to an end for want of prosecution ... It should, however, be regarded as the option of last resort." While the power was to be exercised in the light of the facts and circumstances of each case, the court observed that the delay must be both inordinate and inexcusable and there must be "an added element of unfairness ... specific to the particular factual context".[271]

In *Smith* v *Golar-Nor Offshore A/S*,[272] Lady Paton refused to dismiss an action arising **24.123** from an industrial injury where, although there had been a period of inordinate delay, it was excusable.[273] The delay could be explained by the pursuer having to await the replies of busy medical professionals to his enquiries, by the need for legal aid sanction for a new medical expert and by the pursuer's working offshore. Moreover, the delay had not occasioned any additional element of unfairness to the defender in the factual context of the case.

Similarly, in *Cameron* v *Hughes Dowdall*,[274] the temporary judge refused to dismiss **24.124** a professional negligence action where the delay involved was excusable. Difficulties had been experienced in respect of legal aid and in obtaining a favourable expert opinion. Moreover, there was minimal prejudice to the defenders. Although the partner whose conduct was allegedly negligent had since died, the basis of claim remained unaltered and the relevant files were still available.

In *D's Curator Bonis* v *Lothian Health Board*,[275] in which the plea of *mora* was **24.125** considered (see discussion above), the defender also sought to have the action struck out on the basis of unreasonable delay. Lady Clark took the view that there was nothing inordinate in the delay. The issues involved were complex, a curator bonis had required to be appointed, there had been delays with regard to legal aid and several consultations with experts had taken place. Some of the difficulties experienced by the pursuer were attributable to the defender – in particular, the failure of the relevant midwife to write her notes in a manner which enabled her to be identified. Even if there was inordinate delay, her Ladyship took the view that it was excusable in the context of a complex case such as this.

---

[267] 2011 SC 20.
[268] Note that in terms of the Act of Sederunt (Sheriff Court Rules) (Miscellaneous Amendments) 2009 (SSI 2009/294) provision is now made in the Ordinary and Summary Cause Rules for applications to dismiss an action on the basis of inordinate and inexcusable delay.
[269] 2008 SC 1 at para 116.
[270] *Ibid* at para 123.
[271] *Ibid* at para 136.
[272] 2007 RepLR 127.
[273] A similar conclusion was reached in *Mackay* v *Edmond* [2008] CSOH 92. There, a 4-year delay between a sist and its recall in a professional negligence action was held to be inordinate although not inexcusable in the particular circumstances.
[274] 2008 GWD 40–591.
[275] 2010 SLT 725.

THE ROLE OF INSURANCE AND OTHER COMPENSATION SYSTEMS AS METHODS FOR THE COMPENSATION OF VICTIMS OF DELICT

25

INTRODUCTION

It is important to remember that only a tiny proportion of all the parties who are the **25.1** victims of delict are granted a remedy as a result of a judgment in a civil court. The Royal Commission on Civil Liability and Compensation for Personal Injury, under the chairmanship of Lord Pearson,[1] reported that in 1973 there were about 250,000 tort/delict claims for personal injuries or death in the United Kingdom in that year, of which 215,000 received some form of financial settlement with or without a trial.[2] The evidence produced to the Commission showed that 86 per cent of the claims were settled without a writ having to be issued, 11 per cent were settled after a writ but before any hearing in open court, a further 2 per cent were settled before trial, with only about 1 per cent of cases proceeding to a judgment. Those 99 per cent of cases that do not proceed to a judgment, and the other forms of "compensation" that may be significant in relation to those cases, will be the subject of this chapter.

POSSIBLE REASONS FOR THE SMALL NUMBER OF SUCCESSFUL DELICT ACTIONS

There are many possible reasons why the victim of a delictual act decides not to pursue **25.2** a case through the courts. Possibly the person has received trivial injuries, or for private reasons does not want to pursue the person who caused the injury or damage, perhaps because the two parties are in a relationship. A victim of a delict may decide that the time and expense of having to instruct counsel and attend court are unjustified in economic terms. In other cases, the person may have been the victim of a delict of a particularly

---

[1] Cmnd 7054 (1978), vol 2, pp 18–20.
[2] For a more current figure, the Compensation Recovery Unit of the Department for Work and Pensions gives a figure of 861,325 cases for 2009–10 where compensation had been paid.

traumatic kind, such as a rape, or involvement in a rescue case that did not have a successful outcome, and has suffered post-traumatic stress disorder[3] and may not want to give evidence for fear of having to relive the traumatic incident. In some cases, such as a "hit and run" road accident, the person whose negligence caused the accident may not be traceable. Some people may not be aware of their right to raise an action. The potential pursuer also has to weigh up the chances of success: since the court may order the party who loses the action to pay the expenses of the winner, the pursuer must be reasonably confident of the strength of his or her case to risk the financial consequences of losing it, especially where the law or the facts of the case are complicated, and the case would be likely to be lengthy. Also, in all civil actions, a case in which damages are sought would only be worth raising if the defender appears to have sufficient means to be able to meet a damages award. There is no point raising an action against a "man of straw".

25.3   The party whose fault or negligence is alleged to have caused the loss or damage may also have good reasons for preferring to deal with the case in a way that avoids a court judgment. The potential defender may not be confident of winning an action, and may fear an expenses award going against him or her. Also, if the potential defender might be about to face many other similar actions following the first successful case, he or she may be unwilling to allow a precedent to be set in the first case, and may prefer to reach an out-of-court settlement without having to admit liability. When 3,000 South African asbestos workers were allowed to bring a case in the UK against the parent company of their employer for compensation for asbestos-related injuries, the case was eventually settled out of court for around £10.7 million.[4] This avoided any issues of setting a precedent for future cases. By contrast, various insurance companies lost a case recently in the Inner House of the Court of Session in Scotland to challenge their liability to meet compensation claims from victims of pleural plaques, which are benign lesions that indicate that there has been exposure to asbestos. The Scottish Parliament had passed the Damages (Asbestos-related Conditions) (Scotland) Act 2009 to provide compensation following earlier unsuccessful court action.[5] The case has been appealed to the Supreme Court by the insurance companies. Whatever the final outcome of the final appeal, similar cases in future would be expected to be dealt with in accordance with the eventual legal precedent. This case is discussed in more detail later in this chapter at para 25.19.

SYSTEMS OF COMPENSATION FOR INJURY OR DAMAGE OTHER THAN ACTION IN A CIVIL COURT

25.4   It is important to realise, too, that an award of damages from a defender in a civil action is not the only compensation system available in cases of delict. In the United Kingdom, the injured person will receive from the National Health Service (NHS) medical assistance which is funded through tax and national insurance but generally free at the point of need. Some employees may be able to rely on sick leave paid by their employers, or, in cases of serious injury or illness, may be awarded early retirement on medical grounds and an enhanced pension. Such persons may assess

---

[3] Usually referred to as "nervous shock" in the case law.
[4] *Lubbe v Cape plc* [2000] 1 WLR 1545.
[5] *AXA General Insurance Ltd v Lord Advocate and Ors* [2011] CSIH 31.

their position and conclude that they have received sufficient compensation without resort to the courts.

Other compensation systems that may be available are the social security system,   **25.5** the Motor Insurers Bureau, the use of compensation orders in criminal cases, and compensation from the Criminal Injuries Compensation Scheme (CICS). The rest of this chapter will be devoted to an examination of these sources of compensation.

SOCIAL SECURITY BENEFITS

If the injured person is an employee and is not fit to continue working after the injury,   **25.6** he or she can receive assistance from the social security system. The person may need time off work to recover. In such a case, if the employer funds short-term absence from work by paying statutory sick pay, there is a limited right for employers to recover the amount from the state under s 159A of the Social Security Contributions and Benefits Act 1992 and regulations made thereunder.[6]

If an employee is so sick that he is unable to work in the longer term, there is a range   **25.7** of other state benefits that may be claimed. These benefits may apply to others who are not employees. Some are dependent on having a contributions record, and some are means tested. The principal benefits that may apply are Jobseeker's Allowance, Employment and Support Allowance and Disability Living Allowance.

However, where the victim of delict who has been receiving benefits is successful   **25.8** in claiming damages, the state demands the repayment of benefit payments. Under the Social Security (Recovery of Benefits) Act 1997, the person paying the compensation must deduct the gross amount of certain social security benefits paid to the victim in respect of the injury in the 5 years following the injury before paying the compensation payment. The deducted benefits are payable to the Compensation Recovery Unit of the Department for Work and Pensions.[7] The defender is given a certificate of recoverable benefit by the Compensation Recovery Unit, and the defender is not allowed to make any payment until a certificate has been supplied. From 1997, when the Social Security (Recovery of Benefits) Act 1997 came into force, recoupment no longer relates to awards of solatium. These rules are discussed further in Chapter 22 on Remedies.

The justification for recovery of benefits is that the pursuer is in a sense being   **25.9** compensated twice. However, the rules may cause hardship if a large part of the damages payment has to be paid to the Government before the pursuer can receive the award.

Similar rules on recoupment also apply to the cost of emergency treatment for   **25.10** injuries under s 150 of the Health and Social Care (Community Health and Standards) Act 2003.

INSURANCE

There are two types of insurance that are important in the compensation of victims   **25.11** of delict. The first is *first party* or *loss insurance*, under which the insured holds a policy of insurance against a risk which affects himself. Examples of this type of insurance are fire insurance, life insurance, accident insurance, and permanent health

---

[6] Currently art 2 of the Statutory Sick Pay Percentage Threshold Order 1995 (SI 1995/512).
[7] www.dwp.gov.uk/other-specialists/compensation-recovery-unit.

insurance. Some people hold insurance against the expenses of litigation should this prove necessary. The second type of insurance is *third party* or *liability insurance,* under which the insured holds insurance against the risk of causing injury or damage to third parties through his or her own fault or negligence, or through the fault or negligence of those for whom the first party is vicariously liable. An example of this is motor insurance against injury to third parties through the fault or negligence of a driver. In some cases, such as the one quoted in this example, third party insurance is compulsory, while, in other cases, the policyholder has judged the risk of the event occurring to be sufficiently high, or the consequences, if it does occur, to be sufficiently serious that he or she has decided voluntarily to hold insurance.

25.12   Third party insurance, covering risks of accidental injury or damage to third parties or their property, is very common. There are some special cases where third party insurance is compulsory under statute. This is the case in relation to the liability of employers towards employees arising out of or in the course of employment, following the enactment of the Employers' Liability (Compulsory Insurance) Act 1969. Failure by an employer to hold this insurance is a criminal offence, but has been held on a construction of the statute not to give rise to a right for an employee to claim damages,[8] although in the Scottish case *Quinn* v *McGinty,*[9] the sheriff principal on appeal allowed a right of action in favour of an injured employee against the directors of a company for failing to arrange this insurance. By s 143 of the Road Traffic Act 1988, every driver must hold third party liability insurance. Insurance is also compulsory for nuclear installations under the Nuclear Installations Act 1965, and for merchant shipping against liability for oil pollution, under ss 163–165 of the Merchant Shipping Act 1995, which give third parties direct rights under these policies.

25.13   Professional persons may be compelled to hold insurance by the rules of their professional bodies. This is true of solicitors in Scotland, who have to subscribe to the master policy held by the Law Society of Scotland in respect of all solicitors practising as principals.[10] Since 1990, hospital doctors (though not GPs) have been indemnified by the NHS local health board employer against liability incurred in medical negligence cases, rather than holding insurance. The doctor may also be a member of a medical defence organisation.

25.14   Third party insurance is often also purchased voluntarily, where a person's own assessment of the risk of causing damage to others or the cost of liability is such that it becomes economically sensible to do so. So, for example, it may be commercially sensible for a manufacturer to insure against liability to the end-user should manufactured products prove defective. Public liability insurance is often taken out by occupiers of premises to which the public have access, to cover the risk of liability under the Occupiers' Liability (Scotland) Act 1960.[11]

25.15   The availability or otherwise of insurance is often a deciding factor as to whether or not to litigate in respect of a delict, since the pursuer knows that, if successful, a damages award will be funded by insurance. Evidence given to the Pearson Report[12] showed that employers' liability was the most common type of personal injury claim

---

[8] *Richardson* v *Pitt-Stanley* [1995] QB 123.
[9] 1999 SLT (Sh Ct) 27.
[10] Solicitors (Scotland) Professional Indemnity Rules 2005.
[11] See Chapter 19.
[12] See fn 1, vol 2, pp 19 and 22.

in 1973 at 46 per cent per total number of claims, followed by motor vehicle cases at 40.9 per cent, with occupiers' liability at 4.9 per cent and a miscellaneous category of "other" categories at 5.6 per cent. Other cases including medical negligence and product liability came in at less than 1 per cent of all cases. The evidence also looked at successful cases where the victim received some form of compensation through the civil courts. Here the evidence showed that the victims of motor vehicle injuries were the most successful category at 25 per cent, followed by the victims of injuries at work at 10.5 per cent. It will not pass unnoticed that employers' liability and motor insurance are two areas in which compulsory insurance is demanded by law. Evidence to the Pearson Commission showed that in personal injury cases, 88 per cent of claims, and 94 per cent of the damages paid, were covered by insurance.[13]

Although it will be more likely that a pursuer would raise an action for damages **25.16** where the liability of the defender is covered by insurance, the judges are supposed not to have regard to the existence or otherwise of insurance in a particular case before them when assessing whether or not a delict has been committed, or when assessing quantum of damages. In *Davie* v *New Merton Board Mills*,[14] where an employee sustained an eye injury through using defective equipment which had been bought from a reputable source, but which had a latent defect, the court refused to grant a remedy despite the existence of insurance. Viscount Symonds stated:[15] "It is not the function of a court of law to fasten upon the fortuitous circumstance of insurance to impose a greater burden on the employer than would otherwise lie upon him."

By contrast, the availability of insurance did appear to influence the court's **25.17** decision in *Nettleship* v *Weston*,[16] in which a learner driver drove into a lamp-post, causing a knee injury to the instructor. The decision to impose liability on the learner driver appears to have been influenced by the existence of insurance, and has been doubted in some later cases. Lord Denning stated:[17]

"The learner driver may be doing his best, but his incompetent best is not good enough. He must drive in as good a manner as a driver of skill, experience, and care, who is sound in wind and limb, who makes no errors of judgement, has good enough eyesight and hearing, and is free from any infirmity ... The high standard is largely a result of the policy of (requiring) every driver to be insured ... we are ... moving away from the concept: 'No liability without fault.' We are beginning to apply the test 'On whom should the risk fall?' Morally the learner driver is not at fault: but legally she is liable because she is insured and the risk should fall on her."

When an insurance company pays out on an insurance policy, which is held by the **25.18** victim of a delict, the insurance company is entitled at common law to step into the shoes of the insured person, without the need for an assignation. The insurance company can then exercise any remedy that the insured person might have had against the wrongdoer. This is the principle of subrogation, discussed in Chapter 24. This can arise also where an employer is vicariously liable for wrongs done by an

---

[13] Cmnd 7054 (1978), vol 2, para 509. From a survey carried out by the British Insurance Association based on claims in November 1973.
[14] [1959] AC 604 (HL).
[15] *Ibid* at 627. See also *Lister* v *Romford Ice and Cold Storage Co Ltd* [1957] 1 All ER 125.
[16] [1971] 2 QB 691.
[17] *Ibid* at 699–700.

employee: in such a case the employer's insurer can seek damages from the employee at fault, although this is rarely done: see *Lister v Romford Ice and Cold Storage Co Ltd*.[18] This case took place prior to the enactment of the Employers' Liability (Compulsory Insurance) Act 1969.

25.19　　　　Often the insurance company may be the only person available to the pursuer as a source of recompense. It may be that the pursuer has developed an industrial injury, which may not manifest itself until many years after the events that caused the injury. By that time the employer may no longer be in existence. However, in such cases the insurance remains alive. In *AXA General Insurance Ltd v Lord Advocate and Ors*,[19] various insurance companies sought to challenge the passage of the Damages (Asbestos-related Conditions) (Scotland) Act 2009 as being in breach of the insurance companies' right to enjoyment of their property contrary to Art 1 of Protocol 1 of the European Convention on Human Rights and hence not within the legislative competence of the Scottish Parliament. Although there had been earlier successful actions in England and Scotland based on having contracted pleural plaques through working with asbestos, the court in England had held in a previous case in the House of Lords[20] that there was no evidence that pleural plaques acquired through exposure to asbestos did not go on to lead to illness and so would not give rise to a right of action in tort. Thereafter the Scottish Parliament had passed the Damages (Asbestos-related Conditions) (Scotland) Act 2009 to allow a right of action, because of the psychological distress resulting from the knowledge that a person had developed pleural plaques which might be an indicator that they would go on to develop asbestosis or mesothelioma. It was held in the Inner House of the Court of Session that although the 2009 Act did interfere with the property rights of the insurance companies, the interference was justified by the public interest in rectifying what was seen as a social injustice, and the decision to put the financial burden on insurance companies rather than the public purse lay within the Parliament's margin of appreciation. The decision has been appealed to the Supreme Court by the insurers.

THE MOTOR INSURERS BUREAU[21]

25.20　　When a road accident is caused by the fault or negligence of a driver who does not hold insurance, cover is provided through the Motor Insurers Bureau, which has operated a scheme since 1946. This is a system of insurance of last resort under which cover is provided by law under the Road Traffic Act 1988 by all the motor insurers acting together to ensure that the victims of road accidents receive compensation where they have been injured by road users who should have held insurance by law. The scheme covers not only accidents where the road user who caused the accident was uninsured, or held invalid insurance, but also "hit and run" drivers who cannot be traced. The scheme covers personal injuries and damage to property in accidents on the public road.

---

18 [1957] 1 All ER 125.
19 [2011] CSOH 31.
20 *Rothwell v Chemical Insulating Co Ltd* [2008] AC 281(HL).
21 www.mib.org.uk.

COMPENSATION ORDERS

Under the Criminal Procedure (Scotland) Act 1995, compensation orders can be **25.21** awarded by the criminal courts in Scotland in both solemn and summary proceedings. The compensation goes to the victims of crime. A criminal court can make a compensation order requiring the accused to "pay compensation for any personal injury, loss or damage caused, directly or indirectly, or alarm or distress caused directly to the victim".[22] The courts can enforce these as if they were fines, and these orders can be made in addition to fines. They are generally used in minor cases where small compensation payments are appropriate. They are not competent in respect of death or personal injury or in cases of loss or damage in road accidents, except where a vehicle is driven without insurance or has been dishonestly taken and driven away. Compensation orders have the advantage to the victim of criminal conduct such as minor assaults, or criminal damage to property, that he or she does not have to raise a separate civil action to obtain compensation.

Where a compensation order has been made, and later the victim seeks damages in **25.22** a delict action, the assessment of damages is done by the court without reference to the existence of the compensation order. However, once the award of damages has been made, the damages payable are the difference between the amount of the compensation order which has already been paid, and the amount of the damages award.[23]

STATE COMPENSATION FOR CRIMINAL INJURIES

If a person is injured physically, or suffers psychiatric injury, or dies as a result of a **25.23** crime of violence, a claim can be made to the Criminal Injuries Compensation Authority for compensation which is funded by the state. The rationale for this is that it is an expression of sympathy for the victims of crime.[24] In many ways this is anomalous, in that the victims of criminal violence are singled out for state compensation from other victims of delictual acts who may be equally deserving of public sympathy.

The Criminal Injuries Compensation Scheme[25] was first set up in the United **25.24** Kingdom in 1964 as a non-statutory scheme with the object of providing some state compensation to the victims of violent crime. The scheme is run by the Criminal Injuries Compensation Authority and was eventually given a statutory basis in the Criminal Injuries Compensation Act 1995, and the scheme in its current form dates from 2008. The sums that can be awarded range from £1,000 to £500,000, with a limit of £250,000 for a single case.

An applicant submits a claim within 2 years of the violent incident. There is a **25.25** tariff showing standard amounts of compensation for particular types of injury. The applicant can also claim for loss of earnings, which can be claimed from the 28th week, but may not exceed one-and-a-half times the median gross weekly earnings published by the Annual Survey of Hours and Earnings. Special expenses for special equipment, or for private medical care, can be claimed. In case of fatal injury, close relatives can claim by way of compensation, a bereavement payment of up to £500 or £11,000 if

---

[22] Section 249.
[23] Section 253.
[24] Quoted in the Report of the Royal Commission on Civil Liability and Compensation for Personal Injury (the "Pearson Report"): see fn 1, vol 1, para 329.
[25] www.justice.gov.uk/guidance/compensation-schemes/cica/index.htm.

there is only one claimant. Children under 18 can claim for loss of parental services up to £2,000 per annum until majority.

25.26   If an applicant has received social security payments, they are not deducted from the standard award paid according to the tariff, but they *are* deductible from any award in respect of loss of earnings and special expenses. The difference is explained by the fact that the tariff is a flat rate determined to reflect the net amount of compensation after deductions, whereas loss of earnings payments and special expenses reflect the circumstances of the particular person.

25.27   The decision of the claims officer can be appealed to an appeals panel and thence to a first-tier tribunal.

25.28   The Annual Report and Accounts for the Criminal Injuries Compensation Authority for 2009–10 states that over 70,000 cases were dealt with and over £209 million was paid in tariff compensation in that year.[26]

---

[26] For further reading on the issues discussed in this chapter, see P Cane and P Atiyah, *Atiyah's Accidents, Compensation and the Law* (7th edn, 2006).

INDEX